NEVA AGAIN

HIP HOP ART, ACTIVISM AND EDUCATION IN POST-APARTHEID SOUTH AFRICA

Edited by Adam Haupt, Quentin Williams, H Samy Alim and Emile Jansen

HSRC
PRESS

Download the #IntheKeyofB EP, featuring music by some of Cape Flats' finest Hip Hop MCs, poets, instrumentalists and producers. The music is available as open content to readers of this book.

Published by HSRC Press
Private Bag X9182, Cape Town 8000, South Africa
www.hsrcpress.ac.za

First published 2019

ISBN (soft cover)   978-0-7969-2445-2

Copy-edited by Lee Smith
Typeset by Ismaeel Grant
Cover design by Ismaeel Grant
Cover photograph by Ference Isaacs
Printed and bound by Novus Print Solutions

Distributed in Africa by Blue Weaver
Tel: +27 (0) 21 701 4477; Fax Local: +27 (0) 21 701 7302; Fax International: 0927865242139
www.blueweaver.co.za

Distributed in Europe and the United Kingdom by Eurospan Distribution Services (EDS)
Tel: +44 (0) 17 6760 4972; Fax: +44 (0) 17 6760 1640
www.eurospanbookstore.com

CONTENTS

SHOUT OUTS

ADAM HAUPT

First things first, my own contribution to this book would not have been possible without Incentive Funding from the National Research Foundation (NRF) in South Africa and the University of Cape Town's University Research Committee (URC) in the Faculty of Humanities. I was able to generate momentum for this project by steadily accumulating and generating scholarly work as well as purchasing media production equipment that helped me to document practically every encounter with Hip Hop artists and activists at a number of events.

Thanks to Soraya Abdulatief, who joined me at my Prophets of da City interview in 1994 as my camera person and co-conspirator on many subsequent missions. This will probably sound like hyperbole, but that first interview with Prophets of da City was life-changing. It marked a turning point in my development as a young scholar. My extended exchange with DJ Ready D and Shaheen Ariefdien helped me to imagine a future for South African cultural studies beyond the confines of disciplinary boundaries.

My gratitude to the entire Prophets of da City crew for being generous, critical and accommodating. Thanks to Ghetto Ruff's Lance Stehr, who trusted me with a copy of the banned *Understanding Where I'm Coming From* and popular *Neva Again* music videos in 1994, long enough for me to convert them to the VHS video format from Betacam SP. This gave me rich material for a groundbreaking MA research study at the University of the Western Cape that paved the way towards South African Hip Hop scholarship.

Thanks to Emile Jansen, who welcomed me just as Heal the Hood was being established and as I was beginning to work as a freelance journalist while holding down an assortment of tutoring, lecturing and research assistant positions to fund my music habit. My friendships with Black Noise, Heal the Hood, Brasse Vannie Kaap, Godessa, Bush Radio's *Headwarmers*, ALKEMY, DJ Eazy, DJ Azuhl, DJ E20, Nazli Abrahams, Shaheen Ariefdien, DJ Ready D, Shameema Williams, Eavesdrop, King Voue and Prophets of da City paved the way for many new friendships and partnerships in the Hip Hop community, both locally and internationally. My thanks to them.

Thanks to all of the book's contributors, especially because the process of writing, revising and reframing took many twists and turns. Thanks for your patience and faith in the editors.

Thanks to Nadine Mathews-Nunes, Nathan and Bradley Lodewyk, who set off the #IntheKeyofB EP recording project with me in 2017 and special thanks to H Samy Alim's Center for Race, Ethnicity and Language (CREAL) for providing the necessary funds to cover studio costs (and for the many high-energy brainstorm sessions over good food). We have come a long way from our Sunday morning coffee and *koe'siester* jamming sessions in the Centre for Film & Media Studies staff room at the University of Cape Town. Bradley's contacts on the music scene were crucial to bringing together a talented assortment of instrumentalists and MCs, many from the Cape Flats. Thanks to all of the artists who joined us in the studio and at live performances. They include: Bradley Lodewyk, Nadine Matthews-Nunes, Naftali Solomons, Eavesdrop (aka Monishia Schoeman), Shameema Williams (ex Godessa), Natasha C Tafari, Emile Jansen, Amy Brown, Imie Vannie Delf, Dirtypro Agape Tadana, Stefan Benting, Razeen Haupt, Nathan Lodewyk, Zama Jimba, Eddy Strings, Grant Phillips, Robin Thompson, Matthew Lenting, Renstan White, Nathaneal Bartez, Chloe Rezant, Leroy Muller, Desmond Blake and August West.

The process of composing, recording, producing and performing together was humbling and exhilarating. Thanks to them all and thanks to Gary Erfort (aka Arsenic) at Metalloid Lab Productions. Gary's reputation as a dope Hip Hop producer is well established on the Cape scene and we had the benefit of his technical and creative guidance as Bradley and I navigated the process of composition, arrangement and production with a wide range of instrumentalists and MCs.

#IntheKeyofB is a testament to the creativity and critical consciousness of the Hip Hop artists who contributed to the EP and the book. While not all of the book's contributors feature on the EP, or vice versa, the EP serves as an indicator of Cape Hip Hop heads' ability to engage critically, energetically and creatively with the socioeconomic challenges that they face.

Thanks to Quentin Williams, who found my MA research in the library thesis repository at the University of the Western Cape as he kick-started his PhD. Q wasted no time in reaching out to me. I have learned a great deal from you, Q. May our collective creative and intellectual mission continue, Pastor!

Our love to the Hip Hop artists we have lost over the years: Contro'Versy, Mr Devious, Mr FAT, Ben Sharpa, ProKid, Mark Heuwel, Panaiks, Jaak (*met sy Flêtse maniere*)…

QUENTIN WILLIAMS

This book has grown on me. And I have grown with it. It comes from the heart, and the energy that I gave for it would not have come about without the support of all the people involved. I'd like to thank my co-editors for bringing all the energy to complete this book and the album! This book has its beginnings in a conversation with Eavesdrop, Adam, DJ Eazy and DJ Azuhl, just before Adam created the online Hip Hop forum *Staticphlow*. It then gained momentum when Adam, Emile, Samy and I initiated the first Heal the Hood Hip Hop Lecture Series, hosted by the Centre for Multilingualism and Diversities Research (CMDR) at the University of the Western Cape. And dammnnnn!! Only a few years later, we have *Neva Again*! Brothers, thank you for riding with me on this project, and supporting what is now a major feature of the African Hip Hop Indaba.

To every Hip Hop artist who agreed to present at the first Hip Hop Lecture Series, I express my sincere gratitude to you for coming through and sharing your knowledge. I hope what you hold in your hands is proof of your sacrifice, labour and commitment to the culture. I also thank you for putting aside your time to write your chapters, allowing us to hound you and keeping us honest on any inaccuracies. If there are errors and omissions that remain, sorry nuh, we'll catch them in the second edition.

To help get the book into its initial shape, we recruited a small army of students to transcribe video and audio recordings, and to double and triple check final transcriptions. A huge shout out to Jason Richardson, Tara-Leigh Cornelissen, Shanleigh Roux, Madelynne Madell and Veronique Williams for working on the transcriptions, bringing a disciplined labour and energy I have never seen! You guys were lit with them transcribing! Thank you for helping the editors see what is possible and produce what is arguably the first book of its kind for Hip Hop on the African continent!

Reader, the final product you hold in your hands is also the result of the care given to our vision by the HSRC Press staff. And the cover photo! Daamn! All thanks goes to our brilliant director of photography Ference Isaacs for taking such a dope picture at the African Hip Hop Indaba. And thank you b-girl Loren Lee Langenhoven for granting permission to reproduce the picture for the cover!

Along the way, we received generous financial and material support, locally and internationally. I am grateful to the director of the Centre for Multilingualism and Diversities (CMDR), Prof. Christopher Stroud, and the staff and students at the CMDR for supporting the organising and planning of the initial lecture series. I'd like to thank H Samy Alim's Center for Race, Ethnicity and Language (CREAL) for the generous funding that secured labour, materials, studio time and the final production of the album. Also, I'd like to thank the National Research Foundation (UID: 99241) for funding that went towards the authoring of this book project and the printing of branded USB credit cards for the #IntheKeyofB rap album. If you listen to the album carefully, you'll hear me spit some bars! I Pastor(ed) the shit out of my verse!

Finally, a huge shout out to my wife! There were many nights where I sat up with this project till very late, going back and forth with my fellow editors. We wrote and rewrote, brought visions and produced revisions. We worked hard until we got this shit right! We spent mornings chasing down contributors for their chapters, and daaays checking if we dotted every i and crossed every t. We jumped in and out of Dropbox folders, sent way too many emails and drank large cups of coffee EVERY DAY! In the final push to finalise the book, we freestyle battled the title in a Facebook message chat! The *Neva Again* title won! And throughout this process, my wife was a solid supporter all the way, cheering me and us on. Thanks, Mrs Williams, for your support – not only for this project but also for understanding the art, activism and educational practice and potential of this thing we call Hip Hop!

H SAMY ALIM

Neva Again. This book is a testament to the power, brilliance and creativity of the Cape Town Hip Hop community, as well as their commitment to resistance, disruption, justice and transformation. *Neva Again*. This book is a living document, dedicated to a dope-ass community of artists committed to bringing about the kinds of social, political and economic changes that we need, both in South Africa and beyond. *Neva Again*. This book, as Adam Haupt says, is a park jam, reminding us that our lives are not defined solely by our oppression. *Neva Again*. Hip Hop heads know that our revolution gotta have the right beats per minute, and that our collective joy – that feeling we get when the park jam reaches its climax – is, in fact, the moment when we are most alive, when everything seems possible. So, first, thank you to all the heads – the dozens featured in this book, and more – who have breathed life into all of us over the years and transformed us with your vision.

For all of those who know me – who know how these past five years of living and working in Cape Town, on and off, for months at a time, have changed my life – you know that I could never express enough gratitude for all of the Hip Hop artists, activists and scholars involved in this project, many of whom I consider my friends, even family. Words just can't do my heart justice. For Adam, Quentin and Emile, especially, y'all know without my saying it, that it has been a true honour and privilege to work with you over the years. For me, to work with some of the most brilliant, committed, dedicated and *by far* the hardest-working crew of Hip Hop artists–scholars–activists in the game has been among the most profound learning experiences of my lifetime. I am lucky to have been included in this project and I am beyond grateful for all of the love, kindness, wisdom, and yes, the patience you showed me as you continued to push through this groundbreaking volume, to reshape the academy's stilted and often anti-democratic conventions, and to make sure that we all kept it movin the whole way through. Above all, you are the reason Cape Town has become 'home'.

Last, but not least, shout out to the Center for Race, Ethnicity and Language (CREAL) and all my colleagues at UCLA who have always supported this work, the scores of folks across the University of Cape Town and the University of the Western Cape who made this book possible, and the HSRC Press team for knowing what's up. One Love.

EMILE JANSEN

'Never and *Neva Again* will it be that South African practitioners of all the elements of Hip Hop culture, do not get to speak or write for themselves.' I am so proud of this book and its insistence on giving voice to the practitioners. I would thus like to start by thanking Adam Haupt, Quentin Williams and H Samy Alim for helping to change that narrative and getting all of these voices heard. The more I read what others have contributed, the happier I feel about our mission. We have achieved what we set out to do. I hope that the next generation will learn from our eagerness to document and share our experiences for generations to come. Adam my bro, it's been a long journey of sharing and learning from each other. Thank you for being patient and willing to endure a sometimes emotional Hip Hop community. Quentin, *dankie virrie relaxed way dat djy altyd koenek met 'n man*. (Thank you for the relaxed way in which you always communicate with me.) Meeting you after *Afrikaaps* and seeing you and Adam put in work over the years, really inspired me to help out wherever I can and when requested. I know I'm always doing a million and one things, but try and squeeze in what I can, where I can. To H Samy Alim, I would like to say thanks for seeing the greatness of the work being done by the Cape Town Hip Hop community within the global context. As Credo Mutwa says, 'A people living on a beautiful mountain can only see its beauty when they leave the mountain.' You have helped us and continue to help us see the beauty of the people's work around this mountain that rose from the sea, Hoerikwaggo (Table Mountain). I have been able to see you showcase our work in the USA and seen how people respect what we do. Thank you.

Our initial African Hip Hop Indaba Lecture Series ensured that conversations continue and that locals see the power that Hip Hop has in the academic world. These sessions made many young people rethink how they saw Hip Hop and they continue to do so online. I look forward to many more lecture series about the content of this book and how we can encourage future generations. I want to thank Heal the Hood Project, Tanswell Jansen, Shaquile Southgate, Fabian Petersen, Andre Bozack, Stefan Benting, Charlton Eftha, Nicole Plaatjes and Klein Fortuin for making these events happen annually. I would also like to thank Ference Isaacs for taking the most amazing pictures at our events and contributing them to this book. To members of 'Key of B', I am so thankful that you embraced this concept and ran with it. I am honoured to have been able to contribute my voice to these concepts that became songs and I see so much potential for what Adam, Bradley and Nathan initiated *innie Bontas* (in Bonteheuwel). Thank you to all involved and especially Gary Erfort (aka Arsenic) for the relaxed recording vibes. I can't wait to hear the final EP and share it with everyone.

Lastly, I would like to give a shout out to all those in Cape Town who contributed to the foundation of this culture, which has become a fundamental part of our lives. Every second you contributed is like the droplets that fall from above //Hui !Gaeb (Cape Town, 'the place where the clouds gather') onto Hoerikwaggo ('the mountain rising from the sea') into the streams and waterfalls that flow into the Camissa (//amm = sweet waters) river and finally the ocean.

THANK YOU.

ART BY MAK1ONE | Source: Heal the Hood

INTRODUCTION

NEVA AGAIN

HIP HOP ART, ACTIVISM AND EDUCATION
IN POST-APARTHEID SOUTH AFRICA

Quentin Williams, Adam Haupt, H Samy Alim and Emile Jansen

This book is the culmination of decades of work on Hip Hop culture and Hip Hop activism in South Africa. It speaks to the emergence and development of a unique style of Hip Hop on the Cape Flats – the outlying township areas located within a 25-kilometre range of the city of Cape Town and housing largely working-class black[1] and coloured residents – and, in the case of one chapter, in the Eastern Cape. A distinctive feature of this book is that it weaves together the many varied and rich voices of this dynamic Hip Hop scene to present a powerful vision for the potential of youth art, culture, music, language and identities to shape our politics. These voices have never been read together before, often featured separately in newspapers, opinion pieces and academic essays.

As a challenge to the constraining, colonial nature of academic research and writing, this volume presents academic analyses side by side with, and sometimes privileging, the brilliant insights from the creative minds behind this transformative cultural movement. Throughout the book, we share original artist interviews, panel discussions, and essays written by both the

---

1. In this book, we define the racial categories of black and coloured as colonial and apartheid constructs created to design an unequal South African society.

   As with Haupt's book, *Static*, the editors of the volume view race as socially and politically constructed. We take our cue from Zimitri Erasmus, the editor of the seminal work *Coloured by History, Shaped by Place: New Perspectives on Coloured Identities in Cape Town*. In an editor's note prior to the introduction of the book, Erasmus frames the work's exploration of 'coloured' identity politics in the following way:

   There is no such thing as the Black 'race'. Blackness, whiteness and colouredness exist, but they are cultural, historical and political identities. To talk about 'race mixture', 'miscegenation', 'inter-racial' sex and 'mixed descent' is to use terms and habits of thought inherited from the very 'rare science' that was used to justify oppression, brutality and the marginalisation of 'bastard peoples'. To remind us of their ignoble origins, these terms have been used in quotation marks throughout. (Erasmus 2001: 12)

   Erasmus refutes biologically essentialist thinking on race that was employed to justify racist oppression during the colonial occupation of Africa as well as during 48 years of apartheid in South Africa. In order to make her position clear, she elects to include the editor's note as well as to use a number of contested terms in quotation marks throughout the edited volume. Neva Again does not employ the use of quotation marks throughout, but the editors hope that this note suffices to signal its position they view racial identities as culturally, historically and politically constructed.

pioneers of Hip Hop in South Africa and the next generation of Hip Hop heads who are active in the culture today. Within these pages, and given the multi-genre, polyvocal nature of this text, we are particularly concerned with understanding how activism comes to shape and define Hip Hop culture in post-apartheid South Africa. Some of the questions we asked as we launched this project were:

» What is the history of Hip Hop activism in South Africa?

» What are some of the strategies that Hip Hop heads employ to sustain their art and activism?

» How do Hip Hop artists rethink the relationship between language, education and power? And how do they transform those relations through their sociolinguistic and educational engagements?

» What are the race, class, gender and sexuality politics of South African Hip Hop? And how do Hip Hop heads deal with the intersectional and transformational politics of the present?

Hip Hop activism can be understood as a form of activism that employs Hip Hop to engage communities critically and creatively with regard to their respective social, economic and political contexts, either through live performance and artistic production (e.g. graffiti, poetry, lyricism, turntablism or breaking) or through educational practices within and beyond conventional schooling (e.g. conducting workshops or developing curricula for alternative forms of education). In a recent work, we contend that 'hip hop has become a meaningful way for diverse sets of artists, activists and a range of other types of hip hop participants to seize agency in the ways in which they are represented and to make sense of their respective contexts' (Haupt, Williams & Alim 2018: 13). It is a form of practice that challenges the oppression and homogenisation of individuals, groups and communities. It embraces the concept Each One, Teach One – a motto that was taken to heart by young activists during the struggle against apartheid, particularly during the apartheid state's repression of freedom of movement during the states of emergency.

During that historical moment, youth themselves took responsibility for their education in modes of engagement that dispensed with the traditional teacher–pupil hierarchy that was associated with regressive, apartheid-era education. It was during this time that some young activists first realised that 'conscious' Hip Hop could be used as a vehicle for them to express their political beliefs. At the same time, young people who were not necessarily politically engaged came to be politically active via the music as well as through their interactions with more politically aware Hip Hop heads, in meeting places such as The Base, which used to run Saturday Hip Hop matinees during the final years of legislated apartheid. The focus was on how to raise the critical consciousness of the Hip Hop community and facilitate ways for artists to exercise agency in the face of social, economic and political restrictions. For South African heads, Hip Hop activism involved translating the culture locally, but also teaching aspects of Black Consciousness, the principles of the Nation of Islam and the fundamentals of the Zulu Nation, among other influential ideologies.

In many respects, this book speaks to how Hip Hop artists, activists and educators have built upon the work of earlier heads to make sense of life in post-apartheid South Africa, a context that continues to struggle with racialised and gendered class inequalities as well as with various forms of interpersonal prejudice – be it gendered, racialised or class-based.

GRANDMASTER DJ READY D | Source: Ference Isaacs

NEVA AGAIN

The book takes its title from Prophets of da City's (POC's) song 'Neva Again', which was a single on *Phunk Phlow* (1995), the album released after their third album, *Age of Truth*, was banned in 1993. The song references the first democratically elected president of South Africa, Nelson Mandela, in his 1994 inaugural speech, by sampling the most famous portion of this speech at the outset of the track. The music video opens with grainy footage of the crew walking the city and then moves into a small lounge where they are watching TV. The camera pans from the TV set to the crew as they watch Mandela intently while he delivers the lines: 'Never, never and never again shall it be that this beautiful land will again experience the oppression of one by another.'[2]

Unlike tracks from *Age of Truth*, 'Neva Again' was aired repeatedly on SABC TV (at the time, the South African Broadcasting Corporation acted as a mouthpiece for the apartheid regime, but made the transition to being a public service broadcaster with the advent of democracy), no doubt in celebration of the nation's first democratic elections and the victory of the African National Congress (ANC). Shaheen Ariefdien's opening lines in the song suggest that what is at stake is leadership that truly represents the interests of citizens:

Excellent!

Finally a black president!

To represent

The notions of representation and authenticity are key themes in Hip Hop; artists are expected to authentically represent their experiences and the communities from which they come. Often, the kind of authenticity that is celebrated is linked to representations of working-class black neighbourhoods, or 'the hood' (Jeffries 2011). Ariefdien celebrates the authenticity of the president because he represents the interests of black citizens after a hard-fought struggle by youth to both free Nelson Mandela from imprisonment and to secure a democratic state that will serve the interests of civil society – in other

---

2. https://www.youtube.com/watch?v=vhN_GzCbH0I

words, leadership that is representative. In Hip Hop terms, the president *represents*. In this regard, DJ Ready D raps that the process of securing and maintaining the gains of the struggle is one that requires constant vigilance and continual revision:

> Books and pens are great, Now knowledge awaits Seeka the believer and
> the believer will become the achiever and the achiever needs to pass it on,
> knowledge of self is gonna make us strong
> You made a choice you took the vote Madiba spoke and said 'NEVER AGAIN'
> yes yes sure, we should help the man to make sure that the future stays
> secure or…REVOLUTION

Ready D's reference to books and pens alludes to the return to school after years of school protests, boycotts, the detention of youth and skirmishes with riot police and intelligence operatives, as well as to the concept of Knowledge of Self – education is essential to pursuing freedom.

What is worth noting here is that, despite the celebratory nature of this song, Ready D's verse – which precedes the outgoing chorus's reference to R&B/funk/disco band Skyy's celebratory song 'Here's to You' – contains not-so-thinly veiled undertones of the defiance that characterised *Age of Truth*, which was unyielding in its refusal to accept both the ANC's and the National Party's calls to 'forgive and forget' in the build-up to the elections (Haupt 1996, 2001). While Ready D raps that citizens should assist the president in securing the nation's future, he invokes the threat of revolution. This aligns with *Age of Truth*'s call for revolution as a means of rejecting calls for reconciliation that are not accompanied with a clear plan for distributive and restorative justice in post-apartheid South Africa. When the elections produced a victory for Nelson Mandela and the ANC, they celebrated this victory but also indicated that if the ruling party were to falter, they would not hesitate to engage them critically. The invocation of revolution in the event that citizens do not play an active part in democratic processes could thus be read as a healthy measure of scepticism on their part.

The scepticism in this song as well as on *Age of Truth* was justified, in retrospect. Mandela's statement that 'this beautiful land should [never] again experience oppression of one by another' is ironic in light of the fact that the ruling party proceeded to embrace neoliberal economic policies. These policies have done very little to reverse the racialised class inequalities that legislated apartheid, produced largely because they place a low premium on public spending and adopt a laissez-faire approach to state regulation of markets (Haupt 2008, 2012). In fact, Africa Check reports that white South Africans are least affected by poverty by a very large margin, while a very large percentage of black and coloured South Africans live in poverty (Table 1).

TABLE 1: NUMBER OF PEOPLE LIVING IN POVERTY IN SOUTH AFRICA BY POPULATION GROUP

POPULATION GROUP	NO.	%
AFRICAN/BLACK	28 267 530	64.2
COLOURED	1 989 304	41.3
INDIAN/ASIAN	79 460	5.9
WHITE	47 494	1.0
SOUTH AFRICA	30 383 788	55.5

Source: Wilkinson (2018)

These statistics challenge the claims made by white right-wing interest groups, such as Solidarity, that white South Africans are living in poverty and that they are being marginalised by a black-led government. They also challenge claims by coloured nationalist interest groups, such as Gatvol Capetonians, that African/black South Africans are being afforded more opportunities than coloured South Africans and that coloured communities are therefore being marginalised.

It is ironic that Africa Check uses apartheid-era racial classifications to demonstrate that inequalities that were produced by apartheid continue to operate along the same racialised lines well after apartheid. For this reason, those apartheid racial categories are useful as indicators of the progress South Africa has made since the fall of legislated apartheid. However, we contend that we should always be wary of using these racial categories without thoughtful consideration of the ways in which race continues to be culturally, politically, socially, legally and economically constructed. It is also ironic that white and coloured nationalist interest groups employ the same categories used to reinforce the apartheid state's logic of racial segregation to assert that they are being marginalised, while the empirical data clearly undermine their claims. Citizens in the African/black category make up 64.2 per cent of people living in poverty, coloured citizens make up 41.3 per cent, while Indian/Asian make up 5.9 per cent and white South Africans account for just 1 per cent. The figures for African/black citizens are dismal, while the figures for citizens in the coloured category are also cause for concern. While the disparity between coloured subjects and those in the African/black category is significant, it is also apparent that citizens who fall in both categories have a great deal more in common when it comes to class struggles – this has not changed since the decline of legislated apartheid. In effect, the commonalities along class lines make Steve Biko's (1978: 48) definition of Black Consciousness compelling:

> We have defined blacks as those who are by law or tradition politically, economically and socially discriminated against as a group in the South African society and identifying themselves as a unit in the struggle towards the realisation of their aspirations.

This definition illustrates to us a number of things:

» Being black is not a matter of pigmentation – being black is a reflection of a mental attitude.

» Merely by describing yourself as black you have started on a road towards emancipation, you have committed yourself to fight against all forces that seek to use your blackness as a stamp that marks you out as a subservient being.

Biko rejected biologically essentialist conceptions of race; instead, he recognised that race serves political and economic functions in a capitalist economy and that it is shaped by these factors. The assertion of blackness is therefore a political one that rejects the internalisation of racist interpellation and dehumanisation, as theorised by Frantz Fanon in *Black Skins, White Masks* (1967). Biko therefore calls for solidarity between diverse black communities in efforts to oppose racism and systemic processes of marginalisation. His work is thus essential in a context where racial divisions endure and where racialised class inequalities continue to shape the spaces that citizens occupy as well as relationships between communities that still view each other along apartheid-defined racial lines. Further, Biko contends that blackness reflects one's mental attitude and that one's emancipation comes from within. This resonates with Hip Hop's conception of Knowledge of Self – freedom and creativity come from critical introspection and self-affirmation before engaging any given context critically or creatively.

Returning to POC's sample of Mandela's historic speech, it is clearly ironic. Their album was banned for advancing a revolutionary message that rejected calls for reconciliation when they rapped lines such as 'Forgive and forget?/Naa! It's easier said than done 'cause you stole the land from the black man'. The issue of the land and restorative and distributive justice, along with critical reflections on state violence and repression, are key themes that run throughout the album – and this book. These themes prefigure current debates about gentrification, land reclamation, the assassination of social movement activists, political activists' so-called 'land invasions', state repression of protests in places like Marikana, various township service delivery protests and university protests, the latter having been the site of movements like Fees Must Fall in recent years. A quarter of a century after making it, Mandela's statement, 'Never again', serves to highlight these failures of the state. The oppression of one by another is being experienced again. It is happening again in service of white global capital privilege at the hands of the black elite, 'whose mission has nothing to do with transforming the nation; it consists, prosaically of being the transmission line between the nation and a capitalism, rampant though camouflaged' (Fanon 1968: 122).

Despite these challenges, Hip Hop artists and activists are exercising their creative and political agency on stage, in the studio, on social media, in workshops, classrooms, panel discussions and in any other available learning space, much like they did in the late 1980s and early 1990s. As we witness throughout the pages of this book, Hip Hop plays a key role in assisting them to redefine themselves on their own terms as well as to renegotiate their relationship with spaces, institutions and hierarchies that position them in ways that potentially limit their agency. Perhaps it is in this regard that the appellation 'never again' rings true on an aspirational level. Thanks to transgressive countercultures such as Hip Hop, black subjects (in the inclusive Biko sense of the term) should never again be silenced by repressive practices.

OUTLINE OF THE BOOK

This book includes photographic work by Ference Isaacs to present examples of the visual and performative modalities of Hip Hop. It also includes images supplied by Emile Jansen and Heal the Hood, given their intimate relationship with artists and activists over the years. In this regard, the book is also associated with music produced by a collective of Hip Hop and jazz musicians who call themselves #IntheKeyofB. The recording project began as a community event that was produced by former Brasse Vannie Kaap (BVK) b-boy, Bradley Lodewyk (aka King Voue), to lay claim to his neighbourhood, Bonteheuwel, as a creative space in the face of ongoing gang violence and negative press coverage that largely associated it exclusively with violent crime. The recording project led to the production of an extended play (EP), co-produced by Gary Erfort (aka Arsenic), Lodewyk and Adam Haupt, and explores themes such as gun violence, toxic masculinity, racialised poverty, racism, gentrification, government corruption, and language and identity politics. Many of these themes speak to aspects of the book and feature a range of MCs as well as instrumentalists who perform jazz and R&B. The project is unique because it brings Hip Hop artists both into the studio with and onto the same stage as instrumentalists and singers from other genres. Despite the key artistic differences in this collective, all artists have one thing in common: they are from the Cape Flats, a space that has hegemonically been represented in racially stereotypic ways. In many respects, this creative collaboration defies those stereotypes.

The other parts of the book are introduced below.

PART ONE: Bring that beat back: Sampling early narratives

The chapters in Part One provide a decolonial perspective on our present times. Hip Hop is intricately bound up with the story of enslavement and colonisation and is profoundly political. It has been politicised from its inception and its precursors, the cultural practices that preceded Hip Hop, are signifyin(g), as Henry Louis Gates Jr theorises it in his books *The Signifying Monkey* (1988) and *Figures in Black* (1987). Signifying and playing the dozens. Verbal insults, verbal duelling, wordplay, the punchline – all of these things are not actually specifically Hip Hop cultural practices; they precede Hip Hop. They come from playing the dozens.

POC ALL ELEMENTS JAM | Source: Ference Isaacs

In this section, there is a strand of Hip Hop activism that is closely tied to the black nationalist narrative associated with places like the South Bronx, narratives that played an important role in uniting people across a range of boundaries in South Africa. Blackness became a unifying signifier that brought together people who were undermined, who were exploited and marginalised by colonialism. Black nationalism unified diverse groups under a broad, inclusive banner of blackness. Thus, if in Cape Town, for example, the apartheid state positioned people as either coloured or black (Zulu, Xhosa or Sotho), black nationalist narratives rejected what they viewed as 'divide-and-conquer' strategies by, as Public Enemy's Chuck D famously rapped, 'the powers that be'. For many Hip Hop heads at the time, even if they self-identified as coloured, they also recognised themselves as being part of the broader black experience – that is, colouredness was viewed within the spectrum of blackness, not separate from or superior to blackness.

In reading the chapters in Part One, it becomes evident how groups like Prophets of da City, Black Noise and Godessa were able to tap into the concept of Knowledge of Self as they developed their various Hip Hop artistic practices. The chapters not only inform the reader about the importance of Knowledge of Self, and Hip Hop art and activism, but they do so while exploring the role of the DJ, MC, dancer and graffiti writer. The aesthetics of Hip Hop are not separate from its politics. In fact, as Tricia Rose argues (ironically, in 1994), the aesthetic is political in Hip Hop because Hip Hop privileges black cultural priorities where whiteness insists on hearing only 'black noise'.

The insightful interviews conducted by Adam Haupt with the pioneering artists of South African Hip Hop open up a range of conversations about life under apartheid, and the role Hip Hop played in the development of a distinctly local style that served to celebrate life under, as well as resist, those oppressive conditions. Interviews with POC, and pioneering DJs Azuhl and Eazy, demonstrate that while often DJs are the most underrated standard-bearers of Hip Hop, they nevertheless push the culture to sample new ways of art(ing) and engaging in activism. From developing a new performance of 'baby scratch', 'landing a toe' and 'nose on vinyl', to new ways of sampling, the DJ is, as DJ Ready D explains, invested in the advancement of Knowledge of Self and focused on dispelling ignorance through performance. While the MC's job is to advance Hip Hop through the word, what is clear from the interviews is that DJs are also known for their lyrical ingenuity and linguistic creativity. This interplay between the DJ and the MC – both functioning as ethnographers of Hip Hop culture, if you will – is produced through various artistic genres and modes that both archive and evolve particular politics and knowledges. A prime example of this kind of artistic work – this aesthetic activism of sorts – is Godessa's pioneering music and lyricism. As an all-woman Hip Hop crew, they not only contested the sexual politics of Hip Hop, but also challenged sexism, racism and classism in the broader society.

Today, breakdancing is a dominant element of South African Hip Hop. This is in no small part due to the exhaustive efforts of Heal the Hood, and its pioneer Emile YX?. In a trailblazing chapter about the history and future of breakdancing as a Hip Hop element, Emile YX? demonstrates vividly that South African Hip Hop developed into a versatile culture during apartheid, producing new genres of breakdance pops, locks, top rocks, and contemporaneously krumping or jerking, while uniting diverse participants into inclusive dance circles, and conceiving of this circular arrangement as a metaphor for social inclusion. The future of Hip Hop culture in South Africa, as Emile YX? points out, will require the next generations to redouble their activism by putting thought into action.

The photographic work about Mak1One's graffiti, compiled by Ference Isaacs (with assistance from Heal the Hood) and interspersed throughout the book, reintroduces the reader to the multimodality of graffiti, the one element of Hip Hop that through pictures has always conscientised the larger South African public. Graffiti artists provide a stylistic image comprising icons and figures, guiding the viewing public toward the stylistic repertoires and political messages of Hip Hop art and activism. And nowhere is this made clearer than in the ALKEMY interviews that Haupt conducted with Nazli Abrahams and Shaheen Ariefdien.

The graffiti artist is, like every participant in Hip Hop, self-critical and self-reflexive about the objects in their 'throw-ups' and 'pieces', focusing always on stylistic clarity but subtly (or explicitly) underwritten by challenging symbolic power. Graffiti artists are concerned with a Hip Hop ethnography of ocular aesthetics: how to conduct research from an empty canvas to producing a beautiful graffiti piece that stimulates our visual repertoires. And through this process, graffiti artists paint the diversity of our urban landscapes and provide the air to Hip Hop art and activism as a novelist would.

PART TWO: Awêh(ness): Hip Hop language activism and pedagogy

In an interview with Marlon Burgess (Ariefdien & Burgess 2011: 235), Shaheen Ariefdien said the following in relation to Hip Hop language style and politics:

> [Cape Town] Hip Hop took the language of the 'less thans' and embraced it,
> paraded it, and made it sexy to the point that there is an open pride about
> what constituted 'our' style...to express local reworkings of hip-hop.

These words provide a cogent and concise definition of South Africa's Hip Hop art, activism and education with respect to language. For decades, Hip Hop artists have honed, through individual effort and community gatherings, a South African style of Hip Hop based on 'the language of the "less thans"'. This was an important phase in the localisation of the culture. Once the local scene found its voice, the artists who then became activists both interrogated and embraced the marginality of that voice, and they began to remix and amplify that voice.

But what happens when you really take on the plight of voiceless people, the language of the less thans, and make it form part of the principles and values of your art, activism and education? The chapters in this section, a rich collection of interviews, essays and panel discussions, dig into the linguistic, pedagogical and meaning-making systems of South African Hip Hop culture – not only in various distinctive styles but also reaching across cultural and racial borders to connect with other voiceless people. Contributors open up debates about supporting the culture's multilingual speakers, South African Hip Hop rhyming for a global stage, and methods of developing the agency and voice of the marginalised via transformative language education and policies. Take for example the reflections on South African Hip Hop's multilingual activism, that is, the process of establishing and identifying translingual means to produce new voices. The first few chapters demonstrate that various ways of speaking, used across a variety of languages, spaces and places, can be meaningful tools for empowering people of colour in contemporary South Africa, and for counteracting the raciolinguistic profiling and discrimination faced by many of the nation's citizens in educational and other institutions.

As artists explain in these chapters, historically multilingual activism has always been a feature of South African Hip Hop. It has increased the mobility of Hip Hop artists, and allowed them to transcend borders and boundaries. Often, artists had to move across geographical locations to share in the inter-/cross-cultural voices and speech varieties of their neighbours and other communities. As Alim, Ibrahim and Pennycook (2009) argue in *Global Linguistic Flows: Hip Hop Cultures, Youth Identities, and the Politics of Language*, this kind of linguistic sharing, combined with Hip Hop's demand for linguistic innovation, creativity and a broader 'rule-breaking' ethos that eschews tradition, has made for some unique challenges to education and language policy-makers. Just as artists have and continue to 'remix multilingualism' (Williams 2017), educators will have to develop new, innovative pedagogies that allow communities to sustain these rich, globally influential language practices. Contributors in this part argue for a break from the eradicationist pedagogies of the past (those that erased our language varieties in the name of upward mobility) and a move towards the sustaining pedagogies of the future.

PART THREE: Remixing race and gender politics

What happens when you speak out on racial and gender discrimination through Hip Hop art, activism and education? This question is answered by a number of sharp and critical intersectional reflections by some of South Africa's Hip Hop artists, activists and pedagogues. The chapters provide strategies on how to counter the hegemonic forces of racism, sexism and homophobia and how to challenge discrimination across society. Contributors demonstrate in detail how Knowledge of Self helps keep the oppressive politics of race, class and gender in check. However, as with all cultural practices, inward reflection on race and gender is sometimes overlooked, which is often the case when it comes to gender and sexuality in the male-dominated domains of Hip Hop. Within these pages, however, artists move beyond characterisations of Hip Hop culture as inherently sexist and misogynistic. Artists and activists have begun to take the intersections of race, gender and sexuality seriously and are arguing for a Hip Hop that is inclusive of all bodies: straight, queer, dis/abled and non-binary.

With the success of artists like Andy Mkosi and Dope Saint Jude, along with community-organising efforts by Natasha C Tafari (all featured in this part), among many others, Hip Hop culture continues Godessa's earlier efforts to remix gender mindsets, reframe the way we talk about gender and sexuality, and the way we represent the body. As we witness throughout these pages, a new generation of Hip Hop artists has emerged and is committed to taking an intersectional approach to race, class, gender and sexuality through a re-engagement with the histories and legacies of Hip Hop culture and our broader communities. This powerful, transformative work within Hip Hop has the potential to influence social transformation beyond Hip Hop, for, as Andy Mkosi warns in her interview with H Samy Alim: 'Everywhere you go, all these spaces, they're problematic. We all problematic.'

PART FOUR: Reality check: The business of music

Part Four of the book provides participants' views on the ways in which aspiring artists can navigate careers in a music industry that, historically, has been shaped by unequal relations of power along the lines of race, gender and class, both during and after the colonial era. It ends with a scholarly reflection on the ways in which the challenges in the music industry resonate with those faced by scholars in the academy. Ultimately, foundational changes need to be made on a macroeconomic level to address inequities in both the music industry and the academy. Provocatively, the final chapter in this section argues that the problem of corporate monopolisation in the music industry is similar to the problem of corporate monopolisation of scholarly publishing, to the extent that democratic rights to free speech and academic freedom are undermined. Ultimately, it argues that if calls for the decolonisation of knowledge are to be heeded, knowledge needs to be decommodified.

CONCLUSION

In conclusion, it is important to note that this book is unique precisely because it decentres the voices of the scholars who have long been writing about Hip Hop. This is a first for South African Hip Hop scholarship. The book's multi-genre approach, which arranges writing by theme and not by genre, is intended to decentralise the authority of the scholars in this edited volume – to place academics alongside the contributions of the artists and activists who have cut, mixed and remixed Hip Hop politics, activism and aesthetics to speak to their specific respective locations and agendas. We recognise, as Alim – influenced by Spady's (1991) 'hiphopography' – wrote, that Hip Hop artists are not merely cultural producers and consumers. They 'are "cultural critics" and "cultural theorists" whose thoughts and ideas help us to make sense of one of the most important cultural movements of the late twentieth and early twenty-first centuries' (Alim 2006: 11). This is why we insist on direct engagement with the cultural creators of Hip Hop.

Multiple voices, which appear as authors and co-authors, feature here in the tradition of Hip Hop's polyphonic approach to music production – from the lyricist dropping 16 bars of verse, which feature multisyllabic rhymes that are often intertextual and layered, and who may share a track with other MCs and singers (itself polyphonic); to the producer who samples music and media from a range of sources to create new music and media forms (more polyphony); to the DJ whose turntablism cuts, mixes and scratches a range of sounds and voices to move the crowd (yet more polyphony); to the graff artist whose textual and iconic styles of production often reference a range of media and texts (polyphony of a visual and textual kind, cutting across modalities); and to the breakdancer interpreting and remixing a range of cultural references, histories and dance styles (polyphony in yet another modality).

This volume is therefore like a park jam or block party, bringing together many voices, styles and modalities in ways that can be both celebratory and unpredictable. We have designed it this way in an intentional effort to claim public spaces that appear to be hostile to black, working-class subjects, the academy included. Or better still, as is the case with the #IntheKeyofB EP associated with this book, we present a polyphony of voices and styles in order to sample, cut and remix what counts as scholarship in a context where scholars are debating what it means to decolonise the academy and challenge hegemonic approaches to knowledge production, distribution, teaching and learning. Like the block party and the park jam, this edited volume is meant to produce scholarship that claims hegemonic spaces that are historically hostile to black modes of thought and articulation in an effort to rethink and remix our understanding of scholarship.

REFERENCES

Alim HS (2006) *Roc the mic right: The language of hip hop culture*. New York: Routledge

Alim HS, Ibrahim A & Pennycook A (eds) (2009) Global linguistic flows: Hip hop cultures, youth identities, and the politics of language. New York: Routledge

Ariefdien S & Burgess M (2011) A cross-generational conversation about hip hop in a changing South Africa. In PK Saucier (ed.) *Native tongue: An African hip hop reader*. New Jersey: Africa World Press

Biko S (1978) *I write what I like*. Gaborone: Heinemann

Fanon F (1967) *Black skins, white masks*, trans. Charles Lam Markmann. New York: Grove Press

Fanon F (1968) *The wretched of the earth*, trans. Constance Farrington. New York: Grove Press

Gates HL Jr (1987) *Figures in black: Words, signs, and the 'racial' self*. New York: Oxford University Press

Gates HL Jr (1988) *The signifying monkey: A theory of African-American literary criticism*. New York: Oxford University Press

Haupt A (1996) Stifled noise in the South African music box: Prophets of da City and the struggle for public space. *South African Theatre Journal* 10(2): 51-61

Haupt A (2001) Black thing: Hip-hop nationalism, 'race' and gender in Prophets of da City and Brasse vannie Kaap. In Z Erasmus (ed.) *Coloured by history, shaped by place*. Cape Town: Kwela Books & SA History Online

Haupt A (2008) *Stealing empire: P2P, intellectual property and hip-hop subversion*. Cape Town: HSRC Press

Haupt A (2012) *Static: Race and representation in post-apartheid music, media and film*. Cape Town: HSRC Press

Haupt A, Williams QE & Samy Alim H (2018) It's bigger than hip hop. *Journal of World Popular Music* 5(1): 9–14

Jeffries MP (2011) *Thug life: Race, gender, and the meaning of hip-hop*. Chicago, IL: University of Chicago Press

Rose T (1994) *Black noise: Rap music and black culture in contemporary America*. Middletown, CT: Wesleyan University Press

Spady JG (1991) Grandmaster Caz and a hiphopography of the Bronx. In JG Spady & J Eure (eds) *Nation conscious rap: The hip hop vision*. Philadelphia, PA: Black History Museum Press

Wilkinson K (2018) FACTSHEET: South Africa's official poverty numbers. *Africa Check*, 15 February. Accessed September 2018, https://africacheck.org/factsheets/factsheet-south-africas-official-poverty-numbers/

Williams QE (2017) *Remix multilingualism: Hip hop, ethnography, and performing marginalized voices*. London: Bloomsbury

PART 1

Bring That Beat Back:
Sampling Early Narratives

POC PERFORMING AT THE CAPE TOWN INTERNATIONAL JAZZ FESTIVAL, 2017 | Source: Ference Isaacs

BRING THAT BEAT BACK: SAMPLING EARLY NARRATIVES

The first part of the book samples a look back at Hip Hop dating back to the early 1990s, from Emile YX?'s foundational work with Black Noise and Heal the Hood; Prophets of da City's battles with censorship; DJ Eazy and DJ Azuhl's accounts of how they came to Hip Hop and the mentorship they received from leading Hip Hop figures, such as the late Mr Fat and DJ Ready D; to Godessa's point of entry into a largely male-dominated music scene. A key issue that threads through the interviews, panel discussion and opinion piece in this part of the book is that the artists in question seem to agree about the potential that Hip Hop has for engaging young people critically in their social, economic and political contexts. Another significant aspect of the exchanges here is that many of the early accounts of artists entering the Cape context of Hip Hop is that a great deal of mentoring seems to have taken place, whether informally between established artists and younger Hip Hop enthusiasts, or in formal programmes at Bush Radio or Heal the Hood's projects. While the narratives presented here are not meant to function as a definitive history of Cape Hip Hop activism and art, and while we do not want to reproduce myths of origin, the participants provide meaningful insights into how they came to Hip Hop, grew as artists and young adults and started to explore the ways in which Hip Hop can be employed to engage people both on and off stage. The chapters in this part of the book also offer meaningful insights into questions about agency in a country that grapples with apartheid-era racialised and gendered inequalities. They provide critical perspectives into the failure of the ruling party to develop a schooling system that creates and sustains learning environments that help marginalised youth to overcome dire economic realities. Likewise, the contributors to these chapters also offer the reader insights into the ways in which artists and activists have negotiated poor state support of the arts, arts education and youth development. The accounts by Godessa, Emile YX?, Prophets of da City, DJ Eazy, DJ Azuhl, Nazli Abrahams (ALKEMY) and Shaheen Ariefdien (ALKEMY) provide essential reading for practitioners, policy-makers, scholars and artists who would like to gain a sense of how Cape artists have exercised agency in the face of severe systemic limitations. They also provide essential reading for newer generations of

LEGENDARY POC READY TO PERFORM AT CAPE TOWN INTERNATIONAL JAZZ FESTIVAL, 2017 | Source: Ference Isaacs

Hip Hop heads who may not be aware of Hip Hop's long contribution to public discourse on South Africa's transition to democracy, as well as the role of heads who played a key part in co-creating Hip Hop culture in the Western Cape.

What is worth noting is that the chapters speak to a period from the late 1980s/early 1990s and into the early 2000s as Hip Hop scholarship was taking shape in South Africa. During the late 1990s and early 2000s particularly, European, British and American scholars began to take an interest in African Hip Hop, whilst a fairly small number of Africans were writing about this area of research. Much the same is true of South African scholars – very few postgraduates were researching Hip Hop at doctoral level. It was for this reason that Adam Haupt's (2015) and Quentin Williams's (2012) PhD research on Hip Hop was significant, both being South African scholars located at South African universities, as opposed to institutions located in the global North. For both scholars, it was important to push the boundaries of their respective disciplines on their own terms from the position of the global South. For both, questions persisted about whether developing research interests in Hip Hop was viable as a career path; they pushed through regardless, and began to lay the foundations for collaboration. These collaborations took the form of an online project named Staticphlow, lectures, workshops, a special issue of the Journal of World Popular Music (2018) with H Samy Alim, and this book project.

LOREN HENDERSON, AFRICAN HIP HOP INDABA, 2011 | Source: Ference Isaacs

CHAPTER 1.
POWER TO THE PEOPLE:
AN INTERVIEW WITH PROPHETS
OF DA CITY IN 1994

DJ READY D AND SHAHEEN ARIEFDIEN WITH ADAM HAUPT

Adam Haupt and Soraya Abdulatief interviewed Prophets of da City (POC) in 1994 after their third album, *Age of Truth*, was banned. The interview is Haupt's first point of contact with the crew as he commenced postgraduate research on Cape Hip Hop. This interview vindicated Haupt's hypothesis that Cape Hip Hop was becoming a meaningful tool for political self-expression and for challenging the ways in which the apartheid state had positioned black and coloured subjects. For Haupt, this moment was a key turning point as a postgraduate student in English Literature. This research helped to establish South African Hip Hop as a viable field of research, regardless of disciplinary location.

Adam: What do you think about the South African music industry at this point; has it changed?

DJ Ready D: Well, the South African music industry is fucked up, and it hasn't changed one bit and everything has become worse. I mean, just looking at the way using POC as an example…and the experiences we had with a record company…I don't wanna mention names, but we were just totally…

Shaheen: Tusk.

DJ Ready D: Ja…

Adam: What happened?

Shaheen: Fuck pop, ja. I mean, you know to me I don't mind fusing music. I actually think fusing music is actually brilliant because, why, if you can fuse let's say reggae with jazz with Africa music with whatever, I think it's cool to just like mixing cultures and stuff like that. But as soon as the pop element comes in then it fucks everything up, you know what I mean, 'cause that, means that…that there is more gimmicks involved, there's more like marketing strategies and shit involved. They taking the what you ma call it out of the music, the art out of the music. It's just now product, basically. You know what I mean, that's fucked up.

DJ Ready D: And we not only speaking from a POC point of view. We speaking about jazz as well, about African music.

Shaheen: Reggae.

DJ Ready D: Reggae even, you know. They basically suffering the same things and are gonna suffer the same things. So we believe that [the] record company out now and some talent scouts or search or whatever…and if we can just warn those people, watch out. Or just watch your backs, you know, get yourself a lawyer or whatever when dealing with these people, you know, just to secure yourself as well and then just study the contracts, whatever. Just do what you think is best for you and just watch out 'cause there is a lot of snakes within the South African music industry, you know, because they are always dictating to people. If you, if you, even if you look at the TV, you see something like Snoop Doggy Dogg on TV, so when someone else comes around and says, 'Okay you gotta educate yourself.' They quick to ban the shit, but they quick to put someone on who speaks about bitches and hoes slapping bottoms and shooting niggas. Stuff like that…that just goes to show the type of mentality. So as long as they can just clock the capital, just make money they don't give a fuck…They don't believe in putting money into an artist…

Shaheen: Ja, ja, you check what happens normally. Let's say whoever Tusk or whatever… they get a package from overseas whether it be, uhm, George Benson or whatever they get the video they get the masters types you know what I mean, they get their photos they get the whole shit so all they have to do is go to the SABC [South African Broadcasting Corporation], go radio, go to the media blah, blah, blah, blah with local artist you need to put money into them you know what I mean, you need to be there, have their backs, the music videos the, the, the recording costs or whatever you know what I mean and they just a bunch a lazy-ass motherfuckers, you know what I mean.

Adam: Can I ask you about your experiences with the SABC, especially in that regard? What was the last video who had…?

Shaheen: Banned.

Adam: …banned.

Shaheen: Uhm, *Understand Where I'm Coming From*. That was from the what you ma call it album, *Age of Truth*, and that was even released in an overseas compilation realised by Tommy Boy and shit was playing out there in the world and that shit was banned here.

Adam: Did they give you a reason?

Shaheen: Okay, wait, the first time we had something banned…Okay, on the first album, they didn't wanna play 'Roots', hey, 'cause you know because that was a black upliftment, a black pride type of song. They didn't wanna play it, they didn't give no reason, you know what I mean, and…and, okay, on the what you ma call it album, *Boom Style*, it was 'Ons Stem' because we used 'Die Stem' and we fucked around with it, you know what I mean. So the SABC the, the, censorship board, sent us this letter: they disgusted at the way we disrespected the national anthem and shit. We just laughed at the letter. We didn't even take that shit seriously. We were just like, 'Yeah, whatever, whatever.' And then off *Age of Truth*, I mean a whole bunch of songs, I mean…
Ja. You must check man the SABC…they got a CD there and the amount of stickers next to the songs…They have this avoid stickers like to avoid the songs because of whatever like avoid, avoid, avoid, avoid…We were like, 'fuck!' Now where's the, you know, like, 'Can you play…Oh, okay. Look there. Oh, like look here.' You know what I mean? So to us it was like, damn, you know this is like supposed to be the new South Africa. They, they said, the first time they banned it was, they said that…

DJ Ready D: The images.

Shaheen: Ja, the images promoted violence and shit like that. And we took news material, I mean shit that actually happened. I mean there was no, uhm, acting and shit like that, the whole shit was…

DJ Ready D: It's like a documentary.

Shaheen: Ja, a reminder, look to the believer. Whatever's in the lyrics is portrayed on the screen and after the whole elections, whatever, our manager went back like to appeal this shit again to, to get the shit played on TV. So they said, '*Naai* [No], we still not gonna play it.' So what's your reason? What was the reason?

DJ Ready D: Uhm, they don't ban things no more. They just don't play it, to sum it all up.

Shaheen: I don't know, man. They covering their backs, I don't know.

DJ Ready D: Just to sum it all up, that video was banned in the old South Africa and it's being banned in the new South Africa and, I don't know. So hopefully the album we just completed…they gonna play it because this album is more relaxed, you know. We just hope they gonna put the album out because basically what I can guarantee you basically is that the next album we gonna do, I'm sure the motherfuckers are gonna definitely ban that shit again.

Adam: Do you think that, do you think that censorship boards should be, uhm, scrapped? Do you think some alternative should be…?

DJ Ready D: All that people on the censorship board are all over 40 year old; they don't know what's down on the street level with modern pop music, whatever the case might be, even to a certain extent modern art because I mean things are constantly changing. People got different ways and terms of expressing themselves…

Shaheen: Ja, and interpreting things.

DJ Ready D: So I mean that's still part of the legacy of the old South Africa. I mean dictating to people what they should see what they should listen to, you know. Maybe one day they gonna come and make a law: you shouldn't sit like this on the toilet. You should maybe, you should put your head in the pot and shit like that, you know. If they don't catch you doing that, they gonna give your ass a fine. That is basically what it boils down to, basically still dictating to people, still doing the old South African shit. I mean, they basically undermined intelligence, whatever the case may be. If you know you don't wanna listen to something, you don't wanna see that, leave it alone. Simple as that, you know I mean. You can maybe warn people. Okay uhm. This most probably won't be right for a kid under the age, whatever the case might be, and then…

Shaheen: Age restrictions, ja.

DJ Ready D: Okay, cool. I'm down with age restrictions. You can understand that shit, but don't ban the shit. I mean, it's up to you to come there and decide what you wanna listen to or not. I mean otherwise it's just like some mother acting like a grandmother, grandfather, mother or father telling you, 'Look here, you not allowed to do this you not allowed to do that, don't take that, don't take this. We want this for you 'cause we think it's best.'

Shaheen: And you know what's fucked up? Because they keep this shit away, the shit becomes big, you know what I mean? I mean there is a lot of shit that, that they say, '*Naai, naai.* This shit's fucked up.' It's like the whole *Body Count* thing with Ice T.

DJ Ready D: Ja.

Shaheen: I mean there was whole shit on his ass and 'Cop Killer' and shit like that. The album sold because of the controversy, because they didn't want people to listen to it, so kids went out there and people were like, 'Okay, okay, what the fuck's this?' So they playing themselves.

Adam: Do you think the same thing happens in this country? I mean your videos didn't get airtime and…

Shaheen: No, no. South Africa, they control shit like this, you know what I mean. They control the radio station, TV station, media, boom, boom, boom, boom. They cut your ass off and they programme the audience. If something doesn't come on TV, then the shit doesn't count anyway, you know what I mean. So your ass gotta be on TV or somehow in some spotlight or whatever in some high-profile shit before people take note of you because they programme the audience as well. Do you think your Kylie Minogues and all that shit sells because the shit is creative or artistic? The shit gets forced down the people's throats; they got no other choice. This is the shit, this is the shit you have your radio…All over you see this thing; you bound to say, 'Okay, this is the shit.' If you even look at the mind states of the people, you know what I mean…the way we being programmed. I mean if you look at South Africa, even the audience themselves, we being programmed, man. You go to Joburg and places, the amount of cover bands there are in South Africa, man. Damn, it's frightening, man, and some of those bands they got their own material that's nice man. It's because the people are programmed and shit like that and people on top are dictating to them boom, boom, boom, boom, boom, boom. So now you gotta do your own shit or whatever gotta…Start playing some fucked-up shit on stage because you know because of whatever, you know what I mean. I mean the mind states gotta change. They gotta reprogramme the people man, you know what I mean, to respect other music and stuff as well. I mean when we went to Demark…It's a small-ass country, man, a small-ass country in Europe. I mean, damn, I mean when we went there we were like, fuck, they gonna have Hip Hop here. There's people, man…the same person who's heavy into Hip Hop, heavy into rock, heavy into reggae, heavy into jazz. You don't have that shit here in this country because people aren't exposed to those things. That's why you can have people either just into Hip Hop, just into rock, just into pop and just into some house shit, you know, whatever, I mean. Because people don't get exposed to things to say, 'Okay, this is good, this is good.' So…you know my taste in music is therefore not my taste in jazz only, not my taste in pop only, you know what I mean. So I think people need to be reprogrammed.

Adam: So what is your position right now? The ANC [African National Congress] is in power. You say nothing has changed with the music industry. You say nothing has changed with the SABC. Do you think that change…?

Shaheen: I think that in the SABC there is a couple of people who's got a little power now who's on the right track, you know. I think it's the motherfuckers on top there…

DJ Ready D: The one who's above them…

Shaheen: There the shit should happen because I mean I know people at Radio Metro and whatever that I've met, like producers, who's down with the programme, who support like local music and want to support black artists and stuff like that as well. And I'm glad to see that, you know what I mean, but it's still who's on top, man, 'cause I mean you can say your shit or stand for whatever at the bottom, you know. But if they cut your ass off and whatever and blah, blah and blah, blah, you know what I mean, a little is gonna get done as well the people right on top that's where the shit should happen also and to us shit has gotta change and people's gotta go for self as well, you know. Go do your own shit don't rely on…

DJ Ready D: 'Cause what we are basically saying is to the kid in the street, if you wanna call it, the people at the bottom is…you gotta work your ass to the top and knock that motherfucker off 'cause he's making all the decisions. He's dictating your life. He's playing you like puppets. So I mean, if you look at the situation, things didn't change because we still have people calling themselves coloureds and they proud of that shit. We still have people believing they a kaffir. They still a couple of levels below the white man and shit like that, you know. So as long as we got those problems, things are always gonna be fucked up, you know. I mean these white motherfuckers, they basically know us. They know our habits. They study our asses 'cause that is the only…they can control and dictate so until basically we can understand that and rise above that shit and we can basically say there is changes. Because as long as we trapped in the townships with gangsterism, fucking shebeens, drug dealers, corrupted police, fucked-up politicians, inexperienced people to deal with public relations and shit like that, inexperienced social and welfare workers and all that shit, we still trapped. We still trapped in the ghetto. We trapped in the township and that's no change because to me straight up I don't care if some French president white motherfucker comes and switches on electricity for 70 000 people. What the fuck's that? It just means that now they can use a stove and now they can switch their heater on in winter, but still their mentality…they are still crippled upstairs. So as long as your mental state is fucked up it doesn't matter whether you got electricity, whether you got a fucking BM [BMW], whether you got money, whether you got this, whether you got that. But if you crippled upstairs, you fucked for life. You can forget about it.

Adam: Can you tell me about the Rapping for Democracy tour?

Shaheen: Voter education, ja.

Adam: Did you use anything from *Age of Truth*?

Shaheen: We used 'Understand Where I'm Coming From', yeah, 'Power to the People'. You see, to us it was really important that kids know as well at the same time you know we support the whole voting thing and whatever. I mean people been dying, people been detained for all of that shit you know. At the same time, if you vote, it doesn't mean that your ass has got to be just about forgiving or whatever. One of the reasons I voted was to get that assholes out of power, you know what I mean. So whether the people wanna look at it and say you went around to schools and told people to vote…Ja, we went around. People should vote, you know, if you unhappy with whoever is in power, do that shit, you know what I mean. Use that x that you got. *Yakit* [Write it/put it] on a piece of paper. Get whoever the fuckers in power…if you don't want them there, get them out of there, you know what I mean.

Adam: So you don't think it was a contradiction?

Shaheen: No, not at all. I wouldn't say that at all because, I voted. I know who I voted for, you know what I mean, to get their ass out of power. Their ass is out of power, you know what I mean. So whoever fucks up now, you know, use that shit. Boom! Get them out of power if they fuck up, you know what I mean.

Adam: So if the ANC fucks up, would you vote to get them out of power?

Shaheen: Yes, why not? I mean the truth is impersonal. Just because…why their ass got credibility and shit like that doesn't make them infallible, you know what I mean. Just because blah and blah and blah…I mean if you – I think they actually got a lot of pressure on them, you know what I mean, because why they gotta rectify all that shit that was done by the NP [National Party].

DJ Ready D: They basically gotta clean up the slave master's shit because that's what the new South Africa is about. Some white motherfucker came along. He came all over the country and now you gotta stand with a fucking mop and broom.

Shaheen: And you know what's the fucked-up part to me, to be honest? I voted and all of that. What's the most fucked up part is that there is still NP motherfuckers that's got positions. Still this puppet-ass motherfuckers that played their own people, you know what I mean. Who? What's this dude's name? Patrick McKenzie…

DJ Ready D: Ja.

Shaheen: I mean, I don't know what the fuck they doing in there man, really man.

DJ Ready D: And he's got a position in the police. No wonder those fucking cops are still corrupt and shit because those are the motherfuckers who can't put their foot down and say who, who and who, get the fuck out because you corrupt. I mean if you wanna be a minister of a law and order, whatever they call those motherfuckers, you gotta do a job. You got a responsibility to, don't say you gonna look into the matter and investigate it or fucking send it to the higher court or whoever's above and discuss it. If you hear about it, you gotta be on that shit today 'cause every single day people are dying. They are still dying at the hands of the police because the fucking police are gangsters in the township. They fucking drug-dealing shebeen runners. They fucking doing all the crazy shit, you know. No wonder the gangsters can get away with anything because they have total support from the police. And I mean, if you a minister or whatever the case might be, it's your fucking job to make sure those things are rectified and that the police are there to protect us, not to gangbang against our asses. So that's also one of the things deteriorating the situation and the relations with the police…I mean they put across this whole friendly image: 'We playing with the children, we coming, we give you food stamps.' Fucking help paint the township. Fuck that. We don't wanna see that. You gotta work your ass and fucking protect us from these gangsters and shit. Some of these motherfuckers, you know, this Western Cape Patrick McKenzie, whoever the fuck he is, he's not doing his job properly. He can get the fuck out.

Shaheen: And to me that's a bad *gedagte* [idea] just for justice, you know. It's that people can get away if they fucked up in the past. They still got positions and stuff like that, so justice and equality, that shit does not mean a lot in South Africa.

DJ Ready D: So if I come along tomorrow and shoot a motherfucker in the head, they gonna hang my ass. But, I mean, all these guilty motherfuckers, they still got positions in government. So it's just like forgive and forget. I'm your brother now, you know, and they were responsible for the death of millions, millions and millions of innocent people, blacks, whites, coloured, Indians whatever the fuck may be. Ja and, like he says, they still got positions there, so I mean what are we actually talking about?

Shaheen: And what's scary to me, those are people who have had power for a very long time, you know, and they probably know all the ways and means to fuck all the red tape… They probably got their millions stashed away. I won't be surprised if there is still CCB [Civil Cooperation Bureau, a covert apartheid intelligence entity] shit going on.

Adam: About the album *Age of Truth*, what were you trying to do with it? Correct me if I'm wrong, but it's radically different from what you done before at all.

Shaheen: Uhm, yes and no, yes and no. Okay, musically I would say that, that it's different from anything we done before, but then again, so was *Boom Style* different to *Our World*, you know what I mean. And we just felt, fuck that. We gonna do a Hip Hop album, lyrically, musically, you know what I mean, and at the time it was crucial because we could see our people were suffering from amnesia that time already, you know. Forgiving shit just like that so we were like okay the elections are coming up. A reminder is good to the believer, you know. There is a lot of shit and all of that. I mean, you look at the outcome of the elections even just in Cape Town. It really hurt us, so we were just saying whatever we felt at the time. I mean we would programme a beat and we just in the studio: 'Okay, what do you feel? Just write what you feel. Okay let me write.' There was no concept thing behind this shit and whatever, you know, there wasn't a whole lot of planning involved. It was just whatever we felt at the time because I mean there was a lot of anger as well and stuff like that. So to us it was just about saying whatever we feel 'cause I mean, there is [a] lot of artists or in the artist field who feel the same way, you know, but due to censorship and people in power whatever, they got to tone down their shit, you know what I mean, and to us it was like, '*Naai*, it can't go on like this.'

Adam: I spoke to some people and they said *Age of Truth* is so American. It's so Public

Enemy. It's so like harping back to that sort of hard core rap kinda stuff. How do you repond to the charge that it's so American?

Shaheen: Ja, ja, I fully understand. I won't say it at all. I mean, if there is any reference… if the shit sounds, if we talk about police or whatever sounds like Public Enemy, I would say what the fuck. They probably suffering from the same shit, you know what I mean. That means we can relate to whatever. I mean if they have police brutality, we have police brutality. So if we talk about police brutality, does it make us sound like, you know what I mean. I think fuck that 'cause why I mean if you even look at the music on the album – that time everyone was tripping off this Naughty by Nature type of thing, the leader of the new school, we were like, 'Aah, no we not gonna go into that shit because that's like that flavour of the month type of sounds.'

DJ Ready D: Even like sounding Public Enemy or whatever the case might be, if you listen to the accent, listen to the sound of the music, you just listen to the samples, you listen to the way the production is put together, it's definitely not Public Enemy because Public Enemy came out with all the screeches and Flavor Flav shouting over every track, 'Yeah, boyee,' and that shit…

Shaheen: Ja, I think people tend to generalise when you have a message, you know what I mean, or you have some shit to say…

DJ Ready D: Ja, we speaking about our experiences, the way we see things…

Shaheen: And we went through some shit on that album, I mean damn, hey.

Adam: Tell us about that.

Shaheen: I mean we were just finished recording. The day we left, the master types were confiscated.

DJ Ready D: From the recording studio…

Adam: The recording studio?

Shaheen: The recording studio.

Adam: Why?

Shaheen: 'Cause why, we recorded at BOP Studios. That's like the best studio with the best facilities in like South Africa, in Africa for that matter. Apparently, they got the best equipment in the world, so we were recording there, 'cause why, lucky we came up with some shit to record there, uhm whatever…It was like, 'Sure, we record here, but still fuck him,' you know what I mean. 'Cause we want the best product available. I mean even if we record it in South Africa – I mean it's still South Africa, but I mean Joburg or Cape Town – we will still say fuck the NP or fuck FW [de Klerk], you know what I mean. It doesn't matter where. So when they heard that shit, they heard some shit we were saying on the album and all of that they were like, 'Ah, ah, ah, we can't have this.'

Adam: So how did you get it back?

Shaheen: We stole it. We stole the shit back, man. So we had to come with some other shit there and negotiate and shit like that. We were like, fuck that, you know what I mean. And then there was the whole censorship board thing. I mean, they banned tracks without any actual lyrics on it. I mean like instrumental type of tracks. So they banned that shit. It was fucked up. I mean, when we had to go through uhm; when we went on air, when we went to Tusk and all of that we were like, 'Okay if we gonna do interviews or whatever, you know what's said on the album. You know what we stand for, we gonna say our thing. Is that cool?' Cool. We on this radio interview once in Joburg and this one dude of, uhm, Tusk was along. We were like, 'Okay we gonna say our shit.' And blah, blah and blah. We were gonna play 'Dallah Flet'. In the last verse of 'Dallah Flet' we warning people against the NP and the whole apartheid era – that shit, you know. So we were like, 'Okay we gonna play that shit on air. So if they press play, we just gonna try to start talking to the interviewer and stuff like that so they don't listen to the lyrics.' So just start talking and they forget about the lyrics and shit. You know how they are. So they press play and we gonna start talking and we gonna keep them busy. So they press play and this dude is like, 'Yo, yo, don't try and fuck this shit up and blah and blah.' We were like, 'Fuck this. You know what the album is about, you know what we stand for and stuff.' The dude walked away! He walked away, went to don't know where, heard the interview and shit and came back, he was like, 'I'm not responsible for this shit,' you know. You supposed to have our back if you believe in the artists and you believe…I mean, we didn't come to them and propose, 'Give us some money to record an album.' We came with the master types, they heard the album, they were jumping up and down, you know what I mean. We had like – from the censorship board, uhm, from family members to friends and all that shit that bombed us about certain things. We said on the album, you know what I mean. Like, how the fuck can you say this shit, and this shit and this shit. We like, you know the thing is you either agree or you don't agree. You see, there is a lot of people, artists and stuff whose got shit to say, you know, but it's, because why, a lot [of] people – they wanna be praised and stuff like that. They wanna get their props and shit. They don't wanna go against the grain or not go with the flow type of shit, you know, and it's because why, they probably don't want no enemies in the industry and stuff like that. I mean, fuck, the industry itself is basically the enemy.

DJ Ready D: But now you got this record company, ridiculous publishing shit where you gotta pay like thousands of rands just to use a sample, and I mean Hip Hop is basically about fusing all types of stuff – scratching, you know, mixing, that is what basically Hip Hop is about. So you get this white motherfuckers doing all sorts of ridiculous shit and, at the end of the day, they just say its business, you know. And I mean, fuck that, if someone wants to come along and sample our record, it's fine by me. It's cool, sample whatever the fuck you wanna sample because, it just goes to show, they respect the music. Our music has some sort of influence or encouragement on the artists that want to use it, you know it.

Shaheen: What is strange to me, first of all, is that people call Hip Hop American because it started in the Bronx and stuff like that. That shit comes from Africa way back, you know. And even if they wanna argue that shit started in America, it's not American. It's African because it was started by African kids. Whether you call them African American, they are African kids. They were stolen from Africa, brought to America, you know. Bob Marley said that shit. So they are African kids, so that shit is African, you know what I mean. You can look at it from that angle. The shit's African. That's why we can relate to it here, you know what I mean. It's about Hip Hop is just about expressing yourself. It's ghetto language, it's township vibe, you know what I mean. There's everything in there that kids can relate to.

You don't need blond hair, straight hair, light skin, rich ass, nice car, Ford, Ray Ban-wearing, leather jacket shit. It's about being yourself, it's about, uhm, doing your shit, saying your shit, you know what I mean. That's what it is about. As far as this whole publishing thing goes, it's like a whole circle the way I see it. I mean, when jazz started out and all of that, black people created that shit, the soul, the flair was there, you know. They watered the shit down. Even rock and roll – the Chuck Berrys and all that. I mean, if you look at rock and roll, you think rock and roll, you think white music. That to me is fucked up. They steal cultures and, shit, that's why when Vanilla Ice came out, everyone was like, 'Fuck that. We not gonna have that.' At the end of the day, in a couple of years down the line, people gonna look back and say it's white music 'cause that's what happened to rock as well with Jimi Hendrix and all of that people. Like starting the shit, you know, being there on the forefront, they inspired how many white kids?

DJ Ready D: They calling Elvis [Presley] the king of rock. Fucking bullshit.

Shaheen: You know what I mean, fuck that. So now what they doing; so now you sample old shit whether it be soul or rock or whatever. Now you gotta pay the man on top for using that shit whether you use a little sound whatever. If they can hear that shit is from there, even if you change it around and sample it backwards, they want a piece of the pie, you know what I mean. They gonna try to play you. That's why we say fuck all this. Ja, we down with the new South Africa, but we need power, you know what I mean. And I do believe in black cohesion, you know, 'cause I mean if you look at kids at school, the average black girl's room or so-called average coloured girl's room, it's almost guaranteed, if you find posters there, it's gonna be some hunk-ass white motherfuckers with long-ass hair or blue eyes and shit. 'Cause that's what we been told on TV. This is what beauty is, you know what I mean. Your Lux ads are whatever. So you have a *bietjie* [little bit] of *kroes kop* [curly/kinky head] and whatever; fuck, you gonna hate yourself. You gonna think, '*Naai*, I'm not beautiful,' and all this shit. So that's why to us, keep this shit street. Keep the shit where the kids can relate to it. That's why we want to be street. When we do interviews and shit like that, or whatever, and we use like *gamtaal* [Cape Flats Afrikaans dialect] or whatever, that shit's on purpose so the kid at home can say, 'Fuck, they talking my language.' They representing what's coming out of the townships and shit like that. So if some mid-class ass motherfucker thinks *skollie taal* [gangster language], the shit's not for them. This shit's not for them, you know what I mean. I don't care if some white-ass dude at home thinks, 'Oh look at this, you know what I mean, uncultured,' or whatever. Fuck that. I want the kid in the ghetto to say, '*Naai*, we can relate to that.'

POC, ALL ELEMENTS JAM, 2017 | Source: Ference Isaacs

CHAPTER 2.
AGE OF TRUTH:
TWO DECADES OF DEMOCRACY

DJ READY D, SHAHEEN ARIEFDIEN, DJ AZUHL, DJ EAZY
AND ROBYN CONWAY WITH ADAM HAUPT

DJ Ready D, DJ Azuhl, DJ Eazy and Robyn Conway joined Adam Haupt at the University of Cape Town's Summer School Hip Hop activism lectures in 2014 to discuss POC's banned album, *Age of Truth* (1993). Speaking via prerecorded video interview, Conway recalls the circumstances under which she edited the music video *Understand Where I'm Coming From* at the SABC's edit suite in the early 1990s, a context in which the freedom of the press was constitutionally protected. Shaheen Ariefdien's video interview and Ready D's lecture offer some hindsight on their earlier experiences as young artists in a time when Hip Hop was emerging parallel to an emerging democracy.

Adam Haupt: We will discuss *Age of Truth* using the banned video *Understand Where I'm Coming From* as a point of entry. We're going to play the video. Then we're going to cut to an interview with the filmmaker who actually directed and edited the video. I only discovered the director after I wrote a blog about *Age of Truth* for *Thought Leader*.[1] I discovered that very little material about Prophets of the [da] City is actually on YouTube. I obtained the music video for *Understand Where I'm Coming From* about 20 years ago and had it digitised recently. I then decided, 'Well, nobody's actually going to put this up, it has historical value. People should be sharing this.' I uploaded it onto YouTube and wrote an article about it for *Thought Leader* and *Staticphlow*. Robyn Conway then contacted me after reading the article. So that's the story. And then we cut to an interview with Shaheen. Actually Shaheen and Ready D, but, for the interest of time, I cut D out as D's here to speak for himself. So without further ado, I think we should cut to the video to give you a bit of context if you haven't seen it already.

---

1. https://thoughtleader.co.za/about-thoughtleader/

[Plays video: Prophets of da City's *Understand Where I'm Coming From* off *Age of Truth* (1993, Ghetto Ruff). *Age of Truth* was banned during the build-up to South Africa's first democratic elections in 1994. This video is being shared non-commercially due to its historical, cultural and political significance.

An interview with Robyn Conway about the making of Prophets of da City's *Understand Where I'm Coming From* music video in 1993.]

Robyn Conway: I came back when the ANC was unbanned and with the intention of helping prepare for elections. So I was based at Shell House [former ANC head office in Johannesburg] under *bra* Wally's [Serote] team and we had a very difficult agenda, which is hard to actually grasp in this day of, you know…high media, almost a constant stream of media of different flavours that people can choose. We came into an environment where we were a government in waiting in one office block, with no access to the media. In fact, the opposite, with a media that was intent on suppressing our message. So…when Lance [Stehr] approached me, obviously I had to run it past the channels, because they didn't have any budget. I think they had like R2 000, or something like that, and…I got the go-ahead to use the resources that we had to make this video. And, at the time, I mean…what people don't realise is the context. That when you walked into the SABC, there were armed guards…that when you walked into an edit suite, there were guys, armed guards, standing often at the doors…that – there – everybody knew the suites were all bugged, you know. That was the context that you were in and…we had no access to any of the facilities without permissions and paperworks and these kinds of things and we had no access to the archives. So for me to use archive footage in that climate was a statement in itself, because, you know, what's the point of being unbanned if I can't show you *Sharpeville*? Right? So the only way I could show that imagery, was to do it subversively.

So…at the time, [Eddie] Mbalo, who had been in the ANC underground film unit, he had formed the first black-owned production company. There I was, you know, the one white girl, it always was this thing. I was always the one whitey in the black production company [laughing] at the cultural desk, or whatever, and more militant than anyone, this was always the problem. But, anyway, I got Eddie with some of Wally's help, to agree to produce this bloody video. So, it involved like a whole lot of…underground grapevine channels to get that footage out of that archive and into my hands. So we had a whole system that involved the SABC canteen, where we would go into the canteen, we would have put in like an innocuous request for, I don't know, CNN footage on spaceships or whatever. We'd filled out the requisitions, we'd hand it to our guy, and he, of course, would bring me back Steve Biko, or whatever else I wanted. Anyway, this went on for about three weeks. I sat – I couldn't sit and cut that video during working hours, right? Because you had like ears everywhere. You had people everywhere. They would like come and just, oh, open your door, listen to what you are cutting. No, it wouldn't have even seen the light of day. So…I would like sit from like six in the evening 'till six the next morning, or that kind of…shift, to cut the bloody thing. And I liked it rough. Like I liked the rough cut that I'd made and wanted to polish. But there were certain things that I wanted to do with that footage that at that time you couldn't do in a regular edit suite. You needed like the first computerised suite, which at the time, in the SABC, was called Henry. And one of my good friends, Michael Becker, was the main editor of Henry, so a little bit of arm twisting, there we sat three o'clock in the morning again polishing the POC video. And at that time I think Henry was like R5 000 an hour or something like that, which was a huge amount of money at the time. And the irony was that at a similar time I was about to make Johannes Kerkorrel's video, but I spoke no Afrikaans, at all. And there I was doing POC's and Johannes' and not really understanding the language, but understanding their essence, so to speak. So, we polished POC and it had to go to a final mix. And I tried very hard to get the sound dude that I thought was the least, you know, racist, the least inflammable, to book for that final mix, and…he was sick on the day or I can't remember what happened, but I walked into the sound suite, the guy stuck the tape in. We started the first verse. He threw his hands up and said, 'I refuse to cut this. I refuse to mix this.' I won't go into the expletives that he used in Afrikaans [laughing] but just to say that he refused to do the mix. So, Eddie had to pull a few strings. We actually did the sound mix OUTside of the SABC. We had to pay with our own money. We got followed by guards to our cars, with our tape boxes. They were searched. I mean from that moment on, every time we walked into the building, it was an ongoing search. Not to mention that we had people outside of our houses. But I think we always had that because we were working at Shell House so I can't say it was linked [laughing].

Anyway, now we had our little prize. The guys loved it. Wally loved it. And we had to think about how we were gonna get this on air, because what people don't understand is, the media of the country was entirely state-run. So, where am I gonna show you this stuff? Okay, so the guys wrote great tracks; okay, so I made a great video about marching to Pretoria with MK [*uMkhonto we Sizwe*, armed wing of the ANC], but where am I gonna show this thing? And there the kinda underground network again stepped in. Before I knew it, Eddie – one morning I remember waking up and there was *Good Morning South Africa* [TV programme] or something. I can't even remember what it was called. Was it that? *Good morning South Africa*?

Adam Haupt: I know that I saw it on the *Toyota Top 20*.

Robyn Conway: Yes. That was Lawrence [Dube]. But first, it went out on breakfast TV.

Adam Haupt: Good grief.

Robyn Conway: There, over their corn flakes at seven-thirty in the morning, was everybody watching *Understand Where I'm Coming From*, right? 'Cause one of the guys had slipped it into the playlist. When it came to Lawrence, Lawrence and I were like very, very close friends, so you know that was easy. Even though he risked his job in doing that, but I think it's not so much that as youth we were fearless, as much as we were ready to stand up, you know? That was what you were measured by. You were talking about tape measures. In that time, for us as part of the movement, we were measured by being willing to stand up. No one was measuring you sitting down and crumpled.

[Shaheen Ariefdien and DJ Ready D talk about Prophets of da City's banned album, *Age of Truth* (1993).]

Shaheen Ariefdien: When we actually recorded the album, we found out that the reason for BOP's studios to be built was part of the Bophuthatswana's government to kind of – as part of broader publicity, marketing kinda thing. They wanted to present Bophuthatswana as a kind of sovereign state, distanced from South Africa, and so they built the best studio in the southern hemisphere, and the idea was to attract the Michael Jacksons and whatever to record, you know, in, in, in 'the heartbeat of Africa' [mock deep voice], you know, that kind of *kak* [shit]. So this kind of curio shop thingy, where it's like you know, 'Don't look for creativity in the hustle bustle of New York or London.' You know what I mean? 'You wanna come to the home of the drum.' You know all of this kind of curio shop kind of colonial kind of shit. They tried to – tried to attract all the big artists. And they felt that if they recorded there…because they couldn't perform in 'South Africa', you know what I mean, due to the [sanctions] campaign there, that – that it would help boost Bophuthatswana's reputation on the world stage and all of that, so we heard about this while we were recording, and that made it to the lyrics, right? Because Luca – Lucas Mangope was the kind of 'head of phony state'…

DJ Ready D: …so-called president of the puppet states…

Shaheen Ariefdien: Exactly [laughing]. Ja, he was the class prefect [Ready D laughing]. And so, yeah class prefect and so the *gedagte* [thought] there was – in one of our lines we were like, 'Fuck Mangope even if we record here.' You know, that type of – that type of thing. And the guy who ran the studio at the time, like he was fuming. He called the two of us into a meeting. This long-ass table, with all our masters there, the master DATS [Digital Audio Tape master copy] and fortunately we made backups…uhm like second-generation backups of all the mixes. And so Ramone [de Wet] managed to get hold of the box, remember [to Ready D]? Ramone managed to get hold of the box with the, the, the backup mixes, 'cause they held the masters back, and so Ramone managed to grab the *beweging* [DATS/the thing], while they were threatening us with stuff. What was the one thing he *wys'd* [showed] us? 'B-bite the hand that feeds you. Why would you bite the hand that feeds you? Use our studio equip… gear. We give the studio uh to you to use.' So, so basically Mango Groove, us, and I think it was Stimela at the time [to Ready D]? Because Ray Phiri was there, right?

DJ Ready D: Ja.

Shaheen Ariefdien: We could have access to the studio, uhm, at like a *crazy* discounted rate, to, to test out the studios and also to, to, to basically use the music that came outta that to kinda entice the quality of the mixes, and stuff like that, to entice other people to record there as well. So we were kind of like…part of the experimental group. Anyway, so he was like, 'We gave the studio space to you for almost next to nothing and blah blah blah blah blah.' Like, 'How do you explain that to yourself? How do you live with yourself?' And what was the *gedagte* that we said [to Ready D]? 'In the same way Biko and [Nelson] Mandela does when they went to university [laughing] to get that information to flip it.' We were like *kak harregat* [extremely hard-assed]! Yoh, that *bra* was angry, *ne* [to Ready D]? Yoh!

DJ Ready D: Look, here this is a *bra*, a white *bra* who's running the studio. He's just trying to cover his ass.

Shaheen Ariefdien: Ja.

DJ Ready D: That's it. Because he's *bang* [scared] that if Mangope hears the stuff that we are saying, they're maybe gonna send a couple of their…you know, their freakin *manskappe* [men/crew/comrades], raise hell with this *brasse* [brothers/bros]. He was obviously trying to protect his job, and just to cover his own ass as well.

Shaheen Ariefdien: And I think – from what I recall now, I – it's kind of vague, but I think the reason – 'cause we basically *spat* [left/escaped] with the backup masters, right. Uh, 'cause we, remember, we rushed out of that *gedagte* just to get to the border. We were like '*KAP AAN!* [keep going/push hard]' to get to the border of so-called South Africa so they couldn't call in anyone. And I think they didn't make a whole fuss about that 'cause they didn't want that kind of negative publicity, do you know what I mean? To kind of go after us legally or something. I think that's kind of what I recall. BUT – but – so we felt at that time, when the album was released and everything, like 'Okay, *naai* [no], we won this *beweging*', but we really underestimated the relationship between the state and corporations, because what happened was, like, like, like D said, we…every single major festival we were booked on, we were cancelled [makes swooshing sound]. It was, uhm, Mitchells Plain's Musica had like what? Five copies of *Age of Truth* and like 100 copies of Guns and Roses, or something like that. Like you couldn't find it in stores really and we were…it was very difficult to make a living then as Prophets of da City after that album came out because those relationships were very, very, very tight and it was like, 'Okay, you're gonna *dala* [do] that? *Kwaai. Snipe die gedagte* [Cool. Check this response/thought].' So we were in some ways forced to go outside of the country. And I mean – I'm not saying we wanted to be provincial or anything like that. Like you wanna explore the world. But you wanna at least wanted to explore the world on your own terms. And, and, and we made music for the Mitchells Plains and the Gugs [Gugulethu], you know? And the Lavender Hills and the Langas and stuff like that. And to NOT have that kind of engagement or to have that music – have access to our brothers and sisters. Tsk. It was – it was BLIND painful in very many ways.

You know some of us have gotten a lot of flak by negating and rejecting colouredness, you know what I mean? And embracing blackness in the way that we did – that it was like, 'Yoh, you don't have any coloured groups. You have just like this one coloured group that people identify with and like, *jarre* [gee whiz], you're ours and now you *wys* [say] like no coloured.' Like, you know what I mean? It was a – a kind of militancy in the way that we rejected colouredness, that at times was very clumsy in the way that – in the same way that you know like when you get like, uh, uhm some lefties, you know? That are – that are like *lamming* [chilling] with Marx, *en wietie wat alles nie* [and don't know what all], and then they treat other people that might not have read those things almost like, 'Ja, you don't know shit.' You know like that kind of *beweging* [thing/situation/mindset]. Like they were born – they came out [makes crying baby noise]. 'Means of production' or whatever. And not realising you have this…racial category. You know, that was in many ways hammered into people, do you know what I mean? You're talking about parts of history where the conditions under which identities were created was extremely, extremely brutal, and the options people had to counter that were very *zalties* [minimal/difficult] or *dala ma* [go with it, rather].

[Q&A session]

Geneva Smitherman: Just a quick comment. Uhm, I was really drawn to how the issue and 'he is black, he is coloured', I was really drawn to how that thing played out over here.

H Samy Alim: I got a question for, uhm, for the artists and thinking about this – Ready D, specifically. So in Hip Hop in the States at that time, blackness was so front and centre, and black identity was everything. You know, almost every song that you heard, even if it was a song about the club or partying, it had a verse that was about blackness or Africa or something, right? It was about being black. And so I wonder, when we talk about Hip Hop moving all around the world, one thing that I notice, and that scholars write about, is this shifting the way local paradigms of race and constructions of race and systems of race gets shifted through ideologies of race that move in through rap music, you know, or Hip Hop culture, so in what ways were you thinking about – I mean were you thinking about, 'Oh, the US has a different system of racial classification than ours, but let us adopt and adapt blackness to our circumstance'? Or what was the process? Were you thinking about that specifically?

DJ Ready D: Uhm, thank you for that…our connection with Hip Hop as a culture…We – we're sort of from the first generation of Hip Hop heads in South Africa, if you can call it that. So we obviously had quite a deep connection with the likes of Afrika Bambaataa, Afrika, Islam, and, uhm, those types of personalities, using Hip Hop as a medium to broker peace between gangs and that's how the birth of the Zulu Nation sort of came together, and I think that was probably our interpretation of Hip Hop's first entry point into the consciousness realm, and from that we then learned about the Black Panthers, the Five Percenters in New York, as well as the – the Nation of Islam as well and then, uhm, there's various other groups through Hip Hop that were delivering very strong if you wanna call it, uhm, Black Consciousness or proud-to-be-black messages and of course KRS-One with his Temple of Hip Hop and the Stop the Violence movement. We could relate to all of those things, and at one stage we were so deep into what was coming from the US and with Hip Hop stuff that was going through the Black Conscious phase, we were taking a very deep look at ourselves, because at that stage we were trying to emulate what was coming from the US, and at this point in time it was so serious, we thought, 'Well, if the brothers and the sisters in the US are all sporting the African medallions and wearing the dashikis.' And, you know, all those types of energies and messages are coming through…we should actually be taking, uhm, more…we should be taking note of what's taking place right here on our doorstep. We are African, *ne*? So we are being celebrated abroad as well and I think that was the turning point for us. And with, uhm, the country slowly going through this transition, and with the turmoil, the harassment, the flak…uhm, the type of imagery, bombs going off, people being assassinated. You know, that even drew us closer to, if you wanna call it becoming more conscious and aware. So you start reading through the literature. You start coming across, uhm, Marcus Garvey, you start reading, uhm, Steve Biko. You know, guys are pulling literature from all over, there's discussion groups, we had the whole, uhm, uh, lecture sessions where there's like four, five, up to ten of us sitting in my mom's living room on a weekly basis, just trying to get ourselves educated because as we said in the video, we didn't…You can't expect that type of education, uhm, behind the school benches. That was non-existent. You know the type of things that WE were taught, the messages that were…that we were fed, is the thing of us as being inferior because all the images was white. It's the white God, the white Jesus, Boet and Saartjie, Mark and Kathy…those were the type of stories we grew up with from, uh, kindergarten, if you wanna call it that, you know if the – uhm and the level of demoralisation…if I think about it, it's still beyond belief that human beings could actually do that to other people, you know? The way that they, they, they segregated us, right through from your hair texture, the size of your lips, your skin colour. You had to go there and they measure your lips. They would measure and roll their fingers and put pencils through your hair to establish whether you're African, whether you're coloured, whether you're Malay. It was those types of things – and they'd stamp your pass – uhm, your ID documents, and you needed a pass to go from one area to the other area, so growing up as a, as a young boy not aware of these things and all of a sudden, it's almost like an overnight switch. A switch went on, it's just like overnight, 'Oh my Lord…Look what's happened to us,' you know? We really, really need to deal with this issue, point blank, because it was almost like the apartheid government put a state of emergency in place. We also felt like we needed to counter that with our interpretation of the state of emergency to counter that as well, and I guess thinking back and looking at the images, that's probably what that was, you know, in one sense.

Adam Haupt: Can I just explain very quickly, uhm. D mentioned *Boet and Saartjie* and *Kathy and Mark*. For those of you who don't know, who are not South African, *Kathy and Mark* was a reader. If you were Sub A, the equivalent of Grade 1. If you were Sub A, in English class you get a *Kathy and Mark* reader and, of course, for Afrikaans, *Boet and Saartjie*. Saartjie and Boet, you know, brother and sister. Uhm, Saartjie is the – what do you call it, *verkleining* [diminutive] – what is *verkleining* in English?

DJ Ready D: Don't wanna go there. Didn't pay attention [laughs].

Adam Haupt: Sarah, basically. Little Sarah. Little Sarah. Can't believe I can't translate something from Afrikaans into English. Funny. I used to be Afrikaans speaking [laughter], so – not anymore so much. Now I'm also theory speaking. Theory speaks me, right? So the point I'm making is these readers – the Afrikaans readers, *Boet and Saartjie*, were…the characters were white, the family was white, it was a heterosexual nuclear family. There [were] no black people in the narrative. If you were Sub A, coming into this imagining…you know, coming into literacy, becoming literate, learning to read…you had to imagine these white kids, these white protagonists, Afrikaner protagonists. If you were in the English class, *Kathy and Mark*. You had to imagine a white American middle-class family. 'Cause that's what Kathy and Mark was. White American, right? Uhm, heteronormative, race-specific, a whole lot of stuff. So that sort of socialisation, that…that's what we're talking about…So, uhm, for me specifically and I think D as well, we're about the same age, uh, you would have come out of '76 in the townships, into schools, learning about *Kathy and Mark*, or *Boet and Saartjie*, right? Having just gone through '76 and seeing that kind of brutality. The first white people you encounter are men in boots with rifles, right? And then you get *Kathy and Mark* and *Boet and Saartjie*, those sorts of contradictions, right? So, that's one part of it. What I also wanted to point to, is, I think for D – I think people's experiences will – experiences will differ. Uh, for D, am I correct in saying that the conscientisation running through Hip Hop…the exposure to people like Shaheen, was already down that road?

DJ Ready D: Yes, that's correct.

Adam Haupt: So someone like Shaheen…Shaheen was the class clown, co-opted into the Students' Representative Council [SRC], I believe, right? 'So you think you're so funny. Why don't you go to the SRC, get involved?' Right? 'Put your money [where] your mouth is.' He was like, 'All right. I will. I will make them pay for it.' Right? So obviously he seized the opportunity to use Hip Hop. Already his father was of a generation of jazz musicians who come out of this Black Consciousness era, right? And what was jazz doing? Jazz was defying colonial segregation. Racial segregation. So places like District Six [in Cape Town] and Sofiatown [in Johannesburg] were places…they were melting pots. People would come there for their music. There would be people of all races and classes. [Hendrik] Verwoerd did not like this at all. Sophiatown had to be broken down and became Triumph, Triomf, right? Triumph. Triumph of what? 'We kicked your ass, that's what.' White supremacy, right? Triumph. That's what it becomes. Segregation. Everyone goes off to their locations. White folk, you must bugger off. Uh, there's this story about a journalist who had an affair…a *Drum* journalist with a white woman. And I think she ended up in Australia or something like that. They were just completely vilified. Same thing happens in District Six. The place gets broken down. The musicians, the artists who come from those spaces, they all get sent off and dispersed. My great aunt was one of the people sort of, uh, drew diverse people to her and it was one of the 'Hands off District Six' campaigners. Her parental home was one of the last homes to be demolished. She ended up in Rylands basically, uhm, in a council flat. That's where she died. So that's the sort of narrative. So the jazz generation was already embracing these things. Was already mobilising. It was a site of resistance. And then, you know, that's Issy Ariefdien's generation. And his son, Shaheen Ariefdien, becomes a founding member of Prophets, so there's already this continuity. It's just generations coming in at different levels, setting things off. And as I suggested in, you know, one of the earlier lectures, what had happened before Prophets existed, or Black Noise existed? There was Sandile Dikeni, there was Lesego Rampolokeng. A lot of other poets, uh playwrights, uhm novelists, Wally Serote, Wally Serote who, who gets referenced in one of the early interviews, you know, doing great poetry, uh to – uhm *To Every Birth Its Blood*.[2] One of…probably one of the most phenomenal novels, uh, to come out of this country. Totally underrated. Uhm, so there's this sort of history. It's not as if people discovered Hip Hop and it set off. We were inspired by these Americans, and, you know, American Hip Hop can save us. Kanye [West], come and save me with your dress sense, right? That's not what happened. It's just a bunch of people seeing the opportunity, look – recognising the resonance and, you know, culture is bricoleur. You draw on the means at hand. So jazz musicians did that. Ironically, if you look at the work by Dave Copland and Veit Erlmann you see that American, African American jazz musicians looked to Africa for inspiration, and it was a two-way thing. So the [John] Coltranes and the [Charles] Minguses of the world, it was a two-way thing already that was going on and part of that was an ideological orientation, this notion of blackness which is ideological, not founded in biologically essentialist notions of identity, which is what I think you were getting at. Ja.

H Samy Alim: I really like that, that last point you were making and it helped me sort of think of something else that I maybe wanna explore a little bit more that I've been thinking about, because I've written some stuff on the relationship between Islam and Hip Hop culture and I – I think it's interesting. I don't know, of course, all the stuff that's out there that's written about,

---

2. See Serote (1981).

uhm, Capetonian or South African Hip Hop…but it seems to me like a lot of the connections we're talking about blackness and race, a lot, or a lot of the connection was also Islam. In that moment – in that particular moment, I – I – I'm a little bit surprised by almost how dominant Islam was in the sort of early Hip Hop, you know, community here. Of course, the same thing was in the United States where so much of Hip Hop was, you know, Islamic oriented, in various communities, as Ready D mentioned. Uhm, but we always talk about the race and the race connections and I wonder about what were the sort of religious connections, or spiritual connections? 'Cause there's – there's a very spiritual movement at the core of blackness and Black Consciousness for African Americans. But it's not just a political movement, or whatever, like for people involved there was also a spiritual movement, and so I wonder – the resonances. Adam, you mentioned the resonances and so I wonder what resonances were also seen in that way now. That's a big question…yeah.

DJ Ready D: That, uhm, that's quite a big question. Uhm, it's gonna take quite a bit of assistance. But just from my perspective, I embraced Islam because of the consciousness that came through Hip Hop and the reason why I did that was also learning a little bit more about my roots, in terms of where, you wanna call it, uhm, my family, my ancestors come from as well. Although we got this European African connection, we also have connections that goes [as] far back as Java, if you look at the East, you look at India, you look at all those places, and because of the Dutch East India Company, uhm, that was one of the companies, if I…I stand to be corrected, but they obviously had certain routes that they dominated, spice routes and so forth. Uh, Cape Town was one of the stopping points and they would bring in quite a lot of slaves from abroad, and it was a lot of Muslim slaves that came to settle in Cape Town, as well as slaves coming from elsewhere in Africa as well. And, uhm, I thought it was very interesting that I have Muslim family members and Christian family members and I was a little bit confused about everything. My dad was Muslim, converted to Christianity. My sister's Muslim, so it's all these things taking place and just learning a little more about that and my personality and character at the time, uhm, I felt I was – I couldn't – I couldn't, uhm – in layman's terms I couldn't find my bearings within Christianity, kinda learning about its history and how it was enforced upon our people and if you trace it back to the days of slavery, you know there were certain – there's certain stories that if you wanted your freedom, you had to become Christian, and you had to buy yourself out of slavery as well, so it was certainly – there was a huge – uhm uh you, you, you couldn't budge. That was it. And also, kinda learning a little bit about the links when it comes to the Muslims joining forces with the local or should I say the indigenous Khoi people of southern Africa as well. They formed various, uhm, movements and militias to counter what was happening as well. And that's a lot of information and a lot of history that's not freely available, unfortunately. You know, you gotta go to a mosque. You gotta sit with the elder, or dig deep. So for our general, if you wanna call it a general uhm community, unfortunately you know, that information, it's not circulating, unless you come to, you know, these types of environments as well, to come and, you know, learn a little bit more about that. But for me once again I felt like it made sense, because I needed to understand… my history a little bit more, and knowing my ancestry came from the – from the uhm from the East, you know ten to one they were Muslim and that's what I needed to embrace. You know, I couldn't embrace anything else that meant oppression to me, so that was…

H Samy Alim: That's deep so it's 'Understand Where I'm Coming From'…is a message to people and also an understanding of where I've come from…

DJ Ready D: Yes.

H Samy Alim: …at the same time.

DJ Azuhl: I just wanna latch on to what D was saying. Another factor, uhm, to that was also the religion that we've got, you know, because there was a figure known as King Jamo where we used to get information, alternative information from the Universal Zulu Nation. Uh, you know, in New York and he's one of the figures that doesn't get mentioned in South African Hip Hop, and he's a figure that, you know, shared…this information with us. Uhm, furthermore, you also have to understand we also had a Nation of Islam back in the days of The Base [a nightclub] and stuff like that. Uhm, and – I mean me also, not coming from a Muslim household, 'cause I come from a staunch Catholic, I had a staunch Catholic upbringing. Uhm, I mean, I got influenced by that as well, you know.

Student: Ja, my question is for D and Azuhl. Just in the context of Adam mentioning that, uhm, Shaheen's dad was like a jazz muso, uhm, I'm just wondering, like how explicit was the connection in the '80s and '90s between, uhm, Hip Hop and jazz in Cape Town? 'Cause – like on the Cape Flats or whatever. I mean now you've got guys like Jitsvinger playing Afrikaan – Afrikaaps with Kyle Shepherd. It's like that, like that coming together of Cape jazz tradition and Hip Hop tradition. So, ja, was it just like sons and daughters of jazz musos taking that sensibility forward into Hip Hop or were there like jams going on with young guys who were playing jazz as well, or like what was the vibe?

DJ Ready D: I would say with, uh, Shaheen's dad playing a very important role in POC as a producer, that was the first link between jazz and Hip Hop in our country.

Adam Haupt: And he played on the album.

DJ Ready D: That's correct.

Adam Haupt: Basil Coetzee playing on 'Cape Crusader'. One of the coolest Cape Town songs ever.

DJ Azuhl: Uhm, I shall correct you, as an avid POC fan [laughter], actually the first…

Adam Haupt: …Robbie Jansen, sorry!

DJ Azuhl: Actually, the first South African Hip Hop, uh, and jazz track was actually on the second POC album, and the track was called 'Musical Madness'.

DJ Ready D: Oh ja!

DJ Azuhl: That is actually South Africa's first, you know, jazz meets Hip Hop for the first time officially.

DJ Ready D: I would have to counter that [laughter] 'avid POC fan' [laughter]. Is, is 'Roots' on that album? Or was 'Roots' on the first album?

DJ Azuhl: 'Roots' is on the first album. 'Roots' was the first one…

DJ Ready D: I just got to tell the story very, very, very quickly…

DJ Azuhl: Damn.

DJ Ready D: Uhm, we, we were sitting in Shaheen's dad's little studio, uhm, producing music, and I always tell the story because I think it's a really phenomenal story and I'm still trying to make sense of it...knowing Shaheen's dad and his dad's record collection, but I didn't quite understand jazz music. I heard it in the community, but I didn't understand it and my motivation for getting involved with Shaheen is, I wanted to be a ghetto superstar. When I met him, I heard his dad had a studio and I'm like, '"Dude, uh when can I record an album?" because I need to make some money. You know? I need cars. I need clothing. I need the whole story.' 'Rappers Delight.' That for me was – that was the word right there. Nicks playing, basketball, and it's colour TVs and it's swimming pools, those things were foreign to us. And I'm like, 'I like what these guys are saying, and the way I'm gonna get that is to get into a recording studio and record that stuff.' Anyway, we're in the recording studio, and I'm checking out Shaheen doing his thing and writing his lyrics and Shaheen's talking to me about Mandela and Biko and what's happening on school and I'm like, '*Bra*, don't talk about those things...basketball and colour TVs. Let's talk about that' [laughter]. You know that's kind of the vibe because I'm in a hurry over here, you know. We were selling beer bottles, I'm selling scrap iron to afford sneakers so that we can style and profile when we go back on the streets because we started off as b-boys. And while sitting in the recording studio one night, uhm, Shaheen flipped out these records, and on the turntable he drops this vinyl and he drops the needle, and there's a jazz song. An Afro jazz song that plays and it's on Abdullah Ibrahim, better known as Dollar Brand. His song plays, 'The Boy.' I don't know what happened to me personally. Everything changed. My whole life changed; my perspective, everything changed. And right there and then, the lyrics, everything just transformed at that point in time, and that was probably my entry level, once again, into becoming conscious and it wasn't – the music, the artist, wasn't related to Hip Hop whatsoever. There was an energy, there was a truth, there was a level of persuasion, you know, that changed everything for me. So that was kinda, you know, the first, uhm, connection, and then we wrote a song called 'Roots Resurrected' on our first album, that uhm, that sort of – it's a tribute to Afro jazz, the likes of, uhm, Hotep Galeta, Abdullah Ibrahim, Robert Jansen. That was some of the, the local jazz musicians and, of course, Pacific Express, the band that, uh, Shaheen's dad belonged to.

Adam Haupt: We were going to run through the entire album with you, quickly, but we can't.

But can you give them a taste of 'Cape Crusader', at least? At least the introduction. It's off *Ghetto Code*…The saxophonist is…?

DJ Ready D: 'Cape Crusader'…Uhm, I think the saxophonist on that track was – *sjoe* I stand to be corrected. It could be Robbie Jansen.

Adam Haupt: I thought so.

DJ Ready D: That…we sampled that track from a Pacific Express album and the original version was recorded in the early '70s, and the guys didn't write the track. It was a jam session. That's what that was all about. And they just decided to record the jam session, and we were listening to some albums for interesting samples to use and when we latched onto that thing…we didn't have lyrics to the music. The music dictated everything.

Adam Haupt: Check it out.

[DJ Azuhl plays track.[3]]

VERSE #1

They don't understand the man now they wanna let the style seize

They planned against the band with propaganda and banned our LP's

7 years of blood, sweat and tears

It's like only the wack crews are getting theirs

My pockets are broken, 'cause the Prophets are outspoken

They say mindless topics only get the crowd open

they even said you've got to sound like this one or that one

Silence is golden, even platinum

And drop the knowledge trip and politics

and holler shit to get the rand and the dollar quick

---

3. Lyrics from http://www.africaserver.nl/geto3000/content/lyrics5.html

> Life is kinda funny with the gospel it sends me
> Money can test your morals, if your tummy's empty
> being desolate can tempt a kid for duckets
> and say anything to benefit the pockets
> I just hope I stay true for later
> and remain a Cape crusader

Adam Haupt: So an appropriate link back to the censorship thing...what I really want us to talk about. So, the verse is, 'My pockets are broken, 'cause the Prophets are outspoken/ They say mindless topics only get the crowd open.' Uhm, in the very, very beginning he talks about seven years of, you know, having to deal with censorship and the difficulty of being an artist in this climate where you're gonna get banned doing this, that or the other. The losing proposition: the easiest thing to do is to go for mindless topics that get the 'crowd open', crowd-pleasers. The culture of censorship, and do you want to speak to that quickly?

DJ Ready D: Ja. It's sad to say that…the censorship issue started internally with management. As Shaheen has said, uhm you know, in his first verse, and a lot of issues that we had to deal with was trying to fight for what we believed in, the type of music we wanted to produce; on the other end, uhm…with a lot of attention coming from the SABC and the censorship board starting to reject certain tracks, you know. We were kinda pushed into – into the direction where the music had to become a little bit more commercial and on *Boom Style* that's quite evident because there's quite a lot of commercial-sounding songs, other producers were brought in. We were muscled into using other recording studios because management believed that this was the way to go. If you wanna survive in the industry, you wanna eat, you wanna be successful, unfortunately you're gonna have to tone down everything. And on that album, we…decided, 'Man, we can't do that. It just doesn't feel right. Morally, it doesn't feel right.' And we squeezed in a track called 'Ons Stem' and that was kinda our counter to the previous apartheid government's national anthem called 'Die Stem' at the time. That was the last track we recorded in Cape Town. Everything else was recorded in Joburg. And we had to fight tooth and nail to get that track onto the album. At least you got to have some degree of principle, you know, with putting music and expression out into the arena over there. Then there was a song that appeared on the album called 'Kicking Non-Stop'. We recorded that, uhm, music video, uhm, in the SABC studios. Again, MC Hammer was the rage, C&C Music Factory, all those types of poppy songs and then the SABC decided to bring in some really jiggy dancers in the music video. They had these tight leotards, pulling MC Hammer moves, and those type of things, and uh we couldn't – we couldn't cope with that. And we thought, 'Okay, why don't we at least, you know, somehow, some way, we gotta say something.' And right at the end of that music video, there was a refrigerator standing in the – in the studio at the – at the SABC's television recording facility, and we decided – and there was a picture of former president PW Botha hanging on the wall as well, and we thought, 'Man, can't we just take the picture off the wall very quickly, and maybe put that pic inside the refrigerator, close the door, saying, "Chill out, Homeboy".' And that's exactly what we did [laughing]. This really poppy music video went out and everybody was like, 'Ja, "Kicking Non-Stop". Cool dancing. Wow, look at the cool dudes now.' You know? And at the end, you see the fridge door open, the picture goes in, and boom, the door closes. And right there and then, that music video was banned [laughter] and that portion of the video, and 'Ons Stem' that was banned as well, you know that – we got this hectic letter from the SABC, you know, and from there, one thing led to the – another, we recorded the third album, *Phunk Phlow*, that didn't get any…Sorry it was, uhm, *Age of Truth*, and when…after we came from Bophuthatswana, after the story that Shaheen delivered in the clip, I think the whole country was terrified of Prophets of da City. Probably thought, 'These guys have gone terrorist mad because they're firing shots left, right and centre.' And we were scheduled to perform at, uhm, former president Nelson Mandela's inauguration. On the – on the morning of the event, we received a call. 'You guys can't perform at the event anymore.' And our manager fought. We fought. We were threatening with newspaper, every single channel at our disposal we were gonna use to expose these people. Then they decided, 'You guys can perform, but you're not allowed to set up your decks, and you can't use your music.' And we were like, 'Oh, Lord. What are we gonna do?' We actually had a journalist from *The Source* or *Rap Pages* following us to cover the story and then we were like, 'Oh my gosh, but we got Jazzmo.' Jazzmo was one of the members. He was a beatboxer. And we thought, 'Okay, that's the way to go. Jazzmo, you beatbox. We'll rhyme. We're still gonna do our thing.' So that's the way we pulled off that performance at Mandela's inauguration. So that was, you know, just some of the censorship stories from, from our perspective.

Adam Haupt: So even as we're making the transition into democracy on paper, the fact is, *Phunk Phlow* post-election and then *Ghetto Code* definitely post-election…

DJ Ready D: *Universal Souljaz* as well…

Adam Haupt: …*Universal Souljaz*, it was just like – it was – it was you know, roadblocks all the way…

DJ Ready D: Ja. And, uhm, *Understand Where I'm Coming From* won a foreign music – a foreign music video award…

Adam Haupt: Midem? Was it Midem?

DJ Ready D: Yes. Midem, ja. And we, we, we got exposure, but it was a very small little story in the newspaper…And for any artist in that point in time to achieve anything, even if you got a gig, it was a big thing for South Africans at the time and, you know, that was just swept under the carpet as well because I think people still felt that threat. And we were still seen as a 'coloured group from the Cape Flats' and the National Party had a strong hold on the Western Cape, so for an outspoken/militant voice – and it's young guys coming from the Cape Flats, and the National Party still fighting for votes in the Western Cape – it was very dangerous for them to allow a group such as Prophets of da City to become sort of more, uhm, successful or more vocal. So that was also part of the reasons.

Adam Haupt: I wish we could speak some more, but what I want to do is draw your attention to the present day. For those of you who don't know, that's a painting by Brett Murray [points to Murray's *The Spear* on slide presentation]. It appeared in the Goodman Gallery…This exhibition went down in Joburg. Whole seas of critiques, parodies of Zuma – but critiques basically of corruption, nepotism, lack of transparency, consumer culture in the ANC… *The Spear*, literally, it references the Lenin poster, right? So, of course, it makes reference to communism, the history, the so-called communist history, socialist ideology in place by the ANC completely being flipped over by this neoliberal turn, the flaccid penis referencing the rape trial and the remarks Zuma made during his rape trial – he was acquitted, but the remarks that he made during the rape trial, sexist remarks, the assertion that, you know, he's a traditional Zulu male…all of those things being referenced in here. The remarks he made were more damning than possibly being a rapist. He was acquitted. So I think…it produced a whole lot of critiques, spin-offs, spoofs…[laughter]. So what happens is, you know, in the gallery, the painting gets defaced by two people, unrelated to each other – that's the one thing. But while this is going on, you know, court action is launched to sue, but in order to pull this painting and maybe to get newspapers to stop publishing pictures of the painting, you needed to prove that it was defamation. So it was going to be a long road. First, you had to prove that it was defamation…There's a good defence. He's a public figure, everything he does, you know, uh, news and critiques are protected by section 16 in the Constitution, which guarantees free speech. Artists are covered by this, journalists etc., etc. There probably weren't going to win. So instead of pursuing that court action, they basically abandoned that and took to the streets. Rolling mass action. Let's use '80s and '90s rhetoric. 'We will march on the gallery. We will pressurise the editor of *City Press*. She must take this picture down from her website.' So it was intimidation. Eventually, the editor of *City Press*, Ferial Haffajee, says, 'You know what, I'm very intimidated. My journalists now can't work in the field. They can't access trade union meetings, because they've been locked out, threatened, etc., etc. For the safety of my staff, and just to get everyone to chill the hell out, I'm just going to take the picture down from the website.' After the fact, she said, 'I regret doing that.' But at the time it was really, really difficult. Press meeting, uh, press conference with the – with the gallery owners, uhm, saying like now, you know…basically taking a step back. And it all looks like they've been muscled to actually, you know, capitulate, right? Uhm, so it's all very threatening. So even though legal channels weren't used, intimidation was used, right, to actually shut this whole thing down. Now I'm thinking to myself, 'How different is the outcome of, you know, *The Spear* and journalists' coverage of the issue, how different is that to the experience of Prophets of da City, right?' There are damning parallels that are really, really, really, really, really tricky. And, of course, one of the lightning rods in the media context is someone named Zapiro, who has produced a number of critiques. The original critique, uh, that he offered was the rape of Lady Justice with members of the Tripartite Alliance[4] holding Lady Justice down as Jacob Zuma, uh, is about to violate her, right? And here we have, you know, free speech being violated as well. This is his critique of what happened, uhm you know, during *The Spear*

---

4. An alliance between the ANC, the Congress of South African Trade Unions and the South African Communist Party

debacle. But here's the catch. Zapiro…the critique of Zapiro's critique is that he's banalising rape, gender-based violence. That gender politics takes a backseat to the politics of the ruling party. That…he is replicating the problem from a gender perspective. So there are all sorts of levels of complexity that are worth considering. If you wanna read up a little bit more about this, yes this is also a plug for something that I wrote, like yesterday. See a thread here? Check out a book called *State of the Nation 2014*. The HSRC Press publishes something called *State of the Nation* on a yearly basis, and it's something like, you know, a thermometer. How's the country doing in a range of areas. So there's an article about this very issue in *State of the Nation 2014*.[5] Also…I think in the first chapter. Three thousand words in the first chapter of the book *Static*,[6] also discussed in this; it's worth looking at – especially in relation to this story of censorship. Thank you so much, and thanks to Prophets of da City.

---

5. See Meyiwa, Nkondo, Chitiga-Mabugu, Sithole & Nyamnjoh (2014)
6. See Haupt (2012)

SHAHEEN ARIEFDIEN, POC REHEARSALS | Source: Ference Isaacs

LEGENDARY BEATBANGAZ: (FROM L TO R) DJ E20, DJ AZUL AND DJ READY D | Source: Ference Isaacs

CHAPTER 3.
COMING TO HIP HOP
IN THE EARLY '90S

DJ EAZY AND DJ AZUHL WITH ADAM HAUPT

Founders of Hip Hop Education South Africa, DJs Eazy and Azuhl, talk about how they came to Hip Hop and found points of entry into Hip Hop activism. This interview took place on the University of Cape Town (UCT) campus in 2007 when Mr Fat, Eazy and Azuhl used to run a Hop Hop radio show at UCT Radio. At the time, Azuhl was still involved with Brasse Vannie Kaap (BVK), but had begun to work on his solo career. He, Eazy and Fat had also been working on community arts projects. Hence, this interview took place just as Eazy and Azuhl were beginning to establish themselves as sought-after DJs and media personalities.

Adam Haupt: So, Eazy, how did you first come to Hip Hop, or how did Hip Hop come to you? How did you become involved in the Hip Hop scene?

DJ Eazy: Sure. Uhm, I can think of two things. The one was just some girl's house that I wasn't supposed to be at. I was at her house and when her parents came home I was thinking of an excuse why I was there; it was to pick up the cassette and it was a cassette with some Hip Hop stuff on, 'My Philosophy' by KRS-One…I was listening to the music and it was some music that I thought was the next big thing, or whatever. And that will be my intro to the music because I was kind of…not sheltered, but I wasn't exposed to it. I was a very good Christian, home, whatever, no bad TV.

I lived in Bonteheuwel. But, Mom and Dad worked. And you know I had two bigger brothers who looked out for me. So, go to school, come home from school and then that's it. No PlayStation, no computer. No pool table. They always promised we'll get those things when we get a better house, or whatever, big house. So some of the crazy stuff that other kids will do, go to the dam and do stuff…I wasn't allowed to do stuff like that. I was taught when I was [a] kid not to play in the park because the park was a dangerous place. You get robbed, stabbed, and do other kinds of stuff, so, and I'd be kept away. And I am not even sure that if I was there that I'd actually get those things you know, because it was the early days. So, in '85, *Breakdance 2*. You know, I knew what *Breakdance 2* was about but didn't know what Hip Hop was about. I started breaking with some friends, whatever. '86, '87, '88, '89...I would say, yeah. A competition on radio for a big chips company happens and some girl in my school says, 'Why don't you enter?' Because I was making fun in the class, always writing little rhymes, or whatever. So I write about 10 to 12 rhymes at that time. This was before I met Mr Fat, who taught me about verse or whatnot, right? Like 12, 13 lines or whatever...I entered the competition. But a month later, I was like a celebrity in Bonteheuwel. I won the rap competition, which was a big thing to Mr Fat, that's how we met, because someone told him, 'Oh, a guy from Bonteheuwel won the rap competition,' And he was like, 'Who is this guy? Why is he winning the rap competition?'

He was actually Fat MC then, not Mr Fat. He was Fat MC. This was before BVK. This was Jam B days. Just another miracle from Bonteheuwel, which he had done with Marchant. So, that happened and, because of the competition, Fat is now looking for this Tyrone, which at that time was Eazy T, looking for this Eazy T guy who won the rap competition on radio. And then, South Africa still celebrated Red Nose Day at the time, which was at March some time, where people go and have a concert somewhere, buy a nose for five bucks, or something, and it goes to Red Cross. So Prophets of da City was performing. But by then I had, like, every news article they were in, you know, whether it be *Plainsman*, *Metro Burger*, *The Jelly Bean Journal*, whatever it was. If there was an article with music...Organized Rhyme was in there, AK47 I think was in there, so was Black Noise, Caramel and White Boys, as well as Prophets of da City, which was, for me, the group because they just rapped my song, which was DSA. And they rapped the song that I wrote. I then met them at that Red Nose Day concert, which was a big thing for me, and we exchanged numbers, which was kind of impossibility. It was like saying, 'Okay, what are you doing?' And I was like, 'I'm trying to get my rap thing together so...'

Adam Haupt: So that was 1989?

DJ Eazy: Yeah, I'm trying to figure out when I went to school and when...It could have been 1989 or '90. But yeah, so up until then it was just...whatever radio was calling rap music at that time, I had the same access everyone else had, but I never had CDs, never had records, never had tapes, none of that. It was only after that...

Adam Haupt: Which station was that competition on?

DJ Eazy: Uh, Alex Jay was the guy that gave me the check, so that would have been…

Adam Haupt: Five? Radio Five?

DJ Eazy: Ja.

Adam Haupt: Okay, so Shaheen, Prophets, basically performed your rhyme, basically.

DJ Eazy: Ja, basically there were guests in the studio and they got the rhyme and they obviously recorded it somewhere, wherever. So, they made a beat that they made somewhere and Shaheen just rapped it. And then I was like, 'Oh my goodness, that's the song.' But when they announced the winner, I didn't know about that. It wasn't until the next day at school people telling me, but for like a week…You try to come home in the afternoon trying to tune in to that show because you wanna know…Other guys were also entered into the competition, so…So, I meet Fat or Fat MC at that time, which is like this big dude with the jeans that he basically just bought two hours ago, but it's like with, full of writing with kokis, or whatever. That was like Fat's signature in Bonteheuwel: the big dude with the Air Force Ones. We meet at the Bonteheuwel library area, which was like a game shop and people were gathering there and even that was like a very unlikely thing for me to do. Like I said, I've never walked around Bonteheuwel because it was like dodgy. My folks will just be freaked out by it.

So I'm there and I meet this guy Fat and it's like for me, it's like a big thing because this guy is famous, so to speak. And Fat then won the…I don't know what name the competition was, but they won the competition at The Base [nightclub] as Jam B. And not long after that the Teenage Classics tape came out, which was a collection of other artists from Cape Town. But being kinda brought up in the church, and with all the, you know, Godly principles, Hip Hop is from the devil, or whatever the case may be. That tape also introduced me to a guy called Brother A, which was a dude with a big record round his neck [laughs], or CD, I think. He told us, he was like, 'Cool. If you did the one thing, do the next thing.' So we entered at the Westgate Mall Talent Search blah, blah-blah. Shaheen commented in an article, I think it was [in] *The Plainsman* or maybe even the *South*, on Christian or gospel rap where there was a group…the picture was of a group called, uh, Faith Heroes. And Shaheen was commenting on just international, you know, like just music in general, and how some people should not call it Christian rap because it's kinda like selling God or…they weren't selling music they were selling Jesus, but their medium was like flaky, was bad or the beats were junk or the guys didn't have any skill or any flow so that made me…no, I don't want to go there, you know. But I want to definitely go and delve in this whole circle of things, and then I was like, okay, but now I have a story to tell. So, through an English teacher at my high school, I said, you know, 'I want to write stuff.' And I think it was actually, I wanted to write like LL Cool J [laughs] because I was a fan. And she said, you know, blah, blah, blah in Woodstock just before you hit the Good Hope Centre, there's an office there. The *South* newspaper, I think, was based there. Go and talk to them and tell them you want to do something. So I go there, 14, 15 years old, maybe ja, maybe 15, 16 years old. I go there and I'm like, 'Hey, you know, I'm this guy, I won the rap competition. I have a thousand rand. Put me on a Karaoke Boom Box. I'm like the dude. I've hung out with Mr Fat, I've met Prophets of da City and, like, I've been to The Base once, but I never see any of your people there.' They're like, 'No, they don't go there.' And I was like, 'I'm there. You wanna tell the people what's going on there. Why don't you let me tell the people what's going on there?' They're like 'Okay, if you wanna contribute.' Dude, like I said, I'm like 15 years old, you know. A thousand bucks is a lot of money. There wasn't ABSA. I think it was Volkskas Bank…gave me my first bank card and whatever.

So I went to the *South* paper. They were happy. I had to put pen to paper and went to The Base and bumped into a guy called Craig aka Falko. I've seen his name all over Cape Town, even when I'm in the train going to town or whatever. Went and met him in his house in Mitchells Plain and interviewed him. And, obviously, when it was in the paper and it was like a big thing again because there was his picture, with some of the graffiti he's done, the story and my picture. Now, it's like not just my name is on the radio, my name is on the picture. So now in Bonteheuwel, I'm like, you know, the dude who was all over the place. And obviously it's cool because now I know Falko. And now, when I go to The Base, it's not just that Fat's there, he's my friend now because we live in Bonteheuwel. I just walk in for free because people think I'm his brother. I also know Falko. And I also shake hands with Ready D and whatever. And then I was like, okay, but these people who don't know me, the other people, and so that's really not cool so I have to show off to some other people. So, I went back to church and got some church things to give and I was like, you know, like you guys are preaching to the choir or whatever. Or, you guys are hanging out with the wrong people. Come to the other side and I'll show you the other side.

Adam Haupt: Come with me to the dark side…

DJ Eazy: [laughs] Come with me to the dark side, type of thing. So, ja, I took some guys there. And these dudes were obviously like, because they went to Cedars High School; I think Shaheen attended. Was it Cedars, I think? No, but I mean the school knew a lot about him. Hip Hop was like hectic at Cedars High.

DJ Azuhl: He did workshops in that school…

DJ Eazy: Okay, that's probably what happened but I knew that for them, the best rapper, the greatest rapper of all time, was DSA, uhm, you know. When their *Kicking Non-Stop* music video came out and Shaheen had that big black jacket on with the fur thing, like those dudes like wanted to sell their arms to get a jacket like that because Shaheen owned a jacket like that in the video. And some of those kids or guys from the church were from Westridge High, I think, as well, which was like their entry into it was graffiti and then it ended up being rapping; which, as Azuhl was saying, because of the workshops. So for me, it was doing like one, two, three Jesus loves me type of thing you know, which was just like, I dunno, telling Bible stories or Sunday school stories to a beat now. But, I want to do this thing. Then, when I met D, when I went to D's house with Fat, which has nothing to do with Hip Hop or the music; it was just that Fat was gonna visit him. Fat had a car at that time and I went with him. Fat was asking, you know, how are things going, blah, blah, blah, because we were performing to other people's beats. Like, I had a couple of shows with youth and that was a cool thing to do. And he was like, you know, Martian just bought a machine. Martian can make beats for you. But, if you want, I can also make a beat for you. I was like, what? Because now these people are in the Top 20. They are…there was a show every Saturday morning called *File it in the F*. I don't know if you remember that show. You know, these dudes are on TV like twice a week or every other week. They're in the newspaper. It's like you know, if you were them, you know, you should be thinking America. That's what you're thinking [laughs]. You are thinking Statue of Liberty, Central Park, McDonald's, gold chain, LL Cool Js from sitting in the park, or whatever. So that kind of stuff was interesting because yeah, as a *laaitie* [youngster], it was also like hearing the music like I was…I didn't know who the hell Fidel Castro was. But I heard a song by Jeru the Damaja and he was like, 'Control the mic like Fidel Castro.' I was like, what does he control? You know, I mean, I wanted to find out what the deal was. Hearing songs by KRS-One saying 'no chicken or no hamburger' or talking about whatever. Now I was like, what's up with these dudes? It's music now they're telling me what to eat, they're telling me about [Louis] Farrakhan. And it was like pretty scary to my folks because I came home once with a photocopied thing that was about this much paper and it said something like brainwash to whitewash or black wash to…I don't even know the name, but when I had that it was like I had like a satanic bible in my hand, basically. And there was this other messed up dude that had meetings on a Saturday morning that I bumped into through a girl at school. And she was like, 'Hey, these dudes are bring[ing] Public Enemy to South Africa.' And I was like, what? So, I was like, 'Forget Sunday school, subs.' This is like, you know what I mean? Forget that…And I mean, because like I said, the family, my family situation has contributed a lot to it because there was the protection element where it, like kids would hang like. I don't know if you know from the area where you grew up but if a bakkie, that little thing that sells the fish cart or they sell the cooldrinks or the woods for a price, when they come pass, they don't go on a fast speed you know because a dude will be shouting off you or blowing the trumpet, so for the kids, you know, an activity in the afternoon would be hanging at the back of that. That's way before train surfing. They will be hanging on the back of the truck or the bakkie but I couldn't participate in stuff like that because if my parents saw me I'd be dead, you know what I mean. So, I never did that. Didn't climb on roofs, or whatever. Didn't smoke, stayed away from that because we were told that was wrong thing to do. Although we had lots of freedom. My friends could come by the house, you know, eat meals or hang out with us. So, it was a good, I mean, there was a true thing to it. But with the music, it was like, they took an interest in it, like what are you doing? Like, who are these people?

I remember now, like '93 when Prophets of da City did the Rapping for Democracy tour and Fat came to my house to pick me up, I was like, what? I'm going with these dudes to a school? It's like are we gonna rap to these people or whatever? I mean, I didn't rap with him on the tour, I just went with…I was just like, you know, a guy that Fat, you know, liked to hang out with, whatever. So they picked me up in this Combi. And the dudes who owned Club Vibe, the Collins brothers, they used to have a sound company. So we go there and it's like after the show, you know, we were the important people because we had the sound equipment. You know, we had the cables and without us there is no show. So we're carrying speakers back to the place, blah, blah, blah…Then Fat said, 'Oh…' I don't know who it was; one of the guys gave me a t-shirt and it was a white Rapping for Democracy t-shirt, and I was like, 'Dang, I'm wearing this to school tomorrow.' And wearing it to school made the kids go nuts about the t-shirt and that's how I got them to come to our school. And then I was also like the big shot at school because I brought these dudes to school. And when they arrived at the school I took them all into the office.

Adam: And what school is that?

DJ Eazy: Arcadia in Bonteheuwel. So I took you know Shaheen and these guys into the office to meet the principal. But it's kinda like not these are the people performing, these are my friends who's coming to preach the school about voting blah, blah.

Yeah, it's like, you know, it was kinda like, Rapping for Democracy would probably be where the light went on in terms of how the music could be used, you know…That was like my thing. It was like I could, you know, do this, and like people are voting, but you know what's going to be the big next thing next year? You could talk about something else when it's not the voting thing. Uhm, so in '94 to like, I think; yeah '94, '95, the one dude I was friends with, we still had a little bit of beats. I bought over Martian's old drum machine which was a Boss DR-550, or something…Dr Rhythm 550, you know. And the next thing, I'm introduced to this guy called Patrick Hickey aka Caramel. So I'm on the train going to his house because he was going to record a demo. My dad worked for a company that was making and selling CD players, so Caramel never had a CD player in his studio and I was like, 'I can hook you up. I'll give you a CD player in exchange for like three demos'…He still owes me two demos [laughs]. I'm gonna go get it some time.

So, that was like my exposure to Caramel. And through Caramel, he introduced me to a guy called Mike Hattingh, which opened up another door, like you know, the whole sound aspect. He told me to buy, not just the drum machine, to buy the S50, which was a machine that was a hundred dollar and seventy or something at that time. So I bought that. Then it was also the guy was rapping, was studying, so he was like hectic dude. He got like 98 per cent for his motor mechanics or diesel trade or whatever. So he was like a hectic school-studying type of cat and that always made it impossible for us to do lots of shows. And I was like, 'How far can I go with this kind of thing?'

Adam: Who was he?

DJ Eazy: Quentin Bailey, a friend of mine. We called him MC Q. You know how everything was MC something back then. It had to be some letter. You were either a number or a letter. You were A1, or Z3 or MC something so…Yeah, he was MC Q. So with him doing that I was like no forget this. So, in '96 a friend of mine who had a band…there were two girls and two guys…I think the government endorsed or commissioned something called 'Addicted to Life'. Yeah, that was the name of the tour. So they did that tour and they wanted someone to do the sound while they were on tour and I was like, 'Hmm, this is it,' you know. This is the break. So I had to give up eight to nine months of my life to do that thing. So five of us were in a microbus and…a trailer and we just go like from Swaziland to Johannesburg to East London to PE [Port Elizabeth] to George, Nigel, whatever. We see 90 schools, or whatever, but now it was like Prophets of da City's Rapping for Democracy because I was trying…because I'm…listen these kids never had…those exposures again…they went to model C type schools. No one in the Hip Hop community knew who they claim they were. But I mean they knew who Ready D was, they knew who DSA was…So I was like okay, cool. Now, this thing, and you know I'm still doing my thing that I said in '93, you know, if I get the chance I'm gonna use music at that time. Uh, you know I didn't think Hip Hop because I couldn't tell what they were doing. Hip Hop was more like dance music, and a little bit of rapping. But then on the tour, we get there and they wanted to do a sound check and they had a very limited repertoire at that time. So you don't want to play a beat to a song that they were gonna perform 20 minutes later. So you just play a thing and none of them could freestyle, you know. And I would take music with me. And then I would start playing music. And then we were in another city and I had two CD players and I was like okay cool, let's do this. Let's DJ.

Yeah. From Eazy T to DJ Eazy because you know they would say we're gonna be here for two hours and then the next time they say we're gonna be here for five hours…I'll be like, 'I'm easy'…I mean, between all that, there's lot of small details I could…but I would say Falko was very instrumental because I mean I don't…I can't ever remember…I can't remember ever picking up a spray can, but I must've at home messed with kokis and paints, like writing my name or maybe also on my jeans because that's what Fat did. And Fat was, from the day that we met, it was like everything changed about my perceptions…I mean there was another guy

I met, they call him DJ Sinus…This guy was like the dude who had mixed tapes. And he was friends with Rozanno and B Side was another friend of his…Shamiel X was referred to him as Bob at that time. He had a brother…Yeah, and that dude had Peace Radio and I used to get recordings from this other girl in Mitchells Plain, because I couldn't listen to Peace Radio at my house because if my parents knew I was listening to a guy called Shamiel X, they'd totally wouldn't like me listening to Shamiel X…to an underground radio station…So I would get the tapes from them and listen to it. That was like my porn stash so to speak.

I would listen to Peace Radio, that's like, and not get caught. But I mean, he wasn't only playing Hip Hop. He was playing from Dr. Dre's *The Chronic* to Public Announcement, Vibe or whatever, you know. That was like the songs he was playing. MC Lite or whatever. So it was like a lot of music to take in and, yeah, I was just like trying to know. I mean, go to town and not buy lunch or buy burgers at a place called…there's a place…not to buy food there, Captain Dorigo's, and rather buy *Right On* magazine…You know, or *Rap Pages* or *Yo!* Buy those magazines and cut it out and then check their hairstyles. Then wear your clothes back to front and criss-cross or whatever…I wore a chain and lock it around my neck because I thought that's what dudes of my nature did. You know I had rap-style boots, and the whole thing, because you do like whatever the magazine would say…I spent a lot of time with Martian learning how to work some of the equipment from the drum machine to the S50. Like I said, Fat kinda schooled me with the whole Boss thing and, you know, how to, I mean, how to rhyme and how to write stuff. Because obviously, now it's like I did one little verse and it won me a prize on radio. Fat then won the competition at The Base for, yeah, the rap…I don't know what the battle was called. I don't know what the rap competition was called, but they were, I mean, they were called Jam B and they won it…

When POC came to my school, I took, you know, I listened, you know, 'cause they were talking about stuff that was relevant to me. They were educating me at the same time and it was in a fun way that I could enjoy it and, at the same time, it sounded very close to the stuff that I listened to when I am out of school…And my brother was a salesperson in a bookshop, like a Christian bookshop, so he was selling whatever types, the Sandi Patty types of music. So he was not exposed to that. I know somebody who was a DJ who has got lots of records and I can remember going with him to parties…When the song was running we'll just change the record. There was no mixer or nothing. For like a while we did it that way, but it was just cool, like you know, going out with my brother because he was a DJ. And at that time it probably just crossed, you know, I might have thought, you know, one day I will DJ, but it wasn't up until…You know, the whole thing: you had to be rapper first and then figure out, 'Okay, cool, but I don't want to be a solo rapper. I'm rapping with this guy and when it didn't work out with him I'll try do collaboration with a couple other people.' And then it was like, 'No, I want to be the brain behind the beat.' I want to be the guy that makes the people move kinda thing, you know. But yeah, so, and I think up until now, I still look forward to the Faculty of Hip Hop. It's like if there are people that want to wear chains around their necks, or wear the inside-out clothes, or whatever, I don't dislocate that from Hip Hop. I don't say that's not Hip Hop; it's just not my Hip Hop. And I'm trying to, from all the stuff that I got, you know, to take certain things out of that and apply it in my own situation. It will be the same whether it be religion or be it salvation issue, or whatever. Try to work it out for yourself. And that's what I'm trying to do with the Faculty of Hip Hop. Now it's like there's no like 'this is it', you know. The mission is obviously to kind of eradicate or set the records straight on…we won't say what Hip Hop is but we can say what it's not in terms of like, you know, it's not about that, and it's not about this…So for us, music is just…if jazz was the biggest selling music in our country, because, you know, because in our country Hip Hop is its music so, if jazz was the biggest selling music we'd be called the faculty of jazz, you know. But it was Hip Hop that's for me, what started, what I saw, the people's mindset. If Prophets of da City came to my school and did jazz and taught kids about voting, maybe I would have thought of jazz also…But it was kinda of, yeah, like, yeah, I can expect those from them, to the other crews. And also understanding how the elements came together like I said, you know, the face of Hip Hop and like the sound or whatever; like Falko doing his graffiti thing.

So I did that one time with Fat, with Fat…the DJing thing was more appealing. I just thought that you know, you could, it's kinda more vibe. Because for DJing people don't remember your name because you know it's always MC this, MC that, or whatever. But for DJ, they might not remember your name but they remember the way you make them feel. And it's also…like… I've been exposed to the vibe where I go to The Base and the guy puts on a song like 'Gangsta Gangsta', you know, and like when it comes to a certain part, like Ice Cube and 'I'd like to say that I'm a crazy…' and like the DJ could fade the song and the whole Base would sound to the lyrics and I was like, 'Hm.' Because that was power, you know what I mean. And I was like a referee making a whole stadium have a moment of silence for people who died in the stadium or whatever. It's like that same kind of power. One person could control it. So me, when I was exposed to that at The Base, that was like the DJ thing…and not just The Base, other places as well. And even other forms of music, I've seen it happen. So, I think that's why I went to the DJ…And the Faculty of Hip Hop – the DJ thing is so that I can have the respect, so to speak. So, if I am saying I'm Mr So-and-So from the Faculty of Hip Hop the school might be, not be as keen as when I am saying I'm DJ Eazy. And even though the teacher doesn't know me, it's like 90 per cent of the kids know who I am…So it's like using that, I don't know what you call it, but using that to get into the school, to get into the community, to get into the church youth group, or getting to whatever…yeah…[chuckles]. So, yeah, that's it man, that's me [laughs]. And Hip Hop. Boy meets girl or boy meets Hip Hop. Yeah, Eazy T…

I mean, sex for me, what's his name? Luke taught me sex education. You know, *Banned in the USA*. That was like my sex educ…(*Azuhl: 2 Live Crew*) 2 Live Crew, yeah. You know, but I mean, there was a song in there…'it's like on the count of three nailed my DJ', when he did the 'one-two-three get loose'. That was like crazy but the only other person you ever hear do that was Ready D and he did that at your school, but I'm talking way before there was like turntablism or we even knew what a DMC competition was, listening to 2 Live Crew. And that's the thing. It's like there were songs on the record that was cool, and back then the song like 'F tha Police'…because you knew that your brother was…My brother was detained because he was in a struggle, he was part of a youth movement in our community, and he was detained. So he was one of those people that would agree with the song like 'F tha Police', you know, or whatever. But there were other songs on the record that was 'Express Yourself'. You know. And that was kinda like 'I don't smoke because smoking gives you brain damage/ Brain damage on the mic it don't manage'. That's like cool, I can agree with that.

I go to church, I pray. I don't do this. I listen to this music but look at it, it's actually saying, you know what I mean. So it's cool to take those type of things off the record instead of saying stay away from it. And that's what a lot of organisations in churches are doing. It's like, I get upset when even churches or people say yeah, but loveLife is all about condoms, but what are you doing? You know what I mean? You're not doing anything, so don't say loveLife mustn't come; give the kids that. Don't say the Faculty of Hip Hop is just the Faculty of Hip Hop. Like, where are you? You know what I mean? We go to kids and to schools and someone says, 'Oh, we need more people like you to go out there. You guys should actually come to this school and that.' And I'm like, we'll go but will you put your hand in your pocket actually, you know what I mean? To actually fund it or to kind of say, 'Azuhl and Eazy, can I get you something to drink? Can I get you something to eat? How will you guys get there? Can I carry something for you?'

So, we have a mandate, so to speak. Or, we have a vision to, not save the world, you know, because we can't save everybody, but Azuhl's a father, I am a father. And it's like if I'm not here, I'd love for my child to experience the friendships or be exposed to the same kind of recruitment that I was exposed to through the Mr Fats, Ready Ds and even like Azuhl and other people. To have that kind of friendship that was about the music but you know, it was more, you know…There were very hectic times in my life when these guys were there for me and vice versa as well, you know what I mean. So, I would want my daughter to be exposed to that kind of thing, you know. If she doesn't want to have anything to do with Hip Hop, that's also fine. But I'm just saying that for me, I found something like a place, I found like a vibe that I could fit in. I was like, you know, my church group or my youth friends were cool on a Friday, on a Sunday, but on a Saturday I was at 88 Shortmarket Street [location of The Base] and you know, walked to the parade to go by the Gatsby, walked back 24-hour jam, wear pyjamas to a nightclub, watch *Malcom X* and have a break for five hours and watch the rest of the movie. I was part of all of that nonsense but no one knew who I was. I wasn't Eazy T then, I was Eazy T before then, you know what I mean? I was then just the dude that came with Fat; Fat's brother, Fat's cousin, something. You know, I was the something related to Fat. I'm the dream team everybody thought, you know, this dude was always with Fat, and that was it. People saw me in the street, just the guy who goes with Fat. And then, you know, after that, a lot of those dudes that I even saw there, they don't care. They got married, they had babies, they worked, they don't want to know anything about Hip Hop but it's like a lot of them was part of my, you know, I would say growth, or part of being the person that I am now. Because you know, of what I saw them do there, so yeah…[laughs] The Base. The book's coming out [laughter]. Watch the screen. Yeah, that was the vibe. Its home away from home for some people, so…that's the vibe.

DJ Azuhl: For me basically, Hip Hop started, for me, it started with the love of music. The area that I lived in, Rocklands…At that time we were fortunate, my mother was in the medical profession and my daddy was in civil engineering, worked at Swartklip. And we were fortunate at that time to get the first VHS video machine in our neighbourhood. Because that was the time when they just phased out the Betamax machines, you know. (*Adam: That was in the late '80s?*) Late '80s? That was about, no. That was '83. '82…'82, '83. And what my dad…because my dad had a nice, like…I'm so sad because of that…He had a very nice vinyl collection because he loved music. So obviously we grew up with that, you know, music in our house, you know, my mother as well. And one of the bonding sessions that I had with my dad is what we used to do was we used to record music videos, like the songs that we had, they used to have *Solid Gold* [TV show], they used to have TV2, *Nonqombela*, something like that. They used to have another programme, can't remember the name, we used to record those stuff. Sit up late nights. And then one day, this random video came up [singing – Hey DJ, tanananan, keep me dancing all night long]. It was the World Supreme Team and the song was 'Hey DJ'. It was a singing song but this guy would use to spin on their heads [laughs]. And like, I was hectic because every word from them they would like have, you know, Hip Hop videos, but I mean I didn't know it was Hip Hop music. They used to have another one, 'There's No Stopping Us'. It's a singing song but these guys are like tight tracksuits and these guys are spinning on their heads and spinning on their backs and stuff like that. And the first rap video that I saw like rap, rap, rap, I mean, we've seen…what was this other song? There was another famous song, which was a disco song, which had b-boys in. But the first rap song that I saw on TV was LL Cool J, 'I'm Bad'. [Raps – No rapper can rap quite like I can…] He had on a red Adidas top and a Kangol and he was rapping on the bonnet of a car, stuff like that. That was a hectic video and I used to write the lyrics of that song down. And you know, practise to that, you know. Just rewind it every Saturday morning when my parents are not there. [Raps – No rapper can rap quite like I can…] And from then on with the influx of videos that we got…because like the time that these videos came on TV that was the time that we were supposed to sleep, you know. I was still on primary school, you know. But in that time there was such a lot of music videos and raps that we got because, I mean, we just had one rap song and a bunch of, whole lot of maskandi music, you know, or '80s pop, you know, like the Madonnas or whatever was big at that time.

Just kind of write down the lyrics in my little book and practise it then, you know, do my own vibe. Practise breakdancing groups. At that time there was nobody in the area that did that that I was aware of, you know, til I got to Standard Five [last year of primary school] and there was, you know, we had…I don't know what we had at school, American Day or something where the kids can wear whatever they want to for that one day. Wear casual clothing and there was a group on stage and they kinda did the same stuff that I saw on the videos. So there is a couple of guys, you know, and I approached these, like, kids and made friends with them. And they were the guys that would introduce me to groups like the Fat Boys; groups like who was this, what's his name…Steady B. Steady B. But much like early rap stuff man. And Fat Boys because at that time the Fat Boys had about seven cassettes, you know, Fat Boys, and they used to have like the guy, that cool…making beatbox, you know. And I was like damn, the guy is making music with his mouth, you know. And from the rapping, I was introduced to beatboxing and I would do that. And the following year I would be in a group. That was Standard Six. I would be in a group. And then I would go to this guy's house, his name was Neil, he was in my class. And we would form a group, learn how to breakdance. He introduced me to a guy in our school, his name was Mak1One. He used to be in art school…

Adam: What was your group called?

DJ Azuhl: Ah, us…group's name was called Suicide Funk, and I was in a group called H2O, and I was in a group called Dev Dragon Bombers and I was in a group called…Man, it was like every month…You know, the guys will be together for three months and the group will break up. And then maybe the three that were closest friends will form a new group. And then you guys will break up and then the two will go to another group…That was like how it was like for a period of three years, you know. But I mean, there was a lot of groups in Cape Town. When I was exposed through that people, to what they were doing, when I was exposed to these, all these cassettes and stuff you know, it was like a new world opened. Because it will introduce you to other guys in your neighbourhood that you weren't aware of, just a few streets from you, and they were doing the same stuff.

At that time also, my best friend also, because I was an altar boy, since…I was an altar boy for 12 years, so I was an altar boy since I was 10 years old, yeah, since I was 10 years old. And my best friend at that time, because I mean we used to go to mass in the morning, half-past-eight mass, do the service then I used to stay there for the following mass, which was of half-past 11, you know. And there was a mass on a Saturday also, so I used to go to mass on a Saturday also. And on a Wednesday you go to the Legion of Mary and on a Sunday afternoon at six o'clock you go to youth group. So for me it was just church, church, church. Other than that, in my spare time, I mean my mom obviously didn't know about it, I was practising my Hip Hop on the side. And also I was a fairly good academic student as well. I was also good at sports so I used to practise sports as well. And also, I was doing martial arts at the same time, so it's like a whole lot of stuff.

Man, that's like a whole lot of stuff that's being hurled at you like this…And my friend, his friend actually gave me a Public Enemy cassette and I was not into this because it was too heavy for me, man. It was like heavy vibes. That cassette, I just threw on the side. I didn't listen because my vibes was like Fat Boys. Run-DMC was my favourite group actually at that time also. And when I was Standard Five my parents split up and we moved to another section in Rocklands. And when I went into high school, Standard Six, that was just like a new world because…at that time freestyle dancing was big as well, you know, on the Cape Flats because there used to be groups like… (*Eazy: Juvenitics?*) No, not Juvenitics. (*Eazy: Dynamics?*) Dynamics! The Dynamics. Yeah, they were very, very good. You know, there was like this beef between breakdancers and freestyle dancers, you know. The freestyle dancing they were like the pretty boys, who used to dance in the paisley t-shirts and stuff like that, you know. And at our school, I attended Cedar High School, the activity of Hip Hop was very, very big there. There were breakdancers, there were graffiti artists, there were MCs. And at that time, I kind of just developed into my MCing, I would say. So I joined this group. I was the beatboxer, I was the dancer and I was the MC, you know. We were a crew of seven, and at that time it was like a dope thing to have a female, you know. If you have a female in the group that was like 'it', you know.

And the way you would battle at that time was the way you would battle kids at carnivals, you know. And also like when your school, like you had presentations. Every class would have a group. A rap group, or a sing group. Your vibes was just to take them out, you know. I didn't mingle because at that time we were the best at our, at school, you know. You kinda develop this ego that you're the shit and stuff like that you know. And we managed together a gig on the town centre. They used to have this little stage in the town centre on a Saturday and people used to perform there. I think the MC's name was Luigi or something. A funny dude. Yeah, Radio Luigi, a funny dude. And we used to do our thing there you know, Thursday, Friday evening. No sleeping just practising the move, the sequences. The rappers got to be on point, the vocalist got to be on point. And if we had no show then we just rapped there. And at the same time, on a day you know, there was a whole lot of breakdancers and people from other areas around the Cape Flats, especially like Westridge and especially Beacon Valley, you know, because they also had a very, very strong Hip Hop scene there, in their little areas you know. That was also the time we witnessed the battles among the areas would happen because Westridge was known for the graffiti and the breakdancing, you know. Rocklands was known for the kinda, the vibes in between and like versus like Beacon Valley they had very, very nice MCs. And that's the first time I heard about something like the Zulu Nation because we were there for just one day and lots of guys were just…the Zulu Nation, the Zulu Nation. What's the Zulu Nation? And I met the guy there, uhm, I can't recall his name…Riley was his name, Riley was his name. He was from my school. (*Adam: What year was this about?*) This…man…this is probably… (*Adam: '89? '88?*) '89, '89…'88…'89. This guy's giving me stuff, like the same thing Eazy was…black out or whitewash or something…Black Consciousness material…that's in the library room…My father had a vibe where if I had questions he'd always tell me, 'Okay, you have a question for me. Go to the library. Go read it up yourself. Come back to me and then we can discuss it.' And I can also in my own time, you know, try to find out what this is all about if I don't understand it. So my parents were fairly kind of open in that regard, you know. And now I get this Black Consciousness thing and at the same thing this guy's telling me, 'Look at here, there's this place in town. You know [what] happens there? They play Hip Hop music, you know, they just play Hip Hop music.' Because you know that time we were hard core, our…or whatever our version of hard core was like, true to the culture you know. No radio songs, you know, just Hip Hop 24/7. And he was telling me, 'Yo, this is the place in Cape Town you have to go to. You know, the people, they dance on the speakers, you know. And they just dance on the speaker, they're just breakdancing.' I'm like, 'Okay, but we can't go to nightclubs, you know.' We were at Westridge City, you know. And Westridge, what they used to do is they used to have matinees, but I can't go to that. My mother will kill me if she is to, if she were to find out I went.

And I mean, I heard about The Base and I can recall I heard about it for about a year and I didn't go. 'Ja, you guys are good but you must come to The Base.' And in that time also, there was an article about this guy Ready D, or something, you know. And I was like okay, cool. Those guys are the top group. And then, that was about the time when *Our World* dropped. I was in town you know. And you know, like, POC and Ready D and all of that stuff. It was like even if we didn't know them or have seen them, it was like an urban legend about this group and about this guy that was so good at turntables or whatever, you know. And we were at this place in town called Vibes. And that was also the advent of CDs, I think. The CDs just came in, but I mean, they had vinyls at that time. And I can still recall I bought an LL Cool J record 'I'm Bad', the 'I'm Bad' record with my crew at that time. And we walked and my friend was like, 'That's that Ready D guy.' And we went to him and we stopped him. I wonder if he can still recall this. And he was still, yeah, actually Malikah was still with him at that time. D had this long freaking tail on his hair; black cap – a cap that said SWAT – Specialist With A Turntable, you know.

I don't know man, he's got African medallions, black jacket, you know. I was like, 'Ja, we heard about The Base, blah, blah.' And he said, 'No, no, no, no, we can all take the train together, you know. You just…where do you stay…no…' Naa, we stay in Rocklands and he was, 'No, no, just take the train to Lentegeur station this and that time and we can, you know, all go together to The Base.' But then, you know, at that time we're young. Our vibe was like we want to battle this group called Prophets of da City. They have a *kwaai* [cool/dope] DJ, they have a *kwaai* rapper, *kwaai* dancer, everything was *kwaai* you know. What is it that we…can contribute that can be different? We must get a vocalist but we don't have a DJ, you know. Okay cool, we're gonna have to work that out somehow. And when I went to The Base, the first time I went, my deceased best friend, Ronald was his name. He went with me because he was actually the guy that taught me how to dance. He was a brilliant dancer. We went to The Base. Man! It was just like you come into this dark place…Like when you stand outside you see all these guys, you see a guy on a wheelchair, you see a fat dude with hair that's wet that's still here like a Steven Seagal haircut. You know, and standing with a baseball bat, you know. And you see another dude with that pants that's over, you know. You stand in a long line and you kinda feel, you feel intimidated because this is like new territory you know, and then…We've heard about stories about guys that they just chase away…They just chase you out of the line. If they don't like you, they just chase you. And I mean we didn't know anybody by then, you know. Because our vibe was like we begin our little community, you know.

And we went in and you know this DJ was playing a song and this DJ was like scratching the same thing, you know, that I saw on videos, you know. The thing Jam Master Jay was doing this guy was scratching. But besides scratching…he's scratching and then there's a b-boy battle there and then this dude comes behind the turntables and he actually dances and I was like, 'Damn!' You know. And that was Ready D by the way, you know. Damn! That is hectic! You know. And this dude goes back and this dude plays and then there's a section in the vibe where guys come up to rap, whatever, whatever, whatever. You know, at that time you're like, okay cool, maybe I'm not the shit [laughs]. Maybe I'm not the shit because there's a lot of guys doing this actually. You don't feel so special anymore, you know. Because, I mean, I'm sure the capacity of The Base was plus 200, I'm very sure of that, you know. It was a big place, you know. And you know, then for me at that time there was almost like…I'm like a little child, I'm just gonna absorb whatever was happening here you know. I used to go down, I used to go, and obviously I used to tell my parents I'm going somewhere else. Go to The Base.

And at that time, because also in my class I was a good student…though I belonged to a crew, I was very…I was an introvert man, you know. The only time I would kinda…you'd see my personality was when I step on the stage, basically. That's like my vibe, you know. But other than that, I was a good student, never in trouble, you know. Yeah. And there was this guy in my class called Neil, and he told me one day…it was also when this other group… we broke up and stuff. He told me, 'Come to my house. We can start a crew. You're a nice rapper, you know. I'm a DJ.' Yeah you're a DJ, there's only one DJ. There's only one DJ. That DJ's the shit! I went to his house and this is a true story…I went to this guy's house, I mean he was a very silent dude. And he's like, 'I'm gonna show…' I don't know what happened man but he said, 'I'm gonna show you…' I think I asked him to DJ for me, or something. And this guy had a hi-fi, you know the hi-fi with the two-deck tapes? And he put on…I can distinctively remember because, like after that I went to go and buy those two records. It was Tone Lõc…Lõc-ed *After Dark*, or something. And on that record, there's a certain section that's a vocals, that's like an interlude where it just talks and he put the needle on that part of the record. And this guy was scratching and I mean he used the balance, the balance knob, he was turning it up and down like this and it makes 'cause his…What it does is the same function that a fader does by cutting off…eliminating the sound when you pull the record back, you know. He did the same thing and it sounded like scratching and I was like…Damn! I saw that dude in the club do this DJing thing with two turntables and a mixer and you're doing it with your mom's stereo and I mean, it's exactly the same…the same sound and the same pattern and I was like, I want to do this. I want to be a DJ, you know. I was still doing the MCing thing but my thing was always I wanted to be a DJ. And moving through high school, I belonged to SRC. And obviously with the advent of the conscious rap, you know, like with the BDP [Boogie Down Productions] and Public Enemy and stuff like that… and the stuff that they were saying. Because I never knew who Farrakhan was, and I never knew what Black Power was and all of that stuff…And the SRC does, was the type of stuff that you will hear of, but you would not understand because our vibe was all about, 'We can now go to the 'lectric station and they're gonna burn the 'lectric station.' I want to be part of that team to see what's happening there. I mean, when I'm in front of my parents I'm like an angel but like at school I'm rolling with people like my mother will not appreciate, you know. But I would want to be part of this team because I want to see what all these throwing stones and stuff like that was all about. I mean, the struggle didn't kind of affect me, though. One day in Rocklands they had a…they sent over…they were cordoning off one section and there were helicopters that flew over and people were checking tires and stuff like that. Actually, a friend of mine got shot there at the back with a rubber bullet. I mean, he was next to me so that could have been me. I think that kinda just showed…that swayed my whole perception of what this thing was about. It's not about throwing and having fun. And in the same time, I found out that my father was actually very active in this struggle thing. You know. And he didn't ask anything. You know. And because I can distinctively also remember, I think I was playing something because what did happen – I come from school, do my work, clean the house, make sure five to six that the kettle is boiled. Because if I come from work, I'm the guy that must make tea for them, you know. But in that time that music was like plus 10, you know. It's like Black Power, blah, blah, blah, blah, blah, blah. I think he came from work early or something. And he asked me, 'What are you listening to?' My dad would always use to tell me put the music softer please, put the music softer. And he's like, you know, 'The stuff you're listening to is very dangerous stuff, you know. Do you know what this is?' Blah, blah, blah, blah. And he kinda schooled me on that side of what the struggle is, and all of that.

So taking that kind of consciousness with me through school, through my school life and also the Hip Hop thing, because I had to make decisions when I was Standard 10, Standard

9, 10. I had to decide whether am I gonna, how can I say it, am I gonna choose an academic life for myself because you know I was a good student and I can get into a university and a technikon. I was actually gonna do food technology, and…or am I gonna pursue an athletic career because I was also good at that. Or am I gonna do music? So, I mean, music, obviously, at that time for people was just a hobby, you know, but my vibe was like, I wanna do this because there's groups like Prophets of da City that were on the *Toyota Top 40*. I mean, these guys were performing with Quincy Jones! You know, these guys were like touring Europe for a year. You know. Because – just to come back because I'm going back and forth – in my school, I used to go to D a lot, to Ready D a lot. And if you have to know where Ready D stays, he lives in Lentegeur. I live in Rocklands. I used to walk from Rocklands to Lentegeur, which was a 50-minute walk. A 50-minute walk just till there. Sometimes I'll get to his house because I used to bunk school also, you know, just to go sit there and watch this guy make beats for their next album called *Age of Truth*. I mean literally sit there and have this guy Fat MC come in there and, you know, you come in there and there was a song on the album called 'Here We Go', and that was a Jam B song. Because D made the song for Jam B, you know. And I was there that day when Fat came through and asked, 'Yo, I want the song now. Me and Martian want to write.' And D's like, 'Shaheen said we must use this song for our album.' And they went into a tussle: 'No, D, you can't do that because you see, blah, blah, blah!' 'No, but Shaheen said we have to use the song,' you know, and that song appeared on the *Age of Truth* album. 'Here We Go.'

Also, at that time, I mean, D was making beats for the crew that I also belong in.

I used to see him work on the S50 just to, you know. I mean I wasn't into making beats. I wanted to DJ, that was my…I wanted to DJ. But I never kinda had the courage to ask this dude, 'Let me show you some of my skills.' Because by then I also know how to use my little tape deck, you know, because of the skills this other guy taught me…I can remember it was two years I went to D religiously like I…It almost like I went to a church, you know. And nothing… This dude wouldn't even tell me, 'No, you can't touch the decks.' Nothing. I would just sit there. At six o'clock: 'Damn, I have to go home.' And go. That time I think D had a black Ford, or something; he used to take me home sometimes, you know. Because at that time I also belonged to the Zulu Nation because I used to get information from the States and I used to give it to him. So, that was like my vibe, you know. Yeah, you know, I've got this cassette, you know. I was like cool, cool, cool and…I've got my access to be there and check out the whole vibe, you know. So, yeah, I went there for two years basically. And one day D said, I think [it] was '96. 'No, no, no I think it was '95. It was '95.' He said, 'You can have a shot…do your thing…you want to scratch?' I was like, 'Yeah, I want to scratch.' And I sounded whack, you know. Because it was my first time on SL turntables, and obviously the torque is different. I'm not used to a mixer and like, 'Damn, I'm embarrassing myself in front of this dude.' And I can remember that he just walked out. And you know D can be very serious in front of you; I'm sure he's making fun of you behind your back. Because that's just how he is, you know. As he came out, this other dude was sitting in the lounge and that happened to be E-20. I'm like dude, this is my competition? That's the dude I have to take out? No, I didn't say it, but I was just thinking this is the dude. I know, because I've heard about this dude and I've actually seen him, you know. Because D, Shamiel and E-20 was kinda like the first guys that did the, I would say, team or group DJ thing where three DJs would do things, you know. And E-20 was also the guy POC used to take with to Germany or stuff like that when they'd do POC tours, you know. So, I'm like damn, this dude…After that D would kinda let me on the decks, kinda like show me techniques, stuff like that. I mean I didn't have my own turntables. He'd show me stuff and I'd like go home to nothing, basically [laughing]. I'd go home to nothing. Until this other guy that used to belong to the TVA crew. He was also in our crew; his name is Angelo. He actually told me let's buy a set of decks together. He bought the turntable, I bought the mixer. Bought it from some house DJ. I mean, that mixer, three months and it was dead. At the same time also I've known Falko for a while. Falko used to come over. We practised, do DJ stuff. We'd go dance, because I mean besides graffiti, Falko was a b-boy as well so he danced as well.

And then since then, I would just like, you know, this is actually what I want to do. I don't want to be a rapper, being in the forefront because it seems so hard to write raps for a whole album – 23 tracks and you have to come up with brilliant concepts, so I'd do the DJ thing. If I fast-forward a bit, I also met a girl by the name of Eloise Jones through this guy Angelo.

Adam: Which Angelo was this?

DJ Azuhl: It's not Angelo from Black Noise. Anyway, he was a graffiti artist for TVA. I met this girl…'96. I met her through him because he matriculated and, at his matric ball, she was the waitress. And he was like, 'This was the girl I was talking to you about.' Her name is Eloise.

She can rap in French! And she does French and she can rap in French. I was like, 'Can she rap? Bring her to the house.' And he brought her, this girl was like rapping. I was like damn, this is heavy. And we started a crew, myself, Eloise, him and another dude. I can't remember the name of the crew, I have to ask her what the name of the crew was. And then it just so happened that Angelo took his studies more kinda serious, blah, blah, blah and we kinda fell apart then. It was only me and EJ [Eloise]. And then we were like, 'Cool, how are we gonna be a crew?' I still have our last pictures together. Are we gonna be a crew? She was like, 'No, no, no, I know this guy John. I've also seen John from around. He can make beats.' We hooked up with him and we formed this group called Neophytes. So it was me, John One and EJ – from Godessa now [laughs]. We formed the crew, '96. We recorded. I have to get those tracks. But we recorded an EP [extended play] for three songs. Actually, the first time…I mean because he was very…he studied music, so that kind of just…he taught us more of the technical aspects of music, you know. And he was a qualified sound engineer as well. And I mean, we went in and we recorded this demo in Strandfontein. I don't know what the studio's name was at that time but it was like knobs and like, 'We've made it! We made it! This is like woah! Big studio not in a room!' We recorded this demo. Got nice airplay on the community radio stations and even radio group, I mean for that time, '97. I think it's called Energy or something like that. But we recorded material for an album, we most probably had about 50 songs to record already, you know.

But what happened in '97…I always had this thing with…because at that time also…such a lot of things, sorry for being so long…Around about '96, we started with this, with the park jams where we just used to practise outside and people used to walk past, and my vibe was, 'Why don't we just make this a whole lot, a big party for the people to enjoy?' And I mean I had whack turntables, or whatever, you know, at that time, and we would just bring it out. The tree still exists where we had our park jam. It still exists. So, you know, it's in my quarters, it's like a little tree with a shade and it's like a big circle to dance there, whatever, whatever. I used to take it to my friend's dad because he used to be a mobile DJ, whatever. So we used it for park jams. It was the summer of '96. I'll never forget it. The following year we kinda started this organisation called Vision Productions, you know. We're gonna take park jams across Mitchells Plain. That vibe. That was our big goal, besides other stuff that was happening at that time. Because the b-boy scene at that time was just big. Big, big, big, big. So myself, this guy called…this guy who normally used to come to my house, his name was Wesley. We would later be the producer of a group called Parliament. And we met this guy from Namibia that was on holiday. He said, 'You guys must come over to Namibia and do what you do there.' Okay, cool, you know. Myself, Mak1One, this girl Melinda, Wesley, a guy called Terence, a guy called Ronald, and another dude, we went over. It was a DJ, an MC, a vocalist and b-boys, and a graffiti writer. When we went to Lüderitz; we went to Swakopmund, we went to Walvis Baai. There were other two places we didn't perform at. Where we were based was in Lüderitz. That was the summer of '97. That was the first time, the same time when the Neophytes thing kinda blew up.

So, what happened was John's mother was like the manager. She was like very strict you know. Every week when we go we used to pay subs. I think that was two rand at that time. So we used to rehearse on a Friday, a Saturday and a Sunday. So remember, we get together, we get to his house, we write our songs, you play a beat because he has a week to produce a beat. Sit down, write the lyrics, write concepts. In a matter of that whole weekend we'll have two songs, you know. And his mother became…set us up with shows and stuff like that you know. So it became kinda hectic because it's like, 'Damn, we have a manager now.' And stuff like that. And at the same time, I had to make a decision to go in this thing and I was like, 'Dudes, we're busy with this whole Vision Productions thing that you guys wanna go with to Namibia. We can do this at home.' It's like cool, cool, cool, cool, cool. But I think John's mother wasn't so happy of the whole idea for her own reasons. And I rebelled. I just bounced…That was like December holidays…and I just bounced from my three weeks and when I came back I just heard, 'You're no longer in the crew.' I was like, 'What did I do?' Yeah, but…because we had all this manifesto vibe, you know, that we had that. You know, thou shalt not do this, thou shalt not do that. I kinda broke the rules…Damn! That was like sad, you know. We just went our separate…not separate ways, but we kinda stopped the Neophytes thing. And I know that John still wanted to continue with the thing, but I mean, his mother, you know. His mother has rules, stuff like that…We were still in contact and stuff like that but by then, I mean I was sick of this crew thing, blah, blah, blah, and I was just like I'm heavily gonna concentrate on this DJ thing. And I can remember we pushed the park jams back hard to the core. We had like…I think it was '98, '99. We had park jams every month, we had like two for the month, so we were serious about this Vision Productions. I still have the flyer also, 'Pushing the Real Hip

Hop', you know, in the box. And I think that's the thing that kinda...because I always wanted something like that. You know, because I used to read about stories about Kool Herc, you know, putting his sound system through the block parties and doing all that.

When we started the Faculty of Hip Hop, and when I read about the idea of the Faculty of Hip Hop, I was like I wanted to be part of that, you know, because my thing was like I always wanted to...if it wasn't Faculty of Hip Hop, I would have come up with my own thing in any way. It will be something else but it would be something that would be ghetto, would [be] grassroots, Hip Hop activism, if I can use that word. And also development, you know. But at the same time '98, while we did the Boogie Down Nights...I think, was it at that time? I can't recall...No, it was not Boogie Down Nights yet, D asked me if we can do something together. If I can play at this party in Johannesburg and EJ von Lyrik would go with us, blah, blah, blah... Actually I lied. I was in Johannesburg before then because I was in Joburg for a competition, but this was as a DJ, my first job with D! And we did a gig there and afterwards, when we were in Yeoville, I was called into this office. It was the first time I've been to a rap office. I think it's as big as your office and there used to be these little tapes, Betamax tapes and VHS tape. And it was marked, it was marked Amsterdam. It was marked UK. It was marked practice session. POC footage. And there's one wall just dedicated to POC footage. Like we're talking probably footage from '88, you know, because there's pre-POC stuff in there. I'm like, damn, what is this? I was called in by this guy called Lance, and he's like...And prior to that Fat spoke to me, actually. This is '98, yeah, this is '98. Actually no, not Fat, D spoke to me. D was like, 'You know we may want to maybe give you a trial if you're interested to do this thing with this group called Skeem.' I'm like, 'Skeem?' 'Ja, it's a new kwaito group with Ishmael and stuff, and if you wanted to DJ for them.' I'm like, 'Ja, but I'm not prepared to move to Johannesburg, you know.' So I'm like okay cool, cool, cool...And then one year he asked me, 'We're looking for a DJ for BVK,' you know. That was '98. '98, '99. Because, by then, the DJ at that time, E-20, he decided to put his energies into his business at the time.

Adam: I think his father passed away.

DJ Azuhl: So, he was also going through a lot of personal stuff at that time as well. Because they gave another DJ like the chance...It was Big Dre. He did the tour with them...That was not what they were looking for. And it's like...*naai* [no], because they wanted somebody live and with energy and all that stuff…Okay, I'm gonna give this a shot, you know. Because I mean, I was like, 'Okay, cool, I'll just join this group, it's fine.' I mean, BVK was big, but I mean for me my long-term plan at that time was I wanna start my own thing, concentrate on my DJing and do this Vision Productions thing. I don't want to do anything with people anymore. People are problems, you know. And, like I say, I just wanted to be a DJ in BVK, nothing serious because I didn't want to handle stress with rehearsals or money or stuff like that. I was just happy to get to the venue, show off, do my scratching and bounce, that's my thing. And, ja, was with BVK since then, that was '98. You know what I mean, that's a blessing because that opened up other kind of doors for me. BVK was also kinda responsible for me coming out of that shell, you know, because having an MCing background and stuff, you know, at times I had to fill in for members and stuff like that, you know. So, it kinda forced me to kinda pick up my pen again and scribble stuff, whatever, whatever, even though sometimes for the most part until I think it was last year, I still did own lyrics and stuff, you know. I had to introduce new stuff. So, at that time, it was since…'98, '99, it was leaving the Neophytes. They're asking me to join BVK because they have another plan for this girl called EJ von Lyrik they wanted to join POC, you know. And they speak to us in separate rooms, you know, and we come out, 'Ah, man. What do you think about this?' I was just like, 'Don't know, what do you think?' I'm like, 'Okay, do your thing with POC, you do your thing, I'll do my thing with BVK, and somehow we'll meet again and we'd do whatever we wanted to do. Do our own group or whatever.' You know. It's been 10 years. Nothing has happened yet but we're still in contact because we belong to the same record label called High Voltage, so that's good.

So, it was BVK, it was just doing the park jams in Mitchells Plain and then it was like 2002, 2003 when, you know, because we had the Boogie Down Nights parties as well, which was like landmark Hip Hop parties, I would say. I won't even say parties. I would say events, you know, for groups and DJs, you know, like the Dead Prezes…So it was doing those parties, if I could fast-forward, I think it was 2003, was getting a call from a guy, a white dude, Richard, asking me…Actually I lie, before Richard there was this other guy called Baby. I get weird phone calls from this guy and this guy would go, do you want to do a show? What show? He said a radio show, I have a radio show at UCT Radio every Saturday. I'm like, radio, spinning on radio, that would be cool. Because I always envied to play on Bush Radio, but I never had the guts to say give me a slot because at that time Dre was doing a show, you know, give me a slot too, you know. And this guy called me and say, 'You can come in and you can play whatever you want to. I'm gonna give you an hour slot.' I was like, what? An hour of my own stuff? Hell, yeah, you know. For a year, actually, eight months, I used to travel, take two taxis from Surrey Estate, you know, change in Mowbray, get here by the Main Road, by the Baxter [Theatre]. I'd walk up and I used to have this DJ Syndicate freaking bag. And that's probably, I'm not telling you a word of a lie, I think that's 25 to 35 kgs that I have to carry because my whole stash is in there. I carry it up and you know like, it's *opdraands* [uphill]. Carry it. Get there. Play the show. Go home. For eight months I did that.

Eight months was done, and the guy called me again and he was like, 'We're doing it again this year.' I'm like, 'It's cool, you know.' Because, at that time a whole lot of other things was working out for me as well. You know. Thing with the DJ name just kinda grew. A whole lot of other things were happening. I was getting paid for gigs and stuff like that, you know. So, until, I mean, I love radio because that is what I used to do as a kid – go home, switch on the radio, Dimitri Jegels, *Two-Thirty Date*. And I mean also like, one of those *Two-Thirty Dates*, POC was in the studio. I did a thing for Childline also, for a radio, Good Hope, I think. Dial 800-123-31 toll free, something like that. Yeah. So, 2003, I think 2003 I was speaking under correction, I get a call from this guy. Actually, Fat told me first that this dude wants me to come in for a guest slot as a guest on his radio show that he's giving with this girl called Kate. *The Ghetto Pimp Show*. It's all good. We went – myself and Eazy, we went and did a couple of sessions. I don't know like for me I think that Eazy also kinda had the same vision at that time also because, like I said, my thing was I wanted to be a part of an organisation that does grassroots stuff, you know. And obviously I have my own agenda also to push, but what I mean, which is also positive you know. And Richard told us what this Faculty of Hip Hop kinda stands for and stuff like that. And I was like cool, you know. And we did like small, little projects, but in essence if you think about it, I think it's big projects because at that time nobody was doing that or even thinking about the stuff we were thinking about, and still to this day, you know. The concepts and stuff like that.

So we came up with the, one of the stuff, one of our main projects is called the Ghetto Bootlegs, where we take the recordings of an artist and put it on a CD, make a compilation CD and sell it for 20 bucks. If you sell it for 20 bucks, you can make as much copies of that music, but you're not to change the format or anything, you know, just pass it on. The aim of that project is just for the music to float around, basically. What I mean, I think that we have given out more bootlegs than even selling them, you know. I mean from that CDs we had guys, Jitsvinger on there, we had a group like Ancient Men. We had a guy by the name of Scully and Garlic Brown. Even from Volume Three onwards, there's more international groups from Germany, even the States, even Thailand, you know. So the whole idea had just kinda grown. What was funny for me if I go overseas, you know, because you kinda don't realise the magnitude of the thing you're busy with, man…for the first three years, it's like cool yeah, we're doing stuff, we're doing different stuff, but you don't comprehend the magnitude. You go overseas like a place like Belgium or France even, and you tell people, 'No I'm busy with this.' Because they interview you, 'So apart from DJing, what are you doing?' Oh I do…I'm busy with Faculty of Hip Hop blah, blah, blah. 'What is it, blah, blah, blah. Wow, we don't have something like that here.' What? You know.

So that kinda opened my eyes to kinda push our agenda and just fulfil the kind of, the goals and aims that we have as an organisation, you know, which is access to opportunities. Something that Eazy always kinda mentions you know. And just using Hip Hop as the tool because, it's not like we're going to school and we want to convert people to become DJs, graffiti writers, MCs, beatboxers, you know. It's just using it as a tool so that they can, you know, be aware of their leadership skills, whether it is to show you how you can discipline yourself to attain your goals, you know, whether it is to spread a message, you know. Those are the type of stuff that we've kinda presented in schools. You know, we've had other programmes where we had facilitators come in and share the knowledge on music software, even lyric writing, how to exist as an artist within the music industry. What is publishing, music copywriting, all of those stuff, you know. So that is kinda our mandate, if I can put it as such, as an organisation. So it kinda fits in to my character, to…while I'm striving to be as a human being. And also it perfectly fits into the projects and groups that I'm affiliated [to] and that I'm [a] member of like the BVKs, like the High Voltage stable, so to speak, you know, Beat Bangers, all of that stuff. So it just falls into that. So, it's not something that is in isolation, I would say. I carry it with me every day as I would carry being a member of BVK or just being DJ Azuhl, or whatever, whatever, you know.

DJ Eazy: His radio show was on Monday, we were the guests. I think we came the last Monday of every month or something, for like four months in 2002. And then like he said, 'Oh, this is what's going to happen towards the end of the year'…And then, like you were saying and what we're doing now is simply what we are doing to reach it because we gathered that we didn't have like a hectic background. He didn't know people, like, I don't know, like Mak1One was. You know, you heard his name come up in conversations, you knew him from media but he didn't know a lot of people like who the big players were. He knew about Emile, but they didn't know, you know, like their music or such…So, we would talk about stuff like that and say look, he had the Vision Productions, and the people, like I said I was friends with his crew and some other you know, similar…back in space and time we had something called like the CRA, which is like the Christian Rap Association, and everybody had to come to our thing. If you weren't part of us you were like blaspheming. You weren't rapping for Jesus [laughter]. And we'd do the same thing, go to the Town Centre and rap. Pay, the church pays 50 bucks for that space. I can't believe they charge 50 bucks for that space, you pay 50 bucks and you can use that four hours. The platform of the Town Centre, the PA system, and there's the Westridge Mall talent searches. And you know, just as he's talking, there's lot of stuff that comes up and we were saying like Vibes was the one place…but Ragtime Records was the spot. And I knew people who bought their records there and passed it on to their younger brothers who were my friends…So for us it was like, look, there's a bunch of places out there, but we actually had to work with all these other people because they have access. Because by then, we knew about this brilliant shop called High Five. You know, it's like they import records blah, blah, blah. So it's like you know a lot of kids on the Cape Flats didn't know you can go there and get Public Enemy stuff there. A lot of kids don't know Ready D actually make beats for MCs. A lot of kids don't know that there's a guy named Hipe who makes beats. So we said, if you have all this information, you actually want to be the Yellow Pages of Hip Hop.

DJ Azuhl: That's how it started, yeah.

DJ Eazy: You know, that's how it started, Yellow Pages of Hip Hop. So we wanted to like say, you know because, between us, like if you wanted something done, if he didn't know, I mean if I didn't know, we knew someone who could get it for us. And if I have 10 phone calls, nine of it would be looking for – someone will be looking for [a] graffiti writer, looking for a b-boy…Shamiel X introduced me to the Each One, Teach One people, you know…People arrive here and say, 'Hey, I'm doing the internet *Vibe* magazine can I get an interview? What's your comment on this?' And it becomes a big thing…The Department of Education has a career guidance festival, if you want to call it that. It's called the Learners Expo, hey? The Cape Learners Expo. It's like a career guidance festival. Over three days, like 80 schools, like from the greater Western Cape area; it's like every day whatever, buses come up every day, like 20 schools show up between nine o'clock to four o'clock. And the final day is their last because everybody is exhibiting career choices and you can come and say, 'I want to be a fireman, what subjects must I do?' You can do marine biology and you can do botany, there's lots of government stuff. You can go to the army, you can go to the hospital. And this lady calls me and she says, 'Hey, some people that we know through an events company…just talked to Mr Fat and he said there's a thing called a Faculty of Hip Hop. Aren't you exhibiting at the career expo? Because the kids want to know what subjects must they do to study at the Faculty of Hip Hop.' It's like going to the law faculty or the science faculty. So, obviously I was like, what?…

CHAPTER 4.
GODESSA'S ENTRY INTO HIP HOP IN THE EARLY 2000s

BURNI AMAN, SHAMEEMA WILLIAMS
AND EJ VON LYRIK WITH ADAM HAUPT

Godessa spoke to Adam Haupt in Woodstock in 2002 as their career as a crew started to take shape. The crew broke new ground as the country's most prominent female hip crew, which went on to initiate international collaborative projects, such as Rogue State Alliance.

Adam: Godessa – as in Burni, Eloise and Shameema – how, why, when did this thing come about? How did it happen?

Eloise: Where did Godessa start out?…We started in April 2000, around that time – March.

Shameema: Early 2000.

Eloise: Uhm, we basically got together because Shameema was the coordinator for this whole, this soundtrack of this documentary called *Tomorrow's Heroes*. Basically, it's just about gangsterism on the Cape Flats. And then she called Burni up, she called me up and a bunch of other artists as well. And we were initially gonna do a track each, but then we decided to collaborate on one track. And we just felt that the energy, the vibe was very good between the three of us and we thought about getting together as well. But it was also Shameema's dream for a long time to get a female crew together, so maybe she can say a bit more.

Shameema, in retrospect:
The artist we worked with was Mr Devious, who at the time had formed a crew with producer Bradley Williams and Duanne Jacobs called Untouchable Fellas. They were all from Beacon Valley and Bradley became our producer after the project once we formed as Godessa. There was also Marco Polo, a very talented freestyle MC and beatboxer from Lavender Hill. This all happened at Black Beach Studios in Muizenberg, owned by Jonathan DeVries, and

the documentary was directed by John Fredericks, now known for his biographical movie *Noem My Skollie*. The project came to me while working as a creative-writing facilitator for CRED [Creative Education for Youth at Risk] at Pollsmoor Prison with John.

On the formation of Godessa, looking back at it now, it happened very naturally, like it was supposed to be the three of us. I always wanted to be in a crew with Burni since I first heard her at Angels [nightclub] during the mid-'90s; she had a raw energy that I loved, and when I heard how EJ [Eloise] had been slaying dudes at battles I knew she would have the tenacity for it. I think I was looking for strong women I could go into battle with. And that's exactly what those years felt like and I don't think any other women would have had the strength to endure what we had to face as the years passed by.

Shameema: I think you know pretty much what happened. We met around about the time also that I was trying to get, uhm, like some kind of crew together when I was at Bush [Radio]. Uhm.

Adam: I think we first met '98, '99.

Shameema: Ja.

Shameema: And I'd known Burni for a couple of years by then and we tried to do something. I don't know, at that time I guess everybody was still very young, finishing school, uhm, never ever took Hip Hop serious in any way. It was just about going like to parties and that kind of thing. That was the general vibe, uhm, at the time. And I just started connecting with the people from the Hip Hop generation before us – that having grown up listening to the stuff from that generation, it kind of informed this drive to not just a female crew just rapping, whatever, although that it seems like we do. Now we're labelled a politically conscious type of group and essentially we, I think we have become that, although not everything we say is necessarily – like people think that we're political, but my argument always is that anything in this world, anything related to our situation, uhm, the way we grow up, just like anything is related to politics. So we've kind of taken on that role to deliver commentary on what's happening around us and to show what's happening and to show the youth what the political situation is in this country. So, I think a couple of years ago when I was trying to form a crew, that that didn't really come across because you're so young, because the last thing on your mind is, is how fucked up the country, or whatever. Now we're much older and we realise that, that something needs to be said, someone needs to say it. Prophets of da City could do it and they made a very big impact on especially the coloured community in general and especially the Hip Hop uhm community. So their time has ended and there hasn't been a group in that time up until, I think, us now, that has been able…to have that sort of impact, to make people think about their situation. For me, Prophets of da City made me think how, as a coloured person, talking about the political history of the country. So we can kind of take on that type of, that role as well. We can teach, uhm, similar things that they did, you know? That's where I mean I think from the crew – I mean when we recorded our first song we didn't know we were going to be Godessa, uhm. We just clicked so well together and we realised we're on the same wavelength and we want [to] use this thing for more than just music and that we've grown up in this Hip Hop culture very positively that we need to use this to take it out to like show people that you can use this movement to have a positive impact on people's lives. And I really think we have, every show that do, uhm, interviews or, we always get feedback from people and it's always been positive. I think just once we had this fucked up attitude – Hip Hop Indaba. This fucking white boy came walking up to us after we performed and – at the Indaba – it was at the breakdancing dancing champs and we could only do just one song. So we did 'Affirm to the Action'. That song was a very Black Conscious song. When we wrote it we like, okay, we going to write with the perspective that we're affirming ourselves, uhm, our identity, uhm, we're not recognised as black people in this country – we're called coloured people. We think we're African, we're black, so we're gonna say that with this song. We got attacked by this white boy saying that we're excluding…that we're excluding people when we do a Black Conscious song and we almost got into an argument with him because all that we were doing with this song was affirming our identity. And the fact that he had a problem with that, that a white person came up to us and told us that this is [a] problem is like, you know, just, 'Just fuck off.' Step back because this is who we are and like we're sick and tired of having people – just in general any coloured person, that we've been labelled as coloured people, that – we're very proud of being so-called coloured, but don't have to be called coloured. I find it derogatory. I'm an African, I'm a black person because I'm not white. You know what I mean? So I mean like sometimes we run into those sorts of issues where recently we performed, we perform to crowds that are like 80 per cent white because now it's like 80 per cent of people who listened to Hip Hop, that buy Hip Hop, that can afford to pay 40 bucks at the door at the club, is fucking white.

Eloise: And also I think this guy, this guy's only heard this song once and with the messed-up sound that we had, people couldn't really exactly hear what we were saying. So it was really a situation where he was just attacking us for the sake of doing that and not really what you actually say. 'Please explain to me what this song is actually about.' And it's also basically about making black people feel proud of themselves because for years people like, so-called coloured people especially, have always looked up to whites and thinking about white is better than black. So that's wrong to me, you know, and that's part of the reason I wrote that verse for that specific song and nobody's gonna tell me that's wrong, you know what I mean.

Shameema: We've grown up in a society where, where like my mother them, like they vote NP and I've lived in communities where the majority of coloured people around me would say, 'Fuck the ANC.' And you grow up hearing your grandparents say, '*Kyk daar gaan 'fokking kaffir daar* [Look there goes a fucking kaffir there].' Like, you know growing up with those types of things. Like I lived in Kraaifontein for a while and I was walking to the station one day and this fucking *snotgat* [snotty-nosed/snippy] small little white girl – I walk past and she calls me a kaffir. And it's like, you know, that same situation happens in like coloured communities where, where coloured parents teach their kids things like that. I see it happening with my little nieces growing up now, where my grandparents and my sister and them say those sorts [of] things in front of them and they then learn that. So with us doing a song like that, for instance, like she was saying this is who we are and we must stop…

Eloise: …thinking less of ourselves.

Shameema: …thinking that we're in the middle 'cause that's how we're never going to move forward as coloured people, we're never going to have, we're never gonna get what we want if we don't stop thinking like that.

Eloise: And also like in the past we were all so box that in our communities like coloured people just amongst the coloured, like black folk and that type of thing and since '94 or so, you know, [Nelson] Mandela's release, like nothing has really changed. There hasn't been a real integration of people, especially in Cape Town in the Western Cape. So people who are still really insecure about who they are and when they hear something which is positive and, you know, you're speaking out about how you feel about yourself. I'm a black person, I'm a coloured person then it's like, okay, whoa. It's a bit too much, a bit too soon for them, and, uhm, which is sad thing, it's been quite [a] couple of years since so-called…

Shameema: …democracy.

Eloise: Ja. Democracy and stuff like that. Uhm, people need to realise that just because, you know…apartheid was more [than] just your skin colour. You know what I mean? Or your hair colour. It was an, an economic oppression of most people, you know what I mean? So it's about whether you're black on the outside or whatever. It's about – these days it's about how much money you have. It's a class system right now. So people still need to recognise that and they need to fight against that because, you know, if we don't work together, then we're never going to get anywhere.

Shameema: I think it's like quite a plastic thing that has now happened since '94 where again I would use POC as an example – and this is the kind of thing that came up in the panel discussions we had – and it's like before POC had emerged on *Age of Truth*, for instance, where they were speaking out against the NP government. Uhm, and the ANC backed it – they supported it so much up to the point that they used it as a vehicle to go around to schools to teach them about the elections and whatever. And they did that under the ANC banner. Now you have like a group like Skwatta Kamp doing a song about politics and dissing the ANC government and now it's a problem and I think the general vibe is people are scared to speak out against, against the government because the government is run by the ANC. That is pretty fucked up because we, like everyone, fought against the Nationalist government and it changed the country so drastically and now people are scared [of] the ANC government and what's happening in the government right now is, it's making people feel insecure because all the years they fought these people and within the media every day you see the faults in the government, all the fraud, all the stuff that they catching on, man. Daily buying jets and fucking Mercedes Benz, importing it from overseas where people are like in shacks and when their shacks burn down there's like nowhere to put them type of thing. So people are scared to fight against the government – I think it's sad because the only, because that the ANC and the black people in this country were able to get that democracy, to kick the NP out of power was because they actively fought for that, they died for that and people just won't do that now because they think they fought for this government and they still [think] things are going to change. They still have this hope that things are gonna change and I don't see that happening because it's been six years already and things have gone from bad to worse for people like physically in this country. And it's so sad. Like I understand why people are moving out of South Africa, uhm. There's too much corruption in this country at the moment… Nothing is gonna change. That's why I say, like when we write a song everything comes down to politics at the end of it. No matter what we write about, it comes down to politics at the end of it because it's just like nothing in this country is gonna work. The AIDS situation isn't gonna change if politicians [don't] change their fucking mindsets or, you know what I mean, their beliefs. Poverty is not gonna change, just nothing, the economic situation, none of that is gonna change with the politicians that run this country right now with the way they think. They've abused their power and they let down so much people; that people that supported them to be able to get that power in the first place. This is turning a bit political.

Adam: This is pretty cool – completely what my mission is about, actually.

Shameema: And we're very young still. Let me add on there. Because we've been told we sound very young and I guess part of that is because we're very passionate about this country, we're very passionate because we've grown up in this country. We've come to love this country and to see what is happening in this country; to be a coloured person in this country right now is not like the coolest thing. You're always left behind. It's difficult for a coloured person to get a bursary to get a decent education. It's, like you must have Xhosa now, now to get a fucking job, you know. Those types of things is like…so now there's a black government and, 'So fuck everyone else,' you know what I mean. 'We're gonna help the black people a little bit, we're going to do a little bit for the coloured people so that they like don't completely feel left out.' But then why are those coloured people still – like I mean I know the whole party things has changed now – but why were they still voting NP and DP [Democratic Party] when there still was NP and all of that after '94, you know what I mean. Because they do realise that they are in a marginalised position and they're still being left out. So it's just like it feels pathetic to be a citizen of this country. You can't do anything. It seems like you can't even freely express yourself without having something like the ANC bladdy Youth League being offended by something that kids are saying and it's something that they see, something happening all the time and they're something on it. So now it's wrong to comment on something, on something like that as well.

Adam: What is that Skwatta Kamp song called now again?

Shameema and Eloise: 'Politics.'

Adam: Oh, ja.

Shameema: Do you want to listen to it?

Adam: Ja, cool, but maybe afterwards. I think I should hear it. I mean, I don't have it. Let's just talk about that – that idea. Given the present context, given the difficulties that one has with expressing oneself, how do you position yourself as Godessa, given that Hip Hop in Cape Town seems to be taking off a lot more – well seems to have taken off a lot better – than it has in the early '90s, given that you can go into what used to be white clubs, play to white audiences, white kids, R&B, Hip Hop, etc., etc. And it seems to be a bit more possible than when POC was around. Uhm, how do you manage that? You guys are with African Dope [independent record label], you're playing nationally, etc. etc. How does that, you see those dynamics affecting your ability to get your message across? Or…

Shameema: I think it's helping it.

Eloise: Ja, that's what I was going to say as well. Because just like we were talking about the whole mainstream issue and how we want to get those messages out to a bigger audience, rather than just having it to ourselves and to the underground community. I think going with a record label definitely helps that. They can put our music onto the mainstream, but that doesn't necessarily mean that the message is gonna change. So we're still gonna do the exact same thing independently over the years as individuals, but at the same time get it out, get it out on a bigger scale.

BURNI AND SHAMEEMA, CAPE TOWN, 2007 | Source: Adam Haupt

Shameema: And we don't write specifically for one target market. Uhm, what we write about. And we don't specifically for anybody because we write for ourselves. If we go out on stage and people like what we're saying, then fine, cool. That's just a reflection of what we said, you know what I mean? So that's all that we do. It's not like if we play a white club we're not, some of the songs we'd play in the ghetto or you know, that type of thing. I don't think we need to…uhm… place ourselves in a certain situation where if you perform to like someone who comes from a different background that you have to kind of change yourself or change your position or how you think, you know, and when you communicate with those people.

Adam: Okay. Three words. Ja. The globalisation tracks. Those are three words. I counted them.

Shameema: How much syllables? [everyone laughs]

Adam: Let's talk about that. I heard one globalisation track. You tell me there are two more… Uhm, what's with that? You tell me about the background to that. A documentary series…

Shameema: Okay, cool.

Adam: Will we see that kind of content being put onto an album?

Shameema: Of course. We've been performing it. Like we've been performing the globalisation tracks. We just decided like, 'Fuck the…? Why can't we perform this?' We did it for the documentary, but it's a song that we have. We wrote it. We believe it. It's like any other song that we have, so we need to perform it.

Eloise: Even at our launch we perform one of the songs. Because most of the times…because our launch was the first like Godessa gig like we…not many times have been able to perform in Cape Town. We haven't been able to perform a full set. So normally we would choose the most hyped tracks, whatever, to perform at the club. So here we have the opportunity to perform everything that we want to do and we did the one song. And while we were performing it we heard like…you know, you hear these responses of people to a particular line that you say or whatever. So we know like we can…those songs don't have to be just for just that. We can do it anywhere else. We know people listen when we perform. I think that like most crowds recently know that they're not just gonna come and dance when we're performing. So a lot of times we're in a situation where people are standing and looking at us like that. And it feels weird because you're in a club and people are supposed to be dancing and jumping or whatever. People are standing and listening to us.

Adam: Ja, I'm one of those people. '…and shut up. I'm listening to the words.' [they laugh]

Shameema, in retrospect:

On our content and being labelled as politically and socially conscious, I stand by what we said even though my personal political views may have changed since then. I believe that we were necessary during that period of our country's transition and we may not have had the impact on a generation like, say, Public Enemy did, we did inspire other groups not to be afraid to be outspoken as youth who were not happy with the decisions our country was making. We did not choose content to be controversial; we wrote what we felt was pertinent in that moment. When 'Mindz Ablaze' came along, a clear departure from what we became known for, some saw us as sell-outs; we wrote what we heard in the music with the idea that could still inspire people without political content and responded to the shift in the consciousness of our youth, of the city, moving more towards putting the past behind us and reaching out for the doors that were now opened to us.

Shameema: So…I mean the whole background with doing these tracks. The first one we did was just myself and EJ and we hooked up with Devious, only because she wasn't available to do the recording. And we hooked up with Devious. It started out…I mean Shaheen was the cat who started this whole thing where he was connected with these people from the States and they were looking for somebody from South Africa. Uhm, we…globalisation at that time was like something that was very, very strange. Just the term 'globalisation', although we know it's something that's been around fucking years, this term was new to us when we wrote the first track. So Shaheen brought in some academics and stuff for them to, to, to you know just teach us the basic terms, explain a little bit what it was about and then we wrote that first track. It was called 'How Low'. Just to take you through, 'cause you haven't heard the song. The chorus is something like, 'Is life really worth the profit?'

Eloise: 'Is your heart really worth the duckets?'

Shameema: 'Is your heart really worth a duckets? Would it put an end to the hardship?' You know, those are just some of the key things in the song where we…when we decided to do the other tracks after doing that first song that was saying things like that, you realise like, 'Fuck, this thing globalisation actually affects the whole fucking world. It affects all of us right here and we need to understand what the effects of globalisation are on our lives.' In the same way we came to realise…like we didn't start out being a political group – we just naturally got labelled as that. But then you started to realise how much these politics has to do with your everyday life; so does globalisation. And therefore just doing the other track is just being able to have something that is cool to listen to – so now people now listen to us, so then write something that is worthwhile listening to, you know.

Eloise: Just to also educate people about this thing because a lot of people, especially…that come from poorer communities, they don't really give a damn about this thing because the term already is so, you know, it's such a big thing for them to fathom already that if somebody's not gonna explain it to them, how they going to understand it? How they going to know that it's actually not such a good thing for them as poor people, as people where it only benefits the rich, you know what I mean? Instead of helping the poorer African countries or whatever country in the world whose economic, economy is not as, uhm, what do you call it, whose economy can't sustain the people of the country really, but still want to enter into this whole thing called globalisation. That fucks up the country more and the people of the country. So people that don't understand it, they're not going to fight against it 'cause they don't know what the hell is going on. So through those kinds of songs we're trying to educate people, to just make them understand, man, that this thing is not really as glamorous as CNN tells you it is.

Adam: What is the name of the documentary?

Shameema: I'm not even sure what the documentary is called. You see, we just give the tracks to Shaheen and he just sends it off. But it's a project, it's project, uhm, called Hip Hop Artists Against Infinite War. I'll see if I can find some of the emails, check the emails there. 'Cause there is an email that explains the project a little bit more.

Adam: Ja, I'd like to see the final product.

Shameema: No, they haven't because these guys, they came down now, earlier this year and they…'cause that's when we did the final song for them so I guess they're still busy with the whole thing, you know what I mean.

> **Shameema, in retrospect:**
> Nas has a copy of this track…will get you a copy…it's on cassette! It's the only song we ever got to do with Devious, we were gonna do more.

Adam: There are two more tracks for the same project?

Shameema: Ja. So also it's the same with the HIV song that we've done and then there's an argument that comes in that how effective is, like you'd call it edutainment. How effective is it really? And I mean like say when we had the HIV Hop concert, for instance, why [did] kids come to the concert? They knew it was a HIV Hop concert – it had to do with HIV/AIDS. Why did they come to the concert, you know what I mean? So obviously there is that they don't want to sit down and watch a programme about HIV/AIDS, they don't want to read about it or whatever, but they'll come to a concert. So like if there's 50 people at that concert and one person [is] understanding and listening to what you're saying it's cool. Like, you know, 'cause you know you've at least, you've touched one person's life, you've had an influence on how they're going to think when they use that route. So I think that's what it's about at the end of the day. It's that you're able to influence someone's decision on something that they didn't necessarily think about or take seriously before. Very serious issue and we need to…I think that's one of the great things about the *Headwarmers* [radio] show, man. That it's not just music – that Shaheen brings in all these discussions. He forces it on the heads, man. He decides, 'Okay, there's shit going on in…like we need to speak about it and get a response from people.' And the fact that throughout the years of the show that people call in and participate in the discussion – and it's young kids that are into Hip Hop, you know what I mean – that is like proof for me that we can make this thing work. We can make it work on a level of more than just music.

Adam: So for you – just to get back to what you were saying before, you…you do think, as Godessa, it is possible to engage people critically on the level of performance as well as workshops, community activism. You don't see a conflict there?

Shameema: No. I think other people, I think other people, other heads and stuff might see, 'It's fucked up. How can you like have your shit playing on Good Hope [radio station]? How can you have like a music video on Channel O [TV channel]?' Because those mediums are seen as the devil, you know what I mean?

Adam: Sell-out media.

Shameema, in retrospect:
Hey look, D has a show on Good Hope now and everyone be scrambling to get on it! Just shows how far local Hip Hop has come!

Shameema: Exactly, but how can we be selling out if we have such a positive song like 'Social Ills' being blasted every day, getting so much attention and people come to us after they hear the song. They just come to us and tell us, 'That's a fucking great song. I really like what you're saying with it.' Whatever. How can that be selling out? You know what I mean? We're simply using that medium. You were asking earlier about, uhm, you know the white kids falling in love with Hip Hop and all of that. That's something that I can't understand. I looked at the Dead Prez concert the first time that they came here and I know they went back home saying, 'Fuck, that place was full like of white people. Eighty per cent of the crowd was like filled with white people.' And of the crowd that was the white people was jumping up and down when Dead Prez was like saying all these anti-white things, you know what I mean? So that's like really difficult to understand, but I think that there's this new conscious with the next generation of white people growing up, that's like our age, that are trying to understand, uhm, that we've had like really difficult lives growing up as non-white people in this country. And if we're able to make white kids more compassionate through our music and make them understand, uhm, where we're coming from a little bit, they could possibly grow out of the

GODESSA, AFRICAN HIP HOP INDABA, 2007 | Source: Adam Haupt

racist, uhm, mindsets that they [have] grown up with in their homes. That also becomes a very positive thing. The other thing is us being with a record label that is white-owned, uhm, I know that also becomes quite an issue for people like, you know, record label. That's also supposed to be selling out, whatever. Then again, it's like how are we going to get music out? There are no other labels that want to put Hip Hop out. Here is a label, even though they're white, in having people express themselves any way that they want to. So we're using that opportunity. They're giving us that opportunity and we're gonna use it. We're going to put our shit out. At the same time, we're gonna do everything else that we want to do, so then people can't say that we're selling out. I think over time, uhm, the general community will realise that they need to get into this media thing. They need to get into the mainstream. It's the only way we can reach our people like all over. Hip Hop can't stay just here in Cape Town. We can't stay just here in South Africa. It needs to go all over Africa. It needs to go all over the world.

Adam: The danger of compromise? I mean how do you see that? As soon as something goes into the mainstream media, it goes into…

Shameema: It depends on you as an individual. It depends on us as individuals and as the group Godessa. We're not prepared to compromise what we believe. So we make decisions at the end of the day when opportunities are offered to us and if it's not something we like, we say, 'No fuck this. This is not something that we want to do,' we'll say no to it, but when [we] see an opportunity to, to remain ourselves – like with 'Social Ills' where we're still able to be these conscious people about everything else, everything in life, about all the songs that we write about. We can do both. We're not prepared to compromise our values and morals to, to get the kind of media attention that kwaito has or whatever. Just like maybe something off the record…

Shameema, in retrospect:

Hip Hop's audience throughout SA [South Africa] was very underground and limited so instead of seeing us as sell-outs, we saw our activity as groundbreaking, not for us but for the movement of Hip Hop, which very quickly became an industry because of groups like us, Skwatta Kamp, Tumi, H20, etc. Godessa was recently honoured at the SA Hip Hop Awards for exactly this contribution to the growth of Hip Hop's audiences and I watched Cassper

Nyovest receive an award for selling out the Dome [venue in Johannesburg] with 50 000 seats. A remarkable achievement today, unheard of even just 10 years ago because we struggled to fill venues meant for 1 000 people, we had no sponsors and MTV ads and we had no publicists and business managers. If Skwatta didn't take the Gallo [Record Company] deal, if we didn't sign with Dope and release 'Social Ills', if Outrageous Records didn't push out compilations and if YFM [radio station] didn't have Harambe, Hip Hop could very likely still be underground.

Shameema: It's a difficult thing.

Adam: Can I sum it up? You elected not to go with a white manager any longer because of your sense of the person was that she didn't have a sense of what Hip Hop was about, what the black South African experience was really about and, possibly, she wasn't open to the idea of learning what the black South African experience was really about, what Hip Hop was really about. You didn't feel such a person – black or white, in this case white – could represent what South African Hip Hop was about.

Shameema, in retrospect:

We fired our white female manager because she was not the right person for us. She was very good at what she did, but our vision was not the same. She wanted to take the band in a direction that we were not comfortable with. I think all of the above is true to a certain extent, but this drove our decision more than race or experience.

Shameema: Ja, for sure. Ja, that's another problem I have calling it South African Hip Hop. I think that's the next issue we can maybe go into.

Adam: Let's talk about that, while we are on about that. And anyone beside Shameema feel free to say something. This reminds me of…I once shut Skin up in a Skunk Anansie interview and I told the drummer – I forget his name – and I said, 'Maybe you want to say something now.' The bass guitarist and Skin were just like [sound effect] and when I turned to her like, 'What do you think?' 'Fuck that you shut me up. This interview's over' [they laugh]. So maybe I shouldn't say that. Er, ja. Hip Hop. What is your sense of what Hip Hop is? What it is on this continent? And what value it has?

Shameema: Can I please just say something?

Adam: Ja.

Shameema: Because I did bring it up, so I should speak about it.

Adam: You did bring it up.

Shameema: Uhm, that I truly believe that Hip Hop is universal, that it shouldn't be labelled. Hip Hop in America is not labelled American Hip Hop. Why should South African Hip Hop be labelled South African Hip Hop? So, why I believe this is because fundamentally Hip Hop is universal. It is a culture. It's not something that belongs to me or you. It's something that we all share. It's something that is like where language doesn't necessarily become an issue. If you understand the essence and the foundations of Hip Hop, then nothing, not DJing or breakdance or anything, any of those other elements become…Those are just tools, you know what I mean, to be able to spread this thing with. But anywhere in the world you should be able to connect with any head because you have this basic understanding and, you know what I mean. When it becomes music, when it becomes, when people think of Hip Hop as music they label it. But when you speak of it as this culture, it is just Hip Hop because it is one thing we all share throughout this world.

Shameema, in retrospect:

I still firmly believe in this. Since we did this interview, we spent a lot of time in Europe and met heads from all over, many of which did not speak English, but we were connected through the culture. Rogue State Alliance is an example of this; French, Italian, Swiss-German, Xhosa, Zulu, Afrikaans and English-speaking MCs and musicians recorded, toured and developed friendships that have outlasted the project. I know there is always a need to define everything, especially with popular culture, but if you view Hip Hop as a culture and not just a form of music, then this connectedness will make sense.

Adam: And what is that?

Shameema: This is a difficult question because you always get asked, 'What is Hip Hop? What does it mean to you?' You know what I mean? You always get asked that. It's not something that you can explain because it's something that you've grown up with and has groomed you into, into the kind of person you are, into the way you think and then you meet another person on the other side of the world who thinks exactly the same like you. And it's this like understanding of, of what…of what this culture is about that brings people together. I really, I don't know how to put it into words. It's like this feeling inside that you have that someone, the fact that someone else on the other side of the world who has grown up in a completely different place than you, that you can connect with that person within seconds of meeting them. You know what I mean? That's why I think it's fucked up to label Hip Hop in terms of the different countries. 'Cause it's just that something that's inside all of us that we learned as we were growing up with this culture that we all share.

Shameema, in retrospect:

Having grown up a bit, past the naivety of my youth, away from needing to prove I am Hip Hop with the way I dress or what music I listen to, having different priorities and with the career choices that I am now faced with, I believe in it as [a] way of life even more now. I can be chilling in hijab and still feel a beat and feel different to the people around me because Hip Hop is at the core of my being. It raised me, educated me and fed me. Like I can embrace my new career and still be an MC.

Eloise: And also like what you were saying about the core of Hip Hop, it's the essence as you put it, is basically trying to first of all through being an MC spreading positive messages, trying to educate people [phone rings]. Can I go on? And also just to basically trying to get people, spreading knowledge about anything, helping people out, making them see things that they never even thought twice about, you know. That, those kinds of things. It's not just the music, you know what I mean? Music can be used, Hip Hop music can be used to do all those things. And that is what people like Shaheen is doing through his workshops…using the music, but it's not the main element in Hip Hop. It's not the main thing.

Shameema: So forget like music, forget South African Hip Hop or, or African Hip Hop or European Hip Hop or whatever. Forget all of that because it's not about that. It's not about music at all.

Eloise: Because there's a lot of DJs and MCs and even certain b-boys in most of the countries that I've been to that does a lot of other things except just the DJing element or the breakdancing or whatever trip they're on. They do workshops, they do radio shows to educate people and sometimes to discuss things. So it's not just about that.

Adam: It's about activism.

Eloise: It's about activism, ja.

Shameema: Ja.

Eloise: Exactly.

Shameema: Burni?

Burni: Ja, I guess we've been fortunate to be in the whole sort of Hip Hop community and the Hip Hop culture. It's not like it's a lifestyle or anything. And we didn't choose to be in Hip Hop, you know. Personally, I didn't choose to be in Hip Hop. It's like Hip Hop kind of chose me.

Adam: How did you get into it? Let's talk about really personal stuff now because, uhm. Shit. Let's talk about personal stuff. I hear, for example, that you've got a day job and you've got heads to support.

Burni: Ja.

Adam: People rely on you and you're into this not because you love being on stage, not necessarily. There are other reasons that drive you.

Burni: Ja, there are other reasons and I mean at first [I] started like going to Hip Hop clubs and stuff like that, I didn't know that like a couple of years later I'd be actually going into it like, you know, uhm, committedly and things like that. Uhm, it's, it's very like an eye-opener towards a lot of things because I don't think that I would be as aware of as much that I am involved in now if I hadn't been involved in the culture. And if I hadn't been exposed to the people that I've met, you know, being involved in the culture and that, so uhm, I'm grateful for that, man. And, and like uhm it is like a positive tool. I think that I've been fortunate because now I am able to communicate with other people what I felt and what Hip Hop has meant to me, you know, over a couple of years that I've been involved in. So, uhm, ja.

Adam: I want to talk about the idea of, you know, day, daily reality versus what got you into Hip Hop culture and why you do it. Surely there are easier things to do, uhm…

Eloise: I do it simply because I like it. There's no other, there's no reason other than that.

Burni: There's no reason other than that. The reason I have a day job is because I have a family to support and right now I'm the only one that…that's in the position to take on that responsibility and, uhm, the reason why I'm with Godessa is because it's given me a way of expressing myself and, if I wasn't given that opportunity, I don't think that I would be able to…I don't know. It's like…I mean like in a sense I'm a very quiet person and I am to myself and they've been able to like being on stage and being able communicate with people. I've been able to do that via Godessa and that's why I'm with them. You know? Uhm and uhm and the community. I love Hip Hop. I love the culture.

Shameema: It's like for me also, man, this is something that has saved me from becoming a lot of things that I didn't want to be. Things that you're supposed to be because that what your family thinks you're supposed to be, but it has like, taken me to a next level of understanding life and that is something you will never be able to get if you were sitting behind a desk all day or if you were working in a store. It's like impossible to understand life in any way or to have an impact on life because you just become a part of like the norm and that's why I really feel like Hip Hop has saved me from becoming a really boring person. Like she said, I would have also probably shot myself by now because it's the only thing I think that – it's a medium for me that keeps, that makes me look forward to waking up each day. Not just Godessa, but the fact we Hip Hop has given me this other understanding that's made me realise a whole lot of other things. You must understand I grew up in a very like Cape Malay type of household where you like, I was saying earlier you, you grow up hearing your parents speaking about people being kaffirs. When a black person comes to your day asking for something to eat – I see it now with my niece. She will run away. She's become scared of black people because of what you hear in your home and we haven't gone outside of…like I'm completely different to everyone else in my family and I look at life completely different to all of them. Uhm, where there are a lot, a lot of them that are important to me where I was still thinking like the rest of my family I would definitely be working as a receptionist, or a cashier or something like that because the important thing in that situation is that you bring money in every month. And I know money's important because like Burni has to support her family, she need to have that salary where she brings money in every month. But I've become a better person because my main focus in life hasn't been to, to bring money in every month, to support a family. It's really tough to be in that situation. I've taken myself out of that situation because I realised that with what I had the potential to do with my life was bigger than that. What I can do for other people is bigger than the day job.

Eloise: The other issue is supporting yourself as well, which is fucking difficult when you're doing this because the point that Godessa specifically is in right now is, it's hectic to have your day job and do this 'cause there'll have to be time when you have to go away and your boss is never going to understand…

[The discussion is interrupted as we run out of tape on the recorder, but soon kick-starts again.]

Eloise: And it's just that you have to sort of try and find other ways to sustain yourself because nobody else is gonna do that for you and that's just reality. Like Burni's situation is quite difficult. I can understand, but I've also been in the position where my father left, my brother had a baby before his time which he had to support and I was then left over as the second eldest in the family to, to be the breadwinner to support my mother and my other two brothers that were still on school. And for a couple of years I've done that and just look for a job in this country, for instance, is so damn difficult. Finding one…

Shameema: Can you imagine, she was working in a factory, in a clothing factory. She would still be working in a clothing factory…

Eloise: Straight out of school, like I just matriculated the end of that year I matriculated. Two weeks before Christmas. I got this job and then I got, I was…uhm, included as a permanent and I mean it's so hectic to do that. But I mean at the same time trying to balance doing your music and that, it somehow clashes, man. Because getting money is so difficult you still have to do that. What are you gonna do? Then I decided to, to take something and learn a skill, which is music production. I've thrown myself in at the deep end, I just started learning it. And also working at Bush Radio for a while also helped a lot in that respect. I mean I was, we were working with, uhm, before Godessa hooked up I was working with this guy called Bradley Williams in Mitchells Plain. He's also a producer. He was still working on really old-school equipment and stuff, but that's where I first got to taste the music production thing. And I got really interested in the whole thing and I thought, well, maybe this could also be some kind of, if I really wanted to learn the skill I can support myself through this skill. And fortunate, I've been fortunate enough to hook up with people like Grenville. And I mean there's been a lot of others that's been supporting me in this whole thing, uhm doing music production and stuff like that I mean; I've learned quite a lot through reading things in magazines. You don't necessarily have to also go to an institution to get this knowledge. You can get it from the internet, get it from everywhere, you know what I mean. It's in books. It's everywhere, just as long as you're willing to do that. And I mean you don't really need to pay that much money to get that kind of knowledge because it's everywhere, it's freely available. And at the same time, also being fortunate to have someone like Grenville sharing his equipment and stuff where I can now make money from what I've learned. So I'm making money now doing music production and recording because I've pushed myself to learn that skill. But it's difficult for a lot of other people.

Shameema: I think with like all arrogance aside, we're very intelligent and talented people and the fact that she would've still been working in a factory now, I would have still been working at a fucking security company, uhm, that none of this would have been a realisation, we wouldn't have been able to, to like be who we really meant to be and this is who we need to be. So, you know, imagine this potential having been wasted like in a fucking clothing factory or, you know what I mean. It's like ridiculous when I think of that. I'm so glad that Hip Hop became a part of my life…that I was able to look at life differently because I find like my friends like that I was at school and I look at what they're become. It's so fucking boring. I mean I was like, I was like the dropout – not the dropout. I was expelled from high school.

GODESSA | Source: Adam Haupt

All of them finished matric, went to university or tech or have like cool little office jobs, or whatever, like I'm still running around taking taxi and you know what I mean. But I can fucking go to America without having to pay a cent, but it's, it's like something they could only dream of doing and I didn't have to go and [get] an education or anything to be able to do, to be able to, to, to share what I have with other people all over the world. Like you're stuck in your fucking office with your certificate and that's all you're gonna be for the rest of your life.

Eloise: A lot of people become tunnel-visioned as well because they, their circumstances dictate who they are at the end of the day and what they think about. You don't see jack shit sitting in an office from nine o'clock till five o'clock every single day for a year and years on end. You never get to learn anything besides that. You never get to learn anything besides that, that you're doing right now and just moving up the ladder in that specific area that you're working in. And there's a lot of other things that's also important.

Shameema: I mean also what, with, in our case, we were looking as individuals before Godessa. We were looking for something more that we could do with our lives and I think it's an example of what we've become, is an example of creating things for yourself other than…So anyone has the potential to become anything and they only need to look inside of themselves to realise that what that is. When you're in high school you make the decision, 'Okay, fuck. I'm gonna do matric next year. When I finish, what am I gonna do after matric?' Then you start panicking. 'Fuck, what am I gonna do? Because this is it. I don't have to go to school anymore, but I have to do something.' So a lot of…

Eloise: Family's also putting pressure on you. Soon as you leave school, you're gonna have to bring the pay cheque in somehow.

Shameema: So like, what you gonna do? You rush into a decision to do something and you're stuck with that for a couple of years and you become unhappy. You become a miserable person or whatever, you know. Most people make the wrong decision at the end of high school and end up changing their…like halfway through their studies they either drop out or they change their course. You know, that sort of thing. So even for us, if we decided to go and study now, we would know what we want to study 'cause we've had these years of experience to know. If we have to get the certificate…exactly what it would be.

Shameema, in retrospect:

It should be noted that it took a long time for our families to believe in what we were doing, that we weren't just fucking around and when we started to earn a living from it they eased up. But there was very little support from our families, and I can understand why; they wanted us to have regular jobs. It was always a fight in my home getting my family to believe in what I was trying to do. At some point during the first three years of Godessa, I had two jobs and I was managing the band and supporting myself. It was incredibly tough for all of us to constantly keep the peace with our families and keep believing in what we were trying to do. Sometimes we were broke as fuck, eating beans from a tin and it was hard to stay on the path, but we always had each other to keep reminding ourselves that we were onto something and we were doing something with real purpose.

Adam: So cool. I dig talking to people in the Hip Hop scene because you just ask them one question…

Eloise: You get a million answers! [laughs]

Shameema: Look, we're MCs. We gotta rock the stage.

Adam: If I were talking to like rock musicians as a journalist…talking to rock musicians and jazz musicians – no rock musicians are actually more eloquent. You'd have to prod them all the time. They're so not articulate. 'Come on, dude, you wrote these lyrics. What the fuck do they mean?'

Shameema: He's thinking notes, man. It's about the music [they laugh].

Adam: Uhm, just about that. I never knew you got into the music production via Grenville and other cats like Bradley. I think I know him. I met him.

Eloise: He was our first producer before Grenville.

Adam: Uhm, I want to talk about that idea – the idea of technology, that it gives you access. Here we are in your, you know, luxurious [they laugh], luxurious…

Eloise: Well, not really.

Adam: …apartment-meets-studio and we have the multimillion-rand studio a few feet away [they laugh]. I'm sure if I go in there I'll be impressed by the massive desk, 24-channel…

Shameema: No…

Eloise: Only the speakers will impress you 'cause it's NS10s. We're still working on our hi-fi amps.

Adam: Let's talk about that technology – and maybe I should talk to Grenville as well. But, I mean, we're talk[ing] about PC-based software… Some software probably costs about R15 000.

Eloise: And I mean like going through a recording studio, for instance, you're gonna pay a thousand rand a day from 10 o'clock to five o'clock not getting anything done, really, because you're always running into technical problems anyway. And also just studios, if you want to do a demo, for instance, studios charge you something like R750 for six hours or R200 an hour. That all amounts to so much that we that, you know, that are doing this kind of thing won't be able to survive. We're very grateful for having this opportunity, but Grenville has also been – he's also had a vision, man, if he starts doing a thing. He didn't just want to be a musician playing for nothing, you know what I mean? He's also…started seeing the potential of having a studio, charging very little so that a lot of other people that want to do things – well, not just Godessa – can also come in for a very little, for very little money and do their thing and get higher quality out of it without having to pay that much at a big studio. And most of the time when you listen back to the stuff that you've gotten, the, the time that you spend on the stuff, the time that [the] engineer spent to mix the stuff is so little that you won't get a very good quality, like sound quality out of it. So and also most of the time it's not about the equipment. It's about the person sitting behind the equipment and having that knowledge because sometimes it's people that have studied at City Varsity or here and there or the other, spending that money, now trying to make a DAT [Digital Audio Tape] working at the studio and still they have very little understanding of how it actually works. That's what we've experienced.

And I mean he also works for years to get the stuff together. Like he built that damn PC with his hands, you know what I mean. Like buying the hard drive, buying the console, buying the motherboard separately. Everything comes in little boxes. You have to put it together yourself and that's what he did. And I mean it took him quite a while to get it to the level that it's now. And like just in this year he was working last year till when we met him, he was working with fucked-up speakers, like hi-fi speakers and now the, the, the, because he saved up, he could buy better monitors to listen to the music, which means the sound quality is also gonna be better at the end of the day. And, er, ja, I mean just things like that, man, making things possible for yourself and not having to look to the next person to do it for you. Learn the damn skill if you want to get into production. Don't be arrogant or egotistical and think, 'I can't learn things from anybody.' Because I think that's also something that gets in the way of people growing, man. Like you really have to sit and think, 'Listen, I have to do this, but I have to also be open to criticism and things.' Because I mean I get criticised a lot. 'Why did you do the hats like that? Why does the kicks sound so fumbled?' Or this kind or that kind of thing. But I listened and I ask him, 'Why do you think because this frequency's not like…that's the frequency that you have to take out. So you do EQ [equalise] the stuff properly and then go listen back to it.' I mean that's how you learn. You have to be open to, to all kind of other things.

Shameema: It takes time to build, to build the shit the way you want it and then it's also like it's too expensive to go to the studio to get that quality and you're not necessarily guaranteed that quality like she said. And then also just people's performances are poor. They don't know how to handle a microphone properly. They believe if you're a Hip Hop artist you have to close the mic like your shit has to sound all muffled. Like what's the point if people can't hear anything that you're saying? Like, do you now understand why people don't want to watch you perform, you know what I mean.

Eloise: Or ja, I mean, like Shameema said now, clarity is an important thing. Like people enjoy music if it sounds good, right? And like if you are a so-called conscious Hip Hop artist, or whatever, and if you want to spread those messages, getting people to listen to your stuff, you're gonna have to learn how to handle a mic properly first of all. If you're not clear, people are not gonna hear what you have to say. So what's the purpose of saying it anyway? So you have to learn all these things and you have to be open, like open to criticism and learning things, otherwise you're not gonna, you're not gonna get it.

Shameema: And also like just going back to the whole record label thing…Putting yourself in a position where if you have to be with a record label. Now you know that record labels are gonna take as much as they can from you, but now we've begun to understand how this whole thing works – how the percentages work and all of that – so we know, for instance, that the fact that the, normally the record label would pay for your recording, right. So because the record labels are paying for your recording, they own the recording of your work, so therefore you get the smaller percentage because now the money goes into recording, it goes into advertising of the product, the pressing, the distribution. Like any, everything that needs to happen to get that one product out, the record label pays for that. Like with us, with African Dope for instance, because our music is the quality that it is, they don't have to, we don't have to go to them for a recording. So already that makes our percentage bigger at the end of the day. So advertising – we decided to go like half-half with them. Okay, you need to advertise because [it] is a product on your label, so this is something you need to do anyway. But we also need to advertise, so there again we can make the percentage a bit less because normally Sony or whoever would have someone there that would take care of all of that shit for you, you know what I mean. So people go, people have this mindset when you're gonna sign with a record company, they're gonna own you. They're gonna own everything and you're gonna make 1 per cent. And, true enough, your percentage is very small, but there are ways to make those percentages bigger and the cats just aren't thinking like that. They don't understand enough of how a relationship between an artist and a record company work. So because they've heard all these things, or whatever, they inevitably make this decision that it's fucked up to go with a record company. It's selling out – but if you know what's happening, what the relationship is, how the percentages and all of that, then you will know that fuck it's actually not bad and there are ways to get around it to make our percentages bigger.

Eloise: And I find that a lot of cats don't understand like contracts and stuff, man, and they don't make, they don't make the effort to take these contracts to people that clarify things for them, you know. That's where they also just look at the contract, 'Okay, cool.' They're all excited about this deal they're gonna get now that they just put their signature down and sign their whole three years away or five years of their life away to this record company. The complaining afterwards when they can't get out of this deal because their signature's on paper already, which makes things more fucked up already. So that's also some things that cats need to learn, man, that it's not really – the industry is a bit fucked up, there a lot of things going on there, but there's ways for you. You can make it better for yourself. And like the way we've been going about contracts and stuff, getting somebody who understands the legalities and stuff like that. 'Can you explain to us exactly what this contract says and then we can go around and change it.' And all this asking for advice and stuff, it's like...

Shameema: 'Cause that's the fucked-up thing. People confuse you with the language. Immediately you see that language, you don't understand it. You like pull from it. We've made it our mission to understand what is in contracts. Uhm, the way things are said in contracts is meant to fool you. So nothing is said like, straight, straight out. Uhm, also like say, for instance, we had got our managing contract for the first time from to read. And it was like thick and we went through it – there was a whole lotta shit that we didn't like. And there was some shit we didn't understand. Like what is it actually saying? So we first took the contract to someone to understand what was in it, so we were clear on everything that was in there. Everything that we weren't happy with we took out and we made it into a contract that we felt happy with. So now we have that contract to give to our manager. But what it comes down to is that everything is negotiable. You're led to believe that everything is standard. These are all the misconceptions we had when we first started dealing with record companies and stuff that, what it is said is law. It's actually not like that. And that's the fuck up that a lot of artists make, whether Hip Hop, kwaito, jazz or whatever kind of art. They make that mistake – they don't believe that they can be in a position to negotiate because you like, you signing a part of your life away when you sign a fucked-up contract that Sony is gonna give you or you know what I mean. So you must like us trying to understand exactly what's happening. And that's why we don't feel we're selling out because we know exactly what we're doing.

Eloise: Also, we're not signed to a major label.

Adam: It's an independent label.

Eloise: It's an independent label, which makes us semi-independent partly. Because they're not paying for recording, paying for a lot of other stuff. Like Sony, for instance, or EMI or whoever would pay for. We still pay our own way.

Adam: Shameema has a problem with academic work. What is your problem, Shameema?

Shameema: The fact that, uhm, things are researched and analysed and it is shared amongst academics. So what is the point because the things that you're researching and analysing should be shown to other people. So when you do show these things to other people who aren't academics, they fucking don't understand it because it's in their language. It's the same like a contract. When you receive a contract that you get turned off by what is written in that contract because you don't understand it. And, I mean the language that academics use baffle me so much because there's like words that I've never heard of before in my life and I'm a well-read person. I have three fucking dictionaries and [laughs], you know what I mean? It's like hectic to have to sit and read something and then go to the dictionary every time and – like just that one word can throw off the whole paragraph that you've just read. So now you have to spend like an hour analysing that one paragraph that was written, which, which is a good thing for you like, but I don't mind it. But now, I don't mind reading academic stuff because I would spend the time trying to understand what it is about, but just for other people, man. I think that when you're writing, when you've researched something that is important and other people need to know about it, not just academics, you know what I mean? That it becomes a problem – you exclude people from, from understanding this research that you've put into this project. So it's just for you and the rest of the lecturers at the university or the students that you gonna give this talk to or whatever. And I bet you half the time the students don't even understand what the fuck it going on and understand the language. Maybe in five years' time they will, but right now they don't. So that's my problem [chuckles]. I mean, even with the thing that you wrote, was cool uhm, but I thought like if someone else reads this, like who's not on the level and who doesn't have the interest that I do in writing – not just writing rhymes, but in writing and literature and then they not gonna even bother to read this thing finished because it's gonna throw them off. You check? What do you have to say about it? I mean, do you understand like where…where I'm coming from? I mean I don't mind the academic shit because I'm interested in learning the language and stuff, but, uhm, she might not necessarily be. She might be thrown off by it or whatever. So she's not gonna even bother to understand what is written. You know sometimes you have to give things to people on a plate, you know what I mean.

> **Adam, in retrospect:**
>
> This discussion echoes the views expressed by my fellow postgraduate students when I was working on my honours and MA degrees. As graduate tutors, we were teaching English literature to undergraduates who were negotiating academic literacy and critical literacy as second-language English speakers, a context in which competence in English was largely read as an indicator of academic competence. It also speaks to the rationale for this book. We wanted to offer a range of readers multiple points of entry into the text and the field of Hip Hop studies.

Eloise: Spoon-feeding. I'm not quite cool with that.

Shameema: This is one of the reasons we take on issue like globalisation and break it down into simple language and stuff because the language that this thing is spoken about on CNN or whatever is too hectic for other people to understand. So we need to break it down and make people understand it because it's an important issue. It has an effect on our lives.

Adam: What do you think, Burni? Before I get to a response, I don't think I've got a good defence, to begin with. I can't offer anything [Shameema laughs]. I can't offer anything. I'm defenceless here. Uhm.

Burni: I don't think people should like, you know. I mean that argument is good that maybe academics should try and simplify things a bit more, but it's good as an individual if you are interested in something, uhm, enough then you will take it upon yourself.

Shameema: For sure. Ja.

Burni: You know what I mean.

Shameema: Like myself. That's why I said like I, I, I would take the time to learn what is written there, but we know the nature of our people, man.

Burni: But then maybe we should instil that type of culture where they should learn…

Shameema: That's what we…no, that's what we as Godessa try to do with breaking – we first get people interested in something by breaking it down to them and then afterward you can deal with it on a, on a, on a bigger level. But when you're introducing something, you know what I mean, to someone then you kinda have to spoon-feed them just to get them interested.

Burni: Like sometimes people, sometime people…

Shameema: Lazy.

Burni: We think that other people don't understand or we take their intelligence like…

Shameema: Undermine it.

Burni: Ja, undermine it and think that it's minimal and when really it's not. It's…

Shameema: I know.

Burni: Just ignore it.

Shameema: Ignore it. I do think. But I do think. I really do think and from reading because what I do is I ask a lot of students to pass papers and like their, the stuff that they're busy with and I'm interested in, that I ask them to pass their papers to me. And uhm I read like a lot of university shit because I can't afford to go study, but I'd love to go and study. That's why I'm gathering like a lot of university papers and stuff. But I don't like understand half of that shit, Burni, you know what I mean and I'm not a stupid person.

Burni: But what I'm also saying is, you think that other people. Like you know, we undermine their intelligence. You don't think that we'd be able to communicate with them on that level. When maybe if we really do try, maybe we'd be able to find out, you know what I mean?

Shameema: Hmm. No, I definitely think there are. There definitely are people that do understand, but I know also that there's a lot of people that don't just by the way they speak, just by like the kind of books that they read or what they're interested in, you know what I mean. That it's like just that general vibe of people we know, uhm, and the community that we're from that there isn't that and academic language, the way these papers are written is fucking hectic. It's like so fucking hectic. That's why most fucking students drop out of university after a year, or lose interest in their course, or you know what I mean. That's my problem. That it just becomes like on such a level that you can't understand it. You have to sit down and really go through the shit word by word. If one word can throw you off, like in a whole fucking paragraph, you know what I mean. It's just that for me [chuckles]. It's hectic, I think.

Adam: I suppose you want me to offer a response.

Shameema: Ja, it would be good. It would be good.

Adam: Uhm, I don't think I can. Uhm, I think you're right. I think you're like spot on. I mean when I did my honours at UWC [University of the Western Cape] I first really started to talk about my difficulty with theory, literary theory specifically. The year before I was really confronting stuff and for me it was easier because I had done a course which made the stuff even more accessible than many other honours students. Uhm, and one key criticism that we levelled at our, some of our mentors, our lecturers, was the stuff is not accessible. 'If this is what this person is saying, why couldn't he just say it?'

Shameema: [laughs] No!

Adam: Because the point that the person is making is not revolutionary. It's not an earthquake. It's a simple point. Why did we have to spend an hour about what this stuff is meaning if this is all he's saying? [they laugh] He's not contributing to the debate in any way. He's taking a wank! I'm talking about one person in particular. Someone I know who wrote an impressive analytic article on film, you know what I mean? And…

Eloise: It was just the language that was impressive but not the content as such.

Adam: A lot of academic language oftentimes is about that. It's about fronting.

Eloise and Shameema: [chorus] Exactly!

Shameema: That's what I'm saying. That you can say things like for the lesser person to understand it, you know.

Adam: But maybe that's a part of what one needs to remember about academia specifically, uhm, is that a lot of it – I mean universities are essentially quite elitist and this is why someone like…

Shameema: UCT [laughs].

Adam: Well, ja. This is why it's revolutionary for me that someone like Shaheen has…

Shameema: For sure.

Adam: …is actively pursuing tertiary education and is doing well and can play the game…
Shameema: For sure. Exactly. Exactly. Exactly.

Adam: That's powerful. But does it have to be that way? I don't think so? I think it can be simpler, but for it's like this difficult thing. There are like people like – I don't know if you read something by [Gayatri Chakravorty] Spivak. Sort of postcolonial feminist person. She's from India and she's based in the States. She's at a major [university]. Spivak's language – your average Indian person at university from India seriously [has] difficulty understanding this shit. What does it mean if someone from, you know, a third-world country goes to an American university [and] produces such dense, dense academic language?

Shameema: For sure. I think that's what we have to do. Like that's what I'm trying to do like, you know what I mean.

Adam: Part of it is quite fucked up at the same time because only so many people are going to get the core of what the game is about and really play it well and everyone else is not going to access it.

Shameema: For sure.

Adam: And I think that's how the knowledge game works. Uhm, what makes you powerful in any context is your access to knowledge…

Shameema: For sure.

Adam: …and what you do with that knowledge. And I think this is why academic discourse plays that game because it's about who gets access and who doesn't.

Shameema: That's what pisses me off because that's what it comes down to at the end of the day. It's the exclusion. Uhm, so…

Adam: It's quite a contradiction. I mean, in a way, I mean, the question is that are you the black academic…are you selling out if you're playing this game?

Shameema: No, but you want to be able to, to…You want to be able to like – I see Shaheen as that, man, where he can be in a position to, to argue things exactly, with exactly the same language and shit the way any other academic would. He like comes and tells us stories about arguments he has with his lecturers at school because he is able to argue the opposite of what the lecturer's saying, but because he's using the language and all of that, he's arguing it so well that like the lecturer ends up failing him because he's black. He knows what he's talking about, he's using the correct terms and language and everything, you know what I mean, so they end up like failing him. But obviously Shaheen doesn't leave it there…So we need to get into that kind of position that he's in to be able to cut it. I think in America Hip Hop could become something, uhm, could become like a part of the curriculum at school, university, it could become very useful, uhm, if they wanna, if they wanna. I mean they draw this new curriculum – there's again this new curriculum – 2004, 2006 or something. There's again a new curriculum, you know what I mean, and they're trying to make the curriculums more creative and stuff like that. Why the fuck can't they just, you know, use Hip Hop in the new curriculum as part of that new curriculum. But that's another thing. Uhm, so ja. I do think that we need to be in that position to, to become as – this tape is running out now – as, as knowledgeable as any academic, but not all of us are able to get into university, don't have money to go into university to learn.

Adam: Ja, you're absolutely right. It's partly what worries me as well…

Shameema: I look at just politicians sometimes on TV when they're doing their speeches and stuff and how many of them did not go to university. Like are in the position that they are in because they pulled with the ANC, you know what I mean, and naturally pull into parliament. So they have this fucking page that someone else wrote and I'm sure half of the time they don't even understand what they're saying because they just, they never went to go study. They don't know the language. I know that because they don't write their speeches. You know what I mean. So half of the time they standing there. You can just hear, man, by the way, the way someone says something, the way you say a sentence, you would…

Eloise: …where the emphasis lies.

Shameema: …where the emphasis is on certain things or how you would say a certain word or whatever, you know what I mean. So even if like when I listen to people talking or whatever, I can hear how much they believe in what they're saying, you know what I mean. So when I look at the politician reading something from a page, like then I don't believe what they're saying because I don't believe that they believe and understand what they're saying. Especially those talks like in parliament in the day and stuff like that. The debates and sometimes when like the higher MPs come in to parliament and all of that with a page and stand up there and talk *kak* [shit] for 45 minutes, then it like pisses me off all the time because I can hear by the way they're talking that it's not, it's a page that someone gave them. They say, 'Okay, this is what I'm gonna talk about,' and whatever, you know. I've also met like one or two people that write speeches in parliament for some of the MPs and stuff, I got a little bit of info from them as well and language is a hectic thing it seems as well. And that's just English! How many languages? Eleven languages [laughs].

Adam: How do you feel about someone coming to you as an academic, taking your shit, coding it in a way that makes it difficult for you to understand, perhaps not intentionally, and writing for an academic audience and you are accessing that stuff…

Shameema: I think, I think that it's cool in one way because, I mean the reason because the reason why we do these interviews, the reason why I consent to doing these interviews is because I want those academics to understand what this is about, what Hip Hop is about – the power of it and all of that – and that I have this hope that it's going to become, uhm, it's going to become a part of the curriculum here. So if we can offer the time to speak about it, hoping that – even if it's in 10 years' time – that what we've been speaking about becomes a part of the curriculum – simply because I have this hope that it's going to become a part of the curriculum sooner or later and I think academics need to know, especially people researching around popular culture and all of that. They should know from the grassroots level what this culture is about. For you to be able to take it to them in your language is cool because they don't want to sit and hear when you talking Hip Hop standing here, you know what I mean? [they laugh]

GODESSA | Source: Shameema Williams of Godessa

CHAPTER 5.
THE B-BOY IS AN ACTIVIST

EMILE YX?

IN THE BEGINNING WAS THE B-BOY…

Hip Hop culture first arrived in South Africa in the form of the b-boy. A b-boy (breakdancer) turns thought into action. No words are needed. Even when sharing with others in your crew, you are teaching and taking action to grow and improve the culture of Hip Hop in your immediate community (your crew). In the early 1980s, most people had no idea what we were doing. We were thus in charge of spreading the culture ourselves, by jamming on street corners, in parking lots, shopping malls, train stations and so on. This was an act that would benefit the Cape Town scene from day one. B-boys were the first to learn to DJ, do graffiti, MC and finally learn to share Knowledge of Self with the rest of the community. I was with the b-boy crew called Pop Glide Crew, whose core members Mikey, Dean and Edmund joined up with Marley, Warro and Tarro (Supreme Team) to form Black Noise in 1988.

POP GLIDE CREW, 1982 | Source: Author

BLACK NOISE, 1994 | Source: Author

Black Noise members had a special way of doing things for themselves. We toured locally at libraries and shared b-boying with other youth to organise tours to Johannesburg and then internationally. Ready D, Rozanno, Gogga (graffiti artist), Ramone and Jazzmo were the core members of the b-boy crew called Ballistic Rock. Ready D joined up with Shaheen and later Gogga, Jazzmo and Ramone (b-boy Ram1) to form the core of Prophets of da City. It was Rozanno and Ready D that would join forces with Guy Ho and bring a Hip Hop hour to Club Teazers and then The Base. Other b-boys that manifested the thought to action to activism of b-boying included King Jamo. He reached out to Henry Chalfant and Martha Cooper, of the classic graffiti book *Subway Art* (Cooper & Chalfant 1984), who linked him with Afrika Bambaataa who encouraged him to form the Universal Zulu Nation in Cape Town. Caramel, a b-boy from Jam Rock Crew, became one of the first MCs and producers to win a South African Music Award for his production skills. Last but not least, I have to mention b-girl Malikah, Ready D's wife, who is now his manager.

In my communication with b-boys globally, I have realised that some of the biggest Hip Hop events were started by and are still run by b-boys and b-girls. The international breakdance championship Battle of the Year, hosted in France and Germany, was started by a b-boy, Thomas Hergenrother.

The event has run since the 1990s and Hollywood made a movie about it starring singer/actor Chris Brown. Every year 15 000 Hip Hoppers from around the world travel to the finals of Battle of the Year. Freestyle Session's founder, b-boy Cros1, travels to 60 national finals each year. Hooch, a b-boy from England, hosts the UK Breakdance Champs in conjunction with the creator of the PlayStation b-boy game.

THE SYSTEM TRUMPS HIP HOP

I often read about Hip Hop's profound influence on mass mobilisation against apartheid and am unable to recall this. Hip Hop definitely got youth away from the usual negative influence in the poorer communities, but the self-hate and testosterone-packed battles still raged on in the communities. Black Noise and POC had a running feud from the b-boy days that continued into the MC phase and at no point was there any collective desire from either side to observe the content of Hip Hop's collective power in the form of Black Consciousness or Knowledge of Self. We tried to create a movement but the internal divides and self-hate implanted in us via colonialism and apartheid were as strong as ever. But our battles were often seen as healthy competition. Hip Hop had no major impact on the collective mass politically, but individually it did impact the minds of a few, who ironically were already politically active within school SRCs and civic organisations.

INTERNALISATION OF KNOWLEDGE OF SELF

A lot of information remained in the hands and heads of a few. Groups like the Nation of Islam influenced some youth to be apprenticed into Hip Hop, but to many it was associated with Public Enemy and seen as the next cool thing to be involved in. I recall receiving information from Rozanno and then sharing information I was sent from a USA Black Consciousness organisation by the name of Auzar.[1] The information we received encouraged us to act collectively and try to organise under the African Hip Hop Movement and the African Hip Hop Alliance. Neither of these organisations was very successful at collective action. The local Hip Hop reflects this lack of collective action in local Hip Hop until this very day. It remains a reflection of the mentalities created by apartheid and neocolonialism. Very few people in my opinion have internalised Knowledge of Self for self and community. The same b-boys that I mentioned in the beginning of this chapter are examples of the few that internalised the information.

---

1. Auzar was a Black Consciousness collective located in Indianapolis and Dayton, Ohio.

Initially, my immediate reaction to Knowledge of Self was anger at white people and white supremacy. My next reaction was to talk to and share the information with people by any means necessary. I remember making copies of *Blacked out through Whitewash* (Suzar 1999) for Rozanno, who in turn made copies for everyone in the scene. I even hosted talks at Westridge City where some members of the Zulu Nation gathered. It always seemed like the people who attended were suspicious of the sharing that was taking place.

HOW I INTERNALISED KNOWLEDGE OF SELF INTO MY ACTIVISM

My performance name is a reflection of what I was observing within the local Hip Hop scene. I chose Emile YX? instead of Emile X because I wanted to continue to ask why (Y), search for the unknown (X) and emphasise the ongoing questioning with a question mark (?) at the end of my name. This was also a reminder to me to challenge myself about the information that I was reading and sharing. My first observation was that we needed our own newsletter or magazine. I was teaching in school at this stage and created *The Message*, a cut-and-paste magazine which spread basic information about Hip Hop culture. I became aware that Falko had a graffiti magazine called *The Dark Pages*, so I helped him to create a mix of both and then later helped him get more copies of his own out. I decided to also just focus on slowly putting together *Da Juice Magazine* on my own.

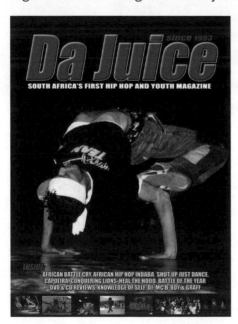

COVER OF DA JUICE *MAGAZINE* | Source: Author

This was initially a cut-and-paste job and demanded that I think mathematically about the duplication, manufacturing and selling costs of the magazine. Knowledge of Self had me questioning the content of what I was sharing as a primary school teacher with the learners in my class. It influenced me to leave teaching and try to create an alternative to what existed. I soon learned the truth about people speaking Knowledge of Self and then living it. I suggested that Black Noise release its own cassette and had Falko design the cover. We were involved in the recording process as well, and considered the content of the album to be a sharing of information. The album was called *Rebirth of Mind & Hip Hop Culture*. I decided to take my pay-out from teaching and to learn more about the Universal Zulu Nation by travelling to the Zulu Nation anniversary in New York in 1994. It was after leaving teaching that I spoke to Afrika Bambaataa personally and met all the people that had sent me information packs about Knowledge of Self. This was a huge leap of faith on my part as I had never before travelled or taken such a huge step in the direction of my destiny.

We released 500 cassettes independently, which were sold out on our first tour to Sweden in 1995. We were asked by the Swedes if we wanted gifts, but we asked instead if the funders could help us print our first CD independently. We made history by doing this as it sparked an understanding of the process of production and challenged those in the group who spoke Knowledge of Self on stage. Unfortunately, some in the group wanted their share of the money.

On our return to South Africa, I suggested that we create our own concerts at which to sell our CDs and encourage others to participate on that platform and pay people. The event was called Do for Self. We even went on to release one of the first Do for Self compilation cassettes.

Earlier on b-boying had taught me that I could earn an income by merely dancing on the streets of Cape Town and earn more than most 'casual' workers for the day. This liberating thought also made me very rebellious towards formal jobs at clubs and malls. I started making button badges, bumper stickers and photocopied posters of Black Noise to help market the group. This later developed into actual posters. All the while I was very aware of the need to expand the Hip Hop community locally in order for us to make a living from it. I set to work spreading Hip Hop through library tours and then teaching mostly b-boying because it was the most appealing to youth. After releasing the first compilation CD, I realised that most MCs were not really into marketing their work or themselves. I focused my energy into teaching b-boying and creating a scene. After our first library tour – at which most of the kids asked 'What is Hip Hop?' – I returned to the drawing board by creating a manual by the same name. It was a photocopied booklet and had a breakdown of all the elements of the culture and information from practitioners like Shaheen and Ready D, whom I interviewed for the manual. I later found out from others that copies of this booklet spread to many parts of the country. B-boying is also my first love and I made that our focus. Aside from teaching b-boying, I was also selling VHS cassettes that contained b-boy footage. I ensured that b-boying spread to areas like Kraaifontein, Kuilsrivier, Bonteheuwel, Mitchells Plain, Retreat, Lavender Hill, Manenberg and other areas on the Cape Flats, and even to places as wide afield as Worcester, Ceres and later to Mossel Bay, Saldanha Bay, Port Elizabeth, East London and of course Johannesburg. On my return from the USA, I tried to help spread the Universal Zulu Nation in Cape Town but soon realised the difficulty of spreading the name of such an organisation in the land of the Zulu tribe. I hosted the first Universal Hip Hop Nation Celebration in December 1996 to help spread Hip Hop culture with workshops; this event became the African Battle Cry in 1997. That same year, I also secured funding for Black Noise to perform and then participate at Battle of the Year in Germany, where we won third place for South Africa. The following year we took along one young dancer. This had a major impact on his life as he saw how his dancing developed and the benefits of choosing to join Black Noise as a career. After that trip, it really encouraged us to host the event annually and send the best dancers as the South African Allstar B-boys to Germany. In 1998, I started the Heal the Hood Project, through which I created more platforms for practitioners and fans of Hip Hop culture. I created events like the African Hip Hop Indaba, Shut Up Just Dance, Our Hip Hop Festival, Freestyle Session, Battle of the Year, Black Noise and Heal the Hood tours, Learn to Surf Day, Up the Rock, Do for Self concerts, Cape Flats Film Festival, Cape Flats Performing Arts Conference, Cape Flats Photo Exhibition and Cellphone Picture Competition. I also raised money for flights to send 193 artists to international events in Germany, France, Belgium, the Netherlands, Sweden, Reunion Island, Denmark, Italy, England, Ireland, Brazil, India, Australia, Norway, Switzerland, Botswana, Zimbabwe, Namibia, Egypt, Korea, the USA and Finland.

Through the Heal the Hood Project, I was also able to create seven compilation CDs and assisted artists to release their CDs – artists like Isaac Mutant, Plain Madnizz, Black Noise, Jamayka

Poston, Conquering Lions, Lionz of Zion, Ancient Men and my own Emile YX? solo CDs. I was also able to help writers get their stories out via a book called *RAPSS* (Heal the Hood Project 2005), which is an acronym for rhymes, articles, poetry, short stories, sketches. I also went on to lead by example by writing and releasing my own books: *What Is Hip Hop?* (Jansen 1995), *My Hip Hop Is African & Proud* (Jansen 2003), *Conscious Rhymes for Unconscious Times* (Jansen 2010a), *B-boy Syllabus 1* (Jansen 2010b) and *RAPSS* (two volumes).

In 2005, I decided to create a regular class at the Cape Flats Development Association to encourage youth from Lavender Hill to attend and grow with the many projects that I created and implemented. In 2009, I created a touring performance crew for the Heal the Hood Project that travelled to Norway, Sweden, Ireland, England and Italy. This Heal the Hood performance involved South Africa's number one b-boy, Benny Burgess, and another b-boy, Daniel van Wyk, and a Hip Hop New Skool dancer, Latitia Fisher. They were shown the reality of touring and in return for monthly salaries, they taught other youth for free. In 2012, I gave four young men from Lavender Hill a similar opportunity, but instead of being involved in a performance to tour internationally, they were supplied with real-life experiences and opportunities and had to make it work. This group is called Mixed Mense. They form part of a Hip Hop practical school for life lessons and personal development.

More recently, I have been creating alternative ways of showcasing Hip Hop dance via plays. In 2013, I created the first dance Hip Hop play called *Mixing It Up*, then the following year *Break 1* and then *Break 2*. I also assisted in creating *Afrikaaps*, a Hip Hopera about the black history of the Afrikaans language. Furthermore, I assisted Natural Justice[2] to create a play about land restitution for the Bushman community in South Africa. It was called *Ons Bou* (We Build). In 2016, I created a garage-style Hip Hop play called *Stompie*.

MAKING THE SAME BLACK NOISE

I started wondering how black was this noise that we were actually making. Was the content of the Knowledge of Self actually impacting the minds of the very members within Black Noise? Were they overstanding the bigger picture and fully utilising their creative ability for weekly, monthly, annual and long-term survival? Was I getting through to them or was I just fooling

---

2. http://www.naturaljustice.org/countries/south-africa/

myself about our growth as a Hip Hop group promoting Knowledge of Self and Hip Hop culture? Over the years, I had earned millions of South African rands for artists that I shared the stage with as Black Noise, or purchased dancers flight tickets to International Battles, had Hip Hop artists that performed at our gigs, or DJs, beatboxers and MCs that toured with Black Noise. I represented our country internationally, taught for free wherever I was asked and never complained about the millions spent driving or the time sharing my knowledge for free. I seldom speak about the inner workings or personal experiences of Black Noise, even though I have heard numerous stories about what people thought of me. Few people know that in the Black Noise Hip Hop group, we all earned the same, except for whoever arranged the shows; that person got an extra 15 per cent of the profit for securing the shows and making payments to each member. There were no EFTs back then. You had to draw the cash and drop it with them at their homes. I have heard remarkable stories to the contrary, yet I have hundreds of signed proofs of payment to prove my case.

BLACK NOISE, 2005 | Source: Author

I was naïve enough to think that trying to share all information about management would help all members of the group to get shows. In fact, our history of distrust towards other people who look like us got amplified. I started to realise that I was the only one running around for shows, even though I was not the manager of Black Noise or the group's agent. I guess the fact that I come from Grassy Park (seen as a more middle-class community) and that I do not spend my hard-earned money on trivial things, made people dislike me even more. I remember when Black Noise was sponsored by Adidas. We went on an international trip and some of the members spent their money from Adidas. I asked them why they would do such a thing. They replied, 'Because we will be the only *ouens* [guys] with that style of Adidas in Cape Town.' Did I fail in sharing Knowledge of Self that would create a group that would empower themselves or is that just too huge a task for one person to do? On another occasion we were given a huge amount of money upfront for per diems and I saved the entire amount by not buying ridiculously priced food. I explained this to the rest of the group beforehand and even explained how they could do the same. I even went on a rant about how we never know when the next shows would be after this. I later found out that one of the group's members had purchased a shotgun on his return home.

I sometimes think that artists are afraid to sound too happy with their girlfriends or wives about their time at shows or international travels, and slowly but surely they make it sound like being an artist is the worst thing that they can do and eventually their partners agree with them and they have to leave what they love. Many Black Noise members had to choose between the group and their partners because of this.

History finally repeated itself when I secured a deal for Black Noise in Sweden (with the help of a friend) and instead of grabbing the opportunity with both hands, some members were tired of touring and wanted to settle down and get married. I always asked what it was that members wanted, on every long road trip through South Africa or during flights between South Africa and Europe or the USA, and it always came down to the same thing: we need a deal and then make enough money from it. Ironically, when it did happen, all things fell apart. It was also ironic to me because I had been at that point before with Black Noise and this time I was sad that it was the same noise we ended up making, but I was realistic about the mentalities of the group members. On my return to South Africa, I told the group that I would no longer look for shows for Black Noise. The noise faded.

GIVE A MAN A FISH: HEAL THE HOOD PERFORMANCE GROUP 1

After my announcement to Black Noise about my intention, I decided to share the reality of touring internationally and locally with new dancers and youth. I had been working with Benny Burgess and Daniel van Wyk and wanted to add two female dancers to the group because it was desperately needed. I created new songs and they had to create new dance sequences. Together we created a show for national and international performances. Each member got a salary at the end of the month and in turn had to teach others. At the very beginning, the one female dancer did not want to dance with the other female dancer and we decided to just go with one. I soon realised that this did not arm the young dancers with the drive or desire to create their own opportunities and, more importantly, collective opportunities for the team. Again, the reliance fell on my shoulders or that of the Heal the Hood Project. It seemed like a duplication of what I did with Black Noise. It reminded me of the Chinese proverb, 'Give a man a fish, and you feed him for a day. Teach a man to fish and you'll feed him for a lifetime.'

I needed to teach young dancers how to take care of their own careers and place more of the organisational workload on their shoulders. To do so successfully, we tried to link up with people internationally to create an international body for dance that was in the control of local people of colour and not in the hands of the same previously advantaged, so-called white community. I had New Skool Hip Hop dancers, Krumpers, b-boys, poppers and even local freestyle dancers lined up for this huge change, but the power of the past was just too much for us to trust each other. The many youth we had taught joined these same previously and currently advantaged dance schools in South Africa to continue to benefit from this dance that they had had no interest in before. The irony was that many of the local dancers were willing to work for cheap at these schools, but were not willing to create their own local, national and international dance organisations. It proved to be an impossible task, as most people opted to help themselves with the new skills and not the entire Hip Hop community. A huge benefit of colonialism, tribalism, race and apartheid for the previously and currently advantaged is the minds of the enslaved and how they do not trust each other enough to work together. I realised that the past had a deep psychological impact on our communities and that we had very little trust for other people of colour and always saw forward mobility as something tied into buying into the controllers of the bulk of Africa's economy. Race and previous privilege truly proved to have a huge impact on what happened to Hip Hop in Cape Town after our sharing of 'how to teach'.

TEACHING OTHERS HOW TO TEACH

In 2009, a member of Heal the Hood was invited to a government initiative aimed at using Hip Hop as a means to address drug issues on the Cape Flats. I attended the meeting and was very afraid of the final intention and control of what we would create. It was a national African National Congress initiative and I was aware that the local government in Cape Town, the Democratic Alliance (DA), would not like to continue with us because they did not want to address the underlying issues in order to bring about real change in the minds of youth. They were only concerned with number crunching and ticking boxes. I took a backseat and instead wrote a syllabus for the teachers, including teaching them how to teach. The way I wrote the syllabus placed the focus on teaching the connection between the first people of southern Africa, the San and Khoi, and the b-boy circle. My aim was to create a sense of self-worth and historic connection to Africa and the elements of Hip Hop: linking DJing to the drummer, MCing to the griot or storyteller, and b-boying to the shaman or the one who goes into trance dance and breaks from this reality. We taught many unemployed youths and they in turn taught a whole new generation of breakdancers that are some of the best in the country today. Amongst the teachers were Angelo van Wyk, Nigel February, Elgernon van Wyk and a few more that have since worked for the DA government in the Western Cape at their school MOD centres.[3] In fact, Angelo and Nigel are leaders of dance in the province. We are proud of arming them with the teaching skills to take these posts, but are sad that Hip Hop has been co-opted to achieve number-crunching exercises, instead of its original revolutionary agenda of freeing the minds of young artists. Intellectual property was never an issue until that happened to Heal the Hood Project and we saw our technique of teaching spread to various organisations that do not have the interests of Hip Hop culture at heart, but instead their own pockets.

---

3. https://www.westerncape.gov.za/general-publication/mod-programme

AFRIKAAPS: BLACK CONSCIOUSNESS BEGINS WITH THE BUSHMAN

At the end of 2009, Catherine Henegan called me about an idea she had about producing a play on the black history of the Afrikaans language. I was busy with things and my mind was too busy to get back to her, because I did not see myself as a theatre type of person. On 7 January 2010, I finally agreed to meet with Catherine and the rough cast of *Afrikaaps* at that point. I kept thinking about these words, 'When you take a step towards your ancestry, it will take two steps towards you.' My work with Black Noise was slowing down and the silence seemed to make space for my ancestors to find me again. It has been one of my dreams to dance with the first peoples of all people, the Bushmen. I have always had a great interest in the unwritten truths about our heritage. It was thus no coincidence that I was contacted to be part of this production about the black history of the Afrikaans language.

I was sceptical about doing a play because I am not an actor but I nevertheless attended the information and research session. I was extremely impressed with the depth of the information and the contributions by Bushmen to the formation of the language, and the untold information about the history of South Africa before the Europeans arrived. As I read and listened to the information, I could not exclude myself from the process of creating the production of *Afrikaaps*. From the start of the production we felt blessed to tell this very important story. Initially, I was very fearful of my level of writing in Afrikaans and kept to what I had already written previously. Compared to the others in the cast, I was the most English speaking of the lot. The other members of the cast were also more spontaneous and uninhibited to make mistakes in public. I questioned my standard of speaking the language silently, and, as I read the information, I realised why I was called to be part of this production and to share in this information. This new journey was more about my growth as an artist, organiser and person than I had even realised. The information was overwhelming and reminded me of the time when I was first exposed to Black Consciousness. Ironically, at that same time, I was finding new books and information about South African history, especially related to the Khoi and the San.

One of my major realisations was my own neglect of early Africans' contribution to civilisation and how my position in southern Africa is directly linked to that greatness. My mind expanded to the greatness of who we are here in southern Africa. My ancestors were present on this journey and were whispering into my ear. I was helping to set this information free to the general population.

We gathered information from Patrick Mallet and I remember jotting down that we would meet with Dr Neville Alexander on 20 May 2010. I then suggested that we travel to a high school to get an idea from the speakers of the language exactly what it was like growing up speaking one version of the language, and then having to write exams in a completely other version that was only spoken in class and nowhere else. One of the breakdancers that attended my free workshops was now in his final year at Lavender Hill High and arranged for the *Afrikaaps* cast to visit their class. One learner explained that he had to concentrate on how he spoke in an interview for a job because one slip-up would have his interviewers associating him with gangsters and all the other stereotypes associated with speaking Kaaps.[4] Hearing this was so profound and exposed me to an unspoken truth about the impact being examined in the standard (white-dominant) version of our language had on youth from the Cape Flats. I left the school invigorated to spread this word of Afrikaaps to the masses on the Cape Flats and throughout the country. Every single day was exciting and nerve-racking all at the same time. It was like I was back in school and the teachers were the theatre practitioners that gathered every Friday to check on our progress.

We finally had something ready for presentation and I was nervous because my usual shows were a million times more physical, while this was very 'heady'. We finally had an opportunity to showcase the content at the Klein Karoo Nasionale Kunstefees (KKNK; Little Karoo National Arts Festival) in Oudtshoorn. Before we left Cape Town, we had a debriefing session with Aryan Kaganof, a South African filmmaker, novelist, poet and fine artist. The cast was very hyped up and ready for the *Afrikaaps* takeover. I, on the other hand, was very sceptical about launching a revolution from a space like the Baxter Theatre, which is associated with UCT. *Afrikaaps* went on to win best production and was nominated for best new Afrikaans production, received a Kanna 2010 nomination for best KKNK debut and a nomination for best presentation. The *Afrikaaps* documentary also won the Audience Award at the Encounters Film Festival[5] as well as the Runner Up Best SA Documentary.

TEACH THEM HOW TO FISH: HEAL THE HOOD PRACTICAL HIP HOP SCHOOL 2

I started Mixed Mense, a practical performance Hip Hop school, with learners from Lavender Hill that the Heal the Hood Project and Emile YX? had been working with since 2008. Also involved

---

4. Cape Flats original version of the stolen language named Afrikaans by colonisers.
5. https://www.encounters.co.za/

were Stefan aka b-boy Mouse and Leeroy Phillips aka b-boy Malis. They were participants in the Ke Moja Project's Each One, Teach One campaign and were then paid to teach for the Heal the Hood Project in various communities. My mission was to share my experiences that I obtained over the last plus-minus 30 years of being involved with entertainment through Hip Hop culture as a breakdancer/b-boy and rapper with Black Noise and these youths. I made it clear that I would share information that I had learned from Knowledge of Self and Afrikaaps with them in the form of rhymes and reading material that I had. The first task I set for them was to write about their experience of attending my class back in 2008. They wrote about that experience and what they had learned over the years. I encouraged them to write in Afrikaaps. We first spoke about what the experiences were like and it was very clear that they needed more opportunities to speak about their thoughts and feelings. I started reading the rhyme that I wrote in Afrikaaps to encourage them to do the same. It was hard at first because they were very aware of the fact that they had spelling and grammatical errors, but as soon as they realised that I was not interested in those things they found it easier to read and rhyme what they were thinking. Our first song was called '*Ek Leer Vir Jou, Dan Leer Djy Vir My*' (I Teach You and Then You Teach Me). Once we had written the song, the next step was to create a music video of the song. The aim of that was to show them the importance of the story spreading to others and how visuals would not only bring the story to life, but also emphasise what they were talking about. Another thing we spoke about was how others would react to them writing like they spoke and seeing them and their community on video.

MY 'B' IN B-BOY STANDS FOR BUSHMAN

I was watching a documentary called *The Freshest Kids* and in an interview with DJ Kool Herc, he said that he named them b-boys because they seemed to break or that their minds broke and that they were going into a trance as the music played. I went silent at this connection between the graffiti and rock art, MCing and storytelling, DJing and beatmaking to the hand clap, and the cyclic chants done for the b-boy or shaman to go into trance or breakdance. Around the same time, I got Mixed Mense involved in the fight to stop the government from building a mall on the edge of a sacred lake/vlei in Cape Town called Princess Vlei. Our journey into this story exposed us to people on the same journey of self-discovery. My intention to turn Mixed Mense into a practical school helped me to create a practical example that can be assessed in the field and developed for various communities. It felt as if everything I had done over the years was culminating in this school. As we spoke to blending various local heritages, we were approached by the British Council to create a Hip Hop dance play. I immediately suggested the idea of mixing things through Hip Hop dance and local sounds. I included Stefan and Leeroy in the production and again the blend between Namastap or Bushman dance and Hip Hop became a reality. We later developed the Hip Hop dance play into a full-fledged play by the name of *Break* and it was performed at Artscape twice. The play, as with all other self-love talks and activities, shares information about Afrikaaps. I was hungry for more information and my ancestors were taking steps towards me to supply me with that information so that I could do this work. I was approached by Natural Justice to tour to the Bushman communities and create a play entitled *Ons Bou* (*We Build*),[6] and perform it for them. Only Janine and Charl from *Afrikaaps* agreed to do it and I asked if I could take Stefan and Leeroy along to participate in whichever way, so they could also enjoy the experience. The tour to the various Bushman communities in South Africa had a lasting impact on all participants. At the end of the tour, we were asked to perform it to the First People Council.[7] Not a day goes by that I don't speak about these great first people of southern Africa.

LET'S MAKE A BLACK NOISE IN THE LAND OF THE FREE, WHERE THE BLACKS CAN'T BE

As I stood at the graveside of Oom Dawid Kruiper, leader of the Khomani San, I suddenly realised that the noise I had been trying to make for such a long time had been silenced from its very origin. I was suddenly inspired to relaunch Black Noise and give this new generation an opportunity to see the group in action again and continue the legacy. As always, that action and intent resulted in an invitation by Nomadic Wax (production company) for Black Noise to be part of an event called One Mic at the Kennedy Centre in Washington DC, as well as the Trinity International Hip Hop Festival in Connecticut. I included the members of Mixed Mense (Stefan Benting, Leeroy Phillips, MC Jean-Pierre Frolick, SA b-boy champ Alfred Burgess aka b-boy Benny, DJ Madfingaz aka Nantel Hopley, myself and videographer Tanswell Jansen) in the squad travelling to the USA. We were ready to do our best.

---

6. The play employed techniques outlined by Augusto Boal (1985).
7. First People/First Nation Council is a collective represented by Natural Justice in issues relating to the various tribes – the Khoi, San, !Kwe and !Kung – in southern Africa.

My activist nature saw the potential for these young men from Lavender Hill on the Cape Flats to show what they had learned. I was both pleasantly surprised as well as saddened by one of them, when he found it impossible to be at peace with new experiences while his family was struggling back home. He left the group soon after. However, before he left, he asked me a question that changed my view of Lavender Hill forever. (A good teacher should always be ready and willing to learn new things.) Leeroy approached me outside Whole Foods in Washington DC and asked me why a military veteran was sitting outside in the winter cold. I replied that he was probably homeless. He then said, *'Die sal nooit innie Lavender Hill gebeur nie'* (This will never happen in Lavender Hill). He asked me if this man had no family or friends. I then asked why he would say so and he said that people would always bring someone indoors, because nobody slept on the streets in Lavender Hill.

Over the years, many Black Noise and Heal the Hood Project members had left us to do something more lucrative and I sensed that I had to prepare for another such reality. The USA trip also served as a great opportunity to see if Stefan, Leeroy and Benny were able to participate in a panel discussion after the screening of the Heal the Hood Project documentary *From B-boys to Men*. If I had had graduation certificates that night, I would have handed them each one, as they made me proud to see them perform with much confidence. These silent boys that I had met in 2005 were challenging their fears of public speaking.

At our final performance at the One Mic Festival at the Kennedy Centre, an older gentleman, who had been working at the venue for the last 45 years, approached the group and said that our performance was one of the most powerful that he had seen at the venue and we should be proud of ourselves. I sat in silence and watched the guys glow in the moment. We then went to the Trinity Festival and there they saw first-hand that international people want to see their local flavour. They taught a 'Mixing It Up' traditional South African dance style with Hip Hop session at Trinity and the locals couldn't get enough. They asked us to show them more. I sat there wondering how powerful it would be for others in South Africa to see this.

At the end of 2015, however, Leeroy decided to leave the Heal the Hood Project and started working as a 'casual worker' at Checkers in Blue Route Mall. I still reach out to him when the opportunity presents itself, but he has become very isolated and sad.

LETS GO FISHING: 'THE TEACHER AND STUDENT' HEAL THE HOOD PRACTICAL SCHOOL 3

At the start of 2016, Stefan Benting was officially a paid staff member of the Heal the Hood Project. He would now learn how to make a living from his creativity. To date, he has taught around 100 learners to rap and dance. He has been practising his b-boying and won 2017's solo dance battle at the African Hip Hop Indaba and was part of the team that won African Battle Cry. He won money for that and wants to save to buy his own house. Stefan also joined a casting agency in Cape Town and was offered some work. We have regular talks about what we can create together and how much he needs to make for him and his family. The biggest lesson I have learned is that teaching has to be in both directions and that we have to be available to each other continuously. In 2017, we worked on our second Mixed Mense album, music videos, a new performance, a regional, national and international tour and figured out enough ways to make a living from CDs, DVDs, club gigs, pubs, events, plays, books, tours, paraphernalia and so on. I feel that if we can make Stefan's life easier and help him to achieve his goals, we could duplicate this for many other youths from communities throughout South Africa. Going fishing is also about making sure that we diversify our income streams; making sure that in the silence of catching the next fish, we save and grow our spaces to fish and, finally, ensure that we practise sustainability in order to always have fish to catch.

…AND THE B-BOY WAS MADE MAN

As I get older, I have become less of a superhero and more of a man. As b-boys we believe that we can fly and we have to think that way or we will fall to the ground and be eaten by the competition. Belief in oneself is a powerful tool to possess and I can honestly say that I did not have this as a kid or as a teacher because of the Euro-cation or mental whitewashing that we are fed as Africans in our places of learning. As parents we internalise that self-hate and feed it to our children, who in turn pass that venom on to their kids. It is a vicious cycle that white supremacy has put in place and which benefits the few and enslaves the many. As a man, I cannot play along anymore and must rebel. The game is everywhere. Those who have spoken out and rebelled have been silenced with death. Knowledge of Self is a powerful tool and can free Africa from its global oppression, but violence will not be the way that this change happens. To quote the leader of the Khomani San, Oom Petrus Vaalbooi, *'Moet nie die Boesman roep as julle wil toyi-toyi en die ondier met wapens veg nie. 'n Slim mens veg nooit mense wat wapens maak, met wapens nie.'* (Do not call on the Bushman when you want to toyi-toyi/protest and fight 'the beast' with weapons. A clever person never fights against people who make weapons, with weapons). On hearing the first section of what he said, I was angry and then, as he explained, it suddenly dawned on me that the Bushmen were the first to face the full wrath of the beast and its many mutations since then. They have seen the world being destroyed by this act of violence and they overstand that a new way is needed. As a teacher and student, I wish to create a new way – one that is connected, that feels the planet's heartbeat and is able to heal the self first. One that is not afraid of death, but wants to *live*.

True healing starts from within and then that healing trickles out to others. As a man, I cannot obtain Knowledge of Self and not internalise it to take action. I cannot perpetuate the injustices and continue to play along. When people ask me what b-boying has taught me, I have to say that it has helped me to internalise the lessons Knowledge of Self has taught me and being able to make a living for the last 23 years, since I left formal teaching. This b-boy has made the circle, the globe and the battle against the opponent, a battle against perception of self. I will always ask why and not fear the unknown. Emile means 'industrious'. So, no one could say that I have not been industriously asking questions to overstand the unknown and then take action to know and share.

B-BOY MOUSE AND MALLIS | Source: Heal the Hood

CHAPTER 6.
BUSH RADIO'S ALKEMY
AND HIP HOP ACTIVISM 2.0

ADAM HAUPT IN CONVERSATION
WITH NAZLI ABRAHAMS

Nazli Abrahams spoke to Adam Haupt in 2003 about ALKEMY at Bush Radio in Salt River, Cape Town. ALKEMY is a programme that she initiated with Shaheen Ariefdien at Bush Radio. ALKEMY was billed as an MC workshop, but was really a point of entry into developing critical literacy.

Adam: Okay, thanks for doing this interview, to begin with.

Nazli: You're welcome.

Adam: My first question is, typically, who are the, who are your students? Typically, who are they in terms of age, where they come from, class, race and so on, gender.

Nazli: Uhm, the gender, unfortunately right now, is mostly male and I think when people hear – for lack of a better term, we called it MC workshops, to start with. When they hear that, it's sort of a male thing. And very few women come to the fore and the ones that have are somewhat intimidated by the whole MC thing because it's not something they've done. This one girl in particular…

Adam: Coslyn.

Nazli: Coslyn, right. She stuck with it. Uhm, she, when she started she hadn't rhymed at all and she felt intimidated, but the group helped her along. What happens in the group is, uhm, a lot of people ask if they can stop by, and if they can just sort of observe, watch what's going on and my thing is, 'No, you can't.' It's a very personal space. Uhm, what we try, what we do in the beginning is we have these sessions. We call it pre-performance preparation. And essentially that is how to use your space. But, apart from that, it's for them to interact with each other away from the writing, away from just sort of talking. They have, uhm, they play a lot of trust games, uhm, where you stand and you have to fall back in and know that someone's going to be there to catch you. Uhm, it takes about three sessions for them to actually do that and feel comfortable with doing it and knowing somebody will catch them. So they build this over a little while. So for someone just to come in and observe, it changes the group dynamic. They don't know who the person is. They're not sure even if you, someone is like here for blah, blah, blah, uhm, you can note the change. For example, if they come in and they go through line by line and they have to explain why they use certain words, why they use certain rhyme schemes, and so on, and the group will say to them, 'Okay, ja, but that's a lazy rhyme scheme. You didn't even think. You just did it because you were lazy. Okay, next.' So they're very critical of each other without being personal. And for someone else to witness that, it's very – they don't take kindly to it. So you have to be very careful, uhm, who can and who can't be part of it. But what we do is, when we have open sessions – for example, when we had the linguist come through, it's a rare occasion when we have someone of that calibre come through.

Adam: Geneva Smitherman.

Nazli: Yes. It's not rare. I shouldn't say that. We've been very blessed. We've had all kinds of people come through and people who are really interested in the programme and are willing to donate their time. She was just one of those people. So when we have sessions like that – because we don't have people like that, because people don't have access to people like that – we make it an open session, where we don't discuss lyrics or anything. We just have everybody come in, uhm, sort of a Q&A, uhm, whatever will come out of it will come out of it. But, ja, it is available to the public in certain instances and, uhm, but not always. And then how they're chosen – the first group of people that we had, they were part of a programme that we had at Bush Radio call HIV Hop, where they were looking at using how to use Hip Hop to educate young people about issues about HIV and AIDS, but beyond messaging sort of the ABC thing that you see everywhere. Uhm, so then there was…

Adam: That was in 2000, right?

Nazli: Yes. Yes, it was. The people who funded the HIV Hop programme put together, uhm, uhm, a Hip Hop theatre production based in Amsterdam. So they said, 'Alright look, put together those…people that you had before. Give them a few sessions on governance, labour issues, crime and something else.' And uhm, alright, so they got six people together and we, we were only supposed to be with them a month, but we ended up going for like six months. And, uhm, then they left and then came back then like, wow, we were like…were way prepared for them in a lot of things we talked about. And nobody had a sense of what we were talking about. They just looked at us like…like they couldn't engage us. So I thought, okay, uhm, why we don't do something a little more structured and see where we can take it. So then, uhm, we did. We plugged it on the *Headwarmers* [Hip Hop radio programme] and, uhm, then we got like all kinds of people calling in and then we had an interview process. Our big thing, a lot of people would hear MC workshops and they come with this whole MC vibe, you know, 'I'm an MC.' Blah, blah, blah. And our thing is, 'Look, we're not looking to further your music career and we're not looking to forward your writing skills. That's gonna be part of it, but essentially, uhm, we want you to be…aware of what's happening around you…and be able to know why things are happening around you, sort of why you are in the place that you are.' Uhm, what's disturbing for me in particular is a lot of the young kids, they don't have a sense of, of apartheid, but their lives are governed by that like, you see, totally. So for them to understand why certain things are available and why certain things aren't. Or even the whole idea of, uhm, I mean, their parents will have a certain mindset or maybe they won't, but have to sort of know where it all comes from. Not that I'm an expert or anything in that, but just the other thing that I find in young people is they're always told they're apathetic. They're not interested in anything; you know they're kind of there. But then on the flip side, oh they're the leaders of the future, they're important and so on, but there's nothing to show, there are no opportunities available to make them feel important, to have their voices heard. I mean, have concerts on Youth Day, having graffiti workshops wherever they're doing it, then next you have JP Smith [DA politician] passing, saying, you know, it's essentially criminalised. So there's all these mixed messages. So we're saying, 'Look, as young people, you can't rely on other people to do these things for you. You have to know where you are and what you about and take it from there. You would be proactive in your own learning and in your own getting ahead.' And for a lot of the kids that we work with, they don't have a sense of the world beyond the borders of Cape Town. And I think that's what we're also trying to change. Is for them to know that there's a lot of more to this than just this, you know, and, uhm, like right now the programme is extended. People still call it HIV Hop, but it's a lot more to it than that. We're looking at scholarship opportunities outside of the country. Like, we're looking at getting their writing published. We're looking at, uhm, all kinds of things, but really opening up doors for them. And I think once we have a foundation or a group of youth that are confident, well spoken – and from all the different, across the board, all different cultures, different economic backgrounds, all kind of things – then we can start developing, start developing sort of a peer mentor, peer tutor type system, but nothing just, 'Okay, I'm going to teach you to write the letter "A" and now you teach 10 other people.' Something really substantial, something really solid, something really…I'm gonna use the word 'sophisticated', but I'm not sure that's the right word to use. But, I'm not sure if you're following me, a lot of the times when youth do have issues, uhm, it's not palatable for an international audience because they're not sophisticated enough – either their English isn't cool or they don't say it…

Adam: Are you talking about a kind of a discursive literacy, being able to play the academic, understanding a kind of academic discourse?

Nazli: Right. Using it to your advantage, essentially that's what it is. We're not talking about saying that, that's what it is and that's sort of what you need to aspire to. We're saying that's there. You need to know how to manipulate it and use it and do what you need to do with [it] and know what it's all about. And I think that's what we're trying to do, really, ja, in a nutshell. I think [laughs].

Adam: Seems like it is, you're getting a lot of it, right, especially after talking to Marlon [Swai] and talking to Godessa as well. Uhm, just the range of things that they know – the fact they can engage with [Noam] Chomsky, for example, is scary.

Nazli: That's one of the required readings. Like a lot of, uhm, we had, for example, like a 15-year-old kid that's part of the workshop, asking him to read *Manufacturing of Consent*.[1] 'Ja, but I don't get it.' 'It doesn't matter if you don't get it, just read it. Later on, when you read other things, the names will start clicking and the places will start clicking and things will start falling in place. But for now, don't concentrate on the fact that you don't get it. Just read it and when you have other things to add to it, it will start building.' So that's what we do.

---

1. See Herman & Chomsky (1988).

Adam: How do you structure that? I mean it's potentially quite tricky. I mean, my experience as someone who did honours, uhm, the first time coming out of a BA [Bachelor of Arts] – for many of us, it was challenging and bewildering. Here you have 16 - 17-year-old kids engaging with theory, uhm, that your average BA or Social Science graduate would grapple with at honours level. I've had students at that level really struggling with the stuff. How do you…

Nazli: See, I think the advantage here is that they're not writing exams and they're not having to hand in papers and they're not being graded and they're not being, uhm – their understanding isn't based on regurgitating information. Right now we're looking at a practical application of that information based on – I mean if you look at globalisation, everybody hears this word. You know, what is it? What was it before it was globalisation? So my thing is, look, if you live in Khayelitsha, what does globalisation mean to you? What does NEPAD [New Partnership for Africa's Development] spell to you? Does it mean…there was a case where a bunch of people died of cholera. Was it really just about the cholera or was it about water not being sanitised and where did that come from? Privatisation. So it's just building on very small – it's not small concepts, but it's building on small chunks of information that is very relevant to their everyday living. And because it hits here [points to heart] and not here [points to head], it makes it more interesting and so they're hungry to read or they're hungry to find out more about it and I think that's the difference. It may be very theoretical, but they, with the practical part, they have a chance to look at the everyday…part of it. So it's not something that's out there. It's something that's very real to them. And I think that's the advantage that we have right now for them to not feel, 'Uhhh, I can't do this.' And the other thing is Shaheen and I are available if they need to discuss anything. The only problem with that is I have to read a lot – a lot because if they ask you pointed questions you have to be able to send them in another direction or, or know what they're talking about and give detail. So that's the challenge for the two of us – is to be able to keep reading and to sort of stay on point with some of the things and to cheat sometimes too. I mean, we read little summaries of some of the things or we talk to other people to get a quick, 'Okay, how do you understand this, okay.' And then we also have a lot of, like I say, elders are available to us. People that have all kinds of information and experience that are willing to come in and share. So we've been really fortunate in that regard. And the people that come in are kid-friendly. They don't speak on a, uhm, they don't deal with theory, I mean they don't deal strictly on a theoretical level. And especially what we call the practical part is emotional vomit. It's a big chance to just spew on paper. Because the processing, like you say, they're dealing with concepts that a lot of people in university are only starting to come to terms with or just the process. So it's new to them and they need an outlet and that's where the lyrics come in. So when they come in for an interview, we try to tell them, 'Look, it's not about the lyrics. It's not about the performance.' And they don't quite get it right away, but eventually they do.

Adam: Where do these…or how many generations of graduates have you had so far?

Nazli: Four.

Adam: Four?

Nazli: Ja.

Adam: Okay, so it's literally every semester you've had a turnover of…

Nazli: Uh-hmm. It's like a semester course, yeah. Uhm, the only thing, the problem with that is, uhm, we haven't found a way really to deal with it, is that when you have people who finish the programme what do, like what do you do with them? You know, like where do they…they just finish and they're sort of wandering around trying to see where they fit in with the things. So a few of them, actually all of them, have come back. Uhm, we've funnelled them in through another programme through Bush Radio called the Children's Radio Education Workshop. Like I said earlier, we tried to develop sort of a peer mentor, peer tutor thing.

Adam: Is that Kidocracy?

Nazli: No, Kidocracy is a part of that. I'll explain about that as well. So we have the kids that go on air. But before they go on air, they need to research their topics. Well, they need to come up with a list of topics, research the topics and know how to present them and so on. So what we've done with the people that have graduated when, if they're interested in continuing, they act as facilitators for the younger kids and help them do the research and go into studio with them. They don't go on air, but they're just there as a guide for them on [the] air process. So right now there's [counts] six of them that are doing that every Saturday. And they still bring in their work, they still read and, uhm, they sign books out once a week. They have to read a book a week [laughs].

Adam: Kind of a book club.

Nazli: Ja. And, uhm, and they exchange the books and they discuss, when they've all read it, they discuss what they felt came out of it. One of the big ones was *Heart of Darkness*[2] and, uhm, the other one…uhm…[Frantz] Fanon. I don't know which one it was…

Adam: *White Skin, Black Masks*.

Nazli: No, it wasn't that one.

Adam: I mean *Black Skin, White Masks* [laughs].[3]

Nazli: It wasn't that one.

Adam: *Wretched of the Earth*.[4]

Nazli: It was *Wretched of the Earth*. So that was also some of the required reading. And some of the other books that they read, they don't necessarily understand why they have to read it – not that they have to read it. Say, for example, we have Bruce Lee's *The Tao of Jeet Kune Do*[5] and they go, 'Oh.' Okay. But I guess the philosophy, uhm, of fighting, or redirecting energies and that type of thing and one of the very first talks that they have is about energy and molecular structures and that type of thing and looking at how as an artist you're not responsible for what comes through. You're just sort of a vehicle and, uhm, that you have to be open to all sort of energies and things and so on. It sounds very pie in the sky, but it makes sense. So by the time they get to *The Tao of Jeet Kune Do*, they're been through the other stuff, so it doesn't freak them out. Like, 'Hhh.' For a lot of kids it's all very new and sometimes it be like, uhhhh, you know, it's for them to decide how's going to, how they're going to make use of it.

Adam: What is your sense of how these four generations of graduates have actually negotiated, uhm, this process and do you think it has substantially shifted headsets?

---

2. See Conrad (1902).
3. See Fanon (1952).
4. See Fanon (1963).
5. See Lee (1975).

Nazli: It has, uhm. If I think of, uhm, for example Coslyn. She…actually all of them. We had an emergency meeting. There was four of them that came one Saturday and said, 'Look, we really need to talk. Like we've been talking to each other and we just found out that we don't relate to anybody anymore. Like, what are we supposed to do now? You know, you guys invited us to this programme. You bombarded us with this information, but now what?' So that's not an easy question to answer. You know. I don't know what now. Uhm, so what we tried to tell them is that they need to be a support system for each other because they're dealing with similar issues. So that's one thing that came out of that, is that there's this really tight little network, if you will, of, uhm, like they share information. Like if somebody finds an article, then they bring it in, photocopy it, give it to everybody. Or they recommend books that they've read or…So they've become this little group, like a really tightly knit group. Uhm, any kind of anything that's happening around town, they bring it, the information here, and sort of, yeah. And then the process that they went through – for example, one of the kids had never read a book before, ever. So he finished his first two books in the programme. When he was finished he bought a dictionary because he wanted to be able to use multisyllable rhymes [laughs] and so on. 'Cause he used to use these really big abstract words, but he had no idea what it meant, but it sounded really nice. And we got to a point when he had to go through it line by line and say why he chose those words, he couldn't. So he said, 'Alright, I need to read, I need to get a dictionary.' So that's what he did. And so for me that was like a highlight. It's like people are getting out of it. So, yeah. The other thing is sometimes even for a split second you can see them making connections and that's, wow, just to see them making the connections. Uhm, and they challenge you. Like our thing is don't believe everything we say. Like make up your own mind, but base it on information that you're getting. Don't just make up your mind. Like know what you're talking about. Read, uhm, and don't also believe everything that you're reading. It's like other opinions. You know, you can't read one opinion if that's what it is. Find other opinions. So that's been, that's been cool and they really do challenge you. Like, uhm, if they don't agree with you they'll say, 'That doesn't make sense.' Or, 'I don't buy into that.' And that's cool because it engages them and also that allows them a chance to, to sort of process what they've learned and also make it make sense to them without you saying blah, blah, blah, finished.

Adam: I'm just thinking that it's very interesting that this is happening now, albeit on a small scale in one small part of the country. It's interesting that this process is happening here with all this talk of how messed up our education system is. Uhm, how do you see that making, I mean, what is the next step? Do you see this approach on a mass scale, for example? How do you see this translating into action on a broader scale or is this just something that you want to manage on a small scale, sort of on a small scale?

Nazli: Well, I think ideally we'd like to see it happening in a much larger, on a much larger scale, but we don't have the capacity to do that right now. Time and skills, uhm. Okay, my long-term goal is to build a school, but looking at alternative forms of education. Because a lot of the kids, if you don't fit into a certain mould at school, then you just fall by the side. And I see that happening all the time with the kids that come here. They're either problem kids or…they just, they have an attitude. And it's not even about an attitude. It's just about engaging them. What I find really disturbing is we really don't give kids a lot of credit for anything. Uhm, we talk down to them a lot as educators. We just assume that they don't know much. Like, for example, uhm, I got a call from this guy not too long ago who had grant money. And he said, 'Look, we need to run some workshops for these kids from Heideveld. Uhm, what can you come up with?' So I said, 'Well, we could try this or da-da-da.' And he goes, 'No, that's way above them. No, we need something really simple. I don't know like, like writing compositions.' I'm like, 'Hallo, no then I don't want to have anything to do with it. What if we try something like this?' and he says, 'No that's too academic for them.' And I'm thinking why, like why won't you try to introduce a little bit of substance or something that the kids really grab onto? It's too academic for them or it's too, too much for them. And that's the thing that we, that's the challenge for me right now. It's for me to get. Like I look at the whole system with OBE [outcomes-based education], there's no way if you have 50 or 60 kids in the class that you can have this holistic, uhm, teaching because you can't facilitate that as one teacher. You don't have the time to spend with a kid. You just don't, you know. I really don't know what they're trying to, how this is all gonna work or where they're trying to go with it. Uhm, in Canada I saw that. Like I was part of the whole Year 2000, they used to call it when I was at school. By the year of 2000 it had to be implemented and, but I mean, the training started years and years before they actually put it into place. But I mean now you have this OBE, which is based on a very similar system, and you only have teachers being trained now by people who don't know what it is. I went to one of the training sessions and the person brought a binder and said, 'Look, I don't really know what this is. Read it and however you interpret it, that's what you do.' And I thought, 'Hhh, you know, this is like a mess.' And this is a representative from the Board of Education. You know, so it doesn't leave me with a lot of faith in the school system.

Adam: Shew. Let's talk about the nuts and bolts of your programme then. I mean, ideally what you say is you'd like to set up a school. Uhm, how do [you] make things work right now on a nuts and bolts level and also how is it that you're able to tap into people like Geneva Smitherman and, you know, both local and international people coming in? How does that work? What kind of network do you rely on?

Nazli: Uhm…we've been fortunate that we've had access to the radio station because the radio station has an international reputation. When people are in town they come through and check it out. So when they're here…we say, 'Oh, well, we have this programme and this programme and this programme.' And then we show them the outline of this programme, uhm, they meet the kids and, uhm, and then they, that's what sparks their interest. And then when they – I'm not sure if a lot of it has to do with the fact that we're based in South Africa or on the continent. People just…I'm not sure what they expect us to be doing. So when they see what we're doing, they'd be like, 'Oh, wow.' And sometimes it's really simple things that they like, 'Oh, wow.' And, uhm, okay let me answer the question first [we laugh].

Adam: Their assumptions are interesting to me as well. You know, people coming from first-world spaces and who have very narrow expectations of what they expect to find in Africa.

Nazli: Right. Like even when they read the lyrics, they'd be like, 'Oh! Oh my God, these guys are thinking like this?' It's like, yeah. Okay. It's not necessarily everybody's thinking like that, you know, but it's, they're capable and, uhm, okay. But how we have access to a lot of the people is that, uhm, first of all through the radio station. Once we make contact with those people, they tell other people. And when those people are in town, then they don't necessarily go through the radio station. Then they have our names and they'll say, 'Oh, we heard about your programme, blah, blah, blah.' I've had a lot of mail from people saying, 'We got your name through so and so. Can we donate books? Or, you know, when we're in town next can we stop by? Can we, you know, how can we help out? Can we, like what can we do?' So we've been fortunate like that. And I think Shaheen and I are both personable enough. So when we're not here and we're elsewhere, we talk about the things we're doing, you know. Who's doing similar things? Can we be in touch with them? See what they're doing? And then we exchange programme information to see. And so, yeah, that's mostly how we do it.

Adam: Hmm. Ja, I've seen Shaheen in action, for one. It's scary: Mr Networker.

Nazli: But you have to. You really do. You have to network, yeah, or you won't go anywhere. And I find that a lot of people here, they don't have vision, you know. Like they just…I think it's one thing to be politicised and another to be political. And I find a lot of people political in – okay, this is just my own distinction, right? The whole idea of struggle politics, I understand it and I know where it comes from, but if you wanna engage a larger audience or you wanna engage a lot of people to be able to get this out, you need to engage them on their level and you need to still throw the struggle politics at them. But they get bored after a while. And their whole thing is like, they become more patronising when you do the whole…struggle thing. And so what we try to do is try to stay away from that, uhm, but at the same time, but once you hook them, introduce them to it – if that makes any sense, I don't know if that makes any sense…

Adam: I'm still with you.

Nazli: I suppose, okay, the people that we work with sometimes don't really – not the people that we work with. The people sort of outside of this. When they want to, uhm, see I don't want to mention names. But, alright, let's try to do this like this. [laughs] There are a number [of] groups in and around Cape Town that are doing very, what they call similar things by way of how they explain what they are doing. So they go to schools and they do workshops, blah, blah, blah. But there's no, that's where it ends. It's not about, it's about, uhm, uhm, imparting any kind of skill. It's like, 'Alright, this is what we do. Da-da, da-da, da-da, finished you know.' Move on and you can say, 'Oh, we had this workshop here. So many kids showed up.' But there's no process. And I find what we also do in South Africa – and I'm not sure if that's just part of the system right now – but everybody wants everything now. You know, I want, everything must be now. And…and there's still, there's still a wariness of education. I can understand it, but at the same time we really do need to try to get people away from that kind of, that kind of thinking. Like I know when I first met Shaheen, his whole vibe was, 'No, I'm not gonna go to school.' Like this whole, you know, white man, uhm, you know the conspiracy against the black man, blah, blah, blah. I'm like, 'Yeah, okay, that's only gonna take you so far' [laughs]. I'm like, 'Look, if you're not going to go [to] school, then I'm gonna have nothing to do with you. But if you wanna do what you say you wanna do, then you need to be able to do it and, unfortunately, you're going to need that piece of paper. And you don't have to put a whole lot of faith in the paper, but if you have it, it opens other doors to you.' And essentially with the programme that's what we're trying to do. Like one kid…I can hit him. But he turned down a scholarship because he didn't wanna sell out…

Adam: He turned down a scholarship.

Nazli: Yeah.

Adam: My God.

Nazli: And so when I heard I was like, 'Are you mad? Like, we've got a lot of work to do with you.' There's that and then there's also the whole idea of keeping it real and this whole [laughs]. My whole thing is keeping it real doesn't have to be synonymous with ff'd up, you know, it can…

Adam: With what?

Nazli: With fucked up. Just because it's dysfunctional, doesn't mean it's real. You know, it's dysfunctional for a reason. It can be real for other reasons, but, uhm. So, just trying to get away from that, that's a challenge, also because people think it has to be very ghetto and that; it doesn't always have to be that way.

Adam: I was just thinking because Shaheen was saying that the Hip Hop movement in the States, for example, a lot of people are actually university educated, actually have a certain set of skills in order to carry the movement forward and that the first generation of Hip Hop heads in Cape Town didn't have the skills to…

Nazli: Hmm, to do that, yeah.

Adam: ...to carry the movement forward.

Nazli: That's what, that's what we're doing. Essentially that's what [we're] trying to do with the group of kids, is that – and it sounds maybe a little bit elitist – but it's not. Initially, you know we were grappling with this whole thing of the Hip Hop movement in Cape Town and sort of the people that – you know, sort of the old-school guys that started everything, getting them involved and my initial reaction was like no, no. Because then it's going to become...I don't know. I think right now the Hip Hop movement is wallowing in very much mediocrity and it's okay because nobody's challenging them. You know, it's okay for them to be doing what they're doing. I have a problem with that. Uhm, they...some people have amazing resources available to them. Resources, I mean they have access to funding, they have structures in place, but they're not doing anything with it. Some people are still very much where they were a few years ago. They haven't really progressed beyond either breakdancing at some concert or graffiti at Youth Day or something. And I figured if we're gonna start a programme like this, we need to start it fresh. Get some like young blood. Get some young people involved and let them be the next wave and the next wave, but just thinking about things beyond just here, you know? The bigger picture being beyond just the border, something like that.

Adam: It's a process above once-off Hip Hop for the sake of Hip Hop little missions and, yeah.

Nazli: Yeah, uhm, yeah. That just doesn't sit well. Like right now, what we, what we're trying to do is just open doors and, uhm, for them to be part of the process where they see their work published and being able to put that on a CV or being able to write away to a school and say, 'Okay, this is what I've been involved in. Here's some of my work. Uhm, what's available to me?' Those kinds of things. Just for them to know there are options and, if we can network a lot of the people that we network with, uhm, hit 'em up, you know. We have so and so coming to your side of the world, you know, what can we do or how can we help? Or do you know anybody we can get them in touch with? So, so yeah. A few scholarship opportunities have come our way like that...

Adam: Really?

Nazli: Like in the form, like internships for, uhm, like, uhm, what is it, like say for a first-year student to, uhm, go to California for six months and be based at a university and do some sort of work programme while they're there.

Adam: That has happened already?

Nazli: Like we had an offer to do that. None of the kids are in first year yet.

Adam: Hmm, ja.

Nazli: So it's just for us to get them there. But to keep those channels open so that when they're ready then we can funnel them. But keep their work going and keep the people on that side – or whoever they are – uhm, just keep them up to speed with what's happening so the kids can go when they're ready. So essentially we're just preparing them to, to take the world.

Adam: So most of the kids are high school kids. People like Marlon is the exception. Marlon has got a design diploma from Cape Tech and Shaheen tells me that there are two people who were actually BA graduates, I think?

Nazli: Right. We've got. Three of the girls that were in the programme dropped out. They didn't feel comfortable with the whole rhyming part and I wished they'd said something to us before. I just heard this afterwards. Because it's not about the rhyming. If they wanted to write anything they could have. It was just for them to put it up. So we've got three girls right now. They were based at UCT. So yeah. I think they're third-year students.

Adam: Shew. And it's a major head rush for them as well?

Nazli: Yeah, total [laughs].

Adam: That's interesting because they are already at a privileged institution and yet they're not getting what they're getting here.

Nazli: Like, uhm, two weeks ago the talk was on…guns and butter, uhm, looking at economics in times of war and times of peace. And also looking why the United States has to go to war in terms of them, of them maybe hitting a recession if they don't and that kind of thing. And they were like, 'Oh really? That can happen?' [laughs] So I'm constantly amazed at what UCT turns out [laughs]. I really am. I have a cousin who's, she's in her fourth year. She did three years of law and then she switched over to sociology and she came home a couple of weeks ago with her first assignment. She had to put down something on globalisation and she had no idea what she was doing. Like she had no clue. She didn't know what it was. Like she was all in this whole buzz about, 'Oh, how you know it's about cultures interacting with each other and blah, blah, blah.' And okay, they got you. We've got some work to do. So she got her readings and, uhm, I said, 'Okay, before you do your readings – 'cause I've no idea what your teacher's agenda is – you need to read this and this. And when you're done reading those readings, then you can at least decide for yourself if it works or if it doesn't.' So she didn't like me very much for that at that time, but, uhm, but yeah. Sometimes you should do that to all your students, but you can't. But, er, yeah I'm always amazed at, at the people at UCT. Interesting [laughs].

Adam: Ja. I should maybe speak last, because I'm there right now.

Nazli: Some of the people [laughs]. *Voices of Change* started, uhm, as a concept maybe about two years ago and then we had two professors visiting. One from Howard University [in Washington] and the other from – she was based in Ohio before, but she's no longer there. She sort of freelances right now, but she started the communications for social change department – her and a colleague of hers – at Ohio University. And then the lady at Howard, uhm, she teaches in the communications department. Radio and television – the other one is just radio. So they came to Bush Radio. They were based here for four months each and they took us through this process of documentary making. Uhm, what we came up with was *Voices of Change*, looking at communication during apartheid. Well, what we're trying is [to] steer away from just the sort of political activists and looking at all the different parts of how it happened. Uhm. Looking at the people who didn't participate. Why didn't they participate? Looking at sort of, uhm, educators during that time, looking at the role of women – any women during any kind of liberation struggle, not as necessarily as part of the liberation struggle, but looking at how it affected them. Right now, the pilot is, uhm…he took it, Shaheen took it to the history department at UCT…

Adam: Mohamed Adhikari.

Nazli: Yeah. And so he had a listen to it. 'Cause he didn't really want to, we asked him if we could interview him, if he could listen to it. And he was like, 'No, no, hhhh.' And then Shaheen said, 'Look, if you don't have any faith in us, why don't you listen to Bush Radio. Tune in at this time and this time?' And there was some Michael Parenti programme on at that time looking at something about human nature. So then he was like, 'Oh, I didn't really know that any radio stations had anything like this on air.' So then he listened to the programme and he was like, 'Oh.' You know, he was impressed by it and he said he volunteered to be the advisor on the project, just for historical accuracy and that kind of thing. And he made us narrow it down to just the '80s, which is what we're doing right now. So [we] finished the pilot, but we're hoping to [do] a 13-part series and that's part of the whole 10-year thing as well, but it's, uhm…if you have some time, you can listen to the intro part of it. We can do that now, if you like.

Adam: Okay, before we do that, I just want to throw something at you.

Nazli: Sure.

Adam: I wanna call this paper – the key part of it – the title should be 'Hip Hop Activism on the Cape Flats'. And I'm thinking, my key point of departure is, 'Yes, it's wonderful: MCing, graf art, b-boying. Great. Wonderful. Uhm, the gold isn't what happens on stage or in the limelight. The gold is in workshops.' And I'd like to talk about what you and Shaheen do here as kind of Hip Hop activists. The sort of struggle continues, process-driven thing. Are you comfortable with that idea or would you like to deconstruct it, topple it?

Nazli: Uhm. I need to think about it. I can't come up with anything on it. But it is essentially like a kind of Hip Hop activism, maybe not…I don't know if I'd call it Hip Hop activism. Like right now we're just using Hip Hop. I mean, if the kids are into something else, we'd probably use that, but for now that's what it is – what works.

Adam: But it's definitely community activism with Hip Hop as a tool.

Nazli: Yep.

Adam: I got that on tape, brilliant, cool [we laugh].

Nazli: But it, yeah, it is about community activism. Just engaging young people, but it doesn't matter where they come from. Like right now the kids are from Lotus River, Grassy Park, uhm,

Langa, Khayelitsha, Rondebosch, Kensington, they're just from, from everywhere. Uhm, like we took them to this performance – I don't know if you went to go and see John ZD when he was here?

Adam: John who?

Nazli: John ZD.

Adam: No.

Nazli: Okay, he's a Hip Hop theatre performer, uhm. He's amazing. I should pass on some of his writing to you. But when you see it with the theatre part it's something different. But anyway, I'll see what I can pass on to you. He was here and he came to do a workshop with the kids. Uhm, they were like, whoa. 'Cause what he did was first he did all the movement with no words and they were like, 'What the hell is this?' And then he did the words and then the movement made total sense. In fact, the movement gave the words more meaning. So then we took them to see the performance and when we came from the performance they were really psyched. They were really psyched up and then we went to, we dropped all the kids home. And one of the kids – he didn't want to be dropped home. I'm like, 'Look, I'm not gonna have your mom come and ask "where are you?" I'm responsible for you. I'm gonna make sure you get home.' And he was really embarrassed because he lived in [a] shack. And I was taking him through that whole thing of not being embarrassed about where you live. But how do you tell a 16-year-old kid not to be embarrassed about where he lives when he knows where maybe some of the other kids come from and so on? So that, sometimes that can be, uhm, painful. But, and that's one, that whole thing about it being a personal space because they get to know each another in a way that they wouldn't know each other outside of here. Uhm, there's also that whole mixing of cultures, socioeconomic backgrounds and so on that wouldn't happen away from a certain setting and as well. So in that way I think we're fortunate, uhm, in as far as exchanging ideas and, and it's almost like a cultural exchange, really, because they come from such diverse backgrounds and religions and races and whatever. It's cool. It's cool to watch them. Actually, I will invite you to come one Saturday, like if you wanna, because it will just put a lot of what Shaheen and I say into context – just to see them interacting.

Adam: If you'd like to exploit my labour in some way, you're more than welcome to. Of course, like I said before, I think last when we spoke about this, uhm, I'm very intimidated by the idea of talking to kids so young. It's just so easy to talk to young adults than teens and people at that level, but I'm willing to try, you know…

Nazli: No, by all means, ja just come and…I'll let you know when the next sessions are, uhm, actually next week, this Saturday coming we're just gonna do some of the pre-performance preparation with the trust games and using their space. So if that's something you wanna check out.

CHAPTER 7.
BUSH RADIO
AND HIP HOP ACTIVISM 1.0

ADAM HAUPT IN CONVERSATION
WITH SHAHEEN ARIEFDIEN

Adam Haupt spoke to Shaheen Ariefdien about ALKEMY in 2002. By this time, Ariefdien had left Prophets of da City and was spending a great deal of time at Bush Radio as he and Nazli Abrahams worked on youth development projects, such as ALKEMY. This project became an important platform for a number of young people – including Marlon Swai, who made a career change to become a performing artist and, later, a scholar with a PhD from New York University.

Adam: The first question I want to ask is where did – just on two levels – factually where did Hip Hop start in Cape Town? Which moment? Where?

Shaheen: I'd say with the introduction – okay for the first generation of Hip Hop heads, so to speak, I'd say it was around the time 'Rapper's Delight' was released in the country or was released on radio. Uhm, key moments like certain music videos that had especially b-boying in…uhm, things like the music videos of Malcolm McClarence. Malcolm McClarence or uhm… That's right at the beginning. And also music videos from…what's the thing called? The movie *Breakdance*. Corny-ass fucking movies, but at that time it was fucking amazing. And er…so I'd say real early '80s. So it would probably be around '82ish. So I think generally for people who had access to television and stuff like that. So they had like very few overseas things – *Flashdance* had like a small moment in, some breaking, you know. There was some bullshit at the Rockefeller Centre that had the Roxette crew perform as well. Uhm…and, er, that was also something that people recorded a video and then…So I think at that moment…roughly around that moment, that the music, the dance and crap that, you know, that all of that stuff probably became. So it's around that time for the first generation and just er, er, er, got more momentum with movies like *Beat Street* and with movies like *Wild Style* you know, uhm, and a lot of kids got into it. A lot of kids got into it. At the beginning it was not, ja, it was a few people that, that found some familiarity with the, with this whole…energy. You know, for me personally, er…I was in the Ciskei at the time – my father worked there – and I was…at this so-called radio station, if you want to call it that. Basically propping propaganda and bullshit like that, but, er because, there was very little substance to the establishment of Ciskei itself, what they counted on was like the very good music programmes – they had all this fucking music. Libraries that you won't believe. And they had jazz programmes from Europe, you have even had rap shit on radio…Some of the DJs playing the Hip Hop stuff, they were there as well – they would make me tapes of all the new shit, you know. All the new shit. So, by the time I got to Cape Town, I was already into the stuff. I was even surprised at stuff that they like, 'Holy fuck, oh God mother.' So just before, uhm, I mean before I left obviously, you know, uhm, this was very early like '80s…three, four. 'Cause you know there was dance first, right? Just like the music and then the MCing took off [snaps his fingers fast] that's when…I mean for at the end we didn't like get to see a lot of the stuff fitting together because a lot of us were involved with whatever. Uhm, it was just like, 'Oh shit, ah, it makes sense.' Er, ja, it fit *nogals alles tesame* [just about all together]. You know? So that was cool. But anyway, to cut a long story short I'd say early '80s.

Adam: Why do you think people, for example AbdouMaliq Simone, I think [Mohamed] Adhikari as well, have written about the idea of Hip Hop catching on among the Cape Town coloured community first and that's where it stayed for long? What is your sense of that claim?

Shaheen: Ja, er. It was a Cape Town thing first. Even if you look at the really influential heads up in Joburg: Gogga, Blaise are *laaities* [youngsters] from Cape Town. There were some b-boys around in the '80s in the Gauteng area and few MCs – mostly guys like Ikraam?…He had a track on *Sydney Sessions 2* compilation – for real. So, ja, I'd say the history of Hip Hop in South Africa is really the history of Hip Hop in Cape Town to a large degree. Okay, I think that when it comes to identity issues, right? And when you look at the coloured thing, you know? And you look at how the government made it a priority to deal with this group. It was creating a reserve and all of that *kak* [shit] is easy. Just throw any black motherfucker for no particular reason – *gooi* [throw] you there. Ciskei, Venda, wherever. What the fuck are you going to do with this group? Some of them can pass for white, some of them can pass for black African. You know, like what the fuck? And it was really difficult dealing with that group, I guess, for…for the government. From what I understand, the term 'coloured' was all non-European people. It was only 1954 that it changed to exclude that – it was totally a divide and conquer type of thing. So you have this fucking group, right, that have all types of identity issues, you know? Whereas on the one hand you are discriminated against, but you know the system is set up in such a way that you can manoeuvre your way in. You get some privilege. That's a little privilege – ja, let's say privilege, you know. Uhm… so you have this really weird psychological thing within this coloured mind where how do you trace your history back, especially the whole black culture thing and stuff like that, you know, when before a lot of coloureds, 'What the fuck can you go back to?' You know? What the fuck can you go back to? Have the blood of the oppressor and the oppressed in you. Uhm, some group, cultural group or whatever is now erased. Like, 'What the fuck?' You know? Like ill baggage. So I think it was one of the ways for young people with such a lot of issues to tap into their Africanness. Because it was one of the ways that made them realise uhm, uhm their roots. You know, to here. And even their roots to, uhm, their individual stories, wherever. But especially because of Hip Hop and I think that – and I said this before – it made a lot of us realise, like as we processed things, that it was African tradition with Japanese technology. You know, processed back. Kidnapped from Africa, stolen and *kom terug* [come back] type of *gedagte* [thought/thing]. So it was necessary for these young people to have this, you know, this type of thing, for this generation. And also I think that because of the political climate in the country it was also necessary 'cause the message and all that type of shit. You know, it spoke to us. It was a bit later, uhm, Grandmaster Flash and the Furious Five, a lot of earlier stuff. Uhm…so, if anything, I think it was necessary to have that. Uhm, and I think that when you look at the history of music – and I'm just freestyling here, just like now as things are coming through – like music and the coloured community is that if you look at the earlier generation, shit, motherfuckers were listening to like jazz. You know, and before that it was doo-wa groups and before that it was a whole bunch of other stuff. There was nothing really besides the whole *klopse* [Cape minstrels/ coon carnival] *gedagte*, which you could also argue is from New Orleans and all of that *gedagte*, you know. So there's a really close connection with, with, with, uhm, the States, as far as music is concerned and also conditions when you look at the Bronx and the Cape

Flats. The forced removals, so to speak, the conditions, the…like I argue that – and I really need to move into this – because of parallel experiences and all these other things, that's why it made it so familiar to here. It's also the conditions that people live under, man, that helps shape the way you express yourself and what you choose. And I come with – not me – but processing things on different people, man. Like its alchemy, man. You know, you're taking, making something out of nothing almost, you know. Lekker old shit. Okay, fucking make a beat with your mouth. Okay, cool. You know? Ja, I didn't do Communication and stuff like that, but I love words, you know. Fuck let's rhyme. Make it technical on our own terms. I don't need to have big, big words to do this shit, you know. We can have our own canon. You know, and shoot *daai* [that] shit, you know? So for me that is what Hip Hop was about. For a lot of *ouens* [guys] like…it was a lifeline…But I think when it came to giving the spark in a lot of kids' eyes it was necessary. It was necessary. It was the thing that didn't have to look a certain way. You had to have blue eyes…blue eyes and blonde hair and stuff. Hell, if you didn't have it at some point, you know? You didn't need to have plastic shit, you know? That was debatable when you look at the whole sneaker culture and stuff like that on the Cape Flats. Uhm…and, and, and, ja it said something about it that was necessary, considering apartheid, considering that young voices were stifled, considering that you were cut off from history and stuff like that…At the one moment you can say, 'Throw your hands in the air.' And the next moment you can say, 'Throw your fist in the air.' You know? And, and, and that was cool 'cause it allowed the young people to tap into those, you know, the wild little rebellious thing and the same time go to your consciousness? So you could party for your right to fight…type of vibe. I dig that and I think that for the first generation of Hip Hop heads, although the lyrics and the vibe here wasn't overtly political and stuff like that, but there was still [that] thing about do we express ourselves, ourselves on our terms type of thing, you know, where you are told what to think and how to think and you are told how to respond, react, keep your place type of thing. And your life was fucking refused on various levels, you know? Fuck this, we'll speak the way we want to speak, we'll do the shit we want to do. Altogether we expressed ourselves. And you know the whole coloured thing? Fuck that too! 'Cause after the, during the '80s the whole non-racialism thing with the UDF [United Democratic Front], stuff like that, the whole Black Consciousness thing was like puh-shew – *verby* [past], right. So what the fuck do you do during the '80s, when you're not supposed to claim anything when you still live in a country where it tells you, you know, that you are a fucking kid, you know. And what the fuck? So in that sense alone they also get fucked on like various, various, various levels. And so…I know I'm like talking a bunch of bullshit and stuff like that, but I'm going all over the show. But I'm just freestyling here.

Adam: That's cool.

Shaheen: For me, I'm just freestyling. And all the things that went you look at the countercultural nature, for lack of a better word. The whole thing about counterculture in South Africa – that it's supposed to be that, especially in a South African context where you have this fucking power – all parties telling you who you are, what you're supposed to do, what is good, you know, what is acceptable and stuff like that. The shit has not been allowed to stay at home…and that's why it's so interesting that you could have the whole Christian thing and stuff like that. That's part of the whole *gedagte*, whether some of us like it or not, you not. You know? I might think it's bullshit, you might think it's bullshit and stuff like that, but to a large degree that, you know…

Adam: Part of the counterhegemonic sort of…

Shaheen: Dêh! [Here! Take this!] Ja. Dêh! Anyway, that's another story. So I think that for the first wave of heads it provided with that. And, I mean, when you look at the US cultural imperialism it, it, it…it's just fucking hectic all over the world and I think especially in South Africa, right, when you didn't hear South African music on the air, you didn't see any television till it was…Design – it was by design that we didn't see that shit, right? It was like keeping you in your place…So the only other alternative was European countries. That was like really *kak*. You know, and some American shit. And the one thing you could somehow relate to was Boyz in the Hood – Bonteheuwel and Mitchells Plain, you know? And I think that also played a part with this…one of the tentacles of US cultural imperialism.

Adam: That was then. Here we are…now. It's tricky now. Where the fuck are we? Because we have a scenario where we have Eminem representing what Hip Hop is about to many people – in many people's mind. We had Tupac, we had Coolio, we had mainstream Hip Hop going on. I listen to Eminem and I think it's just like the *Jerry Springer Show* with a beat, okay? And that is supposed to be Hip Hop now. Now we have stuff in Cape Town happening with, er, very really cool stuff. We've got Godessa on the scene being marketed by African Dope Records, which is an interesting angle. And we still have Devious out there and cats like Caco around and stuff, but if you were to ask the average kid in Cape Town, 'What is Hip Hop?' – it depends, it's not going to be the same answer. More often than not, you're gonna have Eminem coming out at you. Where are we now? Where is Hip Hop now in terms of consciousness?

Shaheen: Okay, okay, okay. You have to be very…this is a tricky thing. This is the fucking tricky thing about when you deal with the commodification of culture, right? It's that you have – the machine hijacks certain things, right, from a subculture, or whatever, and to sell it back to you, uhm, minus the subcultural revolutionary shit. You know, make it nice, you know, to keep you going to the store and buy the shit that young kids, you know – you still have to deal with broken jeans and shit. You buy it like that and it's more expensive. So for…it's interesting because there's almost two problems. The one is what has happened to Hip Hop – like Hip Hop transforming. The other thing is like Hip Hop being hijacked and this mass culture thing, you know, is really the vehicle…uhm…that you mistake that…I'd rather opt for the mass cultural argument. For me, at the moment. It makes more sense to me at the moment. Okay. I use this example of where you have strings, right? Like Mozart, or whatever…they might use strings in a classical piece. Now Britney Spears happens to do a ballad that uses strings – that doesn't make it classical music. Similarly, if you hear this rap thing on radio, it doesn't make [it] Hip Hop just because you have this [sound effect] beat thingy and all this *kak* and then all of a sudden you have this rap verse, or something like that, and all of a sudden it's Hip Hop. Like, fuck, that's my vibe right now. Others don't necessarily see it like that. There's a counterargument I have for myself. And right at the beginning – even with Sugar Hill Gang and stuff like that – it's been about the dancing shit and it's been about the flashy, flashy shit. But I think that the difference between the two is…uhm…in fact, Sugar Hill Gang is a bad example. It's very bad example. I'd rather use Grandmaster Flash and them…Ja, this is the early stuff. There's something…that fifth element, if you want to call it that. That *gees* [spirit] that's missing, you know. And I think it's where that *gees* is that what makes Hip Hop for me. And that other shit is just units, product, you know. Uhm…and that's a tricky argument.

That's a real, real tricky argument. But, anyway. So right now Hip Hop is for a lot of kids whatever they want it to be. I think it's like with religion, like with politics and shit like that, you now...Everyone from Claremont mosque to fucking Achmat Cassiem to *koe'siester* sheikhs[1] to a whole fucking range of people having the same point of reference, but on some totally shit, you know. You have your inner mystical theme, you have...you know. So I think it's a similar thing where you have this vibe thing, energy – whatever you want to call it – and whoever's gonna be in charge of that I think that's where Hip Hop's...a movement's gonna go. And I think that because a lot of kids come from ghetto areas, *kak* backgrounds, you know what I mean, if you can sign a deal to get your mother out of self-help, to get her settled, you know, for you to be okay and you're young and you still want to party and stuff like that – sign. You know, 'Aa'it.' Ja, it would be a really extraordinary human being that could be like, 'Fuck, the principles come first, the art form comes first, this comes first, the movement comes first.' You know what I mean? Uhm, you almost need to be involved with that mentality already to really know that you're doing this. You know? So I think that, uhm...it really depends, yes: partly generational for [a] lot of kids who went through the whole apartheid thing that we went through and a whole bunch of other shit that we went through that kinda shaped the way POC sounds and Black Noise and whatever – the way we see the world, you know? The kids now that get all the information from Channel O or MTV or whatever, you know, Radio Good Hope even, you know, that is the trendy thing. And a lot of people I think they...how can I explain it...they mistake, like, like truly countercultural shit, you know, against hegemony, for just un-PC shit. Like you have all un-PC like all over and it seems like kind of rebellion and stuff like that, you know. Like it's truly against the public system. Really. Or just some un-PC shit. That's all accommodated for – accommodated for in this whole *gedagte*. You know, like [Noam] Chomsky, like that whole thing about Chomsky and them where they said that, er...in order to control people in a democracy, so to speak, you need to set up necessary illusions. You know, like in apartheid or Nazi Germany or wherever. You come fucking late and they throw you ass in jail. You got to set up things in place where there is illusion,

---

1. Koe'siester is a Cape Malay version of the doughnut. A sheikh is a religious leader in the Muslim community, who leads prayers and conducts sermons and religious ceremonies. In this context, a koe'siester sheikh is a leader who is more focused on rituals, traditions and cultural aspects of religious leadership, and not so much on the spiritual or intellectual aspects of religion.

there is this illusion of…that needs to be like accommodated for. You know? So if you say, 'Evil fucker.' Evil fuck whatever. It's cool. As long as anybody doesn't take it too seriously, as long as that shit can be trendy, as long as that shit is still appealing they can still keep the machine moving – like all the units and flood stadiums and stuff like that. Blah, blah, blah. It's cool. Say your thing. Fuck your mother, if you wanna, you know. If your baby's mother…say whatever you wanna say. It's cool. Even that shit is like, there's a stage for that, you know. If there's other cats, 'Fuck record companies because blah, blah, blah, fuck the government because blah, blah, blah. You know what I'm gonna do? If everbody's gonna picket Bush. Like go to your local whatever and picket and make sure that you show up in numbers. Fifty per cent off from my next album. Welcome to the town who has the most support and I'll do a show for free…If you go there, if you go there, that's not accommodated for. Fuck you. They will find you, they will [make sure you know who you're fucking with]. They'll throw you ass in jail. You will get fucked. So I think there's a lot of stuff that a lot of people look at and like, 'yeah, yeah, yeah' against the system…ah, bleah. It's the actual ticket, the thing.

Adam: Okay. Let's get specific here. I'm thinking…

Shaheen: I'm just *gooing* [throwing] ideas out here, *ne*.

Adam: That's cool. I don't know where I'm going with this.

Shaheen: Cool.

Adam: Just so you know, I don't know where I'm going with this.

Shaheen: I'll probably say exactly the opposite to you at a later stage.

Adam: That's cool. That's why I want to talk to you now. Uhm, let's get specific on that very thought that you're picking out. I'm thinking Rage Against the Machine, for example. Are they the true counterhegemonic, counterdiscursive voice of Hip Hop?

Shaheen: Not of Hip Hop. It's where Hip Hop meets rock. I think that right now that type of… fusion and a lot of energy and lot of Hip Hop shit…I'm pretty sure. I don't know a lot about it, from what I heard, groups like Fugazi, groups like Rage Against the Machine and, uhm, some, some…uhm they have leftist organisations at their shows, you know, where people sign petitions, where they have all types of shit. Groups like The Levellers, they have like doccies on McDonald's – the *kak* that they're doing – playing at their show, you know, and all types of leaflets, people talking to other people, shit that's happening.

Adam: A safer Hip Hop example would be Dead Prez.

Shaheen: Er, ja. Or Immortal Technique or there…er…there's quite a bit like Booms and them as well – Booms of the Cool, er. So, I think that I don't know, I always see that, as a movement, things can only be truly effective if there's action as well. And, coming back to that point that we spoke about that time, I don't think that the first wave of heads had the education, the know-how, the organising skills, whatever to pull the movement together the way [they were] supposed to. Like we tried with the African Hip Hop movement, you know. A lot of movements from across the world tried that. It was really essentially to get young people together and not catch on like the type of *kak* that's destructive, but to kind of challenge…to get together and do cool, positive shit, you know. I think that since the whole MTV and Sony – Sonyfication, you know all of that *kak* – uhm there…when I look at the States, a lot of heads there. Remember some of them are still at high school, whatever, some people went to college and university. They studied everything from media studies or whatever. So all of the big things that were very fucked up started seeing crazy organisation and action happening. And the whole anti-Prop 21 Movement in Auckland.[2] You had like Free Mumia[3] Hip Hop movements, all types of shit coming out where, whereas on MTV you had girls shaking their asses, people with diamonds in their cars and shit like that. It was like, 'You're joking. The movement is happening.' You know? As far as getting organised, you know. And I think for the second wave it was necessity again that we saw like there was no learning from your mistakes type of thing and also the more oppressive regime in the country…and I think with Hip Hop it was like, 'Hold up. What the fuck? We really need [to] start doing things.' And I think in the same kind of lessons that the generation, the jazz generation kind of learned. 'Hold on, we need to be mentors to other kids, blah, blah, blah, blah.' So you're going to have a lot more of that happening.

If we look at South Africa, I think that Hip Hop then – the African Hip Hop movement and

---

2. http://www.cyc-net.org/today2000/today000309.html
3. http://www.freemumia.com/

a whole bunch of other things – that was happening, the POC stuff, it was really against apartheid. You know? Against white domination. Fuck this *kak*, you know. We didn't have the sophistication in dealing with our experiences and stuff like that. 'Fuck it. I experienced it. This is the shit I know, this is the shit I talk about. If this falls into whatever theoretical framework, let it be. If I even knew [there] was some *kak* like a theoretical framework, this is the shit, this [is] the shit that I talk about.' You know? And I think now it has been through a period, right, where you have this shift in government – and it was a conscious decision, I know that even for POC when we recorded *Phunk Phlow*, right, and *Ghetto Code*. 'Okay, what shit do we comment on? Like the shit that pissed us off. There is a lot of stuff happening. But okay we know we've got this period, we've got a gap to give this government, a grace period. Because…we'd like to see it work 'cause everywhere, all the info that we've got, anywhere in Africa with decolonisation they kind of fucked up. You know? We can go into the reasons for that, you know, but that's not the point. We're talking about the masses…So how do we deal with this? You're gonna have to get like, for lack of better term, a grace period. Like having to deal with the shit of being a new government. It's not gonna happen overnight and blah, blah, blah, blah, blah. So when you actually listen to things like *Phunk Phlow* you get shit about the Station Strangler,[4] you know, you get things about coloured identity and stuff like that. And it wasn't really aimed at the government per se like with *Age of Truth* and stuff like that. *Ghetto Code* as well…the District 6 thing and the industry and, you know, broad *goeters* [things]. And there we struggled continuously like…'Okay, *wag*' [wait]. But even then it was still very much like, 'Okay.' I can remember us sitting down, 'Okay. Blah, blah, blah, blah, blah. What can we do? Shit that we can write about.' There was an almost conscious decision…like okay, 'Let's see where the thing goes before we rip, you know, before we fucking with it.' Like, let's see where it goes. And I think that was almost a microcosm of the Hip Hop community as well. All the…like when you look at power, when [you] look at history and stuff like that, it was linked to almost in total, it was linked to certain things that was very much apartheid and, and, and so for a lot of heads back then, a lot of people it was in South Africa as well – post 1994 – was trying to come to grips with this thing. You know? This post-apartheid thing. Getting to grips. 'Okay, so I can go live there now.' You know? Type of *beweging* thing. Right now, ja, so I can

---

4. https://en.wikipedia.org/wiki/Norman_Afzal_Simons

go piss there now – duh-huh. And I can go live there, but a little bit of money to go live there. So a lot of people now – you can almost buy your apartheid. You know? There's something interesting about how these things, how if you live in Constantia and stuff like that, if you have the bucks, your high-security fences and shit like that and whatever. You're buying apartheid right now. You know? And I think that what's happening now is that for a lot of heads, a lot of people generally in South Africa, like, 'Holy fuck. *Wag*, hold up…' You know? Er, how do you deal with it? Because it's almost like if you look at hegemony pre-'94 it was boxed in nicely for you, man. You [know] what I mean? It was a lekker nice package that you like… pocket, here. Puh-shew! Now it's like, fuck! Now you have things like globalisation. You have the IMF [International Monetary Fund] – that's always been a part of the thing, but in South Africa, I, energy was directed at someone else. You know? Just there without, with the… whatever the fuck it is. Whatever. Right now you have a whole bunch of different things that a lot of young people – even our generation – are realising. You know, we have fucking big corporations, IMF…Uhm, people getting evicted out of their house, privatisation and fucking water, electricity, like basic amenities and stuff like that. So, I think what you have now is that – and I'm looking at the Hip Hop community – uhm, that what you have is a bunch of people, right, that's looking at this post '94 and like going, 'Oh, *wat nou* [what now]? Shit isn't cool.' You know, and trying to learn from the mistakes the African Hip Hop movement, whatever. So you have people…getting stuff as well, and you try and apply certain things outside, you know, dabbling with things. Checking things out. Uhm, so with that comes a certain amount of experience and almost like anticipating things as well and considering other factors, you know. Uhm, so you have a more…the environment, the climate is right for an African Hip Hop movement. Or South African Hip Hop movement again. You know, I'd say. If you look at stuff we're doing with the workshops…

Adam: Give me the background on that.

Shaheen: Okay, by the time I left the crew, right, my thing was I – 'cause we did like workshops all over the fucking country, prisons, schools all over and I really liked the idea of sharing stuff with the younger generation. 'Cause they really had to go through the same shit. And, more importantly, I think that because of the mentors I had as well that the fact that you're sharing with someone doesn't mean you know shit, you're the teacher. You're sharing. They pump shit back and you're learning as well. It's like learning going both ways, you know? Uhm, and what happened was we did the AIDS thing. The HIV Hop stuff on Bush…

Adam: HIV Hop.

Shaheen: Ja. We kinda worked a way of taking information, like resource information, and then flipping and arranging it into songs. So we worked with Devious, Godessa, a whole bunch of other cats as well. Taking raw data, either from the internet or *gedagte* and dealing with stuff. Er, and uhm it worked really, really well. And when we were supposed to send a group of people to Amsterdam to find out more and learn more about Hip Hop theatre, we had to prepare for beforehand. We said, 'What we gonna do is just a couple of workshops, different things like *gooi* together.' But we didn't want to be purely on a technical writing stuff vibe. You know, multisyllable rhyme schemes, this verse, fuck that. You know? We wanted to *gooi*… stuff in, things to think about. You know? This was 2000…Like what do we think that young people really need to know. Okay, so we started brainstorming ideas, we started talking…as well. No, no, no, that was just throwing things out as well. The connections between slavery, colonialism, apartheid and how we behind, you know. Uhm, things like that. So just had a couple of workshops. That was purely just for preparation for them to *gooi*, you know, to perform thingies and stuff like that. And so we started speaking to them afterwards. You know, 'What do you guys think?' Fuck, and some of the discussions we had. Like that was even better than writing shit. The writing shit is cool because you can always practise on it, but other stuff forces you to think, you know. Makes you realise…'Cause Nazli's background is teaching, you know, my background is Hip Hop and that's one of those – that's one of the reasons I also left the crew because I had to fucking travel and things like that and there was stuff that I really wanted to do and a lot of times I couldn't. Uhm, so for to come up with something really befuck. 'Cause I was also concerned that the older generation, a lot of them are already running out of steam. Some of them are getting kids, the age and stuff like that. There's a lot of attention you're gonna have to give to this organising or this is not gonna happen. You know, at the same time you have all these big companies who want to sponsor certain events. You know? Like, what the fuck? Who's gonna run with it? You know? Get some serious young blood that want to do shit and just give all the shit that they need to know. You know, er, so what we did was try to come up with like a semester curriculum thing, you know, that half the thing is going to be a theoretical thing, half of the thing is going to be the writing thing. And we're going to look at this, uhm, little formula thingie for getting information and sorting it around, pumping it around and that will be the thing. Uhm, and what we would also do is using young kids to write songs around things that affect their lives. We play it on radio as well because things that really affect people's lives – like when you look at the Jayzees and shit like that, they hardly say shit, you know…It's something about giving young people a voice and power, man. Say your shit. You know? When it's not just being played as a song for people, but it's like, yo. People are thinking that [this is what young people are thinking about]. You know?…You don't need to go into a certain mode of like, 'I need to use certain phrases, certain imagery in order to be Hip Hop.' You know? It's a 'I need to use certain phrases, certain imagery in order to be Hip Hop'. You know? So right now we're using some of the kids from Khayelitsha, to take the Hip Hop stuff and *gooi* it into Xhosa. Take all that lyrics, you know. We're working with a group of people that are HIV positive, that are activists and stuff like that, sifting through the facts, the data of the lyrics as well. Besides the slang, the wording and all that type of shit. It's like all the stuff, 'Oh shit, fuck!' Amazing. You know. Uhm, so it's about giving them some things to run with. Anyway, the idea behind it was to, to, to tap into the younger generation, right, that really want to do shit and just to share WHATEVER we know with them and then learn from them as well. And then letting them rhyme. Like a huge part of the thing was documenting our own history. And they've got a paper that's due soon where they have to attach it to what is, uhm, uhm, what is your target audience, someone age a hundred years from now, right? So you could really be a historian, a Hip Hop historian right now. But it's almost like a diary thing as well. The shit that's affecting your life, things around you, because the thing was like, 'Okay, what do you know what happened a hundred years ago with someone your age?' You know? Okay, there was someone a hundred year ago and now they're saying exactly the same shit and let's see where we can go with this. It will be a, a, a, a exercise in, in, in creativity, writing some shit – the target audience is there, right? And also really digging deep. Like you can go like crazy just thinking about how you feel and the world, how you view the world around you and how to write a bunch of verses around that, you know…And then also write a thing on an area in Hip Hop that you're passionate about. You know write a small… proposal and we'll try and get readings and stuff into that *gedagte*. We're already helping them with some research, basic research stuff around the normal essay form, you know? Fuck, we're talking about 14, 15, 16.

Adam: These are kids who wouldn't normally do academic tertiary education-style academic essays. You pump them with Chomsky, Tricia Rose.

Shaheen: Ja. Yes. The whole fucking nine, you know? Paulo Freire and, no shit, I'm not even kidding. You know, just throwing ideas out there. [What] we just try and do is if any of us has like a nice graph of some of the stuff, or you know someone just to *gooi* like the style. Don't use like big words and stuff – just like this type of *gedagte*. 'This is what this *bra* thinks. This is what this *bra* thinks. What do you guys think?' Everyone is brainstorming things around. *Gooi* things around, you know. So for me, I think that's the important thing. Like when we, we, we, we get…it's not supposed to be about personalities. You know like POC – POC is the history of Hip Hop to a degree and the history of Black Noise as well. Fokking *kak*, man. *Ons was gebore daai tyd* [we were born that time] – a particular time, we went through *kak* and we were given the opportunity. We a part of a project can realise that it's easier to be in your dealings with, with, with young people. Because you don't want to be the man. You don't want to be like, 'I'm taking a workshop with Shaheen,' and all of that *kak*. You know? Poes. It doesn't fucking count. This is the right here and now. You guys are gonna do it. If you guys run with it, that's gonna be the shit and pass it on as well. That's gonna be the shit, you know. So, uhm, what we're hoping to do is, with them is to see [how] important it is for them to document their own history and feel comfortable with it. If some of them get to university, that will be fucking intimidating. That is the other thing with kids that are starting now, by the time they get here fucking blow some guys away. You know? That's one thing. Writing your own shit, right. Grappling with ideas and theories as well, fucking thinking about theories, you know, that's the other thing. And then giving them the…like normal skills transferal shit, whether it's like public speaking, organisational skills and stuff like that. But they need to be in a position to assume and feel comfortable in a position of leadership and start doing shit. Like real soon I'll be like, 'Kghh!' backtrack and let them run a workshop and then run shit. Like right now with this conference thing, some of the kids that graduated from our first sessions and let them be facilitators and co-facilitators and just like check the vibe out. So they feel comfortable with, really think like, 'I need to watch what I say.' And you know that type of thing.

Adam: The conference you're going to?

Shaheen: No, no, no the conference I just came from. It was part of, it's called Kidocracy. It's about radio and young people, right, and it's about writing up this whole manifesto thing, [our] rights and stuff like that and also a whole week of sharing ideas. They had like a professor from the States, uhm, who did this whole thing on radio drama for young people so they can use their voice and just the techniques. So we did that there, focusing on radio drama and Hip Hop and poetry and stuff, like expressing your ideas without having to sound boring and *gooing* ideas around. So we used some of them as well for that. We used some of them to help out with the young kids and the radio and stuff.

[The tape in the recorder runs out, but the discussion soon continues.]

Shaheen: There are some people, like hard core community activists like fucking on the gravy train right now.

Adam: Volvo driving, Mercedes, living in Durbanville.

Shaheen: Ja, type of thing. You know, it's like, what the fuck is happening to us? And I think it's, it's, it's our duty, man, you know to do exactly the same as we've had that others have done for us. And I think that right now, and I might be wrong, er, I don't think I am, if I was the voice of this generation as far as – if you look at public demonstrations and accountability. On the one hand, I can shake my ass and kick butt, on the other hand I can argue some really interesting shit as well. You know what's really interesting for me is that I'm really…Some of the Hip Hop kids I've had in some of my classes at school, or just observing some of these kids, they are a lot more critical than a lot of other kids. You know? And, er…

Adam: These are high school kids?

Shaheen: Ja, like even here like it's part of their processing and I know that some of [their] ideas they got from some songs, some ideas that they, because of the whole vibe of looking at something from a cynical approach shit. Like generally, you know? It's just interesting. Uhm, it doesn't really say shit. It could be said about any subculture. You know? Uhm, but I think for this voice right now, this Hip Hop voice, for this generation, I think Hip Hop is the voice for this generation. If we were born like in the '50s, I think jazz would have been like the vibe, naturally type of thing, or blues before that, type of thing. But I just think that right now for various reasons Hip Hop is a very useful tool right for now. You know? Uhm, and I think its effectiveness can be judged by what the younger [generation] is getting out of it and what they do with it. Because we're in the positions of the Miles [Davis] and [John] Coltranes and shit like that where [Charles] Mingus and whoever, when they were mentors to others that came after them. Er, so this is a crucial period, I think, where you have our generation sharing with the younger generation and like letting them run with shit. 'Cause we can't do the shit forever and there is a process that is bigger than Hip Hop and Hip Hop's just a fucking vehicle. That's it. A lot of shit, but just a fucking vehicle. You know, uhm, and I still do think that it is useful, very much, especially now. Now you have kids, right, that we are attracting in the workshops that [sound effect] whatever and they appreciate the technical shit, you know. And that's where they start discovering like other stuff, like, 'Fuck! Oh shit.' There's this one kid that was like pissed off 'cause all the stuff that he has listened to in the past – like there are no heroes for him anymore. You know, he's like, 'Fuck!'

Yo, you're going to have to tap into your own vibe now, you know. You become your own hero. Fuck this…the other side. Now the shit begins 'cause now there's a certain responsibility on you. There's a certain thing where you can't lean on someone else, you know? Like now when you're standing on our shoulders and you're taking shit to the next level – that's what you're supposed to do. And strongly encouraging young people to take – like even the whole education thing is bullshit, if you know what you can get from, from it, you know, whether it's just to help you stay focused and keep you capable and stuff like that – even if that's all you get from it, dallah [do it], and just read the necessary shit outside school. Like, this kid who just wrote a paper and he is at Westerford. Imagine, at fucking Westerford. And he just wrote a paper on colonialism in the classroom, like right now. And he was like, 'Okay, I want to write this thing. I have this theory.' And he took all the stuff that we spoke about at the workshops and he processed it and he threw it at me and I was like, 'Fuck, will you hold up. Wait, wait, wait.' I was like so fucking excited! I was like, 'Fuck, throw it at me again.' And he had like this whole thing [makes scribbling notes sound effects]. 'Okay, now you've got to read this.' And I gave him a couple of things to read. The teacher was like, 'Phew!'…

Adam: Was he black?

Shaheen: Ja, ja, ja, or coloured, you know. So amazing. There was this one kid that called into our show and it was just like, just the most 'what the fuck' stuff on radio. 'I'm the extra-nomical, extra-phonical, phonical, phenomenal!' You know like, 'What the fuck are you doing?' [laughs] You know? And we teased him and whatever. 'Why don't you come to Bush tomorrow? We have some workshops you might be interested in.' You know? Uhm. Oh my God, you should see some of the shit that this kid writes. He's one of the kids that we're using for Khayelitsha. He's from…

Adam: You're using him for?

Shaheen: Translating all the Hip Hop stuff into Xhosa, uhm, giving him, uhm, he's worked, like his thing now. What we're going to do now is, for you to not just get shit, you've got to give back as well. And also every Saturday you're gonna come to Bush and you're going to answer the phone. You're going to work from nine o'clock in the morning to two. You're gonna answer the phone. That's what you're gonna do. Like, like so they can see that you don't just get shit. You need to give some back. And he doesn't have to be there, but it's one way…Ja, obviously. There's things that – imagine living in a shack in Khayelitsha, right, and you're writing next-level shit and you're given the responsibility of doing shit. You know what I mean? You can see like the level of confidence in this kid [makes rocket effect]. I used him for the, the watch-you-ma-call-it as well, er, for the conference, writing points to like, okay now type of thing. I think that for me that shit is where it's at right now, I think. If you can [get] that sparkle back into young people and get them to truly deal with the baggage of the past, if they can feel confident, if they can feel safe, that is the shit that we are encouraging. And I think that we, in my opinion, need to focus on. If we're not going to be…what's the word?…if we can't be helpful, right, to…truly help people where they can take shit and take it to the next level, then it's a fucking wank then. You know. What we've been doing, interesting stuff and stuff like, so you can always say that Hip Hop, ja, inspired them type of thing. And I can tell you one thing, I've seen, like recently I've gone in different parts of the townships where like breaking and stuff like that. Just like kids you don't even know about. It's amazing to see the amount of time, energy, commitment young kids put into it. And I think it's taken for granted that it's a dance, rhymes and stuff like that, you know we're extra super fucking critical when [it] comes to that, but I think like there's something at the core of that that these young kids are learning about commitment, about dedication, about energy. You know you're not going to be in fucking Puffy video, you know, but you're doing this shit because there's something about your self-worth, you know there's something, dignity, that it restores. It brings back the sparkle in your eye. You see like *kaalvoet* [barefoot] *laaities*, man, like fucking dancing, doing shit, going all out. Like, jo-ooo. If you could capture [the] thing that they've learned right here so you could… and you can set up programmes, you know, to tap into that potential so *laaities* could take it somewhere else…And, again, I don't care if these kids say fuck Hip Hop at the end of it, [it's cool] and stuff like that – it's not about that. It's about community activism…it's about the struggle that continues and how we engage with it now and all these other factors involved. These bad fucking whatever, you know, er. What the fuck do we do? I think that's gonna be key, key, key, key. And also linking up with other organisations for individuals that share similar feelings. I think that where Hip Hop is at now, we need to pull our heads out of our arses and see ourselves as like a little island. And that's the whole idea we have for countercultural movements – our voice right now, the way we choose to express ourselves, but the struggle is a global struggle, you know, and there are allies out there. There are people out there who feel exactly the same way you do. You might just be pumping Dead Prez in your head bones or Godessa or whatever, you know, but there's someone else that might be pumping something else in their heads or fuck-all in their head bones, but they're just [as] concerned. They're our fucking allies, you know what I mean? That is what needs to happen. Whether it's dialogue, sharing information, workshops, whatever the fuck it is. If you have people that share similar concerns, get together and start empowering some of these *laaities*. Because whether we like it or not, its two thousand fucking two, right? White kids are still way ahead of the game in South Africa. Whether we fucking like it or not. And for the few black kids that's there, they been so fucking removed from reality…I'm so surprised by some of the shit that I hear in lectures. 'What the fuck. *Waar kom jy vandaan*?' [Where do you come from?] You know? Ja, I think that's gonna be interesting to see that and globally – like even in the States. I was so surprised – I thought [what] we are doing right now is something really exciting that a lot of people in the States should know about as well. And that's part of the reason…

Adam: What's the conference called?

Shaheen: It's Planet Hip Hop. The festival…hey?

Adam: Chuck D is one of the organisers.

Shaheen: Chuck D, he's talking about Hip Hop, race, politics and stuff like that. Bambaataa them all are there.

Adam: This is in New Jersey.

Shaheen: Ja…I was invited to it two years ago. It's a spoken word thing. We were supposed to perform, but they had this panel thing there and they just asked me to say a few words. Fuck, fuck, fuck. Fucking freestyle [laughs]. And I said some shit. They were like, 'Whoa, interesting.' So they asked me to, uhm, come again. No, no, no, earlier the year I was supposed to do something, to perform shit, anything to do with like stuff that I'm doing, I'm down with. But I can't chuck to the states right now. So I got this email about this festival thing, this performance and panel and stuff. If I know else, so pretty much Godessa…and er, so ja, they paid my ticket over there.

Adam: There are obvious global links being formed in the Hip Hop community…

Shaheen: When you look at the project on Hip Hop Against Infinite War, drawing from heads from Palestine, from Cape Town, to Tanzania…Seoul, Mexico, the States, England, New Zealand, all fucking over.

Adam: Who runs that?

Shaheen: It's a by [choice from Hip Hop?] in the world.

Adam: To the Hip Hop community?

Shaheen: Ja, people doing similar stuff to what we're doing? The people that I'm…

Adam: Then how does this happen?

Shaheen: Through the internet. That's how we brainstorm, that's [how] we meet, that's how we…uhm…plan. That's how we connect. You know, there's, uhm, some cats from the Masai community that have a school computer and access to a line, so I mail them.

Adam: Jesus.

Shaheen: Masai Hip Hop heads. You know? Fucking, you name it, all over. Uhm, and with that, like Jackie and them, a bunch of independent filmmakers that did that stuff they're supposed to…, 'Ja, why not'…

Adam: What's that company called again?

Shaheen: Big Noise Film Media. You know…You have a documentary thing that's being filmed, going through different places where there's music – like I just heard the Palestinian crew. Like they couldn't record together. They had send, to send their shit via wave file through the internet because of the *kak* that was happening. So you had one kid dropping a verse at home, sending a wave file to another kid on the other side – Gaza, you know. Someone else sent it back and someone mixed it. They gave a copy to Jackie, they gave me as well…Like hectic shit. So we can have a fucking Tanzania recording stuff and send it up to Holland, where the hottest producer in Holland can take the a cappellas and throw a different beat over it. That's fucking amazing. You know? You have people in different parts of the world connecting. Like-minded people who share similar *kak*, *goeters*, you know? And I think that right there is the possibility. It's kind of hectic when you think of internet and Hip Hop and all of that type of shit. So…for me it's important that those kinds of relationships don't stay in the virtual world…but having a place where we say, 'You know what? In the next few years we'd like to have a summer schools for kids of fucked-up areas. To have kids from São Paolo, from Dar es Salaam, you know, like from Papua New Guinea and Cape Flats and we have a two-week summer school thingie. It will be about Hip Hop and you can freestyle and all this little writing techniques and shit, but also organising people into… [we get interrupted by a knock].

Adam: I'll tell you what I'm thinking. You saying something now?

Shaheen: Oh, it needs to be about interaction and have all these kids from these fucked-up areas, you know, give them the necessary survival techniques, man.

Adam: But already that's beginning to happen…The fact that such interaction and I was saying it already seems to be happening, but you're talking about something that is more…

Shaheen: Global – and local. Okay, it's no use of having all these *goeters* happening globally and…

Adam: None of it comes here.

Shaheen: Ja, or, or, or that our focus is just about trying to establish global links. It's got to be like a lot of activity – like not just regional, like national as well. Like I'm already trying to identify people from different areas in South Africa who could be used.

Adam: I mean, so far the stuff you're talking about seems to be specifically Cape Town.

Shaheen: Ja, for now. Like I say, for now – Cape Town-based and then on some global vibe. I'd like to see it spread out – in PE [Port Elizabeth] there's some *dorpies* [small towns] where kids are doing similar shit.

Adam: Again, the internet is going to be quite interesting.

Shaheen: Ja. You see, the only *kak* about the internet is…uhm, like I can use it, someone in my position, in, in, in Tanzania, somebody in my position in blah, blah, blah, blah. But I think of kids, you know…that *laaitie* from Khayelitsha – he lives in a fucking shack. Where the fuck is he gonna get access to…you know what I mean? Unless you go to…

Adam: It's interesting…in the absence of technology, it's radio that becomes the medium that empowers him.

Shaheen: Ja.

Adam: But then it's community radio and it's limited to the Cape Town region. It doesn't reach Paarl, for example.

Shaheen: No. I think that it's going to be a combination of a whole lot of different things. I think that what also needs to happen is a lot of crews will have to play their part as well.

Adam: …This brings me back to one crew that is still on that mission with reaching schools – Black Noise. Of course, that animal mutated. I mean, the only original member is Emile. But it still stays young with what all of these kids are doing? What is your sense of what Black Noise is doing? I mean, they're the only Hip Hop crew that I know still makes the effort to reach kids and go off to schools and do programmes.

Shaheen: Uhm, I think it's important to do that. I think a structured body needs to be put into place where – because we've been doing that as well, going to schools. Like we've got a clever way of focusing to spread Hip Hop – get kids to breakdance properly, rhyme properly, before it's the other shit. You know, you can't do that in one session – one afternoon or two afternoons where, you know, it pulls through. Uhm, the Hip Hop community needs to be organised to a point where I think [full-on curriculum?] should be the key area that gives you wind. Even if it's to run a full-on series of workshops with people that are going to be facilitators in very different areas so that they can – so they can *gooi* out there and kids can come to their local communities that they can break and stuff like that. But there has to be some reading shit involved, you know, like if it's not that then it's Hip Hop for the sake of Hip Hop. You know what I mean? Just for the sake of, 'Yeah, yeah, yeah!' Uh-uh. I don't see that shit doing anything for anybody. You know? The problem with that is then you start having young kids that want to start recording their album and stuff like that, that want to cut a deal and *kak* like that, now they can rhyme, but all the other complexities and *goetertjies* [stuff] that they're really supposed to think about isn't there. Like a lot of these kids are writing some of the bombast shit…they don't give a fuck about recording. Sure they wanna make proper verse and stuff like that, but in the next couple of years they wanna study, they wanna do this, they wanna do that, you know. Like that's the real shit. Uhm, that not to get yourself into a position where you have to make weird decisions, you know. Er, so I think that – I totally obviously support it on one level. I think it's amazing that there are people out there that's going to schools doing the shit, but I think you almost need to tap into resources of schools and have a collective that can make it an ongoing, very structured befuckte thing where it's not just about the dancing. 'Cause the MCing, all of that, Hip Hop is not just about that. Everything is symbolic for some other *beweging*. You know. And, uhm, if you just spend one afternoon with a kid showing him how to headspin. They spend the 300 and other odd days with the likes of *Bold and the Beautiful*, the *kak* they get at school, the *kak* they get at home, the *kak* they get from newspapers in the evening, you know what I mean? Uhm, so I think that, uhm, because of where the country's at and where it's going and all the other *kak* that's happening on in the world, a lot of us have to get to a point where we understand some of these concepts, we understand some of these arguments, we know exactly where we are at. So start talking. Start getting other people to talk as well. We know…all the things involved, all the things that young people have to consider. Uhm, and I think that's gonna be [the] shit for me. I think that's gonna be it. Because if you look at like the Deviouses and Godessas, the stuff that they write already, you know, they write about globalisation, they write about whatever. You know, just like somebody that said a little thingie and that's it. You know like, okay. They have an argument here, they are saying something here, you can perform this forever, you know. There's, there's, there's…when you look at the poetic value and all of that type of *kak*, that shit's locked down, you know. Look at the data and stuff like that, it's there, you know. So, so that type of shit I think is gonna be important. Er, more heads around performance and recording and I think that when we have workshops and stuff like that, it should be something really comprehensive, not something that's like a little tour thing that's gonna go around – and I know it serves a purpose on one level. That's befuck, but we can fall into a trap where it's for the sake of Hip Hop. And I know a lot of people are down with that as well, it's just not where I am at. You know. It's just not where I am at. I, er, can't just speak for the sake of that. You know, like kicking my shit. You know. And I know that there's an argument that even that in itself is an alternative to blah, blah, blah, blah, but I think that we shouldn't – how can I say – reduce the potential of that type of thing to a 'look what it's doing'. Fuck, a lot more can be done. Let's do a lot more.

Adam: You're expending the energy anyway.

Shaheen: Ja. And, and, and, you see like the thing is it's so fucking easy. All you need is just honesty and dialogue, right? Respecting other people enough to know that, 'Yo, you have an opinion. I respect your opinion, hear that. Let's stretch it out. Let's *gooi*. Okay what are you saying? Uh-huh, okay, now what about that, now what about that. Fuck, okay, good point.' That, that we don't live in the way that we are taught, you know, just one-way fucking thing. *Kak*, man. We're just thinking out loud, all of us. Some of us have some experience and now we're sharing it, now what do you think? You've got to wake up to all this different shit. You know, you weren't around in 1976, or '85 or stuff like that. What are you getting? You know what? I learn all the time and I think that…uhm…we should, ja, like let's all be there. I can't even explain it. It's so fucking key to be able to move beyond just that. Kicking the shit for the sake of kicking the shit.

Adam: On that note…do you have to go soon?

Shaheen: Uh…ja, soon-ish.

Adam: This brings me back. All of this just makes me think, 'Fuck, my mission is actually on the right track.'

Shaheen: You think so?

Adam: I don't know, you tell me.

Shaheen: [laughs] I'm talking *kak* [playfully].

Adam: Fuck you! [laughs] This is the right thing. Remember I spoke to you, whenever I bumped into you I'd say, 'I think I should be writing about Hip Hop activism. Before I used to [be] on this whole trip – like with this chapter with Zimitri's book[5] – I used to be on about Hip Hop nationalism and I thought about how the music and the lyrics pushed a particular kind of agenda.' What you're saying now confirms those initial impressions. It's just that you're working in another realm. Not through the lyrics, not through performance…

Shaheen: That too, hey.

Adam: Not exclusively. But there is a continuity from what you're saying and to what you're doing now. There is that continuity ideologically, except that you're not expending energy in producing as a performer yourself. You're now engaged in some other activity I call activism.

Shaheen: Okay.

Adam: The shit is at – not performance – the shit is actually at the level, actually at skills transfer, developing headsets and giving people the conceptual, creative, technical skills to become informed individuals whether they become Hip Hop performers, or not.

Shaheen: Ja.

Adam: That's what you're saying? What I'm on about is that the whole deal [with] Hip Hop right now is not what you see at The Jam [nightclub] on a Friday…

---

5. See Erasmus (2001).

Shaheen: Not for me.

Adam: It never has been.

Shaheen: Hmmm.

Adam: And it seems…that in Cape Town, well, black people and white people are getting together and the shit is happening and African Dope is doing this wonderful stuff. We've got Moodphase 5ive and Godessa's now signed with them and actually it's happening. You know, and there are trips all over the country doing amazing stuff. On one level it's good, but that's not where the action is at. The action is actually at what's happening…

Shaheen: I think, ja. My thing is – and I know it's not very clear about it – there needs to be a balance, right, between this and Hip Hop…community activism shit. That is also very much a part of it. But, uhm, that's not where I am at. We don't own the clubs where we perform. We don't own the distribution and stuff like that, the record plants where they press shit and all that type of thing. We don't own the community centres where we try to get in to do shit like that. Uhm, I think that…what we do have, right, is, is, is a vibe. That's the one thing that we own. Through that vibe that it…it can [be] immensely useful, you know. I, I…it's dope that Godessa's getting signed and Moodphase 5ive and whoever's doing their shit. It's befuck. Uhm, what is it doing for the *laaitie* in Khayelitsha? And again, I think it's befuck that somebody can identify with, somebody's speaking their language, blah, blah, blah…but we know we can do a lot more. Come on, we know we can do a lot more. Uhm, we don't have to fall into the same…Anybody can fucking inspire you. Anybody that's doing interesting shit, you know. Uhm, so I don't know. I don't know. I think that…it just where it's at. I know for a whole lot of other people as well.

Adam: That's why you spend so much time with Godessa and working with them.

Shaheen: Well, the thing is, uhm, for this project I think that we briefed them and did some stuff. They've been writing already, so we just needed to go through the initial stuff. You know, uhm, it was actually way easier working with them because they were already into reading, already into stuff. For Amsterdam it was just giving them certain books and working with a lot of technical stuff, but I mean like where Godessa's at, the amount of energy and time they put into it, you know…ja, and I think that that's what's befuck about them, that it's this, it's this Hip Hop crew that's saying some interesting shit – and not for girls. You know, that a lot of people fall into with all types of fucking stuff, you know, that…they can and do all their own. Uhm, and that is what's exciting for me. They don't have to be overly aggressive in order to compete with the males, you know. They can *gooi* the lyrical stuff, the technical shit, you know, maintain a sense of themselves, you know. Like if they choose to be sexy one night, 'Fuck it, it's who I want be right now…If I think I want to say this, then fuck it I'll say this.' You know? Like they're performing shit that we've done for some of these projects. Like they will do the globalisation shit or AIDS or whatever stuff at some of THEIR shows, you know, that has nothing to do with the specific things that's being organised or whatever because they need it, you know. So I think that's the cool shit. Uhm. Even Devious is doing shit in Pollsmoor [prison] for a while now. He's doing stuff with CRED.

Adam: Really?

Shaheen: Ja, for a while now. So it's all [makes ticking sound effect].

Adam: I heard this track on Bush Radio yesterday. Erna played. It sounded like a raga track and Devious was in it.

Shaheen: No. It was Eloise and this *laaitie* from Lions of Zion and China…

Adam: Cool.

PART ONE REFERENCES

Boal A (1985) *Theatre of the oppressed*, trans. Charles A. & Maria-Odilia Leal McBride. New York: Theatre Communications Group

Conrad J (1902) *Heart of darkness*. New York: Tribeca Books

Cooper M & Chalfant H (1984) *Subway art*. New York: Holt, Rinehart and Winston

Erasmus Z (ed.) (2001) *Coloured by history, shaped by place: New perspectives on coloured identities in Cape Town*. Cape Town: Kwela Books

Fanon F (1952) *Black skin, white masks*, trans. Charles Lam Markmann. New York: Grove Press

Fanon F (1963) *The wretched of the earth*, trans. Constance Farrington. New York: Grove Press

Haupt A (2012) *Static: Race and representation in post-apartheid music, media and film*. Cape Town: HSRC Press

Haupt A (2015) Stealing empire: Debates about global capital, counter-culture, technology and intellectual property, PhD thesis, University of Cape Town

Heal the Hood Project (2005) *RAPSS*. Cape Town: Heal the Hood Office, self-published. See info@healthehood.org.za

Herman ES & Chomsky N (1988) *Manufacturing consent: The political economy of the mass media*. New York: Pantheon Books

Jansen EL (1995) *What is hip hop?* Cape Town: Heal the Hood Office, self-published. Contact emileyx@gmail.com

Jansen EL (2003) *My hip hop is African & proud*. Cape Town: Heal the Hood Office, self-published. Contact emileyx@gmail.com

Jansen EL (2010a) *Conscious rhymes for unconscious times*. Cape Town: Heal the Hood Office, self-published. Contact emileyx@gmail.com

Jansen EL (2010b) *B-boy syllabus 1*. Cape Town: Heal the Hood Office, self-published. Contact emileyx@gmail.com

Journal of World Popular Music (2018) *Special issue: Hip Hop activism and representational politics* 5(1)

Lee B (1975) *Tao of Jeet Kune Do*. Valencia, CA: Black Belt Communications

Meyiwa T, Nkondo M, Chitiga-Mabugu M, Sithole M & Nyamnjoh F (eds) (2014) *State of the nation 2014: South Africa 1994–2014: A twenty-year review*. Cape Town: HSRC Press

Serote MW (1981) *To every birth its blood*. London: Heinemann

Suzar (1999) *Blacked out through whitewash: Exposing the quantum deception/rediscovering and recovering suppressed melanated*. Oak View, CA: A-Kar Productions

Williams Q (2012) Multilingualism in late-modern Cape Town: A focus on popular spaces of Hip Hop and Tshisa Nyama, PhD thesis, University of the Western Cape

PART 2

Awêh(ness):
Hip Hop Language Activism and Pedagogy

LEFT TO RIGHT: *ELISE 'BLACK ATHENA' FERNANDEZ; MARVIN 'CREAM MACHINE' VAN WYK; YOUNGSTA CPT* | Source: Ference Isaacs

PROPHETS OF DA CITY | Source: Ference Isaacs

AWÊH(NESS): HIP HOP LANGUAGE ACTIVISM AND PEDAGOGY

A quarter of a century after the legal fall of apartheid, the transformational racial politics of the current moment call for South Africa to move beyond the rainbow politics of reconciliation and towards the radical politics of redistribution, including the redistribution and revaluing of linguistic resources. As Adam Haupt mentions in his introduction in Chapter 9, Hip Hop offers us a way to think about 'language politics in a multilingual South Africa, a South African context where linguistic imperialism is very much a reality' and imbricated with economic relations as well as identity politics in a nation struggling to forge a way forward. As the first section of this book made clear, Hip Hop is an art form/forum (Spady 1991) and stands firmly positioned to offer us new possibilities for the future.

Our conversations with founding members of the Hip Hop movement in Cape Town, South Africa – Prophets of da City, Emile YX? of Black Noise, Godessa, members of ALKEMY and others – introduce the idea of Hip Hop culture as a site of cultural production, knowledge production and activism where aesthetics are inextricably linked to politics and pedagogy. In fact, we argue that Hip Hop culture is inherently political and pedagogical. The art form/forum itself – which encourages critical dialogic engagement through the explicit philosophies of Each One, Teach One and Knowledge of Self – is produced, both here and in the US, in contexts that are, at their foundation, anti-poor, anti-black and anti-indigenous.

So, what does it mean to art (as a verb) in these contexts where certain cultures, languages and lives are valued more than others, where, as Alette Schoon explains (Chapter 10), youth experience 'the unpredictability of life' as a constant struggle for survival, and as Emile YX? puts it, the unfulfilled promises of democracy function as a form of demockery? To put it another way, perhaps more plainly, as Alim and Ariefdien ask: What does it mean to resist and transform white supremacist systems of oppression in the face of 'colonial, global capitalist, linguistic hegemonic bullshit'? (or as Ariefdien puts it more accurately, 'white supremacist delusionalism'!) As Paris and Alim argue in Culturally Sustaining Pedagogies: Teaching and

OGs OF SA HIP HOP - DJ READY D, SHAHEEN ARIEFDIEN, EMILE YX?, RAMONE AND PATRICK HICKEY | Source: Ference Isaacs

Learning for Justice in a Changing World *(2017)*, these chapters urge us to consider the question: *How do we understand ourselves and our futures and our cultures outside of the white gaze (as Toni Morrison says), outside of a colonial framework, even outside of a decolonial framework (even though that's a necessary step)?*

The chapters in this section all work together, intertextually, to show how Hip Hop creates 'awêh(ness)' through various forms of activism and education to uplift local communities, and how Hip Hop's on-the-ground movements of racial, linguistic and educational justice have pushed the academy to revamp its notions of race, language, culture and learning. As Hip Hop has spread from the largely Afrodiasporic, post-industrial urban ghettos of the US to nearly every corner of the globe, there is an ever-increasing need for educational institutions to understand this profound youth arts and activism movement. This section brings together leading artists, scholars, educators, practitioners and organisers (many of whom defy and/ or blend these categories) to demonstrate how Hip Hop requires youth to gain knowledge of their communities, histories and cultural practices, as well as the current social, economic and political contexts within which they live. Alongside Hip Hop's cultural imperative towards knowledge, its commitment to racial justice and its insistence on elevating 'the language of the people', the convergence of Hip Hop and education has become one of the most exciting areas of educational scholarship in the twenty-first century, while Hip Hop linguistics has continued to reshape our very notions of language, multilingualism and the relationships between language, identity and society more broadly. Not interested in 'knowledge for knowledge's sake', the contributors in this section think through these politics of language, race, educational opportunity and the production of knowledge in ways that aim to counteract and ultimately transform the oppressive conditions under which the majority of our people live.

The artists and activists in this section begin to answer the questions we posed above by showing how those involved in Hip Hop culture offer us a vision of a radical, emancipatory social movement through their music, theatre productions, community organising and educational curricula, among other activities. Chapters 8 and 9 address the Afrikaaps movement's efforts to rewrite the history of Afrikaans while creating new racial and linguistic futures for Cape Town's black/coloured/indigenous communities. For the artists–activists involved in this raciolinguistic movement, Hip Hop becomes a critical vehicle for raising consciousness through language, developing anticolonial resistance and upending the white supremacist legacies of apartheid through a radical re-education. By grounding themselves in one of Hip Hop's five elements, Knowledge of Self, the artists involved in the Hip Hop theatre production Afrikaaps – including Emile YX?, Jitsvinger, Blaq Pearl, Bliksemtraal, Monox, Jethro Louw, Shane Cooper and Kyle Shepherd, among others – view language as a site for the disruption of colonial domination and the transformation of 'the colonial mentality' in the psyche of communities of colour.

These artists' work produces a new reality for South Africans who speak languages that are racialised and marginalised by white South Africans, who still hold 90 per cent of the wealth in this 'post-apartheid' demockery. In their view, the language variety spoken by most coloured speakers in the Cape is not Afrikaans, at least as it is traditionally understood as the language of white Afrikaner nationalism. These artists remix the creole history of Afrikaans and provide a central and pivotal role to the linguistic contributions of indigenous Khoisan peoples and enslaved Muslims from India, Malaysia and other parts of Southeast Asia.

As Adam Haupt and I have written (Alim & Haupt 2017), Capetonian Hip Hop artists are explicitly revising hegemonic understandings of Afrikaans. They offer a creative rewriting of the language variety they refer to as Afrikaaps (a neologism that combines the term 'Afrika' with the term 'Kaaps', meaning 'from the Cape' or 'Capetonian'). This project of historical linguistic revisionism boldly and creatively challenges traditional, static, colonial definitions of Afrikaans as 'the language of the Dutch settlers' in Cape Town, for example, as well as traditional resistance narratives of Afrikaans as 'the language of the coloniser'. Through a clever, politicised, linguistic move, Afrikaans is rendered Afrikaaps, calling upon everyone to re-evaluate their understanding of this language variety and, importantly, the people who speak it.

As Quentin Williams argues in Chapter 8, the Afrikaaps movement reclaims Afrikaans by extricating it from colonial whiteness and lays fertile ground for the radical reshaping of the future of multilingualism in South Africa. He states boldly and unequivocally upfront that 'Hip Hop artists are the avant-garde, post-national critical thinkers and debaters of language in South Africa', as he shows throughout his book Remix Multilingualism (Williams 2017). Throughout this section, we see that artists have given a generation of coloured Capetonians the necessary knowledge to combat the violent racism about their culture and language, a violence designed to limit their potential, their mobility and their very humanity. In Adam Haupt's Chapter 9, which features Emile Jansen, Stefan Benting, Shaquile Southgate and Janine 'Blaq Pearl' van Rooy-Overmeyer, perhaps no one epitomises and articulates this transformation better than Stefan 'B-boy Mouse' Benting, who was a student at Lavender Hill High School and appears in the documentary film about Afrikaaps:

> I was so quiet because I was afraid of speaking like just my normal language of Kaaps. And after just understanding the concept that they tried to pass on to…it basically helped me get hope for myself. I realised, 'Okay. Stefan, if you wanna do this then like, okay, you can't be, you can't, uh, do what you've always been doing…Accept that the negativity in your life, okay, all your life you've been paralysing yourself by taking in okay all of these negative things that, that's been posted on our poles, that 'you are this, you are that', so 'Okay Stefan. Forget about this. Don't paralyse yourself anymore. Don't paralyse your view of yourself. Don't paralyse – whatever idea that you have of yourself, you can do it. Implement it.' And that's why, ja, I thank Afrikaaps for doing that.

Stefan Benting is now involved in Mixed Mense, Heal the Hood, and various other Hip Hop collectives for social justice and education. He is both a product and producer of Hip Hop pedagogies that, as his Heal the Hood partner Shaquile Southgate says, 'use methods which will make kids feel proud of who they are, where they come from, telling their stories, giving them history and a…sense of self-worth and self-love'.

In much the same way that Williams argues that this form of Hip Hop language activism holds 'significant implications for sociolinguistics in the South African academy', with artists often being 'way ahead of any sociolinguistic theory and knowledge', the same can be said for Hip Hop pedagogies. When taken together, the chapters by Kurt Minnaar (Chapter 11), Marlon Swai (Chapter 12), Hakkiesdraad Hartman (Chapter 13), H Samy Alim and Shaheen Ariefdien (Chapter 14), Geneva Smitherman (Chapter 15) and Adrian van Wyk (Chapter 16) offer us an innovative, emancipatory vision of what education can look like by pushing pedagogical *theory and practice to its limits. As Marlon Swai points out about the 'contentious relationship between formal and informal education':*

> *In many instances, education initiatives that are deemed informal, supplemental or alternative come to the rescue and make up for areas where the government falls short. In my case I can say that Hip Hop came to my rescue; it educated and re-educated me in ways that made me a functional adult and citizen in today's South Africa and beyond; and ironically, it is Hip Hop that, in turn, led me to seek out tertiary education and a graduate programme that would allow me to research the effectiveness of Hip Hop as pedagogical tool.*

In these chapters, Hip Hop education occurs in neighbourhoods, community centres, the streets, primary schools and even in such unexpected places as Stellenbosch University, an institution whose history is loop-linked with the history (and if truth be told, the present-ness) of apartheid. As Adrian van Wyk argues, Hip Hop education and activism were central to movements like FEES MUST FALL and Open Stellenbosch:

> *Over the course of six years, InZync became a platform that voiced people's frustrations. In 2015, once the first bout of FEES MUST FALL protests had taken place, InZync conducted a poetry session themed around free, decolonised, intersectional education. The same happened in November 2016, with a free session around the idea of protest and education. Furthermore, the workshops with young poets focused on various themes that young people face, whether it be around sexual identity or gang violence…One highlight was using poetry as an educational tool to educate these young people around the idea of intersectionality within a South African context.*

Beyond Hip Hop's key role in raising awareness across all of these sites of learning, artists–activists were also pushing for paradigms like 'intersectionality' and 'racial capitalism', for example, to be taught in oppressive institutions of higher learning.

Finally, within the pages of this section, we hear from teachers and teacher educators (such as Kurt Minnaar and Emile Jansen), activists and organisers (such as Janine 'Blaq Pearl' van Rooy-Overmeyer and Hakkiesdraad Hartman), all of whom work within very difficult and challenging contexts which can 'suck your spirit dry', as Minnaar wrote about public school teaching. This work is happening in remarkably constrained, antidemocratic school cultures where there is very little incentive for teachers to work together, to innovate curricula or to push the pedagogical envelope. Despite these stifling conditions, Hip Hop artists–activists–educators are committed to building the next generation and the next movement by using Hip Hop methods. As many of them see it, they have no other choice. As Janine 'Blaq Pearl' van Rooy-Overmeyer made clear, returning us to the central focus on language and language pedagogy:

> Like I say, Afrikaaps is me. It's the language I…dissie taal wat ek in droom,
> die taal wat ek in sing, die taal wat ek in poetry doen, die taal wat ek vi' my
> kind sing an 'ie slap. So is ek, you know. (It's the language I dream in, the
> language I sing in, the language that I perform poetry in, the language with
> which I sing my child to sleep. That's how I am, you know.)

These artists see freedom as 'a constant struggle', to quote Angela Davis (2016), one that requires continuous action, constant thinking and rethinking, because 'dissie taal wat ek in droom' (it's the language I dream in). As pioneering linguist of Black Language and the Black Freedom Movement Geneva Smitherman writes in Chapter 15 – offering an international and intergenerational perspective on these issues – 'teachers, scholars, activists, let's git busy y'all!

B-BOY KASHIEF | Source: Ference Isaacs

CHAPTER 8.
HIP HOP LANGUAGE CRITIQUE AS SOCIOLINGUISTIC ACTIVISM

QUENTIN WILLIAMS
(UNIVERSITY OF THE WESTERN CAPE)

INTRODUCTION

Hip Hop artists are the avant-garde, post-national critical thinkers and debaters of language in South Africa. Like their counterparts around the global Hip Hop Nation, Cape Town Hip Hop artists have learned how to remix the flow of practices and performances (old and new) that have come to define their local 'Kaapse style' of Hip Hop (Alim, Ibrahim & Pennycook 2009; see also Williams 2017). For decades, they have produced countless words, metaphors and similes into meaningful rhymes to counteract prevailing ideologies of language that seek to pigeonhole multilingual diversity. Hip Hop artists have also used language, specifically marginalised language varieties, to develop methodologies to conscientise young multilingual speakers to become aware of their own marginality. Also, through Hip Hop activism, they have used their studio and live performances as modes to stage language struggles around multilingualism.

In Cape Town specifically, struggles around language occur at the intersection of racialisation and racial hegemony, gender and cultural discrimination, and the economic weakening of black and coloured multilingual speakers, mainly on the Cape Flats. In an excellent study, Warner (2007) expresses how the Cape Flats was and today still is viewed as a 'problem space' because it was designed by apartheid architects and city planners to regiment the movement of (not exclusively) black and coloured citizens. The racialised bodies and languages of those monitored citizens became fractured and as a result emerged as fraught identities and identifications (see Ariefdien & Burgess 2011). For years, black and coloured citizens – their bodies, cultures and languages – became racialised through ideological and symbolic repressions, whether in the media, on television, in storytelling, jokes and spaces and places of leisure and institution. Hip Hop artists frequently reflected on these forms of subjugation through the production of bilingual and multilingual lyrics, focusing on the racialised class oppression of the township (see

Warner 2007). Rap groups such as Prophets of da City (POC), Black Noise and Brasse Vannie Kaap (Brothers from the Cape) took it upon themselves to narrate lyrics about raciolinguistic discrimination, particularly how racialised identities of coloured people were portrayed in the media and how limited readings of being coloured were framed (Haupt 1996).

At the time, linguistic labels steeped in racial discourse had already been produced to describe black and coloured bilingual or multilingual speakers' linguistic experiences: in the context of English varieties, we have Cape Flats English, black South African English and Cape coloured English, and in the context of Afrikaans, we have highly stigmatised speech practices such as Kaaps and Gamtaal. These racialised demarcations of language varieties and speech practices and their cultural and political linkage to racialised bilingual and multilingual speakers led Hip Hop artists to launch a programmatic language critique that developed into a form of sociolinguistic activism, and has held significant implications for sociolinguistics in the South African academy. Take for example the following early 1990s interview between Shaheen Ariefdien and Adam Haupt, and consider how Shaheen reflects on the inclusive linguistic character of Gamtaal and what it means to use speech that resembles marginalised speakers who need to be recognised:

> When we do interviews and shit like that and we speak gamtaal, or whatever, that shit's on purpose so the kid at home can say, 'Fuck, they're speaking my language,' you know? They're representing, you know, what comes out of the township and shit. So if some middle class motherfucker comes, *'Oe God, skollietaal.'* [Oh God, gangster language.] The shit's not for them, you know what I mean? I don't care if some white-ass dude at home thinks, 'Oh shit, look at this...uncultured, you know?, I want some kid from the ghetto to think, 'Naa, we can relate to that.' (Chapter 2, this book)

In an interview with Marlon Burgess, Shaheen goes further by critically reflecting on language and power:

> Anyone who has ever faced a language barrier knows that language marks difference. In South Africa we face language barriers daily and it's fascinating to see how language – one of the most contested terrains – plays out in Hip Hop both socially and artistically. Under apartheid, coloured schools were

generally divided into English and Afrikaans. Whether justified or not, an assumption settled into place that English was spoken by middle-class kids while Afrikaans was spoken by children of working-class families. However, in coloured township areas where most Afrikaans speakers live, English speakers were constantly harassed for wanting to be/act white. In schools dominated by English speakers, on the other hand, Afrikaans speakers faced chastisement if their second language skills were not good enough. The irony was that many Afrikaans speakers, like myself, would almost always rap in English, more precisely 'Black American English.' It was only after forming POC and experimenting even more that rhyming in Cape Flats Afrikaans not only became a possibility, but also a discovery of unique rhythm and rawness that suits Hip Hop in surprising ways. (see Ariefdien & Burgess 2011: 235)

Both quotes above are indicative of a Hip Hop language critique as a sustained form of sociolinguistic activism that has been around in public space for decades and, unfortunately, has been circulating outside the radar of sociolinguists, or often just ignored. As Ariefdien and Abrahams (2006: 266) write, '[Cape Town] Hip Hop took the language of the "less thans" and embraced it, paraded it, and made it sexy to the point that there is an open pride about what constituted "our" style…to express local reworkings of Hip Hop' (cf. Ariefdien & Burgess 2011).

This chapter is about how Hip Hop language critique as a form of sociolinguistic activism is accomplished by Cape Town Hip Hop artists. I offer a contemporary example of Hip Hop sociolinguistic activism that not only challenges our notions of what constitutes a language in South Africa, but also addresses the persistence of language stereotypes that historically marginalised speakers still have to deal with. The point of departure here is to ask: How do Hip Hop artists fight racism, particularly linguistic profiling and prejudice, through their sociolinguistic activism? And how can they continue to do so in the turbulent South Africa? To answer these questions, I first review and analyse excerpts from the presentation of the documentary *Afrikaaps* and a subsequent panel discussion at the first Annual Heal the Hood Hip Hop Lecture Series, which was held at the Centre for Performing Arts at the University of the Western Cape, and sponsored by the Centre for Multilingualism and Diversities Research. Secondly, I try to suggest alternative but relevant avenues to recast Hip Hop sociolinguistic activism that would involve busting myths about language and language stereotypes, and focusing more specifically on linguistic profiling and prejudice, and the performance of locality, to continue the fight against raciolinguistic discrimination.

CRITICAL LANGUAGE ACTIVISM: AFRIKAAPS AT THE FIRST HEAL THE HOOD HIP HOP LECTURE SERIES

At the first Annual Heal the Hood Hip Hop Lecture Series, two types of Hip Hop sociolinguistic activism were staged and debated in presentations: at the group level and the individual level. Firstly, one of the goals of the Hip Hop Lecture Series was to recuperate – through debate and critique – Hip Hop's activist ethos, in particular as it relates to the 'fifth element', Knowledge of Self. As organisers, Adam Haupt, legendary Hip Hop artist Emile YX?, MC Adrian 'Diff' van Wyk and I designed a programme that first gave preference to staging the elements: breakdancing, turntabling, rap and graffiti writing, with Knowledge of Self as the overarching theme. Secondly, we also offered for a wide range of issues that directly impact the professionalising of Hip Hop artists to be discussed: radio airtime, music rights, going the digital route, marketing and touring as an artist, and so on.

The majority of the presentations were convened in English, but two presentations that spoke directly to Hip Hop language critique as a form of sociolinguistic activism not only highlighted the politics of language and multilingualism in South Africa, as significantly linked to the racialisation of language and the effects on the speakers of a language that becomes racialised, but also performed a meta-reflection on the power struggles of language use shot through with racial stereotypes of historically racialised people in everyday interactions in institutional and non-institutional contexts. In the analysis that follows, I analyse extracts from the screening of the *Afrikaaps* documentary (directed by Dylan Valley) – a film about the theatre group and the politics of the Afrikaans language as an exclusionary form of discourse – and summarise the questions and answers from the panel discussion that followed with some cast members of the *Afrikaaps* theatre group.

My analysis focuses on selected extracts where speakers engage in meta-reflection on language – as tied to the stereotypes of speech and personae – and thereafter I further unpack some issues raised in the question and answer session which followed the screening. I argue that what

B-BOY MILO | Source: Ference Isaacs

the promoters of Afrikaaps commit to is not only to highlight the politics of Afrikaans but also to problematise the very notion of language and standard language use as a universalising idea. I then bring together the analyses in a discussion section.

HIP HOP AFRIKAAPS ACTIVISM AS LANGUAGE CRITIQUE

Language critique as sociolinguistic activism is often not as direct as civil disobedience through a die-in, or confrontations with police brutality during a peaceful strike for better access to institutional resources and recognition of voice. In most cases, it is a narrative that is constructed about the symbolic nature and character of language and what it does by either including an individual or a small group of speakers and/or excluding a large majority of citizenry or a historically racialised or gendered group of people.

The *Afrikaaps* documentary was created to establish a dialogue about such a narrative and specially to inspire fellow Hip Hop artists and others to engage in Hip Hop sociolinguistic activism. The name 'Afrikaaps' itself problematises Afrikaans as a standard language – particularly the *a priori* norms, derived from white Afrikaans-speaker norms, that underwrite the standard language – because there remains a virulent language ideology that still ties Afrikaans to racism and, of course, to the racist apartheid state. The Hip Hop artists promoting Afrikaaps are engaged in an ongoing Hip Hop sociolinguistic struggle that should force sociolinguists to revisit prevailing knowledge about Afrikaans-speaker *legitimacy*, *authenticity* and *intelligibility*. The importance of Afrikaaps is that it completely rewrites history (see Alim & Haupt 2017). As will become obvious further on, the Afrikaaps Hip Hop sociolinguistic activists are trying to open up a symbolic space to produce an alternative, inclusive linguistic narrative of Afrikaans in post-apartheid South Africa, highlighting what it means to speak Afrikaaps today.

To illustrate how the latter is framed in the documentary, I focus on two scenes: first, a class of high school students engaged in an exercise of meta-reflection on the legitimacy, authenticity and intelligibility of being speakers who command Kaaps as their first language, and second, a discussion among some members of the *Afrikaaps* theatre group.

What do high school students think about Afrikaaps? This is the question posed by Emile YX? as the camera cuts to Lavender Hill High School and moves into a classroom, opening up the discussion on Afrikaans and Afrikaaps.

Extract 1

1. Emile: *Sodra die klokkie lui dan praat julle n ander Afrikaans as wat in die boeke is, nuh? Wat is die maklikste om te praat? Die Afrikaans wat in die boek is of die Afrikaans wat…die Afrikaaps wat julle praat? Afrikaans, Afrikaaps?* (The moment the bell rings you talk a different type of Afrikaans than in the textbooks, right? Which is the easiest to speak? The Afrikaans in the books or the Afrikaans…the Afrikaaps which you speak? Afrikaans, Afrikaaps?)

2. Female Student 1: *Ek gaan Kaapse Afrikaans praat.* (I'll speak Kaapse Afrikaans.)

3. Moenier: *Hoe sal julle voel as dit…as Afrikaaps n legal taal is man, of 'n official taal is? Jou taal wat djy praat by die huis. Djy kry 'it in 'n textboek miskien.* (How would you like…if Afrikaaps becomes a legal language, an official language? The language you speak at home. You get it in a textbook for example.)

4. Female Student 2: *Die hele kinders sal Afrikaans so slaag.* (All the children will pass Afrikaans.)

---

5. Female Student 3: *As amper soes 'n mens dink dit is 'n bastard Afrikaans. Suiwer Afrikaans le boe en Kaapse Afrikaans le onder.* (Almost as if we need to think that we speak a bastard form of Afrikaans. Pure Afrikaans is on top and Kaapse Afrikaans is at the bottom.)

6. Male Student 1: *As iemand nou vir my gaan interview. Nou praat ek en hy. Nou't ek hom nie lekke' gehoor nie, dan gaan ek hom nou sê: 'Jy, sorry broertjie, wat het djy nou net gesê?' Dan gaan hy dadelik die indruk kry. Jy, die is n gangstertjie. Nevermind het ek 'n degree of hoe intelligent ek is, maar hy gat my judge by die taal wat ek nou gepraat het. Vir een vraag gat hy my judge vir dai job, wat vir my, my lewe gaan impak.* (If somebody interviews me. And he and I chat. And say I don't hear him correctly, then I will say: 'Yoh, sorry bru, what did you just say?' He will immediately get the impression, 'Damn, this is a gangster.' Never mind if I have a degree or how intelligent I am, he'll judge me by the language I speak. For answering one question, he'll judge me for the job, that would impact my whole life.')

7. Female Student 3: *Vir my is dit almal moet equal getreat word, maak nie saak waar djy vandaan kom nie. Dai is vir my nie iets kwaai nie.* (I think everybody should be treated equally, no matter where you come from. To be treated unfairly is not nice.)

The extracts give insight into how Hip Hop language activism occurs as an action and an event. Firstly, Emile (point 1, extract 1) broaches the subject of authenticity in language with the students – what type of Afrikaans marks them to be what type of speaker of Afrikaans – and reveals what is at first obvious: that the moment the bell rings for a break, they speak a different type of Afrikaans. When he asks which Afrikaans is the easiest to speak – the Afrikaans in the textbooks or Afrikaaps – one student replies 'Kaapse Afrikaans' (point 2, extract 1), making it evident that the students are aware of which Afrikaans variety they speak.

The keyword is 'speak' as opposed to 'write' in Afrikaans: when the students speak Afrikaans, they do so for the sake of group convergence and the maintenance of their group identity (in whatever form) inside the school. This allows for their voices to be heard and for them to be understood, particularly among their peers, who accept them linguistically 'as is'. Furthermore, it is clear that they do not speak 'standard' Afrikaans in their peer groups but rather the marginalised Kaapse Afrikaans variety, which has been organised in a language hierarchy – encompassing both form and function – as an impure construction and ideologically and normatively unacceptable.

Secondly, when Moenier asks how the students would feel if Afrikaaps became an official, legal language, one used as the language of textbooks, he challenges what is commonly understood by intelligibility in Afrikaans. Female Student 2 replies that every student would pass Afrikaans really well. Like Emile, Moenier problematises the notion of what constitutes a legal, official language. There are power struggles involved in the process of making a language legal or officialising it, but what is significant here is Moenier's attempt to overturn the symbolic hold official Afrikaans has over non-official, 'illegal' varieties of Afrikaans (which are still defined by white linguistic norms).

Thirdly, the students view themselves as illegitimate speakers of an ideologically more privileged language variety, that is, the white-normed variety of 'suiwer [pure] Afrikaans'. There is a self-awareness that they speak a 'bastard Afrikaans' because they know that there is a hierarchy that puts 'suiwer Afrikaans' on top and 'Kaapse Afrikaans' at the bottom (point 5, extract 1). Furthermore, the students also understand the material consequences of not speaking a white-normed variety of Afrikaans. In point 6, extract 1, for example, a male student suggests what would happen if he spoke in his non-prestigious variety of Afrikaans during a job interview. He points out that if he were to ask for clarity on a question in his Kaapse speech variety, he would be stereotyped as a gangster and considered unintelligent, even if he possessed a university degree. He would be judged by the way he speaks. He believes these negative social judgements on his speech would have a deleterious effect on his life chances of success.

The example given by the student in point 6 invites us to revisit and recast the debate around linguistic stereotyping and accent bias. The student is fully aware of what he can and cannot accomplish in life as a speaker of Kaaps. He knows that society and the Afrikaans-speaking community stereotype him as sounding like a 'thug', as being 'too street', like a Cape Flats 'gangster'. After his statement acknowledging raciolinguistic discrimination, a young woman in the class argues that everybody should be treated equally, irrespective of where they come from (point 7, extract 1).

It is fair to argue then that the students' anxieties about being seen as legitimate, intelligible speakers of Afrikaans, without falling foul to stereotypes, are not unwarranted given the Kaaps that they speak authentically. On a daily basis they have to contend with linguistic profiling (Baugh 2003) and stereotyping, including of their bodies and the spaces they move through. The students' reflections complement those of some *Afrikaaps* cast members in the group discussion following the screening of the documentary. This discussion reflects not only on Afrikaans, issues of pronunciation and intelligibility, but also on multilingualism more generally.

Extract 2

1. Moenier: I'm scared to speak like I really do, because, even when I got to college and stuff, you know. And I spoke like I did. I got like looks and stuff. Like. My Afrikaans isn't as nice as Jits', you know.

2. Group: [laughs]

3. Jitsvinger: *Wat mien djy?* (What do you mean?)

4. Moenier: *Nou moen djy wiet nou gat ek in 'n klaskamer waa' Engels die hooftaal is. Nou my Engels is nie soe glad 'ie, verstaan djy. En my, my, my tone en die way ek praat is op 'n relax buzz man. Nou sê die juffrou vi' my,* 'You must try…didn't you go for like speech therapy?' (Now you need to know I go into a classroom and English is the main language. Now my English is not as smooth, you understand. And my tone, my tone and the way I speak is on a relax buzz man. Then the teacher tells me, 'You must try…didn't you go for like speech therapy?')

5. Group: [laughs]

6. Moenier: *Nai ek praat 'ie 'n lien. Ek praat nie. Ek lieg nie, nuh.* (Nah, I'm not lying. I'm not lying. I don't lie, okay.)

7. Catherine: *Watter moedertaal was sy?* (What was her mother tongue?)

8. Moenier: *Sy's 'n Indian…Sy vir my sê.* (She's an Indian…She's telling me.)

9. Group: [laughs]

10. Emile: We inhibit ourselves from speaking because we were taught that how we speak is not good enough to be spoken. And it's our parents and everyone else.

> **11. Blaq Pearl:** So now because I don't speak proper Afrikaans enough, I also don't speak proper English enough. It's like you really mixed up. And I really mix Afrikaans and *Ingils as ek* [English if I]…

After the screening of the *Afrikaaps* documentary, most of the cast members had a panel discussion with the audience. One question posed related directly to the impact of the Afrikaaps movement in facilitating debates on language and what progress has been made in schools regarding recognition of Afrikaaps amongst students and teachers. On the issue of whether any programmes have been introduced to put Afrikaaps into practice, both Emile and Janine Blaq Pearl suggested that there has been little progress in schools and that political will is needed to change the education system. There was also discussion around how the documentary stirs up debate among young Kaaps speakers about authentic speakership, including how speaking standard Afrikaans is considered an important marker for raising standards, speaking properly and respectability. Janine argued that young Kaaps speakers need to reclaim Afrikaans, to give new meaning and value to the voices of those who do not speak the white-normed varieties of Afrikaans, and to ultimately refigure their racialised identities in society. In contrast, Emile argued that the Afrikaaps language activist movement does not intend to restrict how people speak Afrikaans or to impose a necessarily right or wrong way. Rather, the idea is to address a gap in how a certain group of speakers are understood, heard and seen (or not seen) as agentive.

WHERE SHOULD WE BE HEADING WITH HIP HOP SOCIOLINGUISTIC ACTIVISM?

Given the preceding discussion, it is important to recast the larger question of what Hip Hop language critique as sociolinguistic activism might contribute to a South African society in transformation, particularly with respect to racism, gender and sexuality. Specifically, we may ask what role the Hip Hop artist should play in raising questions of racing language in South Africa. How do we continue to use language to fight racism today as we move to examine and interpret the dimensions of a transforming civil society? And, do we need a new form of Hip Hop language critique that focuses on the micro-interactional activities of racist and sexist language?

These questions are not easy to answer since race and doing race and gender/sexuality in South Africa today are problematic. It is an indisputable fact that South Africans remain divided by racial labels and language. One thing is clear, however: there is a pressing need to revisit and recast racial labels and categories that seek to divide us linguistically as a society. Hip Hop language critique as sociolinguistic activism plays a special role here by reflecting not only on the inheritance of social and economic inequality in the democratic new South Africa, but also on how the country remains divided by class, space and, more symbolically, the stereotypes of language.

How then, when we hear linguistic labels like 'Cape Flats English', 'white South African English' and 'Cape coloured English', are Hip Hop heads and academics helpful in assisting marginalised speakers of stigmatised varieties who have to deal with racist linguistic stereotypes on a daily basis in South Africa today? When we use particular languages and perform genres of Hip Hop, are we fuelling the racist linguistic imagination by insisting on those racially and spatially problematic linguistic labels? In other words, when we play to a crowd with language styles and speech varieties and embody stereotypical racialised characters and personae, are we reaffirming the assumptions and conclusions of language purists and racist supremacists?

I am not able to provide answers to these questions, so I pose them here for consideration by Hip Hop artists as they continue to practise sociolinguistic activism. What I propose is that Hip Hop language activists shift their focus to, on the one hand, a continuation (and re-emergence) of the macro activism of busting linguistic myths and, on the other, the micro activism of symbolic, linguistic fights through propagating the effects (material and otherwise) of linguistic profiling. I examine each in turn.

Firstly, it should perhaps not be the responsibility of sociolinguists alone to bust myths about language; that responsibility lies also with Hip Hop activists who are deconstructing marginalisation through language. As I stated in the introduction, Hip Hop activists have for decades critically reflected on the use of language and the effects of linguistic marginalisation. Hip Hop artists have actively argued for the mainstreaming of marginalised varieties such as Kaaps, and large macro-activist fights have given way to the Afrikaaps movement in an interesting sociolinguistic twist. Today, however, there still remain myths of language purity in South Africa, such as Kaaps speakers not speaking 'pure' Afrikaans or black speakers not being able to speak 'proper' English (made painfully clear in Extracts 1 above). These myths reinforce linguistic racism and seek to further marginalise speakers that have for decades suffered linguistic marginalisation. However, these myths should not hold us symbolically hostage in a multilingual country where language – its forms, functions and meanings – travels across borders, spaces and media.

The Afrikaaps movement is an excellent example of challenging linguistic myths, linguistic racism and, more specifically, linguistic stereotyping. The Afrikaaps movement has already entered into a public debate on the difficulty of sociolinguistic description (standardisation and speaker legitimacy), and the recognition of multilingual voices (authenticity and intelligibility). The Afrikaaps movement as a sociolinguistic activist collective strictly emphasises multilingual diversity and argues – through breakdance, graffiti writing, lyrics and rhyme performances – for a return of the respect and dignity of marginalised speakers in order for them to realise their full citizenship in South Africa's democracy. Thus, the idea has been to promote the politics of linguistic redress: taking back linguistic power.

Secondly, at a micro-activist level, the stakes for doing Hip Hop sociolinguistic activism are much more immediate and pressing. It is for this reason I would like to propose that Hip Hop activists continue to dismantle the material inaccessibility that accompanies the linguistic discrimination of Afrikaans language use. An example is the recent upswell in student protest movements: at Stellenbosch University, the Open Stellenbosch movement created shock waves with the release of the documentary *Luister* (*Listen*). In the film, from one narrative to the next, black students retell the horrors of racial and linguistic prejudice. Each student in essence reveals the workings of linguistic profiling. I thus propose that Hip Hop activists interested in monitoring linguistic racism at the micro-interactional level be aware of linguistic profiling as a phenomenon. It emerges in multilingual and cultural contexts where speech and writing are used to linguistically discriminate against an individual who belongs to a predefined linguistic and racial subgroup within a given speech community (following Baugh 2003). To do so in a focused way, we have to become examiners of accent bias (those pronunciation differences and auditory cues that become stereotyped over time), which denies multilingual speakers of a certain racial profile access to material resources as they are evaluated on looks and how they sound. At the same time, those very cues also determine preferential linguistic profiling of particular multilingual speakers (mainly white) and their use of language in certain sociocultural contexts.

This discussion leads us back to the initial question of Hip Hop language critique as a form of sociolinguistic activism today. This activism is useful in that it challenges racist language use, discourses and practices that sociolinguists have hitherto only diagnosed as a symptom of what remains of apartheid sociality. Hip Hop activism has always focused its analytical energies on the inequality and marginalisation that occur in various contexts, often way ahead of any sociolinguistic theory and knowledge. The point I want to make here, however, is that we should try to understand how various meaning-making systems draw on different languages as resources (see Williams & Stroud 2014). But how do we anticipate and study this? One way is to try to understand why and how DJs, MCs, graffiti artists and b boys draw on their multilingualism to challenge the extension and reproduction of linguistic racism in the *performance of locality* (that of being and becoming part of the local space and place), as they acknowledge and 'draw on intercultural voices to stylize a version of their own marginalized voice' (Williams & Stroud 2013: 18).

A focus on the performance of locality lends itself well to a parallel focus on the everyday dynamics of racism, particularly the essentialisation of the linguistic and discursive display and enactments by marginalised speakers because it is their multilingualism that is subjugated with respect to the 'standard' language. Those speakers are often described as deficient in their speech and debates about such speakers often put them outside the larger macro-political discourse about what is actually meant by their multilingual communication in South Africa. Thus, in order for Hip Hop activists to continue the critique of language, particularly in local spaces and places, we need to study the various effects and senses of locality, or what I have called elsewhere *extreme locality* (see Williams & Stroud 2010). A focus on the performance of extreme locality provides an alternative Hip Hop cultural narrative of space – not only about where Hip Hop takes place but also what kind of linguistic and non-linguistic resources are drawn into such a locality (bodily behaviour, visuals in the nearby vicinity) and which frame the locality as necessarily about and for the local. This, of course, also brings into sharp focus the forms and functions of multilingualism not yet described by sociolinguists interested in the study of Hip Hop-related multilingualism, but could also help Hip Hop artists generally (for more on this, see Williams 2017).

CONCLUSION

In this chapter, I attempted to give due consideration to what I call Hip Hop language critique as a form of sociolinguistic activism. The sociolinguistic work engaged by Hip Hop activists brings to light the complex reflections, ideas, performances and discourses surrounding language use inside and outside Hip Hop communities. In order for Hip Hop artists engaged in the complicated task of deconstructing language to be effective, a number of issues should be considered to sustain such a task in the current democratic context of South Africa. Breaking down myths of language, linguistic profiling and the performance of locality, for example, are just some of the ways that Hip Hop activists could expose language racism as deeply harmful to us all.

NAMA XAM | Source: Ference Isaacs

CHAPTER 9.
AFRIKAAPS AND HIP HOP

EMILE JANSEN AKA EMILE YX?, STEFAN 'B-BOY
MOUSE' BENTING, SHAQUILE SOUTHGATE,
JANINE 'BLAQ PEARL' VAN ROOY-OVERMEYER
WITH ADAM HAUPT

Adam Haupt sat down with some members of Heal the Hood at the Afrikaaps panel at the 2016 Open Book Festival, Cape Town. Adam was standing in for Quentin Williams as the panel chair. This panel is considered a follow-up discussion, in many ways, of the Afrikaaps panel discussion held at the first Heal the Hood Hip Hop Lecture Series at the University of the Western Cape, arranged by Heal the Hood, Staticphlow and the Centre for Multilingualism and Diversities Research.

Adam Haupt: Good evening and welcome to Afrikaaps and Hip Hop panel discussion. We would like to thank the organisers for inviting us. I think the very act of inviting such a discussion into this space is itself politically quite meaningful and hopefully there's time to unpack what that might mean in this context. Just brief introductions. I'm Adam Haupt from the Centre for Film and Media Studies at UCT [University of Cape Town] or should I say the university currently known as UCT. On my furthest left, b-boy Mouse, Stefan Benting, and you might know Emile YX? aka Emile Jansen, one of the founding members of Black Noise, as well as Heal the Hood, and then to his right, Janine van Rooy-Overmeyer aka Blaq Pearl, a poet, MC, singer in her own right, uhm, has worked quite closely with Emile as well as other collaborators on a theatre show named *Afrikaaps* which we will be talking about tonight. And then to the right of Janine, Shaquile Southgate, a key member of Heal the Hood. All of these narratives intertwine in some way and at some point it'll become clear how these different threads come together. It's a great way for us to think about two things, language politics in a multilingual South Africa, a South African context where linguistic imperialism is very much a reality and is tied up with the politics of not just economic change in South Africa, but tied up with identity politics. Over the last week or two we've seen how the politics of language is intimately tied up with other aspects of identity politics – the politics of hair. So at schools recently, Pretoria Girls High and then in Cape Town, Sans Souci, we've seen horrible stories, which seem to come straight out of Ngũgĩ wa Thiong'o's *Decolonising the Mind*.[1] I'm thinking about a particular chapter by Ngũgĩ, the story of his going to a high school outside of his hometown. He goes to one of these mission schools and the rule is that during school hours you speak English, during your down time you speak English, and essentially what happens is when he goes home to visit his family in his hometown, he could no longer speak his mother tongue that fluently, so much so that his family members tease him. They call him 'The Little Englishman' and of course it isn't until he is much older that he realises what a barbed compliment that is, you know? So, the process of assimilation in a context which is multilingual is a travesty and more than two decades after our first democratic election, we still find ourselves in a context where school children are saying things like, 'If we speak our mother tongue, we get fined 10 rand'; 'We have a little *dom pass*[2] or whatever it's called, a book of offences, and you know, marks against our names are made if our hair is inappropriate, if our language is inappropriate, if our bodies are not policed adequately.' So this is the context within which, you know, we find ourselves, and this is the work, ironically, that Hip Hop activists have been doing. Many people who know a little bit about Hip Hop in this context, will know that the first crews to establish themselves as recording artists are Black Noise and Prophets of da City, and incidentally these are the crews which began to embrace mother-tongue expression, embrace multilingual realities, in defiance of the reality that kids were dealing with in school. In school, kids were being told and are being told to this day, 'If you want to get a job, if you want to make it to varsity, if you want to succeed, you must speak the language of power, you must speak a particular dialect of English, a particular hegemonic speech variety. It's not just that you have to speak English, you have to speak English in a particular way.' Enter Hip Hop activists. Hip Hop activists introduced not just multilingual expression through pop culture, but they began to play with the idea of what is an acceptable way for you to express yourself in your mother tongue. So it's not just about embracing your mother tongue, it's also about upsetting your Zulu-speaking parents who have a particular idea of what traditional culture and language and expression constitute and defying those expectations, defying those ideas. So in other

---

1. See wa Thiong'o (1986).
2. The play on words here is *dom pass* versus the dompas book non-whites were forced to carry in apartheid South Africa. Here *dom* (dumb) pass is understood as a value judgement on the intelligence of black, coloured and Indian South Africans.

COLLABORATORS AT A THEATRE SHOW NAMED AFRIKAAPS | Source: Ference Isaacs

words, Hip Hop activists begin to give scholars like myself and scholars like Quentin Williams at the University of the Western Cape – Quentin would say that what Hip Hop artists are doing is, they're forcing us to think carefully about what the term 'multilingualism' means. You're not just multilingual if you speak more than one language. In actual fact, you're multilingual if you speak more than one speech variety, more than one dialect of a particular language. Now think about your own language practices, how you speak at home, how you speak at work, at university, at the store, in the street, etc. There might be variations or there might not, of how you express yourself, in other words, how you police yourself, not just in the way in which you present your body, but in the way in which you speak. Now imagine a child of colour from a working-class background, going to a privileged, historically white English school, and having to deal with messages about what is acceptable in terms of how they police their bodies, but also how they police their speech. Not just what they say but how they speak. So this is the very idea of internalising your surveillance to such an extent that you might, you know, find yourself being dislocated from the communities from which you come. That very process is what drives the activism of people like Emile, Janine, Stefan, Shaquile and…and I'd like for us to unpack what it is they do and what that has to do with [the] politics of language, the politics of expression, the politics of identity generally speaking; but then also where we can go in terms of cultural production generally speaking; but then also within the educational context; what do we do with the work they are doing? How do we actually utilise that work to address key crises in our schooling and higher education context at this very point in time? Is that a sufficient lead-in?

Emile YX?: Yoh. It's a *moerse* [massive] lead-in my bru.

Adam Haupt: It's a *moerse* lead-in.

[laughter]

Adam Haupt: So, for 50 points. No, I'm kidding. So, the first question is the obvious question: Why Afrikaaps? And I'm not picking…I mean the obvious question is directed at Emile, but I think anyone else can answer it. Why not? Now, just bear with me. I'm going to be devil's advocate. I will be asking a few obtuse questions, because it's a way of, you know, surfacing things that you and I might take for granted but the audience might not. So the first question is, why Afrikaaps? Why not Afrikaans? So for example, a few months ago I was at HemelBesem's performance, scintillating performance of a show called *Die Afrikaansvatter*, and his premise is, you know, 'I'm taking Afrikaans, *ek vat daai "kaans". Ek vat Afrikaans. Dis my taal. So ek gan nie van Afrikaaps praatie. Ek is Afrikaans.* [I take that chance.[3] I take Afrikaans. It's my language. So I'm not going to talk about Afrikaaps. I am Afrikaans.] Deal with it.' That's his position, right? And he distances himself from the moniker Afrikaaps. So, what are you doing when you're saying, 'We speak Afrikaaps' as opposed to Afrikaans?

Emile YX?: Ja, I think…it's actually, uhm, Catherine [Henegan]…that came up with the concept, but at that time she'd already spoken to Jitsvinger and he's actually the one who coined the name Afrikaaps. Uhm, most of us know this Gamtaal Kaaps and, uhm, when they first approached me I was like, '*Kyk hie* [Look here], I don't really wanna be a part of this 'cause this is a white *tannie* [aunty] coming with to tell our story AGAIN my bru.'

Adam Haupt: So Catherine is?

---

3. The word 'chance' is a literal translation of *kaans*. However, the artist is playing on the words 'kaans' in Afrikaans and 'kaaps' in Afrikaaps.

Emile YX?: South African?

Adam Haupt: Is she South African or Dutch?

Emile YX?: She's South African but then she's lived in Holland for a long time. It's my own like, you know, thing about the way things work in South Africa. Uhm, but they say that when you seek your history continuously like…you know. Uhm, I've…for years with Black Noise been pushing Black Consciousness and almost towards the latter part of Black Noise, more and more times…the story of the Bushmen and our heritage locally was starting to take shape. I got involved because of the access to, like, Neville Alexander and all this hidden information that they made available…and also expose my own like, you know…mentality about how things… but also the, the truth about like how things work in South Africa. And so like, I was intrigued by the fact that it wasn't actors, because I don't, I don't believe in that 'if you can rap, you can act' *kak* [shit]. That's not the truth, you know, so I didn't wanna be one of those rap…*ouens* [guys] who rap who think they can act. So she said there can just be a bunch of people who will be… performing like the work that they create, you know, which was, which was cool, which made it easier for me to wrap my head around. And so, uhm, within the group, like Jits was…speaks a different version of Kaaps, you know, more closer to the *suiwer* [pure] version of Kaaps. Janine has a like a Mitchells Plain version of Kaaps, uh, Moenier has like a Bo-Kaap version of Kaaps. Me, I'm like a *verdalade* [messed up] version of Kaaps, and you know, so it's…so it was a…and then there's, uh, Jethro, who's also like that, uhm, Beaufort-Wes Boesman Kaaps…which is like a…and also he tells stories that have like five different meanings in one sentence, which is like YOH. And so it's all of these versions of the language that made it extremely interesting, you know, whereas I think to come to…you mentioned Simon. Simon understands the politics of what's going on. In order to get ahead, you need to buy in, and I think…and I'm not dissing him in any way by saying this, but there's…either you…*speel saam* [play along]…and Oubaas is *nog* [still] once allowed *om* in charge *te wies* [to be in charge]. *Djy, djy, djy skoppie teen 'ie kar 'ie. Oubaas gat vi' jou moer op 'n nog 'n* level, you check? [You, you, you don't kick against the car. Oubaas will beat you on another level, you check?] You have to buy in, in South Africa. To this day, it's exactly the same, you know, it's, uh, and…and I think us doing Afrikaaps made people realise that only a certain AMOUNT of truths can be spoken within the context of South Africa because it's a…language is about power, language is about…uhm…ja it's about finance…Media

24…uhm, like that whole like ja…magazines and newspapers and all the, all the big businesses that's attached to the language. And so I think like we…we went into it very naïve I think, about how revolutionary we could be. I always, I don't know why you asked me this question first, because I always put us in trouble by speaking truth. Uhm, ja anyway, I'll stop there.

Adam Haupt: Ja, that's exactly…I mean, cut to the chase. I mean that's…Afrikaaps. For those of you who didn't Google this yet, or haven't seen the theatre show, it's a theatre production that brought together…MCs, poets, brought in theatrical elements, brought in live musicians…the exquisite music direction of Kyle Shepherd, you know…exquisite music and poetry and theatrical elements, MCs, etc. It went through a whole process of workshopping, and the process was documented by filmmaker Dylan Valley, who also made…sort of a personally reflective documentary about his own language history, and his own sort of disconnected, slightly discombobulated relationship with language and Afrikaans-ness, etc. The process of him going through rehearsals and documenting everything changed his own position on his own language politics. It became a way for, for him to think about coloured identity politics in relation to [the] broader history of colonialism, in relation to the history of Black Consciousness.

Emile YX?: I must say something about the doccie. Pearl can back me up on this. Like, just like, I mentioned how naïve we are about how things are done, but there's a piece in the doccie that shifted as far as time is concerned. The visit to the Klein Karoo Kunstefees was the first thing…the play, and we were like, 'How can you do that?', you know, just to show like how…about how things are put together and like the timeline of how things are done correctly. Everyone watching was like, '*Naai* [No] man. This isn't the truth,' you know? Which is kinda – kind of interesting, the way the story gets told from the outside is not necessarily… and it's allowed to be like changed for the benefit of the viewer and like the palatability of the audience versus…do you get what I'm saying?

Janine Blaq Pearl: Ja…uhm, ja. *Kan ek ma' Afrikaaps praat?* [laughing] *Hoekom praat ons Engels?* [May I speak Afrikaaps? Why do we speak English?] Okay so who all understand Afrikaaps here? Ja? The majority?

Adam Haupt: Don't pretend like you don't.

Janine Blaq Pearl: [laughing] Okay, uhm, look…

Emile YX?: *Iemand translate vi' die mense wat 'ie hulle hande opgesit het 'ie.* [Somebody translate for the people who did not put up their hands.]

Janine Blaq Pearl: There's also some level of English amongst the Afrikaaps words so you'll catch it and you'll feel it. Uhm, ja Afrikaaps man, *vi my*, uhm, *was 'n groot* [for me was a great] personal journey man…*deel van my* [part of my] personal journey in terms *van, djy raak groot jou hele liewe en* [you grow up your whole life and] 'bout that time that was probably just before 30 or something when…2010 when we started…if I can do the math now, when we started with the, with the project, so uhm…it was intense because I'm already a conscientised person, you know. Like, I grew up with a lot of consciousness and I have a big Hip Hop influence in my life as an artist, uhm, so you're already conscious and you're outspoken and *djy's* [you're], uhm, creative *oor dinge* [about things], *djy dink* [think], you know, open-mindedly *oor goetes* [about things] and you're as proactive as you can be to that extent of what you know, and so *Afrikaaps* then happened, this production, the process *en wat wat* [and what what], and then, we did like Emile said, we did a lot of research, but throughout that research man, uhm, even I still discovered stuff about this language, and the origin, and the history, uhm, about Afrikaaps, about the way in particular we speak Afrikaans in the Cape, you know, and the history itself related to that, uhm, that – this is actually…Okay what I wanna say, and the point…I'll come back to this maybe later but, uhm…uhm.

Emile YX?: *Praat* [Speak] Afrikaans.

Janine Blaq Pearl: *Ja, dis omdat ek Engels praat nou moet ek dink in in* – translate *is 'n* process so…uhm, *'it- wat kwai was van daai was* [Yes, it's because I speak English now I need to think in in – translation is a process, so…what's cool is about that] we could finally tell our story and we could say we're not waiting on anyone to say *'is okay om te praat soes ek praat 'ie* [it's okay to speak like I speak]. So that's been – I think a underlying, uhm, issue in most of our lives, you know, growing up speaking Afrikaaps and then going into different environments and suddenly you have to change because of the perception and just the way things work and what you're expected to do. So, small things like going to Pick n Pay or going to the mall or going to UCT or going to a bookshop or going to…

Emile YX?: …coming here.

Janine Blaq Pearl: Coming [laughing] you know, any…whichever…establishment. You suddenly change the way you speak, you know? So, *die antie bly af in 'ie pad by my en ons… ek wiet ons praat 'ie…ons groet elke dag mekaa', ons praat dieselle taal, nou skielik…sy werk by Pick n Pay. Ek gan koep iets oor 'ie counter. Ons altwie praat nou somma Engels.* [So, this aunty lives down the road by me and us…I know we're not talking…we greet each other every day, we speak the same language, now suddenly…she works at Pick n Pay. I go buy something over the counter. Both of us now speak English.] Like we both like, 'Hey! How are you? Can I have uhm…can I have some salomie' or whatever you know, so…

[laughter]

Adam Haupt: What do you call that in English?

Janine Blaq Pearl: Salamie, salomie. *So, julle verstaan wat ek mean? So, dis goed soes daai man wat wat net opmos die hele, die hele ding* [So, you understand what I mean? So, it's things like that that messes up the whole thing]. So, uhm, I then went and I challenged that and I actually went to that same *tanie en praat* [aunty and spoke] in Afrikaaps, *order die ding soes ons praat by die huis elke dag* [order the thing like we speak at home every day], and…

Emile YX?: *Wat makee' jou?* [What's wrong with you?]

Janine Blaq Pearl: *Daai antie* [that aunty] is like 'huh?' You know, the reaction I got when I actually started doing it, like really take…breaking my way of doing, in society…how I used to do in terms of speaking this language at home and then suddenly switching. I tested it and, and it…the reaction was, some people…*hulle kyk jou regtig met 'n judgmental oeg an* [they really look at you with a judgmental eye]. They really judge you and you can see and feel it, everything with that reaction just like *'jy, djy praat vekeed'* [you, you're not talking right] you know? *'Iets is vekeed hiesa'* [Something is wrong here] you know. So you internalise that your whole life. That's what really happened and the impact that has…is you start questioning so many things about yourself, *so as ekkie…as my praat 'ie reg issie, dan wat is my worth an? Wat's my plek hiesa?* [so, if I don't…if my speech is not right, then what is my worth? What is my place here?] So you question a lot of things about your existence, your identity. Okay, so ek [I] is so-called coloured. *Ek praatie reggie. Jarrie die odds is against my hiesa*, you know? *So wane, wane is dit dan okay om ek te wies man? En met Afrikaaps vi' my was daai.* [I don't speak right. Damn, the odds are against me here, you know? So when, when is it then okay to be me man? And with Afrikaaps, for me it was that.] Take…taking that step and putting it together as a production. Putting that information in that creative way, you know, was for me a big step in terms of saying, *'kyk hie man, die's hoe ek praat en dis orrait en ek gannie wag vi jou om vi my te sê, "djy kan nou soe praat en dis reg"' nie* [look here man, that's how I talk and it's alright and I'm not going to wait for you to tell me, 'you can speak like this now and it's right]', okay, *ne*, so really reclaiming the language ourselves and to go back to the…

Emile YX?: …It's a challenge.

Janine Blaq Pearl: It's a heavy challenge. If you go back into the history, the perception that Afrikaans, *die regte* [the real] Afrikaans, you know, *is die* [is the] superior. And we were raised all this years thinking *'ons praat 'n, 'n Kombuistaal…'* [we speak a kitchen language…]

Emile YX?: That's a stolen version.

Janine Blaq Pearl: But that IS a stolen version. And so, that's what we learned, you know? *Die Afrikaans wat os praat kom einlik way, way, way trug voorie Genootskap van Regte Afrikaans, etc. gestig was as a structure.* [The Afrikaans that we talk actually came way, way, way back before the Society of Real Afrikaners, etc. was established as a structure.]

Emile YX?: In my previous life as a teacher…I…you're outside at the school, and *'auw, my broetjie pass 'ie ball'* [Yoh, my brother, pass the ball] and you're playing with your kids on the field and you come into the class and you're like *'haal asseblief julle boeke uit'* [take out your books please], *'auw, kyk hoe change meneer nogal'* [Yoh, look how sir changes]…so it's a… suddenly it dawns on you, the reality of you were hiding this true identity of who you really are and how you speak. And I remember…and I've said this I think in the doccie, that when I went somewhere and I spoke Afrikaans, I'd say *'kyk hie, ek praat 'n bietjie verdalade* [look, I speak a bit of a messed-up] Afrikaans, uhm, bear with me'…*en wat wat* [and what what], and uhm, but after the production I was like, *'kyk hie, ek worry nie mee nie. Ek praat vloekwoorde, ek worry nie mee nie'* [look here, I don't worry anymore. I'll say swear words, I don't worry anymore].

So…and it was like a…previously I was angry when I learned this Black Consciousness about how white people have like whitewashed the civilisation that Africa has brought to the world, which has now only been like, you know, recognised for the RHODES MUST FALL uprising and stuff, which is…made me really pissed off…like being forced to learn that my *kroes hare* [curly hair]…there's something wrong with it, or like…and like my blackness, there's something wrong with it, and how this impacts on black people globally, you know. And then to learn like I actually played a role in denying speaking this language of my mother and my father and both versions that they speak because I felt like *naai* that wasn't a good enough language and that was like forced on us, and so we…when we got the opportunity to do the production, like we had all this information, but we were…the amazing thing about it is that it didn't come across preachy, you know, there was so much, like so much pent-up anger. I'm like *'jarre my bru, nousit, nou gat hulle sien my bru'* [damn brother, now, now they will see my brother] and then like…it sort of eased into the audience's mind. Like people were crying in the audience because they felt the pain of like a *laaitie* [youngster]. We went to his school [pointing to b-boy Mouse] and a kid in his school said something like REALLY profound. He said *'kyk hie, as ek praat soes ek praat nou hie innie klas, dan kry ekkie haai jop 'ie. Ek kan die beste wees in accounting en maths, maa' net as ek as…ek opfok en sê 'kyk hie naai my bru, wat sê djy haa?'* [look here, if I speak the way I speak now in the classroom, then I won't get that job. I can be the best at accounting and maths, but if I…if I fuck up and say 'look here nah bro, what did you say?'] And they associate Lavender Hill with gangs and gangsterism and the way we speak has always been…by the apartheid regime and even now with the coloured regime, associated with gangs and with negativity. Even the *Son* and the *Voice* [newspapers] STILL do that same *kak* on every pole, every day. I'm still angry that this is like what our mothers and our fathers and the good majority of the Cape Flats are addressed with EVERY morning on EVERY pole, throughOUT the Cape Flats. And it's okay. They won't try that *kak* here in Constantia [wealthy suburb]. But it's okay because it's *mos net hulle, daai gangsters, daai Gam* [it's just them, those gangsters, that Gam], so we treat them that way, you know? Anyway, *ek raak 'n bietjie kwaad nou* [I'm getting a bit angry now].

Janine Blaq Pearl: [laughing] *Dit is om kwaad te raak* [It is to get angry about] because as, uhm, *die* [the] corruption *en* [and] misguidedness *gan diep* [goes deep] man, you know? Misinformation, *dit gan diep*, and it's broken down and scarred, for lack of another word, generations and generations of people, you know? So, stuff like, uhm, *'my ma en my pa praat altwee Afrikaans'* [my mother and father both speak Afrikaans], and then they have…or Afrikaaps, and they have a child or children and they start raising the kids speaking English…

Emile YX?: …Ja.

Janine Blaq Pearl: You know? But, the catch there is you still hear THEM speak Afrikaaps [laughing]. But I come to *mammie* [mommy], for example, and I'm like 'mommy can I have a sandwich?', *dan* [then] switch *mammie oek nou* [also now], 'yes my – yes my child' *en mammie praat nou* [and mommy speaks now] 'yes my child. What would you like on the sandwich?' Ja, *en mammie praat oekie great Engels 'ie* [Yes, and mommy also does not speak great English], but my point is, that's how deep it goes. So mom is not even thinking or realising what she's now doing to her identity and her language and passing that on to her child because it's been done to her, you know. Most of us eventually we go back to the core and somehow through our up…our raising…through our teens or whatever, or after school, we're just like 'aweh, my bru' [howzit, my brother] you know, so suddenly English is like…so the truth comes out, at some point the truth comes out.

Emile YX?: *Kroes ko' altyd trug.* [Curly hair always comes back.]

Janine Blaq Pearl: *Kroes kom trug.*

Adam Haupt: So back to Afrikaaps. So *Afrikaaps* is kind of a response, you might say…for those of you who haven't seen the show yet and if it does have another run, by all means, catch it. Some interesting historical nuggets to be found in there, for example…that the first written Afrikaans was actually in Arabic, at Madrassa, it was written out phonetically in Arabic. That's the first written Afrikaans, the first manuscripts actually in Arabic script. The first places where Afrikaans was taught, was at Madrassas, right? So the history of Afrikaans is a creolised history. It's a black history. It's tied up intimately with slave histories. I was having this discussion with an archaeologist from Wits [University of the Witwatersrand] recently. We were talking about an archaeologist in the States who had gone into swamps to uncover evidence, actual physical evidence of slaves who had managed to make a living for themselves outside of the States, literally to dislocate themselves. So they live for decades, free, but in the swamps, right, with alligators and what not. The punchline of the discussion was there's very little evidence, if you look at the amount of slave narratives that come out of, you know, literature, out of historical accounts, out of archaeology in the States, and you compare that with the kind of historical sort of research on slave histories in South Africa, on our continent. It's pathetic. So, what's interesting about Afrikaaps is, it points to research by people like Sara [Jappie]…I think you interviewed her.

Emile YX?: Ja.

Adam Haupt: And finds evidence for the claim that Afrikaans is actually a black language and Afrikaans, the hegemonic, dominant version of Afrikaans as seen on…*KykNet* [TV programme], right? That, THAT Afrikaans is actually the culturally appropriated version of Afrikaans and the actual version of Afrikaans is one that comes out of the black experience. Out of…out of black history.

Emile YX?: Funny part about the production, like at the same time we were doing the production, like, this information was finding us. We're like hanging out with Bradlocks [Bradley van Sitters] and Patrick Malay, a lot of different people, and like…

Adam Haupt: …Who are they? Just fill us in?

Emile YX?: Like Bradlocks was learning about like the original Khoi Khoi plan – sharing that information and all of these things were just finding us, you know, like we were searching for our ancestry and like people were finding that this was taking place, and we're sitting in this room and it almost felt surreal. Occasions we were speaking about stuff and like birds fly into the room and we just, we just froze and there's this story that Dianne Ferris…

Adam Haupt: …Diana Ferris?

Emile YX?: …When she's in Amsterdam, gets this, hears this voice, uhm…'come take me home', or, what's the name of that poem? About Saartjie Baartman. We were in Holland and the same time one night the two of us [pointing to Janine Blaq Pearl] are busy looking at her brother's songs online, and we get…we come together the morning and the first thing we say is, *'raak wys'* [keep it real], and out of that, a song was born, so it was like, a very like strange space to be in. It's like you were, you were called to do this, you know, and THEN when you're like…we go to…we go to post the production, the two of us like, this is VALUABLE information. We need to share it. So irrespective of like funding or anything we're going to [the] Cape Flats Film Festival. We're gonna share this information. And you tell a group of kids from the Cape Flats, '*Kyk hie* [Look here], we speak Boesmantaal [Bushman's language] every day.' You say 'uh' and 'huh uh' every day and 'uh' means 'yes' and 'huh uh' means 'no' in Khoi Khoi. And you look at that kids and their faces, they're like 'Oh shit. Really?' because there's a tendency to not be black, to not be Boesman. Then the *ou* [guy] looks 100 per cent Boesman, my bru. BOESMAN. Boesman. Boesman. 'Ha ah, hm mm, *nee. Ons kom van* Germany' […no. We come from Germany].

[laughter]

Emile YX?: And the more you speak about this rich information that you…that was part of the production, stuff that we weren't able to fit into the production, and we're sharing it with those kids. I mean I just did it recently…diversity, commonality conversation, and so like you're sharing this about who we really are, and you see those kids like, 'Oh damn, this whole race thing is a lotta *kak* actually, you know. Like let's have a conversation about that commonality, that history, *die* [the] Boesman *storie* [story], like the first doctors with the herbs, the first like…the first *alles* [everything] my bru. The first to speak, the first to clap, the first to go into trance…breakdancing, voo' breakdancing. You know what I mean? Like this is who we are. The first to write on rocks. Graffiti my bru. The first to tell stories on five different levels in one sentence. Heavy. That's who we come from, you know? But we, our version of that, is what's his name? Jamie Uys. Fucking Coke bottle *God's Must Be Crazy kak*, you know what I mean? Like, the diminishing of that rich cultural heritage that we all belong to, is like…

Adam Haupt: On that note. Mixed Mense. So we've got *Afrikaaps*. You have Heal the Hood doing a number of things and Mixed Mense is one of them, and you took it to an amazing space, prestigious space. Tell us that story. Maybe not Emile…

Emile YX?: …Ja, *ek praat te veel* [I talk too much]…

Adam Haupt: …Because I think we might be getting tired of Emile now so pass on to Stefan and Shaquile. But I just want us, before we move on, I just wanna ask you this quick question.

AFRIKAAPS IN PERFORMANCE | Source: Ference Isaacs

Afrikaaps has been running on and off since 2010. How much media support have you had in all this time, for the work you've been doing?

Emile YX?: Media with money or like exposure?

Adam Haupt: Ja, well exposure is one part of it, but you always need a media sponsor to make anything work, right? If you don't have a commercial partner in the media business, then your amazing production is dead in the water, right? How much actual support have you had?

Emile YX?: A few.

Janine Blaq Pearl: We had actual support when it was funded and supported internationally. We were running it in theatre spaces like the Baxter and Artscape and then also in Holland. We did a tour there for about a month, at like many theatres there, so once you have the funding and there's a good team of management and there's, you know…it's pushed from a different angle, then it goes. The challenge is when the funding's not there, you know? And the significant thing with *Afrikaaps* is, it's beyond waiting on funding and media support. So, when there's productions running, just like anything, any festival, any event, or big production and the director or management got to secure support financially to keep things going, to pay a PR person, etc., then it's there. It happens. It's like booming. You're on all the mainstream channels and newspapers, etc. And so then when that's not there, now what? You know? And so we've really been challenged with that same fact, and, and it's difficult when you, you're artists. We're a collective of artists, you know? Independent artists and so it becomes difficult without all of that, to still keep your passion and YOU going, because my language is me, you know? So I can't separate that and I can't suddenly say, *'Okay, daas 'ie mee geld 'ie, os het 'ie mee' 'n massive budget om te gan toer die en groot sound en alie resources wat ons need om op so 'n kind of stage 'n production te kan doen in die kind of space, so wanne daai op is, you know, uhm, dan moen os ankap.'* [Okay, there's no more money left, we don't have a massive budget anymore to tour or have great sound and all the resources we need to stage the production in the kind of space, so when that is finished, you know, then we need to move on.] Because I can't be defined by that, and that's the beauty I think of what we ARE doing, and going to the next question is like what we did when we toured this beyond *Afrikaaps* being on stages, etc., on big stages, we took…like Emile said, this information and we called it Afrikaaps and pride-building talk, you know, and screening sessions, and we took it to schools. We made contact with schools. We put it out there. Schools contacted us, saying 'please come to us. We want to have you do this'. And, *in 'ie van* [in the van] – add – *gooi petrol geld* [pool together petrol money], you know? Fuel *geld* [money] together. Some schools offered to give us a donation for our fuel, which was super. And the value of what the information…you just can't put a price tag on, you know? We can't put a price tag on, so yes, there's levels and times where you can be like, 'Okay, *die's my art. Awe. Die's my fee'* [this is my art. Cool. This is my fee]. And we all do that. And then there's levels where you continue to do the work, and you, it's your passion. It drives what comes next, the next big project, but it doesn't mean the work stops, you know, so, um, we still doing it. We still doing it. And we do it through all our other various projects. Like I say, Afrikaaps is me. It's the language I…*dissie taal wat ek in droom, die taal wat ek in sing, die taal wat ek in poetry doen, die taal wat ek vi' my kind sing an 'ie slap. So is ek,* you know, *so ek kan 'ie sê, 'Okay, is 'n project en daa's geld in…nou gebeur 'it' nie.'* It still happens. *Dit gebeur aneen.* [It's the language I dream in, the language I sing in, the language that I perform poetry in, the language with which I sing my child to sleep. That's how I am…I can't say, 'Okay, it's a project and there's money in it…now it doesn't happen'…It happens.] [laughing]

B-boy Mouse: Okay. When *Afrikaaps* came to my school, it was, I had the reaction I got from Emile explaining about the Boesman. When *Afrikaaps* implemented that information in my school, I had at the time, I was, I was in matric, ja, and what I knew about myself was very little because school didn't like teach me anything about myself, and all I knew was, 'Okay I'm from Lavender Hill'…The stereotypes and the negative connotations that we know about Lavender Hill, I absorbed it, basically. And I thought that that was all of who I am, and that defined me, okay. And then *Afrikaaps* came to my school and actually promoted something different about me. Something more positive. Something more, that I can be proud of, and, since that day, I've been smiling ever since…

[laughter]

B-boy Mouse: Still smiling.

Janine Blaq Pearl: And he speaks much more than he used to. I was shocked.

B-boy Mouse: I was so quiet because I was afraid of speaking like just my normal language of Kaaps. And after just understanding the concept that they tried to pass on to…it basically helped me get hope for myself. I realised, 'Okay. Stefan, if you wanna do this then like, okay, you can't be, you can't uh do what you've always been doing, or do. Accept that the negativity in your life, okay, all your life you've been paralysing yourself by taking in, okay, all of these negative things that, that's been posted on our poles, that "you are this, you are that", so "Okay Stefan. Forget about this. Don't paralyse yourself anymore. Don't paralyse your view of yourself. Don't paralyse – whatever idea that you have of yourself, you can do it. Implement it".' And that's why, ja, I thank Afrikaaps for doing that. And then after school, I, because school didn't let me know that I was doing the wrong subjects, I wanted to become an architect, and then, when I went to, uh, what was it called? Uh, UCT?

[laughter]

B-boy Mouse: Ja, and then okay they said, 'Okay, Stefan. You were doing the wrong subjects.' What else? What now? And at the time, I was close with Heal the Hood. So I've been, since I was about 16, I've been part of the Heal the Hood…b-boy…and luckily I knew Emile, and Emile had this idea of, 'Okay. So we don't know what you want to do NOW. Why don't we create a group called Mixed Mense, and like this is a way for you to survive from your art, your talent.' And, um, Emile would explain…

[laughter]

Emile YX?: *Naai, kyk hie die's baie praat vi die man, my bru.* [Nah, look here this is a lot of talking for this man, my brother.] B-boy Mouse…

Janine Blaq Pearl: *Julle wiet 'ie. Julle wiet 'ie.* [You don't know. You don't know.]

Emile YX?: *Kêrk muis my bra* [Church mouse my brother]. *Hy praat 'ie baie nie* [He doesn't speak a lot]. Yoh. Now we…the thing about us going to these schools stuck in my mind the whole time. Like, 'Damn!' You know, there's such a need, and so for like four years we put into effect a practical Hip Hop school. So not only like the b-boying, but for them to, when they were breakdancing, they also like say, 'Check here, this is connected to our ancestry. Like, if we don't all clap in the circle, then the *ou* in the middle will feel like, '*Jarre* [damn] my bru, nobody's supporting me.' So the ENTIRE circle was about the education…and they would travel with me to the reality of what a lot of young people that, 'Ja, we gonna be famous now we hanging out with the *bra* with the big hair.' *Kaantie, is 'n struggle, my bru* [Alas, it's a struggle my brother].

[laughter]

Emile YX?: I told them that from the get go, 'Check here, this is the reality of what's it's really like being an artist, you know. Like you're gonna get paid sometimes…don't blow it all in one place. Save your money.' But it was, instead of speaking, it was more powerful for me to just take them along. Wherever we went and did shows they got to see…like I think it was the second or third year? We got to travel to Washington DC to perform at the Kennedy Centre, and the whole time I'm telling them, '*Naai, kyk hie,*' [No, look here] it isn't so *kwaai* [cool] there in the US. You only think it's *kwaai. Daai mense is deurie wind deur my bru. But yous are kwaai.*

Yous are kwaai.' [You only think it's cool. Those people are trouble my brother. But you are cool. You are cool.] And only when a *bra* at the Kennedy Centre told them that they were *kwaai*, THEN they believed THAT *bra jong* [man]…

[laughter]

Emile YX?: I was like, '*Jarre, ouens*' [Damn, guys] and then they…it was deep *ne*?

B-boy Mouse: Ja, it's deep. It's like if apartheid was like a movie, then…then my role in the movie would be basically the sad guy, you know? Ja. So, that's what I grew up with. So that's the idea of myself. So obviously in everything else I would do like, 'No, I'm not that *kwaai*.' Until I had to go to the US and this old guy told me like, 'Yoh, it's been so long, and I haven't seen this, like a good-quality performance like this in years,' and I'm like, 'Oh, wow, *so os IS rerig so kwaai*' [so we really are that cool].

[laughter]

B-boy Mouse: And that also…we basically followed the American way of…because America right, they were the first ones to promote like b-boying and things like that, so…I thought, 'Okay, since America is doing it, maybe I should do it THAT way.' And then Emile always like, *'Naai my bru, jy's van 'ie Kaap. Jy's van 'ie, daa's klomp diverse cultures hie' van jouself, wat jy kan…Incorporate goetes like daai man, dan represent jy jouself daaso. Dan represent jy nie 'n copy van wat hulle kla het 'ie. Dan gat hulle mos vi' jou invite wee, "Ko' wee' na os toe." Diesele ding soes eke: ek en my anne tjommie van Lavender Hill, o's het nou beginner, uhm, like uh Zulu gemix met uh b-boy'ing en Pantsula gemix met b-boying, en al die diverse cultures van, van hie', wat o's het hie' en toe het ek nou ge…alles in een ge-embrace en yoh ons was so amazing daa gewies dat die mense os gevra het om workshops te doen en toe…* [No my brother, you're from the Cape. You're from, there's diverse cultures here about you that you can…Incorporate things like that man, then you represent yourself there. Then you don't represent a copy that they already have. Then they will invite you again, 'Come to us again.' The same thing that I did: I and my other friend from Lavender Hill, we began to incorporate like Zulu mixes with the b-boying and Pantsula and all the diverse cultures from here. We embraced everything. We were so amazing there that they asked us to do workshops and then…]

Emile YX?: *Ja hulle gee mos dollars my bru*. [Yes, they give dollars my brother.]

[laughter]

B-boy Mouse: And the funny thing is, we don't give value to that, but in the US, it's mind-blowing. You know. Yoh. *Ons gee nie value na onse self en goetes nie. Daai's 'ie main lesson wat ek gelee' het.* [We don't give value to our self and things. That's the main lesson I learned.] Like yoh, value yourself, compile your own material…that way you create like a market and things and then you don't need to copy other people…

[applause]

B-boy Mouse: …own stream, our roots, our tree…sent out to that stream, and then we have our own like *appeltjies* [apples] and that's the main thing also. We have to support *appeltjies* and *goetes* [things]. We have books here for R200…

[laughter and applause]

Emile YX?: *Daa's 'it ja. Plug somma daai appels* brother. [That's it yes. Plug those apples for sale brother.]

B-boy Mouse: We have to support from here. We have to support things that's from here.

[laughter]

Emile YX?: Maybe a quick clip. Like the first thing…because they were so quiet. The first task I gave them was to write a song…Coming from a dance background, there's so many times I wanted to say like what I'm feeling and thinking, and you like, '*Naai, 'is orrait* [Nah, it's alright]. Someone with a *kwaai* [cool] accent would be able to say it better than me.' And so…that was the first thing, to like write a song, and the song that we first did was called '*Ek Leer vir Jou*' [I Teach You]. It's about the experience of them coming to the first class…because it's easy to write what you know. Can you play a small *stukkie* [sample] from that? Ja, 'Ek Leer vir Jou.' You can stop it there, it's cool.

[applause]

Emile YX?: So, ja, so there was like a…trying to create a…the education system outside of the education system, you know? And I mean initially there were four guys in the crew. I tried to…all the way through, from the get go…I promised we'd create a music video and get to the studio to record. You'd tour and travel and get to see the country and hopefully even overseas. All those things to date have become a reality, you know, and like for me, this was in my capability, but at the same time I didn't wanna promise them like stuff that I can't do for them…and then also for them to be honest about, 'Can you like – can you really make a living?' And a lot of the other guys were like, '*Naai my bru. Die is te hard*' [Nah my brother. This is too hard]. You know. Too much work and so they left and did what they wanted to do. And I mean he works with Heal the Hood at the moment and earns his salary through the organisation.

Adam Haupt: And at this point…Let's talk about Heal the Hood. Shaquile, I know you've been waiting a LONG time, patiently.

Shaquile: It's cool.

Adam Haupt: So what does Heal the Hood do?

Shaquile: Heal the Hood is comprised of six individuals, including Emile, myself, Stefan, Tanswell, Andre and Nicole. What we do is, in a nutshell, we utilise the elements of Hip Hop to bring forth change among youth. Looking at healing their heads as well as changing minds, changes actions. With that approach we look at different ways where we can firstly activate them through the performances, and then not just show them what is currently available, what they see on television, because that is the, the tool which is used to brainwash the base, the general populace. Coupled with that and what is in the school syllabus currently, is that kids have no sense of identity. I see Kurt's, your post in terms of what is happening on the educational front as a teacher, and what we try and do is, we offer an alternative, knowledge transfer through skills but giving them the real realities. Giving them basically the red or blue pill from *The Matrix*.

[laughter]

Emile YX?: Yoh heavy!

Shaquile: So…

Emile YX?: To quote an American movie…

Shaquile: Ja, to quote an American movie.

[laughter]

Shaquile: Ja, apologies for my voice or my accent. This is used to ACCESS the funding.

[laughter]

Emile YX?: The funding guy. When he speaks on the phone, you're like, 'What the hell?'

Shaquile: That is a deep-rooted thing in terms of being able to code-switch from when I go to the *jaart* [yard] and speak to my *brasse* [brothers] and have a couple of beers to, 'Hi. This is Shaquile. Give me your money.'

[laughter]

Shaquile: And this…

Emile YX?: …*Jy gee jou* game *weg, my bru.* [You're giving your game away, my brother.]

Shaquile: Unfortunately, ja. That is the game we have to play and…but for now, what we want to do is, we wanna use methods which will make kids feel proud of who they are, where they come from, telling their stories, giving them history and a self. A sense of self-worth and self-love. Whether you are African or Cape coloured, or white, whoever you are, your story has not been told. You've been given a version which suits the masters in control. So WE are here to come and tell you, you DON'T have to work within the system. There's no need, that capitalism as a construct doesn't have to be there. There are ways we can coexist with the land, coexist with your fellow man, learning how to do things, and UNlearn things which have been forced down the throats of our forefathers.

Adam Haupt: So you basically…you use performing and creative arts, right?

Shaquile: Ja.

MAK1ONE AT WORK, 2009 | Source: Heal the Hood

Adam Haupt: And you run events like Hip Hop Indaba, African Battle Cry?

Shaquile: Ja.

Adam Haupt: Tell us, how does it work? You organise events. You've got dancers, you've got MCs. You've got all sorts of people coming together, performing elements of Hip Hop. How do you…how do you inject counterpropaganda?

Emile YX?: Most people when they look at what we do, they associate it with dance. Because that's just…like that's the background of what we come from. But like I was saying with Stefan and the other guys, everything about the dance, the circle, the clapping the hands, the connection to who we are historically, you know, it's right there. If we just be quiet for a moment and actually listen to our history, or watch, they'll be able to see, you know? And so we try and create those spaces where people can be quiet for a moment. And it's not very popular. Like a lot of guys, I mean I, I remember saying online one day like my B in b-boy is for Boesman and yoh! *Ouens* were like, '*Naai*, Emile. *Naai*. It's for break and for the break in, in the…'

Adam Haupt: …The BRONX.

Emile YX?: Ja, you know you gotta be…stick to the truth, you know? And it was, it was quite a eye-opener, you know. And so it's, there's different spaces. Like even in the graffiti world, like with Falko or with Mak1One. I mean Mak1One has sort of embraced the whole history of who he is, and even Falko recently went to go and paint with some Bushmen out in the Kalahari, you know? And so there is a initial resistance, but I think, *soes hulle sê* [like they say], '*Kroes ko' altyd trug. Boesman gat jou vind. Jy ka' ma' wegstiek my bru. Hy gat jou vind*' [Curly hair will come back. Bushman will find you. You can hide my brother. He will find you]. That information will find you. It's just the nature of…And so I think with the work that we're doing now…at the moment we're in the schools, we're in eight schools and communities. And so we've given the kids this information. Plus, we're also giving them practical outcomes. You know like, write your rhyme, we organise to record it, we give you a copy, you Bluetooth it to your *brasse* [brothers], we make a music video of that, and you…and you go onto YouTube and that was the illusion of like fame. Pop idol crap. And then they see themselves for the first time. They see their communities for the first time. They rap and speak the way they do on the song and you give that same effect that Afrikaaps had on US to the kids in the community.

CHAPTER 10.
HIP HOP AS A VALORISING PRACTICE

ALETTE SCHOON (RHODES UNIVERSITY)

During the course of my PhD examining the use of digital technology by local Hip Hop artists, I spent a significant period of 2014 and the following year doing in-depth interviews with Hip Hop heads, predominantly young men in their teens and twenties, in the township areas of Makhanda (previously known as Grahamstown). I was struck not only by how the local Hip Hop culture promotes digital skills amongst such marginalised youth, but also by how Hip Hop allows youngsters to reconstruct themselves as people who have value. For these young people, Hip Hop is a valorising practice that recognises their humanity and their right to a voice even though they may be poor, black and unemployed. Here, Hip Hop is defined as the opposite of gossip. By gossip, Hip Hop artists mean public comments related to someone's likelihood of failing in terms of their current efforts. Such comments might be made directly to the individual concerned, to the person's friends or, particularly, to their girlfriend. Young men I interviewed spoke passionately about how disempowering it is if people look down on you, dismissing your hopes – this is frequently the topic of Hip Hop songs. In Azlan's song 'Don't Give Up', he raps about a conversation with his mother, who warns him about false friends and that he should ignore the words and laughter of those who want to see him fail in life. His lyrics illustrate how incredibly emotionally and psychologically debilitating such discourses of failure are. They are also disciplinary discourses that stop people from attempting to do anything to change their situation and, indeed, to step away from nihilistic behaviour. Gossip can also be understood as a disciplinary discourse directed particularly at those who seem to be achieving something in their lives. For Gato, the competition for success in the community can be explained in terms of a zero-sum economy, where you have to ensure others fail so that you can succeed.

Basically in die community as jy like iets goed doen en like iets achieve en jy's
oppad om like ver uit te kom dan sal mense jou altyd afdruk instead of om
jou die benefit of die doubt te gee om jou 'n push te gee sal hulle nou altyd
afdruk. Hoekom? Ons lewe in 'n lokasie in waar die een nie wil die ander een
se sukses sien nie. Die een wil die ander ene afdruk. So gaan dit aan. Van die
een se downfall wil die ander een sy achievement maak, so gaan dit aan.

(Basically in the community if you do something good and you achieve
something and you're on your way to get ahead people will drag you down
instead of giving you the benefit of the doubt or push you forwards; they will
always drag you down. Why? We live in a township where the one does not
want to recognise the other's success. The one wants to drag down the other.
So it continues. From the one person's downfall the other wants to make a
success, that's what happens.)

Such jealousy and envy are not just words – they lead to resentment and emotional distress that make young people give up on their dreams or isolate themselves from others, and sometimes they have actual violent consequences. During the course of this study, a pantsula dancer who had appeared on a television show, and who was a good friend of many of the Hip Hop artists who participated in the study, was stabbed to death. Words, one of the participants, comments:

Like a week ago we had to bury one of the kids that got stabbed there. And he
was doing art and he was singing and dancing on the Fingo Festival. uRocky –
so he got stabbed by one of the kids...they know each other; it was not as if it
was strangers. As a matter of jealousy, or it was a matter of not understanding.

One needs to contextualise such gossip, jealousy and envy within the precarious conditions of life for young people in the townships of Makhanda: a constant struggle for survival, the unpredictability of life, everyday crime, substance abuse and tensions related to material success.

HANGING ONTO HOPE IN THE CONTEXT OF TOWNSHIP LIFE

The rap track 'Imizamo', written by Ako and Black Magic, summarises many of the problems these young people face. Hip Hop artists translate the Xhosa word *imizamo* as meaning either 'making many efforts to achieve something' or as 'hustling'. In this song, a Hip Hop artist reflects back on the troubles of his life, of going hungry every day, being constantly mocked by others in the community, and never being able hold onto a job. It tells the story of feeling enslaved at school, being part of a generation that waited for things that would never happen, and so losing hope and giving up. Desperation drives him to beg for money from white people, only to be robbed of it by thugs on the way home at the railway line. Witchcraft and the mockery of others block his way. However, he holds onto hope and walks the narrow path of rightful action, thanks to music. This song epitomises the frustrations of young people here, particularly in the refrain *Ndakwiqela ela lilindu kuza kukanxele* (I was part of a group waiting for things that would never happen), illustrating the despair of a generation that grew up under the promise of democracy but that finds itself scrambling for a piece of the little there is going around. In this climate of desperation, what characterises the space of the township is the unpredictability of everyday life.

This perpetual sense of chaos results in the township being a very difficult place in which to create a stable home, making it hard for residents to have some sense of ontological security. In cities throughout South Africa, de-industrialisation has meant the disappearance of the power of the working class, especially that of young people, with the Makhanda township youth now more commonly resembling Wacquant's (2007) precariat than a working-class proletariat (Bank 2011). In the absence of jobs, the Hip Hop artists in this study spend their time 'hustling' (Venkatesh 2002; Wacquant 1998), a practice that they don't associate with crime, but rather with engaging in great effort to charm and persuade people in their social network to support them.

As with Anderson's (1994) ghetto, this is a space where the moral value of the street is focused on survival, and young people are forced to adopt a culture that acknowledges the power of the streets and its nihilist culture. When Azlan was in high school, he was one of a few boys who took his studies seriously. However, because it was mostly girls who spent a lot of time doing schoolwork and studying – and who passed each year – he found himself spending a lot of time with them, as did the other boys who were serious about their work. Like Willis's (1981) ear'oles, studious boys like Azlan were taunted by the other boys, who questioned their masculinity.

In the song 'Back to School', the Imin'esidenge crew implore young men to stay in school, to ignore jealous neighbours and those who tell them to be a 'boss' or be cool, and instead to listen to their future and return to the classroom. This song reflects the everyday reality of young people in Makhanda's townships, where going to school is labelled as uncool and, especially if you are older than the others, you are criticised and mocked. Such labelling is also evident among older young men after school, where masculinity is associated with working-class attributes of toughness, as Ithala'lenyani explains:

> It happens a lot…*Ei, uzimzumUmhlungu…*you wanna
> be a white person…If you are clean, ja, it's gay tendencies. Or, they will think
> that you are soft. Ja. So, if you are a man you must be in the overall, you must
> be dirty, you must work hard in the construction. To prove that you are a man
> you must work hard, you must smoke, you must drink…yeah and you must
> sleep around to prove your manhood.

Here the reproduction of class is reinforced through gender policing (Ortner 2006; Willis 1981), preventing young people from attempting social mobility and expelling those who do from the community of acceptable masculinities. What is ironic is that the social structure of a working-class labour market has disappeared, so that toughness and being comfortable with dirt no longer serve any purpose for the younger generation in terms of socialising them for future jobs. In the South African context, where race is conflated with class due to centuries of racial oppression, any attempt at social mobility is seen as selling out your blackness and assuming a white identity. This does not necessarily even mean actual social mobility, but merely adopting a habitus that does not align with nihilism, but is attuned to a different future. Zion Eyes describes the intense frustration that out-of-school unemployed young men experience in the boredom and dead-end of nihilistic routines to get through the day, until the tension becomes so much that they may have violent outbursts in moments of mental instability:

> Because it's like facing the same chain every year – you are not working,
> you are at home, you are around the community, you go back and smoke,
> you end up every day doing the same thing. It's the same chain and it makes
> people mad, actually, frustrated and crazy. They do things now which are

not predicted. Very scary, actually. Like raping an old woman. It's a shock,

actually, how do you get into those thoughts? How did you get into that

feeling of doing that? How do you get into that feeling as a human being?

Of particular concern to Zion Eyes is that the young man in question, someone from his neighbourhood, somehow relinquished his humanity in his rage and frustration and raped a woman he should have cherished as an elder. Zion Eyes struggles to understand why politicians and the country at large cannot recognise the crisis the nation is in when such things can happen and be considered routine. It is as if politicians cannot see the terrible psychic damage this aimlessness and nihilism creates among young people and the effect it has on society. As a poet and Hip Hop artist, Zion Eyes has engaged in long conversations with such young people, sharing their stories in his lyrics and trying to get them to see the value in themselves, but sometimes their feelings about their failures in life are just too overwhelming. He explains:

'I don't care, even if I die,' it's those kind of feelings. When you start to think

like that, 'I don't care even if I die', then you are messed up, you need some

help. Because now you can do anything, because you think you can go to

prison, it doesn't matter, you can die, it doesn't matter, life does not mean

anything to you. So to me, it bothers me and I'm concerned about that.

Sennett and Cobb (1972) describe the feelings of deep hurt and the emotions of sacrifice and betrayal that are an inevitable product of a deeply unequal society, where people are not valued if they are not middle class. In South Africa in particular, with its long history of oppression, including slavery, colonialism and apartheid, black people were for centuries dehumanised as 'waste'. Now again, in the neoliberal era, the masses of black unemployed people are considered worthless (Mbembe 2011). In Makhanda, X feels that the need to blame someone in your own community is very much part of the psychology of oppression. People are still subject to the injuries of apartheid, and the need to blame those around you for the structural injustices you experience is what racism does to your sense of self.

You are told forever since you grow up, your parents were told they're

nothing. They're subjected to work in the garden, that's all they think about.

That's why it's easy for someone to come to the community to say – let's go march, or let's go burn the house that's next door, or let's say this person is against us. That's why rumour is easy to flourish, 'cause it gets to the hearts of the people who have low self-esteem.

Makhanda Hip Hop artists are acutely aware that the post-apartheid upward mobility of thousands of black South Africans into the middle class has passed them by. This has resulted in those who have succeeded expressing attitudes of disdain towards those who have not. Here, superiority and distinction are expressed through material goods such as fashion. According to uLizwe:

The richer people they also have tendency of looking down to other people. I don't want to say poor people but they look down on poor people the way they dress. So that's what I also said is also a classism, you know in the township.

It is the objects of fashion and consumer goods such as digital technology that classify a person as modern, successful and stylish. Such modern style can be summarised in one word: 'swagger'. Dezz and Snezz distance themselves from this, saying 'we don't do swagger'. They are perturbed by the value judgements such displays seem to be making about people too poor to afford these goods. They are particularly disturbed by the isis'kotane – a South African subculture where groups of young township men destroy their designer clothing in public as a sign of distinction. The literature (Howell & Vincent 2014) is just starting to document the isis'kotane's elaborate destruction of designer clothes by pouring liquids such as Ultramel custard or J&B whiskey onto them and then burning or ripping them apart. Despite the notion of 'swagger' being integral to commercial Hip Hop style through its fashion, jewellery and sports cars, Makhanda artists are very much against it. In their Hip Hop, they resist such discourses of distinction and class differentiation.

Hip Hop artists in Makhanda are very critical of the conspicuous consumption that is starting to characterise the town, as it has the rest of South Africa (Posel 2010). They stress the importance of liberating your mind instead of competing with your neighbour for the best sound system or flat screen TV. Many of the artists refuse to engage in such competitions around displays of consumption through purposefully wearing unconventional clothing and expressing their disdain for material things in a quasi-religious manner. One artist, Words, says:

So they accumulate all these things thinking those things are the solution.
But they not the solution those things because they're gonna add to the
problem. Because once you start accumulating, having all those materialistic
stuff, you are gonna have to start building walls because you're gonna have
to protect all that you have. But you can't. You can never protect anything.
What is here on earth will remain here on earth. But the only thing that you
need to protect is the soul and the mind.

While many Hip Hop artists find meaning in church membership, they do not, however, see politics as an affirming space. They cannot understand why political parties do not stand together to address the problems in the township. Some are concerned that municipal projects often do not take into account what is needed, and the local community is seldom consulted. The young people are all very conscious of their parents' struggle against apartheid. They feel that it is their duty to take this struggle forward but, more importantly, to take up their place in the new society. When this promise of transformation seems out of reach or to have passed them by, they feel like they are betraying their parents. The acute sense of personal responsibility and the lack of value young people experience on a daily basis are symptomatic of the post-apartheid neoliberal era, where everything is perceived in terms of individual ability and there is no space for a sense of collective good or for politics. According to X:

There is no political reason why we should care for each other. There is no
political reason to be educated. There's no political reason why we should
be united. The reason for us to be united is so that we don't kill each other,
that's the only reason. You know, we should be at peace, democracy –
they're not saying why. Why, the underlying things, you know. Twenty years of
democracy why we should celebrate.

While X acknowledges that South Africa has fundamentally shifted from the apartheid state and that this has created new possibilities that did not exist before, he is worried about the lingering mental damage that apartheid caused. He is particularly concerned about communities' lack of responsibility in challenging social ills or imagining a different type of society, and their perpetual dependence on officials and government. In essence, his complaint is related to the neoliberal condition of the 'end of history' (Fukuyama 1992), where there is no vision of a different future but instead an acceptance that things are no longer considered in terms of whether or not they are a public good, but simply in relation to their market value. In contrast, Hip Hop is often a practice of solidarity with others, a way of practising empathy. Azlan spoke at length about composing a song about young people who have ventured into crime, a song focused on understanding and coming up with solutions in the community.

> Like, I put myself in the shoes of someone else…like why he is doing this,
> and also turn it, like – the parents for the guys, like how they would support a
> guy to change it – like stop going into prison, again and again and again – like
> what he needs to do…or how he needs to be helped, like to be like a normal
> person, like me and you and someone else.

Azlan's composing of 'truth lyrics' is therefore a practice of empathy, where the artist suspends judgemental moral categories that circulate in the community – particularly amongst those who attempt respectability and see others as 'useless' – and tries to experience the world from the point of view of the other. Instead of seeing the world as the outcome of a struggle between morally superior and morally corrupt individuals, these Hip Hop artists recognise the importance of social circumstances and misfortunes and how these can change the options available to a person overnight. Azlan's belief that the gangsters could change if only one could unlock the key to their psychological injury evidences a sense of hope. Here in Makhanda, the experiences collected on the streets provide the basis for the 'advices' and the lyrics that provide guidelines for how to sustain your dignity and integrity in a difficult environment. In some ways, they are like a self-help guide to being a moral person in a society where the social fabric is torn apart. Hip Hop reaches out to everyone, believing in their ability to set aside the devaluing injuries of oppression in terms of race and class, and also expresses a sense of loyalty that distinguishes artists from those who have assimilated into the middle class and now consider themselves 'better' or who 'forgot where they came from'.

INTELLECTUALISM

Hip Hop provides a way of asserting an intellectual identity in the face of devaluing discourses that associate blackness in particular with physicality, sexuality and violence, and not the intellect. It is this attribute of intelligence which has historically been denied to black subjects since colonial times (McClintock 1995), and which has resulted in frequent attempts by black men to prove their intellect (Fanon 2008). Foregrounding the intellect instead of raw emotions is arguably an expression of control, of being able to hold it together while your sense of worth is destroyed by the dominant discourse. The Fingo Revolutionaries initiated a project in Makhanda in which Hip Hop artists visited schools and encouraged young people to read books about African history, use dictionaries to expand their vocabulary and write their own verses. This affected some young Hip Hop artists profoundly. Main Event, for example, started visiting the library on a regular basis and improved his English to such an extent that he started doing so well in school that other children asked him to complete their homework for them.

> **Main Event:** If you talk about consciousness you have to go to the library.
> And then have a card there, and then take books, go to your house…

> **Zion Eyes:** And share with other guys books.

> **Main Event:** We used to read like about the South African apartheid era, and
> then write verses about that, and have a talk about that. So that's where it
> came about, this consciousness, this type of style.

Here we see a new kind of masculinity arising, where toughness is associated with mental toughness, an eclectic knowledge and eagerness to learn.

AFRICANISING HIP HOP: CULTURE, LANGUAGE, BLACKNESS AND VALUE

Validating South African indigenous cultures, particularly black South African culture as opposed to American culture, is another way in which Hip Hop artists attribute value to their own experiences, and thus their sense of self-worth. Hip Hop artists recognise Hip Hop as emanating from ancient African cultural forms. However, simply recognising this while continuing to copy American Hip Hop forms is not acceptable to local Hip Hop heads. Azlan argues that because African culture travelled to America through slavery and transformed into Hip Hop – 'spicing up' African cultural forms in the process – in order for local Hip Hop to be truly authentic, it needs to align more with local culture rather than copying American Hip Hop.

It is for this reason that Makhanda Hip Hop heads are not particularly concerned about replicating specific genre features of global Hip Hop. Instead of mimicking the poses and gestures of international Hip Hop artists, local artists like Ako and Njilo, for example, incorporate the gestures and voice patterns of Xhosa *imbongi* poets into their rapping. In terms of clothing, Hip Hop artists also commonly wear traditional African clothing in their performances, or incorporate traditional instruments like the mbira. In Africanising Hip Hop, they are not merely localising it, but affirming the value of local customs. The general intellectual disposition also extends to a mastery of the isiXhosa language, so validating and celebrating its speakers and their rich heritage. Hip Hop artists research old figures of speech and words that have fallen into disuse in the township, and resuscitate them in their rhymes. Artists see it as their duty to revisit the colonial history of dictionary production in South Africa, and to particularly question Xhosa words derived from colonial languages.

Hip Hop artists in the so-called coloured area not only rap in Afrikaans, but frequently combine Afrikaans, English and isiXhosa in one track, so celebrating their multilingual capacity. Instead of considering themselves neither black enough nor white enough (Adhikari 2005), they are proud of having knowledge of 'many cultures'. DJ Kamma prides himself on his Eastern Cape Khoisan roots and traces integration in the Makhanda community back to the tradition of intermarriage between Xhosa and Khoisan royalty in precolonial times in the province. Many of the Hip Hop artists who live in the coloured area have also undergone the Xhosa initiation into manhood, and are scornful of the separation between Xhosa and coloured Hip Hop communities in Cape Town. Nova has visited Cape Town and regards the integration in the Makhanda Hip Hop community as a state of progress and superior social harmony akin to socialism.

> *Ons sê maar ons is sommer ahead of hulle, when it comes to socialism. Of saam werk. Samewerking. So is dit. Ons is like ahead, way ahead, want ons kan mekaar verstaan, maar cats van daai kant kan nie regtig mekaar verstaan nie…As ek kan Xhosa praat, kan ek easily blend met die ouens.*

> (We say we are ahead of them when it comes to socialism. Of working together. Cooperation. It is like so. We are like ahead, way ahead, because we can understand each other, but guys from that side can't really understand each other…if I can speak Xhosa, I can easily blend with the guys.)

Like the Hip Hop artists in Haupt's (2001) study, these artists embrace their blackness as their primary identity. However, unlike the Cape Town artists, this is expressed not only in a black identity, but also in terms of adopting language and traditional culture. Hip Hop artists in Makhanda often see traditional culture in terms of a spiritual dimension, relating their work to that of the traditional healer or the praise poet. Many of the artists refer to their tracks as having healing power, and consider their ability to rhyme as a gift from the ancestors.

INDIVIDUAL CREATIVITY AND ENTREPRENEURSHIP

Most of the Hip Hop heads in this study think of themselves as artists – as creative persons generally able to engage in a range of innovative activities. In claiming this identity, they both challenge and co-opt neoliberal discourses that situate the sole source of agency and innovation in the entrepreneur (Read 2009). They challenge these discourses as poor people by showing that innovation is not only situated among rich company owners, and that being an entrepreneur can be more broadly defined as running a survivalist micro business, or just having an attitude to future success. In this way, the definition of an entrepreneur is extended to include people who live precarious lives, or what Wacquant (2007) calls the precariat, and their everyday 'hustling'. Here they are clearly using neoliberal discourses to validate the struggles of poor people. However, in defining themselves as (aspirant) entrepreneurs, and defining their art not only as dedicated to their community and to transforming society but as integral to building their own brand, trademark and style towards achieving commercial success, they also take on board the ideas of neoliberalism and validate its focus on the power of the market and individuals working according to market forces. In this way Hip Hop in Makhanda, as in the rest of the world, is a cultural form that developed inside neoliberalism and is trying to adapt to its contradictions. Thoroughly disillusioned with the power of politics inside a neoliberal economic system, young people doubt the power of conventional politics to make any difference in their society. Oziris sees politicians as simply engaging in talk, manipulating people into believing promises they cannot keep. As one of the more successful Hip Hop artists – he established a small events company that markets artists at student events – Oziris sees his ability to give local Hip Hop artists a commercial opportunity as much more meaningful than mere political talk.

> Promises don't really come true when people just talk. Like if you do
> something about it that's when you change. And if you do something about
> it that's when you actually...cos the whole point of an entrepreneur is to be

> somebody who wants solutions for people. So you find solutions – at the
> same time you are creating employment. The same time you're taking people
> out of situations where they can help themselves to help other people.
> So you creating a change, really like…as far as activism goes [makes fist
> salute]…I'm not that kind of kid.

Many of the participants in this study set up small companies with Hip Hop artists as directors or created small non-governmental organisations. While several were indeed relatively successful and made some money selling designs or running projects, the vast majority, like Busta, mainly sat at home. They had done what they understood to be their side of the social bargain: stayed in school, remained on a 'narrow' moral path, worked hard to improve their skills and market themselves, but they saw very little pay-off for their efforts. With school results that offered very few options, no money to set up businesses or go to trade schools, they were essentially stuck. I believe that this really shows the failure of our society and that we owe it to these young people who are trying so hard to help them find a way not only to be symbolically valued in society, but also to find some way to earn a living. These Hip Hop artists are doing all they can to be agents for their own futures and the future of their societies. This is best explained in their understanding of the message of Black Consciousness, as elucidated by X:

> You know, we sit here and talk about Steve Biko…the message that he said
> to us was 'build what is broken'…So we are building a broken society and
> this is no joke.

CONCLUSION

We owe it to the next generation to try to meet them halfway and give them the respect to help 'build what is broken'. But what is it that is broken? What this chapter has shown is that inequality creates more than only material deprivation. Being the most unequal country in the world not only creates a generation of young people growing up with poorly resourced schools, and with little access to nutrition and opportunity – these inequalities also convey messages about people's humanity, dignity and value. They break young people symbolically, resulting in despair and nihilism, which can lead to violence and other destructive behaviour. Although people are sometimes able to recognise inequality as injustice, more frequently it is misrecognised and legitimised through discourses that Bourdieu (2003) describes as 'symbolic violence'. The symbolic violence that underpins South Africa's structural inequalities makes injustices and inequalities seem inevitable and acceptable. People are thus frequently portrayed as getting what they deserve. Colonialism justified the extreme exploitation of black people by equating blackness with brutality, lack of culture and human empathy and, through the imposition of colonial religion, language and education, made black persons complicit in accepting their dehumanisation (Oliphant 2008). Bourdieu (2003) and Sennett and Cobb (1972) show how class inequalities in Europe and the USA were often legitimised by representing working-class people as crude, vulgar and less worthy. Telzak's (2012, 2014)research in South Africa shows that even the black middle class now distinguishes itself from its poorer compatriots by emphasising their lack of effort or initiative. In this way, symbolic violence debases people and strips them of any worth, attributing their lot to a lack of merit. Hip Hop in Makhanda, which draws extensively on the intellectual tradition of Black Consciousness, can thus be understood as a project to reclaim dignity, and to attribute worth to the cultural and social life of township communities. It is a way of negating the symbolic violence or gossip that often hounds those who do not resign themselves to their lot. Instead, Hip Hop artists reclaim African cultural expressions, defying the colonial symbolic violence that dehumanised everything related to blackness. They reconceptualise themselves as artists and entrepreneurs, identities that are generally denied to those living precarious lives. Hip Hop here involves a process of conscientisation, that is, taking responsibility and taking charge of one's destiny (More 2008), thus reclaiming one's life, symbolic representation and sense of worth. In this sense, Hip Hop is a valorising practice that recognises the value, humanity and dignity of these young people in the face of great inequality and the symbolic violence that accompanies it.

TAG OF MAK1ONE | Source: Heal the Hood

MAK1ONE PAINTING | Source: Heal the Hood

CHAPTER 11.
HIP HOP NEVER SAVED MY LIFE, BUT IT CHANGED MY LIFE

KURT MINNAAR

WHEN THE BEAT CHANGES

Like most teachers entering the workplace for the first time, I was excited, hopeful and ready to change education. Little did I know that the education system would suffocate my creativity, limit my individuality and render my four-year BEd (specialisation maths and entrepreneurship) teacher training degree inadequate. Before I knew it, my spirit was sucked dry and my intention to make an impact in education vanished. I literally did not care about anything regarding school. I just wanted the school day to end so that I could get home and do as I pleased. At this point I did not see my Hip Hop lifestyle and knowledge as a tool to incorporate in my teaching and learning. I saw it as separate from my school career. It was about five years later that I realised these two worlds could become one and, when that happened, my entire teaching career and experience changed. In this chapter, I highlight some of the problems I encountered as a teacher. I discuss how I started seeing Hip Hop as a tool to bring into my classroom, along with its limitations. Lastly, I look at how I practically used Hip Hop in my classroom to solve problems and achieve my goals.

SOMEBODY SHOULD'VE TOLD ME IT WOULD BE LIKE THIS

My first few days before the learners arrived at school were an information overload: meetings on top of meetings and a long to-do list to get through before the learners arrived at school. I was completely overwhelmed and felt lost most of the time. Soon the learners entered my classroom and I battled. I struggled with discipline. The learners would not listen to me even though I had done everything I was taught to do during my studies. I kept learners in during break, wrote them up for detention, put them out of my classroom, called in the principal to address my classes, shouted and said things I never wanted to but nothing worked. I clearly remember arguing with one of my learners and he ended up telling me, 'Sir, your ma se poes.'

Another challenge was getting the learners to understand the work. They lacked the foundations to master the more complex work, which, I'm sure, frustrated them. I tried to go over the basics, but the curriculum is so packed that as a teacher you are stuck between a rock and a hard place. It's either you go over the basics and fill in the gap, knowing that you are not going to complete the curriculum, or you fly through the curriculum and complete it, knowing that the learners won't have understood most of the work. Also, when it came to teaching the content, I struggled to connect with the learners. For the most part, I used the prescribed textbook but the examples in the textbook were wack and never got the learners or myself excited. I taught the content in a very traditional way, which only catered to the read–write learners and left the visual, kinaesthetic and auditory learners on the sidelines. In other words, I failed to engage the learners and teach in a way that served them all. What made things worse was my tiny prefab classroom that didn't look like much either inside or out. I put up a few posters, but they weren't really attractive and nice to look at. In fact, most teachers' classrooms were dull and some were completely bare. I was operating in a space that was uninviting and not nice to be in. Plus, the administration killed me: marking books and scripts, checking attendance and collecting monies, completing all the department forms, keeping track of all the learners in one extramural programme – the list goes on. This, coupled with a lack of support, is a horrible combination. I recall drawing up my first Grade 9 examination paper, which was not up to my head of department's standards. And instead of assisting me, he left me to figure it out for myself. Upon completion of that year's June exam, after finding out that my learners did not do too well, I learned that it was a norm and that teachers shouldn't feel too bad because that's just how it was. The learners are blamed regardless of the teachers' poor efforts and lack of urgency. Sadly, I started to hate teaching. I became the type of teacher I despised, the boring, rude type that did not care about the school or the learners.

I JUST WANT TO DANCE

On the flip side, while all of this was happening at school, I was truly enjoying my Hip Hop dance life and being part of the culture. I performed solo as 'Pinkurt' and was part of a Hip Hop dance crew called Release Dance Crew. We had an incredible work ethic, practised four to six days per week and pursued perfection in our routines. We were mostly

PART OF KURT'S INTERACTIVE MATH TEACHING METHOD | Source: Kurt

on time for practice and didn't mind practising till the early hours of the morning. Before we choreographed our routines, we would spend a week together working on concepts, selecting music and deciding on our dance attire. When we choreographed and practised, we were strict and put measures in place to ensure we knew every single move and that it was fire (extremely well rehearsed). If you did not meet the standard, we would put you out of the crew. In 2008 we became the first African dance crew to secure a place in the top 12 in the World Hip Hop International Dance competition in Las Vegas. Later on in my Hip Hop journey, I started learning how to capture dance using videography. And because I was a Hip Hop dancer myself, I understood how to capture dance, which many people get wrong. I then used this skill of videography to film people operating in the various elements of Hip Hop. I collaborated with the BeatBangaz to create video content for their scratch series. I filmed *Bo-Kaap* and *OWN 2015* for YoungstaCPT, worked with Emile YX? on a Khoisan short film while doing a short course at the School of Audio Engineering Music Institute, and captured graffiti artists and Hip Hop dancers in action.

THE APARTHEID OF MY BEING

At this point of my teaching career, and in the following few years, I never saw the link between my passion (Hip Hop life) and my teaching. The two existed simultaneously, but not as one. It was right in front of me, but I could not connect the dots. On the one hand, I was arriving late at school and leaving early, and on the other, I rocked up early at dance practice and didn't mind pushing till the early hours of the next morning. I couldn't keep my class quiet or hold their attention but when I hit the stage I could get 'oooohhhhh, ahhhhh' and control the crowd with a single dance move. I hated preparing for lessons and drawing up lesson plans, but I would take my time to create a dope dance piece or study the person I was to battle. I found learning new maths knowledge a painful experience, but would go through hell to learn a new dance move with a smile on my face. I failed to teach my content in a relevant way, but I could think up incredible dance moves and concepts that literally got audiences on their feet, going mad. I later learned that because my academic development ran parallel to my creative/Hip Hop development, I was empowered to think creatively.

LESSONS FROM THE HIP HOP CULTURE

A few years later, I got to the point where I had had enough of the same old, same old, and thought about why I had started teaching. I also wanted more of my Hip Hop life experience in my teaching and learning because it was really exciting compared to my school experience. I then decided to up my game and change things, and that's when I decided to bring my Hip Hop life and skills into my classroom. One of the most valuable lessons I learned from the Hip Hop culture is that you have to bring something new to the table. You have to be creative. In a Hip Hop dance battle, you cannot do the same move over and over and expect the same results. Yes, you can have your signature move, but it's not enough to take you to the top every single time. On the contrary, you have to showcase new moves or new ways of combining moves to get the crowd to throw their hands in the air and to gain their respect. I brought this way of thinking into my teaching practice, in that I had to bring in a new teaching style, new pedagogy, new materials and new ways to engage learners. In hindsight, this was the leading thought process that guided my teaching practice and what I created.

One of the first things I changed was the way we greeted. Instead of greeting the class in the traditional fashion, 'Good morning, class,' 'Good morning, sir,' I created a piece of Hip Hop choreography to charge things up. Once I completed it, I did the routine for the class and, because dance is my thing, I executed it perfectly. The class was entertained, shocked and excited to learn. It was as if my learners became my audience at a Hip Hop dance competition and then my students at a dance class. The best part was that all the learners paid attention and wanted to participate. When I greeted my learners in the traditional fashion, I had to ask them to stand up, to stop talking and so forth. Now when I entered the classroom, I counted the class in aloud, '5, 6 ,7, 8', and they would do their routine. As soon as the learners sat down, they were focused and ready to work.

This new Hip Hop dance greeting method gave me more control over the class and helped me with discipline. In addition, it made me realise that as a teacher I can change things. It's truly liberating. As teachers we can greet our learners in a different way, whether it's a Hip Hop dance routine or something else. Teachers can create a method that is linked to something their learners love. They can use greetings in the morning to learn sign language or something else which is completely out of the box. And doing something new boosts your confidence and makes you realise that you can add value and not just do what you were taught.

The next thing I looked at was helping my Grade 8 learners to learn their basics, which they should have mastered in primary school. And, because most of them listen to Hip Hop music, I started creating maths Hip Hop tracks. I focused on multiplication. I contacted my friends to produce beats. I then went to the studio and laid down the vocals. Then I came to class and asked my learners to say their multiples of seven and most of them could not go as far as seven times ten. They battled and paused for a long time before moving to the next multiple. Then I asked the kids to listen to the track a few times then rap along, as they always do with the music they listen to in their personal time. Within minutes, my kids knew their multiples of seven. I then moved from the actual track to playing the backing track and the kids rapped the multiples to it with ease. Then I had them go a cappella and it worked. I did not stop here – I used this method in addition to teaching them more ways to do their multiples. But I definitely started using this method when introducing multiples because it got the entire class involved and they loved it. It created a dope vibe and I could see how they enjoyed getting their multiples right. The class would rap together then we would go solo. Furthermore, I asked the class to create their own tracks and then encouraged them to use them in their other subjects. Plus, this better served the auditory learners, who often get sidelined in the traditional classroom set-up.

After Hip Hop artists create their tracks, they create music videos and that was my next step. We used the track and shot a dope Hip Hop dance video to it, which I used in class to introduce the multiples tracks. And music videos have a lot of power; I've sometimes hated a track, but then flipped and fallen in love with the very same track because of the music video. Also, adding the music video added a visual aspect to the lesson. In the multiples of seven video, the focus was a dancer but it also featured a BMXer, which meant that when learners worked on the multiples of seven, they related it to something cool because of the video and not to the boring, difficult side of maths that we are so used to. In short, we would start off watching the music video, then listen to the track, rap to it and then look at different methods of doing multiplication.

The last part of the process was choreographing the track. Once the kids had rapped to the track, we choreographed it. In doing this, I served the read–write, visual, kinaesthetic and auditory learners. I used one or two tracks for this part of the process, as choreographing them is extremely time-consuming and could be difficult for some educators. The learners can choreograph it as well but planning needs to be on point; it takes quite a bit of time to choreograph a one-minute dance piece. Also, you will find the uncommon learner who is not too excited about various parts of the lesson structure or method, and who will have to be encouraged to participate. Not all kids want to rap or dance, but the results are way better doing this than sticking to the traditional method and only serving the read–write learners.

In addition, redecorating my classroom and creating dope posters for it was really important. Most posters in classrooms are boring, especially maths posters. They are always shapes on paper – a pain to look at. They do not draw the learner in or make the class visually pleasing. Also, most of the posters do not give the learner any context and they cannot relate to them. In Hip Hop culture, designs and graffiti look dope. I've always loved graffiti. It has the ability to draw you in and make you stare at it for a while. And that's exactly what I wanted my posters to do. They had to have creative and artistic value yet be straight-up mathematical. I got a creative crew together: photographer and dancers. I asked the dancers to put their bodies in specific positions to represent certain angles and then had the photographer capture it. Once we completed that, the images were sent to a graphic designer to overlay the graphics. The posters came out perfectly.

When learners look at the posters, they actually trip (go crazy) on them long enough to get the concept. In creating these posters, I learned that attractive educational materials have the power to command attention, which in turn draws the learner in and helps with discipline. Also, because the image is beautifully designed, they remember it and the concept sticks. It makes the classroom look better and creates a gallery-like effect as well.

My next concept was creating a way to teach maths using purely Hip Hop-inspired dance moves – no talking and no writing. This was something I'd always wanted to do but I battled with getting it right. I then realised that I could create maths symbols and numbers using dance moves. So I created these maths symbols using Hip Hop-inspired dance, took pictures of them, made a number line and more designs.

So instead of writing 4 + 7 = 11 on the board, I danced it using the dance maths symbols and the kids answered the question in the same way. The best part is that it can be done to a beat, although using music can get tricky at times. This technique helps with fitness, coordination, focus and can be used alongside the traditional methods of teaching these concepts. Teachers are well aware that we have kinaesthetic learners, yet many do not know how to teach certain lessons, like addition and subtraction, using movement/dance. This method can be used to show teachers how it can be done, which will in turn help their practice and get them to think differently. Many do not use movement in the classroom and, when they do, it's separate from the topic at hand. This method, which is definitely pushing the envelope, is a combination of maths and dance and the two cannot be separated.

I hope to develop it further so that in the future we can dance more complex maths concepts. We can already do exponents using this method, which is freaking awesome. Moving forward, I would like to use the same approach, but with sound and touch. I've already connected with DJ Ready D on the sound project and look forward to implementing it once we successfully create the sound maths symbols.

Something I'm really inspired by is the energy and power of a dance cypher. When dancers are busy doing their thing, they are focused and not worried about the world around them. The individuals creating the circle, whether they are dancers or not, are fully committed to the dancer in the circle. Also, when you are watching, it makes you want to dance. You start tapping your foot or moving and the energy actually pulls you in. As a dancer watching, there are times I move away to execute a dance move myself and then come back to watch. If I can get my class to operate like this, we will win. Like the audience in the cypher, the kids would be focused, committed and want to participate. Also, the respect is incredible. When someone is in the cypher, the rest of the dancers wait till that dancer is done. They won't just barge in and do their own thing. It's much like waiting your turn to speak when someone else is speaking in the class.

What I've realised is that bringing Hip Hop culture into my teaching has forced me to stretch myself. Learning new skills and growing in one's teaching happens naturally when you want to bring something new to the teaching space. With every single idea I executed, I learned something new. From conversations with the incredible people I collaborate with, to researching things online, to watching people in class teach, I'm always learning. And this, in turn, has helped me remain a lifelong learner, which in my opinion is a characteristic of a great teacher and school leader.

ON TO THE NEXT MOVE

At the end of March 2016, I left the mainstream teaching profession. One of the reasons I left is because I wanted my methods of teaching to spread, and if I stayed in the classroom under the conditions I was working in, it definitely would not have happened. Also, I figured that I would be able to create new materials and methods more rapidly if I had way more free time. When you are working for the department (of education), time is in short supply. Since leaving, I have realised that the system changed me. I lost myself and got pieces of myself back when I started doing me. Three months after resigning, I felt like a new person and it's priceless. A new excitement and craziness came over me, which I'm guessing is who I was when I started teaching. I've been visiting schools a lot to train teachers and learners using my methods. If I had never left the system, I would not have had the opportunity to do this. It's not as if I was in a school where the leadership would have worked with me to spread this method in the school and then create a way for us to get it to other schools. Unfortunately, that's not how many schools work. Plus, I would like to believe that if we had been a tightly knit staff, we could have developed these methods together and tested them in our space, but colleagues were often just encouraged to focus on themselves.

During my sessions at the schools that I visit I'm always amazed at how open the staff are to learning what I have to offer. Yes, you get your odd teacher who is not keen, but that's to be expected. On the flip side, when it comes to the learners, they always love it and that's the magic. Seeing most of the kids eager to learn maths is incredible because most kids in South Africa frown upon the subject, and I don't blame them. Also, quite a few schools have invited me to give their learners motivational talks and advice on bullying. Motivational speaking is something I did in class all the time and I still love it. I've been invited to speak at educational summits all across the country, which is pretty awesome. I share with my audience the importance of connecting with the learners and building valuable relationships, how Hip Hop is a tool, a gateway and a lifestyle that we should incorporate in our practice. I'm always amazed to see how well they take to it. You can see that they never knew that Hip Hop can be used in the class and have a positive impact. When they see me rap the maths tracks live, they actually lose it and you can see the lights going on. The best part is when I teach them; they get the multiples quickly and really vibe to it. I'm sure many people I've addressed have frowned upon Hip Hop and the negative connotations attached to it. However, I can honestly say I never knew that teaching differently and just being my Hip Hop/creative self in the classroom would result in my story blowing up in the media, locally and internationally, and then have me travelling throughout the country doing what I love. And this experience in itself has taught me quite a bit. I was one who spoke about what we need to do as a country to change education, yet, in hindsight, I was operating from a very narrow-minded, one-province perspective. I've learned that Limpopo province is doing some great work in education despite the media always painting a negative picture. I've learned that the non-governmental organisation (NGO) sector has a lot of its own issues and not only government. I mean, you have people in the NGO sector leading programmes that have no experience in education. I have seen the corporates that provide social investment have their staff members involved in key educational decisions despite not having a clue about what's happening in the classroom.

Finally, I have learned that I am working within very difficult and challenging contexts, but I have also learned that we have no choice but to transform how we educate our youth. We must keep building the next generation and the next movement by using our methods.

CHAPTER 12.

PEDAGOGIES OF THE FORMERLY/ FORMALLY OPPRESSED: HIP HOP EDUCATION IN CAPE TOWN

MARLON SWAI (UNIVERSITY OF CAPE TOWN)

INTRODUCTION

I completed my elementary school education during apartheid and secondary school education afterwards, that is to say, after 1994, which marks the year after which we're supposed to say 'formerly' – formerly disadvantaged, formerly classified as, and, in light of *Pedagogy of the Oppressed* (Freire 1970), formerly oppressed. As many have stated in various ways, oppression did not stop in 1994 (Ariefdien & Abrahams 2006; Fataar 1997; Fiske & Ladd 2004; Haupt 2012). In this chapter's title, I play with the words *formerly* and *formally* while also making the obvious reference to Paulo Freire's *Pedagogy of the Oppressed*, originally published in 1968.[1] The English translation of Freire's book inspired educators, students and variations of critical pedagogy movements in many countries, including the Black Consciousness movement in South Africa and many Hip Hop-based education programmes around the world. As with formal and informal economies, there is a contentious relationship between formal and informal education. In many instances, education initiatives that are deemed informal, supplemental or alternative come to the rescue and make up for areas where the government falls short. In my case I can say that Hip Hop came to my rescue: it educated and re-educated me in ways that made me a functional adult and citizen in today's South Africa and beyond, and, ironically, it is Hip Hop that, in turn, led me to seek out tertiary education and a graduate programme that would allow me to research the effectiveness of Hip Hop as a pedagogical tool.

To me, Freire's concepts of 'reading the world' and his prescription for dialogic action are in one way or another pervasive in most of the Hip Hop that resonates with me, which, for brevity's sake,

---

1. The title of this chapter is a variation of the title of my PhD dissertation. See Swai (2017).

I will simply label as 'conscious Hip Hop'. It is a term that has by now lost much of its intended meaning due to its blurry definition and disagreement around what separates Hip Hop that promotes misogyny, racism and ignorance from Hip Hop that promotes critical self-awareness. At the risk of oversimplifying the issue, let us assume that conscious Hip Hop is the kind of Hip Hop that implicitly or explicitly adheres to the so-called fifth element of Hip Hop – Knowledge of Self. An intrinsic part of Knowledge of Self is knowledge about the world we inhabit and how this world shapes or affects the way we see and know ourselves. Conscious Hip Hop thus orients the individual's as well as the group's attention to the very fabric of systemic social injustice.

This chapter is taken from a larger project that traces the ways in which several Cape-based Hip Hop education practitioners work to cultivate critical consciousness in learners. Having provided this disclaimer for my use of the phrase 'conscious Hip Hop', I would simply like to show how Freire's concept of reading the world and dialogic action is evident in the work of two initiatives I worked with: ALKEMY, an acronym for Alternative Kerriculum Mentoring Youth, and the INKredibles writing workshops.

READING THE WORD AND THE WORLD

The English term 'conscientisation' originally derives from Frantz Fanon's (1967) adaptation of a French word, *conscienciser*, in his book *Black Skin, White Masks*. Freire eventually popularised the concept in his *Pedagogy of the Oppressed*, which was quite specific to the Brazilian context but included a theoretical framework around critical consciousness, conscientisation or *conscientização* (Portuguese), which is universally applicable to situations in which an individual obtains a comprehensive understanding of the world that allows for the discernment and uncovering of sociopolitical contradictions. Importantly, critical consciousness also entails translating this understanding into action against the oppressive aspects affecting one's life (Mustakova-Possardt 2003). As such, Freire found formal education systems in his context to be sorely lacking and his critiques thereof resonated widely, not least in South Africa during the 1970s and 1980s.

While some consider Hip Hop to be antidotal to formal education, most artists and programmes that I know of do not encourage youth to turn their backs on school. Take the late great Cape MC, Mr Devious aka Mario van Rooy (RIP), for example. To him, the cultivation of a sharp intellect was the primary way for a young man to survive the odds that are stacked against him. His songs are riddled with appeals to the youth to stay in school and pursue education in addition to taking a critical stance towards it. Consider these lyrics from his 2006 song 'Still Breathing':

> To the youth, stay in school keep on breathing
> Stay motivated, keep on believing
> Higher learning's how you reach your achievement

Devious recognised that 'school' is part of a larger world for which youth need navigation skills. Crouching at a street corner, surrounded by dreadlocked compatriots in his home township of Beacon Valley, the 2006 bio-pic *Mr Devious: My Life* shows him saying:

> We not good guys, we not bad guys
> We are somewhere in the middle
> We the balance between negative and positive
> We can switch at any moment
> So to maintain that balance we have to be conscious of what we see around us
> and how it affects us and our people

'To be conscious of what we see around us and how it affects us and our people' means to develop a certain literacy with which we can 'read the world' in order to become active agents within it. Freire's notion of 'reading the world' posits the world as text that can only be deciphered through a critical kind of literacy. A major 'literacy skill' is the ability to see one's self in (con)text while also activating one's agency to write and rewrite this text. Literacy thus means much more than the ability to read; it means learning to read *and* reading to learn. Literacy includes writing and rewriting, seeing, observing, but also interpreting and intervening. Literacy means access to the world in the first place; it fundamentally alters consciousness and irreversibly changes our ways of knowing, how we process information and how information processes us. Critical literacy complicates, but also demystifies, the power to write versus the power to read, and the power to produce versus the power to consume knowledge. Being 'conscious of what we see around us and how it affects us and our people' directly speaks to the difference between seeing versus comprehending how the seen affects us, shapes us, (in)forms us.

Critical literacy thus demands at least two levels of decoding. This decoding of multiple layers of reality is a skill that I distinctly learned through my engagement with Hip Hop as a youth. Then we all entered the age of mass mediation technologies. Now oral traditions have transcended and transmuted clan, village, skeem, kasi,[2] borough, hood or block in the context of endless mass-mediated sodalities.[3] We are now dealing with a global public literary environment that meshes so tightly the 'real' and the 'simulation' that the frequency, intensity and reach of the reading and writing practice of more and more individuals means we're increasingly spending time engaged in multiple and multimodal acts of literary production and consumption. Whether we're reading or writing pages (inked or Instagramed), listening to or conversing with sages (on stages or SoundCloud) or skimming or scribbling on walls (temple, toilet or timeline), we are producing knowledge even in the act of consuming it. Positioned between tough circumstances and the possibilities opened up by the pursuit of artistry, Mr Devious articulated the nuances involved in existing in the interstices between street life and poetry, between a life seemingly overdetermined by history and economics and the agency to change it, and he reinterpreted these nuances emphatically so his audience could understand the stakes.

DIALOGIC ACTION

Freire argued that through the process of communication about what we see and how we see, we produce and reproduce ourselves through being in perpetual dialogue with others. According to his theory on dialogic action, the educator must make a choice between dialogue and non-dialogue. For Freire, to choose dialogue is to endorse critical learning, and in order to do this, the educator must foster the circumstances for dialogue to occur that animate the learner's epistemological inquisitiveness. Hip Hop is increasingly being recognised as an indispensable tool for creating the kind of learning environments that stimulate learner curiosity and nurture pedagogies that are not only culturally responsive, but also culturally *sustaining* (Paris & Alim 2014; Petchauer 2009; Runell Hall 2011).

---

2. 'Skeem' and 'kasi' are distinctly South African terms which function in much the same way that the word 'hood' does in the US. They signify the discursive reclamation of geopolitical spaces and places inhabited by marginalised communities. Just like 'hood' is appropriated from the word 'neighbourhood', skeem has its origins in the notion of the housing scheme and kasi is from lokasie, the Afrikaans word for location, both designated for black and coloured communities under apartheid-era legislation.

3. For Arjun Appadurai (1996), the onset of the age of mass media has amplified the messiness that historical mass migrations have caused for the idea of nationhood and nationalist conceptions of citizenship. This messiness is represented by 'mass mediated sodalities', vast groups of people whose experiences of belonging and affiliation beyond the nation state are facilitated by mass media.

The objective of dialogic action is to constantly expose the truth through interrelating and interacting with others. Relatedly, Hip Hop education has emerged in the last two decades as a key strategy for bringing the world of the students into the classroom and for inspiring self-regulated learning outside of it. In his dialogic action theory, Freire emphasises the difference between dialogical actions, which stimulate empathy and insight, cultural invention and freedom, and non-dialogic actions, which negate dialogue, distort communication and replicate uneven power relations (Freire 1970). Of course, Hip Hop is equally capable of non-dialogic actions, but again and again it proves to be a set of practices that are endlessly generative for promoting dialogic action.

ALKEMY

ALKEMY was a programme hosted by Bush Radio between 2000 and 2007. Explicitly leaning on Freire's contributions, its aim was to train participants in actively reading and rewriting the world. ALKEMY used music, and Hip Hop in particular, as a means to facilitate the imagining and reimagining of social change. Through a series of seminar sessions, workshops, field trips and a mentorship component, the programme prepared youth for active participation at the civic level, but also for meta-cognitive and self-regulated learning. ALKEMY conscientised youth by proposing a critical lens through which they/we could deconstruct some of the information they/we were receiving in the media and their/our environment, including school.

There was a strong focus on developing close reading skills and producing both creative and analytical writing. The syllabus included texts like *Manufacturing Consent* (1988) by Edward S. Herman and Noam Chomsky, Paulo Freire's *Pedagogy of the Oppressed* (1970) and Frantz Fanon's *Black Skin, White Masks* (1967). A unique feature of ALKEMY's pedagogic approach was to elicit connections between Hip Hop albums and the readings. It so happens that several albums are named after texts, for example, *Things Fall Apart*, Chinua Achebe's famous novel, inspired the Philadelphia-based Roots crew's 1999 album of the same name. Chicago's Common called his album *Like Water for Chocolate* (2000) after Laura Esquivel's 1989 novel, while Bone Thugs 'n Harmony's *The Art of War* (1997) made reference to Sun Tzu's (2005) philosophical treatise. Tupac's *The Don Killuminati: The 7 Day Theory* invited listeners to find out more about *The Prince and Other Writings* by Niccolò Machiavelli (2003). ALKEMY took advantage of these book–music pairings in order to make reading more attractive to youth who were already hooked on the music. ALKEMY

PART TWO

B-GIRLS LOREN AND SHAMI | Source: Ference Isaacs

participants would read these rather advanced texts, discuss them in both facilitated and informal settings, and usually a writing module would bring exposure to a text full circle, for it is through writing that one deciphers text, extracts the lessons most applicable to one's own world, and it is through writing that one inscribes oneself into the world of the text, making its innermost insights knowable. A long-standing member remembers a part of the process:

> ALKEMY…provided us with tools that prepared
> and taught me to navigate the world around me. It
> was in those sessions that I first heard of agency…it never made sense until I
> started applying it to my world. (Oko Camngca interview, 2016)

Oko's twin brother Ade spoke in more explicit terms about the way in which the programme provided him with tools to read and reread:

> In retrospect I saw the programme as a 'legacy project' that was reminiscent of
> the [underground] youth
> struggle movements of the '70s and '80s. I saw this programme as a continuation
> of this [political activism] 'tradition' – because it challenged what I was taught by

providing an alternative narrative that was more plausible than what could be found in the prescribed literature of government schools; again, this doesn't mean all the literature was bad, but made me think why were we made to read *The Great Gatsby* instead of *Things Fall Apart* – subversive cultural domination at its best... (Ade Camngca interview, 2015)

During my participation in ALKEMY, as with my brief involvement with programmes like a series of comic-book writing workshops at the District Six Homecoming Centre, or the Young in Prison's lyric-writing workshop series or, most recently, the INKredibles workshops presented by the Stellenbosch Literacy Project (SLiP), and during numerous interviews and conversations, an underlying theme is the intention to produce a new generation of readers and writers of the world that operates in diverse and multimodal literary forms, including dance, visual arts and other forms of scholasticism. In order to address the deeply systemic problems facing their constituents, these programmes provide training in visual literacy, media literacy, political literacy, transcultural and diasporic literacy, and more. With this multisensory approach to 'reading the world', these projects not only complicate public discourse in a context of hegemonic media culture, but also provide their participants with the means to inscribe themselves into – i.e. reread and rewrite – the world.

The programme facilitators and developers of ALKEMY used the word 'conscientisation' in a direct nod to Freire's *Pedagogy of the Oppressed*. ALKEMY facilitators were both aware and mindful of Freire's (1970) 'banking concept' of education, which he used to critique how formal education treats learners like blank slates and empty vessels needing to be filled. Rather than recognising and building on students' prior knowledge, their life skills and their diverse interests and expertise outside the classroom, the banking model assumes that information can simply just be 'deposited'. Freire argued that the 'banking' approach to education will never 'propose to students that they can critically consider reality' (Freire 1970: 61).

INKREDIBLES

In 2011, three years after ALKEMY ended its official institutional run[4] at Bush Radio, Pieter Odendaal and Leon de Kock, two students in the English department at Stellenbosch University,

---

4. Unofficially means without the original institutional support of the radio station and NGO. However, ALKEMY members have continued to work together on various projects up until the present.

initiated the SLiP as an events and media platform 'to fast-track issues in South African literature and culture'.[5] Their project aimed to create public literary–cultural platforms, which they believed were essential to writers and performers on the 'creative edges of an emerging democracy', seeing themselves as stimulating spaces in which artists can serve as 'mirrors of society'.[6] In 2012 they were joined by Adrian 'Different' aka 'Diff' van Wyk and the vision began to gain traction, particularly with their launch of the InZync poetry sessions and the INKredibles youth poetry workshops.

> Our country has a proud history of using words to critique the status quo,
> to imagine new and more humane ways of living together. In a time where
> money and guns seem to hold sway over the future of our communities, we
> believe that words are the best and most powerful defence against corruption
> and violence. We believe that the poetic word emancipates and enlightens,
> that it dances on the tongues of the dispossessed, refusing to be silenced.[7]

I first met Odendaal and Diff in 2013 in Kalkfontein at Jethro Louw's holiday arts programme, which he hosted for about 50 to 60 primary school-aged children. I learned about SLiP and the InZync poetry sessions from my co-facilitators and became very interested in their work, especially because of the resemblance it seemed to bear to ALKEMY. SLiP has been very successful since its inception in 2011. It has developed three distinct branches/platforms. Firstly, it began as a website, SLiPnet.org, consisting of blog entries, audiovisual material and literary criticism, and continues to serve as a rich repository for translingual and transcultural literary production and appreciation. When Diff joined in 2012, his long wish to someday see 'the little student town of Stellenbosch be rocked by the beats and words of Hip Hop infused wordsmithery'[8] articulated powerfully with Odendaal's love for translation, and the collaboration resulted in the creation of SLiP's second core platform – a monthly poetry slam in Kayamandi,[9] now famously known as the InZync poetry sessions.

The logical next step for a group interested in garnishing stages for new literary voices would be

5. http://slipnet.co.za/about/
6. http://slipnet.co.za/about/
7. http://slipnet.co.za/view/community/
8. http://slipnet.co.za/about/
9. Kayamandi is a suburb of Stellenbosch in the Western Cape province of South Africa. The name means 'nice home' in the Xhosa language – from *khaya* meaning 'home' and *mnandi* meaning 'nice'. It was founded in the early 1950s as part of the apartheid regime's segregation policy.

to work with youth in a pedagogical setting. They set about offering community workshops in local schools, drawing in poets from the InZync sessions to mentor and teach writing skills. This was the missing puzzle piece to truly start to achieve their goal of fostering 'new conversations… across a diversity of cultures and languages, bridging gaps between academia and civil society, performance and publishing…'[10]

Chrystal Williams is one of the outstanding products of the InZync youth poetry workshops – the INKredibles – in Kayamandi. I first came across her on YouTube on a video of a live recording at one of the InZync events. She was captivating for the authority with which she spat in Afrikaaps and the maturity of her content and delivery at such an ostensibly young age. The video captured an INKredibles feature at the InZync session in September 2013 when she professed:

As ek soe skinner

Oorie Antieke Meneere

Met ereksies verleeders

Langer as sy top leeders se traane

Innie klinik's preek kamer

Of voor die uit heem se winkel baas[11]

(When I gossip like this

About the antique Sirs [male teachers]

With erections' pasts

Longer that his top student's tears

in the clinic's prayer room

or when I'm in front of the corner store boss)

By the time I was able to participate in an INKredibles workshop (2015), she had already passed through the programme and had gone on to complete two years of her law degree, but I was subsequently able to interview her and see her give a riveting performance at an InZync festival at the Fugard Theatre in early 2016. In 2012, when Chrystal Williams was in Grade 9, she was invited to take part in a series of poetry workshops hosted by some students

---

10. http://slipnet.co.za/about/
11. http://slipnet.co.za/view/inzync/inzync-poetry-session-27-sept-13-with-the-inkcredibles/

IMMORTAL STYLE VS HANDBREAKTURN | Source: Ference Isaacs

in the English department at Stellenbosch University at one of their high school outreach events. She remembers being sceptical at first because her experience of poetry at school was that it was 'boring'. But the fact that there was free food on offer and the charisma of the facilitator who did a presentation made her and a few friends curious. Diff was the facilitator who performed a repertoire during their school assembly, and what surprised her and piqued her interest was that he delivered his poetry in Afrikaaps. The defiance of this public act shook Chrystal who, up until that point, dared mostly only to speak '*suiwer*' (pure) Afrikaans. Noticing Williams's enthusiasm amongst her peers, Diff called her aside at one of the first sessions she attended and casually asked her how school was. A conversation ensued that would eventually lead to her joining Diff and Odendaal's breakaway project, the SLiP, and becoming one of its success stories. She remembers the encounter as such:

Na die eerste session het ek gecheck 'okay die bra's cool, hy's Afrikaaps, os gat mekaar lekker verstaan'. Ek het toe lateran besef that hulle nie a groot deel is van die klasse nie. Maar ek het toe altyt gegaan. Ennie poetry was nog altyt baie boring. Want ek het toe suiwer Afrikaans geskryf. Want niemand het vir my gese dat ek kan toe Afrikaaps skryfie.

(After the first session, I thought 'this bra's cool. He's Afrikaaps, we're going to understand each other nicely.' I realised later on that they [Van Wyk and Odendaal] were not a big part of the classes. But I still went. And the poetry was still boring. Because I wrote in pure Afrikaans at that time. Because nobody told me that I could write in Afrikaaps.) (Chrystal Williams interview, 2016)

Through SliPnet, Williams felt she had received permission to write in Afrikaaps, which was an act that caused a shift and transformation in her. As for the ALKEMY participants, being encouraged to read and write not only classic western texts, in resistive ways, but also to read and produce oral and written texts in their own vernaculars produced a powerful effect for Williams and others – they were empowered to name the world on their own terms. This resonates distinctly with another Freirean approach to literacy. For Freire, 'To exist, humanly, is to name the world, to change it. Once named, the world in its turn reappears to the namers as a problem and requires of them a new naming' (2000: 88).

CONCLUSION

This chapter investigated the extent of Freire's influence and relevance for Hip Hop-based programmes in Cape Town. It started by asking how various individuals, networks and programmes promote and inspire their participants to a critical 'reading of the world'. The two short case studies illustrated how various programmes nurture a new generation of readers and writers of the world in a spectrum of multimodal literary forms by providing a breadth of multisensory stimulation and training in critical thinking. The multiple literacies targeted here include transcultural and diasporic literacy, media literacy, visual literacy, political literacy and more. With this multisensory approach to 'reading the world', these projects provide their participants with the means to inscribe themselves into (reread and rewrite) the world.

The chapter also articulated Freire's concept of dialogue, which is contrary to what he named 'the banking system of education'. I showed how Hip Hop-inspired programming instantiates dialogic action on several levels. In the broader project, I discuss dialogue in its most literal occurrence, for example in the methods used during a workshop, and I also expand the notion of what dialogic action looks like in a cipha/cypher or when activists take advantage of interlinking networks of artists that organise across geopolitical borders.

In conclusion, one major takeaway from this chapter, especially in relation to themes discussed in the rest of the book, is this: the degree to which these programmes and the work of Mr Devious, for example, are able to activate a rereading of the world and dialogic action is directly related to the extent to which they move beyond culturally relevant pedagogy (which encourages educators to teach in ways that are relevant to students' cultural worlds) and into the realm of what Paris and Alim (2014) call 'culturally sustaining pedagogy'. The latter, simply put, reimagines schools as sites where the cultures, languages, literacies and lifeways of students are sustained as necessary goods unto themselves. After learning how to reread their worlds, these pedagogies equip students with tools and strategies to overcome and transform their conditions.

CT B-BOYS | Source: Ference Isaacs

CHAPTER 13.
HIP HOP ACTIVISM

HAKKIESDRAAD HARTMAN

My roeping as digter sien digkuns

(my calling as poet sees poetry)

As 'n verpligting in die wee van Mohammed en Christus

(as a priority in the ways of Mohammed and Christ)

'n Straat joernalis met beginsels wat dien as 'n spraakbuis

(a street journalist with principles that serve as a spokesperson)

vir sy gemeenskap in tye van teenstand

(for his community in times of hardship)

Met 'n waarheid woorde is kragtig

(truth be told words are powerful)

die toepaslike aanwending kan swakkes bemagtig

(the appropriate application can empower the weak)

Sienswyses verander, kwellinge behartig

(change points of view, address issues of concern)

so verantwoordelikheid op skrif en deur spraak bly 'n verwagting

(so responsibility on paper and through speech remains a necessity)

Wees 'n aanwins vir jou mense

(be an asset for your people)

'n Vakkeldraer vir beste wense en voorspoed in alle tye van teespoed

(a torch bearer/carrier of best wishes and good fortune in times of strife)

Maar ken jou perke binne die wette vir knegte wat veg vir reg en geregtigheid

(but know your boundaries within the laws for servants that fight rights and righteousness)

Verbreed jou kennis, bemoedig met erens en bearbei

(broaden your knowledge, motivate with urgency and cultivate)

slegs daai regte egte rymklets wat se

(only that real rap that says)

If you are good at something, never do it for free but do it to free your people!

LANGUAGE IN HIP HOP

I see language and Hip Hop in the same way I see education. Any individual reserves the right to be taught in a language that she or he wishes to be taught in. English is considered the international language but MCs from all countries are now performing and practising Hip Hop in their mother tongue. Languages are mashed up and variations of languages are being developed in the process, but it's been happening for centuries. Afrikaans is such a language. Elements of Afrikaans are already present in South Africa's other official languages as a result of contact. Individual language preferences and also certain languages are worming themselves into acceptance through the process of cross-pollination and language contact. Even though English might dominate the international music scene, foreign-language music has always had the potential and capacity to compete in an English-dominated market. We have examples in Pavarotti, Angélique Kidjo, Enya, Bjork, Marc Anthony, Celine Dion, MC Solaar, Die Antwoord, Mandoza and Brenda Fassie.

Afrikaans has exactly the same potential and even though it might not be welcomed by certain groups in South Africa, if the content of any song is inclusive and speaks beyond the borders of prejudice it can change the perception of how a language is viewed and understood. With the rich history of Afrikaans and all its contributors, it has forged elements to secure its future and, considering it will always be an evolving language, it will thus remain relevant. The manner in which Afrikaans lyricists present their subject matter will decide their lifespan as a relevant artist. I cannot remember who said it, but when I heard 'music is timeless when it is honest!' it dawned upon me: 'Truth is a presence that stays, BS [bullshit] a sensation that passes.'

MY INSPIRATION

Dr Zilla North, a medical doctor I met in 2014, is the curator and coordinator of National Science Week (NSW) George. One morning in August 2014, day one of NSW, I was addressing primary and high school pupils at the Botanical Gardens in George. I did the welcoming, included poetry and Hip Hop in my greeting, and explained that the host of Science Week, the NSW team, would be facilitating the course. Zilla approached me afterwards and said that she recognised the educational value and the weight of my Hip Hop-focused subject matter and further stated that what she had heard from me in my welcoming speech had broadened her understanding of Hip Hop. Thus, a friendship began.

Zilla, as she prefers I call her, without the doctor title, is a mother of two, a wife, a medical doctor at public hospitals and a community worker. She ensures that meaningful educational programmes about science are implemented in the community and at hospitals. She hustles sponsorships, donations and resources in her spare time. She is proactive and dedicated to creating a better world. She has a profound understanding of people, specifically brown people. She bends over backwards and figures out ways to accommodate our people's way of thinking. She is an educator through progressive and positive action and has zero tolerance for prejudice. She proved this when she severed ties with some white folk that said, to quote, 'transformation is happening too fast' – a remark pointing to brown people's involvement with Science Week. She ensures artists get paid and that people recognise our value and contributions towards education and society. I can say for a fact, without a shadow of a doubt, that she is a genuinely good person. But what steals my heart, and I say this with honesty, is that she loves my Hip Hop. Since meeting her, the amount I have learned from her has equipped me with so many tools to be a true and genuinely conscious MC and edutainer, stretching my experiences beyond the limits of Hip Hop.

Another influence in my life has been Estelle van Rooyen. She was a teacher at the high school I attended, George High, and after more than a decade retired early from teaching and became a librarian. During her time at the George Library and my involvement with a project there, we have grown in our professional relationship. She showed genuine interest in and fascination with the educational aspects of my Hip Hop and it is through conversations that I became aware of her love for the visual and performing arts. She plays a silver flute, the organ in church and her humbleness might hide what else she can play. She is part of a book club. She tutors English and prepares matriculants for their year-end exams. She is a wife with one daughter but is mother to many other children, an attribute she manifests through her actions. She is invested in positive action, with so much zest her aura cannot help but be infectious in a manner which only love can manifest. The total sum of her nurturing capacity is what made me – or should I say my conscience insisted – get her involved in Surge et Insta, a project under construction. Estelle inspires me and for a woman who bumps (plays) choir music, I never thought Hip Hop is the type of music she would listen to.

I am blessed with some exceptional friends, worthy of credit. Friends that motivate me, friends that ensure my attention remains vested in my intentions, friends with words of wisdom in times of hardship and friends with levels of interest that cultivate the growth of Hakkiesdraad Hartman. They are few. They are select. They are worthy of praise and they inspire me. It is this inspiration that allows me to script my thoughts into the words my material is weaved from. It is this inspiration that completes me as an artist, the inspiration that calibrates my balance and it is this inspiration I have an obligation to. Every craftsman needs a master; a partner to spar with and an authority that ensures you do your katas. I have that in these friends. Each One, Teach One. What we have learned from each other by teaching each other is to always remember the cardinal rules of Kung Fu, which is practice, preparation and endless repetition. But if there is a lesson you need to take from this paragraph, it's this: If you are surrounded by friends that bring out the best in you…dramatic pause…Brudder (*of is dit Bra-Duh* [or is it Bra-Duh]), *ek se vir jou* (I'm telling you): 'Inspiration for days!' So a special thanks to Reggie Wesso, Llewellyn Bruwer, Hershel Witbooi, Roual de Reuck, Marco and Lorette Gelderbloem, Warren Jacobs, Garold and Rowena Fouche, Elton Septoe, Fabian Meyer and Byron Botha. They kept me alive, sane and inspired enough to keep grinding for every centimetre, get over the advantage line, go down in the tackle, place the ball, spread it wide, skip pass, first out then a step inside, dummy pass and if you know anything about rugby, you guessed it, wait for it…I wanna play my Hip Hop like the All Blacks play rugby.

I am inspired by beats produced by Nahps, Rude Boi, Ludick, Che Monu, Lance Luger, Nino and Clint Miller. They have inspired all the music I have written thus far and they all have personality traits that are inspiring and worthy of praise. I dare not elaborate on their quality attributes just yet for their stories are still being written. However, for all the nosey people out there, just so you know, my indigenous DNA allows me to accurately smell rain coming, hours before the time, and it is this sense of smell I trust when I tell y'all, their futures are scented with the aroma of greatness.

I am also inspired by the groundbreaking work done by Prophets of da City in their construction of what is now blossoming South African Hip Hop. Every album from *Our World* to *Ghetto Code* was a module in the curriculum that taught Hakkiesdraad Hartman how to rap. The only other artist that has provided me with such educational extrasensory tutorials is KRS-One. Formerly known as a DJ, Grand Master Ready D aka X-plode (but you have to say 'X-plose', it's just Cape Flats phonetically correct), now he, I am telling you, is like my ultra-HERO. *Ga-niemand ka my stry nie!* (Nobody can argue with me!) He's got superpowers, I tell you, but formulating this theory with scientific accuracy might require a PhD in rocket science. 'How he earned the goenja (title) Grand Master' could be the title of my thesis. Somebody once suggested I write a book and I thought to myself: '*Hoor vir die bra!* [Listen to this brother!] A book? *Dus dan Grand Master Ready D my ou* [That is Grand Master Ready D my brother]. His technical skills alone would require an encyclopaedia series you imbecile.'

Other inspiring people are: Bruce MF (mother fucking) Lee magic. Ice MF Cube genius. Hansie Cronje and Herschelle Gibbs. The writing and delivery capacity of Damian Marley, including his humanitarian work; the performance savvy and talent of Michael Bublé; the lyrical skill level and progressive thinking of HemelBesem and Jitsvinger; the writing, the music, the being of Bob Marley, Kurt Cobain, Freddie Mercury, Sade, Michael Franks...On a storytelling tip, Kingsley Holgate and Tolla van der Merwe, hands down. The late Kotie Grove. He might be a sports commentator but he is like my favourite comedian. Ever heard of the 438 match, the greatest cricket game ever, between South Africa and Australia, played on 12 March 2006 at the new Wanderers Stadium, Johannesburg? Now get your hands on the Afrikaans commentary and hear Kotie Grove in action. The humour matched the intensity of the game. Ever since that day I have not heard spine chilling that funny and it wasn't even a joke. You go Kotie!

Then there is my Oupa, the late Oom Daantjie Hartman. Hartman is my real surname because to be a Hakkiesdraad you need to have a hart man...LOL! My Oupa is a legend. There is no title definitive enough to describe him because the word 'Oom' in Oom Daantjie alone carries more weight than Dr, Sir or Your Excellency, although the latter might work because he was an excellent grandfather. He's a classic man. That's my Oupa.

Lastly, I am inspired by typical Hip Hop style. Don't judge me, nuh. I would like to give a special SHOUT OUT to Nama Xam, Bradley Kanasashi, Jerome and Adele Rex, DJ Jeff FX, Tor-C, Rashid Kamalie, Ben 10, normaN$mily, Real Rozanno, YOMA, Die Hooflig, Roché Kester, Shirmoney Rhode, Gaireyah Fredericks, DJ Azuhl, Mak1One, Tribal Echo and Churchill Naude.

HAKKIESDRAAD HARTMAN, AFRICAN HIP HOP INDABA MC BATTLES, 2011 | Source: Ference Isaacs

YOUTH PROJECTS

Since 2014, I have been part of the Eden Knowledge Project, a group of people promoting mathematics and science in George and the Garden Route area. Every year we facilitate NSW in the first week in August. The programme is based on the international theme for science. In preparation for this, I write theme-related rhymes, chants and humour and perform it at the opening of each day of the week for the targeted schools. In 2015, I put together a 45-minute theatre production, performed at the George Arts Theatre for four nights during NSW. This production included a vocalist, a BMX trick artist, a visual artist and me, together with Hip Hop and poetry to illustrate the theme, International Year of Light. In 2016, the Eden Knowledge Project worked with the International Year of Sustainable Living company to improve the quality of life and work towards establishing a science centre in George that can facilitate weekly programmes and assist in developing maths and science in our communities, and broaden the scope of our yearly NSW.

I am also a Friend of the Library and make myself available to all George libraries during Library Week and/or to any other activities during the course of the year that promote reading and writing. One day I had an epiphany. I realised, 'Hakkies, if you wanna be a writer, you have to ensure people can read and have access to reading material, especially children.' I thought that that was not a bad idea. I thought that to myself and ever since then I have been a Friend of the Library. What does it mean to me to be a Friend of the Library? It means FREE education...you read me? You get access to free internet, membership and a free bookmark. Don't hand in your books late and don't come here with your Fees Must Fall *gedagtes* (ideas).

Every first Friday of the month, since September 2015, my team and I organise and host Expression Sessions George (ESG). This is a monthly platform to develop, promote and support local talent. We offer a space where artists from all creeds and genres can mingle and mix, present or show off talent and grow the art of live performance. I mentioned earlier that every craftsman needs a master, a partner to spar with and an authority to ensure you do your katas – voilà, ESG! ESG also stands for:

» Elevating Social Grades: If you consider yourself a respectable artist you must know your responsibilities towards your community. It's not about the old school or the new school; it's all about the schooling.

» Electromagnetic Science Gatherings: Birds of a feather flock together. Positive energy activates constant elevation. The magnetic flux is so much stronger, the power so much more electric when we are gathered in numbers. So if you are hoping to change the world, come let us be honest, you can't do it alone. It's not about me. It's not about you. It's about us.

» Extra Sensory Gateway: Sight, hearing, smell, feeling and taste are the senses allowing the experience of sensation. And believe you me, the talent is extraordinary, sensational and a gateway to experiences that stimulate all the senses at once. We call it: encounters of the sixth sense. The cliché says the proof is in the pudding, but we at ESG say it's in the tasting, because for starters we serve food for thought, a learning experience, the main course and reserved for dessert, Yummy Berry Juice. Kom proe net n bietjie. Plaaslik is smaaklik (Come taste just a little. Local is lekker).

At ESG we have a saying: Everybody wants to be a star. Welcome to the Galaxy! Every first Friday of the month we introduce a new chapter of *'n Duimgooier se gids tot die Sterrestelsel* (a hitch-hiker's guide to the Galaxy). It's almost like a lift club to stardom but you have to pay your dues and talent is the currency accepted. We don't have a grading system and, just for clarity, anyone from novice to professional is welcome. We expect everyone attending to listen without prejudice. You do not have to read between the lines but read the fine print. The terms and conditions that apply are R&D: *Respek en Dissipline* (Respect and Discipline), because to excel in anything discipline is required and to acquire discipline respect is mandatory.

Currently, I am working with George High School on a project called Surge et Insta, which means 'Arise and Shine' (*Styg uit en Skyn*), and that is exactly what we plan on doing. Surge et Insta is the school slogan, my personal motto and the name of the first single from my album *Die Riel Makhoi* – the song features the George High School choir. A music video is in production and together with the school choir it features drama, dance and art students from the school. I have also put together a Surge et Insta committee composed of ex-pupils.

CROSSING LANGUAGE AND RACIAL DIVIDES

Certain genres will always be classed as music from and for a certain racial group, but in the same breath, music in any language and from any cultural background has the potential to cross any racial or cultural boundary. Racial issues are a topic I find annoying, only because of the amount of mindless and senseless racism prevalent in our society. Here is da ting. If the individual takes the leap to cross language and racial divides, that individual is no longer part of the problem. *Ek mean ma* (I'm saying), solutions are the answers of problem solvers through formulae of resolve. But answers I should have, could have, would have are only useful to geniuses who rear their aptitude in retrospect. *As jy die persentasies gaan ontsyfer deur gebruik te maak van die woords om sal jy tot die beseffentjies kom* (If you

BURNI AND JITSVINGER PERFORMING AT KOOLOUT | Source: Ference Isaacs

decode the percentages by using the words then you'll realise), the only maths you need is to love your neighbour like you love yourself. As a matter of fact, I know, it is the snobs that cultivate racism to sustain their classism etter-tude (attitude). Let me tell you that this is Hakkiesdraad Hartman's attempt to cross any racial and language barrier when presented with the opportunity to do so. As long as we agree our milkshakes taste the same, I am hoping that in future my writing can contribute to crossing language and racial divides. My writing still has many mediums to explore and as I am mapping it out, I'm not entirely sure what it will encompass. I hope the direction I choose gets me to a destination that prejudice does not find. My goal is to bridge divides, not continue to create them.

CHAPTER 14.
HIP HOP PEDAGOGIES: BEYOND 'SOUL MURDER', 'LINGUISTIC LOOTING' AND 'WHITE SUPREMACIST DELUSIONALISM'

SHAHEEN ARIEFDIEN IN CONVERSATION
WITH H SAMY ALIM (UNIVERSITY OF CALIFORNIA, LOS ANGELES)

This dialogue between Shaheen Ariefdien and H Samy Alim represents a compilation of conversations spanning from the first Annual Heal the Hood Lecture Series at the University of the Western Cape to electronically mediated conversations from Cape Town to Toronto to California. Together, they provide a comparative US–South African perspective on white supremacy and modes of resistance and transformation through Hip Hop, language and pedagogy. The dialogue is followed by a commentary in Chapter 15 from the legendary linguist of Black Language, Geneva Smitherman.

Samy: Before we talk specifically about Hip Hop pedagogies, I wanna talk about the interrelated issues of language, race, power, discrimination and education. So, for me, a lot of the themes found in the documentary and theatre production *Afrikaaps*, and a lot of what was talked about regarding the politics of race and language at the Heal the Hood Lecture Series, are precisely the kinds of things that I work on as a linguist, anthropologist and educator. So, as someone coming from the States, I wanted to talk about racial segregation to kind of frame our discussion a little bit. And I definitely don't have to tell folks in 'post'-apartheid South Africa anything about racial segregation. Y'all live that shit every day. But I do want us to think about what is happening in Ferguson, Missouri and all over the US actually with respect to racial segregation, state violence against Black people, and Black resistance in the face of that violence.

As I flew and criss-crossed the globe to make my way over to Cape Town for the lecture series, I saw stories about Ferguson, Missouri, in almost every language imaginable, in every newspaper – in Spanish, in German – I was in Switzerland. I came down here to Jozi [Johannesburg] first. And at almost every juncture people were talking about this, but I wanna make sure that when we talk about racial segregation – and language and power and education and Hip Hop – that we delve into the social context, which is really important. So I'll start by saying that I am thankful and I thank God, Allah, the energy of the universe, that I am alive today and that I am on stage and able to be with you. And I say that as someone who, in my country, the police and the state kill over 1 000 of us every year, on a regular basis. Over *1 000* of us. That is not an exaggeration. That is my way of explaining to you in very shorthand what racial segregation is about for us, okay, because we have a town in Ferguson that is on fire right now, straight up on fire. Everybody that I know is flying down to Ferguson right now as we speak and it's going down, okay. People from all over the country are flying to be there, to be present; the hashtag is #BLACKLIVESMATTER, you all know it. We shouldn't have to say that Black lives matter but we clearly still do.

The reason why I bring this up is that the issues of language and power and education are that critical and that important to me. So the battle is going on in the US right now about #BLACKLIVESMATTER because Ferguson is a predominantly Black community, okay, but the police force is 95 per cent white…think about that. There are instances when police officers are actually calling the people 'animals' and 'savages' and they don't care that it's being recorded and seen on TV. That is the kind of situation that we are faced with right now. And whenever the dialogue and the debate happens – and I am about to segue into language right now – Black people in the States are enraged. When expressing that rage, their language and the way that people talk about their own condition, becomes a point to further subjugate them. So, these debates about Black life happen (why are we even debating this, right?) and what do white Americans tell Black Americans who are enraged about the need to have to explain that they are human? They say, 'Why don't you learn to speak English? And then maybe we'll understand your complaints.' This is from an *actual* incident. Okay, so without saying too much more, it should be clear how language and race come together to create a kind of debilitating raciolinguistic discrimination for us.

Shaheen: The history of South Africa reflects the impact of this attitude and language that have negatively affected the lives of millions of people. It's the same mentality that feels comfortable to call people 'animals' or proudly shouts, 'All lives matter!' Our humanity is just not valued on the same level. For me there's a few issues here. First, that language contributes to the normalisation of oppression. While there's an abundance of examples to use from the apartheid era, this kind of normalisation still persists. If we look at the construction of Blikkiesdorp, it was, essentially, a relocation camp that, to varying degrees, evicted people who were considered an eyesore for tourists coming to Cape Town for the 2010 Fifa World Cup soccer tournament.

Samy: Right, to present a poverty-free, 'all is well in this new democracy' kind of image…

Shaheen: Exactly. It's also part of a general approach by urban planners and policy-makers hoping to stimulate economic growth through creating a sanitised environment for tourists and foreign investors. I agree with researcher Tony Samara, who argued that Cape Town's post-apartheid urban renewal strategies maintain the inequalities of apartheid. In the past, people were forcefully evicted to places like Mitchell's Plein. Now it's Blikkiesdorp and conditions there is fucking brutal. It's been described as a kind of concentration camp with over 1 000, one-roomed, zinc-sheet structures. Families are expected to thrive in these substandard living conditions where depression and crime rates are exceptionally high. The City of Cape Town is implicated in this callous treatment that disregards human life. And not just any human – people who are racialised in particular ways and occupy particular spaces on the class spectrum. In the case of Blikkiesdorp, it's to keep people contained as if they were dangerous animals. In fact, one resident, Badronessa Morris, said, 'The police treat us like animals. They swear at us, pepper spray us, search us in public, even children.'[1] The same can be said for the treatment of people in places like Hangberg or any other township. For me, this kind of violence is quite similar to how murderous cops can go free even when their crimes are caught on cellphones in the USA. There's all kinds of other layers when the language of 'animals' and 'savages' are used to describe people of African descent.

---

1. https://www.theguardian.com/world/2010/apr/01/south-africa-world-cup-blikkiesdorp

Samy: Like centuries of other layers!

Shaheen: Exactly. Secondly, you mentioned that some responses to complaints about racial oppression and police brutality were 'why don't you learn to speak English?' Damn. This is clearly a case of what Bronx-born philosofiyah, Desus Nice, would call 'Caucastic gymnastics', when racists use unjustifiable moral and philosophical contortions to vindicate their behaviour. You have conditions that create particular kinds of experiences based on exclusion, marginalisation, exploitation AND just to be able to speak about it becomes another point of marginalisation, because you are expected to learn to speak English in a particular kind of way. In South Africa that has all kinds of other levels to it, because there's the issue of LEARNING TO SPEAK ENGLISH, never mind the kind of English, whether it's considered 'proper' or not. Then there's the way you PRONOUNCE certain words. In one of our songs [for Prophets of da City] we mentioned how 'eloquence is relevant to intelligence. They must be anti the melanin element'. Racism is so embedded in the way that you just FUCKING PRONOUNCE WORDS.

Samy: [laughs] Riiight!

Shaheen: Another layer is how we internalise an expected performance that connects language to race and power. There's a politics of respectability that tells us 'we must act civilised so that we don't get judged' or 'act respectable so that we can progress'. 'Civilised' and 'respectable', in this context, are code words for being compliant to a status quo that expects us to not rock the boat or try and assimilate to the point where…

Samy: …you can be the perfect mimic!

Shaheen: Exactly! It doesn't stop there, though. Once you're able to reach those expected levels, you're regarded as 'uppity'. So that becomes a reason to shut you the fuck up and shut you down because, 'Oh, look at you now, using all these big words!'

Samy: You're damned if you do, damned if you don't.

Shaheen: Yup. Even IF you are invested in making a case for yourself as not 'uppity', does that end up still facilitating the hegemony of colonial values?

Samy: Damn, this is on some Fanon-type shit!

Shaheen: For sure. The assumption is that if you speak English first and articulate it in particular ways, then it's the key to virtual success. Get the fuck out of here!

Samy: Because they stay moving the goalposts, man! Mos Def has that line man, oh, he's got a GOOD line on that man – in 'Mr. Nigga' on *Black on Both Sides*. 'They say they want you successful, but then they make it stressful/You start keepin' pace, they start changing up the tempo!' Like they just change the rules.

Shaheen: Mos definitely! On the one hand, there's external policing plus exclusion from and exploitation in white spaces, right? Self-policing in some spaces is another layer that's also quite traumatic. Notwithstanding how I am implicated in and might be read in relation to patriarchy, it is still deep how I sometimes present myself…

Samy: [laughs] …as, as least scary as possible!

Shaheen: Exactly! There's code-switching in different contexts and it's fascinating how that's related to body language, too. Sometimes my posture, tone and words shift. What makes this switch in white spaces different from code-switching in relation to how I might act with friends, family or in the presence of elders is that my humanity is never questioned with them. Nahmean?

Samy: Awww, man, DO I?? Painfully, painfully, man. Like, I got pulled over by this cop and I was leaving out of the neighbourhood where I was working with youth on critical Hip Hop language awareness. And I was heading over to the other side of town, the wealthy side of town, and I got pulled over right while I was crossing neighbourhood lines. Such bullshit man, you know, it was such bullshit. The cop was like, 'You were talking on the phone,' and I'm like, 'No, what? What did I do officer?' I was like, 'Nah, I wasn't talking on the phone.' And then he was like, 'Yes, you were, I saw you,' and he started inventing this whole story about how I was on the phone. Like, yo, he started just making shit up, just inventing a story that I was on the phone – 'Oh your phone is black, right? You got a black phone.' And I look at my phone – man, 90 per cent of phones are black! 'Yeah it's a black phone but I wasn't talking on the phone, sir.' AND THEN, so forget the fact that he was making it all up, but the SOUL MURDERING aspect of that whole interaction was how I then started to transform my language and body into 'whitey'. Okay, so I started being all corny, submissive and apologetic-like, 'Ohh, oh, officer, I'm so sorry, I just got a ticket speeding

JUST THE OTHER DAY and I just, you know, I DIDN'T EVEN REALISE, I wasn't on the phone but sure I'll wait, here's my ID, here.' And I started performing whitey for this white cop, because I knew, I knew that that would help get me out of this situation, or at a minimum, help him not see me as the 'one of those' that he had just seen me as, whatever was in his head. You understand how sick that is, right?

Shaheen: Absolutely!

Samy: How, how soul murdering that shit is. So I was like – I still can't stop thinking about that shit, because it's like traumatising to the point of…Like, what the fuck, I have to perform for you to show you I'm a human being, you know. I gotta go into this whole other mode so that you can then treat me as human? Because you already pulled me over illegally without warning, and without any justification, so I shouldn't have to say shit to you. But now I gotta perform this whole mode just so that you can see me as a human being and maybe not give me the ticket that I don't deserve in the first place? So, I'm sitting there, right, fuckin crushed because if I don't do that, then what happens, you know? If I don't perform whitey…If I don't perform whitey and do all these cultural shifts linguistically and with body posture, smile and all that shit, what the fuck happens? I call that shit soul murder. It happens often enough that I've developed a whole routine around it, the way I speak, and act…

Shaheen: I'm so with you. We find ourselves in spaces where we feel unsafe to be able to just survive. From township to town hall to ivory tower.

Samy: You know, you have to do that shit and lucky for me I had a Stanford University ID, that now what I do is I pull that shit out on 'accident' whenever they ask me for my licence. I just pull the Stanford ID out, like, 'Oh, oh, oh, I'm sorry, let me get my licence.' 'Cause I NEED them fuckers to see it, you know. As fucked up as that is, I rely on all of the cultural capital that I have accumulated.

Shaheen: Absolutely, and that is so fucked up.

Samy: Yeah, language, posture, power, performance. It's soul murder. And all of that relates to the kinds of language and body postures students of colour are expected to have in schools, because our languages and cultures are constantly policed…

Shaheen: Soul murder through policing happens in all kinds of complicated ways. Earlier we mentioned the soul murder that occurs from the internalisation of colonial values for acceptance and imagined progress. There's also the internalisation of notions of purity or radical alterity that's also colonial, but framed in a so-called counterhegemonic way. The obvious example of how colonial notions of purity and language intersect is how so-called coloureds are DOUBLE OTHERED. On the one hand there's the enduring legacies of colonialism and apartheid that still marginalise the vast majority of folks of African descent. On the other hand, some cultural nationalists deem you not Black enough if you're unable to speak, say, isiXhosa, isiZulu and so on. Othering in both these contexts has broader implications.

Samy: It's political man.

Shaheen: Right. A less obvious example of this kind of othering is what happened to a young brotha I know who was born in Soweto, but grew up in Toronto. His mother was a political activist forced into exile, then settled in Toronto with her kids. He grew up in a city that wasn't kind to his blackness, but he had a bond to South Africa that kept him grounded. Although he spoke only English, a large part of his identity was based on his connection to Soweto. As with many political activists in exile post 1994, his family returned to South Africa to reconnect with their loved ones and contribute to the rebuilding of a new South Africa. He told me he was super excited to return and connect with his family. Unfortunately, his experience in South Africa was extremely traumatic for him. Since he only spoke English, he was ridiculed. He told me he was not seen as a man or a true African. That experience fucked him up. He's back in Toronto and is struggling with a great deal of mental health challenges.

Samy: Daaaaaamn! The very thing that he held onto to survive in Toronto was the very thing that was taken away from him, like he couldn't claim it.

Shaheen: Exactly, and he was constantly reminded of that. Another layer to that story was the jealousy he experienced from family and friends. Again, the complicated internalisation of globally circulated images of North America as this kind of paradise counted against him. They used language as a tool to alienate him, because he got to experience a part of the world they longed to encounter. Also, his person, even as marginalised individual in Toronto, was considered a shorthand target for all the negative shit North America has done all over the world.

SHAHEEN ARIEFDIEN AND H SAMY ALIM, HIP HOP KNOWLEDGE CIPHA, 2017 | Source: Ference Isaacs

Samy: Well you got colonial, global capitalist, linguistic hegemonic bullshit…

Shaheen: Yup.

Samy: But taking sort of its revenge on the individual who happens to be in that context. It's like, 'No, you're gonna have to embody that shit for us,' because that's their only point of contact with all those macro forces.

Shaheen: That's some soul-murdering shit. Although his experience is specific to a particular geographical and cultural context, it's not dissimilar to what happens in the US with Black students who are told to invest in education then learn all the rules to navigate all these hostile white spaces. Once they find themselves back in the hood, they get alienated as well.

Samy: Ja, 'Ohhh, you think you're too good?'

Shaheen: 'You're on some white boy shit.' There's no homogeneity in blackness, but, again, internalising colonial notions of purity becomes tricky if you're not born in the hood or you speak so-called proper English as part of who you are. So, in the same way that some people learn English through Hip Hop music, as I have seen in different parts of the world, some of these kids learn to speak the cultural language through Hip Hop music. It's so fucking next level.

Samy: All kinds of layers to this shit, right?

Shaheen: These colonial and imperialistic notions of purity act in other soul-murdering and nefarious ways, too. In your talk, you used the example of 'hip' and 'okay' being African words but it becomes assumed as English words. For me, it points to the kind of imperialistic character of how English is imagined and presented. In the same way that resources, people and land are annexed and hijacked, the same happens with language. The English language is filled with all this shit that's borrowed – LOOT, linguistic loot from all over. They're like, 'It's our shit now!' Do you know what I mean?

Samy: Yeaaaaah [laughs], linguistic loot maaan, oh shit! First, SOUL MURDER then LINGUISTIC LOOT!

Shaheen: It's deep because English and Afrikaans are these complex spaces that contain all these different linguistic influences from elsewhere to make them what they are. If we take this to a broader scale, this reality flies in the face of the bullshit justifications of protecting some imaginary purity to rationalise xenophobia and racism. Linguistic looting also relates to how it robs us and invades our experiences in the learning environments. If you're from a township area and English isn't your first language and you're fortunate to get to university, it's like you're learning a whole new language. Most educators don't have the cultural and linguistic tools to connect with those students, so it's so easy to feel alienated. When you look at the dropout rates, look at how students are silenced and silence themselves, it's soul murdering. With middle-class white students, there's less of a stretch to overcome the economic, social, linguistic and cultural hurdles. For elementary and high school students in most township areas, the teaching staff is generally folks of colour. While there might be a greater chance for linguistic and cultural connection, the lack of resources, lack of ongoing training and having one teacher to 40 students are also barriers that stifle formalised learning experiences.

Also, in both the US and SA, the education system is also more committed to producing compliant consumers and workers as opposed to engaging citizens. This reminds me of a spoken word piece by Capetonian MC, Marlon Burgess, here he says:

> They force our kids into class,
> Where the principle is

To screw with their heads

And between the periods they plant seeds in our pupils

So at the end of it, all we can look forward to is going into labour

Samy: Yeah, Marlon's always on point! It's crazy because there's one thing that I don't really talk about as much, but that relates to your point about internalisation, and even Marlon's poem. When I was doing this kind of work, language work, culture work, Hip Hop and education in schools, I was first doing it in Philadelphia. And the situation there was, it was a school in the community – all Black community essentially – the school was 99 per cent Black. No, it was 99.9 per cent Black. I think that was actually what was on paper. I'm like, 'Well, what was the 0.1 per cent then?' [laughs] But that's what was on the paper AND the teachers I was workin' with were over 90 per cent Black. And so I come in with these plans, right, like I'ma do this, I'ma do that. Students are gonna produce this and produce that and I'ma use this and that and I'm all excited, right? And it's the BLACK teachers being like, 'Oh, you're not going to get THESE students to write.' 'Some of these students can hardly write they own names.' 'Oh, you're not gonna – don't expect that these students are gonna learn what you want them to learn.'

Shaheen: Right, and you know what, remember with the beginning of Hip Hop, some of the strongest resistance came from Black radio, right?

Samy: Yeaaah [laughs], yeah, I do, and even on the academic level. Because resistance came from some African American studies programmes as well. 'You can't teach Hip Hop in here.' But it was ironic because this resistance just brought out so many interesting and complex dynamics. ONE it brought about the class dimension, right, of language, like the fact that Black working-class culture was resented and really neglected and disrespected amongst a broad swathe of middle-class folks, regardless of race. And these are people who are well intentioned, who go to the community to teach; they're not the people who are sitting on the sidelines being like – 'Fuck this, it's got nothing to do with me.' They're TEACHERS and so they clearly have some kind of thing they want to contribute, but yet at the same time, these ideologies are the same and even more damaging when they come from somebody who 'looks like you', yet because of class privilege harbours these negative attitudes. So that was an eye-opener, you know, because I didn't imagine the class fissure to be expressed so directly on my first day [laughs]. But on the other hand, it's good for us to remember that, also, because of how deep this shit is, right?

Shaheen: It's definitely deep. In fact, we could have the cultural-, linguistic- and class-sensitive educators and the physical environment can still enact micro aggressions on students, because nothing related to them is reflected on the walls of the classrooms, hallways and offices. I've done some work with students in an Afrocentric school in Toronto and the walls are covered with images of Nas, Duke Ellington, Harriet Tubman, scientists and inventors. They have an allegiance to indigenous people of Turtle Island on their walls. When you look around you see Black excellence.

Samy: You mean, you don't see the lines of images of white faces on the wall?

Shaheen: Nope, and while it's not problem free, the students are exposed to Black achievement and resistance as a given.

Samy: Yeah, no, I agree man, I mean the fact that that's even there is huge, you know. And I know you're not saying this, but beyond this space and beyond what's there, it's about what we DO with those representations pedagogically, you know what I mean? Because you could – I've seen people do shit with Malcolm X that's like the oppressor's work, you know what I mean?

Shaheen: Oh ja! I've seen the same stuff with Fanon! [laughs]

Samy: Yeah, it's like what the fuck? So there's also kinda like the space in combination with the pedagogy and how we use that space, you know what I mean? I'm sure there's great examples of it in that school, but I'm just adding a footnote…

Shaheen: Absolutely. I think that's an important point because some might think that physical space and just having a Black face there, in and of itself, will bring about the necessary conditions for a healthy learning environment. Not necessarily.

Samy: Yeah, and developing a space, like you said, that's built around normalising Black political power, intellectual power, just normalising it, like that's just part of being alive right now, you know what I'm saying? So your education is not just knowledge for knowledge's sake, but knowledge for what? And that should be like fucking taken for granted, absolutely taken for granted.

Shaheen: Absolutely, and for me, that has been eye-opening. Imagine if I had gone to a school where Nas and Bob Marley on a school wall is taken as a given. Whoa!

Samy: See, the Nas thing is important – and like there's some places where there's schools centred around Pac, so the Tupac thing is important because it's like, you also don't want the next generation to always be looking back to find greatness, because then they don't see it in themselves, even if it's Black. You know, so I think that Nas and the Pac thing is crazy important, not just because we're Hip Hop heads, but… [laughs].

Shaheen: It's crucial for us to see ourselves in it, yes. It's equally important to put ourselves in it. This brings me to something you mentioned in your talk about Afrikaaps, the stereotype and how speaking it, in and of itself, is considered a criminal act. Afrikaaps is generally viewed as the language of working-class urban coloureds and linked to those regarded as gangsters. The latter [Afrikaaps] generally referring to this intricate communication system that was developed in prison by what's known as the Numbers gangs.

Samy: Yes, it's like Sabela and all that, as Quentin Williams writes about.

Shaheen: Exactly! Sabela, that's exactly one of the influences I was talking about. For many, myself included, the term 'coloured' is a colonial racial category that was constructed as part of a divide-and-rule strategy. I hesitate to use the term, but I also realise that it's an identification that resonates with millions of people. So, Afrikaaps is not only viewed as a language of disempowerment, but also not acknowledged as the language of people with indigenous ancestry. It's coloured. It's disturbing to see how indigenous voices are presented and then also become erased in the way the language is then framed. So, it's a double criminal act by viewing it as a criminal act. Hip Hop heads like Emile YX?, Bradlox and Nama Xam, to name a few, are aggressively educating folks on viewing Afrikaaps as the language of indigenous people. Also, the way Afrikaaps is presented doesn't recognise the heterogeneity WITHIN the language. For instance, the rural–urban divide plays a huge part in how Afrikaaps varieties are spoken, understood, and also the assumptions about the speakers associated with it.

Samy: Yeah, shit, well in terms of the rural–urban divide – and I think that comes up a lot with discussions of Afrikaaps and the regional dimensions of this that get short shrift. Because there's varieties of Afrikaans that are working class, and othered, but they're different right? You get outside of the Cape Flats, and folks like HemelBesem and Vito and others are KILLIN it, right?

Shaheen: Yeah, they definitely do. It's fascinating to see how marginalised groups sometimes mirror and invert the same kind of power dynamics that exist on macro and historical levels. Urban elitism, on the one hand, definitely mirrors the snobbery, minus the political and economic impacts, that exist between the margins and centre of colonial structures. Negative stereotypes usually involve viewing rural people as backwards, uncool, non-intellectual, oblivious to the arts, and so on. Part of urban snobbery flips the relationship of the linguistic hegemonic power dynamics that have existed in South Africa since before apartheid. Since rural Afrikaaps speakers tend to speak a language closer to white Afrikaans, or the Afrikaans of power, it's disparaged. This unfair assessment of our rural family could be a painful reminder of the impact of the racial capitalist and patriarchal systems on our lives. Now here's a flip to that flip that you've alluded to earlier. I think Hip Hop has definitely contributed to a kind of a shift in that urban–rural dynamic. The first time I saw that shift was during a dance battle when some rural b-boys and b-girls really got the respect of urban heads. The first time I heard Jaak and some MCs from Paarl and beyond, I was very impressed and remember thinking this could really challenge the urban–rural dynamic. They were not copying urban Cape Town versions of Afrikaaps; they were spitting that rural shit with so much skill. They didn't sound like POC or BVK [Brasse Vannie Kaap]. It was basically like the southern artists in the US refusing to copy New York or Los Angeles.

HEMELBESEM AND YOMA | Source: H Samy Alim

Samy: That's dope though. I like what you're saying about rural cats just kinda doing their own shit in the same way that, like the Dirty South was just like, 'Yo, ya'll laugh at the way we talk down here, BUT this is how we're gonna do Hip Hop; we're gonna be US.'

Shaheen: And they're doing it dope. They're taking it to the next level.

Samy: That's crazy man, that's crazy. And so, in South Africa, when folks do their shit in the rural areas, when they take that Afrikaans and do that, and Hip Hopitise Afrikaans, is the association with white Afrikaans reduced? Or are they playing with that at all? Like you know how it's perceived as closer to, or racialised as closer to white Afrikaans varieties, what happens to it when it enters the Hip Hop domain?

Shaheen: Based on some of the songs I've heard, there's a wide variety of ideological positions. I think Godessa was probably the first Hip Hop group to explicitly make a case for what came to be known as Afrikaaps. They traced the history of linguistic looting on the song. The earlier songs of Jaak I heard was firmly rooted in an analysis that is very hip to oppression. For many, I think, it's linked to reclaiming a language that was historically associated with oppression. Some MCs might experiment with traditional Hip Hop battle-type verses. It's important to keep in mind that this has never been done with the language before. They are definitely pushing boundaries in that regard. MCs like HemelBesem are also pushing boundaries as a television host, actor and author. I've heard Black Consciousness, Khoi revivalist and dangerous coloured nationalist ideas from MCs who have Hip Hopitised Afrikaans.

Samy: Yeah, so there's a case to be made for multiple varieties of Afrikaaps, so to speak, even though most people wouldn't call it that, but you know what I mean.

Shaheen: I think the case is already there for multiple varieties of Afrikaaps. There's heterogeneity in Afrikaaps in urban areas before we even bring the peri-urban and rural, regional linguistic influences into the mix. Code-switching is present in urban Afrikaaps. The way we speak to our elders is very different to the way you speak to our friends. There's a set of linguistic rules that determine the appropriate words, tones and so on. Groups like BVK have used that in songs when they channel intergenerational conversations. Even within our friend circles there are varieties. Some conversations might involve Sabela and others not. Some Afrikaaps code-switching involves the sarcastic use of white Afrikaans. On our second album we had a song called 'Ons Stem' ('Our Voice') that dissed the apartheid regime's national anthem, 'Die Stem' ('The Voice'). In the song we rhymed in white Afrikaans that was an obvious nod to suggest we can diss you in your own corny language and still do it with skill. After we diss you, we come right back with the song, 'Net 'n Bietjie Liefde' ('Just a Little Love') on some mainstream Afrikaaps.

Samy: Damn, y'all flipped the so-called 'language of the oppressor' AGAINST THE OPPRESSOR and then just kept it movin', like, 'What?! This is *die taal wat ons praat!* [the language that we speak!]' That's not even mainstream Afrikaaps man; that's advanced linguistic layering…

Shaheen: There's LAYERS TO THAT SHIT. There isn't just one Afrikaaps. One of the most gifted Afrikaaps spitting MCs, Isaac Mutant, will use a combination of the varieties of Afrikaaps in one song. In fact, Isaac was part of a crew who had a song called 'Amerikaaps' about the influence of US cultural imperialism on South African Hip Hop.

Samy: Wow, Amerikaaps?! Isaac is ILL with the wordplay.

Shaheen: He is, and Marlon Burgess had a similar take on cultural imperialism and reclaiming marginalised aspects of our language in a song called 'Revenge of the RRR'.

Samy: Oooh, I love it man! That's crazy because it's this: it's the Hip Hop practice of taking the stigmatised aspects of language and just owning it, CLAIMING it.

Shaheen: Yes. What made this piece powerful was that he created a visual art piece around it. He found a discarded drive-through intercom system that consisted of a mouthpiece, speaker and lowercase r-shaped metal bar.

Samy: Was that the 'r'?

Shaheen: That was not only the lowercase 'r', it also symbolised the mouth to the windpipe, because this was where the rrrr resonates the most. It also contained a little speaker that symbolised the mouth. The structure was kept stable with rocks that symbolised the cultural and linguistic roots. The lyrics were placed on the rocks, using a Letraset rub-on transfers. That was some next level Hip Hop visual art shit. So, Afrikaaps-inspired Hip Hop has all these layers to it. Let's take Jitsvinger who hails from Kuilsriver, for example…

MARLON SWAI, CAPE TOWN, 2008 | Source: Gary Stewart

Samy: Northern suburbs.

Shaheen: Yes. It's a peri-urban region so he incorporates the varieties of urban and rural Afrikaaps into his music. In fact, Jitsvinger's music also has a focus on experimenting with cadence, style and flow.

Samy: I love what Jits does with flow and that sing-song style, the way he rides the beat with them complex rhymes, and blends English and Afrikaaps seamlessly. Reminds me of some stuff Pharoahe Monch does, too, in terms of its complexity.

Shaheen: Yeah, he's dope, and MCs like Linkris, Chase Lutron and Niko10Long all blur the boundaries between urban and rural Afrikaaps and they do it well. I think groups like Ancient Men from Uitsig experimented with these urban–rural linguistic blurring in about 2000 already.

Samy: In Hip Hopitising Afrikaans then, these practices change the inflection of it, the social inflection of it. And you gotta be able to decode all that shit!

Shaheen: You need to be hip to it all, because heads are also inventing new words and redefining words. Take the word 'yak', for example. In conventional Afrikaaps 'yak' means 'to wear' or 'gear'. I'm yakking my jacket or sneakers. Check this out. We were on tour in Denmark, I think, sitting outside the hotel with our bags and waiting for transport and take us to the next location. We were all super exhausted. Our lead dancer, Ramone, who loves playing with words, started to tease us by saying, 'Look at you guys, yakking your tiredness.' From that moment, we used 'yak' in all kinds of contexts. I'm yakking my hunger or sadness. In fact, the reworked version of the term made it to record on a song that dealt with the internalisation of racism, called 'Black Thing'. The line went, 'They call me coloured and claim my blood is impure but see/I'm not yakking my insecurity.' After the term made it to record, it totally surprised us how many people on the streets started using 'yak' in its reworked form.

Samy: That's happening with slang, people hearing a particular word on record and then it spreading. But, like, some linguists will say, 'Oh, that just happens with slang,' but linguistically what else is happening? And I'd say it seems like a metaphor for what's happening with language structurally, because when you start combining things differently, right, then those kinds of recombinations and ways of putting resources together become the ways that people are now (trans)languaging it, right, that you have a linguistic restructuring as well.

Shaheen: I agree. Yet, while we find possibilities in the power of language, these possibilities take place in a context where the language of power counts. This brings us right back to navigating those ever-shifting goalposts shaped by broader systemic factors to the point where we consciously shut down parts of ourselves for the sake of so-called progress. I say this because I know of parents and even teachers who might value and celebrate Afrikaaps, but end up policing their kids and students for fear of being two steps behind.

Samy: I think in some cases this makes sense, right, because people hear what I say all the time and they think, 'Oh, what, you're just advocating for our youth to be monolingual or to speak "only" the language of the community?' or whatever. And I'm always saying, 'Man, it's about being multilingual.' Like, it really is, but it's doing it in a way that's CRITICAL and understanding the power relations behind what languages are valued and what languages are not, what it is we need to know and WHY, and developing a pedagogy that really puts languages on par with each other. And not just linguistically speaking, but SOCIALLY: we need to be able to critique where languages are along hierarchies of power and why. Like, how is it that particular languages or varieties of languages come to occupy this space? If you're not dealing with THAT, and you just want people to learn how to speak this way because 'you not gonna be able to graduate' then that's just not enough for me. That's gonna reproduce, not transform, the status quo.

Shaheen: In your context, given the shifting demographics in the States, whites are soon going to be the minority and will actually have to deal with this shit.

Samy: Yeah, that shit is shifting man, that shit is shifting. And now, they're talkin' about white presidential candidates or vice-presidential picks who might be valuable because they know how to speak Spanish, or you know, 'This person also knows how to relate to a particular racial/regional/linguistic demographic.' That's actually part of the explicit discussion about who makes better candidates. So that shift has already happened. You have to be multilingual.

Shaheen: To bring your point back to Afrikaaps, that multilingualism always has to come with owning and valuing ours. In your previous work in relation to Black Language in the US, and I think it applies to Afrikaaps, our linguistic varieties are actually more technically complicated than, say, standardised Afrikaans. It's not a reach to argue that embracing this realisation impacts self-confidence and celebrating who we are as full human beings. Most white (controlled) spaces and outlets tell us, 'You're not worthy enough.' And recognising the beauty of our language is one of the important ways to say, 'Yo, I'm proud of that shit.'

Samy: That's it right there. That's why we must not ever accept hegemony; we must always disrupt it. That's not even a choice for us.

Shaheen: Not a choice, true. Part of the issue becomes how we conceptualise 'disrupt'. Let's take a particular aspect of Hip Hop scholarship, for example. There's a school of thought that's invested in making a case for, say, Rakim's artistic integrity and arguing that he's as poetically worthy as Shakespeare. There's another school of thought arguing that Rakim has value to us and that's where justification lies. Who the fuck is Shakespeare to become the standard? If we take these examples to broader political approaches, I think it's important for us to imagine a future and ways of moving forward that's not necessarily reliant on hegemonic institutions and discourses.

Samy: This is the bigger issue of: How do we understand ourselves and our future and our culture outside of the white gaze, as Toni Morrison says, outside of a colonial framework, even outside of a decolonial framework, even though that's a necessary step? What kind of Black futures then can we imagine that's not necessarily fucking linked to metaphorical Shakespeare? Like, part of the whole reason of doing the Pharoahe Monch poetics work, for me, was…

Shaheen: Still one of my favourite works, yo!

Samy: Yeah, man, there's some ill shit happening in those rhymes and that's what I'm concerned about. There wasn't an argument made to link it to Shakespeare or anything else. If anything, the argument that I made was to link it to the Black Oral Tradition that Geneva Smitherman wrote so powerfully about, right? Just something incredibly dope. And I tell you who peeps this shit – and this is if you're using the Shakespeare metaphor, and it's such a good one because of the way Shakespeare is used even by well-intentioned people that reproduces this kind of link to the white canon, you know, that may or may not be genius or relevant or for our purposes. 'He's not the only fucking genius!' Even if it ain't the only thing, even if Shakespeare's been riddled with criticisms of plagiarism, and all that shit, it ain't the only thing, you know what I mean? So, listen to this. In the same neighbourhood where I'm at, these folks tried to bring Hip Hop to the school, and they thought they were gonna teach kids Shakespeare through Hip Hop, right? And they came in the school and they tried so hard, man. You could tell they've been training and practising and they thought about it and performed it and they put on this great play. And I think it was at the time when Nas was comin' out with one mic and shit like that. And so they tried to link Nas and whatever with Shakespeare. And in the play though there was all these kinds of ways that Black culture and language through Hip Hop was being devalued in relation to European linguistic norms and cultural norms, poetic norms. And you know who peeped it? The students did bro, the fucking students did! So they called them out on that shit and were just like, 'Okay, so why is it the Black kid in the play can only rap – and he raps so good but he can ONLY rap? He doesn't understand Shakespearian poetry. But Shakespeare comes back from the dead, having only his Shakespeare shit and starts rapping easily, like he can rap no problem? It's like rapping ain't shit. Are you trying to tell us he's rapping? Like he can be dead for centuries and come back and just all of a sudden he can rhyme like the ILLEST MC, as if it was just nothing?'
And so, what was great to me about that was the STUDENTS peeped it and deconstructed the levels of whiteness at play THEMSELVES. So you could end up alienating the very students that you are trying to relate to if you've not given thought to how that shit is done. And so that's a

metaphor, you using the Shakespeare metaphor, but that's a metaphor for how you bust and disrupt hegemony; you must be able to see beyond those harmful, condescending linkages that people constantly make in order to legitimise or validate our shit. It's not necessary.

Shaheen: It's sad that in this day and age our young people still have to go through this shit because others are motivated by fear and mental and spiritual illness. It must be done, though, especially in a world infested with ableism, patriarchy, heteronormativity, capitalism and fucking white supre – I don't even like the word white supremacy. There's nothing fucking superior or supreme about whiteness.

Samy: [laughs] The delusion.

Shaheen: White supremacist delusionalism. Ha, flipping the script, practise what you preach, yo!

Samy: We're talkin' about reinventing language and shit, right? What was it that [James] Baldwin said: 'The power of the white world is threatened whenever a Black man [person] refuses to accept the white world's definitions.'[2]

Shaheen: No doubt. This brings us to the work that you and Django Paris write about: *Culturally Sustaining Pedagogy*.[3] It's not enough to be able to use Hip Hop to understand Shakespeare. How does that benefit a community that studies it and the value of Hip Hop and the value of things that are created within that community, right?

Samy: How you just phrased that together is EVERYTHING, because even people who are politically inclined to agree with what we are saying right now lose track of it, of that thought. As soon as we say 'to value Hip Hop', we're talking about more than just Hip Hop; it's the valuing of things that we create, that we produce, that are based in our cultural linguistic experiences, do you know what I mean? Like, that's what Hip Hop represents. It's a metaphor for all of that, you know. So, I'm saying this to the people who are not necessarily relating to Hip Hop, but can understand that 'culturally sustaining pedagogy' is about the idea that what we bring is VALUABLE; it is US. We are valuable, just period. Do you know what I mean? And then, to quote Gloria Ladson-Billings, 'we teach what we value.' We

---

2. https://www.newyorker.com/magazine/1962/11/17/letter-from-a-region-in-my-mind
3. See Paris & Alim (2017).

open up our book, *Culturally Sustaining Pedagogies: Teaching and Learning for Justice in a Changing World*, with that quote for a reason. We teach what we love; we sustain what we love. And that's why schooling needs to be reframed. Culturally sustaining pedagogies can provide us with ways that ultimately move us beyond the soul-murdering, linguistic-looting, white supremacist delusionalism that we've been talking about.

Shaheen: True! So, I've been grappling with this question. What is its relationship to anti-hegemonic PRACTICES? Let me use this example. There's a brilliant rant by George Carlin about the reprehensible behaviour of the United States' 'owning class'. His basic analysis is quite traditionally Marxist on most levels. The bit would likely be considered a good example of stand-up comedy as counterhegemonic expression. However, it actually is quite indicative of hegemony because he goes on to say something to the effect of, 'And that's how shit is, get used to it!' I've seen numerous examples of this in Hip Hop songs. Just because you raise your middle finger to say 'fuck the system', doesn't automatically mean that's anti-hegemonic if nothing can be imagined outside of that said system. I am specifically referring to folks who regard their art as revolutionary or representing some kind of activism. Similar to certain kinds of protests, the conditions under which we produce our art could end up as designated spaces to vent our

DJ READY D INTERVIEWING SHAHEEN, 2017 | Source: H Samy Alim

frustrations, as long as we apply for a proverbial or actual permit to say 'fuck you' between 13h30 and 15h00.

Samy: Yeah, it's also representative of the power of hegemony.

Shaheen: I think the same applies to 'speaking truth to power'. I'm not on some revolutionary purist shit, but I think it's important that we are honest with our critical engagement with 'power', including when we are implicated in certain problematic dynamics. So having said that, not all truth to power is challenging or resistive. Telling an oppressive system the day after Sunday is Monday is, technically, also speaking a kind of truth to power. That's a consciously absurd example I used, but it still boils down to, what exactly are we saying? To whom? For what purpose? What's the use of these seemingly 'fuck you' moments that end up as either self-serving or functioning as safety valves to let off steam. To be clear, not all of us have the privilege or protection to throw around high registers of 'fuck you', but I do think we be mindful of our motivations and impacts of these fuck yous. Again, I'm specifically referring to folks who consider their art or work as activist or revolutionary. Not all fuck yous are created equal. So, for me, it would be interesting to know the relationship between culturally sustaining pedagogy and counter- or anti-hegemonic politics.

Samy: Yo, that's a REALLY good question, man, because one of the things I always hear, time and time again, is the 'that's just the way it is' narrative, okay. Like, 'That's just the way it is, that's the way the world works.' And, you know, these aren't just white teachers telling this to Black kids, as I said.

Shaheen: Nahhh, this is coming from people who consider themselves critical.

Samy: Yeah, it's people who are sorta critical and want to be able to use that kind of discourse to motivate students, but I'm always getting people to think about moving from 'the way things are' to 'the way things can BE'. That's the move. So, in terms of thinking about pedagogy and shit, people are like, 'You can't get this shit into the schools,' or, 'You can't teach this,' or, 'On what scale can you do it?' And I'm like yo, yo, yo, BACK UP, because first we have to create something that lets us imagine what the possibilities actually are before we start cutting off the possibility from even existing. So let's think about what kinds of things can we do differently, how can we imagine this shit DIFFERENTLY, be it pedagogically, etc., and it doesn't have to align with Hip Hop. People think this shit has to align with Hip Hop.

Shaheen: No!

Samy: Or it has to align with youth culture. But there has to be an element where we are also talking about providing this 'loving critique' that me and Django talk about in the culturally sustaining pedagogy work. Where we recognise that there's gonna be some fucked-up shit because youth are only human. We've seen it with the Zulu Nation and all that shit. You know, we talked about that, there are elements that every youth culture, community culture, etc., that's gonna need some loving critique. So the way to get people beyond the 'fuck you' and beyond just throwing up the middle finger, I think, is to start looking at internal sorts of issues and critiquing ourselves and moving to somewhere new, you know what I mean? Going somewhere, like, using and valuing all that we have and all that we've had to fucking do just to be here, right, and then moving in a direction of how things can be. What do we want things to look like? I think that's critical, because it's a good question. You asked a good question, but sometimes the phrase 'culturally sustaining' can make people think we're rooted in some kind of past framework, you know what I mean, like we wanna sustain some shit that we have, period. But you know it's also about evolution, about imagination.

Shaheen: Okay, so that was one thing that I was thinking about. I'm glad you cleared that up for me.

Samy: Yeah, and that part of it is so critical; the SUSTAINING part is so critical, and the IMAGINING part as well. As the homie Mark Gonzales always says, 'What can we do beyond resist?' We can imagine new ways of doing, being, acting, living, loving, etc.

Shaheen: It's about a sustenance and substance.

Samy: Yeah, exactly. Every time we come face to face with an institution, it's erasing and eradicating the things that sustain us, right?

Shaheen: Even if we create the institutions a la the Zulu Nation.

Samy: Yeah, we would wanna be able to sustain those cultures, those languages and also be able to evolve and create new forms and imagine what that would look like. And you know who's really good at that? I'm gonna use this example because I think that he captures both of your examples of the 'fuck you', and the example of imagining something new in one body – that's Tupac. So, if you just look visually at Pac, which a lot of people did, right? White mainstream society just saw the middle finger to the news camera ALL THE TIME and saw the 'Thug Life' tattoo, saw the bandana, saw the whole shoot-out stuff and were just like, 'Oh, this is some bullshit.' But then, when we interviewed him like we did in the book *Street Conscious Rap*[4] and other projects, or you hear him in other interviews, he's trying to spell out like how come these people have this and that [excessive forms of material wealth] and others have nothing. How come you can't have a system where we base things on economic equality, rather than inequality? How can one person have 27 rooms in their house when there's a million homeless people sleeping outside in the streets? How can one person eat at a buffet all day while there are millions going hungry? When all some people saw was a 'Thug Life' tattoo, he told us he was busy theorising social, political and economic inequality through T.H.U.G.L.I.F.E. – The Hate U Gave Little Infants Fucked Everybody. He actually told us this in his interview. So, for Pac, there's a 'fuck you' but there's also a theorising and an envisioning of how we might be able to reorder society and redistribute wealth.

Honestly, I'm also thinking about Isaac Mutant and Dookoom's *Larney Jou Poes* as an example here. One could think of that as 'just' a 'fuck you', but in so-called post-apartheid South Africa – I mean, this video was shot in Oudtshoorn, white Afrikaner, farmer country, man – but we know that's BULLSHIT, because it's really indigenous African territory that was stolen! The farm workers were striking because they're getting paid SHIT for all of their hard work while the whites own most of the land. Getting paid just 69 rand per day, no healthcare, sometimes STILL getting paid with alcohol, despite the tremendous problem of Foetal Alcohol Syndrome in coloured communities from the legacy of the 'dop system', where white farmers paid their workers with liquor. In talking with Isaac, he remembers that the farm workers were terrified to tell the farmer to fuck off. TERRIFIED. He had to get the farmer's permission for them to be able to say that in the video – like, they wanted to be sure they weren't gonna lose their jobs and shit. He makes a point of saying that white folks were treated as if they're gods or some shit, and that he wanted to

---

4. See Spady, Alim & Lee (1999).

provoke some thought as well – he actually says he wanted not only to amplify the strike, and to make the country talk about land and wealth redistribution, but he also wanted the farm workers to feel what that was like for those words to come out of their mouths. And here's the point: he said that folks felt good saying it. They told him that it helped them imagine something new being possible – that you can say things that you thought you couldn't previously say. So, rather than inciting violence, which was the majority white critique of the video, Dookoom wanted to incite thought, a new way of thinking that breaks from the past. To link this back to Pac, Isaac also envisions bringing all the gangs together across the country and fighting the enduring racialised, economic, bullshit legacy of apartheid, or as he says, 'getting all the little people, the oppressed, to understand that we still have one common enemy,' and to figure out what we can do about it. To me, that's more than a safety valve letting off steam.

Shaheen: Right, I definitely don't think of Dookoom's fuck you as 'just' a 'fuck you'; it's a justifiable fuck you. A right-wing Afrikaner group, AfriForum, lodged a hate speech complaint against them with the South African Human Rights Commission for song and video. Not to sound defensive, ha, but I want to be clear that I am advocating for self-awareness to pay attention to the motivation and impact of our 'fuck yous' if we consider our work to contribute to some kind of activist or revolutionary cause, because many of us often end up reproducing the shit we imagine ourselves combating or conflate profanity with automatic revolutionary action. In the examples you mentioned, I see these 'fuck yous' as potentially fuelling a steam engine as opposed to 'just' letting off steam or hot air.

Samy: Yeah, I agree with you. These are more than safety valves that allow the destruction to continue, or that allow for the machinery to keep working as is; they disrupt, they help us rethink, they throw a wrench in the machine. At the same time, if we really are to move forward to some presumably better place, we have to be able to look at Pac and provide a loving critique. If you look at that same interview in the book *Street Conscious Rap*, his gender politics weren't quite thought all the way through at that time, you know what I'm saying – this is what Adam Haupt says about *Larney Jou Poes* as well. Yeah, he may have been revolutionary in terms of his Black Panther spirit and all of that, but remember that even a lot of those organisations – even, as we mentioned, the Zulu Nation and Afrika Bambaataa in Hip Hop – were troubled with problematic bullshit that THIS current generation of activists is trying to work through, trying NOT to repeat that shit, so we can build a truly inclusive, beloved community, you know what I'm saying? Our pedagogies need to be on that vibe, building the kind of world that we wanna see for our children.

Shaheen: Oh, absolutely man. These new allegations and revelations about the Zulu Nation just had my mind like really working overtime in terms of the crucial role of healing, self-awareness, accountability and the role of critical imagination in moving forward. We have so much work to do.

Samy: ALWAYS. That shit never stops. Can't stop, won't stop.

ISAAC MUTANT | Source: Ference Isaacs

CHAPTER 15.
A COMMENTARY ON ALIM AND ARIEFDIEN'S HIP HOP PEDAGOGIES: BEYOND "SOUL MURDER", "LINGUISTIC LOOTING" AND "WHITE SUPREMACIST DELUSIONALISM"'

GENEVA SMITHERMAN (MICHIGAN STATE UNIVERSITY)

There is much in the conversation between H Samy Alim and Shaheen Ariefdien that resonates across time and space, that reflects our common histories and contemporary struggles in the USA and the RSA. The issues raised and the experiences revisited by these dynamic scholar–activists are a painful reminder of the global footprint of settler colonialism and the continuing presence of the past. To remix mid-twentieth-century US writer William Faulkner, the 'past ain't dead and buried, it ain't even the past'.

THE PRESENTNESS OF THE PAST

In November 1959, I received two important documents by mail. One was my official paperwork from the Detroit Public Schools (DPS) informing me that DPS had hired me to teach English and Latin at Northwestern High School, an all-Black academically high-performing school located in the heart of one of the D's long-time Black working-class hoods. The other document was from Wayne State University, notifying me that I had met the requirements for my BA degree, which would be awarded at the university's upcoming commencement in January. I was 18 years old.

I had finished my education years ahead of my girlz that I rolled wit in Detroit's 'Black Bottom'. At the age of four, my father had enrolled me in the primary school, racially segregated by law, located in our sharecropping community in Tennessee, a former slave-holding state in the US South. Then when my family migrated up-South (as Malcolm X called Chicago, Detroit and other northern cities located in the so-called free states of the US), I skipped several grades because my teachers advanced me (called 'double-promotion' in that era). Most of all, my rapid journey through K-12 schooling[1] was due to my father, who had a fervently religious belief that knowledge was power, and thus he was zealously committed to his children getting the education he had never received. I never knew what 'summer break' was because he mandated and funded my enrolling in school during the summers so that I could advance half a grade each year.

I had always felt that teaching was my calling. So I was on a natural high – 'lit', as they say these days – when I assigned my honours English senior class *Native Son*, the 1940 classic novel by Black American writer Richard Wright. In my own high school years in the 1950s, I had sneaked into the closed stacks of our library and read Wright's literary masterpiece. ('Sneaked' because certain literary works were off-limits to students unless they had permission slips from their teachers.) *Native Son* opened up a whole new world to me, helping me understand racial oppression, my family's continuing poverty – despite long, hard hours of work by my father, mother and grandfather – and what in the Black Liberation Movement years later I would come to know as 'class oppression'. As a teacher providing guidance to young students in the 1960s, amidst the profound social changes that were taking place, I reasoned that Wright's novel would have a similar impact on my students and advance their understanding of themselves and the Black condition. Moreover, at that point in the US, school districts were grappling with the profound ramifications of the historic US Supreme Court's 1954 ruling in *Brown v. Board*,[2] which had declared racially segregated schools unconstitutional. In the context of desegregating/integrating the nation's school systems, the educational curriculum was also being re-examined and, in some districts, revamped. For instance, in Detroit public schools, there was a language arts committee working on introducing 'Negro Literature'

---

1. In the US, K12 schooling means from kindergarten through 12th grade. It refers to schooling up to and through secondary education.
2. Brown v. Board of Education of Topeka, 347 U.S. 483 (1954).

into the District's high school curriculum. Thus, this was the ideal historical moment to have Northwestern High School students, among the best and brightest of the D's 'Talented Tenth' future leaders, reading a book like *Native Son*. Or so I naively thought.

A few days after I assigned the book, I got the surprise of my life. Turns out that the parents of one of the students – remember, this was an all-Black high school – had written a letter and later met with the principal to complain about the students reading *Native Son*. A memo subsequently went out to all the teaching staff indicating that *Native Son* was not on the DPS approved reading list and that anyone teaching it would be called to a meeting with the superintendent and subject to contract cancellation. Clearly, it was only a certain kind of 'Negro literature' that was acceptable – only literary works that would not challenge the status quo, and in particular those that would not raise questions about the effect of the socioeconomic system on Black racial and class consciousness, and mos def not works focusing on 'white monopoly capitalism'.

In the 1950s, when US slave descendants began to rise up against centuries of US-style apartheid, and when they were joined in the 1960s by 'Negroes' who had become 'Black',

GENEVA SMITHERMAN WITH SHAHEEN AND SAMY AT HIP HOP KNOWLEDGE CIPHA, 2017 | Source: H Samy Alim

my people stayed believing that 'The Revolution' was just around the corner. It had been a long time coming, but me and my peeps of the Black Power generation knew a change was gon come. Yeah, right. As Samy and Shaheen eloquently and powerfully demonstrate, the mo thangs change, the mo they be stayin the same. Referring to educational systems, Shaheen sums it up like this: 'In both the US and SA, the education system is...more committed to producing compliant consumers and workers as opposed to engaging citizens.' Un-huh, cuz 'engaging citizens' would raise questions about why things are the way they are and would peep how the system manipulates requirements and rules to favour white privilege. As Samy notes, using the Hip Hop work of Mos Def to illustrate, '...they stay moving the goalposts... Mos Def...got a good line...in "Mr. Nigga" on *Black On Both Sides*. "They say they want you successful, but then they make it stressful! You start keepin pace, they start changing up the tempo!" Like, they just change the rules.'

'SOUL MURDER'

A major challenge to the decolonisation project goin down in communities of colour around the globe is the legacy of linguistic–cultural code-switching. As Kenyan writer Ngũgĩ wa Thiong'o (1986) notes, the oppressor devalued the language and culture of the oppressed community in order to control the mental universe of the people. They are then forced to switch to the language and cultural codes of the oppressor In order to establish their humanity and, in instances of police–citizen interaction, their innocence. Samy coined the phrase 'soul murder' to describe the impact of this code-switching. He relays an encounter with a white police officer in the hood, who accused him – insisted, in fact – that he was talking on his cellphone while driving, which is against the law. In order to get out of the grip of this 'soul-murdering' – and, sadly, a potentially body-murdering – situation, Samy is forced into 'performing whitey', relying on 'all of the cultural capital that I have accumulated'. This same scenario occurs 24-7, 365 in communities of colour around the globe.

I recall all too many times in my life, as well as in the experience of so many other sistaz, where I had to take low and go, had to talk and act like a proper 'Negro girl', rather than the angry Black woman I felt like, in order to survive to resist another day. Over the decades, I've often told the story of being arrested in my youth during the Conference on College Composition and Communication's annual convention in Cincinnati in 1971. That story was retold in my interview with Austin Jackson and Bonnie Williams in Blackmon, Kirklighter and Parks' *Listening to Our Elders: Working and Writing for* Change (2011). I recall thinking during that interview that 'soul-murdering' events had become a thing of the past now that I'm at elder status. Ha, naw, it doan stop. Three years ago, in the early afternoon, just a couple of miles from my house in the metro D suburbs, I noticed a cop car that seemed to be following me. But I was on my way to the Whole Foods Market and quickly dismissed that paranoid thought. After all, I was dressed in my professor business casual style (not Hip Hop as I am wont to do at times), everything about my BMW truck was in order, and I was even driving below the speed limit. I pulled into a handicapper space in the Whole Foods parking lot and placed my handicapper placard on my rear-view mirror. That's when the police car pulled right up beside me, and this white cop got out of his car, walked over and asked me if that was my handicapper placard. I said, 'Yes.' Then he asked for my driver's licence, car registration and car insurance. All the while producing the documents he had asked for, politely and in my best Dominant American English (shout out to Django Paris), I asked, 'What's the problem, officer?' He didn't answer, walked back to his car and ran my info through the computer – and of course found nothing, no unpaid tickets, no outstanding warrants for my arrest, nothing. Since my youth during the days of the Black Liberation Movement, I keep all my shit in order cuz I done learned that the PoPo doan play. When he returned to my car with my identity documents, he said, 'I stopped you because you don't look old enough to have a handicapper placard. But everything checked out.' Then he walked away. Say whut? Duh-uh, thass the best lie you could come up wit for fuckin wit me?! Like young people don't be handicapped? It was all I could do to control the anger I felt at that moment, what psychologists Grier and Cobbs (1968) in their research deemed 'Black rage', the tragic result of 'soul murder' caused by constant harassment, cumulative onslaughts on Black dignity and flagrant demonstrations of white privilege and power.

'LINGUISTIC LOOTING'

In Samy and Shaheen's discussion of language issues, Shaheen introduces this wonderful badass phrase he coined: 'linguistic looting'. In my work on African American Language, I have called it the 'Africanisation of American English'. But I love his 'linguistic looting' and am going to start using that conceptual nomenclature because that's just what it is – thievery and looting. Cultural critic Ralph Wiley poses a provocative question about why Black people have no culture. He answers his own question: it's because all 'of it is out on loan to white people. With no interest' (Wiley 1991: 38).

Shaheen's 'linguistic looting' made me think immediately about the 'high five' in the US. This linguistic–cultural practice has a long, honourable history in African America. First off, it wasn't always done 'high'. Rather, originally, the 'high five' involved extending the palm of your hand at waist level, and it was referred to as 'giving/getting skin'. Over time, it came to be known as 'giving/getting five'. According to scholar David Dalby, this linguistic–cultural practice dates to a West African tradition brought to the US during enslavement (see Dalby 1972). It's literally translated as 'put your hand in my hand' – that is, if you agree with what I'm saying or if something I've said strongly resonates with you. 'Giving/getting five' has always been widely used and practised throughout African America by all age and class groups, and by both men and women. Additionally, I have theorised that the Black Church tradition of waving your hand during a church service – for example, the preacher's sermon, choir's singing, deacon's prayer – is the sacred version of 'giving skin/five'.

There was a time when whites commenting on giving/getting skin erroneously associated it with a form of negative 'street' or 'gangster' behaviour, and they referred to it as 'palm slapping'. As a young girl growing up in the 1950s, caught up in the throes of respectability politics of that era, I recall being criticised for giving skin because it wasn't deemed 'ladylike'. In 1972, communications scholar Ben Cooke published his research on giving/getting skin, demonstrating its complex multiple variations (e.g. on the sly; on the Black hand side) (see Cooke 1972). Over time, giving skin/five evolved to the high five – as noted by *Ebony Magazine* in a 1991 article.[3] Today, whites everywhere have taken this Black language–cultural practice as their own. In fact, I have had white students who vehemently deny that the high five originated with us. They are blown away when I show them Cooke's article and Dalby's scholarship – the same Dalby who also convincingly argues that even the good old Americanism 'okay' is derived from African languages.

In 1957, white writer Norman Mailer, in his famous 'White Negro' essay, credited the 'cultural marriage' of white and Black for the production of what was then often referred to as the 'language of hip'. Mailer asserts that this language was the 'child' of the Black–white cultural marriage. Today, Black Language is used to sell everything from snow blowers to shampoo for white folks' hair. As Langston Hughes moaned during the Harlem Renaissance, '[they] done

---

3. See Renee D Turner's article, 'The High Five Revolution', August 1991, at http://findarticles.com/p/articles/mi_m1077/ is_n10_v46/ai_11098726/.

taken my blues and gone.'[4] So yeah, Shaheen, it *is* looting! Whites pay no dues but reap the psychosocial and economic benefits of African American Language – and in South Africa, Afrikaaps – languages born out of our peoples' struggle, oppression and hard times.

'RACIOLINGUISTICS', HIP HOP AND 'CULTURALLY SUSTAINING PEDAGOGY'

Language is a critical running theme throughout Samy and Shaheen's conversation about Hip Hop pedagogies. High five and props to them for focusing on issues of language and language pedagogy in our struggle to bring the next generation of youth to manhood and womanhood. I felt for the Soweto brotha that Shaheen described who grew up in Toronto and spoke only English, having learned, as Shaheen put it, to 'navigate all these hostile white spaces' in order to survive in that environment. But then upon the brotha's return home to post-apartheid South Africa, he was 'ridiculed...[and] not seen as a man or a true African'. We witness similar dynamics in the US, where whites diss Blacks for using African American Language, and then yo own people diss you if you come to the hood wit that white girl talk.

Here's what our work in the vineyard of language struggle has taught us. Language, race and identity are inextricable. After we published our book *Articulate While Black* (Alim & Smitherman 2012), Samy coined the term 'raciolinguistics' to capture these dynamics (see Alim, Rickford & Ball 2016). As Nelson Mandela once said, 'Talk to a man in a language he understands, you speak to his head. Talk to him in his language, you speak to his heart.'[5] The school and public leadership in both our countries are crucial in resolving our linguistic contradictions and ambivalences and in advancing our teaching for decolonisation and linguistic liberation.

Late linguist–revolutionary Neville Alexander left us a legacy of work about what he called 'the power of language' and the 'language of power' (see Busch, Busch & Press 2014). On the latter, he taught us that English would cease to be the 'language of power' if we make it equal, not superior, to the other South African languages which are enshrined in the Constitution and which, just like English, are all recognised as official languages. Alexander contends that language is one of the three major issues that continue to 'shackle post-apartheid South

4. https://www.litnet.co.za/langston-hughes-peoples-poet-revolutionised-african-american-literary-tradition/
5. See, e.g., https://www.iol.co.za/news/opinion/speak-in-his-language-and-youll-speak-to-his-heart-15227807

MAK1ONE PAINTING, AFRICAN HIP HOP INDABA, 2012 | Source: Ference Isaacs

Africa to its apartheid forebear' (Busch, Busch & Press 2014: 76). He argues that in the educational system, the language issue 'is one of the main reasons for much of the failure of the tertiary system in South Africa today' (2014: 76). We need to tackle this problem by using our students' mother tongue as the medium of instruction in school, and not just in primary grades, but throughout the entire educational process. Alexander teaches that:

> Being able to use the language(s) one has the best command of in any
> situation is an empowering factor, and conversely, not being able to do so
> is necessarily disempowering. The self-esteem, self-confidence, potential
> creativity and spontaneity that come with being able to use the language(s)
> that has or have shaped one from early childhood...is the foundation of all
> democratic polities and institutions. To be denied the use of these languages
> is the very meaning of oppression. (Busch, Busch & Press 2014: 96)

The way forward, then, is not English-only, but a language policy of multilingualism with English taught as a subject. As well, the South African languages should be taught as subjects – and to all students, not just Black students. For example, Leketi Makalela, founding director of the Hub for Multilingual Education and Literacies at Wits, has successfully launched experimental courses teaching Nguni languages to Wits students.

But the school all by itself is not enough. As Alexander taught, the language issue calls for public and community leadership. He contends that in South Africa it calls for the 'middle class and its intellectuals [to] find the courage…[and] the imagination to commit class suicide by moving away decisively from the…English-mainly and often English-only language policy, with all its negative consequences for a democratic polity' (Busch, Busch & Press 2014: 111). In a similar vein, activist–scholar Mamphela Ramphele contends that 'African language speakers, both adults and children, are put at a disadvantage by having to communicate in what is a second or third language for them in an environment in which the English language is equated with general competence and sophistication' (2012: 39). Like Alexander, she too takes South African leadership to task for not 'setting the tone'. She notes that South Africa's politicians 'have taken to torturing themselves whilst talking to voters, the majority of whom are not first language English speakers' (2012: 39). Similar to Alexander's challenge to South African political leadership, Ramphele says, 'How I long to see our president speaking eloquently in isiZulu at the UN or at the G20 as East Asian presidents tend to do' (2012: 39).

In the US we grapple with similar linguistic issues and contradictions. And we too have a legacy of scholars–teachers–activists who can serve as guides for our way forward today. Carter G Woodson (1990/1933), historian and founder of Negro History Week, taught us about the 'mis-education of the Negro' (and you too, as I often signify on the white folk). Part of that 'mis-education' involved the way students have historically been taught to 'scoff' at Black Language instead of being made to understand that it represented a 'broken-down African tongue' (1990/1933: 19). WEB Du Bois, in his work on 'the education of Black people', addressed the needs of the 'Negro university' and advocated that students in these universities should be taught in 'the English idiom they use and understand' (see Du Bois & Aptheker 1982: 93).

Teachers can gain guidance and inspiration from work such as the research experiments conducted by Gary Simpkins in the teaching of reading to African American Language speakers. Simpkins and his team created a reading series (which he named *Bridge*) by rewriting folk stories from the African American oral tradition. Teachers were able to bring students who had been several years behind in reading up to grade level in one semester (see Smitherman 1981).

As Samy and Shaheen advocate, we need pedagogies that reflect us, rather than education that causes us to 'shut down parts of ourselves for the sake of so-called progress'. Language teaching, and schooling in general, has to create a space for us 'to own and value' that which is ours. It is insufficient to say that's just the way things are when it comes to language standards. As Samy notes, we need to teach our students (and ourselves, cuz some of us done forgot or ain nevah knew) to critically understand language and power, 'what languages are valued and what languages are not', and 'to develop a pedagogy that really puts languages on par with each other'.

Clearly Hip Hop is a major dimension of our 'culturally sustaining pedagogy' (see Paris & Alim 2017). Drawing on the work of Tupac, Samy illustrates how through Hip Hop, Tupac not only demonstrated resistance but went beyond middle finger-ups and fuck yous to imagine the society we want to strive to build. 'For Pac, there's a "fuck you" but there's also a theorising and an envisioning of how we might be able to reorder society and redistribute wealth.' In the South African Hip Hop context, Samy provides the example of the work of Isaac Mutant and Dookoom's *Larney Jou Poes* as a way for us to rethink current political and economic arrangements and act *differently*, in ways that are self-loving and self-sustaining.

In sum, 'Beyond "Soul Murder", "Linguistic Looting" and "White Supremacist Delusionalism"' reminds those of us in the struggle that, as Samy and Shaheen put it, 'We have so much work to do. That shit never stops. Can't stop, won't stop.' Teachers, scholars, activists, let's git busy y'all!

BRING YOUR PACK, MAK1ONE | Source: Ference Isaacs

CHAPTER 16.
RAAK WYS: COUNTERING CULTURAL ASSIMILATION THROUGH RHYME AND REASON

ADRIAN VAN WYK (UNIVERSITY OF STELLENBOSCH)

Attempting to erase the impact of apartheid on South Africa's population is unimaginable. The country's landscape is riddled with reminders of apartheid's maintenance plan for white minority rule. Around the country, visual cues trigger memories of exclusion and separation. For some reason, these visual hints seem to feel more blatant in the Western Cape. It feels like there is an attempt to erase dialogue and conversation around particular institutions' involvement in this maintenance plan. A grim silence creeps around the landscape, however, and entangled in the South Easter are stories of truth. If the last 365 years were to be painted onto the canvas of a small town, the result would be a town located within the Boland region of the Western Cape – Stellenbosch. A large portion of this town's population is made up of students attending Stellenbosch University (SU). The centre of SU is marked by Victoria Road, lined with oak trees and wandering security guards patrolling the 'fenceless' university.

SU carries strong remnants of the apartheid era in South Africa's history. However, apartheid thought will not necessarily be advertised in the prospectus for students applying to access this institution of higher learning. The greater town of Stellenbosch presents evidence of the mass displacement enforced on people of colour under the Group Areas Act (No. 41 of 1950). The town's urban planning still resembles apartheid's spatial planning (Valley 2014), demarcating areas according to racial categorisation under the Population Registration Act (No. 30 of 1950). Under apartheid, the centre of town was reserved for whites, uprooting people of colour to the periphery (Valley 2014). Dislocated residents were only allowed daytime access to the centre of town for employment purposes. The mass movement of people from the centre to the periphery is still visible today, once the workday has concluded. Stellenbosch carries reminders of colonial settlement with well-preserved Dutch East India

Company-labelled plaques and cannons placed around the town – the same multinational corporation which would eventually play a major role in transporting slaves to the Cape during the eighteenth century (Lucassen 2004).

SU was complicit in the formation and intellectual justification of apartheid. Being the intellectual stronghold of apartheid during the twentieth century, SU produced a variety of thinkers who were the architects of apartheid during its grand era. Some of these men include DF Malan (prime minister of South Africa from 1948–1954), HF Verwoerd (prime minister from 1958 until his death in 1966) John Vorster (prime minister from 1966–1978 and president from 1978–1979) and PW Botha (prime minister from 1978–1984 and state president from 1984–1989) (Moradi 2010). Chris Brink, a former rector of SU, noted in his inaugural lecture that rectors of the university formed part of the *Afrikaner Broederbond* (Fraternity) (Moradi 2010). Furthermore, Malan is cited as saying that 'the Afrikaner *volk* [people] can best realise its ideals and exercise the largest influence...Stellenbosch therefore stands for an idea' (Brink, cited in Moradi 2010: 4). To visitors walking Stellenbosch's streets lined with oak trees, boutiques and cafes, it may seem quiet and serene, presenting a facade that the town has embraced the 'new' South Africa. However, for people of colour, and especially incoming students of colour, residing in Stellenbosch can be a completely different experience. Malan's ideas might be more visible after staying in the town for more than a wine-tasting experience at a farm.

my feet stand steady on this unstable ground

shifting and skutting the soil

engraving my name into the earth's surface

with my big toe.

For too long Malan's legacies

tried to disturb

how we flow and listen

to the earth's biorhythms

Verwoerd's ideas were not wys

that the moon

conveys messages of yesterday's unequal existence

&

our mere presence in these strongholds

Of nostalgic advantage

personifies the phrase never again! (from 'Divided Past' – Adrian 'Diff' van Wyk)

In recent years, ghosts of the past have kept resurfacing at SU. For example, in 2013 a eugenics testing kit belonging to the racial scientist and Nazi eugenicist Eugen Fischer was discovered in an abandoned cupboard at the university (Mail & Guardian 8 June 2013).[1] In 2014, SU's first black rector, Russel Botman, passed away suddenly while trying to champion transformation within SU. Later it was exposed that the final week before his death was riddled with turbulence. At the heart of this turbulence was a controversial policy plan titled 'Strategic Framework for the Turn of the Century and Beyond', which aimed to address SU's tradition of exclusion.[2] In 2015, a collective of students and staff formed in light of the national student movement calling for the decolonising of university institutions as well as free access to tertiary education. The collective, known as Open Stellenbosch (OS), pressured the university to acknowledge that many of the remnants of the past were still alive and that black students did not feel welcome at the institution. OS ignited various on-campus conversations about SU having benefited from apartheid, proposing that the university should compensate the descendants of the forced removals which took place in Stellenbosch in 1964 under the Group Areas Act. It was proposed that academic bursaries should be awarded to high school learners who were descendants of residents removed under the Act. OS disrupted space and occupied various parts of SU, organising protests to address several issues. The collective further produced a short YouTube film called *Luister* (*Listen*), which went viral once it was released.[3]

One student is quoted in the film as saying that, 'The colour of my skin in Stellenbosch is like a social burden...I mean just walking into spaces, there's that stop, pause, and stare where people cannot believe that you would enter into this space'.[4] *Luister* was a reality check for SU,

---

1. Mandisa Mbali & Handri Walters, Rethinking Maties' apartheid past.
2. Thamm M (2014) Revealed: Professor Botman's torrid final week, *Daily Maverick*, 2 July 2014. Accessed 7 March 2017, https://www.dailymaverick.co.za/article/2014-07-02-revealed-professor-botmans-torrid-final-week.
3. Nicolson G (2015) Stellenbosch: 'Luister' could lead to change. *Daily Maverick*, accessed 30 March 2017, https://www.dailymaverick.co.za/article/2015-09-01-stellenbosch-luister-could-lead-to-change/.
4. https://www.youtube.com/watch?v=sF3rTBQTQk4

which publicly stated that transforming and addressing past issues of inequality would be a top priority. Botman made reference to this until his death in 2014, acknowledging the institution's role in the past.[5]

I'm so chilled out

Even though my day begins

In this little town

Where atrocities

Of a racist nature

Are ignored by those who carry stature

Their sporadic concern

At the wrong moments

Makes me question

The manner

In which they perform

&

Pretend

making me

wonder

if I drop out

Will I be another statistic

grouped bunch of numbers represented in the

'Shame they didn't fit in' demographic

Fuck it,

Still i stand strong

With a medium high fist

As i pessimist

Coz i gotta get this degree

While sidestepping these racists.

Call me a hotnot all you want

5. SU website, www.sun.ac.za, 2011

But at the

End of day

I listen to tracks

You could never be about

Because Hip Hop, Jazz and everything good

Taught me to be

So chilled out

I'm so chilled out ('I'm So Chilled Out' – Adrian 'Diff' van Wyk)

From 2010 onward, there were many movements happening at SU before the national student movement and before the viral video about the tradition of exclusion at SU. Residing in Stellenbosch as an artist was a difficult experience, especially coming from a context of having access to expressive cultural platforms in Cape Town central. After returning to Stellenbosch in 2011 from studying abroad, nothing much had changed since leaving in 2008. The dominant student culture of attending nightclubs, which only played pop, *sokkie*,[6] trance and rock music, was noticeable. Nightclubs and listening spaces lacked genres that contained any form of conscious message, such as Hip Hop, jazz, ragga and dub poetry. Sporadic Hip Hop events took place alongside dub gigs organised at the infamous Mystic Boer venue, featuring artists like EJ von Lyrik, Teba Shumba, DJ Azuhl and Crosby. Brasse Vannie Kaap also performed at an event in 2011 which was attended by no more than 30 people.

To state it plainly, there were no consistent spaces of expression that students and community members could attend to either perform or watch as an audience (sometimes university residences would organise cultural evenings, but this was sporadic). This chapter explores the various platforms that came into existence between 2011 and 2016 in the town, alternative spaces of expression beyond the 'normalised' Wednesday nightclub attendance (commonly nicknamed by students as *klein naweek* [small weekend]).

While completing my undergraduate degree at Stellenbosch, the absence of spaces of expression became a personal frustration. This was a contributing factor to my residence room becoming a retreat for Hip Hop headz from SU and the broader Stellenbosch community to

6. http://www.movado.co.za/sokkie-is-lekker-couple-dance/

hang out; a space created for new rhymes and music to be shared. At the same time, I started meeting people from SU who shared similar ideas about artistic expression. Gatherings took place outside the 'normal' activities at night. The basis of this congregation was the common excitement for music, literature, art and films not found within Stellenbosch. Poetry, especially South African struggle poetry, brought a familiarity to the alien context of Stellenbosch. Poets and authors like Keorapetse Kgositsile, Alice Walker, James Matthews, Maya Angelou, Lesego Rampolokeng and Saul Williams fuelled our conversations about South Africa's young democracy and ideas about the country's and continent's future. The soundtrack to these conversations would be Nina Simone, Abdullah Ibrahim, Charles Mingus, John Coltrane, Peter Tosh, Bob Marley and Capleton.

Furthermore, Afrikaans Hip Hop would be circulated between friends who had been connected to the artists creating the music. The music of Brasse Vannie Kaap, Niko10Long, Knoffel Bruin, League of Shadows and Prophets of da City became important avenues of listening within a context that made people of colour feel tolerated, but not accepted. As Shirley Tate (2014: 2480) states: 'Tolerance always points to that which is tolerable, and thus tolerance itself is intolerable!' One important song, which was a retreat from the tolerance of Stellenbosch, was the track by League of Shadows called 'KhoeSunz',[7] with the chorus going:

> Is ya
> Boeta KhoeSunz
> Gaan jou kis dra
> Dis waar
> Voete gooi sand op jou liggaam
> Virdala
> Soos daai jong aiya's innie gwala
> Walaaa
> Spoeg my tong fire tot in
> Ghana
> (Is ya

---

7. https://soundcloud.com/league-of-shadows/khoesunz

brothers KhoeSunz

will carry your coffin

that's true

feet kicking sand on your body

Messed up

Like those young rastas speaking truth

Walaaaa

My tongue spits fire

Till Ghana)

Music and art became a foundation for collectives and crews formed in Stellenbosch. The frustration with SU and lack of performance platforms brought into existence the collective Urban Scapes, comprised of artists, photographers, poets, rappers, researchers, filmmakers and youth workers. Urban Scapes created platforms to confront and convert frustration into conversational points of departure through various artistic interventions, such as setting up impromptu ciphers, usually in spaces of movement such as walkways, on staircases and on the SU student-centre bridge across Merriman Road. These platforms utilised the invitational characteristics of ciphers, inviting people to come and share their ideas in poetic form in spaces that were welcoming and encouraging for young people to express their thoughts.

H. Samy Alim alludes to these characteristics in his book *Roc the Mic Right: The Language of Hip Hop Culture*. Alim (2006: 98) writes that

> The cipher is where all (or some combination) of the Hip Hop cultural modes of discourse and discursive practices – call and response, multilayered totalizing expression, signifying, bustin, tonal semantics, poetics, narrative sequencing, flow, metaphoric and hyperbolic language use, image-making, freestylin, battling, word-explosions, word-creations, word-pictures, dialoguing other voices, talk-singing, kinesics – converge into a fluid matrix of linguistic-cultural activity.

These ciphers became an avenue of empowerment for people to share work, poetry and songs, allowing a space for listening and speaking to happen. In his explorations of the cipher, Alim draws upon the work of James Peterson, who is quoted as writing:

Ciphers are marvelous speech events. They are inviting and also very challenging. They have become a litmus test for modern day griots. Ciphers are the innovative formats for battles (the ritual of rhyming is informed by the physical arrangement of Hip Hop). The concept of the cipher is essential to Hip Hop Culture and to its vernacular. It indicates an epistemology that is non-linear. (Alim, Ibrahim & Pennycook 2009: 98)

The reference to a cipher as a speech event is what made these impromptu gatherings so important in a place like Stellenbosch. There were many occasions when these ciphers were ended by security guards in the town.

The aspect of turning these impromptu gatherings into speech events is what excited rhymers and audiences alike. Having people gather to share their ideas and thoughts through rhyme and reason with minimal planning in a space like Stellenbosch was unheard of. This was a major motivator.

Every week Urban Scapes decided on a different space in Stellenbosch town to disrupt the conventional flow of people moving through those locations. It was also a tactic to draw audiences who were interested in watching rappers and poets converse about various topics suggested by the bystanders. These ciphers laid the foundation for artistic collaborations amongst various disciplines, and the disruption of space was a major part of these events.

Another collaborative exhibition that the collective created was Racebook. From 2011, before the Penny Sparrow racial outburst on social media, Urban Scapes started addressing the growing racism on these forums. They collected statuses, tweets and comments from various social media accounts, printed them out and pasted them on easels that they set up on the Rooiplein, a student gathering space next to the main campus library. A comment section was provided for responses to these statuses and Afrikaans Hip Hop and kwaito music was played to attract people to the exhibition. The comments and responses generated from this formed part of another exhibition illustrating the public reactions to this exhibition.

At the same time, many collectives were meeting up and forming plans to collaborate at the Wednesday ciphers organised by Urban Scapes. In 2011, a group of students and teachers formed a literary collective called the Stellenbosch Literacy Project. SLiP functioned as an online literary magazine based in the English department at SU and provided a platform for various literary conversations. A performance platform of SLiP, called the InZync poetry sessions, was then established. In March 2011, the first InZync poetry event was held in Kayamandi. InZync was purposely curated in the township at the Amazink venue to create two-way traffic between the centre of town and the township. The deliberate aim was to disturb the usual flow of students and residents in the centre of town, who generally would not go into the township at night unless they lived there. InZync became a consistent performance platform in Stellenbosch (and arguably across South Africa), with each event curated according to a multilingual and multi-genre checklist. The purpose of the platform was to celebrate the multilingual landscape of South Africa through poetry and expression. A variety of poets from different poetic genres were invited to perform at InZync, including Jitsvinger, Niko10Long, Blaq Pearl, Antjie Krog, Jethro Louw, Malika Ndlovu, Pieter Odendaal, Toni Stuart, Lesego Rampolokeng, James Matthews, Keorapetse Kgositsile, Mbongeni Nomkonwana and Allison-Claire Hoskins. The open mic segment of these shows continues to be a talking point, attracting people from all over Cape Town who are already creating spaces for performance and cultural expression. InZync therefore became linked to this network of spaces and our sessions became a meeting point for people from different contexts.

MALIKA NDLOVU AND KEORAPETSE KGOSITSILE PERFORMING AT INZYNC | Source: Retha Ferguson

EMILE YX? AND JAMES MATTHEWS PERFORMING AT INZYNC | Source: Retha Ferguson

Multilingual poets came together, sparking conversations around issues that affect the sociopolitical context of South Africa, simultaneously positioning the country within an African context. While working with InZync and doing these monthly shows, as co-curators Pieter Odendaal and I witnessed the excitement around performance poetry and we wanted to create a space for writing and mentoring young poets. This brought about the INKredibles writing workshops in 2012. The workshops hosted young people from the surrounding Stellenbosch region, bringing youths from various backgrounds into one space to write about their individual lived experiences. These sessions are still hosted at the English department of SU and the Amazink venue in Kayamandi.

The InZync sessions expanded the space created by Urban Scapes. This provided a listening space for poets from all genres to be heard and it became a conversation point for activists, creatives and collaborators to start speaking about various social justice issues. Building on the cipher and the concept of one person performing and an audience listening, this ethics of listening was part of the ethos of InZync. This created the frame for performance sessions where audiences learned that providing a safe space for a poet to speak was important. InZync asked no cover charge so we could attract as many people as possible from different backgrounds into one space in Stellenbosch. Furthermore, the multilingual nature of the show created an interesting dynamic, leaving a portion of the audience in silence as they could not understand what was being spoken about by the poets, while another section of the audience would be left ecstatic at hearing poetry in their vernacular language.

ADRIAN, CAPE TOWN 2015 | Source: Adam Haupt

During each InZync session, the programme was bound together by two DJs who selected and mixed tracks that set a particular mood for the event. In the spaces between poets walking to the stage and during intermission, music was played that was definitely not found in nightclubs in Stellenbosch. This was done deliberately to provide the audience with a unique listening experience in between the poetry that was performed by featured poets and open mic guests. The DJs played an important part in giving the audience a listening break after the poetry performances.

In 2016, a self-produced video for Koleka Putuma's poem 'Water' was created, bringing the mediums of video and poetry together.[8] The video, which was released on YouTube, was widely viewed by online audiences. At the same time, an audio collaboration of music and poetry took place, involving producers, musicians and poets who created an eight-track audio recording which was released for free on SoundCloud. The title of the project was InterVerse and it explored intersectionality through poetry and verse.

8. https://www.youtube.com/watch?v=8dfq3C8GNrE

THE FLYER FOR KOLEKA PUTUMA'S POEM 'WATER' | Source: InZync, photograph by Retha Ferguson

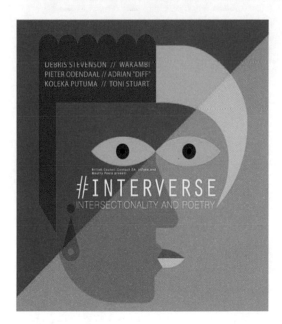

THE COVER OF THE INTERVERSE EP RELEASED IN 2016 | Source: InZync

Furthermore, the posters for each InZync event had bright colours, which drew lots of attention. We had the opportunity to work with Retha Ferguson, who played an important role in creating an online identity because of her unique design techniques, which included, but were not limited to, illustrations and photography. Retha's photos also generated content from every session and were posted on Facebook following each show.

POSTERS FOR THE INZYNC POETRY SESSIONS | Source: InZync

INZYNC AND ACTIVISM

Our artworks occupy corneas

Our poems disrupt eardrums

Our voices protest, demonstrate & activate

Change in an instant

The fact that we are here

Causes the white-supremacist-capitalist-patriarch

To paap.

We are genetically connected to the soil

The lame appliance of pseudo-science

Tried to divorce us from the land

Even R.W. Wilcocks's report

Of 1938

Couldn't separate

My name

From being written

In the Sun's Ray's

By floating dust particles (extract from 'Divided Past' – Adrian 'Diff' van Wyk)

Over the course of six years, InZync became a platform that voiced people's frustrations. In 2015, once the first bout of FEES MUST FALL protests had taken place, InZync conducted a poetry session themed around free, decolonised, intersectional education. The same happened in November 2016, with a free session around the idea of protest and education. Furthermore, the workshops with young poets focused on various themes that young people face, whether it be around sexual identity or gang violence. Each workshop explored the ideas of the young participants. One highlight was using poetry as an educational tool to educate these young people around the idea of intersectionality within a South African context.

The InZync Sessions became a space for me to grow and engage with Stellenbosch's history of forced removals and the attempts at historical erasure, as well as the institution's attempt to only present comfortable histories to students. Poetry and expression became a way for me to remember the past and explore the heritages of people in Stellenbosch who were excluded from the unfriendly corridors of learning.

Drawing inspiration from Prophets of da City and the track 'I Remember District Six', I wrote about the forced removals that happened in Stellenbosch in 1964, the same forced removals that the collective OS held the university accountable for. Reimagining history through creative writing helped me to understand the trauma inflicted on people of colour who have resided in Stellenbosch for centuries.

My writing was inspired by the ability to reimagine the historical context of one place and document it in poetic verse. The story of forced removals from Die Vlakte in Stellenbosch inspired the creation of a documentary, *What the Soil Remembers*, in collaboration with Ecuadorian filmmaking production company Jirafica, as well as a series of poems, including the following poem titled after the documentary. Both the documentary and the poem focus on the mosque that has been in the centre of Stellenbosch since the turn of the twentieth century.

06:30 am

adhan

delivers memories

to ancestors

left destitute

by unhappy histories.

Calls to prayer

Covered in yesterday's

Laughter

Allows the soil,

to

Reflect on its cognizance

Calls to salah (صلاة) for

The morning's fajr (فجر)

& duahr(ظهر) by noon

ASR (عصر) in the afternoon

By sunset it's time

For mahgrieb (مغرب)

Days

concluding with

ESHAAI (عشاء)

Indications of Juma'ah (جمعة)

Calm restless

ancestors

uneasy with yesterdays

anger.

Reminiscence the only comfort

To counter

Decades of trauma

Reminiscence the only comfort

To counter

yesterday's trauma.

September 25 1964

Die Vlakte's

Stellenbosch's

activity

Disturbed

By the Group Areas Act (1950)

3700 souls

spread out amongst

6 schools,

4 churches,

1 mosque

Saturdays at the Geity cinema

Shooooosh, Tarzan is about to start

We bought Fatima's freshly baked Koesisters

Labarang Tafels in

The Malay Kamp

Decorated precisely

With

Pietjies,

Samoosas

Koekies

& KOESIESTERS (x2)

Saturday sports sessions

With a pa brasse

Gat maak

& leftover.......

KOESIESTERS.

A imam's call to prayer

Protects replanted memories

Once

Uprooted in familiar soil

Today,

a fruit hawker's

voice decorates

the lunch hour hustle

calling out seasonal prices

12:00pm every afternoon

a man throws sunflower seeds

in a precise circle

onto the soils surface

attracting pigeons to

what used to be his grandfather's

backyard.

Reminiscence the only comfort

To counter

Decades of trauma

Reminiscence the only comfort

To counter yesterday's trauma.

Cultural assimilation and historical erasure were important for blending purposes within Stellenbosch. Whenever I entered into the claustrophobic, hospital-lit passages of the Arts and Social Sciences building (ASS building), I always felt invisible in these corridors. Whenever I walked the streets of Stellenbosch town on a Wednesday night, I would dream about going to Hip Hop shows in welcoming spaces where security would not interrogate my presence through constantly requesting my student card. I always knew that Stellenbosch was Afrikaans but I could not understand the unapologetic exclusion of people who did not speak Afrikaans. The language debate was a constant topic during my time at Stellenbosch. Sometimes during this language debate some voices felt more included than others. I later understood through research and reading that everything that I was feeling was not just sensitive imagination but actually the maintenance of certain exclusionary traditions.

In retrospect, the frustration about the unwelcoming atmosphere in Stellenbosch ironically connected individuals from various backgrounds, allowing them to create spaces that were safe and promoted creativity. The work that resulted from these spaces created challenging conversations that took place while developing ideas from one another, but also carving out a personalised identity within a South African context. Existing texts and thinkers' work opened up entirely new avenues of self-affirmation intertwined with cultural expression. Understanding the self and unearthing the various histories once almost erased by an academic institution like SU became important in constructing artistic platforms. InZync became a space for conversations to take place around institutional and structural violence inflicted on black people in Stellenbosch. The sessions began countering the spirit of exclusion by including those who were historically excluded by SU. InZync acted as a space for me to understand my own identity within a post-apartheid South Africa. During my first years at SU, it always felt like I was not welcome and that I was merely being tolerated within the space. Working with InZync and Urban Scapes helped provide me and others with a counterspace for expression within Stellenbosch and created opportunities for new collaborations.

Frantz Fanon (1967) references the inferiority complex that the colonised feel with respect to their own cultural practices. Hence, many people at SU acquired new spoken accents to recreate themselves in order to fit in. Working to build a variety of platforms was more than just a performance space where people could experience expression. It played a major part in identity affirmation – creating spaces where people could exist without any pretences imposed upon them; existing without the preconceived idea and, furthermore, performing this preconceived idea.

In *Roc the Mic Right*, Alim (2006: 127) asks a series of questions when linking Hip Hop to black culture, including 'What are the core values of Amiri Baraka and Chuck D that enable them to speak the truth – or be the truth?' I will attempt to answer that question: in contexts that are anti-black, there is an attempt to erase the truth around the black experience, constantly alluding to how much things have changed and that happiness should abound because some basic changes have occurred. However, in a context like Stellenbosch, the truth was moulded to make some people feel comfortable about their historical positioning by excluding certain voices from history and expecting people to assimilate into a system that does not recognise people of colour. What makes artists like Amiri Baraka and Chuck D powerful is that they explore these truths and unapologetically inform their audiences, some of whom latch onto these truths in spaces which have tried to cover centuries of inequality with a veil of ignorance. The truth through these expressions gives energy to those who are feeling sidelined to continue and affirm their presence in celebration of who they are. Years later, I finally understand the reason for helping to build and maintain various platforms in Stellenbosch – they were spaces for us to counter cultural and historical assimilation.

PART TWO REFERENCES

Achebe C (1958) *Things fall apart*. London: Heinemann

Adhikari M (2005) *Not white enough, not black enough: Racial identity in the South African coloured community*. Athens, OH: Ohio University Press

Alim HS (2006) *Roc the mic right: The language of Hip Hop culture*. London: Routledge

Alim HS & Haupt A (2017) Reviving soul(s) with Afrikaaps: Hip hop as culturally sustaining pedagogy in Cape Town, South Africa. In D Paris & HS Alim (eds) *Culturally sustaining pedagogies: Teaching and learning for justice in a changing world*. New York: Teachers College Press

Alim HS & Smitherman G (2012) *Articulate while black: Barack Obama, language, and race in the US*. New York: Oxford University Press

Alim HS, Ibrahim A & Pennycook A (eds) (2009) *Global linguistic flows: Hip Hop cultures, youth identities, and the politics of language*. London: Routledge

Alim HS, Rickford JR & Ball AF (eds) (2016) *Raciolinguistics: How language shapes our ideas about race*. New York: Oxford University Press

Anderson E (1994) The code of the streets. *The Atlantic*, May: 81–94

Appadurai A (1996) *Modernity at large: Cultural dimensions of globalization*. Minneapolis, MN: University of Minnesota Press

Ariefdien S & Abrahams N (2006) Cape Flats alchemy: Hip hop arts in South Africa. In J Chang (ed.) *Total chaos: The art and aesthetics of hip hop*. New York: Basic Civitas Books

Ariefdien S & Burgess M (2011) A cross-generational conversation about hip hop in a changing South Africa. In PK Saucier (ed.) *Native tongue: An African hip hop reader*. New Jersey: Africa World Press

Bank L (2011) *Home spaces, street styles: Contesting power and identity in a South African city*. London: Pluto Press

Baugh J (2003) Linguistic profiling. In S Makoni, G Smitherman, AF Ball & AK Spears (eds) *Black linguistics: Language, politics and society in Africa and the Americas*. London: Routledge

Blackmon S, Kirklighter C & Parks S (eds) (2011) *Listening to our elders: Working and writing for change*. Philadelphia, PA: New City Community Press

Bourdieu P (2003) Symbolic violence. In R Célestin, E DalMolin & I Courtivron (eds) *Beyond French feminisms: Debates on women, politics, and culture in France, 1981–2001*. London: Palgrave Macmillan

Busch B, Busch L & Press K (eds) (2014) *Interviews with Neville Alexander: The power of languages against the language of power*. Pietermaritzburg: University of KwaZulu-Natal Press

Cooke B (1972) Nonverbal communication among Afro-Americans: An initial classification. In T Kochman (ed.) *Rappin' and stylin' out: Communication in urban black America*. Urbana, IL: University of Illinois Press

Dalby D (1972) The African element in American English. In T Kochman (ed.) *Rappin' and stylin' out: Communication in urban black America*. Urbana, IL: University of Illinois Press

Davis AY (2016) *Freedom is a constant struggle: Ferguson, Palestine, and the foundations of a movement*. Chicago, IL: Haymarket Books

Du Bois WEB & Aptheker H (eds) (1982) *Writings by W.E.B. Du Bois in non-periodical literature edited by others*. New York: Kraus-Thomson Organization

Esquivel L (1989) *Like water for chocolate*. New York: Doubleday

Fanon F (1967) *Black skin, white masks*, trans. Charles L. Markmann. New York: Grove Press

Fanon F (2008) *Black skin, white masks*. London: Pluto Press

Fataar A (1997) Access to schooling in a post-apartheid South Africa: Linking concepts to context. *International Review of Education* 43(4): 331–348

Fiske EB & Ladd HF (2004) *Elusive equity: Education reform in post-apartheid South Africa*. Washington, DC: Brookings Institution Press

Freire P (1970) *Pedagogy of the oppressed*, trans. Myra Bergman Ramos. New York: Herder and Herder

Freire P (2000) *Pedagogy of the oppressed*. London: Bloomsbury

Fukuyama F (1992) *The end of history and the last man*. London: Penguin

Grier WH & Cobbs PM (1968) *Black rage*. New York: Basic Books

Haupt A (1996) Rap and the articulation of resistance: An exploration of subversive cultural production during the early 90s, with particular reference to Prophets of da City. MA mini-thesis, University of the Western Cape, Cape Town

Haupt A (2001) Black thing: Hip hop nationalism, 'race' and gender in Prophets of da City and Brasse vannie Kaap. In Z Erasmus (ed.) *Coloured by history, shaped by place: New perspectives on coloured identities in Cape Town*. Cape Town: Kwela Books

Haupt A (2012) *Static: Race and representation in post-apartheid music, media and film*. Cape Town: HSRC Press

Herman ES & Chomsky N (1988) *Manufacturing consent: The political economy of the mass media*. New York: Pantheon Books

Howell S & Vincent L (2014) 'Licking the snake' – the i'khothane and contemporary township youth identities in South Africa. *South African Review of Sociology* 45(2): 60–77

Lucassen J (2004) A multinational and its labor force: The Dutch East India Company, 1595–1795. *International Labor and Working-Class History* 66: 12–39

Machiavelli N (2003) *The prince and other writings*. New York: Barnes & Noble

Mailer N (1957) *The white Negro: Superficial reflections on the hipster*. San Francisco, CA: City Lights

Mbembe A (2011) Democracy as a community of life. *The Johannesburg Salon* 4(1): 5–10

McClintock A (1995) *Imperial leather: Race, gender, and sexuality in the colonial contest*. New York: Routledge

Moradi F (2010) Colour-line: The petrifaction of racialization and alterity at the University of Stellenbosch. *JHEA/RESA* 8(2): 1–21

More MP (2008) Biko: Africana existentialist philosopher. In A Mngxitama, A Alexander & NC Gibson (eds) *Biko lives! Contesting the legacies of Steve Biko*. New York: Palgrave Macmillan

Mustakova-Possardt E (2003) *Critical consciousness: A study of morality in global, historical context*. Westport, CT: Greenwood Publishing

Oliphant A (2008) A human face: Biko's conceptions of African culture and humanism. In A Mngxitama, A Alexander & NC Gibson (eds) *Biko lives! Contesting the legacies of Steve Biko*. New York: Palgrave Macmillan

Ortner SB (2006) *Anthropology and social theory: Culture, power, and the acting subject*. Durham, NC: Duke University Press

Paris D & Alim HS (2014) What are we seeking to sustain through culturally sustaining pedagogy? A loving critique forward. *Harvard Educational Review* 84(1): 85–100

Paris D & Alim HS (eds) (2017) *Culturally sustaining pedagogies: Teaching and learning for justice in a changing world*. New York: Teachers College Press

Petchauer E (2009) Framing and reviewing hip-hop educational research. *Review of Educational Research* 79(2): 946–978

Posel D (2010) Races to consume: Revisiting South Africa's history of race, consumption and the struggle for freedom. *Ethnic and Racial Studies* 33(2): 157–175

Ramphele M (2012) *Conversations with my sons and daughters*. Johannesburg: Penguin

Read J (2009) A genealogy of homo-economicus: Neoliberalism and the production of subjectivity. *Foucault Studies* 6: 25–36

Runell Hall M (2011) Education in a hip-hop nation: Our identity, politics and pedagogy. PhD dissertation, University of Massachusetts Amherst

Sennett R & Cobb J (1972) *The hidden injuries of class*. Cambridge: Cambridge University Press

Smitherman G (ed.) (1981) *Black English and the education of black children and youth: Proceedings of the National Invitational Symposium on the King Decision*. Detroit, MI: Wayne State University Press

Spady JG (1991) Grandmaster Caz and hiphopography of the Bronx. In JG Spady & J Eure (eds) *Nation conscious rap: The hip hop vision*. Philadelphia, PA: Black History Museum Press

Spady JG, Alim HS & CG Lee (1999) *Street conscious rap*. Philadelphia, PA: Black History Museum

Sun Tzu (2005) *The art of war* (special ed.). El Paso, TX: El Paso Norte Press

Swai M (2017) Pedagogies of the 'formerly' oppressed: Hip hop and critical education in South African social justice struggles. PhD dissertation, New York University

Tate S (2014) Racial affective economies, disalienation and 'race made ordinary'. *Ethnic and Racial Studies* 37(13): 2475–2490

Telzak SC (2012) *The tithes of apartheid: Perceptions of social mobility among black individuals in Cape Town, South Africa*. CSSR Working Paper No. 315, University of Cape Town. Accessed 3 March 2019, http://www.cssr.uct.ac.za/pub/wp/315

Telzak SC (2014) *Trouble ahead, trouble behind: Perceptions of social mobility and economic inequality in Mount Frere, Eastern Cape and Newcastle, KwaZulu-Natal*. CSSR Working Paper No. 326, University of Cape Town. Accessed 3 March 2019, http://www.cssr.uct.ac.za/pub/wp/326

Valley G (2014) What's the matter with…Stellenbosch University. *Africa Is a Country*, 8 October 2014. Accessed June 2017, https://africasacountry.com/2014/10/whats-the-matter-with-stellenbosch-university

Venkatesh S (2002) 'Doin' the hustle': Constructing the ethnographer in the American ghetto. *Ethnography* 3(1): 91–111

wa Thiong'o N (1986) *Decolonising the mind: The politics of language in African literature*. London: James Currey

Wacquant L (1998) Inside the zone: The social art of the hustler in the black American ghetto. *Theory, Culture and Society* 15(2): 1–36

Wacquant L (2007) Territorial stigmatization in the age of advanced marginality. *Thesis Eleven* 91(1): 66–77

Warner R (2007) Battles over borders: Hip hop and the politics and poetics of race and place in the new South Africa. PhD dissertation, York University, Toronto, Ontario

Wiley R (1991) *Why black people tend to shout: Cold facts and wry views from a black man's world*. New York: Penguin

Williams QE (2017) *Remix multilingualism: Hip hop, ethnography and the performance of marginalized voices*. London: Bloomsbury Press

Williams QE & Stroud C (2010) Performing rap ciphas in late-modern Cape Town: Extreme locality and multilingual citizenship. *Afrika Focus* 23(2): 39–59

Williams QE & Stroud C (2013) Multilingualism remixed: Sampling texts, braggadocio and the politics of voice in Cape Town hip hop. *Stellenbosch Papers in Linguistics* 42: 15–36

Williams QE & Stroud C (2014) Battling race: Stylizing language and the coproduction of whiteness and colouredness in a freestyle rap battle. *Journal of Linguistic Anthropology* 24(3): 277–293

Willis PE (1981) *Learning to labor: How working class kids get working class jobs*. New York: Columbia University Press

Woodson CG (1990/1933) *The mis-education of the Negro*. Trenton, NJ: Africa World Press

Wright R (1940) *Native son*. New York: Harper and Row

PART 3

Remixing Race and Gender Politics

LEFT TO RIGHT: *B-GIRLS VEE AND FOXXY: AFRICAN HIP HOP INDABA WINNERS* | Source: Ference Isaacs

B-BOY BENNY | Source: Ference Isaacs

REMIXING RACE AND GENDER POLITICS

It should be clear by now that Hip Hop culture in South Africa, and specifically Cape Hip Hop, has always had to negotiate the intersection of race, gender and sexuality, and will continue to do so. In South Africa, where citizens are still dealing with apartheid's patriarchal and racist legacy, race, gender and sexuality are often key themes in efforts to empower the marginalised, whether at the macro or the micro level of society. For Hip Hop culture, race has been an enduring feature that has impacted on the culture and remains a defining marker of difference, distinction and social hierarchy. In the twenty-first century, Hip Hop approaches race as a verb rather than as a noun, with the focus being on racialisation, that is, the racing of interactions and performances. Hip Hop artists nowadays do not critique or try to undo racialisation in isolation from the injurious actions of gender. It is no secret that Hip Hop's greatest limitation is tied to gender politics and the charge often levelled against it for being misogynistic, sexist and downright discriminatory against differently queered people. We see it in rap videos, we hear it in rap songs, and we find it reflected in the participation of women in the culture. A focus on the latter is not enough because there will always be an emphasis on how many women and men participate in the culture. Furthermore, such a focus would be insufficient when it comes to discussions on sexuality. There is thus a need to shift the location of agency and voice to facilitate gender equality in Hip Hop, to recognise the plurality of sexuality that exists in the culture, and the qualitative formation of racialisations that continue to shape racial difference in and outside of Hip Hop culture.

Given these intersecting tensions between race, gender and sexuality in South African Hip Hop, what is the way forward? What can we learn from today's Hip Hop artists in engaging race, gender and sexuality? This intersectionality requires our analytical and moral attention in Hip Hop culture if we are serious about holding ourselves true to the fifth element, Knowledge of Self. We have to be culturally vigilant, too, about how we treat gendered bodies, since it is often the bodies of the historically marginalised that are undervalued, deemed disposable and precarious. We have to remix our practices of

B-GIRLS FOXXY & VEE, AFRICAN HIP HOP INDABA | Source: Ference Isaacs

gender engagement to a level that supersedes our own limitations. In other words, we need to remix our gender mindset, set it ablaze and re-engage the histories and cultural acts that have come to constitute the best of gender respect and love in Hip Hop culture, and guard against the further cheapening of black bodies, of any gender. We especially have to dispense with cis-heteropatriarchal and hegemonic conceptions of gender identity that valorise tough, heterosexist, masculine practices, and that undermine and limit our understanding of non-binary and queer subjects. The chapters in this section – personal narratives, opinion pieces, interviews and academic essays – explore some of these ideas around the intersection between race, gender and sexuality.

In Chapters 17 and 23, for example, H Samy Alim unpacks the intersections of gender, race and sexuality with Natasha C Tafari and Andy Mkosi, respectively. Alim and Tafari, poet, MC and the organiser of Words Worth Saying, talk through the difficulties she experienced in producing a creative space on the Cape Flats. The discussion with Mkosi lays bare the unnerving politics of sexuality for queer, 'other' bodies.

Warrick Moses (Chapter 18) provides a sustained analysis of race and representation in contemporary South African Hip Hop. He highlights the contestations that emerge around authenticity, specifically when questions of race and the racialisation of rap genres are negotiated. Moses argues that the appropriation of signs and symbols in South African Hip Hop by coloured, white and black artists has differential effects, particularly where it concerns the recognition of agency and voice. For Moses, the selection of images and lyrics in rap music videos typically holds implications for the racialised and gendered body politic of South African Hip Hop culture. Although his chapter focuses on the rap music and lyrics of Die Antwoord and Dookoom, he argues convincingly that white Hip Hop artists' appropriation of 'black people's things' does not have the same effect as black or coloured artists' appropriation of 'white people's things', as is often the case in racialised capitalist economies.

In Chapter 19, Ben Caesar brings to light the contradictions and tensions in his masculinity as well as his gendered approach to Hip Hop art and identity activism. This is a refreshing, critical reflection on masculinity, not often found in Hip Hop cultures globally. Caesar narrates his transnational, translingual and transborder experience of South African Hip Hop. His chapter opens with mention of his feminist-activist mother, and moves on to discuss his learning of the precarious dangers of enforcing gender binaries and his introduction to the travails of transgender activists. For Caesar, the gender(ing) of Hip Hop culture intersects with the racialisation of his body. His upbringing by his feminist mother helped him to identify these intersections of race, gender and sexuality. This knowledge has also helped him to 'unlearn' the practice of reducing female Hip Hop artists and fans in his rap videos to mere consumable bodies.

Burni Aman, one of the pioneers of South African Hip Hop, takes a critical stance against gender essentialising in Chapter 20 by disentangling the binary of 'boss bitches' versus 'boss ladies'. Her argument revolves around the deteriorating and racialised effects that come with assigning labels to female Hip Hop artists. Though she pays homage to pioneering artists such as Queen Latifah and others, Aman points out that the hard-fought gender currency in Hip Hop culture goes further than the Iggy Azaleas of the world. Aman argues that women are as culpable as men in the exploitation of black female Hip Hop artists. She claims that although she does not assign the 'boss bitch' label to herself, the use of such labels requires further critical, nuanced reflection.

Chapter 21 is a personal essay penned by one of Cape Town's most active female MCs in the studio, on stage and in her community. Janine 'Blaq Pearl' van Rooy takes us on her intimate, and personal journey into Hip Hop activism, her tireless dedication to social development in the communities where she works, and the language conscientisation of young multilingual speakers through the linguistic activism of Afrikaaps. She is part of a generation of female Hip Hop artists who are deeply embedded in Hip Hop activism and art today and who work hard to transcend gender barriers. Her work suggests new pathways and directions for younger female MCs breaking into the field.

In Chapter 22, Eavesdrop writes about the pitfalls, failures, losses, gains and emotional turbulence a female MC and activist experiences daily in Hip Hop culture. An MC who struggles daily for and on behalf of racialised and classed people, the author documents what it takes to succeed as a female Hip Hop artist. Eavesdrop narrates her reliance on the fifth element of Hip Hop, Knowledge of Self, to keep pushing when the social, spatial and economic decks are stacked against her as an artist. Eavesdrop takes the reader on her emotional journey to bring Hip Hop's message of freedom and its dream as a force of light through lyrics, rhyme and poetry. She reaffirms Hip Hop culture as a counterdiscursive tool against social stereotyping and as a means of escape, if only temporarily, from the hardships of the ghetto.

Chapter 24 highlights the transformative politics of MC Dope Saint Jude. Adam Haupt demonstrates how Dope Saint Jude, in collaboration with Angel Ho, brings to the forefront not only the 'double-coded' gay language of Gayle, but also the queering of city spaces. Haupt's analysis of Dope Saint Jude's music reveals the position that queer bodies hold in and outside of Hip Hop culture and how her work critically unsettles hegemonic and binary conceptions of gender and sexuality. The chapter celebrates the transformative impact that Dope Saint Jude's music has on Hip Hop culture through its critique of gender and sexuality, cultural imperialism, neoliberal economics and, importantly, its resignification of Hip Hop language.

OPEN STREETS, CAPE TOWN | Source: Ference Isaacs

CHAPTER 17.
'THEY TRIED TO BURY US': HIP HOP POETRY, POLITICS AND THE POWER OF WORDS WORTH SAYING

NATASHA C TAFARI WITH H SAMY ALIM

H Samy Alim spoke to Natasha C Tafari, poet, MC, and the organiser of Words Worth Saying, in Athlone in 2017. Words Worth Saying brings poets and MCs into the same creative space and serves as an important platform for building and supporting the Hip Hop underground in Cape Town.

Alim: What music you heard in your household growing up?

Natasha: It hardly played. There's no distinctive music that I can associate my parents with, and they didn't go to church, none of those – I don't know. That is, I guess, part of why – I know people in Hip Hop have this thing where the family just don't understand us. I think that's part of why my mom just didn't understand or don't understand. Myself, even, the involvement with music, I loved Hip Hop. I was more the dancing side than anything else and the culture side of it. The development for me to the music came with poetry, and that was only at 25 because I walked – I was walking one day. Two lines popped into my head, and I said stop. I wasn't at home. I didn't have pen and paper. When I got home I picked up pen and paper, and I wrote freestyle. Then I just wrote. Since then I would – what I did then was, whenever I got angry, when I became angry about something political, then I'd go write. I'd write. There was a lot of like, 'She's a poet, man, she's not Hip Hop. She's a poet.' I used to say, 'I do Hip Hop poetry,' because for me it wasn't necessarily poetry. I was doing commentary on government and politics, just my anger, writing that down.

I remember meeting up with…sister Mariam. This was me then coming back from the States now. We were freestyling in the kitchen one day, and she said, 'Tasha, they'll never put us on. They'll never put on what we are talking about, on platforms that they have around.' I was like, 'So, then let's just create our own platform. Why not?' We went to Chili 'n Lime. We set [up] Hip Hop Poetry in Motion.

Alim: You said you were walking, and two lines came to your head.

Natasha: It was freestyle, something about freestyle. I said, freestyle, your style or freestyle, my style – something like that, that I wrote down. Then 'Warrior' became one of my favourite poems. It's a long poem…Basically, the idea is we are independent beings. The idea is that if each one of us finds who we are, then to bring that into the equation of community contribution strengthens everything. Use your God-given capacity. Use your God-given talent. Work on you. Make you stronger in your role, and then bring that to the table basically. If each of us concentrates on that, it would change the equation. Instead of us looking at each other, breaking each other down, like, 'I do the same as you,' and, 'I'm better than you,' and those kind of dynamics…When I started with it though, what I understood was that I felt like I was healing, and that the power of healing from my side would come through the poetry and through the power of the word at that time and the performance. What I understood was, you can only heal others when you heal yourself. That whole journey was a healing and transformation process for me because you've gotta go through all those things that happen to you; doesn't really matter anymore because it made you who you are. But you need to understand that. If you can't understand it and put it into context, that's when evil comes in because you start operating from a perspective that is clouded by your pain and all of that.

I started looking at that, and I think Carlos Santana said the same thing when he accepted his award, the Legend Award. We do this for the healing of the nation. For me, that's what the role of artists are in many ways, many forms of it. You take what other people feel, and you try to express it in either colour on canvas or in words – what they can't put into words. With poetry and with, even going to freestyle poetry, I'd find that there'd be times that there's no topic, but everybody would be more or less talking about the same topic. In that is where I learned how to share. Even though you're speaking on the same topic, everyone has their own way of speaking about it…You might not hear it from me, but you're gonna get it from that person that says it in that way.

Hip Hop Poetry in Motion then grew. She [Mariam] left, and I continued with it. I would do like – I tried to – at that point I was doing four a year because I would approach venue owners and just pitch it. Then District Six Café became interested in it. It was a beautiful café. You walked in, and then there's just the building. Then you go into another section where it's outside. The mountain was over there. The stage is here. On really lovely nights, you're performing under the mountain like that. It was beautiful. We had our chance – I was brave, man. I walk in, and I'm like, 'Yo, pleased to meet you. I wanna do this gig here.' He says like, 'Alright, bring me the proposal.' Bring him the proposal, and he's like, no compliments to it. I hired a song guy and everything. Next thing I know he is coming to me and he's saying to me, 'No, man, you're just a sister. You're just a face. But actually there's other – there's men behind you. You're not the one that's rolling with this.' That's when I learned how the game of Hip Hop and of entertainment and all of that is not an equal playing field. 'You can't be the one in control. You're a woman,' that's what he was saying to me blatantly in my face. I looked at him, and I was like, 'You know what? Believe what you need to believe as long as I get to do my gig here 'cause this is my gig.' Then the other guy comes to me, and he's like, 'Yo, your sound guy is the one.' I'm like, 'What do you mean?' He's like, 'He's saying it's his gig. He wants to change the name of this gig. He's claiming it's his kind of thing.' I was like, 'Okay.' The sound guy, you know what? Squash you. Go do your own platform, run with your own platform. That's all the kind of little stuff that I had to deal with and that I had to learn with. I'm still sensitive to it because up until today, with Words Worth Saying – Hip Hop Poetry in Motion evolved into Words Worth Saying.

That night that we did there, on Friday night, the venue owner was still running to Isaac [the sound guy] asking him. I don't understand it. I'm the one that's coming to you proposing, talking to you continuously, but you need a male figure…Maybe I just have a hang-up about it as well in this world, but that's the game. You just learn to roll with it, man. This year still I had an MC come to me and say to me, 'For years I've been asking who's doing Words Worth Saying.' I wanted to come in under the radar because the brand must speak for itself. This year that happened, this and last year. People were coming to me in the taxi and they were like, 'You're Words Worth Saying,' which is cool. In fact, they were trying to charge me coming into my own gig 'cause they didn't know who I was, which was cool, because the brand now speaks for itself. Under the radar like that. This guy says to me, 'Yeah, for years I've been asking them. They were like, "Yeah, some other guy, man, is in charge of it".' No, Words Worth Saying has been run by a female. I have built the platform – it took me all of these years. It took 10, 15 years to build this platform. It started with that idea that this is where we do conscious lyrics on this platform. Underground lyrics, we get to do this here. There's strong women. There's a few strong women. Unfortunately, I guess, when you're too strong, you get sideswiped as well because you're too strong. You have to find this balance. You have to be pretty. You have to find the balance.

I understood because it was not just in Hip Hop that I was faced with that. In Islam, Nation of Islam, they were more respectful with similar things. In Rastafari, the same, but what I understood about all three – the culture and the religions or the faiths – the potential for the emancipation of women have always been sitting there and still sits there. If Hip Hop is about strong independence – and that is what is displayed in women as well – why would you have people coming to break that down? That is African thought. This is cultural thought. This is all other thoughts that come and are applied to the equation. But the pure equation of it is for the emancipation of all people. Man or woman. Bring to the table your gifts. That's pretty much it.

Alim: Then when men are in charge of a space, whether it's the mosque or the club, it changes...

Natasha: It's different. I had a conversation with my sister who passed away. When she was diagnosed with cancer, we had a discussion about ego because one day I walked in there. I was so frustrated. I was like, 'This ego thing, I'm gonna let it go, man,' like, 'I'm taking this ego jacket off,' like, 'I don't need this ego jacket.' She said to me, 'Natasha, in Hip Hop we need ego.' Yeah? She said, 'They diagnosed me and told me I have two months to live. Because of my Hip Hop ego, I lived two years, and I went to a party of my own. My Hip Hop ego carried me through that.' I listened, and I was like, 'Okay.' Then I thought about the guys, and I was like, 'That's exactly what they do.' I'm struggling with, 'Am I a poet? Am I a Hip Hopper?' If I'm not gonna say I am a Hip Hopper, then I'm not gonna be accepted as that. It's that kind of arrogance sometimes that is needed, that ego that is needed. That's when I learned you can take the ego jacket off, and you can put it on. The day I tested it – because I remember – like I said, I like to go under the radar. I went to a club, and I was like, 'Okay, I'm gonna walk in with my ego jacket.' The amount of attention that I got walking in that night was something else. Even from the boys, it was a different energy that came. I understand that there's power behind that. But we have to find that balance, man.

Alim: Damn, that's the struggle to navigate it, right?

Natasha: If you have faith, though, then you do find a way to navigate that. It's like art and business. It's similar aspects. Art requires of one certain energy of humbleness. You've gotta give in. You've gotta receive. Then business requires you to be that assertive – have strategy.

Alim: Very few people can do both.

Natasha: God, we're trying, we're trying [laughter]. I think that's what's happened with Words Worth Saying now. I said to Isaac, and I spoke to [someone] who's part of the production with me. I said, 'You know what? It's…' For the longest I retained the host disposition because I felt, for me, what I wanted to create was a space where I would like to go to and I watch because I'd go to events, and there'd be something that I'd be like, 'Ah,' and, 'Mmm, mmm, mmm.' I felt that the energy – we weren't managing the energy well enough. What we did with Words Worth Saying, we have the featured artist. We have the band jam, and then we have the open mic. But we restricted everybody to one song on the open mic. This means you come in with your best. You give it one punch. People must want you again. The bands didn't wanna work with MCs because they felt MCs would go on and on and on. We restricted that as well. Come with 16 bars. Just 16 bars. Keep it concise. Keep it compact. Give us your best shot. What we found was – Trenchtown was a bit undisciplined. I was disappointed in myself because we didn't – it was a new venue, new energy, a lot of different dynamics that night…That's why there were old and new crowd. The older crowd was like, 'Yo, man.' The new crowd was like, 'Yo, we wanna do two or three.' I received a lot of pressure. I started giving in to the two and three, and then I said, 'No. First and foremost we're going back to the formula.' To keep [the] respect of the audience, and I think that's what's happened with Words Worth Saying. The audience has become important. They're part of this equation.

Alim: Absolutely, you can see that.

Natasha: They feel it also. To keep them in there, you give them just so much. You balance that energy, and you keep it moving like that. Back to the formula. And I finally decided to hand over my hosting position because now I looked at it and I was like, 'Okay, I'm not under the radar anymore as much as I wanna be.' It's lifting up a little bit on both aspects, on the artists' side and on the event side. Instead of putting myself too visible on this and making it too much, it's not about me. Take me out of that equation there, concentrate on the event of coordinating this, and put other people on. Have someone else now take over the reins…We'd managed to keep a balance of female energy within the artist, per se. It does get tough because there's more male artists than female artists, but the female artists have represented strongly on that stage as well.

Alim: One of the things I was gonna ask you was a sister who came up on stage, Andy – she had the crowd!

Natasha: She had the crowd. I actually wanted to book Andy…Andy is an interesting phenomenon 'cause Andy has like that kind of soul flow. She had it from a very young age already. She's been on the scene for quite a while. She dips, and then she comes back up. I see she's busy now. In fact, she's releasing. With Andy, I remember from the beginning…You know me. I've been told I'm a feminist. I don't like to claim it because of the connotations that's involved with it. But they say from my actions that that's what I am. I love my women in Hip Hop. I've seen a lot of sad things. I've seen Hip Hop women and Hip Hop men together, and male MCs not being able to acknowledge the power of the female MC. In one household, not being able to see that. Then see how they would then rather back a female MC that is willing to go expose themselves, those kind of dynamics. I understand it. I watched Biggie's movie. I respect my sister, Foxy Brown. She is her. As far as I can see she's being her. She's being real to it. I respect the sisters doing whatever they – and I understand there's evolution of women. You go through periods of where you're sexy, and this comes out in different ways and things like that…I think it's the ego that comes into play, like when very few men are able to really acknowledge, when they're just dope MCs, period. Andy was one of those characters. When she came out, there was a guy, he was pushing the whole – he was pushing and driving this crew, this posse, and she was performing. But you could see she performed like them – and he was up here. After that gig, I went to her, and I was like, 'Yo, man, I'm gonna tell you something now. I don't know how you're gonna take it. But this dude is gonna stand in your way. Drop him. Drop him. Let him go.' Next time I saw her she was on her own. I was very proud of that, that moment for her 'cause I was like, I could see it. She was standing out already, and he was also trying to. There was no way he was gonna let her outshine him, you understand. You can see it from a distance, man.

Alim: She probably felt that shit, too. You gave her the word at the right time.

Natasha: Right time, because any other person could have backed off. She didn't. She didn't. She loves her art. She's evolved. She's grown into her femininity at this point. She does speak about – she's raising the bar on certain issues that's close to her heart right now and her sexuality above everything else. And prior to this, she was speaking about dreams, and the revolution, the way she would bring it. It's so difficult to bring a positive message and not be corny. She can manage that. She manages that, and she's so smooth. She's got a dope voice.

Alim: Dope, that's dope. We were talking before about other artists, and I loved hearing you say that you support your women MCs in the crew. Who else are you thinking about as dope? I know you mentioned Eavesdrop and others, but who's really – who's bringing it?

Natasha: Okay, at this point, I know there's Andy. Eavesdrop, Elise Fernandez, which is Black Athena. YOMA. There's a sister called – there's Amy Brown that's coming out now that I see a lot of hype is happening around her. Dope Saint Jude, of course. There's a sister from Atlantis as well…These are just a few that I know of. There's actually quite a few.

Alim: But people always say, 'Oh, they ain't,' or, 'They can't.'

Natasha: It took so long for the females to get onto the cipher. I know I used to – when it started I went on there a few times. The first time I fumbled, and I had to go back for an audition 'cause I thought I was gonna freestyle on that thing. You can't freestyle – you can freestyle on the radio, but that was a shock. The freestyling feed, and I was like, 'Yo, man. It's cool. I'm gonna freestyle. The shutters are gonna be open. It's on the ocean, I'm sure I'm gonna get inspiration.' Shutters were closed, just the opposite. I was like – [laughter]. The whole week I was like, 'Redemption, redemption.' I thought about what I would rap. I'm going with that, that didn't work. Then I went back the next week, and I was happy, like, 'Okay, I did my thing.' Almost a whole year or so lapsed before females actually started coming up on that cipher. I don't know if it's courage or what it is, but it took a long time for them to…

Alim: Tell me what you thought when you first heard Eavesdrop.

Natasha: She was with League of Shadows, that kind of posse. When I heard Eavesdrop I was like, 'Yo.' She's prolific in how she presents herself, and she's a lyricist. With YOMA I just felt like there's a lyricism there, that sits there. It's not male or female. Yeah, with Eavesdrop it's that intellectual lyricism that comes out, and then the dark, the dark ideas and the underground kind of stuff. Yeah, Eavesdrop was like that.

Alim: She's gritty.

Natasha: She's gritty, yeah. It's gritty grime.

Alim: How do you compare that with YOMA?

Natasha: I think YOMA is smoother. Her concepts and ideas is more palatable towards commercial. But her lyricism is actually – I feel she's got something.

Alim: You're big on the lyricism. What makes a really good lyricist?

Natasha: Well, it's the play of words. It's the intellectual play of words and rhyme schemes. That's what I find and discover. I'm still exploring, and I'm learning through the process. Yeah, play of words, rhyme schemes. Some do sound rhyme schemes. Some do rhyme schemes inside the sentences. Some do rhyme schemes outside the sentences. Then just the play of words and punchlines.

Alim: Damn. You're listening for all of that. What about Dope Saint Jude? What attracts people to her?

Natasha: Dope Saint Jude is breaking out of the box. I think once she understood branding very well, she branded herself very well. When it comes to her music, she has good music. She produces for herself as well, and she's got good lyrics and everything. I don't know. It's a combination there with Dope Saint Jude that really makes it palatable. I think that's what it is. She's actually making a living off art in Cape Town. She's doing very well. She's travelling as well. A UCT [University of Cape Town] graduate. I think she's busy with a doctorate now. She's still busy with her studies. She went back to school, yeah. Somehow I felt like that sort of somehow gave her an edge as well, because I think Amy Brown has studied political science. I think that that somehow affects the approach to maybe the industry side as well. They have the talent, and they have the ability, and it just boosts it to another level.

Alim: That's dope. For you then, I wanted to talk about your music and your poetry and your theatre as much as we can. There was something I'm blown away by which is *Underneath the Poetry*. A 30-person cast?

Natasha: Thirty-person cast. I went to the library one day, and I said, 'I'm gonna write a play.'

Alim: [laughter] Just like that. Just 'cause you're walking in the street.

Natasha: Yeah, just because. Then I looked at the librarian. I was like, 'You're gonna see my name up in lights. I'm gonna write a play.' He just laughed at me, and I was like, 'Okay.' Then my mom saw a scriptwriting course in the newspaper with Roy Sargeant in Mitchells Plain. I attended it. It was a two-week or two-month – no, a two-week thing where you sit and you – there's like a synopsis, da, da, da, da, da. Then I said, 'I'm gonna write a Hip Hop play.' It's like, 'Okay.' For the class you had to do a play thing as well. I wrote it, and he was interested in what I was writing there, but I wasn't interested in developing it because it was about a prostitute kind of thing. For me, I felt like I would have to go do research on this and stuff like that. He wanted me to develop it, and I was like, 'No, but I want to write a Hip Hop play. This is not my play that I wanna write.'

When we finished the course, I was on to my second baby at the time, I think. At that time, being pregnant, I was like, 'Okay, the best thing I can do now is sit down and write this.' I didn't wanna be a wimp about it. I didn't want a one-man play, so I took it on. Part of why I took it on was to prove to myself that I can do it and to make other people, like, 'Here, this is what I'm doing.'

NATASHA C TAFARI | Source: H Samy Alim

'Show me you can do it. Show me you can do this. Come on. Step up.' I did it, yeah, in two parts. We did the one, a quick scene and trance-healing ceremony kind of thing with poetry. The way I wrote it was I wrote it in rhyme scheme, and then I would have – I had actual poets as characters, so I gave them that space to bring in their poetry. Then with the MCs, I did the same kind of thing, so you bring in – I write the script, and then you bring in your personal pieces, like that. The second part was the Hip Hop scene, going from – and, of course, it was – the storyline was 'Underneath the Poetry', a classic Hip Hop story. The storyline is about a woman that has the gift of poetry. Part of her is now an MC, but they told her not to, don't do it, kind of thing. You know, the normal story. She ends up now placing her curse – like Contro'Versey was in this play. It was really nice putting it together and having her a part of this vehicle. Kimosabee as well; Kimosabee actually also passed away. She was instrumental because when I presented the play to her and to Jethro at the time, they were the ones for a year almost, they'd be like, 'Yo, when is this thing happening, when is this thing happening?' They were crucial in me pushing through. This meant I had to go and approach now the theatre. I had to go approach sponsorship and all of this. I wrote, produced and directed this thing.

Alim: Is this Jethro Louw? He was in *Afrikaaps*.

Natasha: Yes, yes, that Jethro.

Alim: Get out of here.

Natasha: Yes, that Jethro, yeah. We had substantial people. On the Hip Hop scene, we had Gogga, who's like the father of graff. He flew down from Joburg. We went to Artscape [theatre venue] because Roy Sargeant was at Artscape. I went, and I was like, 'Yo, man. I wrote this play,' but I couldn't get to him. I got no response, so I went to Baxter [theatre venue], and I presented to Baxter, 'Yo, this is my play.' They were like, 'Okay, we'll give you the Opera House, the big one for three days at a ridiculous price'…What Gogga did for the three days, he would do the piece outside of the theatre during the day. Then when it came to the Hip Hop scene, with the opening…he'd finish up the piece on stage. Then the two, E20 from BeatBangaz and Kato, they were up on the DJ stage. Then we had dancers, and we had everything.

Alim: You had all the elements and all of these people involved.

Natasha: Five elements, I'd say, because the Knowledge of Self was part of it.

Alim: Did you start the story with the Khoi intentionally?

Natasha: What I started with that was the poetry, a healing ceremony. It started out with a lightning strike, the child being born, and then a prophecy kind of thing. At some point, because she's told not to speak, she gets an illness that restricts her, so Jethro does a healing ceremony, and then he used his poetry in the trance dance kind of thing. Some contemporary dancing.

Alim: To heal the child.

Natasha: To heal the woman, the poet, yeah – she has the gift, but she wasn't allowed to practise it. She gets sick from not practising. Then he does a healing ceremony, and that's where it finishes. Then we had a break, and we would then open up with Contro'Versey which is the descendant of this woman who was the poet. She's the MC, and she wakes up and she starts with MCing…

Alim: In modern day. You spanned thousands of years. Wow! What is the second half of the story? Now she can…

Natasha: Well, that's it. She goes through the questioning and the phases of it, and she discovers what's all this art. Then we have this whole big break-out celebration. It's almost like a park jam that we presented right there on stage for that. We presented that. Pro Helvetia still gave us budget. We have always been used to no budget, so Pro Helvetia gave us 50 000 budget. It should have been at 100 000. We pulled it off at 50. It's a Swiss council. He said to me like, 'I take it as project art, and this will be my latest project.' Afterwards when I went to him – because I knew nothing about putting on stage productions. I knew nothing. I directed this thing. We did props. We did all kinds of stuff. I don't know how we did it. I just pulled in everybody. By the time we did it, I was eight months pregnant.

Alim: Unbelievable!

Natasha: Eight months pregnant, yeah.

Alim: That's when the show went on the Baxter?

Natasha: Yeah, eight months pregnant with my second child. Wow, it was so intense. The first night they were like, 'Yo, man, your background is too loud,' like, 'Your stage manager, get him off.' I had to stage manage the next night, 'cause my stage manager was too excitable. It was my husband. The only way I could pull it off was involve him. I put him there, and he was like, '[unintelligible yelling].' He was loud in the background. In the proposal you need to say demographically what you're going to reach, and I said like, 'Demographically Hip Hop reaches from zero, from baby, to 60.' In the audience we had that type of demographics because it appeals. Hip Hop appeals. People love Hip Hop… When I went to him afterwards, and I said to him, 'Feedback on the play?' He's like, 'Look, I will put this play on again. The only thing I would say is get a professional director.' 'It was the small things, he said. It was the attention to detail things that were missed by leaving that out'…There were quite a few people who wanted us to do that, but then I said, 'No.' At that point I went on with my family and so on and so on.

Alim: Let's talk about the new music you're making – you ease on into this album, smooth…

Natasha: Yeah, because I come from a poetic background, I thought that, 'Let me ease in on it.' I thought, 'Okay, I kinda like the surprise element of it.' When you listen to that part, it's either gonna pull you in or it's not. If it pulls you in…

Alim: You get tricked. Right after, what happens?

Natasha: I talk about blood.

Alim: [laughter] It struck me that you were addressing somebody. You said, 'You want me to do…' something. What do you mean?

Natasha: People, people that expect a certain something from entertainment. They want it to be sexy. They want it to be nice. They want it to be pretty.

Alim: Two things happening there. One, you're bringing us in with this, 'You wanna hear me sound sexy on this beat.' Then you say, 'While my people bleed.' You're juxtaposing those things.

Natasha: Yeah. While you were all up in this pretty, pretty image and sexy, sexy image, the reality is our people are hurting. They're bleeding in the streets. This is the reality of what I'm living on a day-to-day. You want me to do this, but this is what I'm experiencing. My people are bleeding literally, like in ghettos, like Delft, recorded a few months ago for the month of – I think it was November – 31 kids died of gangsters shooting, and this is just bullets, stray bullets killing kids. Can you imagine 30 in one area? That's one area of Delft. Every day. Today on the newspaper again, a 14 year old, a Salt River boy, got struck down in Hanover Park by a stray bullet. A 10-month-old baby on their grandfather's lap by a stray bullet. It's happening so often, every single day. Right now it's happening. It's crazy how, when it happens, literally the people say, 'Cops don't wanna go in the area,' because it's such random bullets that they are afraid for their own lives. What about the people? Then all of those questions come up for me like, 'Where are they getting the bullets? Where are they getting the money? Where are they getting the ammunition?' All of this stuff. For me, that's the biggest thing. I think that's most hard. Our kids are dying. Masses and masses of them every single day, and nobody's saying anything about it.

Alim: Damn…

Natasha: You sit in the taxi, and it's a natural conversation. How many people like, 'No,

I'm not gonna go into Hanover Park because they're shooting there. It's not safe there,' that kind of conversation. That's everyday conversation. You go to work. People will come in late to work at one point because they're shooting in Hanover Park, randomly shooting. Hanover Park, Lavender Hill, Manenberg, Mitchells Plain, Delft, just…

Alim: It's widespread. You're wondering how did this get in here? How do the bullets and the guns and the…

Natasha: Yes. Ammunition costs. You will think twice about the ammunition you're shooting if you're paying for it for yourself, you understand. Guns cost. Our kids are not eating in the ghettos. People aren't living. Where are they getting it from? Where are they getting the ammunition from to go shooting, so much that the police won't go in 'cause the gunshots…It's not from ours. It's not BB guns. It's not coming from – dang, if we had a factory, then somebody would be rich. All of those questions come through. It doesn't make sense. What they manage to do is they manage to remove us from our feeling. You become so ice cold to the feeling that you hear, like another child dying, you feel nothing anymore. That's what they manage to do. You have to protect that. We become the same like those people that – the brothers and sisters – the brothers that's shooting. I don't know if there's sisters. I don't know if any sisters are shooting right now. You become like that. You're dead, like a dead soul that, 'Oh, okay, another one got dead, another one shot.' We need to see that like it's painful. It's the next generation that's being phased out. What are we left with? What people are we left with? If we look at the statistics of war, we're not at war, but we have people falling like we are at war. Casualties, it's the numbers that people who are at war are showing. At one point they put in – they send in the army. They send the army in. The army, what did they do, because they were in there for a short while, and they're out again. They'll send [the] Peace Corps to various countries to do what? Here we need something. Sending armies in is like saying we are bad. We're not inherently bad. We're not a bad people. We can't say that. There's something else happening. I don't know what it is, but I just know there's too much blood on the streets, man…They don't have to confine you, send you to camps, and send you into a gas chamber. They don't have to do that because there have been enough numbers dying in the ghettos by the hands of their own people. That's what it's about. Our people are out in the streets. I read the saying in a place called Hopefield (near Vredenburg side): 'They tried to bury us. They didn't know we were seeds.' That was like, 'Wow!'

Alim: I love that.

Natasha: In it, I wanted to bring in something that was very positive, something to fight for, and how to achieve that uplift without being corny. I didn't want it to be just doom and gloom, and then I thought, 'Okay, just put that in there,' like, 'Yo.' Sometimes that kind of message placed like that could sit on the brain better than entirely positive, positive. 'They tried to bury us, but they didn't know we were seeds.' 'Cause we could grow, man. We grow. We're like weeds [laughter]. We grow. Rock, sand, don't matter. We grow. We grow, you know? Even underneath, that's where love bled. We're gonna grow. We grow through that…

B-GIRL FOXY | Source: Ference Isaacs

CHAPTER 18.

THE MORE THINGS CHANGE...: RACE AND REPRESENTATION IN CONTEMPORARY SOUTH AFRICAN RAP

WARRICK MOSES (HARVARD UNIVERSITY)

'WELCOME TO AFRICA, LADY!'

Bold white text against a black screen sets the video's location and timeframe as 'South Africa 2012'.[1] A series of quick edits draws the viewer's gaze from the city skyline featuring the beleaguered Ponte building and Hillbrow tower, to a street-level scene of pedestrians walking through downtown Johannesburg. 'If this is your first time in the concrete jungle,' an enthusiastic voice-over announces, 'just sit back and relax, everything will be o-kay'. This candid allusion to a guided safari through the city is confirmed with a medium close-up of a minibus taxi cruising down the main drag, the lettering 'Big 5 Tours' and images of wildlife painted along the vehicle's side. As a final touch, the narrator gives a little chuckle, setting the viewer/tourist at ease or else providing a sinister foreshadowing of events to come.

At [00'19'], focus shifts to the interior of the vehicle, alternating between shots of an oblivious, unimpressed celebrity client flanked by two stern bodyguards,[2] and their driver/tour guide sporting a pith helmet and khaki outfit. The minibus progresses through the 'concrete jungle' of Joburg, and their guide draws attention to passing attractions: a pair of hyenas pawing at trash bags, 'a shop owner...chilling with his black panther', and another figure sitting nonchalantly on the sidewalk

---

1. https://www.youtube.com/watch?v=AIXUgtNC4Kc
2. With her blonde wig and 'meat-dress' the character portrayed here is clearly US pop star Lady Gaga. Die Antwoord had reportedly turned down an offer to open for Gaga on her 2012 South African tour. The title 'Fatty Boom Boom' is an idiomatic South African children's chant, used here as an allusion to Gaga's highly publicised weight gain at the time.

next to a lion. A little while further he points out a trio of 'local musicians, about to kick some funky tunes'. At this point [01'14'] the video slows to settle on a group rigging together sound equipment for an outdoor performance. Instead of the pedestrians' earlier, more casual glances, the musicians fix their glares resolutely on the passing tour bus and its occupants. On the left side of the frame a black figure wearing a hooded white robe with the words 'Care' and 'Joy' carefully stencilled across the middle beats ominously against an overturned plastic bucket, part of his makeshift drum set. To the right, a lanky male in red and white body paint briefly pauses in his work of adjusting speakers to stare at the camera. In the centre of the image, wearing a sleeveless empire-waist dress and pink high-tops stands a diminutive female character. In contrast to her trademark blonde mullet, she is covered from head to toe in midnight-black body paint...

***

Thus begins the music video for 'Fatty Boom Boom', a single by one of South Africa's most contentious musical offerings to date, the self-proclaimed 'rave-rap' group Die Antwoord (The Answer). The story of the group's rise to fame and notoriety, both locally and abroad, has been related several times over in commercial blogs as well as full-length features by industry tastemakers like Boing Boing, Vice and Spin. Initially posting tracks on the South African alternative Afrikaans-language and -culture website *Watkykjy?* (What are you looking at?), by late 2009 the group had released a video on YouTube entitled *Zef Side*, closely followed by *Enter the Ninja*.[3] Taken together as somewhat of an 'artist's manifesto', both offerings quickly went viral, in no small part due to their highly stylised, carnivalesque visuals, as well as the linguistic nuance employed throughout. Print and related media interviews followed, along with guest slots at respected music festivals like Coachella and Big Day Out. Swiftly thereafter, the band embarked on sold-out international tours as headliners.

As Die Antwoord's public profile increased and details of their backstory gradually came to light, speculation about their relative 'authenticity' – an enduring theme in interrogations of rap-related genres – began to surface. Turns out that frontman Ninja (aka Watkin 'Waddy' Tudor Jones) and his female counterpart Yolandi Visser (aka Anri du Toit) had previously been involved in the short-lived electronic outfits The Constructus Corporation and MaxNormal.TV. Prior to this, Jones had also been a member of The Fantastic Kill and The Original Evergreen.

---

3. http://wewillraakyou.com/2010/02/the-answer-to-die-antwoords-marketing-social-media/

Surely not surprising, for don't all successful performing acts go through a period of maturation on the way to 'finding their voice'?

The problem with Die Antwoord is that detractors questioned exactly *whose* voice was being articulated: the documentary-style introduction and conclusion to *Zef Side* presented the two MCs, along with beatmaker DJ Hi-Tek, as naïve proponents of a home-grown zef aesthetic. Simply put, zef is a South African version of white-trash kitsch, but elevated in Die Antwoord's work to 'next-level' cool. Ninja and Yolandi rap, especially at the beginning of their career as Die Antwoord, in a form of vernacular Afrikaans associated with the Western Cape's working-poor coloured population. The pair engages in a performance genre that took root specifically amongst Cape Town's marginalised, non-white communities. But most audaciously, Ninja's tattoos (the use of his alias throughout is intentional – from the outset the Ninja 'character' was completely subsumed within/supplanted Jones' identity) bear undeniable similarity to the hierarchical inscriptions and physical markings of the infamous Numbers prison gangs, exclusively coloured gangs distinguished in name and function by the numbers 26, 27 and 28.

Numerous scholars have taken up the charge of analysing the complex of influences and signifiers that make up Die Antwoord's exposition, interrogating the degree to which aspects of social praxis imagined to be the exclusive domain of one ethnoracial grouping can plausibly be reproduced and resonate within another context (Krueger 2012; Marx & Milton 2011; Van der Watt 2012). These examples have tended to interpret Die Antwoord's work as a reconfiguration of white Afrikaner identity, with the creative movement between cultural prerogatives occurring primarily at the level of language (in a later section I offer summaries of these proposals). Drawing on Lacan's 'mirror stage' theory, and the interplay between real, imaginary and symbolic registers, I contend that in this instance, visuality precedes language as the process through which identity is constructed and contested (Lacan 1989).

In this chapter, I focus on selected works by South African rap acts Die Antwoord and newcomers Dookoom, arguing that the two groups' relative appeal derives largely from the specular impact of their music videos. It is through the experience of witnessing their videos *accompanied* by the lyrical/language component, and not simply hearing their music in isolation, that the bands have garnered public attention. This is important because despite

CAPE FLATS | Source: Ference Isaacs

NIGHT OF THE BEATBANGAZ. YOUNGSTACPT | Source: Ference Isaacs

the end of formal segregation in South Africa, the 'legacy of apartheid's visualised system of racialisation' remains firmly entrenched (Van Eeden & Du Preez 2005: v). Apartheid-era racial classifications, determined by visual assessment and confirmed via behaviour, remain the primary means by which individuals are socially identified in South Africa. It is therefore impossible to *view* the respective artists' music videos without primarily considering the complicity of race in their performances. From an optic standpoint, Die Antwoord is an all-white group[4] encroaching on a conventionally understood non-white performative space. Dookoom, fronted by Isaac 'Mutant' Williams – a coloured MC and stalwart of the underground Cape Town rap scene – (re)centres the non-white musical and cultural aesthetic using the same technological means, emphasis on visual aesthetic and media dissemination platforms as Die Antwoord.

In a 2011 panel discussion on the persistence of essential racial categories in South Africa, Njabulo Ndebele remarked: '…it seems that each of us, to various degrees, wants to hold onto some notion of purity that has not been tainted by the other. But in fact, it's impossible to find such purity' (Jones & Dlamini 2013: 9). As they evolve, cultures beg, borrow and steal from one another (and the realm of popular musical expression is not immune to these developments). But more than a discussion of cultural appropriation, my concern here is the relationship between visual apperception and behaviour that so preoccupied the apartheid social sphere and its repercussions in the contemporary moment. Deborah Posel (2001) notes how after the implementation of the Population Registration Act (No. 30 of 1950), racial classification came to be determined by 'common sense' appraisals of an individual's lived experience. In addition to subjective vagaries of phenotype (hair texture, relative pigmentation and genital colouration, for example), it was an individual's social behaviour (where she lived, worked, whom she associated with, and how that community generally viewed her) which fixed racial category. This curious logic is explored in much of South African author Zoë Wicomb's writing, but most pointedly in her 2006 novel *Playing in the Light*, which describes the unearthing of the Campbell family's history. Having grown up as a middle-class white individual in Cape Town, protagonist Marion Campbell discovers her parents' collusion as light-skinned coloureds to

4. DJ Hi-Tek is the *nom de guerre* of Justin de Nobrega, although this character is portrayed in Die Antwoord's music videos by a variety of actors.

'pass for white' under apartheid rule. Although Afrikaans-language fluency and sheer dumb luck are contributing factors, it is mainly through physical appearance that Marion's father secures work as a traffic officer, an occupation legally reserved at the time for whites. By conspiring thereafter to adopt conventionally understood white mores, her parents' and ultimately Marion's racial classification is socially confirmed as white.

Wicomb's narrative relates to this chapter in two regards, both underscoring the prioritisation of visual appearance in regards to racial acceptance. In the first instance, Marion is moved to interrogate the long-standing unease she feels about her ancestry through her visceral identification with a photograph included in a newspaper account of Truth and Reconciliation Commission proceedings. The woman pictured bears a striking resemblance to the Campbell family's domestic worker, Tokkie. As the story progresses, it is discovered that Tokkie was in fact Marion's maternal grandmother, and the woman in the photograph a distant relative. Secondly, the deceit that Marion's parents engaged in is colloquially known as 'playing for white'. This epigram demonstrates the prevailing normativity of whiteness in South African society, in that there is no corresponding vernacular phrase bearing the same cultural weight that denotes 'playing for *non*-white'. These instances emphasise the precarity of non-white subjects adopting conventionally understood white social behaviours, in that there is always the danger of being revealed as a fraud, as transgressing in some manner, or to be found out as 'playing in the light'. As Wicomb's patriarch in the novel, John, ruminates:

> Vigilance is everything; to achieve whiteness is to keep on your toes. Which...
> indicates that [the Campbells] cannot achieve it after all; being white in the
> world is surely about being at ease, since the world belongs to you. But [John
> and his wife], it would seem, cannot progress beyond vigilance...beyond being
> play-whites, which as far as he can see has bugger-all to do with *playing*.
> (Wicomb 2006: 152, emphasis added)

Throughout the novel, Marion's questioning of her own racial identity illustrates that the inevitability of 'returning to' or 'uncovering brown-ness' is more psychically destabilising than 'returning to whiteness'. Following this thread, my chapter explores the ease with which white South African musicians who absorb (extra)musical influences widely understood as the purview of non-white subjects, can credibly absorb such influences, and nonetheless still effect a comfortable 'return to whiteness'.

In *Sound of Africa*, Louise Meintjes' seminal ethnography of *mbaqanga* studio recording practice, she describes the 'magician-like status' of white sound engineers in being able to mediate sound and affect through technological means. This in turn highlights the dynamic in the production site between the white technicians behind the desk and the black musicians in the booth. Seemingly abstruse technical skill empowers the white engineers within a black African, Zulu cultural performance space, mirroring the social hierarchy and division of labour inherent to their contemporaneous apartheid context. By Meintjes' reasoning, the black musicians' evaluation of the recording procedure as 'white people's things...propagates the idea that technology...is differently accessible to music-makers on the basis of their class and color' (2003: 101–104). With regard to the music video medium, Adam Haupt argues: 'Whilst *Die Antwoord's* parodies reference white and "coloured" working-class subjects, it is clear that the artists themselves are far better resourced than the subjects of their work. The set design, props, costumes, cinematography, and editing...suggest that a great deal of conceptualisation and expertise went into [their production]' (Haupt 2012a: 419; the *Fatty Boom Boom* 'Making of…' video[5] supports this contention). I propose that the technological means of 'cinematography and editing' can similarly be regarded as 'white people's things' given historically associated constraints of financial and social access. The implication in this instance is that Zulu cultural practice constitutes 'black people's things'.

Although the quality of Dookoom's videos, being examples of coloured working-class prerogatives, stands out as an exception rather than the rule, I maintain that the overall production and visual effect of their work is comparable to that of Die Antwoord's. Another aspect of my writing then is to investigate the implications of non-white musicians adopting the same means of producing and disseminating their work as their white counterparts. I contend ultimately that the emphasis on the spectacle of race, a consequence of both Die Antwoord and Dookoom's performances, created under social conditions where what one looks like, and therefore acts like, continues to have a significant effect on

5. https://www.youtube.com/watch?v=YuGa0wfKfho

the performance and reception of identity in South Africa. If Die Antwoord successfully dabbles in 'black people's things', what are the consequences of non-white agents mobilising 'white people's things'?

THE ANSWER TO WHAT?

Browsing through interviews archived online reveals carefully scripted responses, with Ninja and Yolandi often repeating the same information verbatim in different contexts. Initially maintaining tight control over their on- and off-stage personas, the pair agreed to a tell-all interview with long-time associate Diane Coetzer for the South African *Rolling Stone* magazine. After a standard *mise-en-scène* introduction, Coetzer opens up her line of questioning with the following statement: 'It seems as good a moment as any to bring up the South African critics who accuse the group of cultural appropriation (or worse) and spend hours analysing why two white South Africans shouldn't be stepping over the border to Mitchells Plain or Fietas to mine the lives of those who reside there' (*Rolling Stone* February 2012: 40).[6] Ninja and Yolandi's responses, while irreverent to a degree, are nevertheless instructive, and worth quoting at some length:

Diane Coetzer: Let's go back to your other projects…What do you say to people – it seems to me, only in South Africa who say you never stick with anything?

Ninja: When it comes to music, everything I did before Die Antwoord was me experimenting, messing around and trying to find *die antwoord*. Here's the thing: everything – *everything* – about Die Antwoord is hugely personal. Everything before it was disposable. It was all throwaway…

DC: It surprised many people when you started rapping in Afrikaans. How did that happen?

Yolandi: We were always embarrassed to be from South Africa. I was embarrassed to tell people I was Afrikaans…With Die Antwoord we flipped all that. I had such an Afrikaans background. Ninja said why don't we fuck with it instead of being weird about it – push it out there. And then all this shit came out of it. It was just natural…

6. Mitchells Plain and Fietas are two black (predominantly coloured), working-poor neighbourhoods on the outskirts of Cape Town and Johannesburg, respectively.

DC: And the *zef* thing?

N: ...*(Z)ef* was always everywhere in South Africa. It's the underbelly of South African style. I try to explain it to people overseas and they cannot grasp it...*Zef* is just one element of South Africa that we put a stamp on and now own.

DC: In South Africa, you've been criticised for using elements of gang culture – like Ninja's tattoos. People have written pages and pages about this. What's your view on it?

N: I am a fucking gangster – I'm more of a gangster than anyone. It's because I run my own show and because I don't answer to anyone.

Y: The philosophy of the gangster is to go against the system because they find the system corrupt or it doesn't serve them, so they've created another system...

N: ...[Y]ou're talking about a handful of jealous irrelevant, intellectuals who don't count. They are not making waves, not making noise. They are throwing stones at a tank. (*Rolling Stone* February 2012: 42)

In these exchanges, there is a clear bias against academic scrutiny, a dismissal of critiques towards Die Antwoord's attitude surrounding issues of language propriety, and a disregard for any discomfort some might experience in response to the group's adoption of a specifically racialised visual identity.

As a rebuttal to 'stone-thrower' indictments, the 'Making of...' video that accompanied the release of *Fatty Boom Boom* provides greater insight into the group's overall aesthetic, but operates at the same level of sophistry as the *Rolling Stone* interview. The group's mobilisation in the video of anachronistic 'deepest, darkest Africa' tropes are clearly intended as parody – from the guide's faux-colonial uniform to the 'township tour' deceit, all the way through to the primitivist aesthetic or simplicity of the backdrop imagery and costumes. The group is explicit in acknowledging the contributions and influences of photographer Roger Ballen (who collaborated with them in directing their 2012 music video *I Fink You Freeky*), South African artist Anton Kannemeyer of Bitterkomix fame, and renowned fashion designer Alexander Wang to the production of the video. But Die Antwoord's description of *Fatty Boom Boom* as 'our wild African voodoo anthem' (*Rolling Stone* February 2012: 44)[7] would give even the most casual observer cause to stop and consider questions raised in their work of relative social, specifically racialised, privilege, the stereotyping of marginalised communities, and the potential appropriation of cultural practice and signifiers given the context of South Africa's segregated history and neo-apartheid present.

Indeed, if these are stock-in-trade features of Die Antwoord's output, it could be said that academic responses to the group's oeuvre tread similarly well-worn paths, often rehearsing the same claims and often citing the same sources. It seems almost impossible, for example, to interrogate Die Antwoord's lyrical content and representational politics without referencing: 1) the opening line from 2009's *Enter the Ninja*, beginning with Ninja's assertion, 'I represent South African culture';[8] 2) ethnomusicologist Christopher Ballantine's (2004: 105) essay 'Re-thinking "Whiteness"?' in which he observes white musicians' post-1994 'need for self-reinvention...that is ironic, unpredictable [and] transgressive'; or 3) poet and essayist Rustum Kozain's opinion that the convergence of non-white visual and linguistic inferences renders Die Antwoord's display appropriative as opposed to parodic.[9] Despite these confluences, academic opinions remain divided, as the contributions to a 2012 *Safundi* journal edition entitled 'Roundtable on Die Antwoord' attest.

In his essay 'Die Antwoord's State of Exception', for example, Sean O'Toole dismisses the group simply as opportunists hoping to cash in literally and figuratively at a time of post-apartheid introspection and recalibration of white identity. Their exploration of a poor-white zef ethos, and carefully rendered visual presentation drawing extensively on the vivid worlds inspired by Ballen's photographic collections *Platteland* (1994) and *Outland* (2001), are passing contrivances. O'Toole (2012) maintains that there is nothing to suggest that Die Antwoord's performed tableaux are either motivated by a genuine desire to engage with reconfigured identity politics, or that these representations are at all worthy of serious attention.

---

7. The quote continues: 'It's like a voodoo ceremony where you kill a chicken and cut its head off and swing it around by its legs. There are drums banging and a black mama dancing with no top on while a goat gets killed. There is a cow tied up in the back garden that an old black baba is about to kill so that the mama can eat the heart and drink the blood.'

8. https://www.youtube.com/watch?v=cegdR0GiJl4 – 'Checkit: I represent South African culture. In this place you get a lot of different things...blacks, whites, coloureds, English, Afrikaans, Xhosa, Zulu, *watookal* [whatever]. I'm like...all these different things...all these different people...fucked into one person.'

9 https://groundwork.wordpress.com/2012/01/27/from-the-archive-so-many-questions-so-few-answers/; http://penguin.bookslive.co.za/blog/2010/02/19/richard-poplak-writes-on-die-antwoord/; http://africasacountry.com/2010/02/is-die-antwoord-blackface/

Anton Krueger uses changing perceptions of zef culture as a pivot point to establish Die Antwoord along a continuum of alternative Afrikaner cultural and musical expression initiated in the late 1980s by the *Voëlvry* Movement.[10] He posits the group as champions of a stratum of lower-class white identity that was neglected, or perhaps abandoned, under the heady days of Afrikaner nationalism. On the one hand, Die Antwoord's defiant stance aligns them with erstwhile Afrikaner musicians like Johannes Kerkorrel, Bernoldus Niemand and Koos Kombuis, with whom the formulation zef as resistive to ruling-class conceptions of Afrikanerdom was first associated, and who rallied against hegemonic apartheid conservatism. At the same time, the group's contemporary imagination of zef – 'next level zef', as they put it (Van der Watt 2012: 411) – celebrates poor-white culture in ways that are both ironic and ludic. Die Antwoord rejects pervasive notions of homogenous Afrikaner identity through an explicit cultural affinity with this secondary and marginalised category. Their use of Afrikaans and distinctly South African colloquialisms might spill over into the expressive realm of coloured culture for sure, but this is all to be expected. For it is arguably at the margins of social and spatial delineation that one finds intersections of race and class, hence the previously disavowed correlations between articulations of zef and working-poor coloured culture.[11] According to Krueger (2012), the adoption of a zef ethos therefore ultimately situates Die Antwoord as sympathetic to the concerns of a maligned white lower class, as well as those ethnoracial groupings similarly disenfranchised by apartheid.

In a co-authored paper entitled 'Bastardised Whiteness' (not included in the *Safundi* issue, but useful here as a comparative text), Hannelie Marx and Viola Milton (2011) share Krueger's view that an embrace of zef culture can yield affirmative implications for white Afrikaner identity. An 'indulgence in *zef*' (Marx & Milton 2011: 735), they argue, contributes to a construction of Afrikaner-ness that is no longer primarily thought of as authoritarian and repressive. As with Krueger, the fact that coloured, ostensibly gang, culture is drawn

---

10. *Voëlvry* translates to 'free as a bird,' or 'outlaw.' The word voël meaning 'bird,' is also Afrikaans slang for 'penis,' thus making explicit the connections between the 'free love' sentiment, and 'rock 'n' roll' aesthetic that the movement promoted.
11. In this regard, Sarah Nuttall references Jon Hyslop's 1995 'White Working-Class Women and the Invention of Apartheid': 'In urban slums Afrikaans-speaking poor whites were frequently not demonstrating the instinctive aversion, socially or sexually, to racial mixing proclaimed by government racial ideology...these whites would by no means automatically identify as "Afrikaners" so allegiance to Afrikaner nationalism had constantly to be created.' Hyslop in Nuttall (2009: 26).

upon as a semiotic reservoir, is an inevitable result of legitimate attempts to expand the parameters of contemporary whiteness. Applying theoretical models developed by Victor Turner (1996) and Stuart Hall (1998) – liminality and a shifting or porous conception of racial identity, respectively – this writing dismisses as fallacy the perspective that Die Antwoord's representational strategy constitutes cultural appropriation. Fashioning a version of whiteness at the border of normative assumptions, Die Antwoord not only disrupt conventional understandings of whiteness but destabilise ideas about essential blackness as well. The title and interrogative impulse of Marx and Milton's paper is inspired by well-known South African poet Breyten Breytenbach's observation of Afrikaans, that the language embodies 'the visible history and the ongoing process not only of bastardisation, but also of metamorphosis' (in Marx & Milton 2011: 724). However, the co-authors use the terms 'Afrikaans' and 'Afrikaner' interchangeably throughout their paper, thereby conflating a body of cultural knowledge predicated on language with an exclusively white ethnic grouping. This move forecloses the possibility of acceptance into the *laager* of Afrikanerdom, a cultural template predicated by language *and* race, by non-white subjects who also claim Afrikaans as their mother tongue. This is important, because the teleological shaping of a 'bastardised whiteness' that necessarily incorporates elements of non-white culture, but not non-white subjects, is appreciably problematic, not to mention the unfortunate allusion to miscegenation, 'race mixing' and illegitimacy bound up in the word 'bastardisation'. The formulation proposed here, of 'metamorphosis' leading to a syncretic and hybrid identity, nevertheless reifies essential categories of whiteness and blackness from which a celebratory, alternative vision of white identity comes into being.

The most provocative evaluation of Die Antwoord's work, and the sentiment that corresponds most closely to my contentions in this chapter, is found in the writing of Adam Haupt (2012a), who regards the group's representational moves as wholly appropriative and blatant demonstrations of contemporary blackface. As a point of departure, Haupt interrogates Ninja's admission in an online interview that 'God made a mistake...I'm actually black trapped in a white body',[12] as well as a line taken from Die Antwoord's track *'Never le Nkemise 1'* ('You Can't Stop Me') in which the frontman describes himself as *'die wit kaffir*

---

12. http://www.channel24.co.za/Music/News/Die-Antwoords-Ninja-Im-actually-black-20120217

[the white kaffir]' ('kaffir' being a derogatory term used to denigrate black South Africans). Ninja reiterates this claim at the end of his interview with Coetzer (*Rolling Stone* February 2012), but in another example, the 2010 single 'Fish Paste', he declares: 'I *am* [emphasis added] a fucking coloured, if I want to be a coloured. My inner fucking coloured just wants to be discovered.' Haupt unpacks the way Ninja manipulates coloured gang culture signifiers, metaphorically 'blacking up' with tattoos, for example, and using vernacular Afrikaans to embody the persona of, or literally *to become*, 'the white kaffir'.[13]

This mash-up of essential identitarian markers is nothing new within the trajectory of white Afrikaner South African musical expression. In 1996 Anton Goosen released an album entitled *(Bushrock) of a White Kaffir of Africa*, and in 1997 Koos Kombuis penned '*Almal Kaffirs*' ('We're All Kaffirs') featured on the album *Blameer Dit op Apartheid* (*Blame It on Apartheid*). While Marx and Milton (2011: 730) view such a linguistic inversion as intended rebelliously to 'signal...commonality between the races', drawing parallels of experience between diametrically opposed social categories and histories, these statements only reinscribe relations of power between the two. As Haupt (2012a: 417): notes, despite the artists' intention, the use of such terms reproduces 'racially problematic language that signals white, racist projections of blackness'. Goosen and Kombuis' commentaries inadvertently play to the pervasive misconception that white South Africans caught at a post-1994 juncture have unwillingly and unwittingly been dragged down to the lowest rung on the country's social hierarchy.[14]

---

13. If accepted, the charge of blackface performance, corroborated by the opening sequence of *Fatty Boom Boom*, if only semantically, nevertheless strengthens the alignment of coloured racial and political identity with that of blackness and Black Consciousness. In *Love and Theft*, Eric Lott (1993: 20) notes the 'proto-Brechtian practice of picturing blackface performers out of costume as well as in', since there was a tendency for white audiences of minstrel shows to believe 'that they were being entertained by actual Negroes'. Yolandi's body-paint scene is so obviously an exaggeration that no viewer could 'mistake' her for an 'actual' coloured or black individual. However, there remains the fact that the choice of make-up invariably connotes a manipulation of phenotypical signifiers. In the 'Making of...' video, Yolandi explains this decision obliquely: 'In Africa it's very common to paint your face or your body with tribal tattoos, so we thought it (would) look super fresh to body paint ourselves with different colors for the video [1'12'].' This statement is telling in that it demonstrates their metonymic conception of South Africa as Africa writ large, and, furthermore, as Africans, the members of Die Antwoord are justified in their abstraction of 'tribal' indices.
14. Kombuis' 2008 album Bloedrivier (named for the 1838 Battle of Blood River) features a track entitled 'Die Fokkol Song' ('The Fuck-all Song'). Like the video for 'Fatty Boom Boom', it adopts the ironic stance of a guided tour through the city. In the first verse, the narrator greets visitors at Cape Town International Airport who have arrived to enjoy the 2010 World Cup soccer tournament, and to experience the country's 'friendly democracy'. The tone quickly changes as the chorus announces that the city, and post-1994 South Africa generally, has 'fuck-all' essential infrastructure requirements or expertise to run efficiently. See https://www.youtube.com/watch?v=tVMyUqNbbCg.

But, Liese van der Watt (2012) insists that to read Die Antwoord as perpetrating a modern-day version of blackface (as the *Fatty Boom Boom* video most obviously suggests) is to assess the group's display *only* in terms of race, thereby disregarding the numerous linguistic and socioeconomic codes and types at play in their work. Such a narrow emphasis specifically ignores the defining influence of *zef whiteness* to their aesthetic. To ably account for their contradictory and full range of (extra)musical influence, Van der Watt argues, Die Antwoord must be interpreted vertically as opposed to horizontally. Their aesthetic concern is one of surface representation, inevitably frustrating any attempts to derive significant or deep meaning in their production. The 'relaxed crossing of racial, linguistic and class boundaries' (Van der Watt 2012: 413), flitting from one set of signifiers to another, is a function of Die Antwoord's disregard for historicity, which (intentionally or not), offers a version of white Afrikaner identity unmoored from dominant typecasts. With Die Antwoord, Van der Watt maintains, what you see is what you get. Nothing more and nothing less.

The group's own ambivalence to critical inquiry that Van der Watt picks up on is best conveyed in *Zef Side*. The musical component of this video is framed by sections of interview-style questions addressed to the protagonists by an offstage interlocutor. The exchange beginning at [01'56'] is transcribed here:

Ninja: *Die fokken antwoord!*

Interlocutor: What does that mean?

Ninja: The answer…

Interlocutor: [The] answer to what?

Ninja: Whatever, man…fuck…

This vignette is recalled four years later at the end of *Fatty Boom Boom* [05'20'] with the following dialogue, both an impersonation of, and self-conscious response to, detractors:

> **Voice 1:** *Jeezus, ou, chill net 'n bietjie fokken uit!* [Jesus, dude, just chill the fuck out a little!]
> **Voice 2:** Whatever, man...[15]

And so it seems that every allegation of crass, market-savvy exploitation can be countered with a defence of the group's unparalleled propensity for inventive and inclusive *bricolage*. Every condemnation of non-white cultural appropriation and low minstrel-show (re)enactment is trivialised by hypotheses as to the band's creative reinterpretation of and preoccupation with whiteness. In contemporary South Africa, Sarah Nuttall (2009: 20) acknowledges that 'forms of separation and difference do still occur, materially and epistemologically' – that these cleavages have been the focus of much literary and cultural criticism post-1994. The approach she advocates is to interrogate overlooked instances of unexpected intersection and entanglement, as opposed to conceiving of social sites and histories as incommensurable and wholly separate. Cultural convergences of this type, with non-white individuals situated as the primary agents of their own self-identification, have certainly been investigated (Erasmus 2001; Jones & Dlamini 2013; Nuttall 2009). However, it is important to remember that prior to and after the dismantling of formal apartheid in South Africa, the ability to initiate such interventions, to credibly subsume and explore alternative identitarian modes, has always been the exclusive prerogative of *white* actors. And to remove race from the equation, as Van der Watt's (2012) writing implies, does nothing to mitigate the fact that in South Africa, associations of racialised behaviour accorded to visually recognised phenotype are deeply ingrained.

---

15. In response to Die Antwoord's embodiment of zef, white South African actors Michelle Botha and Andre Odendaal released a parody video questioning the group's 'zef roots' in 2012 entitled *Dankie vir die Antwoord, Maar Wat Was die Vraag?* [Thanks for the Answer, but What Was the Question?]. Sprawled on a sofa (the detached back seat of a minibus taxi) in a low-income caravan park, the pair's opening conversation mimics the exchange between Ninja and his interlocutor (https://www.youtube.com/watch?v=Or0Bf_KSwmQ):

> Odendaal: *Het jy nou gehoor?* [Have you heard?]
> Botha: *Wat gehoor?* [Heard what?]
> Odendaal: *Daar's hierdie ou en sy goose...hulle skeem hulle's 'die antwoord'.* [There's this guy and his girl...they reckon they're 'the answer'.]
> Botha: *Wat was die vraag?* [What was the question?]
> Odendaal: *Weet nie...* [Dunno...]

A case in point: Johnny Clegg, *Le Zulu Blanc* or 'The White Zulu' as he became known during Juluka's and Savuka's heyday, is an obvious example of this racially predicated privilege of cultural exploration. But in a more contemporary frame, a January 2015 *Mail & Guardian* feature entitled 'Blackface, White Guilt, Grey Area' quotes Xander Ferreira of the electronic group Gazelle as saying (without any apparent sense of irony): 'I had more black people around me until I was 13 than white people. Imagine the woman who brought you up, bathed you everyday, you've got a heavy connection with her and her culture. When you were a baby you heard her music. It became a part of *your* culture [emphasis added].'[16] In a complex paradigm where his family's nanny is implicated as a surrogate mother, as a primary agent of socialisation, Ferreira – who is known to perform in leopard print, referencing Mobutu Sese Seko, or otherwise wearing a *Mokorotlo* (conical Basotho grass hat) – positions himself with this statement as an engaged recipient of non-white mores from an early age. Ferreira's transformation is therefore an organic and justified by-product of early exogamous cultural exposure. It is the notion of 'becoming' cited earlier in Haupt (2012a), and 'metamorphosis' of Marx and Milton's (2011) work, which I explore within the framework of psychoanalyst Jacques Lacan's 'mirror stage' proposal in the following section.

THE FAIREST OF THEM ALL

In a famed 1949 lecture, Jacques Lacan presented his 'mirror stage' theory[17] to describe the formation of the ego, using the example of an infant recognising his or her reflection in a mirror for the first time. Between the ages of six and 18 months, children, when placed in front of a mirror, begin to distinguish their own body through movement, mimicry and observation as separate from the specular image or imago[18] before them. Although the infant identifies with or 'assumes' this image,[19] the relationship is fraught, as the subject

---

16. Ferreira, along with Die Antwoord and Afrikaner rapper Jack Parow, were cited in this article for the influence of non-white cultural signifiers and the impact of their work in the construction of an alternative contemporary Afrikaner identity.
17. This theory was first proposed in 1936 at the 14th International Psychoanalytical Congress at Marienbad as *Le stade du miroir* (The Mirror Stage), but revised and presented at the 16th Congress at Zurich in 1949 as *Le stade du miroir comme formateur de la fonction du Je* (The Mirror Stage as Formative of the Function of the I). See Lacan (1989).
18. The image of the subject's body, the specular image, is interchangeable in Lacan's work with the imago/image of the counterpart (the 'imago' is constituted of emotions, as well as visual representation). The term 'counterpart' refers to 'other people in whom the subject perceives a likeness to himself (principally a visual likeness)' (Evans 2006: 29).
19. As Dylan Evans explains: 'To "assume" an image is to recognise oneself in the image, and to appropriate the image *as* oneself' (2006: 82, emphasis added).

itself and the image being viewed are not equivalent (Lacan 1989). There is a discrepancy between the infant's imprecise, uncontrolled physical movements when compared to the wholeness of the 'Ideal-I' witnessed in the reflected image. In other words, the image represents a stable *Gestalt*, misrecognised as a superior form (Mulvey 2006) to which the physically uncoordinated and dependent infant can only aspire. Thus, the Ideal-I, constructed as it is in the fictional context of an inverted reflection, does not provide an accurate depiction of the subject's lived experience, and constitutes the realm of fantasy, a register that Lacan denotes as 'the imaginary order'.

Important to my broader argument is that this mirror developmental stage precedes socialisation with others through language – a communicative domain made up of signifiers – which for Lacan falls under the purview of the 'symbolic order'. Additionally, while the mirror stage refers to a singular period of psychic and early childhood development, it also describes a continuous relationship between primordial subject and projected image. The metaphorical 'man in the mirror' presents the full potential of the subject, but it is a potential that throughout the individual's life can never be realised.

I contend that the formation of Watkin Jones' ego as 'Ninja' can be understood as attempts to realise a fictionalised ideal, one that simultaneously encompasses elements of Afrikaner and coloured cultures, neither of which Jones as an ostensibly middle-class English-speaking South African has plausible recourse to assume. It should be noted that the subject's moment of recognition as independent of his surroundings is not limited to the intervention of an actual mirror, but can also be catalysed through interaction with others. Referring to my previous example: Xander Ferreira might 'assume', in a Lacanian sense, the figure of his black nanny. To identify with an 'ideal self' in her image, Ferreira progresses to the adoption of 'Gazelle' as his ego (Lacan 1989). However, the acts of identification in Jones' case are multiple. As already mentioned, he simultaneously assumes the idealised images of 'Afrikaner', of 'coloured gangster' and perhaps even that of photographer Roger Ballen, given the derivative nature of Jones' artwork, in somewhat of a recursive and additive loop, with each imago continuously providing 'new' imaginative material for the subject to draw on.

In this manner, Jones, who is neither working class nor Afrikaner (Haupt 2012b), might also aspire to the image reflected as such in the figure of Anri du Toit (aka Yolandi Visser). The development of Jones' ego therefore transgresses not only cultural but also gendered boundaries. Of their earliest attempts at working together, Ninja and Yolandi confess:

> **Yolandi:** I was just copying the American thing. I didn't know how to do it in South African.
>
> **Ninja:** Yolandi was trying to do her own voice and it didn't work because she was fronting like she was English. I didn't even know she was Afrikaans. Then all of a sudden she started busting in Afrikaans...Then we just leaned into the Afrikaans thing. (*Rolling Stone* February 2012: 110)

This admission reveals Du Toit's initial unsuccessful attempt to adopt an English-language and US-centric Hip Hop persona – 'fronting' or presenting a façade of Englishness – and her subsequent reversion to Afrikaans as scaffolding for the Yolandi persona. It also illustrates Jones' collusion with Anri to 'lean into' the cultural prerogative of Afrikaans as a potential imago from which to construct the respective egos of Ninja and Yolandi.

In critical appraisals of Die Antwoord, Du Toit's contribution is largely absent, despite the obvious extent of her influence in the group's presentation, her formidable lyrical dexterity and hypersexualised, in some instances disturbingly infantilised, performances as Yolandi (the latter is especially evidenced in the music videos for *Rich Bitch* and *Cookie Thumper*). This lack of recognition can be attributed to the fact that visually, with her shock of bleached-blonde hair, Anri as Yolandi slips more easily into conventional understandings and representations of an excessive South African kitsch aesthetic.[20] The outward presentation of the ego formation known as Yolandi aligns with 'common sense' – to use Posel's (2001) term – perceptions of 'zefness'. Conforming to social expectation in this way renders her in a sense unremarkable and not deserving of further assessment beyond that of female sidekick in a male-oriented performance genre.[21]

---

20. In the 2010 video *Evil Boy*, Yolandi wears a hooded cloak made of faux white rats, evoking the pejorative Afrikaans term for white trash: wit rot (literally, white rat).
21. Laura Mulvey's use of psychoanalysis to interrogate visual pleasure further explains the relative dismissal of Yolandi's character as a topic of analysis in comparison to Ninja's. In her essay 'Visual Pleasure and Narrative Cinema', Mulvey examines the ways in which 'film reflects, reveals and even plays on the straight, socially established interpretation of sexual difference which controls images, erotic ways of looking and spectacle' (2006: 342). The ideas outlined here relating to scopophilic instinct, the transfer of ego libido and circumvention of female threat, could similarly be applied to the visual production of Die Antwoord's music videos, particularly in relation to my proposal of Jones' 'assumption' of a female imago. This investigation, however, is beyond the purview of the current chapter.

By comparison, the ego presentation of Ninja destabilises the 'common sense' visual and behavioural expectations of Jones' ostensibly English-language, middle-class background. Yet despite the violent mullet, rangy physique and faux-prison *tjappies* (tattoos) that all contribute to a sense of racial-/class-signifier play, he is overwhelmingly acknowledged as performing 'a version of whiteness', as opposed to 'a version of brownness/blackness'. This is of course due to Jones' (as an originary subject's) racial categorisation. Hence the assertions of Ninja's performance as an *'alternative whiteness'*. In Lacan's (1989: 3–4) estimation, the point when the analysand/ subject recognises his difference from the mirror image is reflected in dreams of a 'fragmented body', whereas the Ideal-I is represented in dreams by a secure fortress or stadium. Although the figure of Ninja represents Jones' ego, the ability of critics and fans alike to so easily disentangle the composite parts from the whole highlights the inherent instability of this imaginary persona. Here the Ideal-I is compromised by Jones' subject position at every turn. The register of the real (Jones) subverts the efforts of the imaginary (Ninja) even as it progresses through to the adoption of language and into the realm of the symbolic. The dual relation between subject and Ideal-I is inherently one of antagonism. In the 'Ninja ego formation', this conflict is mitigated via the adoption of Afrikaans language, a signifier sufficiently imbued with meaning to affirm whiteness without censure.

Recalling the example of Anri as Yolandi, where an ego presentation matches anticipated visual and social behaviour, the following sections examine the example of Isaac Williams in the ego formation of 'Isaac Mutant', a coloured MC similarly performing socially imagined habits and experience. These analyses expand the metaphor of the mirror stage to address ideas of mimicry and reflection, and especially the similarities between the music videos for Die Antwoord's track 'Zef Side' and Dookoom's debut release *'Kak Stirvy'*; the former's *'Fok Julle Naaiers'* and the latter group's *'Larney Jou Poes'*.

I KEEP ME *KAK STIRVY*

If the video for 'Zef Side' introduced the world to Die Antwoord via digital media, the 2013 video for *'Kak Stirvy'* brought the band Dookoom to the attention of musical and cultural production pundits. Although each offering featured different directors (Sean Metelerkamp and Ari Kruger, respectively), parallels can be drawn between the respective visual aesthetics presented. In both instances, the background setting is a working-class/

working-poor community. Die Antwoord's piece was shot in the white neighbourhood of Ysterplaat (although for an interview with South African lifestyle television programme *Top Billing*, the group recreated the video setting in the coloured residential area of Mitchells Plain),[22] and Dookoom's work was filmed on location in the coloured township of Heinz Park. But whereas the treatment for *Zef Side* tends towards blanched overexposure, *Kak Stirvy* is darker and oversaturated, suggesting a brooding realism lacking from the first example. Isaac Mutant is shown in interstitial spaces – strutting down the main drag, in a stairwell, an informal corrugated-iron dwelling, an empty lot – pointing to transience, a sense of impermanence and disruption more in line with his (real) subject position as Isaac Williams. Ninja and Yolandi are mostly posed against the backdrop of a modest suburban home, implying domesticity.[23] These representations are again in line with 'common sense' assumptions of whiteness as an inherently stable racial identity despite 'playing in the dark' (referencing non-white cultural mores), and colouredness as a rather ambiguous formulation even when mobilising 'white people's things' (employing previously inaccessible means of production).

The phrase *'kak stirvy'* is a vernacular Afrikaans colloquialism meaning 'stuck-up' or 'aloof'. Isaac explains: 'It used to be a negative word in the [coloured] ghetto…it used to mean uptight, snobbish, self-centred even.' But a contemporary interpretation suggests that the term conveys an expression of pride or braggadocio. He elaborates:

> I think coloured people appreciated [the video] more [than white audiences]: 'This dude actually makes gutter look *stirvy*' – that was the idea, you know. And that's how people are in the ghetto *bra* [brother] – *Jy't die kakste skoen, maar **die** ding, jy trap nie op die skoene nie.* [You have the shittiest pair of shoes, but *this* thing, don't you dare step on the shoes.]

---

22. https://www.youtube.com/watch?v=wFGiOqFxE7M
23. From a musical standpoint, *Zef Side* and *Kak Stirvy* both sample tracks popular in the late 1980s: Bronski Beat's 'Hit That Perfect Beat' (1986) and Salt-n-Pepa's 'Push It' (1987), respectively. 'Hit That Perfect Beat' was used as the theme song for Body Beat, the aerobics segment of erstwhile news and variety television show *Good Morning South Africa*. For South African audiences, this parodic reference evokes memories of a decidedly middle-class domestic background: mom doing morning calisthenics before shuffling the kids off to school, and her husband off to work. By contrast, the use of 'Push It' acknowledges a historical indebtedness to Hip Hop's predecessors, and imagines Dookoom as operating within the established conventions of this performance genre. Although Dookoom is a collective comprising both white and coloured members, lyrical content is developed by frontman Isaac Mutant and thus predominantly reflects his outlook and lived experience.

Like *this* [Isaac gestures at his wristwatch], this is *kak stirvy*. I *jak* [wear/
display] this like it's fucking gold *bra*, *dis oorgeblaaste digital, die ding is seker
twee rand* [it's overblown digital, this thing is probably only worth two rand]...
that's ghetto...that *kak* [shit] you have, you gonna bling the fuck out of that *kak*
that you have...Plus it's a South African thing: Rick Ross is 'The Big Boss', Die
Antwoord is *die larneys* [the bosses], we *kak stirvy*. (Isaac Mutant interview)

This latter comment structures the expression '*kak stirvy*' as an inherently coloured
prerogative, as an ethnoracial and cultural perspective equal to the white conception of
zef kitsch adopted in part by Die Antwoord.

Although Isaac Williams has performed under numerous monikers – Ike Deny, DJ Brook Squirter,
Rebel MC, Yucky Stuff (*Rolling Stone* January 2013) – each of these prior ego formations was
resolutely grounded in a vernacular Afrikaans and Hip Hop mode of expression. But it is
Isaac Williams' current ego formation as 'Mutant', together with connotations evoked by the
band name Dookoom (conjurer), that asserts an equivalent authority to manipulate and (re)
fashion signifiers just as white South African artists have done.

Kak Stirvy is certainly not the first South African Hip Hop music video to articulate non-
white sociopolitical concerns; as examples, see Prophets of da City's *Roots* (1990) and
Boomstyle (1991), or Black Noise's *Mitchells Plain* (2011). The adoption of 'white people's
things' – the music video format, and means of distribution via internet and social media
platforms – in this context is nothing out of the ordinary. But what becomes clear when
comparing Dookoom's output to Die Antwoord's is the specific range of visual–dialogic
techniques employed. This is most apparent when considering the *Kak Stirvy* video in
relation to *Zef Side*: from the origin narrative assumed in the localised setting, to the
ubiquitous prefabricated concrete fencing, the cameos featuring bemused locals and the
juvenile, phallocentric humour. With Die Antwoord, these elements contribute to Jones'
movement from originary subject to hopeful realisation of a complete and idealised form
as 'Ninja'. I propose that Dookoom's work, highlighting Isaac Mutant's ego formation,
performs a regressive function, exposing and reflecting the figure of 'Ninja' as simply a
composite, fragmentary entity back to the viewer. Mutant's '*stirvy*-ness' is overblown and

hyperbolised in the same way that Die Antwoord depicts an exaggerated zefness, but Williams' progression to Mutant is more plausible since the Ideal-I appropriately matches 'common sense' assumptions of his racialised behaviour. The order of the real, in other words, is closer to that of the imaginary. Jones' performance as Ninja is too far-fetched, too removed from his primordial subject position to be imagined as a credible ego formation. This impulse, showing up both parallels and contradictions, is taken to a further extreme when analysing Dookoom's video for '*Larney Jou Poes*' and Die Antwoord's '*Fok Julle Naaiers*'.

JY KAN MY NIE VERTEL'IE (YOU CAN'T TELL ME)

'It seems that no...video in the history of South African music,' writes journalist Benjamin Fogel, 'has attracted as much controversy as the Cape Town Hip Hop collective Dookoom's '*Larney Jou Poes*'...'[24] Indeed, several online and print media outlets have commented on the group's 2015 video (the title of which translates loosely to 'Fuck You, Boss!')[25] on account of the hate-speech allegations levelled by a local civil rights watchdog known as AfriForum. A non-governmental organisation that purportedly focuses on the advocacy of marginalised social groups, AfriForum is particularly concerned with 'the rights of Afrikaners as a community living on the southern tip of the continent'.[26] They argue that the track incites antagonism towards Afrikaners and can be read as an encouragement of the 'South African white genocide' as evidenced in (supposedly) racially motivated murders of farmers that have occurred in recent years.[27]

Arguably, the only lyrical reference that could be linked to this idea is included in an adaptation of the Biblical nursery rhyme 'Father Abraham Had Seven Sons'. The text of the introductory section reads:

> Farmer Abrahams had many farms,
> Many farms had Father Abrahams.

---

24. http://africasacountry.com/2014/11/afrikaner-farms-race-relations-and-the-new-south-africa/
25. Jou ma se poes (Your mother's cunt) is a common vernacular Afrikaans epithet that has made its way into the general South African vernacular lexicon. *Larney Jou Poes* could arguably be understood as *Larney Jou (Ma se) Poes*.
26. See https://www.afriforum.co.za/about/about-afriforum. AfriForum has officially brought Dookoom before the South African Human Rights Commission on a charge of purported hate speech. At the time of writing, members of the band were unable to discuss the outcome of the case.
27. https://africacheck.org/reports/are-white-afrikaners-really-being-killed-like-flies/

I work one of them, and so do you,

So let's go burn them down...

Filmed in stark black and white, the video begins with an overhead shot of a farmhouse, followed by close-ups of machinery and livestock. At [00'09'], addressing the camera directly in a medium-close framing, Isaac Mutant delivers the opening nursery rhyme with a menacing sing-song intonation. The first verse begins at [00'20'] with Isaac taking the role of farm owner in his stereotypical khakis and wide-brimmed hat, driving a tractor. On the trailer behind him is a crew of coloured farm workers brandishing scythes and other implements. The scene is easily read as an angry mob armed with pitchforks and flaming torches, advancing on an unjustly accused fairy-tale protagonist.

The video continues, interspersing cuts of farm workers drinking from *papsakke* (spouted bags removed from the inside of boxed wine containers), and rolling discarded, burning tyres through an open field. The video's climax features a white farmer staring in disbelief as the word 'DOOKOOM' blazes defiantly against a hillside. The imagery presented here evokes scenes from an uncomfortable past, specifically the *dop* system[28] and the apartheid-era kangaroo-court penalty of 'necklacing'. In her 1993 essay 'Culture Beyond Color?', Zoë Wicomb draws a comparison between the Afrikaner cultural activity of the *braai*, 'the *bonhomie* of the barbecue', and necklacing, an apartheid-era township practice whereby an *impimpi* (traitor) is made to suffer immolation by having a burning tyre placed around his neck. Wicomb (1993: 31) suggests that:

> Both originate in the need to survive: Boers trekking from British domination relied on shooting buck and eating the roasted meat in the open veld; necklacing eliminates those who endanger the community by spying for the government. Necklacing then is about displacing Boer culture physically and symbolically. It is about positioning; placing the victim as other within an isolating circle of fire and outside of the community...

---

28. The *dop* or 'tot system' refers to the practice of supplementing vineyard farm workers' incomes with alcohol. This often leads to alcohol abuse, Foetal Alcohol Syndrome, as well as a sense of feudal dependency on the part of the workers in relation to the farm owner.

Overall, the video depicts a definitive repositioning of agency, with authority now located in the hands of indentured labourers. The most provocative example of this reversal is found in the visual articulations of the song's chorus. Set against a plain background, the camera offers a succession of close-ups of farm workers lip-synching along with the lyrics: *Jou poes my larney, jy kan my nie vertel'ie!* (Boss, fuck you, you can't tell me nothin'!)

The release of *Larney Jou Poes* coincided with media reports of wildcat strikes, started in 2012 by farm workers at De Doorns in the Great Karoo, which subsequently spread to the rest of the Boland. The strikers argued for a daily wage increase and improved working conditions, but their concerns also touched on historical issues of land dispossession, the legacy of imperialism and white Afrikaner paternalism.[29] Isaac recalls:

> I think '93 or thereabouts, '94, I wrote the second verse...[a friend suggested]
> 'Write about shit that bothers you, that fucks with *you*, like the farm
> workers'[30]...that was even before [the strikes]...I wrote the first verse recently...
> but that was before this whole farm-worker issue...you know...we were not
> trying to even ride on that... (Isaac Mutant interview)

Lyrical structure aside, the concept for the video was the vision of first-time director Dane Dodds, who chose to shoot the production in the farm district outside of Oudtshoorn where he had grown up. Some of the actors featured were farm workers drawn from the area who remembered Dane and referred to him deferentially as *kleinbaas* (little boss). He describes the first day of filming:

> We had this generator with speakers on the back, and we put the song on...we
> couldn't use [the first take], because there were too many smiles...they couldn't
> believe what they were hearing...we had the camera, and I [said] don't imagine
> me as 'Dane', imagine me as all the white people that fucked you over in your
> life, and then you're gonna look me in the eyes, and I'm gonna play the track,
> and then you need to shout it directly at me...I wanted to cry sometimes, some

---

29. http://africasacountry.com/2014/11/afrikaner-farms-race-relations-and-the-new-south-africa/
30. Isaac grew up in Vredendal, an agricultural hub 300 kilometres north of Cape Town, and still has relatives and friends employed as farm workers.

of them *did* cry, it was the most intense thing I've ever experienced, seeing them say that...As soon as I said 'Action', they were in it, as soon as I said 'Cut', they were out of it...they understood that it was a world that was created.

(Dane Dodds interview)

Rasmus Bitsch, Dane's production partner notes:

When we arrived...it was quite difficult for [the farm workers] first to grasp the fact that Isaac and [DJ] Roach...were coloured people who were the bosses, that we were working for them, and not the other way around...I knew that that kind of reality exists, but to suddenly be part of it is a different thing...so I think for the people involved it was a powerful experience... (Rasmus Bitsch interview)

Isaac puts it more succinctly:

These *brasse* [guys] didn't want to say '*Jou poes my larney*', because there's the *larney* that's standing – it's unheard of to say that kind of thing against a white person. [I had to tell them] '*Hier's nou jou kans, hy sal jou nie fire nie*' [This is your chance, he won't fire you]. (Isaac Mutant interview)

These brief examples demonstrate the extent to which roles of dominance and servility are entrenched within the racialised schema of the South African farming community particularly, but also provide a glimpse into the country's broader social dynamic.

For Isaac, media backlash to the video was unexpected, especially since inequitable working and racial conditions in the South African agricultural industry are open secrets:

I was surprised *my bru* [my brother]...2014 and people are *this* pissed off about *this*? Are you *serious*? The issue is there...it's not something we created...I was *kak* [really] surprised...and proud at the same time...It's something that matters...Public Enemy shit. (Isaac Mutant interview)

While not all Dookoom's work explicitly addresses socioeconomic concerns, Isaac's reference to 'Public Enemy shit' situates the track within the lineage of early, politically conscious Cape Town Hip Hop (exemplified by groups like Prophets of da City, Brasse Vannie Kaap and Black Noise), and specifically places it in line with the aesthetic paradigm of late 1980s/early 1990s US-based rap. An iconic collective in the Hip Hop pantheon, Public Enemy's most well-known single is arguably their 1989 effort 'Fight the Power', considered a prototypical anthem in the rap and popular culture canons against authoritarian rule. Discussing 'Larney Jou Poes' alongside 'Fight the Power' speaks to the former track's potentially resistive impetus against contemporary social oppression.

On the other hand, Dane experienced public outcry at a more personal level, since the filming took place in his hometown. He talks of telephone calls from community members offering to pray for him, or otherwise receiving outright death threats for his part in the creation of the *Larney Jou Poes* video. Dane explains that after the video's release:

> I drove to Oudtshoorn to go talk to a lot of the people that were upset about [the video]. It was quite difficult because they couldn't understand that I'm not making the video in praise of farm murders. I grew up as a *laaitie* [youngster] pretty scared...I knew people that were murdered on farms...it's a very *real* thing. What I did want is to show it to people and then let them talk about it, and let them talk about why there's the discontent...it's a *huge* problem, it's not something that's solvable by a music video...but then that sparks more conversations...and then the general consciousness will come together and somehow start working on improving things... (Dane Dodds interview)

While the intentions behind the lyrics and storyboard are clear, AfriForum nevertheless managed to impose a restriction on the video, requiring viewers to sign in and verify their age before being able to access it on YouTube.

The file-sharing site's content guideline section places restrictions on subject matter that might contain 'vulgar language, nudity and sexually suggestive content, violence and disturbing imagery, and portrayal of harmful or dangerous activities'.[31] Curiously, though, some of Dookoom's more risqué videos, interviews and audio files are readily available on YouTube without any preparatory verification. Among these are Dookoom's collaboration with Mississippi rapper David Banner, the chorus of which reads: 'The worst thing to happen to the African is the white man'; the

---

31. https://www.youtube.com/yt/about/policies/#community-guidelines

audio file for *Murrafucker* featuring the coda: '*De La Rey, De La Rey, Ons het die boere verlei*' (We deceived the *boers*/whites), an allusion to Afrikaner musician Bok van Blerk's controversial 2005 single (Haupt 2012b); and the 2016 video for 'Dirty', directed by noted photographer Pieter Hugo, which features simulated sodomy.[32] I contend that the reason for AfriForum's adamant call to censor the *Larney Jou Poes* video rests in the challenge it presents to 'common sense' assumptions of coloured/non-white individuals in a rural setting as a subservient, docile labour force, demonstrated at an explicitly visual level. These assumptions arguably find precedent in the portrayals of labour dynamics in early South African *plaasromans* (farm novels), the form of genre fiction dealing broadly with white Afrikaner experiences of dislocation from urban settings – the 'painful transition from farmer to townsman' (Coetzee 1988: 63) – and at the same time articulating the Afrikaner's deeply embedded cultural sense of stewardship of the land. In Coetzee's (1988: 5) analysis of this literary sphere, he maintains that 'blindness to the colour black' was a *sine qua non.*

Referencing Olive Schreiner's novel *The Story of an African Farm* (1883), Coetzee describes the South African pastoral as a narrative trope obliged to satisfy several complex ideological prerogatives. From a western literary perspective, novelists at the time of Schreiner's writing were hard-pressed to depict the bucolic setting as more than simply a retreat from the pressures of urban life and a wilful descent into idleness. Specific to the South African context was an apprehension that white colonists might 'degenerate' to the level of indolence associated with the region's indigenous population. And despite the historical antagonisms between British and Afrikaner settlers, the failure of the latter group to credibly subdue the wilderness landscape would represent a failure of the colonial project *in toto*. Running parallel to these ideas was the imperial attitude of expansion and 'legitimate' appropriation: whosoever purposefully cultivated the land could justifiably lay claim to its ownership. Thus, pastoral living, and therefore pastoral narratives, had to reflect an ethos of labour. Most importantly though, this labour had to be depicted as being carried out by white Afrikaner protagonists. As Coetzee (1988: 5, emphasis in original) puts it, such conditions led to the inevitable

---

32. The narrative for Die Antwoord's video *Cookie Thumper* (2014) follows a coloured gangster named Bra Anies, who, recently released from prison, rekindles a relationship with a former partner, Yolandi. 'Cookie' is a vernacular term for vagina: The premise of the video is that Anies seduces Yolandi, who plays the role of a young boarding-school student. Anticipating consensual vaginal sex, Yolandi is instead sodomised. Tropes of black masculinity aside, this representation plays on stereotypes of coloureds on the Cape Flats as gang members and criminals. The allusion to male prison rape implicates former inmates as unable to successfully rehabilitate and conform to heteronormative sexual behaviour. The further implication is that coloured individuals are incapable of acceding to mainstream social expectations.

occlusion of black labour from the scene: the black man [became] a shadowy
presence flitting across the stage now and then to hold a horse or serve a meal…
If the work of hands on a particular patch of earth, digging, ploughing, planting,
building [was] what [inscribed] the property of its occupiers *by right*, then the hands
of black serfs doing the work had better not be seen.

The overt visual portrayal of dissatisfied non-white workers in Dookoom's video therefore calls into question long-held notions of the Afrikaner as 'heir to the land' (Coetzee 1988) and, more specifically, turns the ideological basis of landownership on its head.

A BIG BLACK JOKE?

While Die Antwoord's video *Fok Julle Naaiers* (Fuck All You Haters) does not engage the same level of social commentary as *Larney Jou Poes*, there nevertheless exists a visual–dialogic resonance between the two. Both videos are shot in black and white (musically, a descending four-note motif forms the basis of an *ostinato* loop in each piece), but the most striking similarity occurs during their respective chorus sections: a series of close-ups predominantly of coloured individuals emphatically shouting invectives at an imagined antagonist. For Dookoom, the intended recipient of this anger is the 'larney', an individual perpetuating historical class domination through exploitative labour practice. 'Larney' in this instance refers neutrally to an authoritarian figure, but given the context of the video setting, the 'boss man' is implicated as a white character (*vide* Isaac's comparison of Rick Ross, Die Antwoord and Dookoom). By contrast, with 'I Fink You Freeky', one of the few tracks in which Die Antwoord makes an explicit lyrical reference to race, Ninja declares: *'Ek's 'n larney, jy's a gam/want jy sit innie mang, met you slang in a man.'* The word *'gam'* is a derogatory term for a coloured individual, while *'mang'* and *'slang'* are vernacular terms for 'prison' and 'penis', respectively. The entire line immodestly translates to: 'I'm a boss, you're a low-class coloured/you're rotting in prison, committing sodomy.' While his tattoos hint at prison gang culture, this non sequitur occurring at the end of a verse establishes the Ninja ego formation as unambiguously white and heteronormative, superior to the widely accepted stereotype of the coloured Cape Flats criminal from which it is drawn.[33] If these examples suggest clear racial and

---

33. The track begins with Yolandi lying naked in a bathtub, intoning: 'Sexy boys, fancy boys, playboys, bad boys/I fink you freeky, and I like you a lot.' The Sexy Boys and Fancy Boys are notorious Cape Flats gangs, while the Playboy bunny logo and 'bad boy' epithet are common prison tattoo themes. The line simultaneously implies a (white female) fetishisation of race, coloured masculinity and sexuality. See https://www.youtube.com/watch?v=8Uee_mcxvrw.

ideological distinctions, the visual sequences for the introductory and chorus sections of *Fok Julle Naaiers* complicate them again.

The video opens with alternating images of shirtless coloured individuals (one of them covered in prison tattoos), a white subject (an ostensibly zef character typified in Roger Ballen's photographic explorations) and Ninja himself, his tattoos prominently displayed. This visual progression imposes continuity amongst these male characters with all three types as interchangeable, but also reveals the coloured and white figures as component imagos to the Ninja ego formation.[34] This pattern continues with the visual accompaniment to the chorus sections. Regarding the song's title: *'naaiers'* translates literally as 'fuckers', but given the lyrical context – a 'started from the bottom, now we here' type narrative – 'haters' is a more appropriate description. I read the track as a response to those who question the stability of Jones' projection, as evidenced with Ninja's second verse beginning at [02'07']. The relevant section of the text reads:

> ...All hail da great white Ninja!
> Every poes [cunt] wif a phone wants to take my picture!
> Ninja? Jis(laaik), I dig that oke! [Jeez, I love that guy!]
> 'Is it real?' No, it's just a big black joke.
> When dealing wif an idiot, there's really nuffing you can say,
> The next time you ask me: ''Sit real?' I'm gonna punch you in the face!

Throughout this presentation, the dramatic convention of maintaining a separation between actor and audience is disrupted: Yolandi, Ninja, as well as the host of ancillary characters, face the camera head-on, addressing the viewer directly. In line with this strategy, Ninja's promise to 'punch critics in the face' when questioned about the influence of non-white cultural signifiers in Die Antwoord's work (*vide* Diane Coetzer's interview), while simultaneously asserting his own intrinsic whiteness ('the great white Ninja'), is implied through visual and sound effect. Coinciding with the final line of text quoted above, Ninja strikes out towards the camera lens through which he is being viewed. The effect is of the screen being 'smashed', accompanied by the crash of breaking glass as

---

34. Yolandi is featured in the chorus sequences as well, but the focus here is on the similarity in appearance of the male characters.

Ninja punches through 'the fourth wall' [02'37']. Of course, when considered from the subject's perspective, the screen/camera lens can also be interpreted as the metaphorical Lacanian mirror. On realising that the concept of the Ideal-I can never be achieved, that his projection is not accepted by local audiences, Jones lashes out in frustration at the image before him and destroys it.

CONCLUSION

With all the potential avenues available for self-expression in contemporary South Africa, apartheid-era racial typologies are still the dominant means by which individuals are socially identified and measured. One's racial category is initially determined through visual assessment, and then confirmed via social behaviour. Lacan's 'mirror stage' theory demonstrates the process through which Jones has bolstered his career by absorbing exogamous cultural mores, attempting to 'assume' the persona of marginalised subjects. Subverting 'common sense' behavioural expectations, Jones nonetheless fails to realise the idealised version of something perhaps 'other than white' and is always recognised visually as 'an alternative version of whiteness'. Even the contentious aspiration to become *die wit kaffir* is prefixed, is qualified, by an assertion of intrinsic racial identity. But the crucial factor here is Jones and other white South African musicians' ability to 'play in the dark', to playfully draw on a reservoir of diverse cultural influences without censure. 'Whiteness is without restrictions,' as Wicomb's character John Campbell muses, '[i]t has the fluidity of milk…' (2006: 151). The same cannot be said of '*non*-whiteness', as the case with Dookoom attests.

On the one hand, Isaac Williams' performance and visual presentation as 'Isaac Mutant' in the video *Kak Stirvy* embodies historical 'common sense' conceptions of coloured social behaviour: the Mutant ego formation is menacing, confrontational, prowling the mean streets of Heinz Park (a stand-in for all of the Cape Flats). But when Mutant exceeds and disrupts expectation, as with the *Larney Jou Poes* video, his actions must be publicly condemned and his expression curtailed. There is no possibility within this discourse to imagine alternative renderings of coloured identity: Mutant as a farm owner dressed in his khaki outfit, or labourers as anything but docile, servile, hidden in plain sight. For coloured individuals, self-identity may not deviate from socially inscribed identity.

In a surprising turn towards the end of Wicomb's novel, John Campbell remarks: 'Man, in this New South Africa, we can play at anything, mix 'n match, talk and sing any way we like. Because of freedom…' (2006: 213). These examples have shown that the freedom to 'mix 'n match' remains an exclusive purview of the country's white citizenry.

ACKNOWLEDGEMENT

I would like to extend my gratitude to Julie Strand for reading through the initial draft of this chapter and offering her comments.

CHAPTER 19.
A SON OF THE SUN:
A REFLECTION ON HIP HOP
AND MY FATHER

BEN CAESAR

It's funny, almost contradictory, that I'm a Hip Hop artist.

I was raised by a single feminist-activist mother. As a young boy she'd take me to conferences, non-governmental organisation gatherings and marches. Much of my worldview was shaped by all the visits from her variety of friends from all walks of life from around the world, and the discussions we'd have at the dinner table. I was taught to look at society critically and analytically. It translated into my music and had me writing a song against rape at the age of 16. That background contradicts a lot of Hip Hop, as much of it is misogynistic.

My mother was both mother and father to me. Being raised without another father figure, I'd often seek a male role model in older friends. I think I reached to Hip Hop to fill that void, as many of the artists were the fatherless generation dealing with their manhood, black identity and upbringing in all its raw honesty.

My father was black Dominican, my mother white British/South African, trying to get as far away from her colonial history and apartheid South Africa as possible. Identity was a complex issue for me, being born in the Caribbean in Dominica, then moving to St Lucia then living in a squat in London's Brixton, then Amsterdam, then Yeoville in Jozi (Johannesburg) before Cape Town. Identity was a fluctuating concept. I'd had to adapt a few times before I hit high school and as a teen I needed a mould.

In middle school, kids asked if I was adopted when my mother fetched me from the entrance. I identify as black. Being mixed race meant some Capetonians assumed I'm 'coloured' and were offended that I didn't speak Afrikaans, or even speak English like them; some asked if

I'm tryna be white or why I speak like that, as if I was putting up a front. Race in South Africa is an inescapable issue. I had to fit in by standing out.

I found an identity immersing myself in Hip Hop art and culture – it offered room for my voids and gave me a home and tribe where I couldn't find another. Artistically, I was formed by all the places I've lived and travelled. My perspective has been shaped by all the cultures, sexualities, genders, values and people I've been exposed to. All this articulates my music and content.

I love Hip Hop's honesty. Many of the great artists gave you their story with all their glory, tragedy, horror and heart, real heart; the kind of bruises and blemishes only Hip Hop can make space for.

It's one of the few genres that allows for contradiction. A rapper will make a song about blowing money, then right after another about investing in their communities. That's real for me. I understand the world and people to be contradictory; I for sure contradict myself. I don't see how it's avoidable, especially if we're honest with ourselves.

BEN CAESAR BOOK SLOT | Source: Ference Isaacs

Hip Hop gives the space to be three-dimensional. All the most compelling artists are.

While I'm aware that when I'm writing all my choices are political (because one can't create anything apolitical even if you think of it as that), I'm not one for pigeonholes. I don't pigeonhole other people, and certainly not myself. If people ask me what I do, I just say I'm an artist – I don't even say rapper as their understanding of rapper might not be my understanding of rapper. I've had someone say, 'If you're a rapper, where's your bling bling?' Eish. I don't tag myself as a political, commercial, underground, conscious or unconscious rapper, because I could be any or none of those at different times.

With my videos, many women have remarked how much they appreciate that there's a Hip Hop video that has women with clothes on. It's sad that this is remarkable. I remember we were cutting a video of a beach scene and my homegirl was in a bikini. One of the shots was a bit too revealing so I cut it. Harmless as it was, it's about not wanting to be part of the proliferation of videos that use women's bodies to sell products. I make a point to portray women in our music videos as whole people.

Don't get it twisted – there is space for nudity and there are some gorgeous videos with sensuality and I'm planning some of my own. I'd love for women to feel represented, seen and stimulated. However, I'm also aware of the context Hip Hop videos live in.

With massive corporate investment turning Hip Hop culture into a commodity, materialism has become an inflated theme in the music. 'I got this, I got that, and you aint shxt cos you aint got it.'

For this reason, I make a point of not having senseless material in my content. I've been offered luxury cars and mansions for my videos but I don't want to buy into the doctrine that brands and assets determine your value as a person. I think that's a great lie we're sold.

Recently, someone stopped me and said they recognised me, saying, 'Can't mistake that smile, it's in all your videos, you're like the only rapper that smiles in their videos.' I honestly hadn't noticed or didn't actually make it a point to smile.

But I realise from what he said that it's a masculinity issue. I look at these things differently these days as my idea of gender has been challenged.

A few years ago, a trans friend of my mother's was in the process of transitioning. She stayed with us through the duration. It gave me a very real introduction to a world beyond the gender binary. I spent hours going through my mother's work with trans activists and, meeting them, I learned of the risks they took and the many ways they defined gender for themselves in life-threatening circumstances. This gave me new questions to ask and extended my worldview.

Learning the difference between gender and sex, and if there was a whole new world of gender, what was mine actually? What is masculinity even? Is it innate and to what extent is it learned?

Being raised by women, I've been able to form my own masculinity from a different point of reference. But being exposed to the world of trans and more gender diversity, I learned that gender can be self-determined. That we don't have to police or be policed for our genders.

I mean, we're taught in society that you're either male or female – what a sodding lie. In addition, with that there's a whole lifetime of roles, expectations and scripts that are prescribed to you as soon as your gender is determined in the womb. So where is the individuality? This opened up a trapdoor to a tunnel of long reflection.

Here's the rub – last year I started to question and look at Hip Hop's influence on me. Hip Hop my foster parent, my identity. It was like turning on your own tribe. I worked with Adam Haupt on the song 'R.U.SA?' to ask a few questions about where conditioning ends and individuality begins, and the effect of American media (Hip Hop) on specifically South African youth and the identity complexes that come from being raised by this media and content.

It was a process of serious unlearning that started with Hip Hop and broadened to society as a whole. It shifted my paradigm, actually. I stopped taking for granted my opinions and perspectives. I looked at my responsibility as a consumer and the price of my complicity – a price that is paid by the people who are most exploited. I acknowledged my privilege as a male in society. Even with all that analysing, I still have many stones unturned, many of which I only find after I've tripped on them.

There's so much nonsense that we're taught throughout our lives that gets reinforced every single day, from the media we consume to what our food is wrapped in. What's scary is we aren't encouraged to question it. What's worse is we aren't encouraged to take responsibility for our society. Let the government deal with it. Let the environmentalists deal with it. It's disempowering. Our power isn't called upon. So amidst frustration, we point fingers but are made to think that changing the structure we live under is terrifying and beyond our reach.

There's power in Hip Hop, there's fury, rebellion and self-sufficiency. Hip Hop promotes self-promotion; it has a culture outside of the music industry, outside of the red-tape bureaucracy. It maintains its own platforms and revenue streams. Its attitude is do it yourself, do you, hustle hard, show 'em what it is. You don't go to school for that shxt, you learn it in the streets, you learn it by doing it and going out there. And that's what, if I wish for art to do anything, it's to spark the fire.

B-BOY TOUFEEQ IN LONG STREET | Source: Ference Isaacs

IMMORTAL STYLE | Source: Ference Isaacs

B-BOYS POSE FOR A PHOTO SHOOT IN FRONT OF AN ARTWORK | Source: Ference Isaacs

CHAPTER 20.
BOSS BITCHES/
BOSS LADIES

BURNI AMAN

During the time that I have been involved in the Hip Hop movement, the question of who dictates or, more specifically, what dictates expected female norms – whether as an MC or for females in general in various aspects of society or the workplace – has been a strong influence in my music.

I think that how we as females have explored our identity has not only been influenced by societal structures and thinking but also by the restrictions we have placed upon ourselves, willingly and unwillingly.

In the classical sense of patriarchy, we willingly impose views on how we function, speak, think and act, in the sense that we have in place 'male dictatorships', as far as I have come to understand them, in the form of father–daughter relations, sibling relations, community relations and workplace interactions. All of these work in unison to qualify what we ourselves believe to be our own voices, thoughts and understandings and many times speak through our music. Whether it be Godessa, Burni Aman as a solo artist or any other female MC, our music in its basic form is the consciousness or sum of all these various societal views that have over the years become our own. Essentially, at a primal level, we speak more through the voices, ideas and thoughts of others than what we like to admit to ourselves. However, this does not mean that what we have adopted or the beliefs that we were born into cannot and are not able to reflect how we see the world. When Queen Latifah said 'Don't call me a bitch' in her track 'U.N.I.T.Y.', it not only reflected how she wanted to be valued as a woman and person but also reflected the voices of her relatives, community, friend circle and large numbers of black females who wanted the same respect for themselves, their daughters, their sisters and sistas.

So how have we made this leap from willing to unwilling participants in our expression of femaleness? How have we become 'boss bitches' and not just 'bosses' of our own destiny?

Unwillingly, we engage in gender-specific or -targeted warfare. Women are supposed to be strong, act in a certain way and speak in a certain tone. However, there are obviously a multitude of layers within the concept of how women should rep themselves. For the purposes of this chapter, I reflect on one of these layers of womanhood, and that is the different standards between black and white females.

The concept of white women being strong but needing to be protected, for example through protecting her innocence, as happened during slavery. She could not see or was not permitted to see the harshness of what white men were doing to their slaves, but instead had to support him and his subprimal nature by turning a blind eye to his 'seeking out the help' – in other words, using black female slaves sexually to preserve white women's virtue. In Hip Hop today we see white female MCs, for instance in the form of artists like Iggy Azalia, not as active participants in the exploitation of so-called black culture but as cute, innocent, non-threatening conduits who are only role-playing. On the other end of the spectrum, black female MCs are either placed under the banner of 'hard-core revolutionaries' who the whole world should fear, or seen as 'hard-core commercial sluts' who no one should take seriously, since they pose a threat to good old male patriarchal ideas of how females are supposed to be and act. This for me shows again how white female virtue is being protected because obviously they are being presented as only miniscule threats.

This is opposed to the concept of black women being strong, being told to be independent rather than interdependent and doing for self without the assistance of males, whether black or white. In the first instance, this creates a disconnect between black males and black females, since the notion of no or low value has been placed on black females since slavery, thereby affecting their self-worth and image. In the second instance, the black female experiences her world through the eyes of white male privilege, which threatens to violate and dominate her but at the same time wants to revere her nature in some kind of perverse fashion. We see mostly black female images being exploited in Hip Hop videos, mostly in non-wholesome roles as booty shakers and objectified as being hypersexualised.

I have no problem with females choosing to use their image or voice, as in the case of Nicki Minaj and others, as sexual currency. However, I question whether or not their decision to do so is not perhaps unwittingly influenced by gender-targeted warfare specifically aimed at dehumanising the black female body and exposing it as a mere curiosity, as was done in times of slavery. Maybe it's a huge leap or even a sacrilegious thing to say, but have MCs such as Nicki Minaj not become the modern-day versions of Saartjie Baartman? Yes, Sarah was not an instigator or propelling force in the way her image/body was publicly abused by strangers, but are Nicki Minaj and other Hip Hop vixens not also balls being kicked around under the veiled guise of modern black feminism or 'boss bitches' supposedly reclaiming their bodies and sexuality?

In terms of the financial or materialistic side of being a 'boss bitch', has Hip Hop, in the state that it is in now, not become the dumping ground for us postmodern-day slaves? Was Kanye right when he said we are the new slaves? Everything can be sold/marketed in Hip Hop these days. Hell, I don't know a lot of artists, including myself, who wouldn't

BURNI AMAN PERFORMING | Source: Adam Haupt

maybe think twice about doing a shout-out on their tracks to advertise some label in return for a couple of grand. In the past, Godessa took money from Levis (a major corp) to help build our career; it paid for our first pressing. Was that wrong? Were we not utilised as modern-day slaves even though our message was, in my opinion still, very right? Who makes these clear-cut decisions of right and wrong? Where does it leave us in terms of Hip Hop, and, besides the all-important obvious negative in the term 'boss bitch', what influence does this term have on me as I become an elder in the Hip Hop community?

Maybe more importantly for me is whether or not anyone can ever be this term which is being thrown around.

'Boss bitches' aren't supposed to care what others say or think of them, right? So I couldn't possibly be a 'boss bitch'. Are my decisions about how I identify as an MC or as a female MC and, even more importantly than that, as a black female MC, not restricted by societal views and my willingness and unwillingness to enforce them? I consider myself an independent thinker, but what 'boss bitch' doesn't? I choose to use my music as a vehicle for upliftment/ empowerment but in the same instance I have willingly and unwillingly imposed a level of conservatism on my image and music, partly due to my environmental and social upbringing but also because of the voice in my head. Maybe my conscience...lol...won't allow me to overstep the boundaries of what is expected of a good, young, black/coloured, Catholic girl growing up in South Africa. Not only because of that but because I recognise that with me holding a mike as an MC comes a huge level of responsibility. I have dedicated myself through Godessa and various other projects to continue to be a fearless voice of female empowerment and good values and ethics. However, is that not non-boss-bitch speak, for I prefer to be prim and proper and not push boundaries?

So what if we don't all use our feminine currencies in the same way? Nicki Minaj is a dope MC/rapper, Queen Latifah is a dope MC, Lauryn Hill is a dope MC, Godessa were dope MCs. So were, or are, we all not 'boss bitches'? Not based on the vulgarity associated with the term or aggressive behaviour 'unbecoming of young ladies' or using our feminine charms, but based on the mere fact that we were leaders, independent thinkers, young girls working hard. If 'boss bitch' is based on the latter interpretation then yes, I might consider wearing the moniker of 'boss bitch' or 'boss lady' (for the politically correct and feminist sistas who directly and indirectly still uphold patriarchal roles even though they think they don't).

However, who I truly am as a black female is still framed by all the shit of racism, slavery, male patriarchy and societal norms and can't possibly be simplified in a Hip Hop context as 'black, conscious, revolutionary, sista'. In one sense I am all of that and more. In another sense I am none of that, because I am still viewing myself in the context of my work in Godessa or as a solo artist.

Recently, I had the privilege to watch two dope female MCs: one a white, feminist, lesbian, German rapper called Sookee and the other a black, lesbian rapper from the States called Angel Haze. Just including labels because as South Africans we love labels :-). Both were equally aggressive in their demeanour and lyrics on stage; however, the one who was viewed as the most menacing was Angel Haze. What amazed me the most besides their flows, performances and energy was the way in which they seemed to be free to say what they wanted but at the same time I recognise the self-imposed identity norms that even they probably carry. Yes, they had hard-core explicit songs, which I would most probably never choose to do, but in the same instance it was only as a way of pushing boundaries and not necessarily because they felt like writing them. They too were in my view reactionaries to their circumstances and not active participants in defining their femininity or nonconformist feminist views through their music.

There is certainly a dissonance between 'Don't call me a bitch' and what we now so easily throw around as a term of success for women, 'boss bitches', but who am I to judge and who are we to judge what female norms should look like in society or in Hip Hop? It's not a question of what dictates but who dictates – I'm not a 'boss bitch'!

MOTOR SPORT VS B-BOYING (MALIKAH DANIELS AND BRANDON PETERSEN) | Source: Ference Isaacs

NATASHA C TAFARI, AFRICAN HIP HOP INDABA, 2016
Source: Ference Isaacs

BURNI AMAN, AFRICAN HIP HOP INDABA, 2016
Source: Ference Isaacs

CHAPTER 21.
'MY SEEDS MUST PROCEED'

JANINE 'BLAQ PEARL' VAN ROOY

HIP HOP ACTIVISM

In my opinion, 'activism' in this context means, firstly, being an active participant in one or more of the Hip Hop elements, particularly applying consciousness to one's content with the aim to express, share and inform. Secondly, using these Hip Hop elements to bring about positive change in one's life and communities.

I am the sister of the late Mr Devious and I simply cannot speak about my journey and opinion of Hip Hop activism without referring to him. He was and still is described as a Hip Hop activist and icon from Cape Town. Therefore, when I reflect on my journey, the first introduction to Hip Hop was through my brother. He left a life-changing impact on the rest of my life. What I particularly love about Hip Hop is the consciousness it instils and the fact that one can use Hip Hop as a means to express oneself, to relate to another and to share information and opinions in a raw, honest and very creative and skilful way.

Growing up on the Cape Flats, options for positive expression tend to seem limited – until you come across Hip Hop music. It's one of the forms/genres of music that allows you to express your anger and frustrations in just that way! Instead of stabbing, shooting or beating up someone, you can also express love and good times. It can be personal, social or/and political.

DEVELOPMENT WORK

My father was very involved in politics. So, as a child growing up in our household, conversations included society's problems, challenges, social ills, politics, proactive solutions and strategies. My mother was and still is a very loving person. She was and still is very hospitable and we and our friends always had the freedom to make music and listen to loud music in our home.

Communication, education and compassion were key fundamentals in our home. In essence, my first life skills were taught at home as part of our family values.

I was about 10 years old when I started hearing Hip Hop music coming from my brothers' music centre in their bedroom. When I reached 12 and found myself faced with difficult emotions and thoughts about myself and the world I lived in, questioning my purpose, especially growing up on the Cape Flats in Mitchells Plain with its many social ills and crime, I turned to creative writing and poetry to express myself. It felt natural at the time and became my coping mechanism and means to express myself throughout the rest of my life. This was also the age I believe I found myself.

After completing high school, then my bachelor's degree at university with majors in psychology and linguistics, I was already sure that I wanted to contribute positively to society. I also knew that I would be involved in the arts and wanted to make music and create products to sustain myself and, at the same time, uplift my community through my creative work. So, during my studies, I started volunteering at local non-governmental organisations (NGOs) and I really loved it. I worked with youth at risk. I automatically made assessments of the impact the life skills programmes had on them and concluded that something was missing in the approach. My brother Devious was still alive at the time, and we sat down together, like many other times before, started talking and then ended up designing a life skills programme using Hip Hop music and creative writing as the methodology. Time passed by and he started implementing the programme through his work at an NGO called Creative Education for Youth at Risk. After he died and I completed my degree, I continued working with various youth development organisations and also continued using the same approach. The response is always favourable. It's always great meeting participants who have gone through our programme years later and they still thank you.

Currently, I am one of the directors of the Blaqpearl Foundation, a non-profit company established to continue the development programmes, mainly with youth on the Cape Flats. Some of our programmes include the model we initially designed and have now expanded into a broader spectrum in terms of methodology. We transfer life skills and leadership skills to youth, using art disciplines as the methodology. And we've toured with a musical theatre production that includes Hip Hop music. It is a story of identity, challenges and hope titled *Krotoa Van Vandag*, written by me and presented by the Blaqpearl Foundation.

AFRIKAAPS

As an independent artist, I have pursued my career in the arts and entertainment industry full time since 2005. Throughout the years, with much dedication, education and growth, I have successfully managed to sustain myself and my family using my talents and gifts. Starting out as a writer, poet, singer, storyteller, and also classified by others as a Hip Hop artist and now a musical theatre performer and scriptwriter, I am clearly open to exploring various ways of expression and edutainment through this industry. In 2010, I was part of my first musical theatre experience, in a production titled *Afrikaaps*. It was about the true origin of the way we speak Afrikaans in the Cape. We accumulated so much information that we, at least I, had never heard of before. It all started making sense regarding my identity; regarding questions and intuitive feelings about my identity and the language I speak, dream in and express myself through. I felt so liberated knowing and being able to share this information through such a powerful medium as Hip Hop, of course fused with indigenous sounds, jazz and other genres of music. It was a collaboration of mainly Hip Hop artists who created an appealing package that our diverse audiences were drawn to, especially the information, the content. Again, the response was immense – from Cape Town audiences, to Oudtshoorn and even the Netherlands. This journey continues and evolves like the language we speak. It cannot be confined or restricted…

CONCLUSION

I find that Hip Hop music is a tool to reach various audiences and age groups, depending on the content and topic appealing to one's particular market. Now this is where mainstream media play some role. The type of Hip Hop music – content and topics – currently exposed and promoted through television and radio is disgusting, about meaningless content, about materialism and self-destruction, about moving units, about economic benefit only for these artists, record labels and all involved, without responsibility.

The Hip Hop I know and value speaks about identity, Knowledge of Self, issues that are real and relatable. It's a culture of teaching and sharing, it stirs conversation and provokes thinking

AFRIKAAPS PERFORMANCE: JANINE 'BLAQ PEARL' VAN ROOY (LEFT), CHARL 'BLIKSEMSTRAAL' VAN DER WESTHUIZEN AND JETHRO LOUW | Source: Ference Isaacs

that reflects on oneself and one's role in a society, in the world. It's about challenges, survival, theories and offering solutions and healing. This is what I practise. Hip Hop is the foundation to much of my self-motivation and positive actions. It is also within my real-life experiences, good and bad. It's about constant movement and growth of oneself and community.

CHAPTER 22.
MY POETIC PRIME

EAVESDROP

When I first learned about Hip Hop as a culture and movement around 1996, I discovered that one of the most important elements was Knowledge of Self; how unity is the foundation upon which you can build a strong force to fight injustice and conscientise yourself and those you represent. For the first time in my life, I felt ignited by something in the music – it was the way they spoke, the sound of the boom bap beats – the backdrop to my tumultuous world at home and in the ghetto. I had found a portal to escape through; a place where I could learn about the responsibility of freedom.

Because I have always loved language and writing, I naturally gravitated towards MCing. I knew the Knowledge of Self aspect needed to penetrate my lyrics if I was going to bring a message of upliftment and rebellion to the people – the masses of marginalised people of colour in my world.

My world is physically located in Cape Town's Cape Flats, in a small township called Parkwood, populated by all shades of black and brown, where violence and crime, practised by the minority, terrorise the majority of peace-loving, generous people who work hard to survive. Very few services are delivered here and social issues, such as a high unemployment rate, teenage pregnancy, substance abuse and domestic violence, have caused a state of apathy amongst many.

What I've come to learn is that many of the issues we face stem from not having a clear sense of identity, and not knowing or wanting to learn our true stories, which has caused despair. Because of this we feel we do not belong anywhere so we don't unify on a common ground to rebuild what has been broken. The foundation of Hip Hop demands that you look within to discover yourself, and once you find your voice you can use it to shine a light, to create awareness and to speak out on issues courageously and with pride.

Hip Hop is the language of the people; it has the power to completely transform the minds of people who encounter it and its roots come from the struggle, and struggling people are strong people. Around the world, struggling people are mostly black people and Hip Hop is the voice of the black struggle to be recognised as equally human regardless of your socioeconomic circumstances. Hip Hop is the voice of the youth. The youth have energy and vigour, they want to be challenged and they will test boundaries innovatively. Hip Hop speaks to innovation as you need to constantly recreate yourself and keep up with change. We need Hip Hop to gather the attention of every generation, to help people mobilise by using the elements to conscientise. Hip Hop is a force of light!

In 2008 I did my first-ever series of park jams in my township, Parkwood, where I used the various elements of Hip Hop to speak to the people about what I observed. The response was overwhelming: people cried, they laughed, they agreed, they reflected and were entertained – some even tried to destroy it with bad behaviour because the truth brought too much pain, but we soldiered on. This series of outdoor events was called Rebel Arts People's Project.

EAVESDROP IN PERFORMANCE AT HAUS DER KULTUREN DER WELT, BERLIN, 2018 | Source: Quentin Williams

I realised then that we have a responsibility to keep the message of freedom and hope alive because we needed the counternarrative to what the media propagates about us as people from the townships – that we're lazy, destructive, drug-addicted parasites – and I can see how my people have started to believe that, through their behaviour and treatment of themselves and one another.

I have been actively involved in writing rhyme, performing and recording my music for the better part of 20 years and I still feel how the struggle for consciousness continues. But consciousness needs to be coupled with practical ways of surviving and thriving in an ever-changing world, with a system that still sets the ghetto child up for failure. Once a thought seed is planted we need to look at ways through which we can practically develop and sustain that journey for people to create their own positive change. We can capture the attention of anyone, but how will we hold that attention when we compete with their basic need to eat?

I still live in the same township to this day and the only time I really get any attention is when the media focuses on me, fleetingly. The perceived 'fame' makes my people look to me for a way out, but when they realise I am still their neighbour, living in a humble home just like them, they forget and turn away. The very same Knowledge of Self is too abstract for them to identify with and the patience and dedication required for Knowledge of Self to yield any rewards is too distant for the needs of immediate survival. I can't hold this against them because we all need to eat.

So what is the point of fighting for this elusive freedom through Hip Hop as the medium? I would say it is the resilience of an undying optimism and hope that in and amongst the masses, the many, there will be one or two people who will pick up the baton and run with me/us. I think about our forebears and the legacy left for us to study and interrogate – those are our weapons. We must remember them and listen for them as we navigate this complicated, multilayered human landscape, engaging our hearts and minds at all times.

When I write my rhyme, it is a guidance. I believe it to be a spiritual force greater than my understanding, mental dexterity or lyrical skill. It has been a rugged terrain to travel, filled with unexpected hurdles, setbacks and pitfalls, but it has also been rewarding and exhilarating. I still second-guess my ability to move the crowd, but I also remember that this is how I ensure the sustenance of my breath – so I keep braving the unknown.

Living in the world as a creative is not easy, as many know, but it is necessary to learn how to straddle the inner and outer worlds simultaneously in order to keep moving. I work a dead-end job which helps to secure recording/studio time and I observe, reflect and write on my off days. Being a somewhat successful MC has become more important to me over time, as I realise the importance of being authentic in a world of instant gratification. My message needs to be heard because I see from a place that is unseen – the ghetto.

My travels and experiences have given me a perspective that I feel people need to know about and this is why I am an MC. Besides my love for the beautiful power and struggle of the Hip Hop movement, I am curious to know what the next step in this journey will be. I am building my exit strategy to move out of the ghetto sometime soon, and I know it is possible if I keep creating, building, dreaming and acting, regardless of the fear I feel. When I rhyme, I transcend all the limitations of the physical world.

I am certain of nothing, but I do feel that there are many more chapters to be written and lived, and I want to capture those moments in rhyme.

EAVESDROP, BERLIN, 2018 | Source: Quentin Williams

CHAPTER 23.
'LANGA STATE OF MIND': TALKING RACE, CLASS, GENDER AND SEXUALITY

H SAMY ALIM IN CONVERSATION WITH ANDY MKOSI

H Samy Alim interviewed Andy Mkosi in Langa in 2017 to make sense of Hip Hop's engagement with race, gender and sexuality.

Alim: Give us a sense of where we're at.

Mkosi: So Langa is the first township you approach as you leave the CBD [central business district]. As things start getting real, it's the first township you approach. I've lived in between Langa and Gugulethu most of my life. Most of my high school I spent in Gugs and then I moved after matric to Langa and that's sort of where I've spent most of my teens, twenties and so forth. Langa is like a – it's very rich in arts and culture…It's like a community that's very close knit. Everyone knows everyone…There is also a lot of segregation within the township as well. Like in a sense of tribalism. So it's changing, people from the Eastern Cape, people who grew up in Langa, and they claim Langa for themselves. So it's always conflict when it comes to who's gonna receive like government housing. There's always uprisings around it… You'll notice as you drive around Langa there are a lot of units, flats. Langa is a small town and there's not much land. So the only thing that they can accommodate for housing at the moment is building these flats. So when there are flats built, people are always eager to know who's gonna receive what next. People are saying that backyard dwellers are being overlooked. They call people from the Eastern Cape different terms, meaning that they're primitive. 'They don't know anything and why are they being chosen before people who grew up here, people who were born here, people who have parents who've lived in shacks their entire lives?' My issue with that is not the fact that people from the Eastern Cape are gonna get those. It's the fact that there is not space for us to breathe now…So I know there's gonna be an uprising around that. It's almost like an anticipation for it. Yeah.

Alim: Because the space is getting so tight.

Mkosi: Congested. Yeah it is. Very tight.

Alim: I didn't realise that Eastern Cape situation was also here.

Mkosi: Oh, bro, we have a lot of issues here. Black people alone have a lot of issues. I'm not even speaking about Langa now. I'm just talking generally. Even like the arts community. Just black people – you get like affluent black people, you get middle-class black people. You get people who live in the townships who have access to the affluent spaces. So it's levels…Maybe what I don't like is the fact that as affluent blacks we create these spaces for ourselves and we talk about the problems that black people on the ground are facing, not necessarily taking into account that we are not going through those problems. I think that's the problem I have with things like Fees Must Fall, anything that has to do with speaking about the issues of black people. Sometimes the issues of black people are not – what I experience as a black person from Langa is not the same as people from Rondebosch. It's totally split. People in Rondebosch are talking about the issues that people in Langa are having, but they are not involving the people in Langa. How does that work? Talk about it, have wine and then go back home? So some activism is a problem as well here in Cape Town. Everywhere you go, all these spaces, they're problematic. We all problematic.

Alim: How did you become conscious of these dynamics, that we're all problematic?

Mkosi: So I think my fondest memories were made here in Langa, though, 'cause that's where I sort of started understanding things. I became conscious of my environment, what meant what, and who's who and how to go about things. So it's mainly in Langa. I lived in a house that's opposite a park. So you'd go there and even within that park, there were issues that we had as children 'cause there would be these kids that come from the New Flats. That always kids from the Eastern Cape would come play in the park, and it would be an issue. 'Why are these kids here?' 'You guys are primitive, you're not…' It's only now that I'm realising, 'Hey, that was wrong.' We were just following from what we heard at home. 'You're not supposed to associate with these primitive kids. You guys are from the affluent part of Langa.' I had the privilege of living in my aunt's house there. It was like, 'You guys should not play with kids from New Flats.' I'm like, 'Guys, what are you doing?' I'm glad that I'm old enough to understand that is not the way to go about it. We are people first before anything else…Do you know that – the funny thing is that even with the fact that there is an affluent area, the funny thing is the privilege of accessing all these spaces. I have friends everywhere. I can choose who to – according to your economic bracket. The funny thing is that all our parents are the same. They think exactly the same way. In some way they don't have the knowledge that we have as young people. I don't wanna say backward, but they never had the opportunity that we have now. It's almost like you listening in on the same conversation but from a different angle and they don't realise…

Alim: Wow. You mean the class stuff?

Mkosi: …the class stuff. They don't realise that in order to overcome all of that, we need to commune as one. There's no reason for us to be pointing fingers because we're going through exactly the same social factors and they don't know that. It's so frustrating I feel. It's very frustrating.

Alim: They always wanna make distinctions.

Mkosi: Exactly, yeah. It's exactly like that.

Alim: Yeah, so I gotta ask. You speaking about Langa. What does it mean to be in 'a Langa state of mind'?

Mkosi: People in Langa are confident…I think part of my confidence stems from living here and seeing people strive or succeed in whatever they are doing. Having access to all of these homes or people because Langa has a rich history in the arts. I'll always go back to that. It's very deep. To see those people from your area and be successful in it. It's like, why not me? I can do it too. So as much as we're going through stuff, there is the confidence and hope that we can go beyond all these things and rise above them.

Alim: Wow, now, you weren't always that confident though, right?

Mkosi: I was never that confident [laughter].

Alim: It's crazy, but there's some – I was telling you that I was here [in Langa] before. There was one video that you made here that I wanna talk about – the *Camps Bay Township Tour*. How did the idea even come about?

Mkosi: It was a conversation that Onele Liwani, a friend of mine – we used to have – I always used to tell him that, dude, you should come to my township. You won't distinguish whether it's a black township or white township because white people are always here [laughter]. I just don't like that…You see a lot of white people in the CBD and that's enough. Now you're in the hood chillin out and now people are just snapping at you. Taking photos without your permission. I'll go back to my childhood – because in the area that I live in, we used to have exchange students coming in and living within the homes in the area. We'd get excited when, like, 'Oh, a white person is living in your house? [laughter] How's that experience?' It's only now and at that point in – I think it was in 2014 when we did the [*Camps Bay Township Tour*] video that I realised actually this is wrong. It's not cool at all.

ANDY MKOSI | Source: H Samy Alim

Alim: So when you were little, you used to actually get excited when there would be white kids in your neighbourhood.

Mkosi: Dude. Like you would be happy. It was a thing. You know what, I still have pictures of myself and my friends with white people!

Alim: No way. What was in your head at that time? Do you remember?

Mkosi: At that time, it was like oh, these people are coming into our hood and it's a nice thing. 'Oh, "Emily's" living in your house?' I was stoked…It was a cool thing. We never could afford to accommodate those individuals, but I had friends who had the 'privilege' to have the 'opportunity' [laughter] of living with white students in their home. I always used to wonder, 'Do you guys like sit around the table together and eat?' It was fascinating for me. You'd get jealous if Emily was giving someone else a lot of attention, you know, petty things. Not realising that it's deeper than that. We've been made to think that these people are superior than us…So it got to a point in 2014. We were having these conversations consciously now, so this one time it started off. Walking – I don't know from where – and then a group of white tourists were walking past us. I had my camera in my bag and I took it out. So they pointed one at me and I pointed one at them. This was before *Camps Bay*, downtown area. Then they looked at us cocky, like why are you guys pointing the camera at us? We looked at them, why are you pointing the camera at US? Then the idea came about, how's about we go to Camps Bay carrying our cameras and video cameras and make images and fool them without getting their permission. So the idea built up. I was working for a magazine called *Live*…So they gave us the equipment to go do this… Everyone is starting to back up, like, hey, why are we doing this again? I was like – 'cause I'm a shy person. Honestly, I was shit scared. I was terrified, but something in me sort of pushed me to do it…So we get to Camps Bay. We approach this one white guy who's walking his dogs. I couldn't remember what he said, but then he made a remark that these dogs won't – 'they'll bark at these guys 'cause they don't know you…You're strangers'. Something along those lines. Then we carried on. Met a couple of other ladies who were just like, 'Is that camera on? Why are you pointing the camera at me?' So it was various remarks and then I think the highlight of it was the one where we got to this table…So there were these two guys having lunch or whatever – and then they were like, 'Why are you pointing the camera at us?' It became a thing for them…They got upset with us, and then called one of the waiters, 'Come get these people out of our faces.' I was like, 'THESE people.' Like, you know? Then the funny thing is that they use like – I forgot the security officer's name now. They got him to chase us away.

Alim: Oh, this was the big guy, Desmond?

Mkosi: Desmond yeah, yeah, yeah [laughter]. 'Get these people out of here, Desmond!'

Alim: So it was really interesting to me though, to see white people at Camps Bay on that main strip – you know, we all know what that strip is, that's like super-wealthy craziness – calling on Desmond to come get you. Like, the dynamics of that, the racial dynamics of that were…

Mkosi: Exactly. It was crazy because Desmond now could not see that he's attacking his own people, trying to protect these people from his own people. It also goes back to what I was mentioning about Langa again. We are fighting one another…It's crazy. Yeah. People understood. It got a lot of negative responses. The funny thing is that we weren't expecting any responses because I didn't see it as radical or revolutionary, as people sort of saw it after they saw the video. Then we got a lot people applauding us for it and raising it up 'cause it's something that people – everyone had been talking about it, but no one was exactly doing something about it. So it was almost like we ignited a flammable item, you know? We got a lot of flak for it. People were like, why are you going up to white South Africans because it's international people that come and take pictures of you guys in the townships? I mean, valid point, but still. My thing with township tours is that it's like white people placed us in these townships and now it's almost like they are coming back to pity us and make these images of us to come and see how we're doing and take that content. Where do you take that content? What are you gonna do with that content? I think what makes me more angry is that the people who live in Langa are not conscious of the fact that what is being done by these people is wrong. They see it as, oh these people are – they love us.

Alim: I can't believe this shit. So when did this start?

Mkosi: Oh, they've been going for quite some time…Even now as we have this conversation, I'm sure there's a group that just walked in.

Alim: I think I saw a couple [laughter]. I think I saw Emily actually.

Mkosi: Emily's come there every time. I mean, I don't see anything wrong with them coming into Langa or any other township for that matter, but [they] have a way of doing it. Don't come in with your big bus, look through your window, point at us like we're animals. Poverty porn of some sort…I was walking down Woodstock Lower Main [Road] yesterday evening, and they were taking pictures of kids. My thing is, we need permission to take a picture of a kid…The parent does not necessarily know that you made the image of them. So you'd get like tours coming in and then they just grab it. The child is playing on the street. They grab the child, pose with them. Give them sweets. This one time they propped a van next to one of the flats and then they were just dishing out nick-nacks on the side. I'm not kidding you. This white guy was just standing there next to them, calling all the small black children. 'Come. It's our time to come get free sweets.' I'm not kidding you, like a taxi full of sweets. Kids were just running after it…But what I see as problematic, another black person doesn't see as problematic. They came to me. They were like, you don't understand. These people are bringing in business for us and you are speaking against that and all of that. It was intense. A lot of people greet me in Langa because of that video. It's like, you. You try to mess our business up. I kid you not. So black people don't see any problem. It goes back to what you were saying. It's deep. It goes back to you bringing white people in to tell a story about your people and take them into these intimate spaces where they [are] sleeping and where they drink and where – you know, but you don't see anything wrong with that. You're only trying to make money for yourself.

Alim: Does the community benefit from this shit?

Mkosi: They don't…There's also this thing called Open Streets, which I have a problem with. Open Streets is – what happens is they barricade certain streets within a certain area and then all of these activities happen. People are just happy and kumbaya [naively optimistic] [laughter]. There was one time it happened when there was no water in Langa. The city just decided this one weekend that they're gonna cut out our water, but the event wasn't cancelled! It carried on. No one saw a problem with that. People were just – obviously they're gonna utilise some sort of water source, but there are homes. People need to wash. 'But it's kumbaya on Washington Street. People are having fun.' White people do come, yeah. I'm not too, what the intention of the visit is...but the sad part is that they come for this one day and then they disappear again.

Alim: And it's the day that it's barricaded, so it's supposed to be 'safe'.

Mkosi: There are city officials and, you know? So it's not just – that's why I have a problem with it. It's like a sugar-coated experience of the township…What is the purpose?

Alim: Many of us, we came to our political consciousness through Hip Hop, but it seems like it happened earlier than that for you?

Mkosi: So there this one time in high school where I had a mini afro. Then the afro was irritating me, but I asked a friend of mine to plait it. So I went to school with these plaits. They were sort of sticking up like and looked ridiculous [laughter]. Yeah, they were sticking up like dreadlocks. So I went to school…all the girls were looking at me…Then as I'm walking minding my own business, the sister who's in charge of the schools, 'cause it's a Catholic school, she came to me and was like, 'And you, remove that thug hairstyle you have on you.'

Alim: Oh shit!

Mkosi: At first I didn't necessarily – I didn't know she was speaking to me, and then it dawned on me that, hey, this lady's speaking to me actually…She's an Irish white lady. Yo, she was hectic. If you did not pay your school fees, you were placed in a separate room. They called in on an intercom. I was part of that group. Sometimes when you walked into class – there would be a list and then your name would be highlighted in red that you can't get into the class because you haven't paid your school fees. We'd sit in the halls, miss out on classes. Then when your school fees is eventually paid, which would be after like a month or three or two weeks, then you can access classes. Imagine now you've missed out on how many lessons…The other thing that we went through in high school was homophobic experiences…So this one time there were rumours that people were being called into the sister's office and you're being questioned about stuff.

Then it came to me that I might also be called in because they were suspicious of my demeanour and all of that…Then there was a big mass meeting called into the school hall. People were named. 'Stand up. All of these people that you see who are standing are practising homosexuality. They are dating and fornicating with one another within the school grounds.'

Alim: Are you fucking serious?

Mkosi: Yeah, 'These are the culprits. Apparently, the activity is making some of the girls uncomfortable, and parents are complaining about this activity and it's being addressed. Girls you're here for school. You're not to fornicate and lie.' This was in – I was in matric. 2008…It's happening all the time man…Yo, that school was intense on so many levels.

Alim: So you were experiencing institutional homophobia because it was a school telling you. I think it's in 'Childhood' where you mention something like they labelled me – I didn't understand the full line because you talked about menstruation, scarring, scarred for life. Shit that people don't talk about on record hardly ever.

Mkosi: [laughter]

Alim: No seriously. Breasts forming, your relationship to your body.

Mkosi: So when I lived with my aunt and my mom and my cousin, there was a time in my life where I had a group of friends which were girls – and within that group, you know, [you] have to do certain things, and we all get the same hairstyle to relax our hair, sit in the park. You know, it would be the guy and the girl, that side, but I knew deep down that hey, I wanna be with the boys, with the homies. At that point in time – I remember when I started getting my first – when I started menstruating. We were playing in the backyard and I thought I had a tummy ache, but it was period pains. When I went to the loo and saw this blood in my panties, I thought I had a scar. That's why I mentioned that. Literally, I thought I had a scar. I spoke to my – my cousin was around that day and then she said, 'No you're going through this and this.' I'm like,

'Okay cool.' Then I couldn't fathom why now, when I want to be all active, you know? [laughter] Maaan. I wanna be active and then within all of that my breasts started forming. People didn't understand why I was dressing like that and hanging out with girls, and why I was hanging out with boys. If I'm hanging out with boys, am I sleeping with them? Am I homo? Am I dating girls? What is going on with me? People were confused. I don't know if – I wasn't confused. I knew, but it was just a matter of being comfortable in my own skin and breaking out of all that web.

Alim: What was your relationship to your breasts at the time? You talk about it on the track as uncomfortable or…

Mkosi: It was really uncomfortable for me. Not that I wanted to be a boy, but I was sitting in my aunt's place and a cousin of ours had come over. At night we were just chilling. You know, after a long day you're just chilling? Then I said to him, 'You know what dude? I wish I had a flat chest like you.' [laughter] Then he went and told my other friends. So people were laughing at me, like, 'He told us what you said to him last night.' I'm like, 'What are you talking about?' He said, 'You said you wish you had a flat chest like him.' [laughter] People laughing, 'You're a girl, man. Stop trying to act like a boy.' Then there are those types of things that I encountered as well growing up. I didn't see anything wrong with the remark. I didn't understand why people were laughing at that. I just wanted it flat – I don't mind having breasts, but they shouldn't be this big! [laughter]

Alim: Now there's times where you write about love in really vulnerable, painful situations – hurtful situations – that I just find really groundbreaking and honest and true. In 'Zizo', in 'From the Heart'. As I understand 'From the Heart', you fall in love with the girl, but there's not a happy ending. Is that a real story?

Mkosi: It is.

Alim: Get out.

Mkosi: I swear, it was after high school. So I met this person, and then the person like – you know when you met someone and you're convinced that you guys are both on [the] same page? We used to talk to one another and we clicked, and I was like, 'Ah, she's the one.' Only to find out that she was sort of finding herself with me. While I'm thinking that she wants more than a friendship situation with me, she was just looking for refuge within me and I happen to be the person that she was most comfortable with. So it was a situation where I thought she was finding solace in me and love in me, but she was going through stuff, wanting to find her one and only, which is not me. Also I blame myself as well. You don't just assume stuff. You speak about this stuff…I knew. I can't blame her. I think I'm writing those types of songs for me. I was telling a friend of mine. She was saying to me, hey you are a great writer 'cause you write about all of these emotional things. I'm like, but these are my experiences. I think the only way I sometimes heal is if I write about stuff, you know? So those songs become that for me.

Alim: So, your heart was broken basically.

Mkosi: Yeah, it was, like – yeah. I just had to write that down…I recently spoke to her about that. Yeah, we spoke about it and then she was like, 'I understand.' I was wrong as well because she was telling me that the dynamic with her was that her parents were going through a divorce. She was finding herself as well, sexuality-wise. She wasn't too sure, and I was in the picture. All of that. Yeah, so we did speak about it and we're still good friends now as well.

Alim: Oh, that's cool. So then in 'Zizo' you talk about meeting someone who said they were bisexual?

Mkosi: Yeah, this [was] a different woman. Sometimes you get people who are just curious and then they don't hold it back. They tell it to your face that, look, I'm not too sure what's happening, but I do like you. So let's test this out. There's nothing wrong with that. I thought there was something wrong with that at the time. It's just me. I took offence. That person made it out like, yo dude, I want to try some stuff with you, but I'm not too sure if I really am lesbian or bisexual, or I am bisexual whatever the reason…I've been in the weirdest situations…There are a lot of songs about heterosexual relationships as well, so. If anything, there's a gap, a huge gap.

Alim: Of course, there are a lot of gay artists that are NOT out. To talk about this shit and on record, I think, is huge.

Mkosi: It is. Sometimes there's a fine line. There's a song where I wrote intensely about situations that were happening in my family. That's when I became conscious of the fact that there is an interlink with all my stories. If I go through something and write it on record, I sorta need to get consent maybe from my mother because she's involved indirectly. I don't know how she would feel about me speaking about the fact that she worked for a firm that paid close to nothing. It's my experience, yes. I was a part of it, but it's not my story to tell. You know? It goes back to that as well. So sometimes, as much as I'm honest, I need to be conscious of the fact stories are interlinked. You know?

Alim: Yup, I do…There's a lot I want to ask you about. One song in particular I wanna ask you about is 'Monkey'. Okay, that shit was so deep to me…

Mkosi: So the song was written – do you know the story when, I think it was early last year, when Penny Sparrow said something during the festive season, 'It's like all these monkeys are let out and they occupy beach spaces in'…

Alim: I do remember that. I was here, 2016.

Mkosi: Mh-hmm. So she basically called black people monkeys at the beach. Then she even went to court for it…So yeah, the chorus was inspired by that. 'This monkey sees with a third eye. This monkey won't do as you please.' Also the other things that happen within that same space and time, Fees Must Fall and all of these other things that were revolutionary within spaces and occupying spaces. Turning the narrative and not pitting ourselves, and being direct about things and saying we are here and we can speak on behalf of ourselves. We're not going to allow white people anymore to dictate things onto us. So this song speaks to the moment how I see it. It's always been happening, but I feel like in Cape Town at the moment big corporates or even in Joburg, like within the arts and culture scene, black people are driving the narrative of adverts, of whatever. Like I was seeing this other TV add, a beer TV ad, they had black guys in Hip Hop attire rapping and presenting this – Hip Hop is selling man and corporates are using that and are putting black faces upfront to sell the product and stuff. We're influencing a lot of trends and we are being used as well. You get these things called influencers. Sometimes you're given an alcoholic product. They say they're gonna give you that for, say, maybe six months. 'Tweet about us and speak and take pictures about it.' It goes back to the *dop* system. The *dop* system is where you work on the farm and then they pay you with wine. It's the same thing, just in a different context and people, and they don't see it, you see? So this song speaks to that and also it celebrates the fact that we are influencing these things that are happening. We are doing things ourselves with the little resources we have. Creatively. There are people like – there's this girl Jabu Nadia Newman who does a web series, *The Foxy Five*. They speak on feminism and black feminism, and they define that, and they act out scenarios of all these things. These are black women doing it, so this song celebrates that. It speaks to melanin in entertainment. We are the driving force. We're not realising our power within this situation. It also speaks to the fact that we as black people, before we address all of these other issues, in Langa let's address the issues that we have with one another. Before even stepping out of our communities we have our issues, so it mainly speaks to that.

Alim: How did the chorus or the hook come to you?

Mkosi: Yeah, 'This monkey sees with a third eye. This monkey won't do as you please.'...I was basically speaking like from the personal point of view. This white woman is calling me a monkey. I feel like regardless of you calling me a monkey, I'm a smart monkey. I see with the third eye means beyond what you're saying about me. I know more about my situation and things that I go through than you will ever fathom...So that part of the song where the verse speaks on the Penny comment, I play around with – 'Penny dropped words used in your inner circle.' That's how they refer to us when the children are born in the exclusive circles. 'These monkeys.' It's almost like she let it slip on a big platform, social media. She let it slip without realising, but now it's on the public forum and not within the exclusive spaces. 'Penny for your thoughts. The penny dropped words.' It plays around with her surname which is Sparrow. 'The sparrow is out. We are to fly.' So black people are flying now. They're doing their thing. 'It's our time to ape out.' We're doing this thing now [laughter]...

Alim: That's why this song is going to be very powerful, right?

Mkosi: Another part was inspired by Fees Must Fall. The students are speaking on issues that are relevant, but to white people who are seeing it, they're hooligans. 'They're planning to blow up the university one day.' It's all of these other negatives, but they're not getting the point. They're shutting down the point with all of these negative perceptions. 'These thugs. These…'

Alim: There was something that you said here about 'they're gonna say I'm…Watch them twist my words'.

Mkosi: Mh-hmm. Say I'm inciting violence. Yeah. It happens a lot with activists. Especially on social media when they say something or the video clips that they post in situations where – like there was this one where I saw they had barricaded a road at UCT. This lady was pissed off by the fact that your lady was delaying her process of getting to wherever that she needed to get to. Yeah. A white lady obviously. She comes and, 'Why are you guys doing this? Some of us need to go to work and you're delaying us.' 'You're not seeing the point.' 'You guys are acting out. You're acting like hooligans.' 'You're not seeing the point, lady.' The students were just trying to explain to this lady that, 'Dude, you're not seeing the point of what is happening here. You are not in this situation. You don't go through the problems that black people or black students go through.' That's what I'm hinting at there, the fact that when we do react, they see it as an attack, which it's not.

Alim: You're saying they might take your song the same way, huh?

Mkosi: Exactly, yeah…So that part I'm saying that black people have been silent for long. Now we are taking a side, and the side is our side. It's no longer about pleasing the white person. In the midst of all that, we want our land back. Give back the land of our fathers. Does the truth hurt? Is the truth hot? There's an issue of land as well that's happening.

Alim: One of the things that makes total sense is when you're speaking about the shit that they – you said, 'It was always me, bro.'

Mkosi: It speaks about how the system of apartheid, it's not only affected our parents but the granddaughters, the grandsons – it's a generational thing. I'm part of that as well. It inconvenienced a whole generation and generations after that. It's hectic. It's crazy. So that line speaks on that. The legacy of apartheid – it's a ripple effect in that…So when

I say 'It will be about colour in this race', it means that as kids, you're born into a black family or you're born into a white family, but that white kid is one step ahead already in that race. They are already equipped with all the resources to get to where they want to be. You as a black child, you have to gather those resources first. Find yourself first. Know who you are first. That kid is already running with one shoe on and you're still trying to find the sock and – you know? So the race is always the white kid ahead and you trying to catch up. Even in work spaces as well. Regardless, even if you are more qualified than that white individual. The race will always be for the white person. But also I'm speaking to black people specifically. I'm saying, 'Guys. Fine, they are doing all these things to us. How about we focus on us and the good things that we can do. We're already doing them, but we're doing them in islands.' The coloureds are doing it alone. Actually doing it alone. How about we come together and do it together and be more impactful in that? I'm also applauding all of the other individuals that are doing significantly well for themselves with what little that they have. I'm saying we're running things. We're doing it. How about we celebrate that sometimes? We tend to forget and run off with the problems that we're facing, not realising that within all of that we are so successful within the things that we are doing. Black excellence basically, celebrating that. For me it really makes me happy to know of other brown or black people doing well for themselves. That's why I can be vocal about Dope Saint Jude doing her thing for us. It pleases me. It means one of us has opened a door for all of us. So how about we look at it like that?

Alim: Yeah, yeah, yeah. That's right. That's absolutely right.

DOPE SAINT JUDE, CAPE TOWN INTERNATIONAL JAZZ FESTIVAL, 2017 | Source: H Amy Alim

NINJA TURTLES | Source: Ference Isaacs

CHAPTER 24.
QUEERING HIP HOP, QUEERING THE CITY: DOPE SAINT JUDE'S TRANSFORMATIVE POLITICS

ADAM HAUPT (UNIVERSITY OF CAPE TOWN)

This chapter[1] argues that artist Dope Saint Jude is transforming South African Hip Hop by queering a genre that has predominantly been male and heteronormative. Specifically, I analyse the opening skit of her music video *Keep in Touch*[2] in order to unpack the ways in which she revives Gayle, a gay language that adopted double-coded forms of speech during the apartheid era – a context in which homosexuals were criminalised. The use of Gayle and spaces close to the city centre of Cape Town (such as Salt River and Woodstock) speaks to the city as it was before it was transformed by the decline of industries due to the country's adoption of neoliberal economics and, more recently, by the gentrification of these spaces. Dope Saint Jude therefore reclaims these city spaces through her use of gay modes of speech that have a long history in Cape Town and by positioning her work as Hip Hop, which has been popular in the city for well over two decades. Her inclusion of transgender MC and DJ Angel Ho pushes the boundaries of hegemonic and binary conceptions of gender identity even further. In essence, Dope Saint Jude is transforming local Hip Hop in a context that is shaped significantly by US cultural imperialism and male heteronormative imperatives. The artist is also transforming our perspective of spaces that have been altered by neoliberal economics.

---

1. A previous version of this chapter was published in Haupt (2016). The chapter is reproduced here with permission of the journal.
2. https://www.youtube.com/watch?v=w2ux9R839lE

SETTING THE SCENE

Dope Saint Jude is a queer MC from Elsies River, a working-class township located on Cape Town's Cape Flats in South Africa. Elsies River was defined as a 'coloured' neighbourhood under the apartheid state's Group Areas Act (No. 41 of 1950), which segregated South Africans racially. With the aid of the Population Registration Act (No. 30 of 1950), citizens were classified not merely along the lines of white, Asian or black – black subjects were also divided into further categories, with the apartheid state also distinguishing between black (African) and coloured subjects. Michael MacDonald contends that segregation 'ordained blacks to be *inferior* to whites; apartheid cast them to be indelibly *different*' (2006: 11, emphasis in original). Apartheid declared 'African claims in South Africa to be inferior to white claims' and effectively claimed that black subjects 'belonged elsewhere, in societies of their own, because their race was different' (MacDonald 2006: 11). The term 'coloured' defined people as 'mixed race' in order to separate communities that might otherwise have identified as black in the broad and inclusive sense (Erasmus 2001). Racial categorisation was used to create a racial hierarchy, with white subjects at the top of that hierarchy and those classified as black receiving the least resources and benefits. This frustrated attempts to establish broad alliances of black struggles against apartheid. It is in this sense that race is socially and politically constructed and continues to have currency, despite the fact that biologically essentialist understandings of race have been discredited (Yudell 2011). Thanks to apartheid town planning and resource allocation, many townships on the Cape Flats were poverty-stricken and plagued by gang violence (Salo 2003). This continues to be the case because post-apartheid South Africa's embrace of neoliberal economics has failed to significantly address racialised class inequalities (Haupt 2012b).

This was the 1990s context in which socially conscious Hip Hop crews, such as Prophets of da City and Black Noise, came together. They drew inspiration from Black Consciousness philosophy via their exposure to US Hip Hop crews such as Public Enemy in order to challenge apartheid policies, including their racial interpellation as 'coloured' as distinct from the more inclusive category 'black' (Haupt 2001). Prophets of da City – whose co-founding member Shaheen Ariefdien also lived in Elsies River – was the first South African Hip Hop outfit to record an album. Whilst much of their work was performed in English, they quickly transformed the genre by rapping in non-standard varieties of Afrikaans and by including MCs who rap in African languages (Haupt 2001). They therefore succeeded in addressing key issues related to race, language and class disparities in relation to South Africa's transition to democracy (Haupt 2001, 2008). However, as is the case with mainstream US Hip Hop, specifically gangsta rap (Clay 2007), South African Hip Hop has been largely dominated by heterosexual men. This includes the more commercial Hip Hop scene, which is largely perceived to be located in Johannesburg, where male MCs like AKA and Cassper Nyovest became celebrities. However, certain female MCs have claimed the genre, notably EJ von Lyrik and Burni Aman, who are formerly of Godessa, the first female Hip Hop crew to record and perform locally and internationally (Haupt 2008, 2015). Dope Saint Jude therefore presents the exception to a largely heteronormative and male-dominated South African music industry and Hip Hop scene as she transforms it with her queer politics. While queer Hip Hop is not new in the US (Pabón & Smalls 2014), it is new territory for South Africa. Writing about the US MC Jean Grae in the context of a 'male-dominated music industry and genre', Shanté Paradigm Smalls contends, 'Heteronormativity blocks the materiality of the experiences of Black people. Yet, many Black people strive for a heteronormative effect if not "reality". In Hip Hop, there is a particular emphasis on maintaining the rigidity of categories, even if those categories fail' (2011: 87). This chapter demonstrates how Dope Saint Jude challenges these rigid categories.

KEEP IN TOUCH

Dope Saint Jude's most visible entry onto the media landscape to date has been her appearance in an H&M recycling campaign with British Sri Lankan artist MIA (H&M),[3] some fashion shoots, her EP – *Reimagine* (Dope Saint Jude, 2016)[4] – and 2016 and 2017 Finnish, US and French tours as well as her YouTube channel, which features her music videos. As the characters' theatrical costumes suggest, *Keep in Touch* is possibly the most camp and playful music video that she has produced. It commences somewhat comically with Dope Saint Jude walking down Salt River main road to a public telephone, where she and a young woman in pigtails exchange dirty looks. Salt River is located at the foot of Devil's Peak, not far from Cape Town's CBD. Many factories were located there, but the area is also surrounded by low-income housing and was

---

3. https://www.youtube.com/watch?v=f7MskKkn2Jg
4. https://dopesaintjude.bandcamp.com/album/reimagine

designated a 'coloured' area under apartheid. After apartheid, neighbourhoods such as Salt River, Woodstock and the Bo-Kaap became increasingly gentrified and, instead of becoming more inclusive, many parts of Cape Town continued to be influenced by policies that enable racialised inequalities. Dope Saint Jude calls Angel Ho:

> **DSJ**: *Awêh*, Angie! Yoh, you must check this *kak sturvy* girl here by the pay phone. [Turns to the girl, who walks away as she bursts a chewing gum bubble.] Ja, you better keep in touch. Anyway, listen here, what are you *wys*?
>
> **Angel Ho:** Ah, just at the salon getting my hair did. What's good?
>
> **DSJ**: Wanna catch on *kak* today?
>
> **Angel Ho:** Yes, honey. But, first, let me Gayle you this. By the jol by the art gallery, this Wendy, nuh. *This Wendy* tapped me on the shoulder and *wys* me, 'This is a place of decorum.'
>
> **DSJ**: What did she *wys*?
>
> **Angel Ho:** *De*-corum. She basically told me this is not your house.
>
> **DSJ**: I *know* you told that girl to keep in touch!
>
> **Angel Ho:** Yes, Mama! I'm Paula, I told that bitch, 'Keep in touch!' [Points index finger in the air.]
>
> (Dope Saint Jude, 'Keep in Touch')

Angel Ho's name is a play on the male name Angelo and refers to the trope of the ho (whore) in gangsta rap lyrics and in music videos that present objectified women as secondary to male, heterosexual narratives (Collins 2005; Sharpley-Whiting 2007). The queering of Angelo, along with Angel Ho's non-binary styling in terms of hair, makeup and attire, appropriates a heterosexist, sexualised stereotype of women in order to create room for a gender identity that operates beyond heteronormative male–female binaries. Angel Ho's location in a hair salon also speaks to stereotypical associations of salons with women and gay subjects. In a discussion of gender stereotypes about hair salons,

Kristen Barber argues that beauty work has traditionally been 'associated with women and with gay men' and that 'the body beautiful has been tightly linked to the concept of femininity' (2008: 455–456). During the telephonic exchange, Angel Ho and Dope Saint Jude code-switch between standard and non-standard varieties of English and Afrikaans, as the opening appellation '*Awêh*' suggests. In this context, the term is a friendly greeting, which intimates solidarity. *Sturvy* means pretentious, whilst *kak* means shit, but here it is used to qualify *sturvy* and means that the girl at the pay phone is very pretentious or 'full of airs'. To *wys* or be *wys* means to be wise, but it can also mean that you are showing someone something or educating them. The meanings of these terms shift, depending on the context.

The language practices in this skit are in line with the work of earlier Hip Hop crews, such as Prophets of da City and Brasse Vannie Kaap – to validate black, multilingual forms of speech and expression that challenge the linguistic imperialism of standard English and Afrikaans in South Africa, which has 11 official languages (Haupt 2001, 2008; Williams 2016). Henry Louis Gates' research on African American speech varieties and literary practices emerging from the repressive context of slavery is essential to understanding Hip Hop's language politics. Hip Hop artists' multilingual wordplay creates parallel discursive universes that operate both on the syntagmatic axis of meaning-making and the paradigmatic axis (Gates 1988; Haupt 2008). Historically, these discursive universes were those of the slave masters and the slaves, respectively. While white hegemonic meanings are produced on the syntagmatic axis (which is ordered and linear), black modes of speech as seen in Hip Hop wordplay operate on the paradigmatic axis, which is connotative and non-linear (Gates 1988; Haupt 2008). Distinguishing between Signifyin(g)/Signification (upper case, meaning black expression) and signification (lower case, meaning white dominant expression), Gates argues that 'the signifier "Signification" has remained identical in spelling to its white counterpart to demonstrate… that a simultaneous, but negated, parallel discursive (ontological, political) universe exists within the larger white discursive universe' (1988: 49). The meanings of terms and expressions can change, depending on the context and manner in which they are used. It is therefore the shared experiences of speech communities (such as slavery or racist/sexist oppression) that determine the negotiated meanings of certain forms of expression. It is in this sense that meanings can change, depending on the negotiated and shared experiences as well as forms of articulation of these communities.

GAYLE AS A PARALLEL DISCURSIVE UNIVERSE

Dope Saint Jude and Angel Ho's performance of Gayle takes these linguistic practices further. Viewers are offered points of entry into Gayle via the music video's subtitles. We learn that Wendy is code for a white person and that to keep in touch means exactly the opposite. Dope Saint Jude explains that Gayle is

> a very fun queer language that was used to kind of mask what people were saying…It hides meanings and it makes use of women's names…But the thing about Gayle is it's constantly changing…So everywhere you go, you kind of have to pick it up according to the context that you're in. (Ovens, Dope Saint Jude and Haupt interview)

According to Kathryn Luyt, 'Gayle originated as *Moffietaal* [gay language] in the coloured gay drag culture of the Western Cape as a form of slang amongst Afrikaans-speakers which over time, grew into a stylect used by gay English and Afrikaans-speakers across South Africa' (2014: 8; Cage 1999). Given that the apartheid state criminalised homosexuals, Gayle was coded to evade detection and to seek out other members of this speech community (Luyt 2014). Luyt qualifies the term 'language' by arguing, 'The term "language" here, is used not as a constructed language with its own grammar, syntax, morphology and phonology, but in the same way as linguists would discuss women's language, as a way of speaking, a kind of sociolect' (2014: 8; Cage 1999). However, the double-coded nature of Gayle allows one to think of it as creating a parallel discursive universe, as Gates (1988) describes it. Whereas African American and Cape Flats discursive practices function parallel to white, hegemonic discourses, gay modes of speech run parallel to heteronormative communication.

EXCLUSION AND MICRO AGGRESSIONS

The skit brings both discursive practices into play by creating room for one to consider that Dope Saint Jude queers a male-dominated genre that is shaped by US cultural imperialism (Haupt 2008) as a way of speaking back to intersectional forms of marginalisation (Crenshaw 1991), which are created by 'white supremacist capitalist patriarchy' (hooks 1994: 116). This is significant in South

Africa where 'curative rape' of lesbians and other forms of homophobic violence are prominent (cf. Gqola 2015; Hames 2011; Msibi 2009). Angel Ho's anecdote conveys a sense of the extent to which black individuals are subject to scrutiny. Ho's interpretation of the claim that the gallery 'is a place of decorum' is correct: it is not Ho's house. Black queer subjects are not meant to feel at home or feel a sense of ownership of the space. This functions as a racial micro aggression: 'subtle insults (verbal, nonverbal, and/or visual) directed toward people of color, often automatically or unconsciously' (Solórzano, Ceja & Yosso 2000: 60). This speaks to Dope Saint Jude's use of Salt River, Woodstock and Bo-Kaap for the music video, which features black queer bodies in performance – all of these spaces are being gentrified, effectively pushing working-class people of colour out of the city (cf. Didier, Morange & Peyroux 2012; Lemanski 2014). Gustav Visser (2003: 81–82) explains that

> gentrification has come to mean a unit-by-unit acquisition of housing which
> replaces low-income residents with high-income residents, and which occurs
> independent of the structural condition, architecture, tenure or original cost level
> of the housing (although it is usually renovated for or by the new occupiers).

In South Africa this inequity plays out along racial lines because its neoliberal economic policies created a small black elite without improving the lives of the black working class. Instead, the 'new African bourgeoisie, because it shares racial identities with the bulk of the poor and class interests with white economic elites, is in position to mediate the reinforcing cleavages between rich whites and poor blacks without having to make more radical changes' (MacDonald 2006: 158). In a news article about a working-class Salt River family of colour's battle against an eviction, Christine Hogg explains, 'Gentrification often means the poor are displaced as the rich move in or buildings are upgraded by new businesses. In Woodstock and Salt River both are happening at a pace.'[5] Angel Ho's anecdote, as told from a Woodstock hair salon, conveys a sense of what Woodstock's transformation from a coloured, working-class group area to an upmarket, trendy and arty space would mean for people of colour, including black, queer subjects.

One could argue that this reading of the video is undermined by Dope Saint Jude's work with global brand H&M. Was she snared by neoliberal economics? Perhaps, but one response is that

---

5. In Salt River gentrification often means eviction: Family set to lose their home of 11 years, *Ground Up*, 15 June 2016, http://www.groundup.org.za/article/salt-river-gentrification-often-means-eviction/

the seeds of any subculture's commercial co-option lie in the fact it speaks through commodities (e.g. clothing, makeup, CDs, vinyl or iTunes/mp3 downloads) (Haupt 2008; Hebdige 1979). Subcultures have a window period in which to challenge hegemonic ideologies before they are delegitimated or commercially co-opted. Hardt and Negri (2000) contend that the means that extend the reach of corporate globalisation could be used to challenge it from within (Haupt 2008). Dope Saint Jude utilises her H&M work, social media, the Hip Hop genre and international networks to exploit that window period to help mainstream black queer identity politics.

CONCLUSION

Dope Saint Jude speaks back to processes of exclusion from the city, which was transformed by apartheid and, more recently, gentrification, by claiming it as a creative and playful space for queer subjects of colour. She uses Gayle to lay claim to the city as it has a long history in Cape Town. In fact, she says that she is not reviving Gayle but simply 'putting it on a bigger platform' (Ovens, Dope Saint Jude and Haupt interview). The use of subtitles in the video suggests that she wants to mainstream queer identity politics by making the music video accessible to a wider viewership. Dope Saint Jude also transforms Hip Hop heteronormativity by queering the genre and by locating her work within the history of Cape Hip Hop's multilingual wordplay.

DOPE SAINT JUDE | Source: Ference Isaacs

PART THREE REFERENCES

Ballantine C (2004) Re-thinking 'whiteness'? Identity, change and 'white' popular music in post-apartheid South Africa. *Popular Music* 23(2):105–131

Barber K (2008) The well-coiffed man: Class, race, and heterosexual masculinity in the hair salon. *Gender and Society* 22(4): 455–476

Cage K (1999) An investigation into the form and function of language used by gay men in South Africa. MA thesis, Rand Afrikaans University, Johannesburg

Clay A (2007) 'I used to be scared of the dick': Queer women of color and hip hop masculinity. In GD Pough, E Richardson, A Durham & R Raimist (eds) *Home girls make some noise: Hip hop feminism anthology*. Mira Loma, CA: Sojourns

Coetzee JM (1988) *White writing: On the culture of letters in South Africa*. New Haven, CT: Yale University Press

Collins PH (2005) *Black sexual politics: African Americans, gender, and the new racism*. New York: Routledge

Crenshaw K (1991) Mapping the margins: Intersectionality, identity politics, and violence against women of color. *Stanford Law Review* 43(6): 1241–1299

Didier S, Morange M & Peyroux E (2012) The adaptative nature of neoliberalism at the local scale: Fifteen years of city improvement districts in Cape Town and Johannesburg. *Antipode* 45(1): 121–139

Erasmus Z (2001) Introduction. In Z Erasmus (ed.) *Coloured by history, shaped by place: New perspectives on coloured identities in Cape Town*. Cape Town: Kwela Books

Evans D (2006) *An introductory dictionary of Lacanian psychoanalysis*. London: Routledge

Gates HL (1988) *The signifying monkey: A theory of Afro-American literary criticism*. Oxford: Oxford University Press

Gqola PD (2015) *Rape: A South African nightmare*. Johannesburg: Jacana

Hall S (1998) Old and new identities, old and new ethnicities. In A King (ed.) *Culture, globalisation and the world system: Contemporary conditions for the representation of identity*. Minneapolis, MN: University of Minnesota Press

Hames M (2011) Violence against black lesbians: Minding our language. *Agenda* 25(4): 87–91

Hardt M & Negri A (2000) *Empire*. London: Harvard University Press

Haupt A (2001) Black thing: Hip hop nationalism, 'race' and gender in Prophets of da City and Brasse vannie Kaap. In Z Erasmus (ed.) *Coloured by history, shaped by place*. Cape Town: Kwela Books & SA History Online

Haupt A (2008) *Stealing empire: P2P, intellectual property and hip hop subversion*. Cape Town: HSRC Press

Haupt A (2012a) Part IV: Is Die Antwoord blackface? *Safundi: The Journal of South African and American Studies* 13(3–4): 417–423

Haupt A (2012b) *Static: Race and representation in post-apartheid music, media and film*. Cape Town: HSRC Press

Haupt A (2015) Can a woman in hip hop speak on her own terms? Accessed March 2015, http://africasacountry.

com/2015/03/the-double-consciousness-of-burni-aman-can-a-woman-in-Hip Hop-speak-on-her-own-terms/

Haupt A (2016) Queering Hip Hop, queering the city: Dope Saint Jude's transformative politics. *M/C Journal* 19(4), http://journal.media-culture.org.au/index.php/mcjournal/article/view/1125

Hebdige D (1979) *Subculture: The meaning of style*. London: Routledge

hooks b (1994) *Outlaw culture: Resisting representations.* New York: Routledge

Hyslop J (1995) White working-class women and the invention of apartheid: 'Purified' Afrikaner nationalist agitation for legislation against 'mixed' marriages, 1934–9. *The Journal of African History* 36(1): 57–81

Jones M & Dlamini J (eds) (2013) *Categories of persons: Rethinking ourselves and others*. Johannesburg: Picador

Krueger A (2012) Part II: Zef/poor white kitsch chique: Die Antwoord's comedy of degradation. *Safundi: The Journal of South African and American Studies* 13(3–4): 399–408

Lacan J (1989) *Ecrits: A selection*, trans. Alan Sheridan. London: Routledge

Lemanski C (2014) Hybrid gentrification in South Africa: Theorising across southern and northern cities. *Urban Studies* 51(14): 2943–2960

Lott E (1993) *Love and theft: Blackface minstrelsy and the American working class*. Oxford: Oxford University Press

Luyt K (2014) Gay language in Cape Town: A study of Gayle – attitudes, history and usage. MA thesis, University of Cape Town

MacDonald M (2006) *Why race matters in South Africa*. Scottsville: University of KwaZulu-Natal Press

Marx H & Milton V (2011) Bastardised whiteness: 'Zef'-culture, Die Antwoord and the reconfiguration of contemporary Afrikaans identities. *Social Identities* 17(6): 723–745

Meintjes L (2003) *Sound of Africa! Making music Zulu in a South African studio*. Durham, NC: Duke University Press

Msibi T (2009) Not crossing the line: Masculinities and homophobic violence in South Africa. *Agenda* 23(80): 50–54

Mulvey L (2006) Visual pleasure and narrative cinema. In Meenakshi Gigi Durham & Douglas M. Kellner (eds) *Media and cultural studies: Keywords*. Oxford: Blackwell

Nuttall S (2009) *Entanglement: Literary and cultural reflections on post-apartheid*. Johannesburg: Wits University Press

O'Toole S (2012) Part I: Die Antwoord's state of exception. *Safundi: The Journal of South African and American Studies* 13(3–4): 393–399

Pabón JN & Smalls SP (2014) Critical intimacies: Hip hop as queer feminist pedagogy. *Women & Performance: A Journal of Feminist Theory* 24(1): 1–7

Posel D (2001) What's in a name? Racial categorisations under apartheid and their afterlife. *Transformation* 47: 59–82

Salo E (2003) Negotiating gender and personhood in the new South Africa: Adolescent women and gangsters in Manenberg township on the Cape Flats. *Journal of European Cultural Studies* 6(3): 345–365

Schreiner O (1883) *The story of an African farm*. London: Chapman and Hall

Sharpley-Whiting TD (2007) *Pimps up, ho's down: Hip hop's hold on young black women*. New York: New York University
Press

Smalls SP (2011) 'The rain comes down': Jean Grae and hip hop heteronormativity. *American Behavioral Scientist* 55(1):
86–95

Solórzano D, Ceja M & Yosso T (2000) Critical race theory, racial microaggressions, and campus racial climate: The
experiences of African American college students. *Journal of Negro Education* 69(1/2): 60–73

Turner V (1996) Liminality and communitas. In *The ritual process: Structure and anti-structure*. Ithaca, NY: Cornell University
Press

Van der Watt L (2012) Part III: Ask no questions, hear no lies: Staying on Die Antwoord's surface. *Safundi: The Journal of
South African and American Studies* 13(3–4): 409–416

Van Eeden J & Du Preez A (eds) (2005*) South African visual culture*. Pretoria: Van Schaik

Visser G (2003) Gentrification: Prospects for urban South African society? *Acta Academica Supplementum* 1: 79–104

Wicomb Z (1993) Culture beyond color?: A South African dilemma. *Transition* 60: 27–32

Wicomb Z (2006) *Playing in the light*. New York: New Press

Williams QE (2016) Youth multilingualism in South Africa's hip hop culture: A metapragmatic analysis. *Sociolinguistic Studies*
10(1): 109–133

Yudell M (2011) A short history of the race concept. In S. Krimsky & K Sloan (eds) *Race and the genetic revolution: Science,
myth, and culture*. New York: Columbia University Press

INTERVIEWS

Personal interview with Dane Dodds, Cape Town, January 2015

Personal interview with Rasmus Bitsch, Cape Town, January 2015

Personal interview with Isaac Mutant, Cape Town, January 2015

Neil Ovens, Dope Saint Jude and Adam Haupt, One FM Radio interview, 21 April 2016

PART 4

Reality Check:
The Business of Music

LEFT TO RIGHT: *THE READY D SHOW; B-BOY BENNY RUNNING A B-BOY WORKSHOP, AFRICAN HIP HOP INDABA 2016*
Source: Ference Isaacs

JUDGES AT THE AFRICAN HIP HOP INDABA | Source: Ference Isaacs

PART FOUR: REALITY CHECK: THE BUSINESS OF MUSIC

Part Four provides artists' views on the ways in which they navigate a music industry that, historically, has been shaped by unequal relations of power along the lines of race, gender and class, both during and after the colonial era. Their insights speak to the agency of artists who find ways in which to perform and record as artists as well as to position themselves as business people in contexts that have not been geared towards supporting the arts or arts education initiatives. Dope Saint Jude's contribution to the panel on business in Chapter 29 and Marvin Levendal's contribution in Chapter 26 address the ways in which they go about developing business plans and marketing strategies. They provide valuable perspectives on how they create opportunities for themselves as well as other artists. For their part, in Chapter 27 Nicole Klassen and Arthur Price drop knowledge on digital platforms, providing important information for how artists should conduct their digital and mobile media. Adrian van Wyk adds another dimension with his contribution to the panel with DJ Ready D and Ben Caesar in Chapter 25 by talking about his work as an artist and activist who has spent a considerable amount of time promoting business in a marginal but desegregated space, where Hip Hop thrives. Likewise, DJ Ready D and Ben Caesar describe the fine lines they had to walk in order to manage their brand and become a success. For Van Wyk, workshops and educational practices are as important as taking the stage in efforts to break down barriers as well as to create sustainable arts education initiatives for historically marginalised youth. In this regard, Bradley Lodewyk (Chapter 28) reflects on his growth as a b-boy and offers some advice to young dancers on the Hip Hop scene. Like Lodewyk in his early days, many Hip Hop dancers are very young and naïve when they start out – in the absence of formal education initiatives, dancers can become vulnerable to exploitation. Part Four ends with Adam Haupt's Chapter 30, a scholarly reflection on the ways in which the challenges in the music industry resonate with those faced by scholars in the academy. Ultimately, essential changes need to be made on a macroeconomic level to address fundamental inequities in both the music industry and the academy. Haupt outlines the structural issues that limit the production of scholarly knowledge as well as of music. Due to the history of cultural appropriation and

THE READY D SHOW WITH CROSBY | Source: Ference Isaacs

intellectual property regimes that favour white, colonial interests, black cultural production has been exploited and appropriated at the expense of black subjects. The chapter suggests that if calls for the decolonisation of knowledge are to be taken seriously, that knowledge should be decommodified. However, artists such as Ben Caesar, Ready D, Dope Saint Jude, Blaq Pearl and Marvin Levendal find themselves in a post-apartheid context that is shaped by the imperatives of neoliberal economics. For them, the immediate struggle is to find ways to monetise their art on their own terms, with a view to creating sustainable lives as artists. Therefore, while it is laudable to begin to think about how one might decommodify knowledge and cultural production in the interests of social and distributive justice, for them the immediate concern is how to make a living as artists within the parameters of the present socioeconomic context. The key question is how they navigate their trajectories as artists on their own terms and how they exercise agency. This section speaks to these questions.

LEGENDARY BEATBANGAZ | Source: Ference Isaacs

CHAPTER 25.
HIP HOP ACTIVISM, CHANGE AND CREATIVITY

DJ READY D, BEN CAESAR
AND ADRIAN VAN WYK WITH ADAM HAUPT

Adam Haupt joined DJ Ready D, Ben Caesar and Adrian van Wyk in a panel discussion about the ways in which they navigate career paths as performers and activists at the first Heal the Hood Hip Hop Lecture Series at the University of the Western Cape in 2015.

Adam Haupt: So we are here to talk about Hip Hop activism change and creativity and we've got an interesting mix of people. Before I talk about that, I just want to reflect about how interesting – odd some might say – yesterday's session was. We spent quite a good time talking about I suppose artists' integrity and the commitment to using art for social change, but at the same time making a career sustainable as a performing artist as well as an activist. By the time we got to the later part of the afternoon, we had two industry cats talking to us about the reality of the industry…I heard a horrifying tale of how this one label refuses to sign you as a recording artist, unless you also sign up with them for artist management booking your gigs, etc., etc. And I think like 20 per cent – they take 20 per cent…Because you know you don't make money from record sales anymore, so the money is where the gigs are, right? I don't think even the real estate agents charge 20 per cent commission when they sell your property, right? Twenty per cent is a lot of money so…it seems to me it's, you know, this was shocking. It was a good way to end it because we were all getting positive about the power to change, blah, blah, blah. Then we had these industry cats pouring cold water on our optimism…The punchline is that they were not representatives of the major labels, right, labels owned by the major one of the four major holding companies that dominate close to 80 per cent of global market share. They were… independents, southern African independents and they were speaking this speak…How do you retain: (a) your artistic integrity, (b) how do you push your agenda, say if your agenda is to…use your art to, first of all, make yourself happy as an artist, to be happy with what you are doing on an aesthetic and personal level – that's the one thing – and then how do you negotiate market forces? How do you prevent your stuff from being hijacked for purposes…that you do not intend? If you make a feel-good track, for example. I'm thinking of one of Ben Caesar's tracks. How do you make a feel-good track about summer and playing on the beach, your summer outfit, having a good time without doing the misogynist, tired stereotypes of chicks in thongs, you know, adoring men…all the stereotypical, misogynistic things that you see in the mainstream media? How do you prevent that? How do you actually play that game, how do you be sleek aesthetically – solid great production values – and not sell out in terms of gender politics? Those kinds of questions…I'd like us to talk about that. So I think because I'm, I picked on Ben first and I really like his music videos and I like how he somehow doesn't slip into those traps, those potholes…How do you play that game?

Ben Caesar: I think, uhm, hi everybody, firstly! Think it's really how I was raised individually. I was raised by a feminist activist mother who – I was always at the meetings, you know. So feminism's always been a part of, of my story and I was raised to see the struggles that

LEGENDS IN SOUTH AFRICAN HIP HOP: DJ AZUHL, DJ READY D AND DJ EAZY | Source: Ference Isaacs

women go through in the society and how sexist the society is and I know from speaking with my guy friends that they don't see 'cause they were not raised to see it. So I take responsibility in my music, you know, to consciously just not take it there, to not play the same and try just get to portray women in, as more full characters…not just adornments for your video, uhm, but that's just me personally…Wow, that line between doing what people tell you the market wants and what you personally as an artist want to do, I think there are a, a lot of artists who are told and think this is what's hot, this is what's selling and then they try to imitate that. They try to mimic that and…what I've learned is that, that may work even, but it'll work for like this [gesture for small] amount of time…I'm thinking that you really have to tell your own story and you have to be unique. That's why I've, I've made a concerted effort and I told the video directors…because I'm a Hip Hop artist…so when I say I wanna do a video, the first thing they like, 'Okay, let's get some girls, we'll get you some cars, dawg. I got, you know, you know. Yeah, do that, you know. I know some girls. We'll call what agency, what modelling agency.' And I'm like, 'No, I don't want that, you know what I mean.' So, it is a fight. Like a lot of people in the industry as well who think like this…So you really have to identify who you are and ignore the industry. I don't know, that just me, you know, but…

Adam Haupt: On that note, so you are playing that game. How do [you] stay, how do you actually sustain…I mean the stereotypical response to that answer is, 'Well, you have to eat, have to pay the rent…right and…'

Ben Caesar: …Hmm…

Adam Haupt: Let me share this anecdote with you. I was once in a hotel bar with Steve Hofmeyr and he was lecturing me about what he does pays the bills and will sustain his kids… through school and varsity, right, and how me with my principles, my friends with their music and their, their sense of aesthetics and politics, you know…We are not gonna get anywhere, we not gonna pay the bills, you know. Uhm, he's paid the bills. He was lecturing me. He was quite well meaning, I think…Are you paying the rent?

Ben Caesar: Yeah, the music, the way my career it fluctuates, you know what I mean…And I think that's how it is for every artist, so sometimes I have to do other work as well to just feed back into the music 'cause the music's not making enough, uhm, and I think that's also the independent route. I think if we wanted to, we could get signed, but I don't wanna get signed so I'd rather fund it myself so I can make my own decisions.

Adam Haupt: Other things – glad you said that. Other things…I mean this is where you have the stereotypical line, 'Yeah, you have to hustle.'…What are those other things? Are they dodgy other things?… [laughter] Let's move to Ready D. What other things have you done to sustain your passion for music? Those other things…Remember this is being recorded…

DJ Ready D: Yeah, good morning, ladies and gentlemen, thank you very much for having me sit on this panel and for me to get chosen as the guy that must, uhm, react to the dodgy questions [laughter]. Yes, because I come from Lentegeur, Mitchells Plain, so…I'm just gonna do, I'm just gonna do the stereotype [laughter] with regards to the, to the other things. I think that Ben kind of summed up most of what I wanted to say with regards to being an independent artist as well and unfortunately and fortunately to a certain degree, uhm, there's certain…you gonna, you gonna sort of be met with certain hurdles and, on the flip side, you kind of have space to manoeuvre and to practically dictate where you wanna see yourself and where you wanna go at the pace that you dictate as well. So with regards to the other things, so in my case, you know, because of my being and what I gravitate towards, there's a, a lot of stuff, you know, through my childhood that I was extremely passionate about, you know. And I thought, you know, I'm trying to make what I'm passionate about a reality and sometimes I don't really go out there with the intention of, you know, whatever it is, the other things, to kind of find what I do. It's just that I'm passionate. I put my heart and soul into what kind of people can, you know, they see that and they wanna be a part of that. So some of the other things in my case was television presenting and, thankfully, that came through a, another passion of mine, you know, which is cars and motor sport and all those types of crazy things as well. So that happened, so I managed to bring the Hip Hop elements into the show as well because a lot of people were like, whoa, you're a Hip Hop dude! You this scratch guy, the producer, the POC [Prophets of da City] guy…what can we do with you? And they were surprised, 'Wow, you actually into cars and you like other things outside there challenging the system and effing everybody whatever the case would be.' And I'm like, 'Yeah, you know. There's other things…I'm into as well.' Uhm, uhm, I did a couple of television shows. There was one called *Decktales* that was on Channel O as well and, er…through that, that was cool because I could practically do a television show exploring and highlighting the intricacies and the depths of being a, a turntablist as well so with, uhm, sort of going off into different ventures, you kind of form a very strong network base and you meet like-minded people through that networking system as well and that's kind of how you, you become stronger. And I just wanna touch on what Ben said as well and so the energy we give and the more we focus, you know, to whoever or whatever we perceive to be the enemy, we give them more strength. So we focus on us, you know, and we are able to create this environment and this, uh, way of thinking, you know, about supporting what we do as I'm not sure what the name or the title would be for what it is that we do – whether if you wanna call it independent artists…I don't know, the revolutionary artists, the activist artists, the creative artists but I think we need to create the sort of, a, I think…a balance…We need to…create a profile and we need to create a dynamic because within the – I don't know if you wanna call it – a commercial realm or a realm that we see…it's dictated and dominated by enemy forces…There are people within, uhm, you know, I would say that stream that go there because that's the only thing they see and encounter on a day-to-day basis, but there is actually a lot of people in search, you know, of good music, good art entertainment stuff that will enrich the soul. So that's just my take you know on that.

Adam Haupt: So you are multifaceted. You don't just think of yourself as a DJ – that's what I do, I…full stop.

DJ Ready D: No, absolutely not. And I actually wanted to be a stuntman, you know. Growing up, you know, I was very serious about it, you know [laughter]. I was the kid on the BMX doing crazy stuff jumping off rooftops, hanging on trees; that's, that's really what I wanted to be in my day and age. And when I saw karate movies came through, I was like, 'My bro, this is the move. I wanna fly through the air…but I wanna do heavy stuff, but I wanna…do a move, do like that gorilla. Out of the box stuff.' That was me…and the thing that, that really attracted me to Hip Hop was when I saw b-boying or breakdancing an I'm like yoh!…Kung fu and karate moves here to music and this is like cool music. And that was my entry point into the culture, you see, so I'm not sure how we are academically gonna make sense of that or connect the dots, but that was it. So you know, and I was thinking of doing all these little worms and rolls and you know we were doing these moves for about two years and then I learned these moves called Hip Hop and I was like, okay, Hip Hop for me, you can be boss [laughter]. So from there, one thing led to another. POC came into the picture and also being in a group where you have so many different characters, you know, sometimes you have character clashes as well, but it's a good thing if you think about it down the line because we always encourage and we always challenge each other's thoughts. For instance, a person like Shaheen, he was the lead rapper, he was the activist dude. He was on the extreme side of consciousness and I was on the other side of, my bro. Don't tell me about [Nelson] Mandela and Steve Biko. I just wanted to impress the *kinders* [kids] in the neighbourhood. That was like my vibe and I needed to like find a way to get away from ma *brasse* [my brothers] because ma *brasse* were busy stabbing and shooting people and I'm like, this is not gonna be benefit for me, I wanna slack [forget] this Hip Hop move because I can *gooi* [move] my boss moves here. That was my thing, so you meet a person like Shaheen, you know. You meet other people and then there's the turning point, socially, politically all those things are starting to happen in the country as well so how do I see myself in the picture and also because of my circumstance at home and my relationship with my family, I also needed to survive so I think my natural survival instinct kicked in and practically forced me and encouraged me to pursue, if you wanna call it, the alternatives.

GRANDMASTER DJ READY D | Source: Ference Isaacs

Adam Haupt: So your passion was guiding you; you were looking for creative outlets, it was just about following that thing, that curiosity and the thing that motivates you to get up every morning

DJ Ready D: Certainly. I mean, that was the driving force, it was the passion even through, through the days of POC when we were really riding high, we were so focused on performing, on writing, on attending all these different seminars and speaking in the background. We weren't really taught about the business aspect and how the industry works, you know, that came much, much, much later in my years though. So you reach a point where okay, boof, boof, the taxman's coming to, [you] know, on your door, so you're like 'holy crap how did I land in this position and what does this *bra* want with me?' You know, how I'm freaking here pro black and free Mandela and all this stuff, what's this *bra*, can't they see I'm busy doing like some really phenomenal work over here, you not supposed to tax me. They'd be like, aha ha, *bra*, you're a musician, it doesn't work like that, you fall into the, the category as everyone else. So they started to come down on all the likes of Brenda [Fassie] and even [Yvonne] Chaka Chaka and Chico, those were the big, uhm, the high-profile artists…and of course you know that started to trickle down as well because now you riding high, your profile's high as well, so now you need to think about business. Then you have people coming along within the industry, you need endorsements, your music's not selling, how are you gonna survive, how are you gonna eat? Now you starting to be banned, you can't perform, you can't appear on TV, where do you go? You find yourself abroad, now you in that dynamic as well and the way that business works abroad is slightly different to the way business works in South Africa. And unfortunately we had to discover those things in trial and error and the hard way, and we lost a lot of money and a lot of opportunities to make an income because we weren't schooled and educated about how to conduct our business. It's cool to have a manager and it's cool to have a team working with you, but is that the right team, is that the manager you can trust? Is it the agent you can trust, is it, uhm, people that truly have your, your vision, your career, do they have that at…you know, is that their interest as well? Do they wanna grow with that or are they in it because they are self-motivated and they got their own personal agendas? And unfortunately we had to discover and unpack all those things as well. So in my case as DJ Ready D the independent artist/producer I had to walk away from probably one of the most successful business/corporate operations that we've built from the ground up. I just decide one day I am packing my bags and I am walking away from everything…I am giving up everything, I don't want to extract one single cent from what's been generated and I put my wife [Malikah] into the deep end…she agreed. I went all the way down the ladder and she practically, you know, carried DJ Ready D as a artist, practically I've been on her back for all the years and she had no, uhm, knowledge about the industry, no knowledge about reading contracts and conducting business, and that's full proof, you know, that she managed to, to, uhm, to, to, to, to, to take me through all and to all these different platforms and all these different levels because you knew that you had somebody that you could trust, you know, somebody that's got your interests at heart. And through the process you grow together, the network and the opportunities still rolled in and I feel I am in a much, much better place right now, you know, so that's my take…

Malikah: As long as it's working for us, it's fine. I'll wait.

Adam Haupt: I was just reminded that we should actually have Malikah on the panel [laughter]. Uhm, next time we booking you for the Second Annual Indaba Lecture Series. Uhm, and he [Ready D] will do the booking on your behalf [laughter].

DJ Ready D: Don't ask me to book, to do bookings, don't ask me to cook and to garden. I come up short in all those departments.

Adam Haupt: On that note, so you've got a team. So you both have a team, you know, many people look at Ready D as this instant brand. He's a dope DJ. It just happened, right. There's no work behind it. He's an instant brand, uhm. Ready D the brand is, you know, it has a particular kind of currency, you know, of social capital. They don't know the backstory behind what it takes…and you know the team, you know the trust between you and your teammates. That's an important thing.

DJ Ready D: I think it's impossible to be a one-man show. You absolutely cannot do that and you cannot do that without the support of the community. And when I speak about the community, I speak about the people, the fans, the supporters who truly understand you as an artist and somebody that truly represents their interest, you know, whether you gonna be out there rapping and singing in a conscious form or whether [you] come through on an alternative or subliminal level or whatever. But if people aren't able to connect with you…I would say that's one of the ingredients for success…Again, I was lucky. I had a lot of people, like-minded people that we worked with, you know. From POC, we worked with BVK [Brasse Vannie Kaap], you know, all like-minded people – very, very critical people. We had no people… that would stroke your ego. For me that was a good wake-up call as well 'cause at one point, you know, you reach a point where ego kicks in because you know, 'My bro, look what I just did…' You know those things, it's natural. It kicks in, then you have people that, that bring you down to earth very, very quickly and they were constantly, their thumb on top of you, you know, my bro. You know, you remain grounded and that kind [of] keeps you more, uhm, I would say more, uhm, dedicated to the task at a hand and more dedicated to the craft as well. So the more you focus on the craft as well…the music, the culture and all those type of things, I think naturally your mentality and your mind state, you know, it will start to develop, to grow within I would say that setting and, uhm, luckily, I still got people that support me. And I'm in a position where I can exchange and also give that kind of same level of commitment to them as well. So we practically operating in, in I would say in a Indie field, if you wanna call it that, and for that is the…the way forward, you know, the way that I see success coming out of that.

Adam Haupt: So a good relationship with the community out there, a solid team of people you can trust. But not just from the management and business side of things, but on a personal level people who affirm you and keep you grounded – which brings me to BTeam. I always see on your site: #BTeam…

Ben Caesar: …yeah, yeah, yeah…

Adam Haupt: You seem to have a team. You're an Indie artist, but you're connected to a crew of people. You're on the same wavelength, you support each other, but you also somehow keep each other focused…

Ben Caesar: …yeah, yeah, yeah…

Adam Haupt: Tell us more about that.

Ben Caesar: I think it's just the position that I put myself in; as an independent artist you need your own team. I mean the thing is like I was, I came into the game by myself and I know life to be like, I figure things out by myself, so I'm fiercely like independent just within myself as a person. So to work with a team was a learning experience, but I've grown exponentially… just exposure and contact, building a community has grown because of the team. But what D was saying, it's trust and like the team keeps me focused – like Diego my manager keeps me focused all the time. He's like, 'B, you need to be ready.' And your ego gets involved and if you have a team that inflates your ego…I think the ego is the most dangerous thing for artists, you know what I mean. So, yeah, to have a team that you can trust, to have a team that is gonna keep you focused, is essential. So I have a manager, I have a web developer. We recently just started working with a publicist…I think these are some of the essential components, you know, and we started small, you know. Diego's my homie, but over time it developed and we both wanna grow and build something amazing, so…

Adam Haupt: Let me go back to those other things that you can do to sustain your passion for your art now you are doing other things…tell us about that and how those other things are working for you.

Adrian van Wyk: Okay, so I uhm, three years ago…we started an organisation called Stellenbosch Literary Project under the co-foundership of Professor Leon de Kock. There was a need for the university to change its numbers and to change its dynamic of how, you know, black people are coming into the university…We saw poetry as a means to change our society completely through stories, through storytelling that, you know, that ideas can change places and then we eventually got a small team together, a collective of five members…over three years we've transformed into this organisation that is acting as a portal for young writers to come into the university. Uh, we are housed in the English department of Stellenbosch University, so they are also quite keen to give us opportunities for the young people in our programme to come to the university…At the moment we have a group of 10 kids…uhm, 10 young emerging adults, uhm, they'll kill me if I call them kids…And then out of the group of 10, two are currently at the University of Stellenbosch on full scholarships, uhm, so it's about, you know what I mean, it's just like how what we do can actually affect…someone's future and give someone that cream of opportunity…Although these kids come from contexts that are really tough. I mean I would, like I look at some of these realities, it's really tough and it's really an amazing opportunity, an amazing thing what they are doing with their own words, their own poetry, that it's actually giving them this, this, uhm, platform…It's a three-layered organisation where we have a website that covers, uh, literary and cultural phenomena in South Africa and the world. The second one is the InZync poetry sessions…which is our monthly platform where the poetry is mixed – whether you are a rapper or a paid poet, you're all welcome to one platform…We just put it onto one platform, give everyone the same respect. And then the third layer is the bi-weekly workshops with, uhm, the emerging adults between the ages of 15 and 21 using poetry as a means of social uplifting.

Adam Haupt: So you're a spoken word artist. Are you an MC? Do you think of yourself as an MC at all?

Adrian van Wyk: I think of myself as a writer. As a writer. I write, yeah.

Adam Haupt: On that note, you know what I wanna draw on, but I just wanna make this connection here: what I am seeing here is, uhm, people are driven by their passions. There are easier things to do than perform poetry, to rap, to make music. You could be a chartered accountant, you could be a lawyer, you know, you could be a lawyer…What I find interesting is that they use this word to sort of diversify and I think what all participants on the panel are involved in is that they do workshops that share and that is actually one way of generating your brand as well, right – is to share, is to teach and the process of doing that changes the way you learn. You don't just teach. You learn from the people you teach as well and…that helps you grow. It makes you stronger. So it's not unlike being a teacher. You're building relationships when you are on the stage, when you are performing, etc. That's what you're doing. The other thing that Adrian does is he's supporting his nasty habit, academia, you know. Academia's supporting his, his passion for performing, for writing and that's, that's an option and I think that's what Ben and Deon [DJ Ready D] are saying. They teach…They might not have PhDs, etc., etc., but that's what they are doing and for me that was the point of entry when I realised at the end of my third year when I was waking up to what POC and Black Noise were doing, I realised that these guys are teaching. They are involved and they have a level of literacy that I did not have at that time. When I met Shaheen for the first time, I felt like I needed to go straight to the library and find all these books that he is talking about, right. And that's the kind of feeling you'll be getting if you have a supervisor session with, with your postgraduate supervisor. I don't know what she just said. I wrote it down, I go do a keyword search, I have to go to the library...I'm the one with the degree, right! What's this about...So that's the moment when you realise that there's actually a lot going on and if you want to sustain yourself, you have to build that brain, you have to build the word power. And I think that's what's coming through...So Adrian's work is interesting because he's both of those things. He is both the artist and he is the scholar attempting to map it. So those are the other things that you need to do to sustain your career. So this is... the scholar's kind of response to the very sober industry session we had yesterday. There's another way of being in the so-called industry...

GRANDMASTER DJ READY D AND SHAHEEN ARIEFDIEN | Source: Ference Isaacs

CHAPTER 26.
CREATIVE CURRENCY: IS THERE AN ART TO SELLING ART?

MARVIN 'MoB' LEVENDAL

PART I: BACKGROUND

December 2008 at Hi-Point pool club in Kuilsriver. I'm playing an intense game of virtual golf against a fierce opponent, Marvin Seekoei. This is part of our weekly ritual and brainstorming session, and I come out on top again today but only beat him by one stroke. Not sure what my handicap was at that time but I believed I was up there with the greats! I assure you. As we entered our names onto the electronic leader board, me M.O.B and him COW, we realised that we had just entered what would be the name for our record label: MobCow. And just like that our label had been born.

Before the game, and although we had done this on numerous occasions of late, we'd been racking our brains to find a suitable name for our Indie label. It took us a while to realise that actually it had been under our noses the entire time.

Our label name came at a fortuitous time. Suburban Menace, the Hip Hop group we founded with our homies Winston Schereka, Marlin Keating and Clayton Petersen, was about to release a debut album, *Sub-Conscious*, and so it became imperative to launch our Indie record label to promote and register the music. Up until then we had been operating under the banner of Suburban Menace, hosting weekly Hip Hop nights at Club Stones in Kuilsriver. Initially, we promoted our own music and we immediately realised the need to open our platform to the greater music scene in Cape Town.

The Hip Hop nights grew quickly into other types of Hip Hop-related events and soon enough their popularity forced us to branch out and host at popular performance venues like Zula Sound Bar in Long Street, Trinity in Greenpoint and Downtown in Kuilsriver. Several themed nights evolved from this – the most attended one was Lyrical Warfare, where two

MCs battled each other in a lyrical salvo reminiscent of the current Hip Hop battle scene: in other words, you freestyle-battled an MC and all the material you spit had to be put together as you went along, or as we say, had to be spit 'off the top'.

The experience with Suburban Menace Hip Hop nights left an indelible mark on the Cape Town Hip Hop scene. The night of the launch of *Sub-Conscious* featured performances by DJ Ready, Chad Saaiman, Joe Barber and various well-known Cape Town acts to a packed Club Stones in Kuilsriver. The Hip Hop nights themselves drew close to 1 000 patrons and fans on a week night, and we easily sold over 2 000 copies of compact discs (CDs) independently. We tried to bring Cape Town Hip Hop to Club Stones on a Wednesday night. To do so successfully, we asked artists to put aside their differences for the sake of Hip Hop.

It took us two years of strategic planning, public relations (PR), marketing and much blood, sweat, tears (metaphorically speaking) and building of goodwill to be recognised. In no way did our success come about as a random feat, a stroke of luck or because the gods were smiling down on us. We, and I personally, have learned a valuable lesson about

BC ONE SA CYPHER | Source: Ference Isaacs

the arts – that we need to invest in it the same amount of respect, passion, nurturing and investment as any other field, business or sport.

Sure, talent counts, but talent can take you only so far. You need to work hard as a Hip Hop artist, and above all you need to plan because money buys talent.

PART II: FROM NOTHING TO SOMETHING

I was raised in Beacon Valley, a place which played a huge role in the way I identified with Hip Hop as a genre, culture and lifestyle. I vividly remember when I was 10 years old, how I tried to form a Hip Hop group named Prophets of da Valley. Of course, this was a blatant rip-off of Prophets of da City, who made regular visits to our school at the time. In particular, b-boy Ramone 'Ram1' had us all in awe and stiches with his comedic barefoot b-boy sessions in the quad. But specially, I could not forget DJ Ready D on the decks and Shaheen MCing on the mic. At the same time, Black Noise had made major inroads and that group empowered us with a sense of identity and purpose. Our streets were on fire. It was the height of the anti-apartheid protests. The Laughing Boys and Ugly Americans were at each other regularly, locked into street brawls. Still today, I vividly remember the sound of tear-gas canisters ricocheting off the walls. Yet with all of this going on, Hip Hop had me hooked, and as b-boying took off everyone wanted to be or battle the Juvenetics.

Then the era of music videos came and every Friday night I was glued to *Studio Mix* where Bob Mabena and Melanie Son introduced us to all that was happening abroad with Hip Hop and R&B. From MC Hammer, Shabba Ranks and MC Shan to Tupac Shakur, I was transported to a new world, a world where Hip Hop, the arts, music and brands were a serious option to pursue in life.

By 1997, we moved to Kuilsriver and there, at home, I had access to the internet. No one really cared about it but me. My access to Hip Hop improved tenfold with Napster and I started making Hip Hop tapes for DJs in Kuilsriver. Ten years later, in 2007, when the boys and I formed Suburban Menace, I had a clear understanding of how we had to package and execute our Hip Hop brand. Up until then, any relevant Hip Hop brand/act was based in Joburg. Entity was making waves in Cape Town and was pegged to be the next big thing (today rapper AKA still acknowledges that he was a member of Entity).

Developing the Suburban Menace Hip Hop brand was a great exercise for us because from our perspective as artists we had to give careful consideration to our different personae, images and musical styles. It came down to this: we were the bad boys of the suburbs, offering a taste of the township to our suburban audience. And we brought a different experience via our weekly Hip Hop events and tried to transform the sometimes-amateurish representation of Hip Hop that was plaguing the art form in Cape Town.

In order for us to be successful at executing our brand, we brought on board graphic designers, web designers and a public relations team, and utilised new platforms such as MXit, Myspace and Facebook. This process laid down a blueprint that I would later tweak in relaunching MobCow and managing and promoting BazaSon (see Part V). But let's take a step back and consider Hip Hop and its value chain, particularly in the South African context.

PART III: HIP HOP AND ITS VALUE CHAIN

Creative currency? Why that title for this chapter? Well, it was what I titled my talk at the University of the Western Cape's annual Hip Hop Lecture Series. It looked cool on the programme schedule and it sounded dope until I realised I had to flesh it out.

Maybe I should have gone with *'Osse community koepie CDs'ie'* (Our community doesn't buy cds) or *'Wat issie cover charge?'* (What's the cover charge?), seeing as these are constant points of contention in the Cape Town music scene.

For my talk, I thought it prudent to share some key facts about the African entertainment scene, drawing from *Entertainment and Media Outlook: 2016–2020*,[1] according to which the South African entertainment and music industry will be worth a whopping R154 billion by 2018, with a 6 per cent year-on-year growth forecast. The music industry accounts for R2.2 billion of this, with live music performances representing 57.1 per cent of that pie.

If we look at those figures, we can confidently say that a thriving and successful music industry exists, that artists lead successful lives through their art and that we all have an equal opportunity to become part of this music ecosystem. However, the question now is: If you are a Hip Hop artist, what tools, techniques, insights and networks are needed to make the cut?

---

1. https://www.pwc.co.za/en/assets/pdf/enm/entertainment-and-media-outlook-2016-2020.pdf

Independent record labels account for 25 per cent of the music industry growth, but often they do not match the standards of quality and execution offered by the major industry players. In this era of digital technology, we no longer need archaic and expensive systems to achieve quality – what counts is know-how and experience. As the proverbial saying goes, there is no need to reinvent the wheel; all you need to know is how it works and what is needed to make improvements, if need be. The same applies to the quality standards in music. There's a known formula to get the standards right all the time and if we know this we can become more creative. I am not arguing that these systems have to be followed strictly, but as I have discovered, if you know it, your creativity will shine.

I can already hear the naysayers shooting: 'But it's expensive to get your music mixed and mastered professionally.' Of course it is. Professionals have worked in the industry for years. They have perfected the techniques that are still in use today. There is something to be said for this because not anyone can decide on a whim they want to be dentist; it takes years of study and training. Similarly, musicians are always professionals in everything they do.

Besides quality, you need consistent and well-placed marketing and PR. Tagging people in your Facebook posts is not enough. There has to be organic outreach where people are not forced to engage but participate and engage freely with your brand and content. You need to consider that artist managers, booking agents and A&R (Artists and Repertoire) also come into play. Often, when it concerns independent record labels, the artist is the person that represents all these portfolios. Little wonder then that many artists die paupers.

At this point, all of this may seem like too big a mountain to climb, but with careful and considered planning and execution, a certain impact can be made that will in turn allow you to slowly start using more professional services. A clear budget for all these activities also has to be communicated and utilised in order to measure key indicators and actual impact. This allows you to see if funds spent in a certain area get you the desired returns or not.

I see three types of budgets in the area of an independent record label: personal budget, low budget or no budget. As independent artists and record labels, we usually start recording a new album with no budget. We have no idea what it will cost to get the standards or marketing right. We then get frustrated when it takes two years to record 10 tracks, and when we release it no one cares. What about the personal budget? If we are a bit better off and have cushy full-time jobs, we often subsidise our music career with our salaries, but this in turn gives us a false sense of accomplishment. Now don't get me wrong – there is nothing wrong with this. Many successful artists and businesses started this way, but there has to be an end goal because you need to decide to eventually go at it full time. Then there is the low budget: this is where 90 per cent of us remain throughout our careers. We are too afraid of investing too much of our time, money and expertise. It is in this space where we can deliver miracles if we have proper budgeting and strategic planning in place. A little goes a long way, as they say.

In closing, a value chain exists for a reason. If you follow such a chain, you will realise that it provides you with the desired outcome you hope for. You may not be able to afford all the bells and whistles at the beginning, but start with one professional in your value chain. If it is recording in a professional space, make sure you get a track mixed/mastered

MARVIN LEVENDAL OF MoBCow | Source: Author

professionally because this will add more value to your art. As you go along, you add more professionals to your chain and this in turn will get your value on a par with that of the major artists and record labels.

In the next part, I demonstrate a variation of these principles that led BazaSon, a Sotho-based Hip Hop artist managed by MobCow, to score a number one song nationally as well as two international nominations for Best Music Video from a six-track extended play (EP).

PART IV: A CASE STUDY – BAZASON

To avoid the reader saying that these techniques and processes look good on paper and don't really apply in reality, I will briefly elaborate on the processes we followed when conceptualising, recording, mixing, promoting, marketing and launching the *Eclipse* EP by BazaSon & Principlez. They are by no means written in stone as many a time we had to pivot and change strategy, but overall the same principles apply at any given time in the process.

The project flow was very basic, but not easy to execute at all times. Besides, Murphy's Law always rears its ugly head. There were many issues outside the scope of our control. For instance, at the time we had no physical studio space or equipment to mix the project. All we had was the computer that was used to record the project on. Unfortunately, this piece is too short for me to explain why we were in that predicament at the time, but we pushed forward and stayed as close to our original plan as we could. The basics of the project were as follows:

> » We used one producer, namely Principlez;
> » The project was recorded in-house at MobCow Entertainment;
> » The project was mixed in-house;
> » Mastering was done by a professional mastering, in-house;
> » Artwork and design were outsourced to a professional;
> » Two singles were selected beforehand;
> » One music video was shot for one of the singles;
> » PR, marketing and promotion were done in-house by Marvin Levendal;
> » Support from the private sector was sourced for the album launch.

This entire process took us nearly two years in order to release a six-track EP. At the end of it, the impact and response we received was phenomenal. We invested loads of creativity, time, energy, money and tears to make it happen. The aim first and foremost was to make sure we presented a product that was of a certain standard of quality. I live by the mantra that quality will eventually sell. It may take a bit longer to impact the larger music market and be noticed, but in the long run it will sell if promoted and marketed correctly.

We spent almost 12 months on those six tracks, and with all the hiccups, personal problems, technical obstacles and the like, we pushed through. At this point I can add that this entire project was mixed on one speaker, all thanks to DJ Dogg for allowing us to use one of his DJ tops.

After being fairly satisfied with the original mixes it was off to TL Mastering to add a bit of sheen to the mixes. One of the reasons we had to get proper mastering was because the project wasn't mixed to the best of our expected standards because of circumstances. The mastering assisted in lifting the quality of those mixes a bit. As artists, producers and engineers we always attempt to do all of these things in-house, without receiving criticism from a different ear to give us feedback and advice. Usually when the first mixes are sent to the mastering engineer, he will revert with some input around where minor improvements can be made in the mix, which in turn will create a better mastered product.

It is common knowledge that professionally mixing a song will set you back more than mastering it, so this is another reason why we went this route – to keep costs down but not sacrifice quality too much.

The mastering house will also then provide you with a glass master which is used to replicate/duplicate the project for sale purposes. Part of this glass master will include CD authoring information that is embedded into the glass master, consisting of International Standard Recording Codes, track lengths, spaces between tracks, CD text and so forth. All this is important when you submit tracks to radio for broadcast and to online stores for sale. When we finally received the master, we started to promote the first single, 'It's Alright'. The track was very well received and took the number one spot on Good Hope FM, YFM, Bloem FM and Bush Radio, to name but a few. Here is also where we were a bit unprepared because at this stage we had to shoot a music video for the song but didn't have funds available. A music video would have surely increased the footprint of the song and overall project immensely.

The second single, 'Afrika', was a more poignant and revolutionary track. At this stage we secured some funds to shoot a music video and we did so before releasing the track. The track wasn't really a radio song and we knew this, thus we punted the music video and in turn the video got nominated for Best Music Video in Africa alongside Mi Casa and P-Square at the first annual All Africa Music Awards 2014. It was also nominated for Best Music Video at the Ibiza Music Festival Video 2014. We were ecstatic with what we achieved with the project. The video was play-listed by Channel O but because our reach wasn't that big at the time, the video was not put on the regular play list.

Lastly, we had an extensive social media and online campaign, consisting of promoted posts, online surveys, competitions and free giveaways. The background behind this campaign won't be unpacked here, but social media played a huge role in creating impact amongst the youth and online public. Independent sales of the project were also not what we anticipated but the experience we gained was invaluable. If we had another go at this project, it would be the catalyst for all our music careers.

If we had had publishing for the project, I know that the two singles we released would have been placed in ads or movies, and to this day it is still an option that we will pursue going forward. Applying these principles to the new artists we work with has also yielded great results.

PART V: WHERE TO FROM HERE?

I will now speak solely from a Cape Town perspective on how we can create more and improved economic and artistic growth based on opportunities for our music community.

The first thing that everyone always mentions is that the public should buy more local art. I agree but we should also not be of the mindset that because you are from Cape Town the Cape Town public are obliged to buy your product. People spend money where there is some sort of value in the product or project. You would agree that you don't just go out and buy any car. You assess your financial state and then start weighing the pros and cons based on a budget and a quality or feature ratio. We as artists should improve the quality of our products and in order to do this we need to invest! If we are serious enough about the arts, we should go out on a limb and lead by example. The buying public will appreciate it more.

Secondly, we need to play ball nationally/internationally. We don't exist as a country on our own. We need to start working across borders and adhere to some of the practices that exist in the greater industry. As Johannesburg is our media hub, Cape Town acts need to establish some sort of relationship with the powers that be in Johannesburg. Networking and building solid relationships really goes a long way if it is coupled with quality music.

Image, image, image. Although Cape Hip Hop is considered the original source of South African Hip Hop, to be real, we don't want to succumb to the staged version of the music. We need to find a balance somewhere. If you don't want to be the artist that wears formal clothing, grooms regularly and can negotiate, find someone who will to represent you. The majority of people you need to deal with in the industry are not musicians. They follow a formal business approach and you will need to learn how to deal with that and create opportunities. Here I also want to implore for consistency. You can't be a Goth-looking artist today and then be all jazzed up in three months. The buying public needs to become accustomed to you as an artist and you need to be consistent in what you project.

It's time we start thinking outside of the confines of conventional music distribution models. Of late, I see everyone making a fuss if they upload their music on online platforms. That's good. But are you making actual sales? And of those sales, what percentage goes into your pocket? Physical CD sales have decreased over the last couple of years, but subsequently the sale of LPs has gone up. This surely could be an avenue to consider when it comes to distribution. Creating unique opportunities to distribute and sell your music is always welcomed by the bigger distribution players in the market, and here I don't necessarily mean music distributors. Investigate which distributor of products has a national/international footprint and couple your music with their products. This in turn will create reach and upfront sales.

We need to take our music publishing seriously. There are many artists in Cape Town that may not have their so-called hit on the radio but their music is placed in ads, movies or voice-overs. Too many of us have what I call star syndrome. We want to be music stars where our songs are played on the radio all day; our music videos are on high rotation and brands approach us to use our likeness. The brutal honesty here is that only a select few get to live this lifestyle; the other 80 per cent of artists live behind the scenes, and very successfully so.

Understand your publishing and royalty rights. This alone could make you extremely successful or keep you in a constant state of distress. In the past, it was extremely difficult to get a handle on this because you needed entertainment lawyers to assist. They don't come cheap and are very rare in Cape Town. I am happy to report that more people are taking up the challenge of becoming entertainment lawyers, and the costs aren't that high anymore. Consult with one of them. There are also books available now that deal specifically with these issues from a South African perspective.

Lastly, join your music societies and attend their workshops and round tables to stay abreast of the changes in your industry. It is okay to have a manager that deals with all of this but at the end of the day you are the boss, not your manager. You need to be aware of everything that happens in your career, not just the art.

I'm sure there are many other suggestions that can be made. I feel these ones are easier to get a handle on and you don't need wads of cash to implement them.

Since releasing our last official project, the *Eclipse* EP, MobCow has been on a tough journey to bolster tangible relationships with companies and corporates outside of the music industry. We are proud to say that many of these relationships are now starting to bear fruit and we look forward to opening up some of these opportunities when the time is right.

As artists and independent record labels we need to share the spoils and contacts we have in the industry, as this will only come full circle to help us all in the end. Staying shut off and only thinking about yourself has never helped anyone. As MobCow, we are constantly improving our understanding and building relationships that will benefit the industry as a whole. By no means are we a blueprint of what you should be doing; everyone has their own creative ways of growing, their own creative currency, and we hope that you will be a part of our growth.

PEACE!

NADINE MATTHEWS-NUNES, RENSTAN WHITE, EAVESDROP, NATHAN LODEWYK AND RAZEEN HAUPT AT A #INTHEKEYOFB PERFORMANCE, MOWBRAY, 2018 | Source: Gary Stewart

NADINE MATTHEWS-NUNES, RENSTAN WHITE, EAVESDROP, RAZEEN HAUPT, BRADLEY LODEWYK, EDDY STRINGS & ADAM HAUPT AT A #INTHEKEYOFB PERFORMANCE, MOWBRAY, 2018 | Source: Gary Stewart

RAZEEN HAUPT, EDDY STRINGS AND ADAM HAUPT PERFORMING 'STATE CAPTURE' (#INTHEKEYOFB) MOWBRAY, 2018
Source: Gary Stewart

CHAPTER 27.
DIGITAL MUSIC DISTRIBUTION

NICOLE KLASSEN AND ARTHUR PRICE

Nicole Klassen and Arthur Price talk about the potential for digital and mobile media to assist African musicians to sell their music and reach new markets at the first Heal the Hood Hip Hop Lecture Series at the University of the Western Cape in 2015.

Arthur Price: My name is Arthur Price. I own and manage or I am the content manager for a website called *Rymklets Republiek,* which is really a niche activity focusing on the marketing and digital distribution of Afrikaans Hip Hop. When we talk about going viral in music, Afrikaans Hip Hop, with the exception of one or two, is really small from the industry perspective. But what I hope to achieve is…if I have 10 artists with a fan base of 10, then they can start getting fans from one another; we can take this activity, which I try to market within boardrooms and stuff, to grow and I get an answer where they say it's a niche of a niche. So it's not even really qualified yet to be in this room to discuss, but to maybe boldly take it to be graduated to a niche where maybe people can recognise it as an art form and not a guinea pig within the Hip Hop arena.

Nicole Klassen: You know what Marvin [Levendal] was saying about having your creative currency and where you go to sell your products, and so forth, and some of the problems Sipho Sithole pointed out in terms of distribution are the very reasons why we started Bozza [a mobile platform to distribute content]. We were like so there's so much art, there's so much creativity. How do we find it 'cause it's definitely not on mainstream media, whether it's TV or radio or anywhere else? We are not finding it where we want to find it. For the artists themselves, how do they get through these traditional barriers to entry? So Marvin again pointed out sometimes where there's PR you've gotta have the right PR person; they can open those doors for you, but what if you don't? What if you don't know that person at the broadcaster? What if you don't have that pay check to pay somebody off to do something? What happens to all those stories? What happens to all that music and that content that could really make a contribution to our society, on one hand, but also give people an opportunity to live from their craft? These are big questions that we were asking ourselves and, really from a deep philosophical point of view, how can we bring change to this environment? We're passionate about the arts. I myself come from the film industry. I've had relative success in the film industry, but I realise that that's not available to everybody. It became more and more important for me to bring my skill and bring the opportunities that I had to the people and to the stories where things were creative and the energy was. So I teamed up in 2011 with Emma K. She had a vast amount of experience in the mobile industry, specifically. She was like, 'Nicole, you've gotta go mobile. You've gotta go cellphones 'cause that's where people are and that's where they are going to be in the next few years.' The first time I met her and she was talking about mobile, mobility of the mic as well…so she was talking to me and I was like, it's a little bit crazy and it felt like she was a little bit ahead of the curve. But it felt so important and I was like, we have to actually try this. We have to do this now. Some of you may know us through the various stages that we've gone through, but we've really created a kind of a digital ecosystem where artists from wherever you are in Africa…you can upload your work via your mobile phone or by your desktop and that can be poetry, music, film, whatever your craft form is. We have illustrators and animators and all…even an artist that is a shoelace artist. Whatever is available to create great products. There's a variety of artists at different levels in their careers that are on the platform, so there's a bunch of artists that are completely unknown and emerging and there are, of course, people that should not be artists and…they're just expressing themselves. There are those. It's an open platform. There are artists that are there in the emerging stages and I find this word 'emerging' is such a grey word because there's a lot of talented people in there that have been emerging for years and, and it feels like it's the wrong term. It's more like unexposed or something…something else or I haven't been given opportunity yet, uhm, so…we look at what's the value chain then? What are the things we need – and Marvin again I keep quoting you [laughter]. You articulated it so clearly – what are services? What are the prices that you need to be able to develop your product to such a point that it is then ready for sale? So what we've created is a digital toolbelt and we reward the hustle. So everybody has time to go to Facebook, everybody has time to go onto Twitter. What if we make that time count for something? So we have a Bozza profile. Everything, every view, every share, every listen, every read actually unlocks opportunities for you that you can use for your career. So, for example, you're producing an album, you are going to need mixing and mastering; how do you use your views and shares? Okay, I'm gonna need 1 000 views and then I can get mixing by X producer. I need my album artwork from a proper graphic designer, again, photographers. How do I get that done to such a level? I need X number of views on my images – that helps you again unlock the next step of what you need so these are available. So every month we are adding these onto the site where the artists can actually go for the hustle and for sharing your work, it actually starts to become valuable. So instead of having your… a little bit of work on YouTube over here and this on Facebook and this here on Twitter, you're actually, you're aggregating all your digital views onto one place. You use those social networks to actually build your career and open up opportunities for you; to that extent we also obviously have distribution. I feel like distribution is almost like the Achilles' heel of the creative industry sometimes 'cause we have so much talent and there's so much opportunity for the industry to grow itself. And, I mean, it's interesting that we are at 2.2 billion rand for the music industry in South Africa…It's the entire industry which is great, right, and we say we want a sliver of that for the rest of us. There's a few people making that much money, but what if we could expand the industry so it's not just taking a piece of that sliver? But now then we start to expand this chain so there's more people in this industry bringing more money into the cycle and so we build a bigger creative industry so then more people could benefit. Very ambitious [laughter], very ambitious! We are not in this to play small, right? So, again, we look at distribution. I suppose, like a lot of other platforms, we don't look at ourselves as the end digital platform. We actually see ourselves as the gateway, as kind of the beginning of your distribution cycle. So you use Bozza to build that stuff that you need and grow and get your mentorship and whatever else. You need mixing, mastering, clearances, legal advice as well, and then you get to the next step. Now you're ready for distribution. You've got a product that you feel and people feel and people have told you; industry people have given you advice on this, that, now is the time to go to market. We then unlock distribution and we look at a combination and again it's also about strategy. Distribution is not just about putting your work on iTunes and hoping for the best, you know? Most of the digital stores don't work for African artists and I say African because we work across the continent. Unless you're Ice Prince and you're known in the American market and you're being punted by a US company, your digital, international digital stores generally don't work and there's a couple of reasons for that. While it's inspirational to be on those places, it's not mobile friendly. We are a mobile-first market and we are still on feature phones; we're not necessarily on iPhones and android devices. So, yes, there are new android devices coming up and there's a 50-dollar android that's coming through to the market. It's a bit of a game changer. It's very exciting, but for a large amount of the population on the continent, we are still on BlackBerrys, we are still on Nokias, Nokia X2. I don't know how many artists I see with Nokia X2s [laughter]; it's like it was a really popular phone at one point or something and those Samsung flip ones as well, C 320 or something. Those first early phones that you could get, basic phones that you could get the basic amount of media content, are still prolific and they're still selling. We are still on the continent selling about three times more feature phones than we are selling smartphones because the battery life, because the data cost…data is extremely expensive on the continent. South Africa is leading the way; we're still the world's third most expensive data centre. How cool is that? So when you are consuming content and there are various elements that are

GARY 'ARSENIC' ERFORT AND BRADLEY LODEWYK WORKING ON #INTHEKEYOFB EP | Source: Adam Haupt

challenging in the ecosystem that you as artists are trying to thrive and data sensitivity is one of those things. So, yes you're a Hip Hop community and the, the willingness to buy stuff in the Hip Hop community is difficult, but you're coming up against a number of other factors. I think one of them is again ease of access to the content that I want, when I want it, how I want it and the other thing is the data sensitivity and then the price points. The other thing about distribution is, do you have an audience before you really do start selling? If you have 10 fans on Facebook and you wanna try digital sales, the two don't match. Your digital community as well as your offline community have to come together. So sometimes people are not so strong, but when I look at their offline community 'cause they're performing, they're huge. So they can get up, they've got festivals, they're touring, they're going from Kenya to Nigeria to Joburg to wherever and they're moving a lot. So when they getting up on stage and say, 'Buy my stuff, sms 37616 and get my track right here.' Right? So we look at multiple digital tools. So it's the online store, then we look at sms 'cause those are very difficult to get for local artists. So we open up all those avenues and then another interesting component I'd like to put forward to this community actually is mobile community, a place where your fans can experience your content, some free, some paid for, in one place on their phone. So we've just done the first experiment of this with Slikour up in Joburg. He's created the South African Hip Hop store, where you can buy content from various artists in Hip Hop. He's got very commercial artists in his store, which is great for the market that he's targeting. But I think there's a lot more opportunity here. I think creating mobile communities open so much more. We can start to now have a conversation about loyal fans and loyal fans buying content at the right price points in a way that's accessible for them and then I think that starts to become interesting. I'm still nervous about the Hip Hop industry buying content, but think if we can come in at low data points, at the right price points and at least we need to be as fast as the piracy market. We're always blaming that piracy market for all kinds of things, but really at the end of the day they are just people trying to make a living at the best of times. We cannot sell higher than them if your price unit, units are selling at a higher cost than the guys on the street. They are way more accessible a lot of the time than finding, what, a Look & Listen or Musica. You just have to go to the taxi rank in Cape Town, or any of the taxi ranks, to see how much content is selling. There's local content videos. I even saw poetry the other day, a whole CD of audio poetry. I was, like, really? Selling for 20 bucks, 40 bucks, so the price points are important and also they have speed with digital. We also have the speed; we have immediate access. Upload, play your work, upload and, boom, it's out. Share, move your content, build your community. Your fans must know. When you drop something and you are ready to sell, that community's been waiting, they know that thing's been coming. There's an artist here from Delft – in fact, there's a couple that are now using particularly the sms and the mobile short codes and things like that in the mobile communities. This guy is unknown, like he really is unknown to a lot of people, but he has a very loyal fan base. His name is Rebronx. You must check his hustle and Bozza's all about rewarding the hustle. He took time out to produce this stuff, he took time out to promote it, so you must be rewarded. You must be able to use your hustle. He, for example, he'll warm up his fan base. So he starts it like…he'll start with a picture and then he'll start with this and then a little bit of that…like 'get your R7.50 ready [laughter]. My track is coming', you know. He sometimes sells it for R3, he sometimes sells it R7.50. He chooses. That's the kind of flexibility we provide. He'll drop his track and he can make sometimes between R750 to R1 000 in a day just from dropping a new track. It spikes up for him and

BC ONE CT BREAKS BY BEAR | Source: Ference Isaacs

then he'll start dropping around 500, 400 per day. But that's okay for a guy that's unknown. He's producing from [a] kasi studio. I would say the quality levels that he's pushing out are not fantastic, but what he's doing with that money, he's reinvesting it in a new studio and reinvesting it in his work and that for me is very interesting. Now we are contributing to the growth of a bigger, much bigger, creative industry.

Arthur Price: It's cool, it's really cool you've got an expansive product…

Nicole Klassen: Can I see your niche? I want your niche community on Bozza, please?

Arthur Price: It's possible, we can chat. What we basically have is a hybrid not-for-profit venue and the problem with that in South Africa, if you say a hybrid profit, not-for-profit venue, everybody is like, 'Why hybrid?' The problem is I'm not going to go look for funding because I believe in the product, but there's an exchange to it. I don't do it for profit. The cost that I charge literally runs at a loss or break even if I gave economies of scale. You come with a track, like you do, create your pay form, decide what you want to upload to be available for a fee, decide what you want to sell and there's a 15 per cent commission. It's a simple product to help expand and to help consolidate the Afrikaans Hip Hop industry, which has graduated. I actually just took the name on the streets, they call it *Rymklets*. But Simon 'Hemelbesem' Witbooi will speak on all the stuff like that. He knows it, but I wanna talk about the digital distribution aspect of it, just like what we've heard about between yesterday and today is the high entry barriers within the music industry, and what *Rymklets Republiek* together with Bozza aim to do is to remove that entry barrier. So now you don't need your music mastered, you don't need the brand because you're backed by a stronger brand which you really piggyback on. You get your music out and the public can access it fast, which is the key before the pirates get out there. So maybe you have a small window of opportunity where the people can download your music. So what we basically do is we take this concept and all this product and we go from place to place to place to pitch it and come up with alternative concepts. We've only been around a year. The single biggest threat to [the] music industry is digital distribution, but it can be the most powerful thing if you can tame it to make money and to grow your brand individually.

Nicole Klassen: So maybe let's talk about that 'cause taming digital distribution…I'm not so sure we can. I think we actually have to turn it up a bit before it's gonna ease into a pattern. Let's put it in context. So it's very difficult to make money through digital distribution. How many of you have tried? And? Successful, would you say? Worth it? Right, but everybody is talking about this big digital revolution, right? Your work must be on digital. It cannot work alone. It cannot work in isolation. It's not just about putting your stuff online and I had to learn this hard and fast. So you've probably had this experience as well. We started looking at communities and we started looking [at] all the other areas of the media ecosystem. So digital distribution is one area. If that one artist can't perform, if that artist can't get on radio or can't get their music videos on Channel O or MTV, nobody is going to know, so we've now had to open up a whole other tier of networks and then doors. That's partly why I moved to Joburg as well, so I can go and knock on those doors all the time, so that really is that gateway, so your stuff is available for distribution. You can hustle it on one hand, but we'll open all the other channels for you so we've opened up broadcast, so obviously your stuff has to be TV-broadcast quality so that it can actually

REMY E, AFRICAN HIP HOP INDABA | Source: Ference Isaacs

have a chance of getting on air. But the channels are open. So, for example, on radio we are looking at slots, specific radio stations for artists that are on Bozza. We've created our own online radio station now and we are looking at satellite TV broadcasting as well to really fulfil that ecosystem because in the media industry it doesn't work in isolation. DJ Cleo sells the way he does digitally because people know his name, because he's performing. Therefore, all his work always ties together. So in his music video it tells you where to go get his tracks, for example. From his mobile access to TV access to radio access, he's plugged them all together so that they form a loop all the time. So you can see him perform, so you know exactly where to go get his track. From his track, you know when to find him at the next event. Even when he's on radio, and so on and so forth, so he's working constantly to close that loop. We haven't got it perfect in any way, but that's what we are trying to do all the time with artists.

MAK1ONE, AFRICAN HIP HOP INDABA, 2016 | Source: Ference Isaacs

CHAPTER 28.
'DIE BLIKKIE SE BOEM IS UIT': A B-BOY'S REFLECTIONS

BRADLEY 'KING VOUE' LODEWYK

I started dancing at the age of 11 back in 1997. At the time, POC was quite a popular Hip Hop group in South Africa. My first encounter with them was on television on a show called *Geraas* (*Noise*). At the time, I didn't pay attention to what they were rapping about; the dancing had my attention. That is when I decided I want to do breakdancing.

I formed a little crew with a few friends from the same street in my neighbourhood, Bonteheuwel. We called ourselves Mind Blowing Assassins. Our area was a particularly dangerous neighbourhood, which saw the fall of one of the biggest drug lords (Rashaad Staggie) on the Cape Flats and the rise of a vigilante group, People Against Gangsterism and Drugs (Pagad). Gunshots rang out every day. Amidst all this violence, we found something positive that kept us out of harm's way.

My first challenge back then was accessing information. We knew nobody other than ourselves, so all we could do was copy whatever dancing we saw on television – be it in a music video or on talent show. That was all the training I had in the first year – from Michael Jackson to New Kids on the Block. Every little bit helped. As word about our dancing spread, we met Angelo Jansen, who was the nephew of Emile Jansen, founding member of Black Noise and Heal the Hood.

Heal the Hood eventually came out in March 1999 to Angelo's backyard and gave us our first formal breakdance lesson. This was to prepare us for our first breakdance competition, the very first African Hip Hop Indaba, in August 1999. That same year, we formed a new crew called Crazy Hip Squad. We went on to win every competition in South Africa. On the back of this, many other crews became interested in joining our crew or trying to poach some of our key members.

At the time, we were very young and we were not prepared for this kind of spotlight. Our main mission was to survive the ghetto, to travel and just do what we love, breakdancing. But with the gigs and the money came a different set of dynamics. Now it turned into surviving the corporate world, where your mindset becomes about you as an individual and no longer a crew. Nobody warned us that some of us would sell out our crew for money. When big groups approached, they were not invested in our future, only in what they stood to gain from us and, as a youngster, it is easy to get swayed. This really had a negative effect on our Cape Town Hip Hop culture and was a perfect example of the culture killing the culture. Looking back, I realise how very important it is to guide and offer support to up-and-coming youngsters.

At the time I started to dance, there were over 50 breakdance crews. Today, you can't even get four crews together for a breakdance competition. What the established groups did not know is that by selecting youngsters from up-and-coming groups to join their already established groups, they were killing the next generation and creating this individualist mindset of youngsters starting out just with the hope of joining a big group. This really breaks my heart, to think of all the crews that were around in the 1990s that all just slowly faded away. And, in an ever-growing entertainment scene, kids start out today with fame and money on their minds and many fall through the cracks as they are not able to sustain themselves due to a lack of knowledge.

It is very important for any b-boy or b-girl to know the culture's history, and by history I do not mean the basics of breakdance, but the history of Hip Hop as a collective. Back when we started,

B-BOY BATTLES, FAMILY FEUDS 3 EVENT | Source: Ference Isaacs

we knew who the best graffiti artists were and who the dopest MCs and DJs were. You were never just a b-boy. You were part of the Hip Hop culture.

THINGS THAT ARE ESSENTIAL TO YOUR GROWTH AS A B-BOY/GIRL

1. Dance and feel the music.

2. Be creative; think outside of the box, outside of breakdance. This is what makes this dance so beautiful. You can add anything from martial arts to ballet into your moves.

3. Breakdance is divided into three parts: footwork, power moves, and popping and locking. Our bodies are made differently – some of us are strong and some are not so strong. Find a style that you are comfortable with and perfect it; practise every day.

4. Foundation: it's important to have the basics down (six steps, windmills, glides, etc.), but it is also important to know that we do not have to do everything in the same way. Be innovative and create your own foundation. Build your empire from the ground up. Some of the greatest b-boys and b-girls of this generation are famous for their own unique style – from Hong Ten and b-boy Junior to b-boy Pocket.

SAMUEL CONRADIE, GANIEF SALIE, AMBROSE UREN AND BRADLEY 'KING VOUE' LODEWYK | Source: Adam Haupt

5. Because breakdancing is very physical, it is important to always be well protected. Always try to wear knee and elbow pads. As you will knock them a lot, this helps to prevent injuries.

6. It is of utmost importance that you warm up and stretch properly before you start your practice. It is important to write down your practice routine from start to finish, that is, stretches, warm-ups, short sprints, quad burpies and push-ups.

7. Also write down what you want to work on each day. Do not practise everything at once. Your progress will be slow this way because, essentially, you are training your muscles to remember certain movements, like a six step, one step at a time.

8. Study world-class b-boys and b-girls and, once or twice a week, try to practise with those who are better than you – not to test yourself, but to learn and observe.

Hip Hop is all about being authentic, so it is not difficult to stay relevant in the corporate world media. The sound of music may change, but the sound of true Hip Hop stays the same.

B-BOY CREW – HANDBREAKTURN | Source: Ference Isaacs

CHAPTER 29.
BUILDING AN INTERNATIONAL PROFILE AS AN ARTIST

DOPE SAINT JUDE, BLAQ PEARL,
BLACK ATHENA, JEAN-PIERRE,
LYRICAL DEEZY WITH EMILE YX?

Emile YX? joined Dope Saint Jude, Blaq Pearl, Black Athena, Jean-Pierre and Lyrical Deezy in a panel discussion about the ways in which they negotiate obstacles in the local music and media industries, especially when it comes to establishing an international profile.

Emile YX?: So everyone else that is supposed to be on this panel, they [are] stranded at the airport [laughter] and I'm not travelling anywhere…so I'm gonna hand over to…to you to start off so then, uhm, if you have questions about like the reality of an artist, whether you a dancer or singer or whatever, travelling overseas, you know maybe after she's explained that, what the experience was like, then you could ask whatever questions you like, the mic's yours.

Dope Saint Jude: Hi, everybody. My name is Dope Saint Jude, but you can call me Catherine. Uhm, ja. So I'm from Elsies River, do you know where Elsies River is, does anyone know where Elsies is? Elsies River is on the Cape Flats in between, uhm…it's in front of Bishop Lavis and Gugulethu and between Goodwood and Bishop Lavis; it's like a little area over there. So, ja, that's where I'm from and I'm just gonna talk a little bit about how I got in the position to travel overseas with my music. So I started making music, uhm, in Cape Town. I first linking up with the producer, some to make beats and no one really wanted to work with me at first [laughter]. Uhm, no one really believed in what I kinda wanted to do with my music, so I taught myself to make music, so on my computer I download Ableton. It's a music-making program and then I sat every single day and I watch videos on YouTube every single [day] to teach myself how to make my beats because every time I would go the people would tell me, uhm, I must rap like this on this song. I didn't like how everyone was telling me how I must do my stuff. I wanted to do it my own way, so I learned. It took me a year. I struggled and then eventually I learned how to do a song and then in 2011, I released one song. It was the only song I produced; it took me one year to produce that song and it was only two minutes long, but I was very proud of the work, uhm, and…like, uhm, 200 people like listened to it. Me in the first like three months [laughter]. Not so many people listened to it and then after I made, I started making more and more music, like just producing and still like, like some people ask can I perform at your gig or whatever and they be like, uhm, because I didn't have anything behind me. I didn't have any real music so people wouldn't let me perform at their gigs, uhm, so eventually I make more and more music, I put it on the internet…that was a very important step, to put my stuff on the internet because then you have a profile of things that people can look at, they can see this is your body of work, you are doing something. I put my work on the internet, uhm, and then eventually I scraped enough people together and we had a camera and we made a music video. So I made my, uhm, I made two music videos and then they became quite popular and I shared them with a lot of people, uhm, and I got people to share it and people liked it. And then I like started to [be] able to book gigs in Cape Town so people would say, okay, you can come, you can come perform here, you can come perform there. And any gig I got, I went to, I always, I made sure I was on time and I would perform at every single gig I could get, even if they didn't pay me I would perform; maybe they pay me, uhm, 200 rand or 300 rand and, uhm, I would perform because it's a chance for people to see me. I did that for like a year and a half and eventually I got a bit of a name in Cape Town. People started seeing me at the events and, uhm, I was very broke, uhm, I was doing four things at the same time because I believed in what I was doing. I was making my music, I [was] working as a waitress, I was working as a bartender and I was doing a film course and I was broke, I had no money. I use to eat two-minute noodles, my friends they into that, ja, so it was a struggle and I worked really hard. There were times I wanted to give up on it because it was a stupid idea, like now I want to be a rapper, like everyone wants to be a rapper, what makes you different? But then I learned what makes you different is your ability to continue and not give up on something, so I kept on working on it because I just felt this is something I must do…uhm, I kept on working, got some more gigs, uhm, and then finally I got my first opportunity to perform overseas…someone came to Cape

Town and, and I had a, enough of a name in Cape Town and these people were throwing a festival overseas and they said, okay, we wanna see you perform. And also because I work very hard. I also worked with dancers to make my, my live performance better because I always thought, how can I make my performance better than the next person, like what's gonna make me stand out, and I noticed all the rappers come on stage and they rap on stage and sometime it can be a bit boring just to see one person. You want movement on stage and so I started working with dancers, and because I thought about that in the past when the people came to South Africa to come look for people they thought I was different and I had dancers. They booked me for a show in France and then straight after that I got a phone call, uhm, I got an email…people in America saying, hey do you wanna come for a tour, I mean will I come do a show and then I said okay, if I'm gonna do one show there why don't we turn it into five shows…they hooked it up and I was able to travel from San Francisco and Oakland and Hollywood to Los Angeles and I did five shows there and then I came back. And I still kept on, uhm, doing gigs in Cape Town and now I'm going to be, I'm going to New York in two weeks and in the next few weeks, in the next few months, I will be travelling to about three or four different countries. And I never ever travelled before, never ever before I did my music, I never ever left South Africa. I never thought it was possible because no one in my family could travel and couldn't afford it… seemed like something that rich people do, you know [laughter]. Uhm, so it's crazy. I was able to move from something that, uhm, that didn't seem like a possibility, now I'm doing it every week. Like, I'm actually getting a bit, not like tired of it, but it's like it's a lot of work now. But like at first it's very exciting; it is still exciting, but it's like becoming a job now to move around. So ja, uhm ja, so that's how I got from point A to point B. I hope I gave some great information. Do you wanna ask me any questions about?

Audience member 1: Uhm, I wanted to ask is it a good thing to be nervous before you go on stage like perform or is it a bad thing?

Dope Saint Jude: Uhm, before I perform I always feel a little bit nervous. I think it's a good thing, I think it's a very good thing…it shows that you care about your work. If you don't feel nervous you just gonna be like, haaaa, I'm just gonna go on stage. I think it means something when you get nervous but you must turn that nervousness into something amazing. Sometimes when I feel nervous I look in the mirror and I pump myself up. Sometimes I say stupid stuff like, 'I'm the best' or like, you know, 'I'm powerful'. I'll shout things like that but you gotta get yourself into that mood because the thing about Hip Hop, it's about confidence, so if you go on the stage and then you like this and then…no one wants to see a rapper who's like this… all our favourite rappers, AKA, Casper, Kanye, Jay Z, they confident, they come on stage with that power so you gotta find it inside of yourself…

I'm right now an independent artist, uhm, I think it gives you a lot more freedom but the thing about being an independent artist is that you don't have that many resources. So for me I have to pay for my own music videos, but when you with a label they pay for it, but then you end up paying for it in the long term. I mean it depends how far you wanna reach, uhm, I think it give you a lot of freedom. I think there is a lot of nitty gritty about signing or whatever, but I think being an independent artist in this day and age with the internet, it's like that's how far I've gotten and I'm now able to make [a] living out of my music and I haven't been played really on South Africa radio, uhm. But I'm able to make a decent living from my music being an independent artist just because I have my stuff on the internet, uhm. How many, how many of you guys on the internet like using Facebook, using any platform…it very important as an

BLACK NOISE ANNIVERSARY | Source: Ference Isaacs

artist to put your stuff on the internet because maybe you can't get it on the radio, maybe you can't get it on TV but if it's on the internet people can access it, they can see you have a body of work, they can search your name – they just type it into Google and all your stuff comes up. So that's a really, really important thing because the internet isn't limited like the SABC [South African Broadcasting Corporation], because only South African people see it; the SABC is amazing, but when you on the internet people in Spain can see it, people in the US can see your work, people in France can see your work…it's not limited to a small audience.

Adam: Tell us about relationships you built up. What kind of gigs are they? Are they festivals, are they university engagements or [are] they a mixture of both?

Dope Saint Jude: I do any gigs like, uhm, next month when I go to New York I will be performing at an art gallery so, uhm, it's like, I try to keep my, I don't try to limit it just playing at festivals – any opportunity really to build an audience I go for, so whether it's for a university or to speak on a panel somewhere or to, uhm, do a sound spec at an art gallery, I'll take the opportunity as long as it doesn't conflict with my own vision. I even, I did, my first time travelling was actually going [to] Senegal to do an advert for H&M so like that's another opportunity like that's not really what I do, but it was like, uhm, a gig and I got paid for it so I took it and it didn't conflict with my own beliefs. So ja…I think it's important to say yes to opportunities, it's very, you mustn't turn it away. Like this very weekend I performed at a gig and I didn't really, I wasn't…excited about performing at this gig and when I got there, there was all these people who did really look like they would like my music, uhm, and then I performed and then at the end of the gig someone came up to me and said, okay, I'm gonna book you to go to Switzerland in January. And at small things like that you don't know when you gonna meet someone. Last year here at Hip Hop Indaba I met someone who I took with me to France because they were a dancer and I met them at the Hip Hop Indaba so I'm very glad to [say] yes to every single opportunity that comes my way, ja.

Adam: On that tip, how do people engage with you apart from the fact, you know, people see you at events and want to invite you to other events. I'm thinking about the States, I'm thinking about…you were in Norway or Demark was it?

Dope Saint Jude: Uhm, Finland…

Adam: Finland, oops, uhm. How do they speak about what you do? What sense do they make of your work?

Dope Saint Jude: I mean it's, if you an African artist going into Europe, like people there are always excited about your work because you are different and you [are] REAL because you from AFRICA [laughter], so that is *lekker* [good, nice] and also for me I always try to keep my power in the situation because I also realise that Europe has taken a lot from Africa. So when I got there I remember that and I remember that I'm in control – they invited me, I'm the one who's bring the life to the party, so I'm like, I make sure my needs are met. But it's also nice…people are generally very lovely and friendly and also what's nice, you travel, move overseas, and you get there [and] because you from other country you suddenly the most popular person, you know [laughter]. That [is] always nice, people be nice, 'Can we get you this, can we get you?' It's really nice, ja, it's wonderful, it's really…I've never really had a problem when I've travel overseas with the way people treat me or the way people engage with me. But I think it also has to do with how you carry yourself, you always, you teach people how to treat you, so ja.

Emile YX?: Do [you] feel like it's a conflict? You go over there and people, they treat you…well and then you come back here to South Africa and you can't get a song on the radio?

Adam: I was just gonna ask that question…like that disjuncture between the big deal people…whether you in Oakland or whether you in Paris versus, 'Who's Dope Saint Jude? Never heard of her. *Wie's die?* [Who's this?]'

Dope Saint Jude: It's crazy. I had to go overseas to book more gigs in Cape Town, like serious gigs. Like people didn't, I mean in Cape Town we were starting to develop it, but there isn't really a culture of paying artists or taking the art very seriously. So people want you to do stuff for free all the time and I understand that; I did pay dues. I've done enough things for, uhm… For me it's about where am I gonna earn a living? I mean in an ideal society I wouldn't have to stress about that, but I have to pay my school fees. I wanna be able to support myself and support my family. So if South Africa isn't willing to give me that, like I mean I'm still here, like the Hip Hop Indaba…I'll go to all the things…you have to think about how you gonna earn a living. So I mean it is a bit of a conflict, but it's something you have to deal with. But I'm happy I'm doing gigs in Cape Town, so that's *lekker*.

Emile YX?: For those [of] you [who] just came in right now, uhm, this conversation is about international travel or artists who had the opportunity to travel internationally and also how they did it and how they can maybe give you advice…and what the experience was like. So it's a very valuable conversation, I think, for people who actually wanna travel internationally…For those who only came now, we been speaking with Dope Saint Jude. Clap your hands. And then right next to her, this is Blaq Pearl. I don't wanna run through her CV 'cause it's a *hele vrag* [whole load] stuff [laughter]. And next to her is Black Athena, female MC and singer and radio producer. And walking in right now, this [is] Jean-Pierre, JP, MC from here, *almal van die Kaap. Klap julle hande* [everyone from the Cape. Clap your hands] [applause].

Blaq Pearl: Thank you so much for the opportunity. Uhm, this is a *kwaai* [cool] topic to actually be sharing and I'm very excited to be able to share my experiences with all of you. It was 2006, my first time when I travelled, my first time ever on, on an airplane and I travelled all the way to the Netherlands. So in 2005, I got contracted by an organisation at a festival…and it's about youth and music, you know, bringing youth together through music…It was scary and exciting. Uhm, the invitation and news only hit home when I was on the plane. Like, okay, this is really happening now. 'Cause until that point it's a lot of admin. You have to get your visa sorted out. It's just administration, you know. Go to the embassy and all of that and they sorted out everything. So I just had to do my part from this side, also getting my sets together. Gonna sell CDs, you know. That kinda stuff. It was very interesting, though, because I'm still very involved in doing my art and performing and then I get this booking and it was a very profound process because, 2004 my brother, my late brother, was killed. Then I went through a personal struggle and journey, and as part of my healing, I made it a point to get out there and establish my name as Blaq Pearl, an independent artist. And soon after that, like I said 2005…My music got found online and this organisation researched me well and thought, 'You are the right candidate to represent your country.' And that was amazing for me. It was a big step so I went there, like I said. When I got on the plane, it only hit me like, 'Oh my gosh I'm really doing this.' And so I never been on a plane before. I just started a band before…and they were like, 'We only wanted you Blaq Pearl. We can only afford to pay for your trip…' Can I bring one person with, like the percussionist? So…they said, 'Yes, you can do this.' Moral of that part of the story: don't just take it as it comes. Try to get out of it as much as you can for your own experience and your music. And so I asked China. I don't know how many of you know China – DJ, rapper, MC…It was great because China has been travelling before many times, so he knew Europe very well…I felt more secure and more safe, you know, having someone who is experienced with me…I was booked for a weekend festival and I managed to extend my flight through the organisation for another two weeks…My brother used to travel to Europe, especially to Amsterdam, all the time, so for me it was an important part of my personal journey to explore and meet the people he met and, and experience, you know, Amsterdam for myself based on the stories and conversations I had with him in the past… It was a beautiful experience…I…was networking and building up relationships, you know, making the best out of the trip. So that's important information I can share with you. So every year after that I got invited to go to the Netherlands and not only that but also other places like Germany…Berlin. Next month, I travel to Paris. So I've been to various places and…I think the key for me, the great outcomes for great experiences is having an open mind, not going all with certain expectations. Okay, this is how I see it going. This is how it should be. You can't do that because you meeting people, you going to go tour a new country for the first time. So for me I am going to go there without a set of expectations in my head. Of course I'm gonna have set expectations in terms of my professionalism and about my music and about how I am going to conduct myself or what I wanna bring across. So that's what, you know, I prepare for, but I can't prepare for other stuff, you know, the experience, the place and people's response to me. I can't prepare for that, so I go with an open mind and that positive attitude and all the time with that I get, I promise, I've had the best experiences that I can bring home with me. That's it for now, thank you [applause].

Black Athena: Okay. Hi, everyone. As Emile said, my name is Elise. I am also known as Black Athena. I have a little bit of a different story to everyone else sitting here, uhm. I haven't really travelled overseas to perform. I'm basically re-emerging. I'm in the Hip Hop scene again. Put out some music and I'm also much older than my, what do you call it, my Hip Hop brothers and sisters. We're a few generations sitting here. I'm in my forties and I'm a MC and been an MC for more than 20 years, but I never really recorded or released any material. And now that both my sons are out of high school, I'm getting back into my passion and taking a step further. I'm with a band, a group, an urban music group known as Kamissa. I'm part of the group with Jean-Pierre and Garth Links…so we are planning to travel this year. We are planning to go abroad and see some African countries where there are opportunities for us, so I actually don't know what to expect. All I know is I got some good music. I got some REALLY GOOD content. I'm talking about issues of parenthood, uhm, single parenthood, Fees Must Fall. All this issues that we are experiencing in our city, in our country. That's the type of stuff we talking about in our music, so it's gonna be a first for me this year and I'm just gonna go in very open mind. Uhm. Ja, so that's me.

JP: Hey, good afternoon everybody, my name is JP. Like Elise said, I'm a member of the crew with her…Kamissa…there is a lot of black around this table today: Black Athena, Blaq Pearl, Black Noise. Listen, I just wanna get a feel from everyone out here, uhm, any singers, uhm, emerging singers or MCs, uhm, rappers in the audience today? Okay, that's awesome. Look, I've some experience travelling abroad with Black Noise, but I wanna touch on something else today. More, uhm, how do we even get to that point where you get the opportunity to travel abroad. Uhm, so it's something that you earn, isn't it? It's not something that comes by your way and let's chat a bit about that today. Let's be real with ourselves: every *bra* [brother] and his mother wants to rap today and a lot of us are good. A lot of singers and MCs are really good, especially in Cape Town, the level of talent here is amazing, but do we know how to channel our talent correctly in order to allow opportunities to open up for us? And today I wanna share a few very, very practical tips and some advice I've used myself over the years. I wanna impart with you in hope that it will help you on your development journey as a musician. So I wanna start with the music itself and Elise was mentioning a couple of things on content in your music. I know Dope Saint Jude is an advocate of certain social rights, uhm, in the LB – how do you – in the queer community. And so it seems to me when you attach a certain ideal to your music, it carries a bit more weight, opposed to speaking about your new set of rims that you put on your car or, uhm, you know what I mean, or the six girls that you and your friends were trying to sleep with last night and all that, that type of thing. So that's the first point I'm gonna…Make sure like your music is really relevant and that you got something worthy to say. The, the other thing I wanna talk about is how do, do you, now that you got dope music, how do you get it out there, right? Because you want people to hear it and it's important that you get as many people to hear your music as possible. But, uhm, sharing it on your friend's wall on social media is not really gonna cut it anymore, so let's become professional. Let's have some pride in our music and let's get to the point where we even design artwork for songs, right, credit the producer on your artwork and then put it in a nice presentable cover and approach radios and say, 'Listen…' [someone hands JP a CD]. Oh, okay. This [is] an example, you know. Blaq Pearl, *Against All Odds*. That's her album she's got out at the moment. You can get it for R99.95 [laughter]. Sorry, I'm just joking, but this is what I'm talking about. Let's make our product, even if it is just a single, as professional as possible. And as artists in the country we got an advantage where our government has pushed majority local airplay on our radio stations, which can also help us get our music out there, uhm. So that's, that's from a music point of view, getting it onto radio. But, uhm, you as an artist also needs to get out there and it's cool really. I love performing at park jams. It's awesome, you are there. I saw a flyer for a park jam that's happening today and I think there is about 40, about 40 other rappers that's gonna be there today with you included. You rapping with that 40, so it's alright. You wanna get your brand as an artist out there to the public, so you need to start distinguishing yourself from

ELISE 'BLACK ATHENA' FERNANDEZ PERFORMING LIVE AT THE AFRICAN HIP HOP INDABA, 2016
Source: Ference Isaacs

EMILE YX?, BLACK NOISE ANNIVERSARY
Source: Ference Isaacs

your peers because it's about you. It's not about the other 39 artists. So you need to find out what are the events that's happening in and around my city. Are there monthly events? Are there weekly events that's happening? Can I approach the organisers of these events and ask them if they would consider me, uhm, to be one of their headline acts at these events because I have now got this professional-looking CD out and it's not just on Facebook? And I've got relevant topics that I'm talking about so I've done all that and I feel like I should be considered for an actual event. And you will be so surprised what it does for your career as a musician because you're now credible. You can now show your friends and family, 'Look here. This event happens every month and, look here. There's my name. I'm performing here.' And, uhm, if you do that you, you starting to build more than some street cred for yourself, but now you starting to build yourself as a brand, as a musician. So these are some tips I am sharing with you, some practical things on how to develop as an artist…so that you consistently doing those things…the opportunities like Dope Saint Jude and like Blaq Pearl and Emile has had where they perform abroad will also start presenting itself to you. So I hope that has been some help to you. Thank you, guys.

Emile YX?: We wanna open for questions to everyone on the floor so maybe someone wants to ask more specific [things] about travelling. But before I do, I don't know if you know b-boy The Curse, Brandon Peterson. B-boy The Curse was unable to make it today, but he, he did mail me…this is the thing about him. When people see him he's very like slick. He manages himself very well and even when I asked him, he immediately wrote back. He apologised he can't make it himself, but he will mail me something. That is very rare to find: b-boys who follow up and who actually mail…I'm just gonna read some of the stuff he said. He was saying that in order for him to be at that level where he can perform internationally, he actually has to be serious about who he is as a dancer, you know. Unless you serious about yourself and take yourself serious, you not gonna achieve any of things people here talking about, you know. So that's the first thing. The second thing he says, like even when you are not feeling up to it, you gonna make sure you practise every single day. You need to push yourself to that level and then the other thing is the package that you selling people, you know. What is that package? When they see you, what makes you different from everyone else they could have hired? Like what makes you stand out from all the other b-boys that there are? And then he says once he's at the gig internationally, he uses it as an opportunity so he can travel to the next place, you know. So when you there, you don't, 'Oh, my goodness, I've made it.' You make sure you connect with who you can. Be open and to also go to places where there are other free gigs in that community because, like Catherine, Dope Saint Jude said, you never know who's in the audience. Now when you go to a rap in a park in, with 40 other MCs, who knows who's in the audience. Nobody is coming from Switzerland to come book you. There is only other *bras* who would like you to perform for free in a community where 50 rappers will rap for free, you understand. So it is about putting your work in…places that are different from the norm, you know…When there's a Hip Hop gig…most of the time go to support, but I don't expect it to be any different from most of the other gigs. When someone says, 'Emile, come to a book fair,' then I'll go because chances are there may be a MC there that's rhyming or reading his songs from a book. Now that really intrigues me because it's different, right? Or, like you mentioned, you were at a gallery opening, right, and people that go to [the] gallery, they got money there. CD, my bro. There in the park, they gonna make you download, *Aweh, kykie jy* [Yoh, look here you]. Maybe a freebee *daar* [there], you understand. So if you about expanding your audience…because you can always perform for free in the park. I'm not mocking it. I'm just saying, think about expanding your market beyond: man, there's 40 other MCs trying to get on and they parking in the crowd and they probably not gonna clap for you because they wanna be the *ou* [guy] or the person who's getting the attention, right…So think about that. So this is what The Curse was trying to get across – *daar verloor ek my spot van my man se speech*, ja [there I lost my place in my man's speech]. He also mentions that if you mess up, like if you mess up once internationally, chances are you not gonna get a chance to come back. So make sure you well prepared so that you deliver something that's really good so that they want to bring you back there next time…Ja, I mean that's the crux of his sharing. He also said, unlike the old school guys, you dress well. He says the old school guys have nothing to prove, so they just go the way they are. The bastard…[laughter]. He's probably talking about me. Yeah, but he's right, you know. You young and up and coming. You gotta deliver a package that is slick. When you older, you don't give a damn. I better get a suit and tie next time [laughter]. Okay, so that's what The Curse…would like to share with other dancers. You know a lot of the dancers…like Dwayne have set up their own competitions that would also be able to send people to France, you know. So opportunities are there, but if you gonna be like, you know, in your room until it's your turn to dance, you not gonna be able to connect with people and try... and actually go out there and speak to people...

Audience member 2: I'm a Xhosa rapper...what can I do to access international audiences?

Dope Saint Jude: So you say you a Xhosa rapper. Uhm, some of my raps use a lot of colloquial slang, so a lot of people overseas also don't understand a lot of my raps. Anything that you might think is a challenge, you must in fact always see it as an advantage. So the fact that you a Xhosa rapper, that is a selling point. It makes you different. Everyone else is rapping there with an American accent. How could you be the different one? So as a Xhosa rapper you gotta promote and push that you are different and talk about the fact that you are a Xhosa rapper and what makes you significant as a Xhosa rapper. For [example] I am now in the queer community. I am a woman. There are a lot of things like maybe...that people might see that don't, that might work to my advantage...those are precisely the things I say that will put me ahead of the next person because I'm different. So anything you might think is a challenge, you flip on its head to make it work for you, ja...

Adam: So I'm getting two very different accounts: one is Facebook sharing and putting your stuff online versus deliver a product, etc., the CD nicely packaged. But we have at least one example of an artist who went the other route – doesn't have a physical item like a CD, hasn't gone that formal route using her video, using her friendship networks to produce really interesting artistic and politically interesting music videos. And that has actually catapulted her career for her – how she has built a network through alternative means. I'm not doing this to put you under pressure. That is what a lot of my research is about. I'm looking at artists who actually try to do things that actually haven't been done before – you don't go to mass media, you don't rely on SABC. Here is an artist who has travelled and hasn't gotten airtime on TV and who already has a journal article in an Australian journal about her work. So she is kinda the exception. Can you engage with that? What is your sense of that?... They're just different models...Are the two mutually exclusive, for example?

JP: Sorry, brother. I didn't get your name.

Adam: Adam.

JP: Adam. Okay, no look here, Adam, it's a good point that you bring up here and as a musician, uhm, in Cape Town we face a lot of challenges, opposed to our peers in other areas of the country because, specifically, the majority of us are, are independent musicians in Cape Town. So we don't really have the luxury depending on record labels, etc., to help us develop our careers and, uhm, with that said, every opportunity that we have to promote ourselves to push our brands, I would say that is the, you know, the opportunity that you should make use of whether it's on social media, whether it's your, uhm, network of friends that are all in the media field and they can help you push your brand – whether it's appearing at park jams, and…whether it's, uhm, being very proficient, uhm, on social media, whether it's, uhm, about being able to be at a lot of different events and regularly…Whatever, uhm, the opportunity is that we have at our disposal, we as artists in Cape Town don't have the luxury of turning anything down. We must make use of every opportunity that we have. So just to answer your question, in short, I think it's a, ja, I think a combination of different, of different strategies…

Dope Saint Jude: Uhm, ja, I totally agree because remember if you an independent artist and if you don't have someone managing you, you don't have…you, your own producer. You have to be your own manager, you have to be your own publicist, you have to be your own social media marketing whizz, you have to do everything. You have to be a like, basically you have to be a superhuman. You need to be professional on all fronts, so if you want to book gigs with like Adidas or whoever, then you must think, does Adidas want you to send them a link to Data File Host? No! They want a SoundCloud page. So you must think on that level…think they want, if that's the level they want, think about the approach. They don't want you to send them a WhatsApp number. You must email them. And don't email them from your [personal] email address, 'I love golfs' and 'women at gmail.com'. It must be… [a] professional name, your artist name at gmail.com. It looks better and when someone sends you an email, respond the next day. That's the latest, or in the same hour. You must be quick like that. Think about how they work. Think about how professional they are. They have a marketing director. They have [a] publicist. You must be that person, must show you [are] on that level. Some people might even be fooled and might even think you have a team with you and you doing everything by yourself. So you must be on top of your Facebook, be on top of it when it comes to the way you dress, be on top of it when it comes to your performance. You show up on time, you dress well, your set is ready. When people email you, respond. You don't still send WhatsApps, you don't send Data File Host links. You send a SoundCloud link and you say this is what I do and you have professional pictures. If you do all of those things on every single front, you look professional. People will, people will be fooled into thinking you of that calibre and then next thing you know, you in New York. So on every single front, you don't slack, don't slack. And even for me, one of the things I do every single day is I exercise every single day because I know in every single way I must try and be the best I can be, ja.

Emile YX?: So I just wanna get the brother that just came. He actually had a class, that's why he's late. This is Lyrical Deezy. He is a dancer and the topic is about travelling internationally. I think his story is actually amazing and I want him to share that with you.

Deezy: I'm just speaking about international travelling…

Emile YX?: Ja, how you set it up. How you went there, how you made money.

Deezy: Okay, what's up everybody. Thank you so much for coming through. Thank you so much for having me…my name is Dansleigh. I'm also known as Lyrical Deezy within the dance community. I am 23 years old. I am a dancer, a choreographer. I'm so excited to be here today, uhm, just speaking about travelling internationally. I was super fortunate or rather honoured to travel. Uhm, it was my dream to travel…I did this competition called Hip Hop International. It was my very first time. It was in my matric year. I was 17 years old and I managed to get a silver medal in SA. I competed in the world Hip Hop champs in Las Vegas in the USA in, uhm, that was 2011, and ever since I've been going for four consecutive years. It's 2016 now. I've been to USA four times and I just got back in July. August I came from Europe – Switzerland and Germany. I attended, uhm, a dance camp called Urban Dance Camp and just a little bit of information I wanna share with you guys in regard to me heading overseas…I had to raise all the money by myself…I'm from Seawinds, Lavender Hill, which is not too far from here. So, ja. I'm pretty sure you know what our community is like, what our, what we are faced with every day. But, uhm, that didn't turn me down, anything like that. I just had to push, fund-raise for myself. Really nobody assisted me with anything. I literally had to pay for everything by myself. Like it took me like eight, nine months like to pay every trip off, but I was determined. Like I had a vison in my mind. I had a goal [in] mind and I just pushed to make that happen. So, ja, I travelled internationally. I got placed like top nine in the world out of 250 dancers…That was one of my biggest achievements and also going to Urban Dance Camp. It's a master camp in Germany. It's only for up and, uhm, like advance dancers…at the master level you get invited to the camp…I was the only one from South Africa attending that camp in Europe and…so that was pretty cool. That was amazing. It really shifted my mind, the way I see dance as an art. I treat myself as an artist. I now, ja, I really just think people, people treat you as the way you present yourself. Like the lady here says, we are our own brand. How you present yourself to the public, that is how they perceive you. That is a little background about my international travelling. It was next level. It was amazing – like from all the dancers from around the world battling…there will be like 150 students they teach. They will choose the top five in the class who does it cool or who does it *kwaai*, whatever, and [it] was literally [like that] in every single class I took that, that was really amazing for me so, yip, I don't know if there is anything else I can say or that's just really my experience with international travelling. I can tell you one thing, it is not easy at all. Like you can have three, five fundraisers, it won't be enough, but [I] encourage some of you guys, a young dreamer, keep dreaming and do what you have to do, ja. Thank you so much.

Emile YX?: All those with a passport, raise your hand. Thanks for that. Ironically, at every African Hip Hop Indaba we, where we send a team overseas, we always had to find passports for some *ouens* [guys], can you believe it? I'd like to thank the panel for their contributions.

CHAPTER 30.

DECOLONISING KNOWLEDGE: READING HIP HOP SAMPLING IN RELATION TO SCHOLARLY PUBLISHING

ADAM HAUPT (UNIVERSITY OF CAPE TOWN)

My pockets are broken

'cause the Prophets are outspoken

(Prophets of da City, 'Cape Crusader' off *Ghetto Code*)

This chapter poses the following questions: What can a brief consideration of Hip Hop sampling tell us about the commercial co-option of countercultures as well as about cultural appropriation? Is there a parallel with scholarly publishing? A key point of entry is the argument that mainstream media rhetoric on piracy serves narrow, corporate interests at the expense of the public interest. An interrogation of some of the fundamental assumptions that inform modern legal conceptions of intellectual property reveals flawed understandings about the commodification of cultural expressions, such as music. Specifically, John Locke's arguments about the principles of natural justice, as taken up in the Statute of Anne, point to racialised and gendered exclusions that were built into legal thinking about the ownership of tangible and intangible property. Ultimately, these exclusions coincided with the expansion of western imperialism and colonial projects and can be read in relation to Quijano's (2000) concept of the 'coloniality of power'. A consideration of Hip Hop sampling as a challenge to the history of cultural appropriation and mechanisms of exclusion in knowledge production and dissemination allows us to consider challenges to the 'coloniality of power'. This speaks to debates about the commodification of knowledge in the age of corporate globalisation, particularly in a global context where leading industries have framed piracy as a threat to economic prosperity. I argue that the commodification of knowledge goes beyond the context of music and media production and should be read in relation to debates about the far-reaching influence of neoliberal economic imperatives in scholarly publishing and conceptions of 'excellence' in scholarly contexts. Ultimately, I contend that in order for knowledge to be decolonised, it needs to be decommodified and, thereby, neoliberal economic assumptions about knowledge and cultural expression need to be deconstructed.

Sampling refers to the process of grabbing snatches of audio from a variety of media sources for reuse in new music or sound productions. Source material may include music obtained from vinyl, cassettes, CDs, film, videos or recordings from radio and television broadcasts. In a discussion of Hip Hop in South Africa, sociolinguists Quentin Williams and Christopher Stroud (2013: 22) explain that the 'notion of "sampling" stems from the idea of sounds and styles being meshed together by selectively adopting various existing sounds, beats, styles and personae in order to produce mimesis and hybridity'. With the transition from analogue to digital sampling, hardware such as the E-mu SP-1200 Akai MPC-60 became integral tools in Hip Hop production (cf. Schloss 2014), setting Hip Hop on a collision course with the major music labels, which accused Hip Hop producers of copyright violation (Haupt 2008) – notwithstanding the fact that a legal precedent was set in *Campbell v Acuff-Rose*, in which Two Live Crew successfully argued that their use of Roy Orbison's 'Pretty Woman' was parody and should therefore be recognised as fair use (Haupt 2008). Ironically, the threat that Hip Hop sampling purportedly posed to the music industry amplified substantially with the uptake of the mp3 file format and the development of peer-to-peer file-sharing platforms by the early 2000s (Haupt 2008). Essentially, anyone with access to a computer could rip, mix and share music, hence the mainstream media industries' 'way on piracy', which included legal action, media campaigns against piracy as well as lobbying in efforts to protect their established revenue streams (Haupt 2008). However, substantial research led by Joe Karaganis (2011) challenged the industry claim that the uploading and downloading of media files and software automatically equated to lost sales and revenue streams. Instead, Karaganis (2011) contends that so-called piracy (or a less restrictive approach to intellectual property regimes) played a significant role in stimulating emerging economies. In other words, former colonies from the global South are able to exercise a level of economic agency that would not be possible in a context that strictly enforced US legislation like the Digital Millennium Copyright Act or copyright term extensions (Haupt 2008; Karaganis 2011). This speaks to the issue of agency in Africa in a global context, where four music holding companies dominate 80 per cent of global market share (Osgerby 2004), as well as to the extent to which many of the Hip Hop artists who have contributed to this book are able to sustain themselves as musicians. The issue is racialised. As early as 1994, DJ Ready D had already recognised as much:

> But now you got this record company, ridiculous publishing shit where you
> gotta pay like thousands of Rands just to use a sample and I mean Hip Hop
> is basically about fusing all types of stuff – scratching, you know, mixing
> that is what basically Hip Hop is about. So you get this white motherfuckers
> doing all sorts of ridiculous shit and, at the end of the day, they just say its
> business, you know. And I mean, fuck that, if someone wants to come along
> and sample our record, it's fine by me. It's cool, sample whatever the fuck
> you wanna sample because, it just goes to show, they respect the music.
> Our music has some sort of influence or encouragement on the artists that
> want to use it, you know it. (Chapter 1, this book)

Ready D's remarks were made in a context where the immediate threat to POC's work as 'conscious' artists was censorship by the apartheid state as well as the emerging democratic state. However, he recognised that the music industry with which POC had to contend was dominated by white corporate power brokers who had the power to limit free expression by gatekeeping access to sampled material, which was monetised from the perspective of corporate rights holders. What is worth noting here is that the industry argues it is acting in the interests of composers, producers and artists when it issues legal challenges to uncleared samples or online piracy, but the fact is that the rights holders of the media materials in question are not necessarily the producers of that material (Haupt 2008). In the case of sampling, the source material is often located in the back catalogues of corporate vaults. The contention that the rights of artists are being furthered is questionable given that the artists themselves are not necessarily rights holders. Likewise, the Lockean principles of just reward for labour and stimulus for creativity, which inform the rationale for copyright protection (Davies 2002; Haupt 2014), hardly seem applicable, for the same reason. In his discussion of

Locke on the US conception of copyright, KJ Greene (1999: 345) contends,

> John Locke's philosophical legacy deeply influenced the thinking of our
> Constitutional founders, who consistently equated liberty with property
> ownership. For example, Alexander Hamilton, a vehement stalwart for property
> protection by the State, asserted at the Constitutional Convention that the 'one
> great object of government is personal protection and the security of property.'
> Locke's theory of personal property asserted that 'every man has Property in
> his own Person [and thus] the Labour of his body and the work of his hands is
> properly his.' Taken literally, Locke's philosophy is the antithesis of slavery, as a
> slave, by definition, does not own the labor of her or his own body.

However, it is questionable whether rights over tangible and intangible property were ever meant to be extended to black subjects – or women, for that matter. In this way, we see a level of continuity between apartheid and post-apartheid South Africa – corporate interests prevail despite key political changes. The fact that Ready D sees sampling as a form of respect, influence or encouragement is significant because Tricia Rose (1994)

MUE CREW FROM MANENBERG | Source: Ference Isaacs

positions Hip Hop sampling as a form of alternative historiography that challenges listeners to explore forgotten histories of black cultural expression. From this perspective, the act of listening is anything but passive. Hip Hop producers and DJs dig through the crates of basement record stores to source music material that is long forgotten in order to sample rare sounds, create innovative break beats and mixes that will inspire MCs to write new rhymes or to freestyle over their beats, as well as to rock crowds on the dance floor. Following Rose (1994), it is clear that being a successful producer or DJ involves doing a significant amount of research into black cultural history. Hip Hop fans are challenged to do the same. They are encouraged to discover the sources of the samples and remixes that move them. In fact, Ready D reflects on his own sampling practices and the process of his music education:

> And while sitting in the recording studio one night, uhm, Shaheen flipped out these records, and on the turntable he drops this vinyl and he drops the needle, and there's a jazz song. An Afro jazz song that plays and it's on Abdullah Ibraham [Ibrahim], better known as Dollar Brand. His song plays, 'The Boy'. I don't know what happened to me personally. Everything changed. My whole life changed, my perspective, everything changed. And right there and then, the lyrics, everything just transformed at that point in time, and that was probably my entry level, once again, into becoming conscious and it wasn't – the music, the artist, wasn't related to Hip Hop whatsoever. There was a energy, there was a truth, there was a level of persuasion, you know, that changed everything for me. So that was kinda, you know, the first uhm connection, and then we wrote a song called 'Roots Resurrected' on our first album, that uhm that sort of – it's a tribute to Afro jazz, the likes of uhm Hotep Galeta Abdullah Ibrahim, Robert Jansen. That was some of the the local jazz musicians and, of course, Pacific Express, the band that, uh, Shaheen's dad belonged to. (Chapter 2, this book)

It was the previous generation of jazz musicians that inspired DJ Ready D and Shaheen Ariefdien and this was reflected in their sampling. They paid homage to Cape jazz artists, who were overlooked by mainstream apartheid-era media as well as music scholars from that era. The decision to sample the band thus affirms black cultural priorities in a context shaped by white supremacy. You might say that their production practices served as a form of Hip Hop pedagogy or that they were engaged in what H Samy Alim and Haupt (2017) frame as Hip Hop's culturally sustaining pedagogy. As Ready D's comments about sampling suggest, the affirmation of black cultural history goes beyond nostalgia for forgotten black sounds. It speaks to the history of racism in the music industry. In the South African context, the story of Solomon Linda's 'Mbube'[1] speaks to the extent of racist exploitation of black musicians in both apartheid South Africa and the USA (Haupt 2014; Ovesen & Haupt 2011). Linda, whose song is one of the most commercially successful pop songs to be covered by a number of mainstream American musicians, was not justly rewarded for his composition (Haupt 2014; Ovesen & Haupt 2011). Leading intellectual property expert Owen Dean took up the case *pro bono* on behalf of Linda's daughters in order to secure a settlement with Disney, which used the song in its box-office hit *The Lion King*. The song's commercial success and the failure of the US music industry to locate Linda with a view to compensating him fairly may have been an oversight made in good faith, but one has to take into account the difficulty black artists experience in negotiating their careers in a racist context:

> For a rhythm and blues release to become a pop hit, it had to 'crossover'
> from the rhythm and blues charts to the pop charts, which is to say, it had
> to first sell well in the black community. This is the essence of the concept
> of crossover; by and large African American artists must first demonstrate
> success in the black market before gaining access to the mainstream. It is a
> process which holds black artists to a higher standard of performance than
> white and it is only recently that it has been successfully circumvented in
> any systematic way. (Garofalo 1994: 277)

It is easy to see how cultural appropriation of black cultural expression could be facilitated in such a context, especially when white artists, who have preferential access to white

---

1. See https://www.youtube.com/watch?v=mrrQT4WkbNE. The song is also commonly known as 'The Lion Sleeps Tonight'.

audiences with larger disposable incomes, take an interest in performing compositions by black artists (as in the case of Linda's 'Mbube'), or if they take an interest in black genres with a view to performing for white audiences. Rebee Garofalo (1994: 283) makes sense of Elvis Presley's success from this perspective when he argues:

> Even with this degree of cultural conversion there still existed a societal
> need for white interpreters to make the music more acceptable. This
> is precisely why Elvis Presley was so complex and so controversial a
> character. Elvis represented both the triumph of African American culture
> and its vulnerability to the power of white supremacy.

As a white crossover artist, Presley was able to take aspects of rock n roll/RnB to white audiences in a context where the white majority was both politically and economically empowered by systemic racism. Presley was able to appropriate exoticised perceptions of blackness in order to craft performances of white rebellion to young white fans. As Perry Hall (1997: 43–44) contends,

> As had been the case with previous instances of aesthetic appropriation,
> the evolution of rhythm and blues into rock and roll eventually
> overshadowed the connection of the Black music to Black humanity. The
> initial rock-and-roll explosion seemed to energize, even define, a new
> generation of white youth with electrifying dance rhythms.

Hall explains that white attraction to black cultural expression 'is often obscured or distorted by racist habits of thoughts and association that provoke suppression and denial, even while conjuring powerful attractions' (1997: 34). What is significant is the idea of disconnecting black humanity from black music. This speaks to the power to fetishise black cultural expression without having to confront the political and economic hardships that black subjects negotiated as they produced innovative cultural forms. It also speaks to the exercise of power in Jonathan Hart's definition of cultural appropriation. He explains, 'Cultural appropriation occurs when a member of another culture takes a cultural practice or theory of a member of another culture as if it were his own or as if the right of possession should not be questioned or contested' (Hart 1997: 138). It is with this history of cultural appropriation in mind that Tricia Rose (1994:

93) suggests that Hip Hop sampling is a political response to this injustice:

> Maybe rap music represents the real 'big payback'…The very laws that justified and aided in the theft from and denigration of an older generation of black artists have created a profitable, legal loophole and a relatively free-play zone for today's black artists. This creative cul de sac is rapidly evaporating. The record companies are increasingly likely to hold albums until samples are cleared, until publishers and other record companies negotiate their profits.

She therefore suggests that sampling is a response to the music industry's complicity in the dispossession of black artists and that this process of dispossession continues via the industry's responses to what it sees as a threat to their revenue streams and control over the music market. In effect, we see a continuation of racialised marginalisation through legal and economic mechanisms. Nelson George confirms Rose's claim that the industry has managed to use its gatekeeping power to ensure that Hip Hop sampling does not present a financial or political threat to its interests when he explains that

MIXED MENSE: B-BOY MOUSE AND MALLIS | Source: Ference Isaacs

sampling hasn't disappeared from Hip Hop, but the level of ambition in using samples has fallen. The high-intensity sound tapestries of [Public Enemy] have given way to often simpleminded loops of beats and vocal hooks from familiar songs – a formula that grossed Hammer, Coolio, and Puff Daddy millions in sales and made old R&B song catalogs potential gold mines. (George 1998: 95)

Building upon Ready D's views on industry responses to sampling and music publishing, Shaheen Ariefdien says,

As far as this whole publishing thing goes, it's like a whole circle the way I see it. I mean, when jazz started out and all of that, black people created that shit, the soul the flair was there, you know. They watered the shit down. Even rock and roll – the Chuck Berrys and all that. I mean, if you look at rock and roll, you think rock and roll, you think white music. That to me is fucked up. They steal cultures and, shit, that's why when Vanilla Ice came out, everyone was like, 'Fuck that. We not gonna have that.' At the end of the day, in a couple of years down the line people gonna look back and say it's white music 'cause that's what happened to rock as well with Jimi Hendrix and all of that people. Like starting the shit, you know, being there on the forefront, they inspired how many white kids. (This volume, Chapter 1)

Ariefdien recognises the racialised dynamics of power that shape cultural appropriation and the extent to which black genres – such as rock n roll and, more recently, Hip Hop – energise white countercultures at the expense of black communities. Of course, the idea of 'stealing' a culture is a misnomer. What is really at stake in these cultural exchanges is the unequal relations of power between coloniser and colonised, in a context where the colonised are not consulted on how they are represented, or how aspects of their culture or scientific knowledge are taken up by more powerful interest groups (Hart 1997). The notion of stealing ideas or cultures creates an analogy between that which is tangible (and therefore rivalrous) and that which is intangible (and therefore non-rivalrous) (cf. Boyle 2003; Lessig 2004). The term 'intellectual property' also employs this analogy and treats intellectual output as if it can be owned; as if it were tangible property and therefore rivalrous, whereas it is, in fact, not rivalrous or scarce.

PROPHETS OF DA CITY – REHEARSALS | Source: Ference Isaacs

This analogy not only works well in media industries that have a vested interest in commodifying cultural expressions, but also in the scholarly context. For example, Samuel Moore, Cameron Neylon, Martin Paul Eve, Daniel Paul O'Donnell and Damian Pattinson (2017: 1) write that the concept of excellence in the academy has 'no intrinsic meaning'. In fact, it 'functions as a linguistic interchange mechanism' that 'combines with narratives of scarcity and competition to show that the hyper-competition that arises from the performance of "excellence" is completely at odds with the qualities of good research' (Moore et al. 2017: 1). Much as the non-commercial sharing of the more fluid format of music, the mp3 file, is characterised as piracy (Haupt 2008; Karaganis 2011) and recreates the perception of scarcity by attempting to drive consumers back to purchasing hard copies of music in the form of CDs or to push them to pay-walled purchases on commercial services – such as Amazon or iTunes – perceptions of excellence recreate notions of scarcity in a scholarly context where it is possible to sustain an information commons that allows for information knowledge to circulate freely. The free circulation of knowledge is further inhibited by proprietary approaches to scholarly publishing. In an article titled 'The Oligopoly of Academic Publishers in the Digital Era', Larivière, Haustein and Mongeon (2015: 1) contend that, '[c]ombined, the top five most prolific publishers account for more than 50% of all papers published in 2013'. Given that scholars essentially submit, edit and referee academic articles for free, it is not clear how publishers justify exorbitant subscription fees in the digital age where production and distribution costs are significantly lower than in the print era. On the one hand, scholars labour for free and effectively work towards producing an information commons and, on the other, the labour of this gift culture (cf. Boyle 2003; Lessig 2004) is monetised via a proprietary approach to knowledge distribution. Larivière et al. (2015: 12) ask, 'What is it that they provide that is so essential to the scientific community that we collectively agree to devote an increasingly large proportion of our universities' budgets to them?' The answer is that journals owned by the publishing monopolies are deemed to be prestigious and publishing in them has implications for *ad hominem* promotions, university subsidies and research grants. The notion of scarcity is therefore integral to scholarly output and systems that reward scholars for 'excellence'. Eve Gray (2009/2010) summarises the structural inequalities inherent in the system:

> In general, journal articles, particularly in journals in the ISI indexes, are
> privileged as the single most recognised and rewarded scholarly output.
> These are for the most part commercial subscription journals with 'all
> rights reserved' copyright, often with high subscription prices and limited
> circulation in Africa. The result is a limitation on the extent to which African
> researchers can create a collaborative base for developmental research
> relevant to African priorities. This is due to the bias of the journal publishing
> indices against work from the developing world and because of the exclusion
> of applied research outputs in the hierarchy of what type of publication
> outputs are recognised and rewarded in most higher education systems. This
> has the effect of pushing much African research to the periphery.

In other words, the political economy of scholarly publishing seems to direct scholarly and institutional trajectories more than intellectual considerations do. The question to pose here is, 'How does one decolonise scholarship when it is so immersed in a political economy that is exploitative?' One answer is to advance open scholarship through open access journals as well as through book publishers with open content policies (cf. Abrahams, Burke, Gray & Rens 2008; Gray 2009/2010[2]). The very terms upon which knowledge is produced and distributed also require critical attention, specifically with regard to intellectual property and proprietary approaches to scholarly publications and education resources. In order for public institutions to be truly decolonised, access to scholarly publications and education resources needs to be democratised. For this to happen, knowledge needs to be decommodified. The scholarly journal system cannot be understood outside of the coloniality of power (Quijano 2000, 2007). Anibal Quijano argues that the

> coloniality of power is based upon 'racial' social classification of the world
> population under Eurocentered world power. But coloniality of power is
> not exhausted in the problem of 'racist' social relations. It pervaded and
> modulated the basic instances of the Eurocentered capitalist colonial/
> modern world power to become the cornerstone of this coloniality of
> power. (2007: 171)

Gray's (2016) arguments about the global ascendance of English linguistic imperialism in scholarly journals due to the collusion of World War Two allies offer an example of one avenue via which the coloniality of power operates:

> The world of modern journals is thus built on the scientific-military-economic
> power of the victorious Allies in World War II. It is in their postwar political
> aspirations emerging in the late 1940s and the 1950s that one finds the
> mechanisms that embedded a big-business ethos in the supposedly esoteric
> sphere of journal publishing. This entrenched the dominance of the English
> language as the language of science, and the English-speaking North Atlantic
> allies as the leading powers in this scientific world. In the universities, this has
> also translated into a highly competitive culture, in which scholars' prestige
> and status and that of their universities depends upon publication of high-
> impact findings in the right journals. It is backed by an ethos that draws on
> postwar English language nationalism and North Atlantic commercial power,

---

2. See Gray's remarks about the HSRC Press's open content strategy.

with the role of research publication being to forge a link between the two.

Gray adds that this collusion effectively sidelines 'research from the developing world, to this day'. In fact, Makia Diko writes that in 2014, 'the Web of Science published a list of over 3000 researchers from across the world with the most cited publications over an 11-year period (2002–2012)' (2015: 1). The overwhelming majority of influential researchers came from Europe and North America (46.89 per cent and 48.8 per cent, respectively), whilst the most influential African researchers came to just 0.3 per cent (Diko 2015: 1). South Africa is the sole representative of Africa and ranks 25th out of 47 countries (Diko 2015: 1). Furthermore, Victor Ray contends that racial bias in scholarly citation patterns 'reproduces and legitimates racial inequality' (Ray 2018). Drawing on the work of Richard Delgado (1984), Ray (2018) explains:

> In the social sciences and humanities, many of these works were written
> during a period when racial and gender exclusion was simply expected and
> taken for granted. What counts as canonical is shaped by who had access
> to existing knowledge and the tools and institutional resources to produce
> new knowledge.

Racialised inequalities between the global North and South (as well as along racial and gender lines) are therefore created and sustained by the scholarly publishing system, which ensures that public funds are used to fund public university research that will be published in 'excellent' journals, which are largely owned and/or distributed by holding publishing monopolies from the global North, with a view to generating state subsidies for universities for research 'excellence'. However, these public universities spend a significant amount of their funds on accessing journals to which scholars contribute for free. The decommodification of knowledge is therefore essential to working towards the decolonisation of knowledge in order to disentangle it from the coloniality of power. Nelson Maldonado-Torres (2006: 115) argues:

> Decolonization not only refers to the critique of and effort to dismantle
> neocolonial relations that continued and renewed in different ways

dependency and vertical relations of power between northern and southern countries, but also to radical transformation of the modern/colonial matrix of power which continues to define modern identities as well as the relations of power and epistemic forms that go along with them.

Both the music industry and the field of scholarly publishing have been shaped by a political economy that privileges what bell hooks (1994) calls white supremacist capitalist patriarchy by ensuring that white economic and cultural imperatives from the global North are served. Very particular conceptions of cultural expression, knowledge and intellectual production serve these interests. For example, the term 'intellectual property' communicates the belief that intellectual expressions can be owned or stolen in the way that tangible property can be owned or stolen and, therefore, embeds in them notions of ownership that are classed, racialised and gendered (Haupt 2014).

Likewise, debates about cultural appropriation that see cultures as bounded, fixed and capable of being owned or stolen – instead of viewing them in relation to unequal relations of power – run the risk of embedding notions of ownership that are classed, racialised and

AFRICAN HIP HOP INDABA LECTURE SERIES, UWC, 2014: ADAM HAUPT, DJ READY D, H SAMY ALIM, EMILE JANSEN, QUENTIN WILLIAMS AND MALIKAH DANIELS | Source: Adam Haupt

gendered. Here, the concept of sampling as discussed from a sociolinguistic perspective might offer a clue about how one might begin to decolonise knowledge and cultural expression – aside from rethinking the processes by which they are commodified. In their discussion of 'multivocal performances of braggadocio', Williams and Stroud (2013: 33) argue that 'each emcee lays emphasis on different ways of doing so – by sampling everyday texts, stylising local forms of language varieties and by remixing into this other varieties of language (such as the use of accented-AAE) and registers such as Sabela'. A range of sources are therefore sampled with a view to remixing them – that is, reworking source material in order to produce new texts, new modes of speech according to new logics. In other words, the process of sampling and remixing is selective in terms of what is appropriated and in terms of how new forms of expression and modes of articulation are created. The terms upon which these processes happen are also remixed, renegotiated or openly defy hegemonic expectations of what constitutes politically and aesthetically acceptable forms of expression, as well as essentialist perceptions of language and culture as bounded. As Tricia Rose (1994: 36) suggests, Dick Hebdige's concept of subcultural style best explains how Hip Hop style 'can be used as a gesture of refusal or as a form of oblique challenge to structures of domination'. She explains: 'Hip Hop artists use style as a form of identity formation that plays on class distinctions and hierarchies by using commodities to claim the cultural terrain' (Rose 1994: 36). Hebdige contends that '[s]ubcultures represent "noise"…interference in the orderly sequence which leads from real events and phenomena to their representation in the media' (1979: 91) – effectively interrupting myths of consensus about what constitutes 'normality' by appropriating, and thereby inscribing, hegemonic signifiers only to subvert them in order to introduce competing discursive practices. In this instance, the discursive practices in question frustrate attempts to posit linguistic and cultural imperialism as normal, given and unproblematic. In the introduction to *Global Linguistic Flows: Hip Hop Cultures, Youth Identities and the Politics of Language*, H Samy Alim (2008: 7) makes the case for the agency of young people in the face of linguistic imperialism and globalisation:

> As we witness…complex linguistic remixing across the globe…the
> multiplicity of indexicalities brought forth by…multilayered uses of language

demands a sociolinguistics of globalization that gives a more central role to
linguistic agency on the part of youth, as their appropriations and remixes
of Hip Hop indicate that…heteroglot language practices are important
technologies in the fashioning of…local/global identities.

The concepts of sampling and remixing are central to Williams and Stroud's and Alim's arguments in making the case for agency of youth in and beyond empire (cf. Hardt & Negri 2000; Haupt 2008), and effectively challenge essentialist notions of race, language and culture. Hip Hop's translanguaging and translingual practices challenge these essentialist understandings of race, culture and language by drawing attention to the hybrid nature of linguistic and cultural practices (Haupt 2017), and present a challenge to cultural racism in favour of the view that language is a commons. An understanding of language and culture as a commons allows one to value the communal nature of knowledge production and dissemination. Thomas Schumacher's work on Hip Hop sampling speaks to the notion of the commons as well. He argues that Hip Hop samplers challenge conventional understandings of the 'ownership of sound and "Rockist" aesthetics which remain tied to the romantic ideals of the individual performer' (Schumacher 1995: 266). He explains that 'copyright is still influenced by the ideological construct of the "author" as a singular origin of artistic works' (1995: 259). Unlike realist modes of representation, Hip Hop samplers draw attention to the constructedness of their work, not intending to incorporate samples seamlessly into their soundscapes. By drawing attention to the 'process of production, we see that technologized music is the product not just of auteur-musicians but of the work of musicians and engineers alike…in the age of digital reproduction the search for a singular musical moment is in vain' (Schumacher 1995: 261). Again, the communal nature of cultural production is emphasised in order to challenge Locke-influenced individualist understandings of meaning-making and ownership of ideas – in other words, cultural expression draws from and feeds into a commons. Such challenges, along with challenges to the logic of neoliberal economics and the commodification of knowledge and cultural expression in favour of replenishing the commons, would help to establish pathways to dismantling the coloniality of power.

PART FOUR REFERENCES

Abrahams L, Burke M, Gray E & Rens A (2008) *Opening access to knowledge in southern African universities.* Accessed October 2018, http://www.sarua.org/files/publications/OpeningAccess/Opening_Access_Knowledge_2008.pdf

Alim HS (2008) Introduction. In HS Alim, A Ibrahim & A Pennycook (eds) *Global linguistic flows: Hip hop cultures, youth identities, and the politics of language.* New York: Routledge

Alim HS & Haupt A (2017) Reviving soul(s): Hip Hop as culturally sustaining pedagogy in the U.S. & South Africa. In Django Paris & H Samy Alim (eds) *Culturally sustaining pedagogies: Teaching and learning for educational justice.* New York: Teachers College Press, Columbia University

Boyle J (2003) The second enclosure movement and the construction of the public domain. *Law and Contemporary Problems* 66(33): 33–74

Davies G (2002) *Copyright and the public interest.* London: Sweet & Maxwell

Delgado R (1984) The imperial scholar: Reflections on a review of civil rights literature. *University of Pennsylvania Law Review* 132(3): 561–578

Diko ML (2015) South African scholars make Thomson Reuters 'highly cited researchers 2014'. *South African Journal of Science* 111(9/10): 1–4

Garofalo R (1994) Culture versus commerce: The marketing of black popular music. *Public Culture* 7(1): 275–287

George N (1998) *Hip hop America.* New York: Penguin

Gray E (2009/2010) Access to Africa's knowledge: Publishing development research and measuring value. *The African Journal of Information and Communication* 10. Accessed October 2018, https://core.ac.uk/download/pdf/29055289.pdf

Gray E (2016) A neo-colonial enterprise: Robert Maxwell and the rise of the 20th century scholarly journal. *Open and Collaborative Science in Development Network.* Accessed October 2018, http://ocsdnet.org/a-neo-colonial-enterprise-robert-maxwell-and-the-rise-of-the-20th-century-scholarly-journal/

Greene KJ (1999) Copyright, culture, and black music: A legacy of unequal protection. *Hastings Communication and Entertainment Law Journal* 21: 339–392

Hall PA (1997) African-American music: Dynamics of appropriation and innovation. In B Ziff & PV Roa (eds) *Borrowed power: Essays on cultural appropriation.* New Brunswick, NJ: Rutgers University Press

Hardt M & Negri A (2000) *Empire.* Cambridge, MA: Harvard University Press

Hart J (1997) Translating and resisting empire: Cultural appropriation and postcolonial studies. In B Ziff & PV Roa (eds) *Borrowed power: Essays on cultural appropriation.* New Brunswick, NJ: Rutgers University Press

Haupt A (2008) *Stealing empire: P2P, intellectual property and hip hop subversion*. Cape Town: HSRC Press

Haupt A (2014) Interrogating piracy: Race, colonialism and ownership. In L Eckstein (ed.) *Postcolonial piracy: Media distribution and cultural production in the global south*. London: Bloomsbury

Haupt A (2017) *Mix en meng it op*: Emile YX?'s alternative race and language politics in South African hip hop. *M/C Journal* 20(1). Accessed October 2018, http://journal.media-culture.org.au/index.php/mcjournal/article/view/1202/0

Hebdige D (1979) *Subculture: The meaning of style*. London: Routledge

hooks b (1994) *Outlaw culture: resisting representations.* New York: Routledge

Karaganis J (2011) Rethinking piracy. In J Karaganis (ed.) *Media piracy in emerging economies.* New York: Social Science Research Council

Larivière V, Haustein S & Mongeon P (2015) The oligopoly of academic publishers in the digital era. *PLoS ONE* 10(6): 1–15

Lessig L (2004) *Free culture: How big media uses technology and the law to lock down culture and control creativity.* New York: Penguin

Maldonado-Torres N (2006) Césaire's gift and the decolonial turn. *Radical Philosophy Review* 9(2): 111–138

Moore S, Neylon C, Eve MP, O'Donnell DP & Pattinson D (2017) 'Excellence R Us': University research and the fetishisation of excellence. *Palgrave Communications*. Accessed October 2018, https://kclpure.kcl.ac.uk/portal/files/63537303/palcomms2016105.pdf

Osgerby B (2004) *Youth media*. New York: Routledge

Ovesen H & Haupt A (2011) Vindicating capital: Heroes and villains in A Lion's Trail. *Ilha Do Desterro* 61: 73–107

Quijano A (2000) Coloniality of power and Eurocentrism in Latin America. *International Sociology* 15(2): 215–232

Quijano A (2007) Coloniality and modernity/rationality. *Cultural Studies* 21(2–3): 168–178

Ray V (2018) The racial politics of citation. *Inside Higher Ed.* Accessed October 2018, https://www.insidehighered.com/advice/2018/04/27/racial-exclusions-scholarly-citations-opinion

Rose T (1994) *Black noise: Rap music and black culture in contemporary America.* London: Wesleyan University Press

Schloss JG (2014) *Making beats: The art of sample-based hip-hop*. Middletown, CT: Wesleyan University Press

Schumacher TG (1995) 'This is a sampling sport': Digital sampling, rap music and the law in cultural production. *Media, Culture and Society* 17(2): 253–273

Williams QE & Stroud C (2013) Multilingualism remixed: Sampling texts, braggadocio and the politics of voice in Cape Town hip hop. *Stellenbosch Papers in Linguistics* 42: 15–36

B-BOY BRANDON, AFRICAN HIP HOP INDABA | Source: Ference Isaacs

INDEX

1994 election 33–34

kidocracy 150, 177

kinaesthetic learners 252, 256, 257

Klein Karoo Nasionale Kunstefees 139

knowledge
        commodification of 504–505
        free circulation of 513–514

Knowledge of Self 5, 8, 11, 14, 143–144, 360, 413, 415
        and conscious Hip Hop 262
        internalisation 129–130

kombuistaal 222

Koos Kombuis 376, 378

kroes 37, 223, 224, 236

L
labels 450–451
        independent 462, 466

Lacanian mirror *see* mirror stage theory

Langa 417–418
        state of mind 419

language 150, 434–435
        activism 196–197
        barriers 202
        as disruptor 195
        hegemony 216
        hierarchy 206–208, 225
        and marginalisation 209–211
        multi-layered 519
        profiling and stereotyping 209–212
        purity myths 207, 210–211, 288
        race and identity 207–212, 314
        race and power 283–285
        racialisation 203
        and upward mobility 14

Larney Jou Poes 305–306, 317, 387
        age restriction 391
        filming 389–390

Latitia Fisher 133

Lavender Hill 133, 142

League of Shadows 323–324

Lee, Bruce 151

Legendary Beatbangaz *61, 449*

life skills programmes 410–411

Linda, Solomon 509

linguistic
        looting 290, 295, 302, 312–314
        restructuring 298
        see also language

Lion King 509

literacy 154
        see also critical literacy

literature and Hip Hop 265–266

local distribution 45–46

locality 203, 212–213

Locke's theory of personal property 507

Loren Henderson *see* B-girl Loren

loveLife 72–73

Louw, Jethro 359–360

Luister (film) 320–321

Lyrical Deezy 502–503

Lyrical Warfare 462–463

M
Mailer, Norman 313

mainstream media 184–185

Mak1One 12, *14,* 75, 84, 89, *235,* 236, *250*

Makhanda 237
        integration of Hip Hop community 245–246

making a living 113, 133–134, 143, 230–231, 248

management issues 133–135

Mandela, Nelson 4–5

Manufacturing of Consent 148

Mariam 351–352

Marlin Keating 462

Marlon Burgess 201–202, 290–291, 296

Masai Hip Hop heads 181

masculinity 399

safe spaces 336

Salt River 435–436, 439

sampling 506
    and black cultural history 508–509
    and commons 519
    and dispossession of black artists 511–512
    as 'fair use' 505
    and music rights 36–37

Santana, Carlos 351

scholarship/s 156–158
    decolonising 514–515
    see also academia

school 251
    curriculums 123–124
    fees 424–425
    programmes 184
    protests 5
    relevance 252–254
    teaching and Hip Hop 254

Schreiner, Olive 392

Science education and Hip Hop 274–280

seeds 364

segregation 282, 434
    township 417
    in US schools 308–309
    see also apartheid

self-affirmation 336

self-awareness 210, 262, 301, 307
    vs misogyny, racism and ignorance 262

self-hate 129, 143–144, 223–224, 229–230

self-knowledge *see* knowledge of self

self-love 141, 196, 234–235, 317

self-regulated learning 265

self-worth 137, 180, 234–235, 245, 315,

selling out 102–103, 240, 484–485
    vs breaking through 104–105

servility and dominance 390, 392

sexism 14, 352, 355, 452
    see also misogyny

sexual orientation 426–427

shacks 161

Shaheen Ariefdien *60, 193, 302, 310, 461, 473*

Shakespeare 299–301

shamanism 137, 140, 246, 360–361

Shameema Williams 91, *98*

Signifying Monkey 9

skills transfer vs performance 186

Skwatta Kamp 95, 96

slang vs linguistic restructuring 298

slavery 224–225, 405, 437

SLiP 267–268, 325–326, 459–460

smiling 399

social Ills 413

social media 236, 325, 330, 478, 492, 500, 501–502
    see also YouTube

social mobility 242
    as selling out 240

Solidarity 6

sociolinguistics of globalisation 519

sodomy 392, 393

Sonyfication 171

soul murder 286–290, 302, 312

Sound of Africa 372

South (newspaper) 65

South African Broadcasting Corporation *see* SABC

Sparrow, Penny 428

Spear, The 58

speech events 324–325

spiritual side of Hip Hop 415–416

sponsorship 135, 174–175, 227–228

star syndrome 471–472